Land Rover 90, 110 & Defender Diesel
Owners Workshop Manual

Mark Coombs and Steve Rendle

(3017 - 9AM6 - 336)

Models covered
Land Rover 90, 110 & Defender Diesel models, inc. Pick-up, Hard- & Soft-Top,
County & Station Wagon, with 2¼ litre (2286cc) and 2.5 litre (2495cc & 2498cc) normally-aspirated
and Turbo Diesel engines (including TD5 engine)

Covers most features of 130 models
Does NOT cover 2.4 litre TDi diesel engine, petrol engine models, or Land Rover Special Vehicles options and conversions

© Haynes Publishing 2008

ABCDE
FGHIJ
KLMNO

2

A book in the **Haynes Owners Workshop Manual Series**

ISBN: 978 1 84425 603 7

British Library Cataloguing in Publication Data
A catalogue record for this book is available from the British Library.

Printed in the USA

Haynes Publishing
Sparkford, Yeovil, Somerset BA22 7JJ, England

Haynes North America, Inc
861 Lawrence Drive, Newbury Park, California 91320, USA

Haynes Publishing Nordiska AB
Box 1504, 751 45 UPPSALA, Sverige

Contents

LIVING WITH YOUR LAND ROVER DEFENDER

Safety first!   Page   **0•5**

Introduction   Page   **0•6**

Roadside repairs

Jump starting   Page   **0•8**

Wheel changing   Page   **0•8**

Towing   Page   **0•8**

Identifying leaks   Page   **0•9**

Weekly checks

Introduction   Page   **0•10**

Coolant level   Page   **0•10**

Engine oil level   Page   **0•11**

Tyres   Page   **0•12**

Brake fluid level   Page   **0•13**

Washer fluid level   Page   **0•14**

Wiper blades   Page   **0•14**

Battery   Page   **0•14**

Electrical system   Page   **0•14**

Lubricants and fluids   Page   **0•15**

Tyre pressures   Page   **0•15**

MAINTENANCE

Routine Maintenance and Servicing   Page   **1•1**

Maintenance schedule   Page   **1•3**

Maintenance procedures   Page   **1•8**

Contents

REPAIRS & OVERHAUL

Engine and Associated Systems
Non-TD5 engines in-car repair procedures — Page **2A•1**
TD5 engine in-car repair procedures — Page **2B•1**
Engine removal and general overhaul procedures — Page **2C•1**
Cooling, heating and air conditioning systems — Page **3•1**
Fuel, exhaust and emissions control systems – non-TD5 engines — **Page 4A•1**
Fuel, exhaust and emissions control systems – TD5 engines — **Page 4B•1**
Engine electrical systems — Page **5•1**

Transmission
Clutch — Page **6•1**
Manual gearbox — Page **7A•1**
Transfer gearbox — Page **7B•1**
Propeller shafts — Page **8•1**
Front and rear axles — Page **9•1**

Brakes
Braking system — Page **10•1**

Suspension
Suspension and steering — Page **11•1**

Body Equipment
Bodywork and fittings — Page **12•1**

Electrical
Body electrical systems — Page **13•1**
Wiring Diagrams — Page **13•17**

REFERENCE
General dimensions and weights — Page **REF•1**
Conversion factors — Page **REF•2**
General repair procedures — Page **REF•3**
Buying spare parts — Page **REF•4**
Vehicle identification numbers — Page **REF•4**
Jacking and vehicle support — Page **REF•6**
Radio/cassette anti-theft system — Page **REF•6**
Tools and working facilities — Page **REF•7**
MOT test checks — Page **REF•9**
Fault finding — Page **REF•13**
Glossary of technical terms — Page **REF•22**

Index
— Page **REF•27**

Advanced driving

Many people see the words 'advanced driving' and believe that it won't interest them or that it is a style of driving beyond their own abilities. Nothing could be further from the truth. Advanced driving is straightforward safe, sensible driving - the sort of driving we should all do every time we get behind the wheel.

An average of 10 people are killed every day on UK roads and 870 more are injured, some seriously. Lives are ruined daily, usually because somebody did something stupid. Something like 95% of all accidents are due to human error, mostly driver failure. Sometimes we make genuine mistakes - everyone does. Sometimes we have lapses of concentration. Sometimes we deliberately take risks.

For many people, the process of 'learning to drive' doesn't go much further than learning how to pass the driving test because of a common belief that good drivers are made by 'experience'.

Learning to drive by 'experience' teaches three driving skills:

☐ Quick reactions. (Whoops, that was close!)
☐ Good handling skills. (Horn, swerve, brake, horn).
☐ Reliance on vehicle technology. (Great stuff this ABS, stop in no distance even in the wet...)

Drivers whose skills are 'experience based' generally have a lot of near misses and the odd accident. The results can be seen every day in our courts and our hospital casualty departments.

Advanced drivers have learnt to control the risks by controlling the position and speed of their vehicle. They avoid accidents and near misses, even if the drivers around them make mistakes.

The key skills of advanced driving are **concentration,** effective all-round **observation, anticipation** and **planning.** When **good vehicle handling** is added to these skills, all driving situations can be approached and negotiated in a safe, methodical way, leaving nothing to chance.

Concentration means applying your mind to safe driving, completely excluding anything that's not relevant. Driving is usually the most dangerous activity that most of us undertake in our daily routines. It deserves our full attention.

Observation means not just looking, but seeing and seeking out the information found in the driving environment.

Anticipation means asking yourself what is happening, what you can reasonably expect to happen and what could happen unexpectedly. (One of the commonest words used in compiling accident reports is 'suddenly'.)

Planning is the link between seeing something and taking the appropriate action. For many drivers, planning is the missing link.

If you want to become a safer and more skilful driver and you want to enjoy your driving more, contact the Institute of Advanced Motorists at www.iam.org.uk, phone 0208 996 9600, or write to IAM House, 510 Chiswick High Road, London W4 5RG for an information pack.

Working on your car can be dangerous. This page shows just some of the potential risks and hazards, with the aim of creating a safety-conscious attitude.

General hazards

Scalding

• Don't remove the radiator or expansion tank cap while the engine is hot.
• Engine oil, automatic transmission fluid or power steering fluid may also be dangerously hot if the engine has recently been running.

Burning

• Beware of burns from the exhaust system and from any part of the engine. Brake discs and drums can also be extremely hot immediately after use.

Crushing

• When working under or near a raised vehicle, always supplement the jack with axle stands, or use drive-on ramps. *Never venture under a car which is only supported by a jack.*
• Take care if loosening or tightening high-torque nuts when the vehicle is on stands. Initial loosening and final tightening should be done with the wheels on the ground.

Fire

• Fuel is highly flammable; fuel vapour is explosive.
• Don't let fuel spill onto a hot engine.
• Do not smoke or allow naked lights (including pilot lights) anywhere near a vehicle being worked on. Also beware of creating sparks (electrically or by use of tools).
• Fuel vapour is heavier than air, so don't work on the fuel system with the vehicle over an inspection pit.
• Another cause of fire is an electrical overload or short-circuit. Take care when repairing or modifying the vehicle wiring.
• Keep a fire extinguisher handy, of a type suitable for use on fuel and electrical fires.

Electric shock

• Ignition HT voltage can be dangerous, especially to people with heart problems or a pacemaker. Don't work on or near the ignition system with the engine running or the ignition switched on.

• Mains voltage is also dangerous. Make sure that any mains-operated equipment is correctly earthed. Mains power points should be protected by a residual current device (RCD) circuit breaker.

Fume or gas intoxication

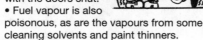

• Exhaust fumes are poisonous; they often contain carbon monoxide, which is rapidly fatal if inhaled. Never run the engine in a confined space such as a garage with the doors shut.
• Fuel vapour is also poisonous, as are the vapours from some cleaning solvents and paint thinners.

Poisonous or irritant substances

• Avoid skin contact with battery acid and with any fuel, fluid or lubricant, especially antifreeze, brake hydraulic fluid and Diesel fuel. Don't syphon them by mouth. If such a substance is swallowed or gets into the eyes, seek medical advice.
• Prolonged contact with used engine oil can cause skin cancer. Wear gloves or use a barrier cream if necessary. Change out of oil-soaked clothes and do not keep oily rags in your pocket.
• Air conditioning refrigerant forms a poisonous gas if exposed to a naked flame (including a cigarette). It can also cause skin burns on contact.

Asbestos

• Asbestos dust can cause cancer if inhaled or swallowed. Asbestos may be found in gaskets and in brake and clutch linings. When dealing with such components it is safest to assume that they contain asbestos.

Special hazards

Hydrofluoric acid

• This extremely corrosive acid is formed when certain types of synthetic rubber, found in some O-rings, oil seals, fuel hoses etc, are exposed to temperatures above 400ºC. The rubber changes into a charred or sticky substance containing the acid. *Once formed, the acid remains dangerous for years. If it gets onto the skin, it may be necessary to amputate the limb concerned.*
• When dealing with a vehicle which has suffered a fire, or with components salvaged from such a vehicle, wear protective gloves and discard them after use.

The battery

• Batteries contain sulphuric acid, which attacks clothing, eyes and skin. Take care when topping-up or carrying the battery.
• The hydrogen gas given off by the battery is highly explosive. Never cause a spark or allow a naked light nearby. Be careful when connecting and disconnecting battery chargers or jump leads.

Air bags

• Air bags can cause injury if they go off accidentally. Take care when removing the steering wheel and/or facia. Special storage instructions may apply.

Diesel injection equipment

• Diesel injection pumps supply fuel at very high pressure. Take care when working on the fuel injectors and fuel pipes.

⚠️ *Warning: Never expose the hands, face or any other part of the body to injector spray; the fuel can penetrate the skin with potentially fatal results.*

Remember...

DO

• Do use eye protection when using power tools, and when working under the vehicle.

• Do wear gloves or use barrier cream to protect your hands when necessary.

• Do get someone to check periodically that all is well when working alone on the vehicle.

• Do keep loose clothing and long hair well out of the way of moving mechanical parts.

• Do remove rings, wristwatch etc, before working on the vehicle – especially the electrical system.

• Do ensure that any lifting or jacking equipment has a safe working load rating adequate for the job.

DON'T

• Don't attempt to lift a heavy component which may be beyond your capability – get assistance.

• Don't rush to finish a job, or take unverified short cuts.

• Don't use ill-fitting tools which may slip and cause injury.

• Don't leave tools or parts lying around where someone can trip over them. Mop up oil and fuel spills at once.

• Don't allow children or pets to play in or near a vehicle being worked on.

Land Rover 90 Pick-up

Land Rover 110 County Station Wagon

First introduced in 1948 at the Amsterdam motor show, the Land Rover was primarily designed for use by farmers as a combined tractor/pick-up truck, and only a limited production run was anticipated. However, the vehicle became a phenomenal success, and by 1951 the Land Rover was outselling Rover saloon cars.

The Land Rover 110 range was introduced to the UK market in 1983, and is basically a more refined development of the previous Land Rover Series III. The 110 name is derived from the 110-inch wheelbase. The 110 models were initially introduced with the 2286 cc normally-aspirated indirect-injection diesel engine, and were available in Pick-Up, Hard-Top and Station Wagon body styles.

In 1984, the 90 range was introduced (90-inch wheelbase), and the 2495 cc normally-aspirated diesel engine superseded the previous smaller-capacity unit across the 90 and 110 ranges.

In 1986, a more powerful turbocharged version of the 2495 cc engine superseded the normally-aspirated engine across the range.

For the 1991 model year, the 90 and 110 ranges were re-christened Defender, and received a heavily-revised 200 TDi turbocharged direct-injection engine, providing a significant improvement in performance over the previous indirect-injection engines. Engine development continued in 1994, when the 300 TDi engine was introduced, to meet revised engine emissions regulations. In November 1998 the TD5 engine was introduced, replacing the 300 TDi engine.

All models are fitted with a five-speed manual gearbox. The drive from the main gearbox is picked up by a transfer gearbox, which provides drive to the front and rear axles, via propeller shafts.

The suspension is of beam axle type, with coil springs and shock absorbers.

A wide range of standard and optional equipment is available within the model ranges, to suit most requirements.

Due to the rugged construction of the vehicle, the number of items requiring regular maintenance (mainly the need for regular lubrication checks) is higher than that found on many smaller vehicles, but the 90/110 and Defender are straightforward vehicles to maintain, and most of the items requiring frequent attention are easily accessible.

Your Land Rover manual

The aim of this manual is to help you get the best value from your vehicle. It can do so in several ways. It can help you decide what work must be done (even should you choose to get it done by a garage). It will also provide information on routine maintenance and servicing, and give a logical course of action and diagnosis when random faults occur. However, it is hoped that you will use the manual by tackling the work yourself.

On simpler jobs it may even be quicker than booking the vehicle into a garage and going there twice, to leave and collect it. Perhaps most important, a lot of money can be saved by avoiding the costs a garage must charge to cover its labour and overheads.

The manual has drawings and descriptions to show the function of the various components so that their layout can be understood. Tasks are described and photographed in a clear step-by-step sequence. The illustrations are numbered by the Section number and paragraph number to which they relate – if there is more than one illustration per paragraph, the sequence is denoted alphabetically.

References to the 'left' and 'right' of the vehicle are in the sense of a person in the driver's seat, facing forwards.

Acknowledgements

Thanks are due to Draper Tools Limited, who provided some of the workshop tools, and to all those people at Sparkford who helped in the production of this manual.

We take great pride in the accuracy of information given in this manual, but car manufacturers make alterations and design changes during the production run of a particular car of which they do not inform us. No liability can be accepted by the authors or publishers for loss, damage or injury caused by any errors in, or omissions from, the information given.

Land Rover 90 Hard-Top

Land Rover Defender

Jump starting

When jump-starting a car using a booster battery, observe the following precautions:

✔ Before connecting the booster battery, make sure that the ignition is switched off.

✔ Ensure that all electrical equipment (lights, heater, wipers, etc) is switched off.

✔ Take note of any special precautions printed on the battery case.

✔ Make sure that the booster battery is the same voltage as the discharged one in the vehicle.

✔ If the battery is being jump-started from the battery in another vehicle, the two vehicles MUST NOT TOUCH each other.

✔ Make sure that the transmission is in neutral (or PARK, in the case of automatic transmission).

Jump starting will get you out of trouble, but you must correct whatever made the battery go flat in the first place. There are three possibilities:

1 *The battery has been drained by repeated attempts to start, or by leaving the lights on.*

2 *The charging system is not working properly (alternator drivebelt slack or broken, alternator wiring fault or alternator itself faulty).*

3 *The battery itself is at fault (electrolyte low, or battery worn out).*

1 Rotate the fastener anti-clockwise and remove the plastic cover from the battery, and connect the red jump lead to the positive terminal. Ensure all electrical consumers are switched off.

2 Connect the other end of the red lead to the positive (+) terminal of the booster battery.

3 Connect the other end of the black jump lead to the battery negative terminal.

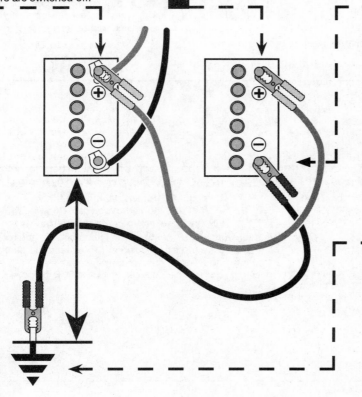

4 Connect one end of the black jump lead to the negative (-) terminal of the booster battery or a bolt or bracket on the engine block.

5 Make sure that the jump leads will not come into contact with the cooling fan drivebelts or other moving parts on the engine.

6 Start the engine, then with the engine running at fast idle speed, disconnect the jump leads strictly in the reverse order of connection, ie, negative (black) lead on the booster battery first. Securely refit the plastic cover over the battery.

Wheel changing

⚠️ *Warning: The handbrake acts on the transmission, not the rear wheels, and may not hold the vehicle stationary when jacking, unless the following procedure is followed precisely. If one front wheel and one rear wheel are raised, no vehicle holding or braking effect is possible using the handbrake, therefore the wheels must always be chocked (using the chock supplied in the tool kit). If the vehicle is coupled to a trailer, disconnect the trailer from the vehicle before commencing jacking. This is to prevent the trailer pulling the vehicle off the jack and causing personal injury.*

1 The jack should always be used on firm, level ground.

2 Apply the handbrake.

3 Switch on the ignition, then engage first gear, and select the Low range in the transfer gearbox.

4 Engage the differential lock, and check that the appropriate warning light on the instrument panel is illuminated. Switch off the ignition, and remove the key.

5 Ensure that any occupants get out of the vehicle before jacking.

6 Using the wheel nut wrench supplied in the tool kit, initially slacken the nuts on the wheel to be removed.

7 Before jacking up a wheel, the chocks supplied with the tool kit should be positioned at the front and rear of the wheel diagonally opposite the wheel to be raised.

8 With the chocks in position, assemble the two-piece operating lever, ensuring that the locking clip engages fully with the corresponding slot.

9 Check that the release valve at the bottom of the jack body is closed (turned fully clockwise).

10 If jacking up a front wheel, slide the jack into position from the front of the vehicle (**not** from the side). Position the jack head so that when raised, it will engage with the front axle casing immediately below the coil spring, between the flange at the end of the axle casing, and the bracket to which the front suspension components are attached (**see illustration**).

11 If raising a rear wheel, slide the jack into position from the rear of the vehicle (**not** from the side). Position the jack head so that when raised, it will engage with the rear axle casing immediately below the coil spring, and as close as possible to the shock absorber mounting bracket.

12 Engage the operating lever with the jack, then pump the lever up and down to raise the vehicle.

13 Once the wheel is clear of the ground, remove the wheel nuts, and lift off the wheel

14 Again using the wheel nut wrench, remove the nuts securing the spare wheel to the carrier, and lift off the wheel.

15 Locate the spare wheel on the studs, then refit the original wheel nuts, and tighten as firmly as possible using the wrench.

16 Lower the vehicle to the ground, and withdraw the jack.

Jack in position under front axle. Check that the release valve (arrowed) is fully closed before jacking

17 Finally tighten the wheel nuts using the wrench, with hand pressure only. Do not use foot pressure or an extension tube on the wheel wrench, as this could overstress the wheel studs, as well as making them difficult to remove subsequently.

18 Fit the removed wheel to the spare wheel carrier, and where applicable, refit the cover.

19 Stow the jack, chocks and tools in their correct locations.

20 On completion, disengage the differential lock and select the High range in the transfer gearbox.

21 At the earliest opportunity, check the that the wheel nuts have been tightened to the specified torque.

Towing

Tow with all four wheels on the ground

1 Turn the ignition key to position II to release the steering lock, and to ensure that the direction indicators and brake lights will work.

2 Select Neutral in the main gearbox, and in the transfer gearbox. Ensure that the differential lock is disengaged.

3 Secure the tow rope/chain (as applicable) to the front towing eye.

4 Release the handbrake.

5 Note that greater-than-usual pedal pressure will be required to operate the brakes, since the vacuum servo unit is only operational with the engine running. Similarly, greater-than-usual steering effort will be required, as the power steering system will not be operational.

Suspended tow by breakdown vehicle

⚠️ *Warning: To prevent damage to the vehicle, the propeller shaft MUST be removed (see Chapter 8), according to which wheels are in contact with the road.*

6 If the front wheels are to be left in contact with the road, the ignition key should be turned to position I to release the steering lock. The steering wheel and/or linkage **must** be secured in the straight-ahead position – **do not** use the steering lock for this purpose.

Identifying leaks

Puddles on the garage floor or drive, or obvious wetness under the bonnet or underneath the car, suggest a leak that needs investigating. It can sometimes be difficult to decide where the leak is coming from, especially if the engine bay is very dirty already. Leaking oil or fluid can also be blown rearwards by the passage of air under the car, giving a false impression of where the problem lies.

 Warning: Most automotive oils and fluids are poisonous. Wash them off skin, and change out of contaminated clothing, without delay.

HAYNES HINT *The smell of a fluid leaking from the car may provide a clue to what's leaking. Some fluids are distinctively coloured.*
It may help to clean the car carefully and to park it over some clean paper overnight as an aid to locating the source of the leak.
Remember that some leaks may only occur while the engine is running.

Sump oil

Engine oil may leak from the drain plug...

Oil from filter

...or from the base of the oil filter.

Gearbox oil

Gearbox oil can leak from the seals at the inboard ends of the driveshafts.

Antifreeze

Leaking antifreeze often leaves a crystalline deposit like this.

Brake fluid

A leak occurring at a wheel is almost certainly brake fluid.

Power steering fluid

Power steering fluid may leak from the pipe connectors on the steering rack.

Introduction

There are some very simple checks which need only take a few minutes to carry out, but which could save you a lot of inconvenience and expense.

These *Weekly checks* require no great skill or special tools, and the small amount of time they take to perform could prove to be very well spent, for example:

☐ Keeping an eye on tyre condition and pressures, will not only help to stop them wearing out prematurely, but could also save your life.

☐ Many breakdowns are caused by electrical problems. Battery-related faults are particularly common, and a quick check on a regular basis will often prevent the majority of these.

☐ If your vehicle develops a brake fluid leak, the first time you might know about it is when your brakes don't work properly. Checking the level regularly will give advance warning of this kind of problem.

☐ If the oil or coolant levels run low, the cost of repairing any engine damage will be far greater than fixing the leak, for example.

Coolant level

⚠️ *Warning: DO NOT attempt to remove the expansion tank pressure cap when the engine is hot, as there is a very great risk of scalding. Do not allow antifreeze to come in contact with your skin, or with the painted surfaces of the vehicle. Rinse off spills immediately with plenty of water. Never leave antifreeze lying around in an open container, or in a puddle on the floor. Children and pets are attracted by its sweet smell, but antifreeze can be fatal if ingested.*

Vehicle care

• With a sealed-type cooling system, adding coolant should not be necessary on a regular basis. If frequent topping-up is required, it is likely there is a leak. Check the radiator, all hoses and joint faces for signs of staining or wetness, and rectify as necessary.

• It is important that antifreeze is used in the cooling system all year round, not just during the winter months. Don't top-up with water alone, as the antifreeze will become too diluted.

1 All vehicles covered by this manual have a pressurised cooling system. An expansion tank is located on the right-hand side of the engine compartment. The expansion tank has a continual flow of coolant passing through it, in order to purge air from the cooling system.
2 The coolant level in the expansion tank should be checked regularly, and the level should always be checked with the engine cold.
3 Wait until the engine is cold, then slowly unscrew the pressure cap on the expansion tank. Allow any remaining pressure to escape, then fully unscrew the cap.
4 With the engine cold, the expansion tank should be approximately half-full, ie, so that

the coolant level is up to the ridge cast into the front edge of the tank. On later models, there may also be an indicator inside the tank **(see illustration)**. On TD5 models the cold level is indicated on the side of the expansion tank **(see illustration)**.
5 If topping-up is necessary, add a mixture of water and antifreeze (see below) through the expansion tank filler neck until the coolant level is correct **(see illustration)**. Refit and tighten the pressure cap.

⚠️ *Warning: 1999 model year-on vehicles must only be filled with antifreeze with OATS (Organic Acid Technology) corrosion inhibitors. DO NOT mix this with any other type of antifreeze.*

6 With a sealed cooling system, the addition of coolant should only be necessary at very infrequent intervals. If frequent topping-up is required, it is likely there is a leak in the system. Check the radiator, all hoses and joint faces for any sign of staining or actual wetness, and rectify as necessary. Coolant leaks usually show up as a white or antifreeze-coloured stain in the area of the leak. If no leaks can

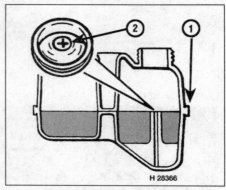

The expansion tank should be approximately half-full, so that the level is up to the ridge (1) on the front of the tank. On later models, a level indicator (2) may also be visible through the tank filler neck

be found, it is advisable to have the pressure cap and the entire system pressure-tested by a dealer or suitably-equipped garage, as this will often show up a small leak not previously visible.

On TD5 models, the coolant level is visible through the expansion tank

Topping-up the cooling system

Engine oil level

The correct oil

Modern engines place great demands on their oil. It is very important that the correct oil for your vehicle is used (see *Lubricants and fluids*).

Vehicle care

• If you have to add oil frequently, you should check whether you have any oil leaks. Place some clean paper under the vehicle overnight, and check for stains in the morning. If there are no leaks, the engine may be burning oil.

• Always maintain the level between the upper and lower dipstick marks. If the level is too low, severe engine damage may occur. Oil seal failure may result if the engine is overfilled by adding too much oil.

1 The engine oil level is checked with a dipstick which extends through a tube and into the sump at the bottom of the engine. The dipstick is located on the left-hand side of the engine on non-TD5 models, and on the right-hand side on TD5 engines **(see illustrations)**.

2 The oil level should be checked with the vehicle standing on level ground. Check the oil level before it is driven, or wait at least 5 minutes after the engine has been switched off.

 HAYNES HiNT *If the oil is checked immediately after driving the vehicle, some of the oil will remain in the upper engine components and oil galleries, resulting in an inaccurate reading on the dipstick.*

3 Withdraw the dipstick from the tube, and wipe all the oil from the end with a clean rag or paper towel. Insert the clean dipstick back into the tube as far as it will go, then withdraw it once more. Check that the oil level is between the lower and upper marks/notches on the dipstick **(see illustration)**. Take the appropriate action as follows, according to the reading on the dipstick.

 Warning: The oil level should never be above the upper mark on the dipstick, as engine damage may be caused.

Non-TD5 engine models

a) If the oil level is between the N mark and the H mark, do not add any oil.

b) If the oil level is between the L and the N marks, add 1.0 litre of the correct type and grade of oil.

c) If the oil level is below the L mark, add 1.0 litre of oil, then wait for five minutes, and recheck the level on the dipstick. Add further oil as necessary to bring the level between the N and H marks, but do not overfill.

TD5 engine models

a) If the oil level is nearer the upper mark than the lower mark take no action.

b) If the oil level is nearer, or below, the lower mark, add oil to bring the level to the upper mark.

c) The amount of oil needed to raise the level from the lower mark to the upper mark is 1.0 litre.

4 To top-up the oil level, remove the oil filler cap from the valve cover, and add fresh oil as required **(see illustrations)**.

5 If the level is allowed to fall below the lower mark/notch, oil starvation may result, which could lead to severe engine damage. If the engine is overfilled by adding too much oil, this may result in oil leaks or oil seal failures.

6 An oil can spout or funnel may help to reduce spillage when adding oil to the engine. Always use the correct grade and type of oil, as shown in *Lubricants and fluids*.

Engine oil level dipstick location (arrowed) – 19J engine

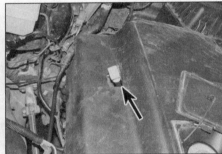

Engine oil level dipstick location (arrowed) – TD5 engine

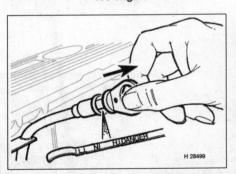

Dipstick markings – 200 TDi engine

Topping-up the engine oil level – non-TD5 engines

On TD5 engines, lift the flap, then undo the filler cap

Tyres

1 The original tyres on this vehicle have tread wear safety bands, which will appear when the tread depth reaches approximately 1.6 mm. Tread wear can be monitored with a simple, inexpensive device known as a tread depth indicator gauge **(see illustration)**.

2 Wheels and tyres should give no real problems in use, provided that a close eye is kept on them with regard to excessive wear or damage. To this end, the following points should be noted.

3 Ensure that tyre pressures are checked regularly, and maintained correctly. Checking should be carried out with the tyres cold, **not** immediately after the vehicle has been in use **(see illustration)**. If the pressures are checked with the tyres hot, an apparently-high reading will be obtained, owing to heat expansion. **Under no circumstances** should an attempt be made to reduce the pressures to the quoted cold reading in this instance, or effective underinflation will result.

4 Note any abnormal tread wear **(see illustration)**. Tread pattern irregularities such as feathering, flat spots, and more wear on one side than the other, are indications of front wheel alignment and/or balance problems. If any of these conditions are noted, they should be rectified as soon as possible.

5 Underinflation will cause overheating of the tyre owing to excessive flexing of the casing, and the tread will not sit correctly on the road surface. This will cause a consequent loss of adhesion and excessive wear, not to mention the danger of sudden tyre failure due to heat build-up.

6 Overinflation will cause rapid wear of the centre part of the tyre tread, coupled with reduced adhesion, harsher ride, and the danger of shock damage occurring in the tyre casing.

7 Regularly check the tyres for damage in the form of cuts or bulges, especially in the sidewalls. Remove any nails or stones embedded in the tread, before they penetrate the tyre to cause deflation. If removal of a nail reveals that the tyre has been punctured, refit the nail so that its point of penetration is marked. Then immediately change the wheel, and have the tyre repaired by a tyre dealer. Do not drive on a tyre in such a condition. If in any doubt as to the possible consequences of any damage found, consult your local tyre dealer for advice.

8 Periodically remove the wheels, and clean any dirt or mud from the inside and outside surfaces. Examine the wheel rims for signs of rusting, corrosion or other damage. Light alloy wheels are easily damaged by 'kerbing' whilst parking, and similarly, steel wheels may become dented or buckled. Renewal of the wheel is very often the only course of remedial action possible.

9 The balance of each wheel and tyre assembly should be maintained to avoid excessive wear, not only to the tyres but also to the steering and suspension components. Wheel imbalance is normally signified by vibration through the vehicle's bodyshell, although in many cases it is particularly noticeable through the steering wheel.

Conversely, it should be noted that wear or damage in suspension or steering components may cause excessive tyre wear. Out-of-round or out-of-true tyres, damaged wheels and wheel bearing wear/ maladjustment also fall into this category. Balancing will not usually cure vibration caused by such wear.

10 Wheel balancing may be carried out with the wheel either on or off the vehicle. If balanced on the vehicle, ensure that the wheel-to-hub relationship is marked in some way prior to subsequent wheel removal, so that it may be refitted in its original position.

11 General tyre wear is influenced to a large degree by driving style – harsh braking and acceleration, or fast cornering, will all produce more rapid tyre wear. Interchanging of tyres may result in more even wear; however, if this is completely effective, a complete set of tyres will have to be renewed at once, which may prove financially restrictive for many owners.

12 Front tyres may wear unevenly as a result of wheel misalignment. The front wheels should always be correctly aligned according to the settings specified by the vehicle manufacturer (see Chapter 11).

13 Legal restrictions apply to many aspects of tyre fitting and usage, and in the UK, this information is contained in the Motor Vehicle Construction and Use Regulations. It is suggested that a copy of these regulations is obtained from your local police, if in doubt as to current legal requirements with regard to tyre type and condition, minimum tread depth, etc.

Measuring the tyre tread depth

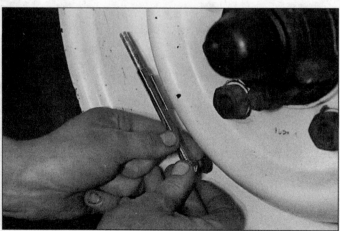

Checking a tyre pressure

Tyre Tread Wear Patterns

Shoulder Wear

**Underinflation
(wear on both sides)**
Check and adjust pressures

**Incorrect wheel camber
(wear on one side)**
*Repair or renew suspension
parts*

Hard cornering
Reduce speed!

Centre Wear

Overinflation
Check and adjust pressures

*If you sometimes have to inflate
your car's tyres to the higher
pressures specified for maximum
load or sustained high speed,
don't forget to reduce the
pressures to normal afterwards.*

Toe Wear

Incorrect toe setting
Adjust front wheel alignment

Note: The feathered edge of
the tread which characterises
toe wear is best checked by
feel.

Uneven Wear

Incorrect camber or castor
*Repair or renew suspension
parts*

Malfunctioning suspension
*Repair or renew suspension
parts*

Unbalanced wheel
Balance tyres

Out-of-round brake disc/drum
Machine or renew

Brake fluid level

⚠️ *Warning: Hydraulic fluid is
poisonous; wash off immediately
and thoroughly in the case of
skin contact, and seek immediate medical
advice if any fluid is swallowed, or gets into
the eyes. Certain types of hydraulic fluid are
inflammable, and may ignite when allowed
into contact with hot components. When
servicing any hydraulic system, it is safest
to assume that the fluid IS inflammable,
and to take precautions against the risk
of fire as though it is petrol that is being
handled. Finally, it is hygroscopic (it
absorbs moisture from the air) – old fluid
may be contaminated, and unfit for further
use. When topping-up or renewing the
fluid, always use the recommended type
(see 'Lubricants and fluids'), and ensure
that it comes from a freshly-opened,
previously-sealed container.*

*• If a leak is suspected, the vehicle should
not be driven until the braking system has
been checked. Never take any risks where
brakes are concerned.*

*• Hydraulic fluid is an effective paint
stripper, and will attack plastics; if any is
spilt, it should be washed off immediately
using copious quantities of fresh water.*

Safety first!

• If the reservoir requires repeated topping-up, this is an indication of a fluid leak
somewhere in the brake system, which should
be investigated immediately.

 HAYNES HiNT *The fluid level in the reservoir
will drop slightly as the brake
pads wear down, but the
fluid level must never be
allowed to drop below the MIN mark.*

1 The brake fluid reservoir is mounted on top
of the brake master cylinder, which is attached
to the front of the vacuum servo unit on the
engine compartment bulkhead.
2 The maximum and minimum marks are
indicated on the side of the reservoir, and
the fluid level should be maintained between
these marks at all times.
3 The brake fluid inside the reservoir is readily
visible. With the vehicle on level ground, the
level should be above the MIN (Danger) mark,
and preferably on or near the MAX mark. Note
that wear of the brake pads causes the level
of the brake fluid to gradually fall, so that
when the brake pads are renewed, the original
level of the fluid is restored. It is not therefore
necessary to top-up the level to compensate
for this minimal drop, but the level must never
be allowed to fall below the minimum mark.
4 If topping-up is necessary, first wipe the
area around the filler cap with a clean rag
before removing the cap. When adding fluid,
pour it carefully into the reservoir, to avoid
spilling it on surrounding painted surfaces. Be
sure to use only the specified brake hydraulic
fluid, since mixing different types of fluid can
cause damage to the system. See *Lubricants
and fluids*.
5 When adding fluid, it is a good idea to
inspect the reservoir for contamination. The
system should be drained and refilled if
deposits, dirt particles or contamination are
seen in the fluid.
6 After filling the reservoir to the proper level,
make sure that the cap is refitted securely, to
avoid leaks and the entry of foreign matter.

Washer fluid level

1 The windscreen/tailgate/headlight washer fluid reservoir is located at the left-hand front corner of the engine compartment. On models with headlight washers, an additional reservoir may also be fitted in the left-hand rear corner of the engine compartment.
Caution: On no account use coolant antifreeze in the washer system – this could discolour or damage paintwork

2 Check that the fluid level is within approximately 25.0 mm of the bottom of the filler neck, and top-up if necessary. When topping-up the reservoir, a screenwash additive should be added in the quantities recommended on the bottle.

Wiper blades

1 Check the condition of the wiper blades. If they are cracked, or show any signs of deterioration, or if they fail to clean the glass effectively, renew the blades.

 HAYNES HiNT *Ideally, the wiper blades should be renewed annually as a matter of course.*

2 To remove a wiper blade, pull the arm away from the glass until it locks. Swivel the blade through 90°, then squeeze the locking clip, and detach the blade from the arm. When fitting the new blade, make sure that the blade locks securely into the arm, and that the blade is orientated correctly.

Battery

Caution: Before carrying out any work on the vehicle battery, read through the precautions given in 'Safety first!' at the beginning of this manual.

1 The battery is located beneath a cover panel under the left-hand front seat (non-TD5 models) or driver's seat (TD5 models).
2 For access to the battery, remove the seat cushion (see Chapter 12), then release the retaining clip and lift out the cover panel.
3 The exterior of the battery should be inspected for damage such as a cracked case or cover.
4 Check the tightness of the battery cable clamp nuts to ensure good electrical connections, and check the entire length of each cable for cracks and frayed conductors.
5 If corrosion (visible as white, fluffy deposits) is evident, remove the cables from the battery terminals, clean them with a small wire brush, then refit them. Corrosion can be kept to a minimum by applying a thin layer of petroleum jelly to the clamps and terminals after they have been reconnected.
6 Make sure that the battery tray is in good

condition, and that the retaining clamp is tight.
7 Corrosion on the tray, retaining clamp and the battery itself can be removed with a solution of water and baking soda. Thoroughly rinse all cleaned areas with plain water. Dry the battery and its surroundings with rags or tissues, which should then be discarded.
8 Any metal parts damaged by corrosion should be covered with a zinc-based primer, then painted.
9 A 'low-maintenance' battery is normally fitted as standard equipment on non-TD5 models, and the electrolyte level should be checked periodically as follows.
10 Pull out the cell covers from the top of the battery **(see illustration)**.
11 Check that the level of electrolyte is no lower than 1.0 mm above the top of the cell plates.
12 If necessary, top-up the level to a maximum of 3.0 mm above the cell plates, using only distilled or demineralised water.
13 Refit the cell covers.
14 Further information on the battery,

charging and jump starting can be found in Chapter 5 and this Chapter.
15 On TD5 models, a 'maintenance-free' battery is fitted, so topping-up is not possible. On the top of the battery is a charge indicator. When the indicator shows green the battery is in a good state of charge, if the indicator is dark (or black) the battery requires charging, and if the indicator is clear, the battery requires renewing.

Battery cell cover (arrowed)

Electrical system

1 Check the operation of all the electrical equipment, ie, lights, direction indicators, horn, etc. Refer to the appropriate Sections of Chapter 13 for details if any of the circuits are found to be inoperative.

 HAYNES HiNT *If you need to check your brake lights and indicators unaided, back up to a wall or garage door and operate the lights. The reflected light should show if they are working properly.*

2 Note that stop-light switch adjustment is described in Chapter 10.
3 Visually check all accessible wiring connectors, harnesses and retaining clips for security, and for signs of chafing or damage. Rectify any faults found.

Lubricants and fluids

Engine

Non-TD5 models . . . . Multigrade engine oil, viscosity SAE 5W/30 to 25W/50, to RES.22. OL.PD-2, CCMC PD-2 or better

TD5 models . . . . Multigrade engine oil, viscosity SAE 5W/40 or 5W50, to ACEA A1, B1

Cooling system

Models up to 1999 MY . . . . Ethylene glycol-based antifreeze

Models 1999 MY-on . . . . Ethylene glycol-based antifreeze with OAT (Organic Acid Technology) corrosion inhibitors

Manual gearbox

Non-TD5 models . . . . Automatic transmission fluid (ATF) to M2C33

TD5 models . . . . Texaco MTF94

Transfer gearbox

Non-TD5 models . . . . Hypoid gear oil, viscosity SAE 80EP or SAE 90EP to API GL4, MIL-L-2105, or better

TD5 models . . . . Castrol Syntrax 75W/90

Front and rear axles . . . . Hypoid gear oil, viscosity SAE 80EP or SAE 90EP to API GL4, MIL-L-2105, or better

Swivel pin housings

Non-TD5 models . . . . Hypoid gear oil, viscosity SAE 80EP or SAE 90EP to API GL4, MIL-L-2105, or better

TD5 models . . . . Texaco EP00 grease

Manual steering box . . . . Hypoid gear oil, viscosity SAE 80EP or SAE 90EP to API GL4, MIL-L-2105, or better

Propeller shaft joints . . . . Multi-purpose lithium-based grease to NLGI-2

Brake fluid reservoir . . . . Hydraulic fluid DOT 4

Clutch fluid reservoir . . . . Hydraulic fluid DOT 4

Power steering fluid reservoir . . . . Dexron IID type automatic transmission fluid (ATF)

Fuel . . . . Commercial Diesel fuel for road vehicles (DERV)

Tyre pressures (tyres cold)

Note: *Pressures apply only to original-equipment tyres, and may vary if any other make of tyre is fitted; check with the tyre manufacturer or supplier for correct pressures if necessary.*

	Front	Rear
90 models:		
Normal use:		
6.00 x 16 tyres	2.4 bar (35 psi)	3.3 bar (48 psi)
7.50 x 16 and 205R16 tyres	1.9 bar (28 psi)	2.4 bar (35 psi)
7.50R16 tyres	1.9 bar (28 psi)	2.8 bar (41 psi)
205/80R16 radial tyres	1.9 bar (28 psi)	2.6 bar (38 psi)
Off-road use (all tyres)*		
Unladen	1.1 bar (16 psi)	1.1 bar (16 psi)
Laden	1.1 bar (16 psi)	1.6 bar (23 psi)
110 models:		
Normal use:		
7.50 x 16 tyres	1.9 bar (28 psi)	2.9 bar (42 psi)
7.50R16 tyres	1.9 bar (28 psi)	3.3 bar (48 psi)
Off-road use (all tyres)*		
Unladen	1.1 bar (16 psi)	1.1 bar (16 psi)
Laden	1.1 bar (16 psi)	1.8 bar (26 psi)
130 models:		
Normal use:		
7.50R16 radial tyres	3.0 bar (44 psi)	4.5 bar (65 psi)

* Vehicle speed must not exceed 25 mph whilst off-road pressures are being used

Chapter 1
Routine maintenance and servicing

Contents

Section number

ABS wheel speed sensor harness check......................39
Accelerator mechanism checking and lubrication..............33
Air cleaner element renewal.................................29
Alarm handset battery renewal...............................49
Auxiliary drivebelt checking and renewal....................14
Axle breather check...23
Axle oil level check..17
Axle oil renewal..52
Brake drum, shoe and wheel cylinder check...................8
Brake fluid renewal...50
Brake pad, disc and caliper check...........................10
Brake vacuum servo air filter renewal.......................60
Brake vacuum servo hose check...............................31
Braking system seal, vacuum servo filter and hose renewal...61
Clutch fluid level check....................................5
Coolant renewal...58
Cooling system and heater system hose check.................20
Crankcase breather hose check...............................13
Drum brake adjustment check.................................9
Engine breather filter cleaning.............................30
Engine oil and filter renewal (non-TD5 engines).............3
Engine oil centrifuge rotor renewal (TD5 engines)...........26
Engine oil filter cartridge renewal (TD5 engines)...........57
Engine oil renewal (TD5 engines)............................4
Exhaust system check..38
Flywheel housing and timing belt housing draining...........41
Front wheel alignment check.................................45
Fuel filter element renewal.................................28
Fuel injector leak check....................................54
Fuel injector spray pattern check (10J, 12J and 19J engines)...55
Fuel sedimenter cleaning....................................25
Fuel tank security check....................................42

Section number

Glow plug wiring check......................................32
Handbrake adjustment check..................................11
Headlight and auxiliary light adjustment check..............44
Hinge and lock check and lubrication........................12
Idle speed checking and adjustment..........................7
Intercooler element cleaning................................62
Introduction..1
Jack and tools security check...............................36
Main gearbox oil level check................................15
Main gearbox oil renewal....................................48
Power steering fluid level check............................6
Propeller shaft joint lubrication...........................37
Propeller shaft securing bolt check.........................39
Radiator and intercooler check..............................34
Rear suspension upper link balljoint lubrication............19
Regular maintenance...2
Road test...24
Seat belt check...47
Shock absorber check..59
Spare wheel check...46
Steering and suspension component check.....................22
Steering box oil level and steering gear backlash check.....35
Swivel pin housing oil level check..........................18
Swivel pin housing oil renewal..............................53
Timing belt renewal...63
Towing bracket check..43
Transfer gearbox oil level check............................16
Transfer gearbox oil renewal................................51
Turbocharger boost pressure check...........................56
Underbody component, pipe, hose and wiring check............21
Valve clearances checking and adjustment....................27

Degrees of difficulty

Easy, suitable for novice with little experience

Fairly easy, suitable for beginner with some experience

Fairly difficult, suitable for competent DIY mechanic

Difficult, suitable for experienced DIY mechanic

Very difficult, suitable for expert DIY or professional

Capacities

Engine oil:
  Sump capacity (drain and refill, excluding oil filter):
    All except 300 TDi and TD5 engines .... 6.00 litres
    300 TDi engine .... 5.80 litres
    TD5 engine .... 7.20 litres
  Oil filter capacity.. 0.85 litre
Cooling system:
  10J and 12J engines .... 10.80 litres
  19J, 200 TDi and 300 TDi engines .... 11.10 litres
  TD5 engine .... 13.00 litres
Fuel tank:
  Rear-mounted tank....................................... 79.5 litres
  Side-mounted tank:
    All models except Station Wagon......................... 68.2 litres
    Station Wagon models .... 45.5 litres
  TD5 models:
    90 models... 60.0 litres
    110/130 models .... 75.0 litres
Main gearbox:
  Non-TD5 models .... 2.67 litres
  TD5 models.. 2.38 litres
Transfer gearbox:
  LT230R type gearbox .... 2.80 litres
  LT230T type gearbox:
    Up to suffix D .... 2.30 litres
    From suffix E... 2.80 litres
Front axle .... 1.70 litres
Rear axle:
  90 models.. 1.70 litre
  110/130 models .... 2.26 litres
Steering box:
  Manual steering .... 0.43 litre
  Power steering box and fluid reservoir..................... 3.40 litres
Swivel pin housing oil (each) .... 0.35 litre

Engine

Valve clearances (inlet and exhaust):
  10J, 12J and 19J engines................................. 0.25 mm
  200 TDi and 300 TDi engines .... 0.20 mm
  TD5 engines .... Hydraulic adjustment

Cooling system

Antifreeze mixture:
  Minimum strength.. 25% antifreeze, 75% water
  Maximum strength .... 60% antifreeze, 40% water
  Protection to -36°C....................................... 50% antifreeze, 50% water

Fuel system

Turbocharger maximum boost pressure:
  19J engine .... 0.64 bar
  200 TDi engine .... 0.78 bar
  300 TDi engine .... 0.83 to 1.04 bars

Brakes

Minimum brake disc pad thickness .... 3.0 mm
Minimum brake shoe lining thickness .... 1.5 mm (typical value)

Torque wrench settings

	Nm	lbf ft
Main gearbox oil drain plug	51	38
Main gearbox oil filler/level plug	30	22
Propeller shaft and rubber coupling securing bolts	47	35
Roadwheel nuts:		
Steel wheels	108	80
Alloy wheels	130	96
Heavy duty wheel	170	125
Sump drain plug:		
10J, 12J, 19J and 300 TDi engines	35	26
200 TDi engines	45	33
TD5 engines	23	17
Transfer gearbox oil drain plug	30	22
Transfer gearbox oil filler/level plug	25	18

The maintenance intervals in this manual are provided with the assumption that you, not the dealer, will be carrying out the work. These are the minimum maintenance intervals recommended by the manufacturers for vehicles driven daily under normal operating conditions. If you wish to keep your vehicle in peak condition at all times, you may wish to perform some of these procedures more often. This applies especially if the vehicle is used in particularly hot or dusty climates, or if the vehicle is regularly used for towing. We encourage frequent maintenance because it enhances the efficiency, performance and resale value of your vehicle.

When the vehicle is new, it should be serviced by a dealer service department (or other workshop recognised by the vehicle manufacturer as providing the same standard of service) in order to preserve the warranty. The vehicle manufacturer may reject warranty claims if you are unable to prove that servicing has been carried out as and when specified, using only original equipment parts or parts certified to be of equivalent quality.

Non-TD5 engine model schedule

Every 250 miles or weekly
- [ ] Refer to Weekly checks

Every 6000 miles
- [ ] Renew the engine oil and filter (Section 3)
- [ ] Check the clutch fluid level (Section 5)
- [ ] Check the power steering fluid level (Section 6)
- [ ] Check and if necessary adjust the engine idle speed (Section 7)
- [ ] Check the condition of the brake drums and shoes (where applicable) (Section 8)
- [ ] Check the brake wheel cylinders for leaks (where applicable) (Section 8)
- [ ] Check the drum brake adjustment (where applicable) (Section 9)
- [ ] Check the condition of the brake pads and discs (where applicable) (Section 10)
- [ ] Check the brake calipers for leaks (where applicable) (Section 10)
- [ ] Check the operation of the handbrake (Section 11)
- [ ] Check the handbrake adjustment (Section 11)
- [ ] Lubricate the handbrake linkage (Section 11)
- [ ] Check the operation of all door, bonnet and tailgate locks (Section 12)

Every 6000 miles (continued)
- [ ] Lubricate all hinges and locks (including the fuel filler) (Section 12)
- [ ] Check the condition of the crankcase breather system hoses (Section 13)
- [ ] Check the condition of the auxiliary drivebelt(s) and adjust if necessary (Section 14)
- [ ] Check the main gearbox oil level (Section 15)
- [ ] Check the transfer gearbox oil level – models up to 1995 (Section 16)
- [ ] Check the front and rear axle oil levels – models up to 1995 (Section 17)
- [ ] Check the swivel pin housing oil level – models up to 1995 (Section 18)
- [ ] Lubricate the rear suspension upper link balljoint (where applicable) (Section 19)
- [ ] Check the cooling and heater system hoses for security and leaks (Section 20)
- [ ] Check all underbody brake, fuel and clutch pipes and hoses for leaks and condition (Section 21)
- [ ] Check the steering and suspension components, including all hydraulic pipes and hoses for leaks and condition (Section 22)
- [ ] Check the front and rear axle breathers for obstructions (Section 23)
- [ ] Carry out a road test (Section 24)

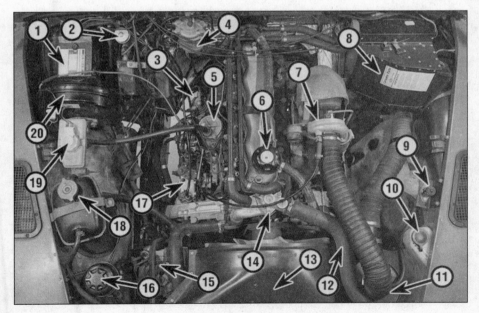

Underbonnet view of a 19J engine model

1 VIN plate
2 Clutch fluid reservoir
3 Fuel lift pump
4 Fuel filter
5 Brake vacuum pump
6 Engine oil filler cap
7 Turbocharger
8 Heater
9 Air filter element condition indicator
10 Washer fluid reservoir
11 Air cleaner
12 Radiator top hose
13 Cooling fan cowl
14 Thermostat housing
15 Steering box
16 Power steering fluid reservoir
17 Fuel injection pump
18 Coolant expansion tank
19 Brake fluid reservoir
20 Brake vacuum servo

Non-TD5 engine model schedule (continued)

Every 12 000 miles

In addition to all the items listed above, carry out the following:
- ☐ Check the transfer gearbox oil level – models from 1995 (Section 16)
- ☐ Check the front and rear axle oil levels – models from 1995 (Section 17)
- ☐ Check the swivel pin housing oil level – models from 1995 (Section 18)
- ☐ Clean the fuel sedimenter (Section 25)
- ☐ Check and if necessary adjust the valve clearances (Section 27)
- ☐ Renew the fuel filter element (Section 28)
- ☐ Renew the air cleaner element (Section 29)
- ☐ Check the condition of the air cleaner dump valve – 200 TDi engine models (Section 29)
- ☐ Clean the engine breather filter (Section 30)
- ☐ Check the brake vacuum servo hose for security (Section 31)
- ☐ Check the condition and security of the glow plug wiring (Section 32)
- ☐ Check the operation of the accelerator mechanism, and lubricate the moving components (Section 33)
- ☐ Check the radiator and intercooler (where applicable) for obstructions, and clean if necessary (Section 34)
- ☐ Check the steering box oil level, and top-up if necessary (manual steering box) – models up to 1995 (Section 35)
- ☐ Check and if necessary adjust the steering gear backlash – models up to 1995 (Section 35)
- ☐ Check the security of the jack and tools (Section 36)
- ☐ Lubricate the propeller shaft universal joints and sliding joints (Section 37)
- ☐ Check the exhaust system for security and condition (Section 38)
- ☐ Check the tightness of the propeller shaft coupling bolts (Section 39)
- ☐ Drain the flywheel housing and timing belt housing (where applicable) (Section 41)
- ☐ Check the security of the fuel tank (Section 42)
- ☐ Check the security of the towing bracket (Section 43)
- ☐ Check and if necessary adjust the headlight and auxiliary light adjustment (Section 44)
- ☐ Check the front wheel alignment (Section 45)
- ☐ Check the condition of the spare wheel (Section 46)
- ☐ Check the condition and operation of all seat belts (Section 47)
- ☐ Renew the main gearbox oil (Section 48)

Every 18 000 miles or 18 months, whichever comes first

In addition to the operations listed under the 6000 mile heading, carry out the following:
- ☐ Renew the brake fluid (Section 50)

Every 24 000 miles

In addition to all the items listed above, carry out the following:
- ☐ Renew the transfer gearbox oil (Section 51)
- ☐ Renew the front and rear axle oil (Section 52)
- ☐ Renew the swivel pin housing oil (Section 53)
- ☐ Check the fuel injectors for leaks (Section 54)
- ☐ Check the fuel injector spray pattern (10J, 12J and 19J engines) (Section 55)
- ☐ Check the turbocharger boost pressure (Section 56)

Every 2 years
- ☐ Renew the coolant (Section 58)

Every 36 000 miles

In addition to all the items listed above, carry out the following:
- ☐ Check the steering box oil level, and top-up if necessary (manual steering box) – models from 1995 (Section 35)
- ☐ Check and if necessary adjust the steering gear backlash – models from 1995 (Section 35)
- ☐ Remove all shock absorbers, and check their operation (Section 59)
- ☐ Renew the brake vacuum servo air filter (Section 60)

Every 36 000 miles or 3 years, whichever comes first
- ☐ Renew all braking system hydraulic fluid seals, the vacuum servo filter, and all flexible brake fluid hoses (Section 61)

Every 48 000 miles or 18 months, whichever comes first

In addition to all the items listed above, carry out the following:
- ☐ Clean the intercooler element (where applicable) (Section 62)

Every 60 000 miles or every 5 years, whichever comes first
- ☐ Renew the timing belt (Section 63)

Note: *This is the manufacturer's timing belt renewal interval. We recommend that the timing belt is renewed at the 36 000 mile interval, especially on those models which are subjected to use in adverse conditions. The actual belt renewal interval is very much up to the individual owner, but bear in mind that severe engine damage will result if the belt breaks.*

TD5 engine model schedule

Every 250 miles or weekly
- ☐ Refer to *Weekly checks*

Every 6000 miles
- ☐ Renew the engine oil (Section 4)
- ☐ Check the clutch fluid level (Section 5)
- ☐ Check the power steering fluid level (Section 6)
- ☐ Check the condition of the brake pads and discs (Section 10)
- ☐ Check the brake calipers for leaks (where applicable) (Section 10)
- ☐ Check the operation of the handbrake (Section 11)
- ☐ Check the handbrake adjustment (Section 11)
- ☐ Lubricate the handbrake linkage (Section 11)
- ☐ Check the operation of all door, bonnet and tailgate locks (Section 12)
- ☐ Lubricate all hinges and locks (including the fuel filler) (Section 12)
- ☐ Check the condition of the crankcase breather system hoses (Section 13)
- ☐ Check the cooling and heater system hoses for security and leaks (Section 20)
- ☐ Check all underbody brake, fuel and clutch pipes and hoses for leaks and condition (Section 21)
- ☐ Check the steering and suspension components, including all hydraulic pipes and hoses for leaks and condition (Section 22)
- ☐ Carry out a road test (Section 24)

Every 12 000 miles
In addition to all the items listed above, carry out the following:
- ☐ Check the condition of the auxiliary drivebelt (Section 14)
- ☐ Check the transfer gearbox oil level (Section 16)
- ☐ Check the front and rear axle oil levels (Section 17)
- ☐ Drain the fuel sedimenter (Section 25)
- ☐ Renew the oil centrifuge rotor (Section 26)
- ☐ Check the radiator and intercooler for obstructions, and clean if necessary (Section 34)
- ☐ Lubricate the propeller shaft universal joints and sliding joints (Section 37)
- ☐ Check the exhaust system for security and condition (Section 38)

Every 12 000 miles (continued)
- ☐ Check the tightness of the propeller shaft coupling bolts (Section 39)
- ☐ Check ABS wheel speed sensor harness (Section 40)
- ☐ Check the security of the towing bracket (Section 43)
- ☐ Check and if necessary adjust the headlight and auxiliary light adjustment (Section 44)
- ☐ Check the condition and operation of all seat belts (Section 47)

Every 24 000 miles
In addition to all the items listed above, carry out the following:
- ☐ Renew the fuel filter element (Section 28)
- ☐ Renew the air cleaner element (Section 29)
- ☐ Renew the main gearbox oil (Section 48)
- ☐ Renew the alarm handset batteries (Section 49)
- ☐ Renew the brake fluid (Section 50)
- ☐ Renew the transfer gearbox oil (Section 51)
- ☐ Renew the front and rear axle oil (Section 52)

Every 36 000 miles
In addition to all the items listed above, carry out the following:
- ☐ Check and if necessary adjust the steering gear backlash (Section 35)
- ☐ Renew the oil filter cartridge (Section 57)
- ☐ Renew the coolant (Section 58)

Every 48 000 miles or 48 months, whichever comes first
In addition to all the items listed above, carry out the following:
- ☐ Renew all braking system hydraulic fluid seals, the vacuum servo filter, and all flexible brake fluid hoses (Section 61)
- ☐ Clean the intercooler element (Section 62)

Every 96 000 miles
- ☐ Renew the auxiliary drivebelt (Section 14)

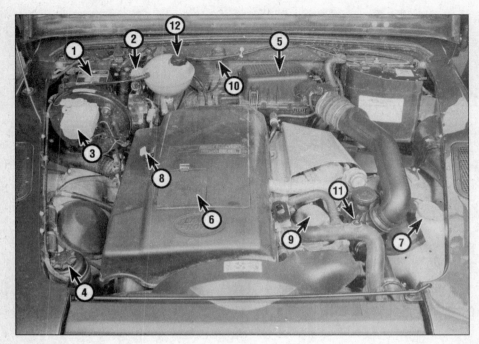

Underbonnet view of a TD5 engine model

1 VIN plate
2 Clutch fluid reservoir
3 Brake fluid reservoir
4 Power steering fluid reservoir
5 Air filter housing
6 Engine oil filler flap
7 Screenwash reservoir
8 Engine oil level dipstick
9 Centrifugal oil filter housing
10 Fuel cut-off switch
11 Radiator top hose bleed screw
12 Coolant expansion tank

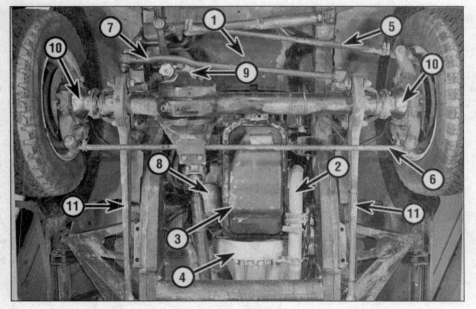

Front underbody view

1 Cooling fan cowl
2 Exhaust
3 Sump
4 Flywheel housing
5 Drag link
6 Track rod
7 Panhard rod
8 Oil filter
9 Steering box
10 Swivel pin housing
11 Radius arm

Centre underbody view

1 *Chassis crossmember*
2 *Radius arm*
3 *Exhaust*
4 *Handbrake drum*
5 *Transfer gearbox*
6 *Rear propeller shaft*
7 *Main gearbox casing*

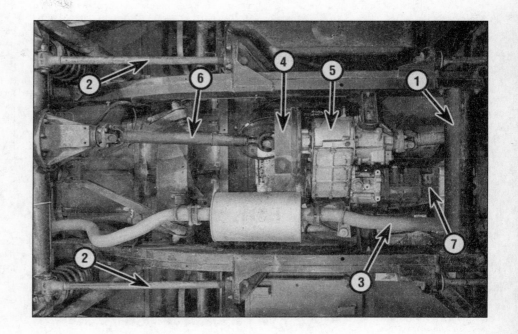

Rear underbody view

1 *Exhaust*
2 *Lower link*
3 *Shock absorber*
4 *Rear axle*
5 *Upper link*
6 *Differential unit*

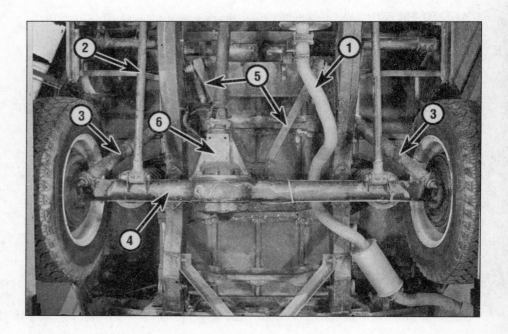

1 Introduction

1 This Chapter is designed to help the home mechanic maintain his/her vehicle for safety, economy, long life and peak performance.

2 The Chapter contains a master maintenance schedule, followed by Sections dealing specifically with each task on the schedule. Visual checks, adjustments, component renewal and other helpful items are included. Refer to the accompanying illustrations of the engine compartment and the underside of the vehicle for the locations of the various components.

3 Servicing of your vehicle in accordance with the mileage/time maintenance schedule and the following Sections will provide a planned maintenance programme, which should result in a long and reliable service life. This is a comprehensive plan, so maintaining some items but not others at the specified service intervals, will not produce the same results.

4 As you service your vehicle, you will discover that many of the procedures can – and should – be grouped together, because of the particular procedure being performed, or because of the close proximity of two otherwise-unrelated components to one another. For example, if the vehicle is raised for any reason, the exhaust can be inspected at the same time as the suspension and steering components.

5 The first step in this maintenance programme is to prepare yourself before the actual work begins. Read through all the Sections relevant to the work to be carried out, then make a list and gather together all the parts and tools required. If a problem is encountered, seek advice from a parts specialist, or a dealer service department.

2 Regular maintenance

1 If, from the time the vehicle is new, the routine maintenance schedule is followed closely, and frequent checks are made of fluid levels and high-wear items, as suggested throughout this manual, the engine will be kept in relatively good running condition, and the need for additional work will be minimised.

2 It is possible that there will be times when the engine is running poorly, due to the lack of regular maintenance. This is even more likely if a used vehicle, which has not received regular and frequent maintenance checks, is purchased. In such cases, additional work may need to be carried out, outside of the regular maintenance intervals.

3 If engine wear is suspected, a compression or leakdown test (Chapter 2A or 2B) will provide valuable information regarding the overall performance of the main internal

components. Such a test can be used as a basis to decide on the extent of the work to be carried out. If for example a compression or leakdown test indicates serious internal engine wear, conventional maintenance as described in this Chapter will not greatly improve the performance of the engine, and may prove a waste of time and money, unless extensive overhaul work (Chapter 2C) is carried out first.

4 The following series of operations are those most often required to improve the performance of a generally poor-running engine:

a) Clean, inspect and test the battery ('Weekly checks').

b) Check the levels of all the engine-related fluids ('Weekly checks').

c) Check the condition and tension of the alternator drivebelt (Section 14).

d) Check the fuel sedimenter – drain off any water, and renew the filter if necessary (Section 25).

e) Check the condition of the air cleaner element, and renew if necessary (Section 29).

f) Check the condition of all hoses, and check for fluid leaks.

g) Check and if necessary adjust the idle speed (where possible) (Chapter 4A).

3 Engine oil and filter renewal (non-TD5 engines)

Every 6000 miles

> **HAYNES HINT** *Frequent oil and filter changes are the most important preventative maintenance procedures that can be undertaken by the DIY owner. As engine oil ages, it becomes diluted and contaminated, which leads to premature engine wear.*

1 Before starting this procedure, gather together all the necessary tools and materials. Also make sure that you have plenty of clean rags and newspapers handy, to mop-up any spills. Ideally, the engine oil should be warm, as it will drain better, and more built-up sludge

will be removed with it. Take care, however, not to touch the exhaust or any other hot parts of the engine when working under the vehicle. To avoid any possibility of scalding, and to protect yourself from possible skin irritants and other harmful contaminants in used engine oils, it is advisable to wear rubber gloves when carrying out this work.

2 Access to the underside of the vehicle will be greatly improved if it can be raised on a lift, driven onto ramps, or jacked up and supported on axle stands (see *Jacking and vehicle support*). Whichever method is chosen, make sure that the vehicle remains as level as possible, to enable the oil to drain fully.

3 Remove the oil filler cap from the valve cover, then position a suitable container beneath the sump.

4 Clean the drain plug and the area around it, then slacken it using a suitable socket or spanner **(see illustration)**. If possible, try to keep the plug pressed into the sump while unscrewing it by hand the last couple of turns. As the plug releases from the threads, move it away sharply, so that the stream of oil issuing from the sump runs into the container, not up your sleeve!

5 Allow some time for the old oil to drain, noting that it may be necessary to reposition the container as the oil flow slows to a trickle.

6 After all the oil has drained, wipe off the drain plug with a clean rag, and check the condition of the copper sealing washer. Renew the washer if necessary. Clean the area around the drain plug opening, then refit and tighten the plug to the specified torque setting.

7 Move the container into position under the oil filter, which is screwed onto the adapter on the right-hand side of the cylinder block.

8 Using an oil filter removal tool if necessary, slacken the filter initially **(see illustration)**. Loosely wrap some rags around the oil filter, then unscrew it. Immediately turn its open end uppermost, to prevent further spillage of oil. Remove the oil filter from the engine compartment, and empty the oil into the container used to drain the sump.

9 Use a clean rag to remove all oil, dirt and sludge from the filter sealing area on the engine. Check the old filter, to make sure that the rubber sealing ring hasn't stuck to the engine. If it has, carefully remove it.

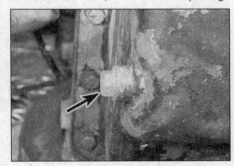

3.4 Sump drain plug (arrowed) – 19J engine

3.8 Using a removal tool to slacken the oil filter (viewed from underneath vehicle)

4.5 Undo the sump drain plug (arrowed) – TD5 engine

4.7 Renew the sump plug sealing washer

valve cover. Check that the oil level is up to the correct level on the dipstick (see *Weekly checks*), then refit and tighten the oil filler cap.

10 Run the engine for a few minutes, and check that there are no leaks around the sump drain plug.

11 Switch off the engine, and wait a few minutes for the oil to settle in the sump once more. With the new oil circulated and the filter now completely full, recheck the level on the dipstick, and add more oil if necessary.

5 Clutch fluid level check

10 Apply a light coating of clean oil to the sealing ring on the new filter, then screw it into position on the engine. Tighten the filter firmly by hand only – do not use any tools. Wipe clean the exterior of the oil filter.

11 Remove the old oil and all tools from under the vehicle, then (if applicable) lower the vehicle to the ground.

12 Fill the engine with the specified quantity and grade of oil. Pour the oil in slowly, otherwise it may overflow from the top of the valve cover. Check that the oil level is up to the correct level on the dipstick (see *Weekly checks*), then refit and tighten the oil filler cap.

13 Run the engine for a few minutes, and check that there are no leaks around the oil filter seal and the sump drain plug.

14 Switch off the engine, and wait a few minutes for the oil to settle in the sump once more. With the new oil circulated and the filter now completely full, recheck the level on the dipstick, and add more oil if necessary.

4 Engine oil renewal (TD5 engines)
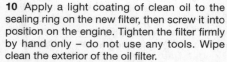

Every 6000 miles

 Frequent oil and filter changes are the most important preventative maintenance procedures that can be undertaken by the DIY owner. As engine oil ages, it becomes diluted and contaminated, which leads to premature engine wear.

1 Before starting this procedure, gather together all the necessary tools and materials. Also make sure that you have plenty of clean rags and newspapers handy, to mop-up any spills. Ideally, the engine oil should be warm, as it will drain better, and more built-up sludge will be removed with it. Take care, however, not to touch the exhaust or any other hot parts of the engine when working under the vehicle. To avoid any possibility of scalding, and to protect yourself from possible skin irritants and other harmful contaminants in

used engine oils, it is advisable to wear rubber gloves when carrying out this work.

2 Access to the underside of the vehicle will be greatly improved if it can be raised on a lift, driven onto ramps, or jacked up and supported on axle stands (see *Jacking and vehicle support*). Whichever method is chosen, make sure that the vehicle remains as level as possible, to enable the oil to drain fully.

4 Lift the flap in the engine cover, and unscrew the oil filler cap from the valve cover. Position a suitable container beneath the sump.

5 Clean the drain plug and the area around it, then slacken it using a suitable socket or spanner **(see illustration)**. If possible, try to keep the plug pressed into the sump while unscrewing it by hand the last couple of turns. As the plug releases from the threads, move it away sharply, so that the stream of oil issuing from the sump runs into the container, not up your sleeve!

6 Allow some time for the old oil to drain, noting that it may be necessary to reposition the container as the oil flow slows to a trickle.

7 After all the oil has drained, wipe off the drain plug with a clean rag, and discard the sealing washer – a new sealing washer must be fitted. Clean the area around the drain plug opening, then refit and tighten the plug (with the new sealing washer) to the specified torque setting **(see illustration)**.

8 Remove the old oil and all tools from under the vehicle, then (if applicable) lower the vehicle to the ground.

9 Fill the engine with the specified quantity and grade of oil. Pour the oil in slowly, otherwise it may overflow from the top of the

1 The clutch fluid reservoir is attached to the master cylinder, which is located on the right-hand side of the engine compartment on right-hand-drive models, or on the left-hand side of the engine compartment on left-hand-drive models.

2 On models with level marks on the side of the reservoir, the fluid level should be maintained between the MAX and MIN marks **(see illustration)**. On models with no level markings, the fluid level should be up to the lower edge of the filler neck on the reservoir.

3 There should be no significant drop in fluid level during normal operation of the clutch.

4 Any significant loss of fluid is likely to be due to a leak in the hydraulic system, which should be investigated and corrected.

6 Power steering fluid level check

All models: Every 6000 miles

1 The power steering fluid level is checked with a dipstick attached to the reservoir filler cap.

2 The fluid level should be checked with the engine stopped, and the front wheels set in the straight-ahead position.

3 Unscrew the filler cap from the top of the reservoir, and wipe all fluid from the cap dipstick with a clean rag. Refit the filler cap, then remove it again. Note the fluid level on the dipstick **(see illustration)**. When the engine is cold, the fluid

5.2 Topping-up the clutch fluid level

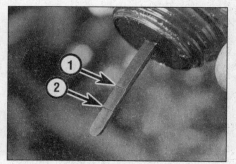

6.3 Power steering fluid level dipstick maximum (1) and minimum (2) markings

6.4 Topping-up the power steering fluid level

level should be between the upper and lower marks on the dipstick. When the engine is at normal operating temperature, the fluid level should be up to the upper mark on the dipstick. **Note:** *Do not start the engine if the fluid level is below the minimum mark, as serious damage could be caused to the power steering pump.*

4 If necessary, top-up with the specified type of fluid, then refit the filler cap securely **(see illustration)**.

5 If frequent topping-up of the system proves to be necessary, this indicates that there is a leak in the hydraulic system, which should be traced and rectified without delay.

7 Idle speed checking and adjustment

Non-TD5 models: Every 6000 miles

Refer to Chapter 4A.

8 Brake drum, shoe and wheel cylinder check

Non-TD5 models: Every 6000 miles

1 Referring to the relevant sections of Chapter 10, remove the brake drums, and check the brake shoes for signs of wear or contamination. Also check the wheel cylinders for signs of fluid leakage. Check the brake drums' inner surfaces for wear or damage.

9 Drum brake adjustment check

Non-TD5 models: Every 6000 miles

1 Chock the front wheels, then jack up the rear of the vehicle and support securely on axle stands so that the rear wheels are positioned clear of the ground (see *Jacking and vehicle support*).

2 Rotate the leading shoe adjuster, situated on the rear of the brake plate, until the shoe is forced against the surface of the brake drum. From this point, back the adjuster off slightly until it is felt to have travelled through two notches of the adjuster snail cam.

3 Check the brake drum rotates freely and, where necessary, repeat the operation on the trailing shoe adjuster.

4 With the adjuster(s) correctly set, depress the brake pedal repeatedly until normal (non-assisted) pedal pressure is restored. Check that both wheels are free to rotate easily, then lower the vehicle to the ground.

10 Brake pad, disc and caliper check

All models: Every 6000 miles

1 Jack up the vehicle, support securely on axle stands, then remove the roadwheels (see *Jacking and vehicle support*).

2 For a quick check, the thickness of friction material remaining on each pad can be measured through the slot in the caliper body. If any pad is worn to the specified minimum thickness or less, **all four** pads must be renewed (see Chapter 10).

3 For a comprehensive check, the brake pads should be removed and cleaned. This will allow the operation of the caliper to be checked, and the condition of the brake disc itself to be fully examined on both sides (see Chapter 10).

11 Handbrake adjustment check

All models: Every 6000 miles

1 The handbrake mechanism is mounted onto the rear of the transfer box assembly. Select a gear, then release the handbrake lever and chock the front wheels.

2 Jack up the rear of the vehicle and support it on axle stands so that the wheels are clear of the ground.

Rod-actuated brake assembly

3 From underneath the vehicle, slacken the cable locknut, then loosen the adjuster nut to obtain plenty of freeplay in the cable.

4 Using a suitable spanner, rotate the adjuster on the rear of the handbrake assembly clockwise, until both shoes are fully expanded against the drum.

5 With the shoes in full contact with the drum, remove all but a slight amount of freeplay from the handbrake cable, using the adjuster nut. Hold the adjuster nut in this position, and securely tighten the cable locknut.

6 Rotate the handbrake adjuster in an anti-clockwise direction until the handbrake drum is free to rotate easily.

7 Applying normal, moderate pressure, pull the handbrake lever to the fully-applied position, counting the number of clicks emitted from the handbrake ratchet mechanism. The handbrake

should be fully-applied on the second or third click of the ratchet mechanism. If necessary, adjust by rotating the adjuster in the relevant direction.

8 When adjustment is correct, release the handbrake lever, and check that the drum is free to rotate easily.

9 Apply a smear of high melting-point grease to all the linkage pivot points, and to the exposed end of the handbrake cable, then lower the vehicle to the ground.

Cable-actuated brake assembly

10 Slacken the adjuster, situated at the lever end of the cable, to obtain some freeplay in the cable.

11 From underneath the vehicle, using a suitable spanner, rotate the adjuster on the rear of the handbrake assembly clockwise until both shoes are fully expanded against the drum.

12 With the shoes in full contact with the drum, rotate the handbrake adjuster one and a half turns in an anti-clockwise direction. Check that the handbrake drum is free to rotate easily.

13 Applying normal, moderate pressure, pull the handbrake lever to the fully-applied position, counting the number of clicks emitted from the handbrake ratchet mechanism. The handbrake should be fully-applied on the third click of the ratchet mechanism. If necessary, adjust the cable setting using the adjuster nut.

14 When adjustment is correct, release the handbrake lever, and check the drum is free to rotate easily. If all is well, lower the vehicle to the ground.

12 Hinge and lock check and lubrication

All models: Every 6000 miles

1 Lubricate the hinges of the bonnet, doors and tailgate with a light general-purpose oil. Similarly, lubricate all latches, locks and lock strikers. At the same time, check the security and operation of all the locks, adjusting them if necessary (see Chapter 12).

2 Lightly lubricate the bonnet release mechanism and cable with a suitable grease.

13 Crankcase breather hose check

All models: Every 6000 miles

1 Check all the engine breather hoses for signs of cracking, leaks, and general deterioration.

2 It is advisable to loosen the hose clips, and remove each hose to check for a build-up of deposits, which may cause restrictions or even a blockage. If necessary, clean the hose using paraffin, but ensure that the hose is completely dry before refitting.

14 Auxiliary drivebelt checking and renewal

Non-TD5 models: Every 6000 miles

TD5 models: Every 12 000 miles

10J, 12J and 19J engines – alternator/cooling fan/coolant pump drivebelt

Drivebelt checking and adjustment

1 Correct tensioning of the drivebelt will ensure that it has a long life. Beware, however, of overtightening, as this can cause excessive wear in the ancillary components.

2 To improve access, if desired remove the cooling fan and cowl as described in Chapter 3.

3 The belt should be inspected along its entire length, and if it is found to be worn, frayed or cracked, it should be renewed as a precaution against breakage in service. It is advisable to carry a spare drivebelt of the correct type in the vehicle at all times.

4 The belt tension should be checked at the mid-point of the belt run between the alternator and the coolant pump. Under normal finger pressure, the belt should deflect by approximately 9.0 mm.

5 If adjustment is required, slacken the bolt securing the alternator to the adjuster bracket, the adjuster bracket mounting bolt, and the front and rear lower alternator mounting bolts (and nuts, where applicable) **(see illustrations)**.

6 Pivot the alternator as required to give the correct belt tension, then tighten the mountings and the adjuster bracket bolt.

7 If a new drivebelt has been fitted, on completion, start the engine and run it for five minutes at a fast idle. Stop the engine, then recheck the tension of both drivebelts and adjust if necessary.

8 Where applicable, refit the cooling fan and cowl as described in Chapter 3.

14.5a Slacken the alternator-to-adjuster bracket bolt (arrowed) . . .

Drivebelt removal and refitting

9 Where applicable, remove the power steering pump and/or the air conditioning compressor drivebelt(s) as described later in this Section.

10 To remove the alternator drivebelt, simply loosen the alternator mounting bolts and the adjuster bracket bolts as described previously, and pivot the alternator sufficiently to slip the drivebelt from the pulleys **(see illustration)**.

11 Refit the belt and tension it as described previously.

10J, 12J and 19J engines – power steering pump drivebelt without tensioner pulley

Drivebelt checking and adjustment

12 Proceed as described in paragraphs 1 to 3.

13 The belt tension should be checked at the mid-point of the belt run. Under normal finger pressure, the belt should deflect by approximately 12.0 mm.

14 If adjustment is required, slacken the power steering pump pivot bolt and the two adjuster clamp bolts. Move the pump mounting plate within the elongated holes as necessary to achieve the correct belt tension **(see illustration)**.

15 Tighten the clamp bolts first, then the pivot bolt.

14.5b . . . and the lower alternator mounting bolts – 19J engine

16 If a new drivebelt has been fitted, on completion, start the engine and run it for five minutes at a fast idle, then recheck the belt tension, and adjust if necessary.

17 Where applicable, refit the cooling fan and cowl as described in Chapter 3.

Drivebelt removal and refitting

18 To remove the belt, simply loosen the pump pivot bolt and the two clamp bolts as described previously, and slacken the belt sufficiently to slip it from the pulleys **(see illustration)**.

19 Refit the belt, and tension it as described previously.

14.10 Removing the alternator/cooling fan/coolant pump drivebelt – 19J engine

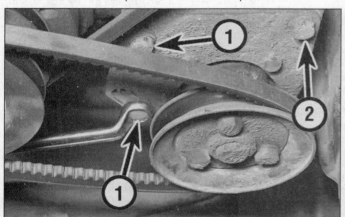

14.14 Power steering pump adjuster clamp bolts (1) and pivot bolt (2) – 19J engine without tensioner pulley

14.18 Removing the power steering pump drivebelt – 19J engine without tensioner pulley

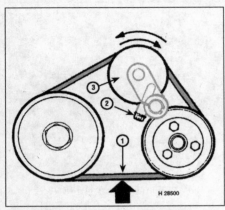

14.22 Power steering pump drivebelt details – 10J, 12J and 19J engines with tensioner pulley

1 *Belt tension checking point*
2 *Tensioner pulley pinch-bolt*
3 *Tensioner pulley*

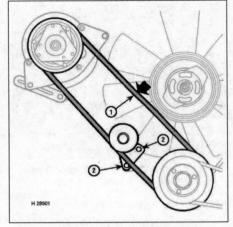

14.29 Air conditioning compressor drivebelt details – 10J, 12J and 19J engines

1 *Belt tension checking point*
2 *Damper pulley pivot and clamp bolts*

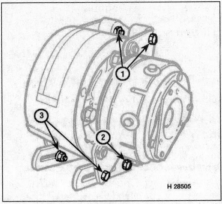

14.30 Air conditioning compressor mounting details – 10J, 12J and 19J engines

1 *Compressor pivot nuts and bolts*
2 *Adjuster link pivot bolt*
3 *Compressor-to-adjuster link nuts and bolts*

10J, 12J and 19J engines – power steering pump drivebelt with tensioner pulley

Drivebelt checking and adjustment

20 Proceed as described in paragraphs 1 to 3.
21 The belt tension should be checked at the mid-point of the run between the crankshaft and power steering pump pulleys. Under normal finger pressure, the belt should deflect by approximately 12.0 mm.
22 If adjustment is required, slacken the tensioner pulley pinch-bolt, then pivot the tensioner pulley as required to achieve the correct belt tension, and retighten the pinch-bolt **(see illustration)**.
23 If a new drivebelt has been fitted, on completion, start the engine and run it for five minutes at a fast idle. Stop the engine, then recheck the belt tension, and adjust if necessary.
24 Where applicable, refit the cooling fan and cowl as described in Chapter 3.

Drivebelt removal and refitting

25 To remove the belt, simply loosen the tensioner pinch-bolt as described previously, and slacken the belt sufficiently to slip it from the pulleys.
26 Refit and tension the belt as described previously.

10J, 12J and 19J engines – air conditioning drivebelt

Drivebelt checking and adjustment

27 Proceed as described in paragraphs 1 to 3.
28 The belt tension should be checked at the mid-point of the run opposite the belt damper pulley. Under normal finger pressure, the belt should deflect by approximately 12.0 mm.
29 If adjustment is required, slacken the belt damper pulley pivot and clamp bolts, and

move the damper pulley clear of the belt **(see illustration)**.
30 Slacken the two compressor pivot bolts and nuts **(see illustration)**.
31 Slacken the adjuster link pivot bolt (the two links are mounted on a common bolt).
32 Slacken the two nuts and bolts securing the compressor to the adjuster links.
33 Pivot the compressor as necessary to achieve the correct belt tension, then tighten the pivot bolts and nuts, the adjuster link pivot bolt, and the two nuts and bolts securing the compressor to the adjuster links.
34 Position the damper pulley so that it is just in contact with the belt, or a maximum of 1.0 mm clear of the belt, then tighten the pivot and clamp bolts.
35 Where applicable, refit the cooling fan and cowl as described in Chapter 3.

Drivebelt removal and refitting

36 To remove the belt, move the damper pulley to one side, and loosen the compressor and adjuster link nuts and bolts as described previously. Pivot the compressor sufficiently to slip the belt from the pulleys.
37 Refit and tension the belt as described previously.

200 TDi engine – cooling fan/coolant pump/ power steering pump drivebelt

Drivebelt checking and adjustment

38 Proceed as described in paragraphs 1 to 3.
39 The belt tension should be checked at the mid-point of the belt run between the coolant pump and the power steering pump.
40 Measure the length of the belt run between the centres of the coolant pump and power steering pump pulleys. Under normal finger pressure, the belt should deflect by 0.5 mm for every 25.0 mm of belt run between pulley centres.

41 If adjustment is required, slacken the front and rear alternator mounting bolts, and the alternator adjuster link mounting bolt at the power steering pump plate.
42 Slacken the bolt securing the alternator to the adjuster link.
43 Slacken the three power steering pump mounting plate bolts, then turn the power steering pump as necessary to achieve the correct belt tension. **Do not** lever against the power steering pump body to move it.
44 When the correct tension is achieved, tighten the power steering pump mounting plate bolts, then recheck the tension and repeat the adjustment procedure if necessary.
45 On completion, adjust the alternator drivebelt tension as described later in this Section.
46 If a new drivebelt has been fitted, on completion, start the engine and run it for five minutes at a fast idle. Stop the engine, then recheck the tension of both drivebelts, and adjust if necessary.
47 Where applicable, refit the viscous fan and coupling as described in Chapter 3.

Drivebelt removal and refitting

48 To remove the belt, simply loosen the alternator mounting bolts, the alternator adjuster link bolts, and the power steering pump mounting plate bolts, as described previously, and slacken the belt sufficiently to slip it from the pulleys.
49 Refit the belt, and tension it as described previously.

200 TDi engine – alternator drivebelt

Drivebelt checking and adjustment

50 Proceed as described in paragraphs 1 to 3 inclusive.
51 The belt tension should be checked at the mid-point of the belt run.

52 Measure the length of the belt run between the centres of the power steering pump and alternator pulleys. Under normal finger pressure, the belt should deflect by 0.5 mm for every 25.0 mm of belt run between pulley centres.

53 If adjustment is required, slacken the front and rear alternator mounting bolts, and the alternator adjuster link bolts.

54 Pivot the alternator as necessary to achieve the correct belt tension. **Do not** lever against the alternator body to move it.

55 When the correct tension is achieved, tighten the alternator mounting bolts and the adjuster link bolts, then recheck the tension and repeat the adjustment procedure if necessary.

56 If a new drivebelt has been fitted, on completion, start the engine and run it for five minutes at a fast idle. Stop the engine, then recheck the tension of both drivebelts, and adjust if necessary.

57 Where applicable, refit the cooling fan and cowl as described in Chapter 3.

Drivebelt removal and refitting

58 To remove the belt, first remove the cooling fan/coolant pump/power steering pump drivebelt as described previously in this Section, then manipulate the alternator drivebelt from the pulleys.

59 Refit both drivebelts (alternator drivebelt last), and tension as described previously in this Section.

200 TDi engine – air conditioning drivebelt

Drivebelt checking and adjustment

60 Proceed as described in paragraphs 1 to 3 inclusive.

61 The belt tension should be checked at the mid-point of the belt run between the air conditioning compressor and the crankshaft pulley (see illustration).

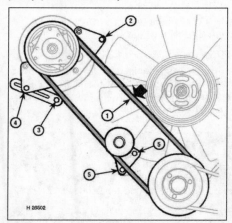

14.61 Air conditioning compressor mounting details – 200 TDi engine

1 Belt tension checking point
2 Compressor pivot bolt
3 Adjuster link pivot bolt
4 Compressor-to-adjuster link bolt
5 Damper bolts

62 Under normal finger pressure, the belt should deflect by 12.0 mm at the mid-point of the belt run.

63 If adjustment is required, slacken the compressor pivot bolts, then slacken the adjuster link pivot bolt, and the compressor-to-adjuster link bolt.

64 If the belt damper is touching the belt, slacken the two damper bolts, and move the damper clear of the belt.

65 Pivot the compressor to achieve the correct belt tension.

66 When the correct tension is achieved, tighten the compressor pivot bolts, and the adjuster link pivot and compressor-to-adjuster link bolts.

67 Adjust the position of the damper so that it just touches the belt, or is up to 1.0 mm clear of the belt, then tighten the damper bolts.

68 If a new drivebelt has been fitted, on completion, start the engine and run it for five minutes at a fast idle. Stop the engine, then recheck the drivebelt tension, and adjust if necessary.

69 Where applicable, refit the cooling fan and cowl as described in Chapter 3.

Drivebelt removal and refitting

70 To remove the belt, first remove the cooling fan/coolant pump/power steering pump drivebelt as described previously in this Section.

71 Slacken the air conditioning compressor pivot bolts and the adjuster link and compressor-to-adjuster link bolts as described previously.

72 Slacken the damper bolts and move the damper clear of the belt, then slip the belt from the pulleys.

73 Refit both drivebelts (air conditioning compressor drivebelt last), and tension as described previously in this Section.

300 TDi engine – cooling fan/coolant pump/ power steering pump/ alternator drivebelt

Drivebelt checking and adjustment

74 Proceed as described in paragraphs 1 to 3 inclusive, noting that it is only necessary to remove the cooling fan upper cowl for access to the belt.

14.79 Levering the belt tensioner to relieve the tension in the drivebelt (viewed with engine removed for clarity) – 300 TDi engine

75 An automatic drivebelt tensioner is fitted, and no checking of the tension is necessary. However, the belt should be inspected for wear and damage at the recommended intervals.

76 The belt should be inspected along its entire length, and if it is found to be worn, frayed or cracked, it should be renewed as a precaution against breakage in service. It is advisable to carry a spare drivebelt of the correct type in the vehicle at all times.

77 Refit the cooling fan upper cowl on completion.

Drivebelt removal and refitting

78 Remove the cooling fan upper cowl.

79 Using a suitable ring spanner, lever the belt tensioner pulley retaining bolt to move the tensioner and relieve the tension in the belt (see illustration).

80 Slide the belt from the pulleys, and manipulate it over the viscous fan blades.

81 If the original belt is to be refitted, mark the running direction to ensure correct refitting.

82 Refitting is a reversal of removal, but ensure that the belt is correctly seated on the pulleys.

83 On completion, refit the cooling fan upper cowl.

300 TDi engine – air conditioning drivebelt

Drivebelt checking and adjustment

84 Proceed as described in paragraphs 1 to 3 inclusive.

85 Correct tensioning of the drivebelt will ensure that it has a long life. Beware, however, of overtightening, as this can cause excessive wear in the compressor.

86 To improve access, remove the air conditioning compressor shield.

87 Loosen the three bolts securing the belt tensioner to the timing belt cover (see illustration).

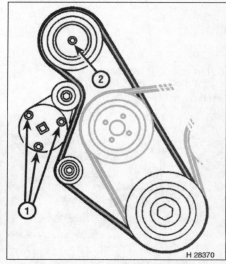

14.87 Air conditioning compressor drivebelt – 300 TDi engine

1 Tensioner securing bolts
2 Air conditioning compressor pulley

88 Fit a suitable square-drive extension to a torque wrench, and engage the extension with the square hole in the centre of the tensioner. A gauge-type torque wrench will be required for this, as a break-type wrench is unlikely to prove satisfactory

89 Apply and hold a torque of 35 Nm, then tighten the tensioner securing bolts.

90 Rotate the engine through two full turns.

91 Again, apply and hold a torque of 35 Nm to the tensioner pulley, then fully loosen and tighten the tensioner securing bolts.

92 Refit the air conditioning compressor shield.

Drivebelt removal and refitting

93 Remove the cooling fan/coolant pump/power steering pump/alternator drivebelt, as described previously in this Section.

94 Remove the air conditioning compressor shield.

95 Loosen the three belt tensioner securing bolts, then move the tensioner sufficiently to allow the belt to be removed.

96 If the original belt is to be refitted, mark the running direction to ensure correct refitting.

97 Refit and tension the belt as described previously in this Section.

TD5 engine

Drivebelt checking and adjustment

98 Proceed as described in paragraphs 1 to 3 inclusive.

99 An automatic drivebelt tensioner is fitted, and no checking of the tension is necessary. However, the belt should be inspected for wear and damage and the recommended intervals.

100 The belt should be inspected along its entire length, and if it is found to be worn, frayed or cracked, it should be renewed as a precaution against breakage in service. It is advisable to carry a spare drivebelt of the correct type in the vehicle at all times.

101 Refit the cooling fan cowl on completion (where applicable).

Drivebelt removal and refitting

102 Remove the cooling fan and cowl (see Chapter 3).

14.103 Rotate the tensioner pulley bolt clockwise to relieve the tension on the belt

103 Using a suitable ring spanner, lever the belt tensioner pulley retaining bolt clockwise to move the tensioner and relieve the tension in the belt **(see illustration)**.

104 Slide the belt from the pulleys, and manipulate it over the viscous fan blades.

105 If the original belt is to be refitted, mark the running direction to ensure correct refitting.

106 Refitting is a reversal of removal, but ensure that the belt is correctly seated on the pulleys **(see illustration)**.

107 On completion, refit the cooling fan and cowl.

15 Main gearbox oil level check

Non-TD5 models: Every 6000 miles

Note: *There is no requirement in the manufacturer's service schedule for the main gearbox oil level to be checked on TD5 models. However, it may be prudent for owners to perform this task at least once between gearbox oil changes.*

1 Ensure that the vehicle is level. On TD5 models, undo the fasteners and remove the transmission undershield.

2 Locate the oil filler/level plug in the side of the gearbox casing, and place a suitable

14.106 Auxiliary drivebelt routing – TD5 engines

container beneath the hole to catch any escaping oil.

3 Unscrew the filler/level plug, and check the oil level. The level should be up to the lower edge of the filler/level plug hole **(see illustrations)**.

4 If necessary, add oil of the specified type (see *Lubricants and fluids*) until the oil overflows from the filler/level hole.

5 Clean and refit the filler/level plug, and tighten to the specified torque. **Do not** overtighten the plug, as it has tapered threads.

6 Wipe any spilt oil from the gearbox casing, and refit the engine undershield (where applicable).

16 Transfer gearbox oil level check

Non-TD5 models up to 1995: Every 6000 miles

Non-TD5 models from 1995: Every 12 000 miles

TD5 models: Every 12 000 miles

Proceed as described for the main gearbox in Section 15, noting that the filler/level plug is located in the rear of the transfer gearbox casing **(see illustration)**.

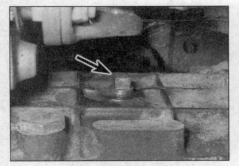

15.3a Main gearbox oil filler/level plug (arrowed) – LT77-type gearbox

15.3b Unscrewing the main gearbox oil filler/level plug – R380-type gearbox

16.1 Unscrewing the transfer gearbox filler/level plug

17.4 Topping-up the axle oil level

18.2 Swivel pin housing level plug (1) and filler plug (2)

(hoses, joint faces, etc) for leaks. Where any problems of this nature are found on system components, renew the component or gasket with reference to Chapter 3.

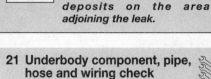

A leak in the cooling system will usually show up as white or antifreeze-coloured deposits on the area adjoining the leak.

17 Axle oil level check

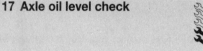

Non-TD5 models up to 1995: Every 6000 miles

Non-TD5 models from 1995: Every 12 000 miles

TD5 models: Every 12 000 miles

Note: *A 13 mm square-section wrench will be required to undo the axle filler/level plug. These wrenches can be obtained from most motor factors, or from your Land Rover dealer.*

1 Ensure that the vehicle is standing on level ground, and apply the handbrake.
2 Working underneath the vehicle, unscrew the front axle oil filler/level plug, which is located in the differential housing.
3 The oil level should be up to the lower edge of the filler/level plug hole.
4 If necessary, top-up with the specified grade of oil, until oil just begins to run from the plug hole. Do not overfill – if too much oil is added, wait until the excess has run out of the plug hole **(see illustration)**.
5 Once the level is correct, refit the filler/level plug and tighten it securely.
6 Repeat the procedure for the rear axle.

18 Swivel pin housing oil level check

Non-TD5 models up to 1995: Every 6000 miles

Non-TD5 models from 1995: Every 12 000 miles

1 Ensure that the vehicle is standing on level ground, and apply the handbrake.
2 Working underneath the vehicle, unscrew the left-hand swivel pin housing level plug. The level plug has a square-section head, and is situated approximately halfway up the housing **(see illustration)**.
3 The oil level should be up to the lower edge of the level plug hole.

4 If topping-up is necessary, unscrew the filler plug from the top of the swivel pin housing, the filler plug also has a square-section head. Top-up the housing via the filler plug hole, using the specified grade of oil, until oil just begins to run from the level plug hole. Do not overfill – if too much oil is added, wait until the excess has run out of the level plug hole.
5 Once the level is correct, refit both the filler and level plugs, and tighten them securely.
6 Repeat the above procedure on the right-hand swivel pin housing.

19 Rear suspension upper link balljoint lubrication

Non-TD5 models: Every 6000 miles

1 On early models where a grease nipple is fitted to the top of the balljoint, using a suitable grease gun, pump the balljoint full of a multi-purpose lithium-based grease.
2 On later models, no grease nipple is fitted, and therefore this operation is not necessary.

20 Cooling system and heater system hose check

All models: Every 6000 miles

1 Check the security and condition of all the engine-related coolant pipes and hoses. Ensure that all cable-ties or securing clips are in place, and in good condition. Clips which are broken or missing can lead to chafing of the hoses, pipes or wiring, which could cause more serious problems in the future.
2 Carefully check the radiator hoses and heater hoses along their entire length. Renew any hose which is cracked, swollen or deteriorated. Cracks will show up better if the hose is squeezed. Pay close attention to the hose clips that secure the hoses to the cooling system components. Hose clips can pinch and puncture hoses, resulting in cooling system leaks. If wire-type hose clips are used, it may be a good idea to update them with screw-type clips.
3 Inspect all the cooling system components

21 Underbody component, pipe, hose and wiring check

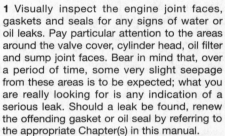

All models: Every 6000 miles

1 Visually inspect the engine joint faces, gaskets and seals for any signs of water or oil leaks. Pay particular attention to the areas around the valve cover, cylinder head, oil filter and sump joint faces. Bear in mind that, over a period of time, some very slight seepage from these areas is to be expected; what you are really looking for is any indication of a serious leak. Should a leak be found, renew the offending gasket or oil seal by referring to the appropriate Chapter(s) in this manual.
2 Similarly, check the transmission components for oil leaks, and investigate and rectify any problems found.
3 Check the security and condition of all the engine-related pipes and hoses. Ensure that all cable-ties or securing clips are in place, and in good condition. Clips which are broken or missing can lead to chafing of the hoses, pipes or wiring, which could cause more serious problems in the future.
4 Carefully check the condition of all coolant, fuel and brake hoses. Renew any hose which is cracked, swollen or deteriorated. Cracks will show up better if the hose is squeezed. Pay close attention to the hose clips that secure the hoses to the system components. Hose clips can pinch and puncture hoses, resulting in leaks. If wire-type hose clips are used, it may be a good idea to update them with screw-type clips.
5 With the vehicle raised, inspect the fuel tank and filler neck for punctures, cracks and other damage. The connection between the filler neck and tank is especially critical. Sometimes a rubber filler neck or connecting hose will leak, due to loose retaining clamps or deteriorated rubber.
6 Similarly, inspect all brake hoses and metal pipes. If any damage or deterioration is discovered, do not drive the vehicle until the necessary repair work has been carried out. Renew any damaged sections of hose or pipe.
7 Carefully check all rubber hoses and metal fuel lines leading away from the petrol tank. Check for loose connections, deteriorated hoses, crimped lines, and other damage. Pay particular attention to the vent pipes and

hoses, which often loop up around the filler neck and can become blocked or crimped. Follow the lines to the front of the vehicle, carefully inspecting them all the way. Renew damaged sections as necessary.

8 From within the engine compartment, check the security of all fuel hose attachments and pipe unions, and inspect the fuel hoses and vacuum hoses for kinks, chafing and deterioration.

9 Check the condition of the oil cooler hoses and pipes.

10 Where applicable, check the condition of the power steering fluid hoses and pipes.

11 Check the condition of all exposed wiring harnesses.

12 Also check the engine and transmission components for signs of fluid leaks.

22 Steering and suspension component check

All models: Every 6000 miles

1 Apply the handbrake, then raise the front of the vehicle and securely support it on axle stands.

2 Visually inspect the balljoint dust covers for splits, chafing or deterioration. Any damage will cause loss of lubricant, together with dirt and water entry, resulting in rapid deterioration of the balljoints.

3 Where applicable, check the power steering fluid hoses for chafing or deterioration, and the pipe and hose unions for fluid leaks. Also check for signs of fluid leakage under pressure from the steering box, which would indicate failed fluid seals within the steering box assembly.

4 Grasp the roadwheel at the 12 o'clock and 6 o'clock positions, and try to rock it. Very slight freeplay may be felt, but if the movement is appreciable, further investigation is necessary to determine the source. Continue rocking the wheel while an assistant depresses the footbrake. If the movement is now eliminated or significantly reduced, it is likely that the hub bearings are at fault. If the freeplay is still evident with the footbrake depressed, then there is wear in the suspension joints or mountings.

5 Now grasp the wheel at the 9 o'clock and 3 o'clock positions, and try to rock it as before. Any movement felt now may again be caused by wear in the hub bearings, or the steering track rod and drag link balljoints. If a balljoint is worn, the visual movement will be obvious.

6 Using a large screwdriver or flat bar, check for wear in the suspension mounting bushes by levering between the relevant suspension component and its attachment point. Some movement is to be expected, as the mountings are made of rubber, but excessive wear should be obvious. Also check the condition of any visible rubber bushes, looking for splits, cracks or contamination of the rubber.

7 With the vehicle standing on its wheels,

have an assistant turn the steering wheel back-and-forth. There should be very little, if any, lost movement between the steering wheel and roadwheels. If this is not the case, closely observe the joints and mountings previously described, but in addition, check the steering column universal joints for wear. The steering box backlash is adjustable, but adjustment should be entrusted to a Land Rover dealer (see Section 35).

23 Axle breather check

Non-TD5 models: Every 6000 miles

1 Ensure that the vehicle is standing on level ground, and apply the handbrake.

Ball valve type breathers

2 Remove all traces of dirt from around the breather, then unscrew it from the axle.

3 Wash the breather in a high-flash-point solvent to remove all traces of dirt and debris, then check that the ball is free to move easily. If the ball is seized or does not move freely, the breather must be renewed.

4 Lubricate the ball with clean engine oil, then refit the breather to the axle and tighten it securely.

Breather tubes

5 Check that both the front and rear axle breather tubes are securely retained by all the relevant retaining clips, and show no signs of damage or deterioration.

6 If renewal is necessary, unscrew the union bolt securing the breather hose to the top of the axle, and recover the sealing washers from the hose union. Free the hose from its retaining clips, and remove it from the vehicle.

7 Position a new sealing washer on each side of the hose union, and refit the union bolt. Ensure that the hose is correctly routed and retained by all the necessary clips, then securely tighten the union bolt.

24 Road test

All models: Every 6000 miles

Instruments and electrical equipment

1 Check the operation of all instruments and electrical equipment.

2 Make sure that all instruments read correctly, and switch on all electrical equipment in turn, to check that it functions properly.

Steering and suspension

3 Check for any abnormalities in the steering, suspension, handling or road 'feel'.

4 Drive the vehicle, and check that there are no unusual vibrations or noises.

5 Check that the steering feels positive, with no excessive 'sloppiness', or roughness, and check for any suspension noises when cornering and driving over bumps.

Drivetrain

6 Check the performance of the engine, clutch and propeller shafts.

7 Listen for any unusual noises from the engine, clutch and transmission.

8 Make sure that the engine runs smoothly when idling, and that there is no hesitation when accelerating.

9 Check that the clutch action is smooth and progressive, that the drive is taken up smoothly, and that the pedal travel is not excessive. Also listen for any noises when the clutch pedal is depressed.

10 Check that all gears can be engaged smoothly without noise, and that the gear lever action is smooth and not abnormally vague or 'notchy'. This check applies to both the main gearbox and the transfer gearbox.

Braking system

11 Make sure that the vehicle does not pull to one side when braking, and that the wheels do not lock prematurely when braking hard.

12 Check that there is no vibration through the steering when braking.

13 Check that the handbrake operates correctly without excessive movement of the lever, and that it holds the vehicle stationary on a slope.

14 Test the operation of the brake servo unit as follows. With the engine switched off, depress the footbrake four or five times to exhaust the vacuum. Start the engine, keeping the footbrake depressed. As the engine starts, there should be a noticeable 'give' in the brake pedal as vacuum builds-up. Allow the engine to run for at least two minutes, and then switch it off. If the brake pedal is depressed again, it should be possible to detect a hiss from the servo. After about four or five applications, no further hissing should be heard, and the pedal should feel considerably firmer.

25 Fuel sedimenter cleaning

All models: Every 12 000 miles

Non-TD5 models

1 The fuel sedimenter is an optional fitment, designed to increase the life of the fuel filter, by removing the larger droplets of water and dirt from the fuel before it reaches the filter.

2 The sedimenter location varies according to model, but the unit is usually mounted under the vehicle on a bracket attached to the chassis, near the fuel tank.

3 Before cleaning the sedimenter element, drain off the water as follows. Remove the drain plug at the bottom of the sedimenter body, and allow the water to run out (see

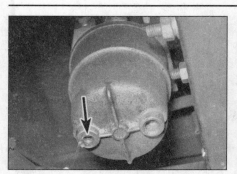

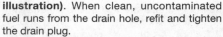

25.3 Allow any water to drain from the fuel sedimenter drain hole (arrowed)

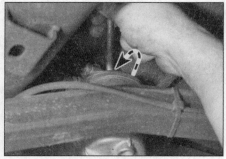

25.5 Unscrewing the fuel sedimenter securing bolt

25.7 Fit a new seal to the top of the sedimenter bowl – sleeve arrowed

illustration). When clean, uncontaminated fuel runs from the drain hole, refit and tighten the drain plug.

4 Disconnect the fuel inlet pipe from the sedimenter, and lift the pipe above the level of the fuel tank. Alternatively, plug the end of the pipe to prevent fuel draining from the tank.

5 Support the sedimenter bowl, then unscrew the bolt at the top of the sedimenter head, until the bowl can be removed (see illustration).

6 Remove the sedimenter sleeve from the bowl, and recover the plastic collar, then clean the components in clean paraffin.

7 Fit new seals to the sedimenter head, fit a new seal to the top of the bowl, then fit the sleeve to the bowl (see illustration).

8 Fit the plastic collar to the sedimenter head, then fit the bowl/sleeve assembly (see illustration).

9 Tighten the bolt to secure the bowl.

10 Reconnect the fuel pipe, and tighten the union.

11 Slacken the drain plug at the bottom of the sedimenter body, and tighten the plug when clean, uncontaminated fuel runs from the drain hole.

12 Prime the fuel system as described in Chapter 4A.

13 Start the engine, and check for fuel leaks around the sedimenter.

TD5 models

14 The water drain tap is fitted to the base of the fuel filter.

15 Position a container under the fuel filter, located on the chassis longitudinal

25.8 Fitting the plastic collar to the sedimenter head – seals arrowed

member, below the right-hand rear wheel arch. Rotate the fastener anti-clockwise and remove the cover from the filter assembly (see illustration 28.16).

16 Place a container under the filter, then rotate the drain tap on the base of the sedimenter and allow any water to run out. When clean, uncontaminated fuel runs from the drain, tighten the tap (see illustration).

17 Refit the cover and tighten the fastener.

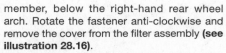

26 Engine oil centrifuge rotor renewal (TD5 engines)

Every 12 000 miles

Note: *This procedure must be accompanied by changing the engine oil as described in Section 4.*

25.16 Undo the drain plug to release any trapped water – TD5 models

1 On TD5 engines, a centrifugal oil cleaner is fitted on the left-hand side of the engine block. Oil enters the centrifuge from the side under pressure, and spins the rotor within at up to 15 000 rpm. Any dirt/particles within the oil are captured on the inner surface of the rotor as the oil is thrown outwards, forming a sludge inside the rotor. The rotor is able to trap very fine impurities that would normally pass through a paper element type filter.

2 Undo the two bolts and remove the centrifuge cover (see illustration). Discard the cover O-ring seal – a new one must be fitted.

3 Lift out the rotor and discard it – a new one must be fitted (see illustration).

4 Use shop rag to clean the centrifuge body and cover.

5 Fit the new rotor into the body, then refit the cover with a new O-ring seal (see illustration). Tighten the cover bolts securely.

26.2 Remove the oil centrifuge cover bolts (arrowed)

26.3 Lift the centrifuge rotor from the housing

26.5 Renew the filter cover O-ring seal

27.4 Adjusting a valve clearance – 19J engine

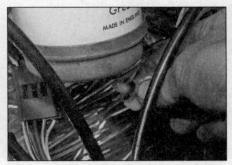

28.2 Fuel filter drain tap (removed from the filter for clarity)

28.4 Unscrewing the fuel filter through-bolt – 19J engine

27 Valve clearances checking and adjustment

Non-TD5 models: Every 12 000 miles

Note: *The following procedure does not apply to TD5 engines, which are equipped with hydraulic valve clearance adjusters.*

⚠ **Warning: If the crankshaft is rotated with excessive valve clearances, it is possible for the pushrods to become dislodged and fracture the tappet slides. To prevent the possibility of damage, turn the adjusters to eliminate all clearance from any loose rocker arms before turning the crankshaft to check the valve clearances.**

1 Remove the valve cover, as described in Chapter 2A.

2 Using a spanner or socket on the crankshaft pulley bolt (the bolt is most easily reached from underneath the vehicle), turn the crankshaft until No 8 valve is fully open (valve spring fully compressed). The valves are numbered from the front of the engine.

3 Using a feeler blade of the specified thickness (see *Specifications*), check the clearance between the top of No 1 valve stem, and the valve stem contact face of the rocker arm.

4 If the clearance is not as specified, slacken the adjuster locknut, and turn the tappet adjuster screw as required to give the specified clearance **(see illustration)**. Turn the adjuster screw clockwise to reduce the clearance, and anti-clockwise to increase the clearance.

5 When the clearance is correct, tighten the adjuster locknut. Hold the adjuster screw stationary as the locknut is tightened.

6 With the locknut tightened, recheck the clearance, and re-adjust if necessary.

7 Turn the crankshaft, and continue to check the remaining valve clearances in the following order:

Valve fully open	Valve clearance to be checked
No 6	No 3
No 4	No 5
No 7	No 2
No 1	No 8
No 3	No 6
No 5	No 4
No 2	No 7

8 When all the valve clearances have been checked, refit the valve cover as described in Chapter 2A.

28 Fuel filter element renewal

Non-TD5 models: Every 12 000 miles

TD5 models: Every 24 000 miles

1 On non-TD5 models, the fuel filter assembly is located on the engine compartment bulkhead, to the right-hand side of the engine. On TD5 models, the fuel filter is mounted on the longitudinal chassis member below the right-hand rear wheel arch.

2 Before the filter is renewed, any water present should be drained from the filter bowl as follows **(see illustration)**:

 a) *Hold a small container beneath the drain tap at the bottom of the filter, then unscrew the tap by half-a-turn.*

 b) *Drain off water and sediment until clean fuel flows from the tap.*

 c) *Immediately close the tap when fuel flows from it – failure to do so may result in the fuel system requiring bleeding.*

3 Clean the area around the filter head, and place a container beneath the filter.

10J, 12J and 19J engines

4 Unscrew the through-bolt from the top of the filter head, and withdraw the filter bowl and the element **(see illustration)**.

5 Discard the old element and the rubber seals (new seals should be supplied with a new filter element).

6 Thoroughly clean the inside of the filter head and the bowl.

7 Fit new large and small sealing rings to the filter head, then push the new filter element into position in the filter head, with the holes in the element uppermost **(see illustrations)**.

8 Fit a new seal to the filter bowl, then refit the bowl, and secure with the through-bolt **(see illustrations)**.

9 Make sure that the drain tap at the base of the filter is closed. Referring to Chapter 4A, Section 5, prime and bleed the fuel system. Start the engine, and check for leaks around the filter.

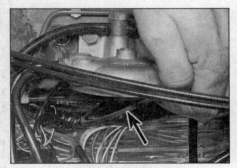

28.7a Fit new large (arrowed) . . .

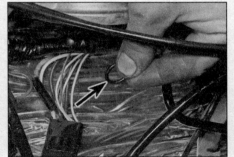

28.7b . . . and small sealing rings (arrowed) to the filter head – 19J engine

28.8a Fit a new seal to the filter bowl . . .

28.8b ... and secure the assembly with the through-bolt – 19J engine

28.16 Rotate the fastener (arrowed) anti-clockwise and remove the filter cover

28.18 Unscrew the element from the filter head

200 TDi and 300 TDi engines

10 Unscrew the filter element, and catch the fuel which is released. A strap wrench can be used to grip the base of the filter element if necessary.
11 Lubricate the seals of the new filter with a little fuel.
12 Screw the new filter into position, and tighten the filter firmly by hand only.
13 Make sure that the drain tap at the base of the filter is closed.
14 Referring to Chapter 4A, Section 5, prime and bleed the fuel system.
15 Start the engine, and check for leaks around the filter.

TD5 engines

16 Rotate the fastener anti-clockwise and remove the filter cover **(see illustration)**.

29.1 Disconnecting the air cleaner condition indicator hose from the air cleaner casing – 19J engine

17 Place a container under the filter, then unscrew and remove the drain tap. Allow the fuel to drain out **(see illustration 25.16)**.
18 Unscrew the filter from the filter head. If necessary, use a filter removal tool or strap wrench **(see illustration)**.
19 Thoroughly clean the inside of the filter head.
20 Smear a little clean engine oil on the rubber sealing rings on the top of the new filter, then screw into position in the filter head **(see illustration)**. Tighten the filter by hand only.
21 Clean out the dirt and debris from the original drain tap, then fit the new sealing washer (supplied with the new filter), and screw it onto the base of the new filter. Tighten it by hand only.
22 Start the engine and check for leaks around the filter. There is no need to prime or bleed the fuel system following filter renewal.
23 Refit the cover and tighten the fastener.

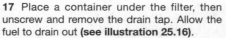

29 Air cleaner element renewal

Non-TD5 models: Every 12 000 miles

TD5 models: Every 24 000 miles

Note: *If a new air cleaner element is not available, it may be possible to clean the old element – consult a Land Rover dealer or specialist for advice. On certain models, an air cleaner condition indicator may be fitted*

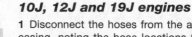

28.20 Apply a little clean engine oil to the filter sealing ring

– the indicator shows by means of a red band moving across a clear aperture that the element requires renewal. Renew the element before the recommended intervals if the indicator turns red.

10J, 12J and 19J engines

1 Disconnect the hoses from the air cleaner casing, noting the hose locations to ensure correct refitting **(see illustration)**.
2 Release the three securing clips, and lift the air cleaner casing from the baseplate **(see illustration)**.
3 Unscrew the wing nut, recover the washer, then withdraw the element **(see illustrations)**.
4 Thoroughly clean the inside of the casing and the baseplate, and check the condition of the casing sealing ring. Fit a new sealing ring if necessary.
5 Squeeze open the air cleaner dump valve, which is located at the bottom of the casing.

29.2 Lifting the air cleaner casing from the baseplate – 19J engine

29.3a Unscrew the wing nut ...

29.3b ... and withdraw the element – 19J engine

**29.10 Air cleaner condition indicator –
19J engine**

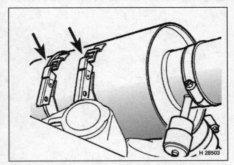

**29.12 Air cleaner securing clips (arrowed)
– 200 TDi and 300 TDi engines**

withdraw the assembly from its mounting cradle (**see illustration**).

13 Unscrew the nut securing the air cleaner lid to the body, then withdraw the lid (**see illustration**).

14 Unscrew the now-exposed wing nut securing the air cleaner element, and recover the sealing washer.

15 Pull the element from the casing, and discard it.

16 Thoroughly clean the inside of the air cleaner casing and the lid.

17 Squeeze open the air cleaner dump valve, which is located at the bottom of the casing. Check that the valve is flexible, and is in good condition.

18 If necessary, pull the dump valve from the air cleaner casing, and clean it. Fit a new valve if necessary.

19 Fit the new element to the casing, with the fins furthest away from the lid.

20 Refit the wing nut to the casing, ensuring that the sealing washer is in place, and tighten to secure the element.

21 Refit the air cleaner lid, aligning the arrows on the casing and lid, and tighten the securing nut.

22 Refit the air cleaner to the mounting cradle, twisting the assembly clockwise to ensure that the securing clips engage with the slots in the casing.

23 Fasten the securing clips, then reconnect the hoses to their correct locations on the casing, as noted before removal.

24 If an air cleaner condition indicator is fitted (see note at beginning of this Section), reset it by pressing the top of the indicator until the red bar is no longer visible.

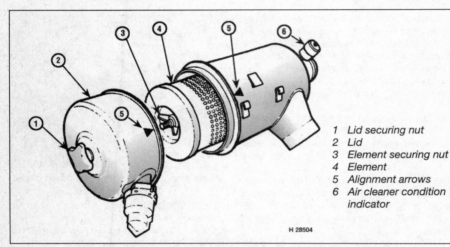

1 Lid securing nut
2 Lid
3 Element securing nut
4 Element
5 Alignment arrows
6 Air cleaner condition indicator

29.13 Air cleaner components – 200 TDi and 300 TDi engines

Check that the valve is flexible, and is in good condition.

6 If necessary, pull the dump valve from the air cleaner casing, and clean it. Fit a new valve if necessary.

7 Fit the new element to the casing, and secure with the washer and wing nut. Check the condition of the sealing ring on the wing nut, and renew if necessary.

8 Fit the casing to the baseplate, and secure with the three clips.

9 Reconnect the hoses to their correct locations on the casing, as noted before removal.

10 If an air cleaner condition indicator is fitted (see note at beginning of this Section), reset it by pressing the top of the indicator until the red bar is no longer visible (**see illustration**).

200 TDi and 300 TDi engines

11 Disconnect the hoses from the air cleaner casing, noting the hose locations to ensure correct refitting.

12 Release the two securing clips, then twist the air cleaner casing anti-clockwise (when viewed from the front of the vehicle) and

TD5 engines

25 Release the clips and disconnect the airflow meter from the air cleaner cover (**see illustration**).

26 Disconnect the AAP (Ambient Air Pressure) sensor wiring plug, and disconnect the rubber vacuum pipe from the air cleaner cover (**see illustration**).

27 Release the two clips and lift the air cleaner cover from the housing (**see illustration**).

28 Lift the old element from place, then

29.25 Release the clips (arrowed) and detach the air flow meter from the air filter cover

29.26 Disconnect the sensor wiring plug and the vacuum hose (arrowed)

29.27 Release the clips and lift the air cleaner cover (arrowed)

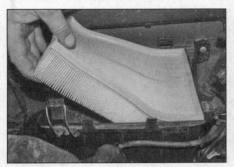

29.29 Fit new element with the seal uppermost

30.6 Engine breather filter (arrowed) – 200 TDi and 300 TDi engines

remove any debris and clean the inside of the housing and cover.

29 Fit the new element into the housing **(see illustration)**.

30 Refit the cover and secure it in place with the clips.

31 Refit the AAP sensor, and securely tighten the retaining screws.

32 Refit the airflow meter and secure the retaining clips.

30 Engine breather filter cleaning

Non-TD5 models: Every 12 000 miles

10J, 12J and 19J engines

1 The filter is incorporated in the engine oil filler cap.

2 Disconnect the breather hose(s) and remove the oil filler cap.

3 Fill a suitable container with clean paraffin, then immerse the assembly in the paraffin to dissolve any oily deposits which have formed inside the gauze filter.

4 Once satisfied that the filter is clean, remove it from the paraffin, and dry thoroughly. **Note:** *It is **vital** that the filter is absolutely dry before it is refitted to the engine.*

5 Refit the oil filler cap, and reconnect the breather hose(s).

200 TDi and 300 TDi engines

Note: *A new gasket will be required when refitting the filter.*

6 The filter is located at the rear right-hand corner of the valve cover **(see illustration)**.

7 Loosen the clips securing the hoses to the top and bottom of the filter, noting their locations to ensure correct refitting.

8 Unscrew the two bolts securing the filter to the valve cover, then carefully pull the filter away from the valve cover, and recover the gasket.

9 Fill a suitable container with clean paraffin, then immerse the filter in the paraffin to dissolve any oily deposits which may have formed inside.

10 Once satisfied that the filter is clean, remove it from the paraffin, and dry thoroughly.

Note: *It is **vital** that the filter is absolutely dry before it is refitted to the engine.*

11 Refit the filter to the valve cover, using a new gasket, and tighten the securing bolts.

12 Reconnect the two hoses to the filter, ensuring that the clips are securely tightened to produce a gas-tight seal.

31 Brake vacuum servo hose check

Non-TD5 models: Every 12 000 miles

1 Working from the vacuum pump back to the servo unit, examine the vacuum hose for signs of damage or deterioration. At the same time, also check the servo unit check valve rubber grommet. If necessary renew the hose/grommet, referring to the information given in Chapter 10.

32 Glow plug wiring check

Non-TD5 models: Every 12 000 miles

1 Where applicable, to improve access, remove the oil filler cap, and unclip the plastic cover from the valve cover.

2 Check all the glow plug wiring for signs of fraying, chafing and general deterioration.

3 Check that the nuts securing the wiring to the glow plugs are secure. Where applicable (200 TDi and 300 TDi engines), also check the security of the wiring connector at the preheating system relay/timer unit (see Chapter 5).

33 Accelerator mechanism checking and lubrication

Non-TD5 models: Every 12 000 miles

1 Check the operation of the accelerator pedal. Make sure that the pedal pivots freely, and if necessary, lightly lubricate the pivot bushes using a little multi-purpose grease.

2 Check the condition of the accelerator cable. Make sure that the cable is routed correctly, is free from kinks, and is clear of surrounding components. Check the cable for signs of chafing and fraying, particularly at the injection pump end, and renew the cable if necessary.

3 Check that, when the accelerator pedal is fully depressed, the accelerator lever on the injection pump moves to the full-throttle position.

4 Check the cable freeplay. Cable removal, refitting, and adjustment is in Chapter 4A.

5 Check the operation of the throttle linkage at the bracket behind the injection pump, and lubricate the pivots if necessary.

34 Radiator and intercooler check

All models: Every 12 000 miles

1 Check that the radiator and (where fitted) intercooler matrixes are clean, and free from obstructions which would reduce the airflow through them. Remove any debris, taking great care not to damage either component.

35 Steering box oil level and steering gear backlash check

Non-TD5 models up to 1995: Every 12 000 miles

Non-TD5 models from 1995: Every 36 000 miles

TD5 models: Every 36 000 miles

Steering gear backlash check

1 If at any time it is noted that the steering action has become stiff or sloppy, the vehicle should be taken to a Land Rover dealer for the steering components to be checked. Adjustments of the steering components and steering box are possible, but specialist knowledge and equipment are needed. Therefore, this task must be entrusted to a Land Rover dealer.

Steering box oil level check (manual steering only)

2 Clean the area around the steering box oil filler plug, then unscrew the plug from the top of the steering box.

3 Check that the oil level is approximately 25 mm **below** the top of the oil filler hole. This can be checked by making up a 'dipstick' from a suitable piece of wire; take care not to use anything which could fall into the steering box.

4 If necessary, top-up the steering box using the specified type of oil until the level is correct. Excess oil should be removed using a syringe.

5 When the oil level is correct, refit the filler plug and tighten it securely.

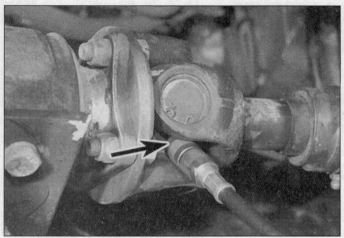

37.3a Greasing a propeller shaft universal joint – nipple arrowed

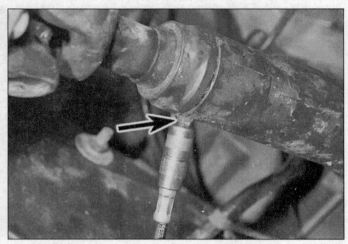

37.3b Greasing a propeller shaft sliding joint – nipple arrowed

36 Jack and tools security check

Non-TD5 models: Every 12 000 miles

1 Check that the jack and tools are securely stowed, and check that the jack is in good condition.

37 Propeller shaft joint lubrication

All models: Every 12 000 miles

Note: *A low-pressure grease gun will be required for this operation.*
1 Working under the vehicle, locate the grease nipples on the front and rear propeller shafts universal joint spiders, and on the shaft sliding joints.
2 Thoroughly clean the around each nipple.
3 Fill a suitable grease gun with the recommended type of grease (see *Lubricants and fluids*), then apply the grease gun to each of the nipples in turn, and pump grease into the joints **(see illustrations)**. Apply grease until it emerges from the end of the nipple, then wipe away the excess.

38.3 Check the condition of the exhaust mountings

38 Exhaust system check

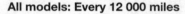

All models: Every 12 000 miles

1 With the engine cold (at least an hour after the vehicle has been driven), check the complete exhaust system from the engine to the end of the tailpipe. Ideally, the inspection should be carried out with the vehicle raised (see *Jacking and vehicle support*).
2 Check the exhaust pipes and connections for evidence of leaks, severe corrosion and damage. Make sure that all brackets and mountings are in good condition, and tight. Leakage at any of the joints or in other parts of the system will usually show up as a black sooty stain in the vicinity of the leak..
3 Rattles and other noises can often be traced to the exhaust system, especially the brackets and mountings **(see illustration)**. Try to move the pipes and silencers. If the components can come into contact with the body or suspension parts, secure the system with new mountings. If possible, separate the joints, and twist the pipes as necessary to provide additional clearance.
4 Run the engine at idle speed, then temporarily place a cloth rag over the rear end

41.1 Flywheel housing drain plug (arrowed) – 300 TDi engine

of the exhaust pipe, and listen for any escape of exhaust gases that would indicate a leak.
5 On completion, where applicable, lower the vehicle to the ground.

39 Propeller shaft securing bolt check

All models: Every 12 000 miles

1 Working under the vehicle, use a torque wrench to check the tightness of the bolts securing the propeller shafts to the transfer gearbox and axle drive flanges.

40 ABS wheel speed sensor harness check

TD5 models: Every 12 000 miles

1 Working underneath the vehicle, check each sensor harness for chafing and damage, and that they are correctly routed.

41 Flywheel housing and timing belt housing draining

Non-TD5 models: Every 12 000 miles

Flywheel housing

1 In production, the flywheel housing plug is not normally fitted. The plug can be fitted to the oil drain hole in the housing, to seal the housing if the vehicle is likely to be used off-road in very muddy conditions, or under severe wading conditions. A suitable plug can be obtained from a Land Rover dealer **(see illustration)**.
2 If the vehicle is regularly used in adverse conditions, the plug should be fitted permanently, but if the vehicle is normally used on the road, the plug should be removed.

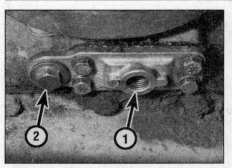

41.5a Timing belt housing inspection hole (1) and plug storage location (2) – 19J engine

41.5b Timing belt housing inspection hole location (arrowed) – 300 TDi engine

3 If the plug is permanently fitted, it should be removed at the recommended intervals, to allow any accumulated oil to drain from the housing.

4 Clean the plug before refitting.

Timing belt housing

5 Refer to paragraphs 1 to 4, but note that the plug should be treated as an inspection plug – there should be no oil in the timing belt housing. If oil is present, investigate the cause immediately, as the timing belt will deteriorate if contaminated with oil. Note that on some engines, the plug can be screwed into a plate next to the drain hole **(see illustrations)**.

42 Fuel tank security check

Non-TD5 models: Every 12 000 miles

1 Working under the vehicle, check the fuel tank for any signs of damage or corrosion.

2 If there is any sign of significant damage or corrosion, remove the fuel tank (see Chapter 4A) and take it to a professional for repair. **Do not** under any circumstances attempt to weld or solder a fuel tank.

43 Towing bracket check

All models: Every 12 000 miles

1 Where applicable, check the security of the towbar bracket mountings. Also check that all wiring is intact, and that the trailer electrical systems function correctly.

44 Headlight and auxiliary light adjustment check

All models: Every 12 000 miles

1 Accurate adjustment of the headlight beam is only possible using optical beam-setting equipment, and this work should therefore

be carried out by a Land Rover dealer, or a service station with the necessary facilities.

2 Basic adjustments can be carried out in an emergency, and further details are given in Chapter 13.

45 Front wheel alignment check

Non-TD5 models: Every 12 000 miles

Check the front wheel alignment as described in Chapter 11.

46 Spare wheel check

Non-TD5 models: Every 12 000 miles

Refer to *Weekly checks*.

47 Seat belt check

All models: Every 12 000 miles

1 Carefully examine the seat belt webbing for cuts, or any signs of serious fraying or deterioration. If the seat belt is of the retractable type, pull the belt all the way out, and examine the full extent of the webbing.

2 Fasten and unfasten the belt, ensuring that

48.3 Unscrewing the main gearbox drain plug – R380-type gearbox

the locking mechanism holds securely, and releases properly when intended. If the belt is of the retractable type, check also that the retracting mechanism operates correctly when the belt is released.

3 Check the security of all seat belt mountings and attachments which are accessible (without removing any trim or other components) from inside the vehicle.

4 Renew any worn components as described in Chapter 12.

48 Main gearbox oil renewal

Non-TD5 models: Every 12 000 miles

TD5 models: Every 24 000 miles

1 Ideally, the oil should be drained shortly after the vehicle has been driven, when the oil will be warm (allow time for the exhaust system to cool, however). Park the vehicle on level ground. On TD5 models, undo the fasteners and remove the transmission undershield.

2 Working under the vehicle, locate the main gearbox casing drain plug, and place a suitable container beneath the plug to catch the escaping oil.

3 Unscrew the drain plug, and allow the oil to drain. If the oil is hot, take precautions against scalding. Allow at least ten minutes for all the oil to drain **(see illustration)**.

4 Similarly, on models with LT 77 and LT77S-type gearboxes, locate the extension housing drain plug, then unscrew the plug and drain the remaining oil from the gearbox **(see illustration)**.

5 Renew the drain plug sealing washer(s) regardless of their apparent condition.

6 The extension housing drain plug (where applicable) incorporates a filter. Clean the filter with paraffin, then thoroughly dry the filter and the plug before refitting.

7 When all the oil has drained from the gearbox, clean, refit and tighten the drain plug(s), using new washer(s). Tighten the plugs to the specified torque, where given.

8 Unscrew the oil filler/level plug from the side of the main gearbox casing, and place a suitable container beneath the hole, to catch

48.4 Main gearbox extension housing drain plug (arrowed) – LT77-type gearbox

any excess oil which may be spilled when the gearbox is filled **(see illustrations 15.3a and 15.3b)**. Note that on R380 gearboxes, a Torx 55 bit may be required to unscrew the plug.

9 Fill the gearbox with the specified grade of oil (see *Lubricants and fluids*), until the oil flows from the filler/level plug hole. It is advisable to fill the gearbox slowly, to avoid a sudden spillage!

10 On completion, refit the filler/level plug, and tighten to the specified torque. **Do not** overtighten the plug, as it has a tapered thread. **Note:** *On TD5 gearboxes, apply a little RTV sealant to the threads of the filler/level plug before refitting.*

11 Wipe any split oil from the gearbox casing. Refit the transmission undershield where applicable.

49 Alarm handset battery renewal

TD5 models: Every 24 000 miles

⚠️ *Warning: Do not remove the battery until you are ready to install a new one. The engine will immobilise 5 minutes after the ignition key is removed from the switch (or 30 seconds after the engine has been switched off and the driver's door opened). If the battery renewal procedure is not completed in this time, the emergency key access code will have to be entered (refer to your Owners Handbook or Dealer/Specialist) before the handset can be synchronised.*

1 Unlock the vehicle/disable the alarm system using the unlock button on the remote handset.

2 Insert the ignition key and turn the key to position II, then back to position 0 and remove the key.

3 Using a coin or small flat-bladed screwdriver, carefully prise apart the two halves of the handset and slide the battery from the retaining clip **(see illustration)**. Do not touch the circuit board or contact surfaces of the clip with bare skin.

4 Press and hold any one of the handset buttons for at least 5 seconds to drain any residual electrical energy.

5 Fit the new battery (type CR2032), into the clip with the positive (+) side facing upwards **(see illustration)**. Avoid touching the flat surfaces of the battery with bare skin as this may reduce the life of the battery.

6 Clip the two halves of the handset back together.

7 Press the padlock symbol button on the handset at least 4 times whilst next to the vehicle to resynchronise the handset, then press the unlock button once. The handset should now be ready for use.

50 Brake fluid renewal

Non-TD5 models: Every 18 000 miles
TD5 models: Every 24 000 miles

1 The procedure is similar to that for the bleeding of the hydraulic system as described in Chapter 10, except that the brake fluid reservoir should be emptied before starting. Either syphon off the fluid, using a (clean) old battery hydrometer or similar, or open the first bleed screw in the sequence, and pump the fluid from the reservoir. Allowance should be made for all the old fluid to be expelled from the circuit when bleeding each section of the circuit. Used brake fluid is usually much darker in colour than fresh fluid, making it easy to distinguish the two.

51 Transfer gearbox oil renewal

All models: Every 24 000 miles

1 Park the vehicle on level ground. Undo the fasteners and remove the transmission undershield (where applicable).

2 Locate the filler/level plug in the side of the transfer gearbox casing, then unscrew the plug (see Section 16).

3 Place a container beneath the drain plug in the bottom of the gearbox casing, then unscrew the drain plug and allow the oil to drain **(see illustration)**. Recover the sealing washer.

4 When the oil has finished draining, refit and tighten the drain plug, using a new sealing washer if necessary.

5 Refill the gearbox with oil of the specified type through the filler/level hole, until the oil level reaches the lower edge of the hole (place a container beneath the hole, to catch any escaping oil).

6 Clean and refit the filler/level plug, and tighten to the specified torque. **Do not** overtighten the plug, as it has tapered threads.

7 Wipe any split oil from the gearbox casing. Refit the undershield where applicable.

52 Axle oil renewal

All models: Every 24 000 miles

Note: *A 13 mm square-section wrench will be required to undo the axle filler/level plug and drain plug. These wrenches can be obtained from most motor factors, or from your Land Rover dealer.*

1 This operation is much quicker and more efficient if the car is first taken on a journey of sufficient length to warm the axle oil up to normal operating temperature. Allow time, however, for the exhaust system to cool.

2 Park the car on level ground, switch off the ignition, and apply the handbrake firmly.

3 Wipe clean the area around the front axle filler/level plug, which is on the differential housing. Unscrew the plug, and clean it.

4 Position a suitable container under the drain plug situated on the base of the differential housing.

5 Unscrew the drain plug, and allow the oil to drain completely into the container. If the oil is hot, take precautions against scalding. Examine the sealing washer for signs of damage, renewing it if necessary, and clean both the filler/level and the drain plugs.

6 When the oil has finished draining, clean the drain plug threads and those of the differential casing, then refit the drain plug and washer, tightening it securely.

7 Refilling the axle is an extremely awkward operation. Above all, allow plenty of time for the oil level to settle properly before checking

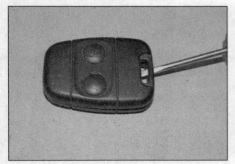

49.3 Carefully prise apart the two halves of the handset

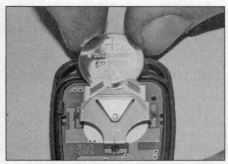

49.5 Fit the new battery with the positive side upwards

51.3 Transfer gearbox oil drain plug (arrowed)

53.5 Removing the swivel pin housing drain plug

it. Note that the car must be parked on level ground when checking the oil level.

8 Refill the axle with the exact amount of the specified type of oil (see *Lubricants and fluids*), then check the oil level as described in Section 17. If the correct amount was poured into the transmission, and a large amount flows out on checking the level, refit the filler/level plug; take the car on a short journey so that the new oil is distributed fully around the axle components, then check the level again on your return.

9 When the level is correct, refit the filler/level plug, tightening it securely, and wash off any spilt oil.

10 Repeat the procedure for the rear axle.

53 Swivel pin housing oil renewal

Non-TD5 models: Every 24 000 miles

1 This operation is much quicker and more efficient if the car is first taken on a journey of sufficient length to warm the swivel pin housing oil up to normal operating temperature. Allow time, however, for the exhaust system to cool.

2 Park the car on level ground, switch off the ignition, and apply the handbrake firmly.

3 Working underneath the vehicle, unscrew the left-hand swivel pin housing level and filler plugs. Both plugs can be identified by their square-section heads (see Section 18).

4 Position a suitable container under the drain plug situated on the base of the swivel pin housing.

5 Unscrew the drain plug, and allow the oil to drain completely into the container **(see illustration)**. If the oil is hot, take precautions against scalding. Examine the sealing washer for signs of damage, renewing it if necessary, and clean the threads of all removed plugs.

6 When the oil has finished draining, clean the drain plug threads and those of the housing, then refit the drain plug and washer, tightening it securely.

7 Refilling the housing is an extremely awkward operation. Above all, allow plenty of time for the oil level to settle properly before checking it. Note that the car must be parked on level ground when checking the oil level.

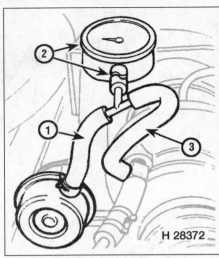

56.2 Turbocharger boost pressure checking

1 Wastegate actuator hose
2 T-piece and pressure gauge
3 Hose to turbocharger

8 Refill the housing with the exact amount of the specified type of oil (see *Lubricants and fluids*), then check the oil level as described in Section 18. If the correct amount was poured into the transmission, and a large amount flows out on checking the level, refit the filler and level plugs; take the car on a short journey so that the new oil is distributed fully around the swivel pin housing components, then check the level again on your return.

9 When the level is correct, refit the filler and level plugs, tightening them securely, and wash off any spilt oil.

10 Repeat the above operation on the right-hand swivel pin housing.

54 Fuel injector leak check

Non-TD5 models: Every 24 000 miles

1 Check the fuel injector seating areas in the cylinder head for any signs of fuel leakage.

2 Similarly, check the fuel supply pipe unions and the fuel leak-off pipe unions.

3 Rectify any leaks without delay. Do not overtighten the fuel unions in an attempt to cure leaks.

55 Fuel injector spray pattern check (10J, 12J and 19J engines)

Every 24 000 miles

This check requires the use of specialist equipment, and must be entrusted to a Land Rover dealer or a diesel fuel injection specialist.

56 Turbocharger boost pressure check

Non-TD5 models: Every 24 000 miles

Note: *A pressure gauge capable of registering a pressure of 1.0 bars will be required for this check.*

1 Working in the engine compartment, disconnect the hose connecting the wastegate actuator to the turbocharger, at the turbocharger.

2 Connect the hose to a T-piece, and use a short length of hose to connect the T-piece to the turbocharger **(see illustration)**.

3 Obtain a length of hose long enough to run from the T-piece in the engine compartment to the passenger compartment, to enable a pressure gauge to be read by the driver or passenger whilst the vehicle is being driven. Note that the hose must be long enough to be routed so that it is not trapped when the bonnet is closed.

4 Connect the hose between the T-piece and the pressure gauge. Carefully lower the bonnet, taking care not to trap the hose. Do not fully close the bonnet (as this will trap the hose), but ensure that the safety catch is engaged so that there is no risk of the bonnet opening when the vehicle is driven. As a safety precaution, it is advisable to secure the bonnet, using a length of string or a cable-tie around the lock and striker.

5 Start the engine, and drive the vehicle normally until the engine reaches normal operating temperature.

6 When the engine is warm, drive the vehicle normally up a suitable shallow hill, in such a manner that full throttle can be maintained, with the engine speed held steady between 2500 and 3000 rpm.

7 Under these conditions, the maximum boost pressure should be as specified (see *Specifications*).

8 If the reading is not as specified, it is likely that there is a fault with the turbocharger wastegate. In this case, have the problem investigated by a Land Rover dealer.

57 Engine oil filter cartridge renewal (TD5 engines)

Every 36 000 miles

Note: *This procedure must be accompanied by changing the engine oil as described in Section 4. Ensure the exhaust pipe is cooled before attempting this procedure.*

1 Clean the area around the filter housing, and place a container under the engine beneath the filter.

2 Using an oil filter removal tool if necessary, slacken the filter initially **(see illustrations)**. Loosely wrap some rags around the oil filter,

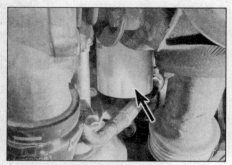

57.2a The oil filter cartridge is located on the left-hand side of the engine, just in front of the exhaust pipe (arrowed) . . .

57.2b . . . using a strap wrench if necessary

57.4 Apply a little clean engine oil to the filter sealing ring

then unscrew it. Remove the oil filter from the engine compartment, and empty the oil into the container used to drain the sump.

3 Use a clean rag to remove all oil, dirt and sludge from the filter sealing area on the engine. Check the old filter, to make sure that the rubber sealing ring hasn't stuck to the engine. If it has, carefully remove it.

4 Apply a light coating of clean oil to the sealing ring on the new filter, then screw it into position on the engine **(see illustration)**. Tighten the filter firmly by hand only – do not use any tools. Wipe clean the exterior of the oil filter.

5 Refitting is a reversal of removal. Fill the engine with clean oil as described earlier in this Section.

58 Coolant renewal

Non-TD5 models: Every 2 years

TD5 models: Every 36 000 miles

⚠️ *Warning: Wait until the engine is cold before starting this procedure. Do not allow antifreeze to come in contact with your skin, or with the painted surfaces of the vehicle. Rinse off spills immediately with plenty of water. Never leave antifreeze lying around in an open container, or in a puddle in the driveway or garage floor. Children and pets are attracted by its sweet smell, but antifreeze is fatal if ingested. Refer to the 'Antifreeze mixture' sub-Section below before proceeding.*

Cooling system draining

1 To drain the cooling system, first cover the expansion tank cap with a wad of rag, and slowly turn the cap anti-clockwise to relieve the pressure in the cooling system (a hissing sound will normally be heard). Wait until any pressure remaining in the system is released, then continue to turn the cap until it can be removed.

2 Position a suitable container beneath the radiator. On early models (where a drain screw is fitted to the bottom, left-hand corner

of radiator) unscrew the drain screw and washer, and allow the coolant to drain into the container. On later models (were no drain screw is fitted), release the hose clip, and ease the hose from the radiator stub. If the hose joint has not been disturbed for some time, it will be necessary to carefully manipulate the hose to break the joint (refer to Chapter 3, Section 2). Allow the coolant to drain into the container. On TD5 models, slacken the clips and remove the intercooler-to-intake manifold hose for access to the radiator bottom hose.

3 To fully drain the system, on non-TD5 engines, also slacken and remove the coolant drain plug from the left-hand side of the cylinder block, and allow any residual coolant to drain from the block. On TD5 engines, there is a drain plug fitted to the right-hand side of the block **(see illustration)**, but the alternator must be removed before access can be gained. When the flow of coolant has stopped, wipe clean the threads of the drain plug and block. Where the plug was fitted with a sealing washer, fit a new sealing washer. Where no washer was fitted, apply a smear of suitable sealant to the drain plug threads. Refit the drain plug to the block, and tighten it securely.

4 If the coolant has been drained for a reason other than renewal, then provided it is clean and less than two years old, it can be re-used.

Cooling system flushing

5 If coolant renewal has been neglected, or

58.3 On TD5 engines, the cylinder block drain plug (arrowed) can only be accessed after removal of the alternator

if the antifreeze mixture has become diluted, then in time, the cooling system may gradually lose efficiency, as the coolant passages become restricted due to rust, scale deposits, and other sediment. The cooling system efficiency can be restored by flushing the system clean.

6 The radiator should be flushed independently of the engine, to avoid unnecessary contamination.

7 To flush the radiator, disconnect the top hose at the radiator, then insert a garden hose into the radiator top inlet. Direct a flow of clean water through the radiator, and continue flushing until clean water emerges from the radiator bottom outlet (the bottom radiator hose should have been disconnected to drain the system). If after a reasonable period, the water still does not run clear, the radiator can be flushed with a good proprietary cleaning agent. It is important that the cleaning agent manufacturer's instructions are followed carefully. If the contamination is particularly bad, insert the hose in the radiator bottom outlet, and flush the radiator in reverse (reverse-flushing).

8 Remove the thermostat as described in Chapter 3, then temporarily refit the thermostat cover.

9 With the radiator top and bottom hoses disconnected from the radiator, insert a hose into the radiator bottom hose. Direct a clean flow of water through the engine, and continue flushing until clean water emerges from the radiator top hose.

10 On completion of flushing, refit the thermostat with reference to Chapter 3, and reconnect the hoses.

Cooling system filling

11 Before attempting to fill the cooling system, make sure that all hoses and clips are in good condition, and that the clips are tight. Note that an antifreeze mixture must be used all year round, to prevent corrosion of the alloy engine components.

12 On early models, refit the drain plug and sealing washer to the radiator, and tighten it securely. On later models, reconnect the bottom hose, and securely tighten its retaining clip.

58.13a On 300 TDi engines, the filler cap (arrowed) is situated on the top of the thermostat housing

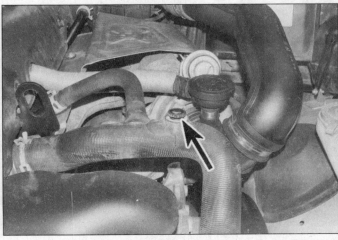

58.13b On TD5 engines, open the bleed screw in the radiator top hose (arrowed) . . .

13 Remove the expansion tank cap. On 300 TDi engines, unscrew the filler cap from the top of the thermostat housing, and recover the sealing ring **(see illustration)**. On earlier models, unscrew the filler cap (where fitted) from the top of the radiator. Recover the cap sealing ring (where fitted); renew it if it shows signs of damage or deterioration. On TD5 models, slacken the bleed screw in the radiator top hose and fuel cooler hose **(see illustrations)**.

14 Set the cabin heater controls to maximum heat.

15 Fill the system by slowly pouring the coolant into the filler hole or, where no filler hole is fitted, into the expansion tank (as applicable) to prevent airlocks from forming.

16 If the coolant is being renewed, begin by pouring in a couple of litres of water, followed by the correct quantity of antifreeze, then top-up with more water.

17 When coolant free of air bubbles emerges from the filler (where fitted), refit the seal and filler cap, and tighten it securely. On TD5 models, when air-free coolant emerges, tighten the bleed screw in the radiator top hose and fuel cooler hose.

18 Top-up the expansion tank to the correct level (see *Weekly checks*), then refit the expansion tank cap. On TD5 models, also refit the intercooler hose.

19 Start the engine, run it until it reaches normal operating temperature, then stop the engine and allow it to cool.

20 Check for leaks, particularly around disturbed components. Check the coolant level in the expansion tank, and top-up if necessary. Note that the system must be cold before an accurate level is indicated in the expansion tank. If the expansion tank cap is removed while the engine is still warm, cover the cap with a thick cloth. Unscrew the cap slowly, to gradually relieve the system pressure (a hissing sound will normally be heard). Wait until any pressure remaining in the system is

released, then continue to turn the cap until it can be removed.

Antifreeze mixture

21 Always use an ethylene-glycol based antifreeze which is suitable for use in mixed-metal cooling systems. The quantity of antifreeze and levels of protection are indicated in the Specifications. **Note:** *On TD5 models, only antifreeze with OAT (Organic Acid Technology) corrosion inhibitors must be used. Do not mix this with any other type of antifreeze.*

22 Before adding antifreeze, the cooling system should be completely drained, preferably flushed, and all hoses and clips checked for condition and security.

23 After filling with antifreeze, a label should be attached to the radiator or expansion tank, stating the type and concentration of antifreeze used, and the date installed. Any subsequent topping-up should be made with the same type and concentration of antifreeze.

24 Do not use engine antifreeze in the windscreen/tailgate washer system, as it will cause damage to the vehicle paintwork. A screenwash should be added to the washer system, in the quantities recommended on the bottle.

59 Shock absorber check

Non-TD5 models: Every 36 000 miles

1 Check for any signs of fluid leakage around the shock absorber body, or from the rubber gaiter around the piston rod. Should any fluid be noticed, the shock absorber is defective internally, and should be renewed. **Note:** *Shock absorbers should always be renewed in pairs on the same axle – never renew just one, or abnormal handling characteristics may result.*

58.13c . . . and in the fuel cooler hose on the right-hand side of the engine (arrowed)

2 The efficiency of the shock absorber may be checked by bouncing the vehicle at each corner. Generally speaking, the body will return to its normal position and stop after being depressed. If it rises and returns on a rebound, the shock absorber is probably suspect. Examine also the shock absorber upper and lower mountings for any signs of wear.

60 Brake vacuum servo air filter renewal

Non-TD5 models: Every 36 000 miles

1 Remove the servo unit (see Chapter 10).
2 Peel back the dust cover from the rear of the servo unit, to gain access to the air filter. Release the end cap from the servo unit, then carefully hook the old filters out of the servo, and release them from the pushrod.
3 Remove all traces of dirt from the servo unit, then install both new filters, making sure that they are correctly seated. Note that it will be necessary to cut a slot in each filter, to allow them to be slid into position.
4 Make sure that both filters are correctly

seated, then clip the end cap back into position.

5 Slide the dust cover back into position, then refit the servo unit (Chapter 10).

61 Braking system seal, vacuum servo filter and hose renewal

Non-TD5 models: Every 36 000 miles

TD5 models: Every 48 000 miles

1 At this interval, Land Rover recommend that all the brake wheel cylinder/caliper seals and flexible rubber hoses are renewed, and the hydraulic system filled with fresh fluid. At the same time, the vacuum servo unit filter should also be renewed. Refer to the relevant Sections of Chapter 10 for renewal information.

62 Intercooler element cleaning

All models: Every 48 000 miles

1 Remove the intercooler as described in Chapter 4A or 4B.

2 Check the element for damage and deterioration, and renew if necessary.

3 If the original element is to be refitted, flush the element with Unicorn Chemicals C Solve or a suitable alternative (check with your Land Rover dealer or specialist, following the instructions supplied with the cleaner.

4 Dry the element thoroughly, then refit as described in Chapter 4A or 4B.

63 Timing belt renewal

Non-TD5 models: Every 60 000 miles

The timing belt renewal procedure is described in Chapter 2A.

Chapter 2 Part A:
Non-TD5 engines in-car repair procedures

Contents

Section number

Cam follower components – removal, inspection and refitting 12
Camshaft – removal, inspection and refitting. 18
Compression and leakdown tests – description and interpretation. . 2
Crankcase breather hose check. . . . . .See Chapter 1
Crankshaft pulley (and damper – 200 TDi engine) –
   removal and refitting. 5
Crankshaft spigot bush – renewal 20
Cylinder head – removal, inspection and refitting 11
Engine breather filter cleaning .See Chapter 1
Engine mountings – removal and refitting 21
Engine oil and filter renewal . . . . .See Chapter 1
Engine oil cooler and thermostat – removal and refitting 22
Engine oil level check. . . . . .See Chapter 1
Flywheel – removal, inspection and refitting 19
Flywheel housing and timing belt housing draining . . . . .See Chapter 1
General information 1

Section number

Oil pump and skew gear (all except 300 TDi engines) –
   removal, inspection and refitting 14
Oil pump and strainer (300 TDi engines) – removal, inspection and
   refitting 15
Oil seals – renewal 16
Sump – removal and refitting 13
Timing belt (all except 10J engines) –
   inspection, removal and refitting 8
Timing belt housing gasket (all except 10J engines) – renewal 17
Timing chain (10J engines) – removal, inspection and refitting 7
Timing chain/belt cover – removal and refitting 6
Timing sprockets and tensioner – removal and refitting 9
Top dead centre (TDC) for No 1 piston – locating 3
Valve clearances checking and adjustment . . . . .See Chapter 1
Valve cover – removal and refitting. 4
Valve operating (rocker) gear – removal, inspection and refitting . . . 10

Degrees of difficulty

Easy, suitable for novice with little experience	**Fairly easy,** suitable for beginner with some experience	**Fairly difficult,** suitable for competent DIY mechanic	**Difficult,** suitable for experienced DIY mechanic	**Very difficult,** suitable for expert DIY or professional

Specifications

General

Engine type. . . . .   Four-cylinder, in-line, water-cooled. Single chain-driven (10J engines) or belt-driven (all except 10J engines) camshaft, operating valves via pushrods and rocker gear

Manufacturer's engine codes:
   2286 cc (2 1/4) normally-aspirated engine (1983 to 1984). 10J
   2495 cc (2 1/2) normally-aspirated engine (1984 to 1986). 12J
   2495 cc turbocharged engine (1986 to September 1990) 19J
   2495 cc turbocharged and intercooled engine:
      September 1990 to 1994 . . . .   200 TDi
      1994 on. . . . .   300 TDi
Bore . . . .   90.4700 mm
Stroke:
   10J engine . . . .   88.9000 mm
   All except 10J engine . . . .   97.0000 mm
Firing order . . . .   1-3-4-2 (No 1 at timing chain/belt end)
Direction of crankshaft rotation . . . .   Clockwise (viewed from timing chain/belt end of engine)
Compression ratio:
   10J engine 23:1
   12J and 19J engines 21:1
   200 TDi and 300 TDi engines . . . . $19.5:1 \pm 0.5:1$
Maximum power (DIN):
   10J engine . . . .   44 kW (59 bhp) at 4000 rpm
   12J engine . . . .   50 kW (67 bhp) at 4000 rpm
   19J engine . . . .   63 kW (85 bhp) at 4000 rpm
   200 TDi and 300 TDi engines . . . .   83 kW (111 bhp) at 4000 rpm
Maximum torque (DIN):
   10J engine . . . .   136 Nm (100 lbf ft) at 1800 rpm
   12J engine . . . .   155 Nm (114 lbf ft) at 1800 rpm
   19J engine . . . .   203 Nm (150 lbf ft) at 1800 rpm
   200 TDi and 300 TDi engines . . . .   265 Nm (195 lbf ft) at 1800 rpm
Maximum compression pressure difference between cylinders
   (typical value) . . . .   5.0 bars (70 psi)

Timing chain
Damper-to-chain clearance . . . .   0.25 mm maximum

Timing belt

Tension (using gauge-type torque wrench – see text):	Nm	lbf ft
12J and 19J engines:		
New belt	24 to 29	18 to 21
Used belt	19 to 24	14 to 18
200 TDi engine:		
New belt	19	14
Used belt	17	13
300 TDi engine:		
New belt	14 to 16	10 to 12
Used belt	11 to 13	8 to 10

Camshaft
Endfloat . . . .   0.1000 to 0.2000 mm
Maximum camshaft bearing running clearance . . . .   0.0508 mm

Rocker arms
Rocker arm freeplay on rocker shaft . . . .   0.1010 to 0.1270 mm

Lubrication system
Normal oil pressure (engine at normal operating temperature
 and operating speeds) . . . .   1.7 to 3.8 bars (25.0 to 55.0 psi)
Oil pump type:
 200 TDi engine . . . .   Double gear-type, driven by camshaft via skew gear and driveshaft
 300 TDi engine . . . .   Rotor type, driven directly from front of crankshaft
Oil pump clearances:
 10J and early 12J engines:
  Maximum gear-to-housing clearance (endfloat):
   Steel gear . . . .   0.0500 to 0.1200 mm
   Aluminium gear . . . .   0.0700 to 0.1500 mm
  Maximum gear lobe-to-housing clearance . . . .   0.0200 to 0.1000 mm
  Maximum gear backlash . . . .   0.1500 to 0.2800 mm
 Later 12J*, and 19J and 200 TDi engines:
  Maximum gear-to-housing clearance (endfloat) . . . .   0.0260 to 0.1350 mm
  Maximum gear lobe-to-housing clearance . . . .   0.0250 to 0.0750 mm
  Maximum gear backlash . . . .   0.1000 to 0.2000 mm
 * **Note:** *Later 12J engines have oil pump gears with 10 teeth.*

Flywheel
Maximum permissible lateral run-out of flywheel . . . .   0.0500 to 0.0700 mm
Minimum permissible thickness of flywheel after refinishing . . . .   36.9600 mm

Oil pump skew gear
Bush-to-thrustwasher clearance (10J, 12J and 19J engines) . . . .   0.0510 to 0.2030 mm

Torque wrench settings

	Nm	lbf ft
Air conditioning compressor mounting bracket bolts	45	33
Air conditioning compressor/alternator drivebelt:		
Idler pulley bolt	45	33
Tensioner securing bolt	25	18
Alternator adjuster link bolt (10J, 12J and 19J engines)	25	18
Alternator mounting bracket bolts:		
10J, 12J and 19J engines	25	18
Models with air conditioning	45	33
Auxiliaries mounting bracket to cylinder block (200 TDi and		
300 TDi engines)	25	18
Auxiliary drivebelt tensioner securing nut (200 TDi and 300 TDi engines) .	45	33
Big-end cap nuts*:		
10J, 12J and 19J engines	34	25
200 TDi and 300 TDi engines	59	44
Camshaft oil jet	7	5
Camshaft sprocket bolt (all except 300 TDi engine)	45	33
Camshaft sprocket hub-to-camshaft bolt (300 TDi engine)	80	59
Camshaft sprocket-to-camshaft hub bolts (300 TDi engine)	25	18
Camshaft thrustplate bolts	9	7

Torque wrench settings (continued)

	Nm	lbf ft
Coolant pipe stub-to-cylinder head (200 TDi and 300 TDi engines) . . .	22	16
Coolant temperature sensor/blanking plug	14	10
Coolant temperature sensor adapter (10J, 12J and 19J engines)	25	18
Crankcase breather cover bolts (300 TDi engine)	25	18
Crankshaft damper bolt (200 TDi engine).	340`	251
Crankshaft pulley bolt (300 TDi engine):		
Stage 1	80	59
Stage 2	Angle-tighten a further 90º	
Crankshaft pulley bolt/nut/starter dog	270	199
Crankshaft rear oil seal housing bolts (300 TDi engine).	25	18
Cylinder block coolant drain plug.	25	18
Cylinder block ladder frame bolts (200 TDi engine)	25	18
Cylinder block oil gallery rear plug	37	27
Cylinder block oil jets	17	13
Cylinder block side cover bolts	25	18
Cylinder head bolts:		
10J, 12J and 19J engines.	123	91
200 TDi engine:		
Stage 1	40	30
Stage 2	Angle-tighten a further 60º	
Stage 3	Angle-tighten a further 60º	
300 TDi engine:		
Stage 1 (all bolts)	Tighten until undersides of bolt heads just contact cylinder head face	
Stage 2 (all bolts)	40	30
Stage 3 (all bolts)	Angle-tighten a further 60º	
Stage 4 (all bolts)	Angle-tighten a further 60º	
Stage 5 (M12 x 140 mm bolts only)	Angle tighten a further 20º	
Dipstick tube bolt	25	18
Engine lifting bracket bolts:		
10J, 12J and 19J engines.	34	25
200 TDi and 300 TDi engines	25	18
Engine mounting bracket-to-cylinder block bolts	85	63
Engine mounting rubber-to-bracket nuts.	85	63
Exhaust manifold nuts/bolts:		
19J engine	32	24
200 TDi engine	25	18
300 TDi engine	45	33
Flywheel housing drain plug.	12	9
Flywheel housing-to-cylinder block bolts	45	33
Flywheel securing bolts:		
10J, 12J and 19J engines.	137	101
200 TDi and 300 TDi engines	146	108
Fuel injection pump rear mounting bracket-to-cylinder block bolts . . .	25	18
Fuel injection pump sprocket nut (12J and 19J engines).	45	33
Fuel injection pump sprocket to hub (200 TDi and 300 TDi engines) . .	25	18
Inlet manifold nuts/bolts:		
19J engine	35	26
200 TDi and 300 TDi engines	25	18
Main bearing cap bolts**	133	98
Oil baffle-to-crankcase breather cover bolts (300 TDi engine).	4	3
Oil cooler pipe-to-oil filter adapter unions	45	33
Oil drain pipes-to-cylinder block	25	18
Oil filter adapter bolts	45	33
Oil pick-up pipe-to-bearing cap bolts (300 TDi engine).	9	7
Oil pick-up pipe-to-bracket bolt (all except 300 TDi engine)	25	18
Oil pick-up pipe-to-oil pump nut (all except 300 TDi engine)	45	33
Oil pick-up pipe-to-timing belt housing bolts (300 TDi engine)	25	18
Oil pressure relief valve plug	30	22
Oil pressure warning light switch	17	13
Oil pump cover-to-oil pump bolts (all except 300 TDi engine).	25	18
Oil pump driveshaft bush-to-cylinder block screw:		
12J and 19J engines (initial torque – see text)	4	3
200 TDi engine	25	18
Oil pump skew gear bush locknut (10J, 12J and 19J engines)	30	22
Oil pump-to-cylinder block bolts (all except 300 TDi engine)	25	18
Oil separator-to-valve cover bolt (200 TDi and 300 TDi engines).	9	7
Oil thermostat housing-to-oil filter adapter bolts	9	7

Torque wrench settings (continued)

	Nm	lbf ft
Power steering pump bracket bolts	25	18
Rocker shaft pedestal bolts:		
10J, 12J and 19J engines	25	18
200 TDi engine	30	22
300 TDi engine:		
Stage 1	5	4
Stage 2	Angle-tighten a further 50°	
Rocker shaft-to-pedestal bolts (10J, 12J and 19J engines)	25	18
Sump drain plug:		
All except 200 TDi engine	35	26
200 TDi engine	45	33
Sump securing nuts/bolts:		
10J, 12J and 19J engines	18	13
200 TDi and 300 TDi engines	25	18
Tappet adjuster nut:		
All except 300 TDi engine	25	18
300 TDi engine	16	12
Tappet guide locating screws	14	10
Thermostat cover-to-cylinder head bolts (10J, 12J and 19J engines)	9	7
Thermostat cover-to-thermostat housing bolts:		
200 TDi engine	9	7
300 TDi engine	25	18
Thermostat housing to cylinder head (200 TDi and 300 TDi engines)	25	18
Timing belt housing-to-cylinder block bolts	25	18
Timing belt idler pulley nut (300 TDi engine)	45	33
Timing belt tensioner bolt (200 TDi and 300 TDi engines)	45	33
Timing belt tensioner nuts (12J and 19J engines)	25	18
Timing chain damper bolts (10J engine)	9	7
Timing chain/belt cover bolts	25	18
Turbocharger oil drain adapter to cylinder block:		
19J engine	25	18
200 TDi and 300 TDi engines	42	31
Turbocharger oil feed adapter to cylinder block	25	18
Valve cover securing bolts/screws:		
10J, 12J and 19J engines	9	7
200 TDi engine	4	3
300 TDi engine	10	7
Wiring harness bracket bolts	25	18

* New big-end nuts and bolts must be used on refitting.
** New bolts must be used on refitting.

1 General information

How to use this Chapter

This Part of Chapter 2 describes the repair procedures which can reasonably be carried out on the engine while it remains in the vehicle. If the engine has been removed from the vehicle and is being dismantled as described in Chapter 2C, any preliminary dismantling procedures can be ignored.

Note that, while it may be possible physically to overhaul items such as the piston/connecting rod assemblies while the engine is in the vehicle, this is not recommended. Such tasks are not usually carried out as separate operations, and usually require the execution of several additional procedures (not to mention the cleaning of components and of oilways); for this reason, all such tasks are classed as major overhaul procedures, and are described in Chapter 2C.

Chapter 2C describes the removal of the engine from the vehicle, and the full overhaul procedures which can then be carried out.

Engine description

Although five different diesel engines have been fitted to models covered by this manual, they are all (with the exception of the TD5 unit) basically developments of the original Land Rover 2 1/4 petrol/diesel engine. The engines have undergone a continuous process of development, and although many internal details and ancillaries have altered, the basic configuration of the engine remains unchanged.

The engine is of four-cylinder in-line, overhead valve type, and is mounted longitudinally at the front of the vehicle.

10J, 12J and 19J engines use indirect diesel injection, with swirl chambers incorporated in the cylinder head. 200 TDi and 300 TDi engines use direct diesel injection, with combustion chambers incorporated in the piston crowns.

On early 10J engines, the crankshaft runs in three shell-type bearings. On all other engines, the crankshaft runs in five bearings. The centre bearing incorporates thrustwashers, to control crankshaft endfloat.

The connecting rods are attached to the crankshaft by horizontally-split shell-type big-end bearings. The pistons are attached to the connecting rods by gudgeon pins, which are a push-fit in the connecting rod small-end bores. The gudgeon pins are retained by circlips. On 10J engines, the pistons are fitted with four piston rings, three compression rings, and an oil control ring. On all other engines, the pistons are fitted with three piston rings – two compression rings and an oil control ring.

On 10J engines, the camshaft is driven by a double-row chain. On all other engines, the camshaft is driven from the crankshaft by a toothed composite-rubber belt, which also drives the fuel injection pump.

The camshaft runs in four bearings pressed into the cylinder block. Each cylinder has two valves (one inlet and one exhaust), operated from the camshaft via pushrods and rocker arms. To minimise camshaft wear, tappet rollers act on the camshaft lobes. The rollers act on tappet slides, which in turn operate the pushrods. The rocker arms pivot on a shaft bolted to the cylinder head, and incorporate adjuster pins to enable valve clearance adjustment.

On 10J, 12J and 19J engines, the inlet and exhaust valves are each closed by double valve springs. On 200 TDi and 300 TDi engines, each valve is closed by a single valve spring. The valves operate in guides pressed into the cylinder head.

On all except 300 TDi engines, a gear-type oil pump is located in the sump, and is driven from the camshaft via a skew gear and driveshaft. On 300 TDi engines, a rotor type oil pump is fitted, and the pump is driven directly from the front of the crankshaft.

The fuel lift pump and the brake vacuum pump (and, on 10J engines, the fuel injection pump) are driven from the camshaft.

The coolant pump is located in a housing at the front of the engine, and is driven by the auxiliary drivebelt.

Operations with engine in place

The following operations can be carried out without having to remove the engine from the vehicle.

a) Removal and refitting of the valve operating (rocker) gear.
b) Removal and refitting of the cylinder head.
c) Removal and refitting of the timing chain/belt and sprockets.
d) Removal and refitting of the sump.
e) Removal and refitting of the big-end bearings, connecting rods, and pistons*.
f) Removal and refitting of the oil pump.
g) Renewal of the engine mountings.
h) Removal and refitting of the flywheel.

* Although the operation marked with an asterisk can be carried out with the engine in the vehicle (after removal of the sump), it is preferable for the engine to be removed, in the interests of cleanliness and improved access. For this reason, the procedure is described in Chapter 2C.

2 Compression and leakdown tests – description and interpretation

Compression test

Note: A compression tester specifically designed for diesel engines must be used for this test.

1 When engine performance is down, or if misfiring occurs which cannot be attributed to the fuel system, a compression test can provide diagnostic clues as to the engine's condition. If the test is performed regularly, it can give warning of trouble before any other symptoms become apparent.

2 A compression tester specifically intended for diesel engines must be used, because of the higher pressures involved. The tester is connected to an adapter which screws into the glow plug or injector hole. It is unlikely to be worthwhile buying such a tester for occasional use, but it may be possible to borrow or hire one – if not, have the test performed by a garage.

3 Unless specific instructions to the contrary are supplied with the tester, observe the following points:

a) The battery must be in a good state of charge, the air filter must be clean, and the engine should be at normal operating temperature.
b) All the injectors or glow plugs should be removed before starting the test. If removing the injectors, also remove the copper washers (which must be renewed when the injectors are refitted – see Chapter 4A), otherwise they may be blown out.
c) It is advisable to disconnect the stop solenoid on the fuel injection pump, to reduce the amount of fuel discharged as the engine is cranked.

4 There is no need to hold the accelerator pedal down during the test, because the diesel engine air inlet is not throttled.

5 The actual compression pressures measured are not so important as the balance between cylinders. Land Rover do not specify compression pressures, but a typical value for the maximum difference between cylinders is given in the Specifications.

6 The cause of poor compression is less easy to establish on a diesel engine than on a petrol one. The effect of introducing oil into the cylinders ('wet' testing) is not conclusive, because there is a risk that the oil will sit in the recess on the piston crown, instead of passing to the rings. However, the following can be used as a rough guide to diagnosis.

7 All cylinders should produce very similar pressures; any difference greater than that specified indicates the existence of a fault. Note that the compression should build-up quickly in a healthy engine; low compression on the first stroke, followed by gradually-increasing pressure on successive strokes, indicates worn piston rings. A low compression reading on the first stroke, which does not build-up during successive strokes, indicates leaking valves or a blown head gasket (a cracked head could also be the cause). Deposits on the undersides of the valve heads can also cause low compression.

8 A low reading from two adjacent cylinders is almost certainly due to the head gasket having blown between them; the presence of coolant in the engine oil will confirm this.

9 If the compression reading is unusually high, the cylinder head surfaces, valves and pistons are probably coated with carbon deposits. If this is the case, the cylinder head should be removed and decarbonised (see Chapter 2C).

Leakdown test

10 A leakdown test measures the rate at which compressed air fed into the cylinder is lost. It is an alternative to a compression test, and in many ways it is better, since the escaping air provides easy identification of where pressure loss is occurring (piston rings, valves or head gasket).

11 The equipment needed for leakdown testing is unlikely to be available to the home mechanic. If poor compression is suspected, have the test performed by a suitably-equipped garage.

3 Top dead centre (TDC) for No 1 piston – locating

General

1 Top dead centre (TDC) is the highest point in the cylinder that each piston reaches as the crankshaft turns. Each piston reaches TDC at the end of the compression stoke, and again at the end of the exhaust stroke.

10J engine

Note: A timing pointer may be required for this operation (see text), and a new timing aperture cover gasket should be used on refitting.

2 Unscrew the two securing nuts and washers, and remove the cover from the timing aperture in the upper right-hand side of the flywheel housing. Recover the gasket.

3 Look to see if a timing pointer is visible in the aperture. If no pointer is visible, a suitable pointer can be obtained from a Land Rover dealer (part No ERC 2250). Where applicable, fit the timing pointer and secure with the two nuts – note that the pointer arrow should be positioned on the gearbox side of the timing aperture.

4 Remove the timing chain cover as described in Section 6.

5 Remove the valve cover as described in Section 4.

6 Using a suitable tool on the crankshaft pulley bolt, turn the crankshaft until the flywheel timing pointer is aligned with the line on the flywheel periphery marked E.P (see illustration).

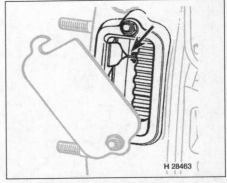

3.6 Flywheel E.P mark (arrowed) aligned with timing pointer – 10J and early 12J engines

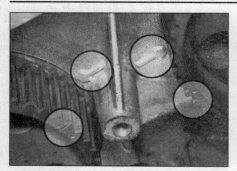

3.13 Fuel injection pump and camshaft sprocket timing marks aligned with arrows on timing belt housing – 19J engine

Note that the marks do not appear to align in this photo, due to the viewing angle

7 If the crankshaft is inadvertently turned beyond the TDC position, do not turn the crankshaft back – continue to turn in a clockwise direction until the flywheel E.P mark is exactly aligned with the pointer.

8 Check that No 1 exhaust valve is fully open. If the valve is closed, turn the crankshaft through a further complete turn, to align the flywheel mark with the pointer. Again, do not turn the crankshaft back if the TDC point is passed.

9 No 1 piston is now at TDC.

Early 12J engine with timing marks on flywheel

Note: *A timing pointer may be required for this operation (see text), and a new timing aperture cover gasket should be used on refitting.*

10 Unscrew the two securing nuts and washers, and remove the cover from the

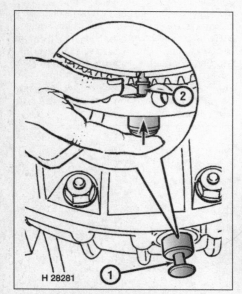

3.25a Special tool LRT-12-044 in position – 300 TDi engine model

1 Special tool LRT-12-044
2 Tool centre pin

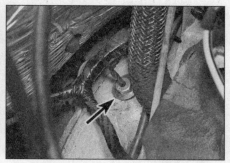

3.21 Flywheel locking tool (arrowed) in position in flywheel housing – 19J engine

timing aperture in the upper right-hand side of the flywheel housing. Recover the gasket.

11 Look to see if a timing pointer is visible in the aperture. If no pointer is visible, a suitable pointer can be obtained from a Land Rover dealer (part No ERC 2250). Where applicable, fit the timing pointer and secure with the two nuts – note that the pointer arrow should be positioned on the gearbox side of the timing aperture.

12 Remove the timing belt cover as described in Section 6.

13 Using a suitable tool on the crankshaft pulley bolt, turn the crankshaft until the timing dots on the camshaft and fuel injection pump sprockets are exactly aligned with their respective timing arrows cast into the timing belt housing (see illustration).

14 The flywheel timing pointer should now be aligned with a line on the flywheel periphery marked E.P (see illustration 3.6).

15 If the crankshaft is inadvertently turned beyond the TDC position, do not turn the crankshaft back – continue to turn in a clockwise direction until the sprocket timing marks are again in alignment, and the flywheel E.P mark is exactly aligned with the pointer.

16 No 1 piston is now at TDC.

Later 12J and 19J engines with timing slot in flywheel

Note: *A suitable tool will be required to lock the flywheel in position during this operation.*

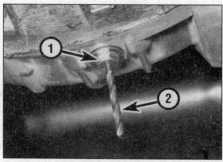

3.25b Improvised flywheel locking tool in position – 300 TDi engine model

1 Blanking plug
2 3/16 in twist drill

The Land Rover special tool for this purpose is LRT-12-044. Special flywheel locking tool can be improvised by obtaining a spare flywheel housing blanking plug, and accurately drilling a hole though its centre to accept a 3/16 in twist drill.

17 Unscrew the blanking plug from the timing hole in the upper right-hand side of the flywheel housing.

18 Screw the flywheel locking tool (see note at the beginning of this Section) into the timing hole. Do not engage the locking tool centre pin at this stage.

19 Remove the timing belt cover as described in Section 6.

20 Using a suitable tool on the crankshaft pulley bolt, turn the crankshaft until the timing dots on the camshaft and fuel injection pump sprockets are exactly aligned with their respective timing arrows cast into the timing belt housing (see illustration 3.13).

21 The flywheel locking tool centre pin should now slide easily into engagement with the timing slot in the flywheel (see illustration).

22 If the crankshaft is inadvertently turned beyond the TDC position, do not turn the crankshaft back – continue to turn in a clockwise direction until the sprocket timing marks are again in alignment, and the locking tool centre pin can be fully engaged with the flywheel slot.

23 The engine is now locked with No 1 piston at top dead centre.

200 TDi and 300 TDi engines

Note: *Suitable tools will be required to lock the flywheel and the fuel injection pump spindle in position during this operation. The Land Rover special tool available to lock the flywheel is LRT-12-044. Special flywheel locking tool can be improvised by obtaining a spare flywheel housing blanking plug, and accurately drilling a hole though its centre to accept a 3/16 in twist drill. To lock the fuel injection pump sprocket, special tool LRT-12-045 will be required – this tool can be improvised using a short length (approximately 50.0 mm) of 3/8 in diameter round bar. A new injection pump hub cover plate gasket should be used on refitting.*

24 Unscrew the blanking plug from the timing hole in the base of the flywheel housing.

25 Screw the flywheel locking tool (see note at the beginning of this sub-Section) into the timing hole. Do not engage the locking tool centre pin at this stage (see illustrations).

26 On models with air conditioning, remove the air conditioning compressor drivebelt as described in Chapter 1. If desired, unscrew the securing bolts, and move the compressor to one side, clear of the working area – **do not** disconnect the refrigerant lines (refer to the precautions in Chapter 3).

27 Remove the three securing screws, and withdraw the injection pump hub cover plate

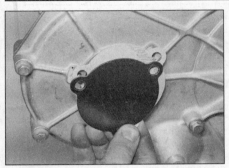

3.27 Remove the injection pump hub cover plate and gasket – viewed with engine removed

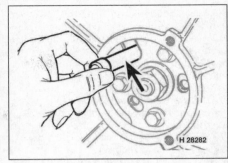

3.28 Injection pump timing pin (arrowed) in position

3.29 Improvised flywheel locking tool centre pin engaged with flywheel (viewed with gearbox removed)

from the timing belt cover **(see illustration)**. Note that on models with air conditioning, the air conditioning drivebelt tensioner pulley is secured to the cover plate. Recover the gasket.

28 Insert the pump timing pin (tool No LRT-12-045), or an improvised equivalent, through the U-shaped slot in the pump hub. Using a suitable tool on the crankshaft pulley/ damper bolt, turn the crankshaft until the timing pin can be slid through the pump hub into the pump body **(see illustration)**. The tool should slide easily into position.

29 The flywheel locking tool centre pin should now slide easily into engagement with the timing slot in the flywheel (if the tool does not slide easily into position, this indicates that the injection pump timing is incorrect – see Chapter 4A) **(see illustration)**.

30 The engine is now locked with No 1 piston at top dead centre.

4   Valve cover – removal and refitting

10J, 12J and 19J engines

Note: *A new gasket will be required on refitting.*

Removal

1 Remove the oil filler cap, and move the

cap to one side, leaving the breather hose(s) connected. If desired to improve access, the breather hoses can be disconnected and removed – note their locations, to ensure correct refitting.

2 Unscrew the three valve cover securing nuts, and recover the washers. Note the locations of any brackets secured by the nuts **(see illustration)**.

3 Lift the rocker cover from the cylinder head, and recover the gasket **(see illustration)**.

Refitting

4 Commence refitting by thoroughly cleaning the gasket faces of the cover and the cylinder head.

5 Further refitting is a reversal of removal, but use a new gasket, and ensure that any brackets are in position on the securing studs, as noted before removal.

200 TDi and 300 TDi engines

Note: *A new valve cover gasket may be required on refitting (the manufacturers recommend that the gasket is re-used a maximum of five times). New securing bolt sealing washers may be required and, on 200 TDi engines, new semi-circular seals and suitable liquid sealant may be required.*

Removal

6 Where applicable, unscrew the oil filler cap, then unclip the plastic cover from the top of the valve cover.

7 Loosen the hose clip(s), and disconnect the breather hose(s) from the valve cover, and from the breather filter on the side of the valve cover, where applicable.

8 Unscrew the three securing bolts (recover the sealing washers if they are loose) then lift the valve cover from the cylinder head.

9 Recover the gasket.

Refitting

10 Commence refitting by thoroughly cleaning the gasket faces of the cover and the cylinder head.

11 On 200 TDi engines, check the condition of the semi-circular seals at each end of the cylinder head, and renew if necessary. To renew the seals, prise them from the cut-outs in the cylinder head; thoroughly clean the cut-outs, and fit the new seals using suitable liquid sealant.

12 Check the condition of the sealing washers on the securing bolts, and renew if necessary.

13 Check the condition of the valve cover gasket, and renew if necessary. Note that the manufacturers recommend that the gasket is re-used a maximum of five times, regardless of condition.

14 Fit the gasket to the cover, then place the cover in position on the cylinder head **(see illustration)**.

15 Fit the securing bolts (with the sealing

4.2 Unscrew the securing nuts . . .

4.3 . . . and remove the valve cover – 19J engine

4.14 Fitting the gasket to the valve cover – 300 TDi engine

4.15 Ensure that the sealing washers (arrowed) are in place on the valve cover bolts – 300 TDi engine

washers), and tighten the bolts to the specified torque **(see illustration)**.

16 Reconnect the breather hose(s) to the cover, and tighten the hose clip(s).

17 Where applicable, refit the plastic cover to the valve cover, and refit the oil filler cap.

---

5 Crankshaft pulley (and damper – 200 TDi engine) – removal and refitting

10J, 12J and 19J engines

Removal

1 Disconnect the battery negative lead.

2 Where applicable, on models with air conditioning, proceed as follows:

a) *Remove the air conditioning compressor drivebelt, as described in Chapter 1.*

b) *Disconnect the wiring from the temperature sensor.*

c) *Remove the bolts securing the air conditioning compressor to the engine, and move the compressor to one side, clear of the working area. Take care not to strain the refrigerant hoses – do not under any circumstances disconnect the hoses.*

3 Remove the cooling fan cowl, and the cooling fan as described in Chapter 3.

4 Remove the auxiliary drivebelt(s) 'as described in Chapter 1.

5 The crankshaft must now be held stationary as the crankshaft pulley nut or bolt/starter

5.8 Removing the crankshaft pulley – 19J engine

dog (as applicable) is unscrewed – note that the nut/bolt is very tight. This can be achieved by removing the starter motor (see Chapter 5), and jamming the starter ring gear using a large screwdriver or similar tool. Alternatively, carry out the following:

a) *Apply the handbrake.*

b) *Engage the differential lock.*

c) *Engage the Low range in the transfer gearbox.*

d) *Engage first gear in the main gearbox.*

e) *Remove the ignition key.*

6 Hold the pulley stationary, and loosen the securing nut/bolt (the securing bolt incorporates a starter dog on early engines), using a suitable socket and extension bar.

7 Remove the nut/bolt and recover the washer, where applicable.

8 Withdraw the pulley from the crankshaft, using a suitable puller to free it if necessary **(see illustration)**.

Refitting

9 Refitting is a reversal of removal, bearing in mind the following points:

a) *Lightly grease the pulley spigot before fitting.*

b) *Tighten the pulley nut or bolt/starter dog to the specified torque.*

c) *Refit and tension the auxiliary drivebelt(s) as described in Chapter 1.*

d) *Refit the cooling fan and fan cowl assembly as described in Chapter 3.*

200 TDi engine

⚠️ *Warning: The crankshaft damper securing bolt is tightened to a very high torque, and both the damper and bolt are coated with thread-locking compound. Ensure that adequate, good-quality tools are used to hold the damper, and to loosen and tighten the bolt. Check the condition of the tools before use, to avoid the possibility of failure and resulting personal injury. Suitable thread-locking compound will be required to coat the threads of the bolt and the damper on refitting.*

Removal

10 Disconnect the battery negative lead.

11 On models with air conditioning, proceed as follows:

a) *Remove the air conditioning compressor drivebelt, as described in Chapter 1.*

b) *Disconnect the wiring from the temperature sensor located in the thermostat housing.*

c) *Remove the four bolts securing the air conditioning compressor to the engine, and move the compressor to one side, clear of the working area. Take care not to strain the refrigerant hoses – do not under any circumstances disconnect the hoses.*

12 Drain the cooling system as described in Chapter 1.

13 Remove the viscous cooling fan and coupling as described in Chapter 3.

14 Loosen the securing clip, and disconnect the intercooler-to-inlet manifold air trunking at the manifold.

15 Loosen the securing clips and remove the radiator top hose.

16 Unscrew the nuts securing the cooling fan cowl to the top of the radiator, and withdraw the cowl.

17 Remove the alternator and power steering pump drivebelts as described in Chapter 1.

18 Unscrew the four securing bolts, and remove the crankshaft pulley from the crankshaft damper.

19 To remove the damper, proceed as follows.

20 A suitable tool will be required to hold the damper stationary as the damper bolt is loosened – note that the bolt is very tight. This is most easily achieved by bolting a suitable metal bar to the damper, using bolts screwed into at least two of the pulley bolt holes. Alternatively, carry out the following:

a) *Apply the handbrake.*

b) *Engage the differential lock.*

c) *Engage the Low range in the transfer gearbox.*

d) *Engage first gear in the main gearbox.*

e) *Remove the ignition key.*

21 Hold the damper stationary, and loosen the damper bolt using a suitable socket and extension bar.

22 Where applicable, unbolt the tool used to hold the damper stationary, then remove the damper bolt and recover the washer.

23 Withdraw the damper from the crankshaft, using a suitable puller to free it if necessary.

Refitting

24 Clean all traces of thread-locking compound from the damper and the securing bolt.

25 Smear the crankshaft contact surfaces of the damper spigot with thread-locking compound.

26 Fit the damper to the crankshaft, then fit the washer and bolt.

27 Using the tool to hold the damper stationary, as during removal, tighten the bolt to pull the damper into position on the nose of the crankshaft.

28 Unscrew the bolt, then apply thread-locking compound to the bolt threads.

29 Refit the bolt, and tighten to the specified torque.

30 Further refitting is a reversal of removal, bearing in mind the following points:

a) *Tighten the crankshaft pulley bolts to the specified torque.*

b) *Refit and tension the power steering pump and alternator drivebelts as described in Chapter 1.*

c) *Refit the viscous cooling fan and coupling as described in Chapter 3.*

d) *On models with air conditioning, refit the air conditioning compressor drivebelt as described in Chapter 1.*

e) *On completion, refill the cooling system as described in Chapter 1.*

300 TDi engine

Note: *Suitable thread-locking compound will be required to coat the threads of the damper bolt on refitting.*

Removal

31 Disconnect the battery negative lead.
32 Drain the cooling system as described in Chapter 1.
33 Disconnect the radiator top hose.
34 Loosen the securing clips, and remove the air trunking connecting the intercooler to the inlet manifold.
35 Remove the viscous fan unit and cowl, as described in Chapter 3.
36 Remove the auxiliary drivebelt, as described in Chapter 1.
37 Proceed as described in paragraphs 20 to 23 inclusive.

Refitting

38 Refitting is a reversal of removal, bearing in mind the following points:
a) *Lightly grease the pulley spigot before fitting.*
b) *Apply suitable thread-locking compound to the bolt threads, and tighten the bolt to the specified torque, holding the pulley stationary as during removal.*
c) *Refit and tension the auxiliary drivebelt as described in Chapter 1.*
d) *Refit the viscous fan, coupling and fan cowl assembly, as described in Chapter 3.*
e) *On completion, refill the cooling system as described in Chapter 1.*

6 Timing chain/belt cover
– removal and refitting

10J engine

Note: *A new timing chain cover gasket must be used on refitting, and it is advisable to fit a new crankshaft oil seal to the cover.*

Removal

1 Remove the crankshaft pulley as described in Section 5.
2 Remove the cooling fan and the cowl assembly, as described in Chapter 3.

6.6 Withdrawing the timing chain cover – 10J engine

3 Drain the cooling system as described in Chapter 1.
4 Disconnect the coolant hoses from the coolant pump. Remove the short hose connecting the coolant pump to the thermostat housing.
5 Working under the vehicle, unscrew the bolts securing the sump to the timing chain cover.
6 Unscrew the nine securing bolts and the single nut, and withdraw the timing chain cover **(see illustration)**. Recover the main gasket, and the coolant passage gasket.

Refitting

7 Commence refitting by cleaning all traces of old gasket from the mating faces of the timing chain cover and the cylinder block.
8 It is advisable to fit a new crankshaft front oil seal to the cover as follows:
a) *Where applicable, drill out the rivets securing the oil seal dust shield to the timing chain cover. Alternatively, remove the self-tapping screws. Remove the dust shield.*
b) *Prise the old seal from the aperture in the cover using a suitable screwdriver.*
c) *Clean the seal seat in the cover.*
d) *Press a new seal into position using a suitable socket or tube. The seal lips should face the crankshaft. Take care not to damage the seal lips.*
e) *Fit the dust shield. Secure the dust shield with self-tapping screws (even if the shield was originally riveted in*

place) – coat the threads of the screws with sealing compound before fitting.
9 Refit the cover to the cylinder block using a new gasket, then refit the securing bolts and nut, and tighten to the specified torque.
10 Refit the bolts securing the sump to the timing chain cover, and tighten to the specified torque.
11 Refit and reconnect the coolant pump hoses.
12 Refit the cooling fan and cowl assembly as described in Chapter 3.
13 Refit the crankshaft pulley as described in Section 5.
14 On completion, refill the cooling system as described in Chapter 1.

12J and 19J engines

Note: *A new timing belt cover gasket must be used on refitting, and it is advisable to fit a new crankshaft dust seal to the cover.*

Removal

15 Remove the crankshaft pulley as described in Section 5.
16 Remove the coolant pump as described in Chapter 3.
17 Where applicable, unclip the coolant hose from the bracket on the cover.
18 Working at the bottom of the timing belt cover, unscrew the four securing bolts, and withdraw the breather cover plate and gauze filter **(see illustrations)**. Recover the gasket.
19 Unscrew the securing bolts (note the bolt locations, as several different lengths of bolt are used), and recover the washers, then withdraw the timing belt cover **(see illustration)**. The cover locates on dowels in the timing belt housing – if necessary, lever between the cover and housing mating faces to free the cover, but take care not to damage the mating faces. Note the locations of any brackets secured by the bolts.
20 Recover the gasket. Where applicable, also recover the smaller circular gasket from the centre cover securing bolt lug.

Refitting

21 Commence refitting by cleaning all traces of old gasket from the mating faces of the timing belt cover and housing.

6.18a Unscrew the securing bolts . . .

6.18b . . . and withdraw the breather cover plate and gauze – 19J engine

6.19 Withdrawing the timing belt cover – 19J engine

22 It is advisable to fit a new crankshaft dust seal to the cover as follows:

a) *Prise the old seal from the aperture in the cover using a suitable screwdriver.*
b) *Clean the seal seat in the cover.*
c) *Press a new seal into position using a suitable socket or tube. Take care not to damage the seal lips.*

23 Refit the cover to the housing, using a new gasket (and a new centre lug gasket, where applicable), then refit the securing bolts in their correct locations, as noted before removal **(see illustration)**. Tighten the bolts to the specified torque.

24 Refit the coolant pump as described in Chapter 3.

25 Refit the crankshaft pulley as described in Section 5.

200 TDi engine

Note: *A new timing belt cover gasket and a new coolant pump gasket must be used on refitting, and it is advisable to fit a new crankshaft dust seal to the cover.*

Removal

26 Remove the crankshaft pulley and damper, as described in Section 5.

27 Loosen the hose clips, and disconnect the hoses from the coolant pump.

28 If necessary, hold the coolant pump pulley stationary by wrapping the drivebelt tightly round the pulley, then unscrew the three securing bolts, and withdraw the pulley.

29 Unscrew the securing bolts, and withdraw the coolant pump. Recover the gasket.

30 Loosen the hose clips, and withdraw the air trunking connecting the air cleaner to the turbocharger. Where applicable, disconnect the breather hose from the air trunking.

31 Disconnect the wiring from the alternator, then unscrew the through-bolt and nut, and remove the alternator from its mounting bracket.

32 Unscrew the through-bolt and nut, and remove the power steering pump from the mounting bracket. There is no need to disconnect the fluid hoses – move the pump to one side clear of the working area, taking care not to strain the hoses.

33 Unscrew the securing bolts, and remove the alternator/power steering pump mounting bracket.

34 Unscrew the nine securing bolts, and remove the timing belt cover. Note the locations of the bolts, as they are of different lengths. Recover the gasket.

Refitting

35 Commence refitting by cleaning all traces of old gasket from the mating faces of the timing belt cover and housing.

36 It is advisable to fit a new crankshaft dust seal to the cover as follows:

a) *Prise the old seal from the aperture in the cover, using a suitable screwdriver.*
b) *Clean the seal seat in the cover.*
c) *Press a new seal into position using a suitable socket or tube. Take care not to damage the seal lips.*

37 Refit the cover to the housing, using a new gasket, then refit the securing bolts in their correct locations as noted before removal **(see illustration)**. Tighten the bolts to the specified torque.

38 Refit the alternator/power steering pump mounting bracket, and tighten the securing bolts.

39 Refit the power steering pump and alternator to the bracket, and reconnect the alternator wiring.

40 Refit the air trunking, and tighten the securing clips.

41 Clean all traces of old gasket from the mating faces of the coolant pump and housing, then refit the coolant pump using a new gasket. Tighten the securing bolts to the specified torque (see Chapter 3).

42 Refit the coolant pump pulley, and tighten the securing bolts. Hold the pulley using the drivebelt, as during removal.

43 Reconnect the hoses to the coolant pump.

44 Refit the crankshaft damper and pulley as described in Section 5.

300 TDi engine

Note: *New gaskets must be used on refitting, and it is advisable to fit a new crankshaft dust seal to the cover.*

Removal

45 Remove the crankshaft pulley as described in Section 5.

46 Unscrew and withdraw the fourteen bolts securing the timing belt cover to the housing. Note the locations of the bolts, as they are of different lengths. Note also that the top two bolts secure the thermostat coolant hose clips.

47 Unbolt the viscous fan pulley if desired.

48 Withdraw the cover, and recover the gasket. Where applicable, also recover the small gasket located around the cover centre securing bolt boss.

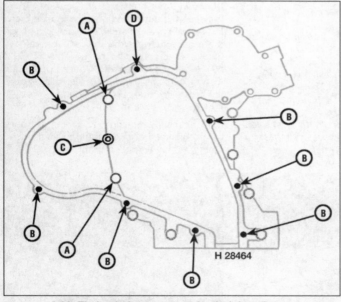

6.23 Timing belt cover securing bolt locations – 12J and 19J engines

| A | 20 mm long bolt | C | 65 mm long bolt |
| B | 25 mm long bolt | D | 95 mm long bolt |

6.37 Timing belt cover securing bolt locations – 200 TDi engine

| A | Stud hole | C | 25 mm long bolt | E | 90 mm long bolt |
| B | Dowel hole | D | 80 mm long bolt | | |

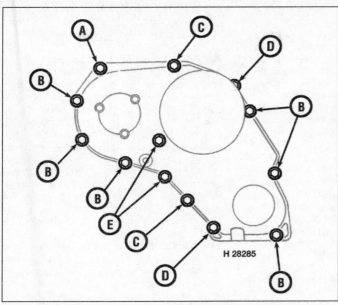

**6.51 Timing belt cover securing bolt locations –
300 TDi engine**

A 25 mm long bolt   C 50 mm long bolt   E 110 mm long bolt
B 35 mm long bolt   D 100 mm long bolt

7.8 Timing chain tensioner and damper components – 10J engine

1 Tensioner ratchet   securing bolt   4 Chain damper
   securing bolt   3 Tensioner   securing bolts
2 Tensioner   securing nut

Refitting

49 Commence refitting by cleaning all traces
of old gasket from the mating faces of the
timing belt cover and housing.
50 It is advisable to fit a new crankshaft dust
seal to the cover as follows:
 a) Prise the old seal from the aperture in the
    cover using a suitable screwdriver.
 b) Clean the seal seat in the cover.
 c) Press a new seal into position using a
    suitable socket or tube. Take care not
    to damage the seal lips. Note that the
    seal fits with the lips facing towards the
    outside of the timing belt cover.
51 Refit the cover to the housing, using new
gaskets, then refit the securing bolts in their
correct locations, as noted before removal
(see illustration). Tighten the bolts to the
specified torque.
52 Refit the crankshaft pulley as described in
Section 5.

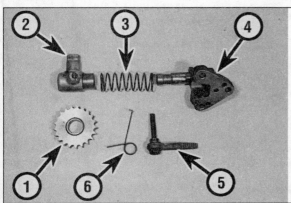

**7.15 Timing chain tensioner
components – 10J engine**

1 Sprocket
2 Piston
3 Piston spring
4 Tensioner body
5 Ratchet
6 Ratchet spring

7 Timing chain (10J engine) – removal, inspection and refitting

Removal

1 Remove the timing chain cover as described
in Section 6.
2 Before proceeding, timing marks must
be made on the camshaft and crankshaft
sprockets to ensure correct valve timing on
refitting.
3 If the camshaft sprocket is to be removed,
loosen the securing bolt before proceeding.
4 Turn the crankshaft to position No 1 piston
at TDC as described in Section 3.
5 Using a scriber and a steel rule, make
alignment marks between the camshaft,
camshaft sprocket, and the cylinder block.
6 Similarly, make alignment marks on the

crankshaft, crankshaft sprocket and cylinder
block.
7 Check the position of the chain tensioner
ratchet in relation to the pawl. This will give an
indication of chain wear. If the last tooth on the
ratchet is engaged with the pawl, the chain is
excessively worn, and should be renewed.
8 Unscrew the securing bolt, and remove the
tensioner ratchet and spring **(see illustration)**.
9 Unscrew the securing nut and bolt (and
recover the washers), and withdraw the
tensioner assembly. If necessary, compress
the tensioner by hand to aid removal.
10 Withdraw the timing chain from the
sprockets.

⚠ **Warning: Do not turn the crankshaft
or the camshaft once the timing
chain has been removed.**

11 Bend back the locktabs, then unscrew
the two securing bolts, and remove the chain
damper from the cylinder block.

Inspection

12 Examine the timing chain. If there are any
obvious signs of wear or damage, renew the
chain. Hold the chain horizontally (link plates
facing downwards) – if the chain takes on a
deeply-bowed appearance, this indicates that
the links are worn, and the chain should be
renewed.
13 Examine the teeth on the camshaft and
crankshaft sprockets, and on the tensioner
sprocket.
14 If the teeth are worn or significantly
hooked in appearance, the relevant sprocket
or tensioner should be renewed.
15 Dismantle the tensioner assembly, and
check the components for wear as follows
(see illustration):

a) *Check the condition of the ratchet and the pawl, and renew if worn.*
b) *Check the tension of the piston spring (by comparing it with a new one if possible).*
c) *Check for excessive play of the sprocket on the cylinder – the bush in the sprocket can be renewed if worn, using a press.*
d) *Check the condition of the ratchet spring, and renew if necessary.*

16 Clean all the components, then reassemble the tensioner. Inspect the rubber strip on the chain damper. If the strip is badly worn or grooved, renew the damper.

Refitting

17 Check that the E.P mark on the flywheel is still exactly aligned with the timing pointer (see Section 3). If the original crankshaft sprocket is being used, check that the marks made on the sprocket and the cylinder block are aligned (if the crankshaft sprocket has been removed, refit it with the larger shoulder towards the cylinder block).

18 Also check that the previously-made marks on the camshaft sprocket and the cylinder block are aligned. If a new camshaft sprocket has been fitted (and the timing mark has not been transferred from the old sprocket), check that No 1 exhaust valve is fully open, then make suitable alignment marks on the camshaft sprocket and cylinder block.

19 If desired, to achieve optimum engine efficiency and performance, the exact mid-point of the exhaust valve fully-open position can be determined by using a dial gauge as follows. This will give optimum valve timing, but it is up to the individual owner to decide whether this is worthwhile, given that chain wear is likely to give a greater error in valve timing than that obtained if the exhaust valve fully-open position is determined 'by eye'. If it is decided not to use a dial gauge, proceed to paragraph 20.

a) *Make up a suitable bracket to mount a dial gauge on the exhaust rocker arm of No 1 cylinder (see illustration).*
b) *Unscrew the locknut from the tappet adjuster screw, then refit and tighten the locknut to secure the dial test indicator bracket.*

c) *Position the dial gauge probe on the head of one of the cylinder head bolts, then push the probe to load the indicator.*
d) *Make up a pointer from a piece of wire, and use one of the timing chain cover bolts to secure the pointer in position on the cylinder block (see illustration). Position the end of the pointer as close as possible to the camshaft sprocket. An imaginary extended line from the right-angled end of the pointer should pass through the centre of the camshaft sprocket bolt hole.*
e) *Turn the camshaft slightly until No 1 exhaust valve is fully open, indicated by the maximum reading on the dial gauge. Because the top of the camshaft exhaust lobes are flat, the camshaft can be turned a further small amount (approximately 4°) without movement of the dial gauge. As an error of 4° in the valve timing is not acceptable, the exact centre of the 4° 'fully open' period must be established as follows.*
f) *Zero the dial gauge, then carefully turn the camshaft clockwise until the dial gauge reading is 0.25 mm. This represents a point on the cam lobe past the fully-open position. Make a suitable mark on the camshaft sprocket, exactly in line with the pointer. If the original camshaft sprocket is being used, ensure that the mark cannot be confused with the alignment mark made before the sprocket was removed (see paragraph 5).*
g) *Carefully turn the camshaft anti-clockwise until the dial gauge reads zero, then continue to turn the camshaft until the reading is 0.25 mm. Again, make a mark on the camshaft sprocket, exactly in line with the pointer.*
h) *Using a rule, determine the exact mid-point between the two marks made in paragraphs f) and g), and make a third mark.*
i) *Remove the dial gauge, and refit the tappet adjuster screw locknut.*
j) *Turn the camshaft until the third mark (see paragraph h)) aligns with the pointer. The camshaft is now positioned with the*

tappet roller at the centre of the No 1 exhaust valve 'fully open' period, and the camshaft is correctly positioned in relation to the crankshaft.

20 Without moving the camshaft or the crankshaft, fit the timing chain over the sprockets, keeping it taut on the drive (chain damper) side. If it is not possible to obtain a taut fit, remove the camshaft sprocket (see Section 9) and reposition the sprocket using one of the alternative keyways until the optimum position is obtained. It is preferable to choose a keyway which gives a slightly tight chain, rather than a slack one. **Note:** *If the camshaft is moved during this procedure, it will be necessary to recheck that the camshaft is positioned with No 1 exhaust valve fully open (see paragraphs 18 and 19) before fitting the chain to the sprockets.*

21 Refit the chain damper (use new securing bolt locktabs), and adjust to give the specified clearance (see *Specifications*). Tighten the securing bolts, and secure with the locktabs.

22 Compress the tensioner piston spring, and refit the assembly to the engine, ensuring that the piston housing locates on the dowels in the cylinder block, and that the spigot engages with the slot in the cylinder block. Fit the tensioner ratchet bolt to retain the assembly.

23 Allow the tensioner sprocket to take up the slack in the chain, then refit and tighten the remaining securing bolt and nut.

24 If a dial test indicator has been used to determine the fully-open position of No 1 exhaust valve (see paragraph 19), proceed as follows. Otherwise, proceed to paragraph 25.

a) *Do not turn the crankshaft until any excessive clearance has been eliminated between the end of the valve stem and the rocker arm.*
b) *Refit the locknut to the tappet adjuster screw, then check No 1 exhaust valve clearance as described in Chapter 1.*

25 Refit the timing chain cover as described in Section 6.

26 Refit the valve cover as described in Section 4.

8 Timing belt (all except 10J engine) – inspection, removal and refitting

Inspection

1 Remove the timing belt cover as described in Section 6.

2 Temporarily refit the crankshaft damper/pulley bolt to the end of the crankshaft.

3 Ensure that the gearbox is in neutral, then using a suitable spanner or socket on the crankshaft damper/pulley bolt, rotate the crankshaft so that the full length of the timing belt can be progressively checked. (Turning the engine will be much easier if the glow plugs are removed first – see Chapter 5.)

4 Examine the belt carefully for any signs of

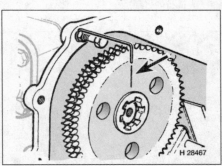

7.19a Dial test indicator mounted on No 1 exhaust valve rocker arm – 10J engine

1 *Tappet adjuster screw locknut*
2 *Cylinder head bolt*

7.19b Timing pointer secured by timing chain cover bolt (sprocket timing mark arrowed) – 10J engine

8.8a Camshaft sprocket timing mark aligned with web on timing belt housing – 300 TDi engine

8.8b Crankshaft Woodruff key aligned with arrow on timing belt housing – 300 TDi engine

8.10 Slacken the belt tensioner pulley bolt (arrowed) and slide off the timing belt – 300 TDi engine

uneven wear, splitting or oil contamination and renew it if there is the slightest doubt about its condition. On completion, refit the timing belt cover as described in Section 6.

Removal

Note: *If the original belt is to be refitted, it must be refitted so that it rotates in the original running direction – mark the running direction before removal. When removed from the engine, timing belts must be stored on edge, on a clean surface.* **Do not** *bend the belt through acute angles (radius less than 50 mm), as damage and premature failure may result. A gauge-type torque wrench is will be required to tension the belt during refitting – a break-type torque wrench is not suitable.*

5 Remove the timing belt cover as described in Section 6.

6 If the camshaft sprocket (sprocket hub on 300 TDi engines) is to be removed for any reason, the sprocket/hub securing bolt should be loosened at this stage, before the timing belt is removed. Similarly, if the fuel injection pump sprocket is to be removed on 12J or 19J engines, the securing nut should be loosened at this stage.

7 Temporarily refit the crankshaft damper/pulley bolt to the end of the crankshaft, then turn the crankshaft (using a suitable spanner or socket on the damper/pulley bolt) to bring No 1 piston to TDC and lock it in place, as described in Section 3. Ignore the references to removal of the air conditioning compressor and the injection pump hub cover plate.

8.11 Unscrew the three bolts (arrowed) securing the injection pump sprocket to the pump hub – 300 TDi engine

8 On 200 TDi and 300 TDi engines, check that the timing marks are aligned as follows:

a) *The timing mark on the camshaft sprocket should be aligned with the web on the timing belt housing* **(see illustration).**

b) *The Woodruff key in the end of the crankshaft should be aligned with the arrow on the timing belt housing* **(see illustration).**

9 Slacken the belt tensioner pulley bolt, or the two nuts, as applicable.

10 Slide the timing belt from the sprockets **(see illustration).** If the original belt is to be refitted, mark the running direction of the belt, to ensure correct refitting.

⚠ **Warning: Do not turn the camshaft or crankshaft once the timing belt had been removed.**

HAYNES HiNT *If the belt cannot easily be slid from the sprockets on 300 TDi engines, unscrew the securing nut, and remove the belt idler pulley.*

Refitting

Note: *During refitting, the timing belt tensioning procedure is effectively carried out twice. This double-tensioning procedure* **must** *be carried out as described, to avoid the possibility of belt failure and resultant engine damage.*

11 On 200 TDi and 300 TDi engines, slacken the three bolts securing the injection pump sprocket to the pump hub **(see illustration).**

8.16 Tensioning the timing belt – 300 TDi engine

12 Carefully fit the belt over the sprockets, starting with the crankshaft sprocket, followed by the camshaft and fuel injection pump sprockets, then the tensioner. Ensure that the direction of rotation marks are correctly orientated if the original belt is being refitted. Take care not to move the sprockets, and make sure that the timing marks are still aligned as described in paragraph 8. If necessary, adjust the position of the belt, so that it sits correctly on the sprockets, with the timing marks still aligned. On 12J and 19J engines, if the belt teeth do not quite mate with the sprocket grooves, move the camshaft sprocket (and if necessary, the fuel injection pump sprocket) slightly clockwise until the teeth engage with the sprocket grooves.

13 On 300 TDi engines, refit the idler pulley, and tighten the securing nut.

14 Tighten the belt tensioner pulley bolt or nuts (as applicable) finger-tight.

15 Engage a suitable square-drive extension with the hole in the tensioner pulley mounting plate.

16 Using a gauge-type torque wrench held vertically, turn the extension to tension the belt to the specified torque (see *Specifications*). Tighten the tensioner pulley bolt/nuts, taking care to maintain the correct torque **(see illustration).**

17 On 200 TDi and 300 TDi engines, tighten the injection pump sprocket-to-hub securing bolts to the specified torque.

18 Where applicable, remove the pump timing pin from the injection pump sprocket, and/or withdraw the flywheel locking tool centre pin from the slot in the flywheel.

19 Where applicable (if the camshaft sprocket has been removed), tighten the camshaft sprocket/hub securing bolt to the specified torque.

20 Turn the crankshaft clockwise through two complete turns, until the timing marks are aligned again with No 1 piston at TDC (see Section 3 and paragraph 8).

21 Slacken the tensioner pulley bolt/nuts, and repeat the tensioning procedure described in paragraph 16.

22 Check the fuel injection pump timing as described in Chapter 4A.

23 On completion, refit the timing belt cover as described in Section 6.

9 Timing sprockets and tensioner – removal and refitting

Camshaft sprocket – 10J engine

Note: *A new sprocket securing bolt must be used on refitting.*

Removal

1 Remove the timing chain as described in Section 7.

 Warning: Do not turn the crankshaft or the camshaft once the timing chain has been removed.

2 Unscrew the sprocket securing bolt (the bolt should have been loosened before the timing chain was removed), and withdraw the locking plate (where applicable), and the washer.

3 Withdraw the sprocket from the end of the camshaft. If necessary, a puller can be bolted to the sprocket, using the two tapped holes provided. If a puller is used, take care not to damage the threaded end of the camshaft (temporarily refit the sprocket bolt, and position the puller screw on the bolt head).

Refitting

4 Refitting is a reversal of removal, bearing in mind the following points:
  a) Use a new sprocket securing bolt
  b) Do not fully tighten the sprocket bolt until the timing chain has been refitted.
  c) Refit the timing chain as described in Section 7, but before refitting the timing chain cover, tighten the sprocket bolt to the specified torque.

Camshaft sprocket – 12J, 19J and 200 TDi engines

Note: *New retaining plate O-rings must be used on refitting.*

Removal

5 Remove the timing belt as described in Section 8.

 Warning: Do not turn the crankshaft or the camshaft once the timing belt has been removed.

6 Unscrew the sprocket securing bolt (the bolt should have been loosened before the timing belt was removed). Recover the washer, the small O-ring, the retaining plate, and the larger O-ring.

7 Withdraw the sprocket from the end of the camshaft. If necessary on 12J and 19J engines, a puller can be bolted to the sprocket, using the two tapped holes provided. If a puller is used, take care not to damage the threaded end of the camshaft.

Refitting

8 Refitting is a reversal of removal, bearing in mind the following points:
  a) On 12J and 19J engines, use a new sprocket securing bolt.
  b) Use new O-rings when refitting the sprocket retaining plate. Note that the

larger O-ring fits between the retaining plate and the sprocket. The smaller O-ring fits between the retaining plate and the washer.
  c) Do not fully tighten the sprocket securing bolt until the timing belt has been refitted.
  d) Refit the timing belt as described in Section 8, but before refitting the timing belt cover, tighten the sprocket securing bolt to the specified torque.

Camshaft sprocket and hub – 300 TDi engine

Note: *The sprocket is bolted to a hub (with 3 bolts and a retaining plate) on 300 TDi engines, and the hub is in turn bolted to the end of the camshaft. If the sprocket is to be removed, leaving the hub on the camshaft, the sprocket retaining plate **must** be locked in position on the sprocket by fitting and tightening two M8 bolts in the holes provided. If this is not done, it is possible for the valve timing to be altered when the sprocket is refitted (the bolt holes are elongated), which may adversely affect the performance of the engine.*

Removal

9 Remove the timing belt as described in Section 8.

 Warning: Do not turn the crankshaft or the camshaft once the timing belt has been removed.

10 If the sprocket/hub assembly is to be removed as a complete unit, proceed as follows. If the sprocket is to be removed leaving the hub in place on the camshaft, proceed to paragraph 12.

11 If the sprocket/hub assembly is to be removed as a complete unit (such as for camshaft renewal), unscrew the hub securing bolt (the bolt should have been loosened before the timing belt was removed), then recover the washer and withdraw the assembly from the end of the camshaft **(see illustration)**. If the sprocket is to be removed from the hub, ensure that the retaining plate is locked in position first, as described in the note at the beginning of this sub-Section.

12 If the sprocket is to be removed leaving the hub in place on the camshaft, refer to the

note at the beginning of this sub-Section, and fit two M8 bolts to lock the retaining plate in position on the sprocket.

13 Counterhold the camshaft using a suitable socket on the hub securing bolt, then unscrew the three bolts securing the sprocket to the hub, and withdraw the sprocket from the hub **(see illustration)**.

Refitting

14 Refitting is a reversal of removal, bearing in mind the following points:
  a) Where applicable, do not fully tighten the sprocket hub securing bolt until the timing belt has been refitted.
  b) Refit the timing belt as described in Section 8, but before refitting the timing belt cover, where applicable, tighten the sprocket hub securing bolt to the specified torque, and/or remove the two bolts used to lock the retaining plate to the sprocket.

Crankshaft sprocket – 10J engine

Removal

15 Remove the timing chain as described in Section 7.

 Warning: Do not turn the crankshaft or the camshaft once the timing chain has been removed.

16 Withdraw the sprocket from the end of the crankshaft.

Refitting

17 Refitting is a reversal of removal, but note that the sprocket fits with the larger shoulder towards the cylinder block, and refit the timing chain as described in Section 7.

Crankshaft sprocket – 12J, 19J, 200TDi and 300 TDi engines

Note: *On 300 TDi engines, a new O-ring should be used when refitting the sprocket.*

Removal

18 Remove the timing belt as described in Section 8.

 Warning: Do not turn the crankshaft or the camshaft once the timing belt has been removed.

9.11 Removing the camshaft sprocket/hub assembly – 300 TDi engine

9.13 Removing the camshaft sprocket from the hub. Note two M8 bolts (arrowed) locking retaining plate to hub – 300 TDi engine

9.19 Withdraw the crankshaft sprocket . . .

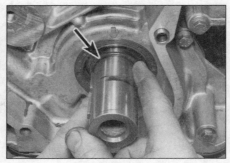

9.20 . . . and recover the O-ring (arrowed) from the crankshaft – 300 TDi engine

9.31a Remove the three securing bolts . . .

19 Withdraw the sprocket from the end of the crankshaft **(see illustration)**. If the sprocket is tight, a suitable puller should be used. If a puller is used, do not allow the puller to bear on the end of the crankshaft – temporarily refit the pulley/damper bolt, and allow the puller to bear on the bolt head.

20 Recover the Woodruff key if it is loose, and on 300 TDi engines, recover the O-ring which fits behind the sprocket **(see illustration)**.

Refitting

21 Refitting is a reversal of removal, bearing in mind the following points:
a) *Ensure that the Woodruff key is securely fitted to the end of the crankshaft.*
b) *On 300 TDi engines, refit the sprocket using a new O-ring.*
c) *If the sprocket is a tight fit on the crankshaft, carefully tap it into position using a soft-faced mallet. On 300 TDi engines, ensure that the O-ring is properly seated.*
d) *Refit the timing belt as described in Section 8.*

Fuel injection pump sprocket – 12J and 19J engines

Removal

22 Remove the timing belt as described in Section 8.

 Warning: Do not turn the crankshaft or the camshaft once the timing belt has been removed.

23 Unscrew the sprocket securing nut (the nut should have been loosened before the timing belt was removed).

24 Withdraw the sprocket from the end of the fuel injection pump spindle. If necessary, a puller can be bolted to the sprocket, using the two tapped holes provided. If a puller is used, take care not to damage the threaded end of the pump spindle.

Refitting

25 Refitting is a reversal of removal, bearing in mind the following points:
a) *Do not fully tighten the sprocket securing nut until the timing belt has been refitted.*
b) *Refit the timing belt as described in Section 8, but before refitting the timing belt cover, tighten the sprocket securing nut to the specified torque.*

Fuel injection pump sprocket – 200 TDi and 300 TDi engines

Removal

26 Remove the timing belt as described in Section 8.

 Warning: Do not turn the crankshaft or the camshaft once the timing belt has been removed.

27 Slacken the three bolts securing the injection pump sprocket to the pump hub.

28 Loosen the pump locking screw, and remove the keeper plate (located at the front of the pump, behind the timing belt housing). Tighten the locking screw to lock the pump spindle in position.

29 Ensure that the flywheel locking tool is engaged with the slot in the flywheel – no attempt must be made to turn the crankshaft

or the fuel injection pump once the pump spindle has been locked.

30 Remove the injection pump timing pin from the pump.

31 Remove the sprocket securing bolts, then recover the retaining plate, and withdraw the sprocket from the pump hub **(see illustrations)**.

Refitting

32 Fit the sprocket to the pump hub, then fit the retaining plate, and the securing bolts. Do not fully tighten the securing bolts at this stage.

33 Fit the injection pump timing pin, and engage the pin with the pump hub.

34 Loosen the pump locking screw, then refit the keeper plate, and tighten the locking screw.

35 Refit the timing belt as described in Section 8.

Idler pulley – 300 TDi engine

Removal

36 Remove the timing belt as described in Section 8.

 Warning: Do not turn the crankshaft or the camshaft once the timing belt has been removed.

37 Unscrew the securing nut, recover the washer, and withdraw the idler pulley **(see illustration)**.

Refitting

38 Refitting is a reversal of removal, but refit the timing belt as described in Section 8.

9.31b . . . recover the retaining plate . . .

9.31c . . . and withdraw the sprocket

9.37 Removing the timing belt idler pulley – 300 TDi engine

9.45a Unscrew the securing bolt and recover the washer . . .

9.45b . . . withdraw the tensioner . . .

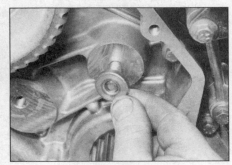

9.45c . . . and recover the spacer washer – 300 TDi engine

Timing chain tensioner – 10J engine

39 Removal and refitting of the tensioner is described as part of the timing chain removal and refitting procedure in Section 7.

Timing belt tensioner – 12J and 19J engines

Removal

40 Remove the timing belt as described in Section 8.

⚠️ **Warning: Do not turn the crankshaft or the camshaft once the timing belt has been removed.**

41 Unscrew the securing nuts and washers, and withdraw the tensioner.

Refitting

42 Refitting is a reversal of removal, but refit the timing belt as described in Section 8.

Timing belt tensioner – 200 TDi and 300 TDi engines

Removal

43 Remove the timing belt as described in Section 8.

⚠️ **Warning: Do not turn the crankshaft or the camshaft once the timing belt has been removed.**

44 On 300 TDi engines, remove the idler pulley as described previously in this Section.
45 Unscrew the securing bolt, recover the washer, and withdraw the tensioner. On 300

TDi engines, recover the spacer washer from the idler pulley stud **(see illustrations)**.

Refitting

46 Refitting is a reversal of removal, bearing in mind the following points:
a) *On 200 TDi engines, make sure that the hole in the tensioner plate locates over the lug on the timing belt housing.*
b) *On 300 TDi engines, make sure that the spacer washer is in place on the idler pulley stud, and make sure that the tensioner plate locates over the stud.*
c) *Refit the timing belt as described in Section 8.*

---

10 Valve operating (rocker) gear
– removal, inspection and refitting

Note: *In order to remove the cam follower components, the cylinder head must be removed. Removal of the cam follower components is described in Section 12.*

10J, 12J and 19J engines

Removal

1 Remove the valve cover as described in Section 4.
2 Slacken the tappet adjuster screw locknuts, and back off the adjuster screws until they are clear of the pushrods.
3 Progressively unscrew the five smaller rocker pedestal securing bolts **(see illustration)**.
4 Similarly, unscrew the five cylinder head bolts which secure the rocker pedestals to the cylinder head, then lift the assembly from the cylinder head **(see illustration)**.
5 Unless the assembly is to be dismantled, invert the assembly, and engage the valve cover securing studs on the rocker pedestals with the corresponding holes in the valve cover. This will prevent the assembly from falling apart.
6 If the assembly is to be dismantled, proceed as follows **(see illustration)**.
7 Remove the locating screw from the No 2 rocker pedestal (recover the washer), then withdraw the spacers, rocker pedestals, rocker arms, and springs from the shaft. Take care not to mix the components up, as they

10.3 Removing one of the smaller rocker pedestal securing bolts – 19J engine. Cylinder head bolt securing rocker pedestal arrowed

10.4 Unscrewing one of the cylinder head bolts securing the rocker pedestal – 19J engine

1 Rocker pedestal
2 Rocker arm
3 Spring
4 Rocker arm
5 Spacer
6 Rocker pedestal
7 Rocker shaft locating screw
8 Tappet adjuster screw
9 Locknut
10 Rocker shaft
11 Spacer

H 28468

10.6 Valve operating gear components – 10J, 12J and 19J engines

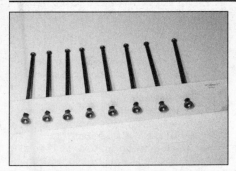

10.9 Store the pushrods in order by pushing them through holes in piece of card

must be refitted to the rocker shaft in their original positions.

HAYNES HiNT

If the belt cannot easily be slid from the sprockets on 300 TDi engines, unscrew the securing nut, and remove the belt idler pulley.

8 Make suitable holes to accommodate the pushrods in a piece of card, then number the holes from 1 to 8 (No 1 at the timing chain/belt end of the engine).

9 Working from the timing chain/belt end of the cylinder head, lift the pushrods from their bores in the cylinder head, and insert them through the holes in the card, in order of removal **(see illustration)**.

10 Where applicable, remove the valve stem caps from the tops of the valve stems. Keep them in order, so that they can be refitted to their original locations.

Inspection

Note: *It is unlikely that individual components will wear significantly, without obvious general wear in all the components. It can be a false economy to renew individual components, and if significant wear is evident, or if the engine is being overhauled after completing a high mileage, it is advisable to renew all the valve operating and cam follower components.*

11 Clean all the components thoroughly, one by one, keeping them in order.

12 Examine the rocker shaft for wear. Check the bearing surfaces, and check that the

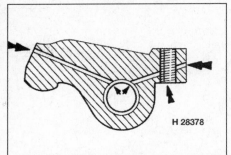

10.13 Check that the oil holes (arrowed) in the rocker arms are clear

oilways are clear. If there is any sign of wear, scoring or pitting on the bearing surfaces, the shaft must be renewed.

13 Inspect the rocker arm pads (the areas which contact the valve stems) for wear. If excessive wear is evident, the rocker arms must be renewed – it is not permissible to grind the pads to compensate for wear. Check that the oil holes in the rocker arms are free from obstructions **(see illustration)**.

14 Check the freeplay of the rocker arms on the shaft. This is most easily accomplished as follows:

a) *Clamp the rocker shaft horizontally in a soft-jawed vice.*

b) *Slide the rocker arm onto the shaft.*

c) *Position a suitable dial test indicator to read from the cylindrical section of the rocker arm.*

d) *Grip the rocker arm and move it laterally on the shaft, reading off the freeplay on the dial gauge.*

15 If the freeplay is outside the specified limits (see *Specifications*), the rocker arm bushes can be renewed, but this is best entrusted to a Land Rover dealer.

16 Examine the tappet adjuster screws, and check that the ball-ends are not worn or pitted. Also check that the oil holes are clear. If any wear is evident, the relevant adjustment screw should be renewed (bearing in mind the note at the beginning of this Section).

17 Examine the pushrods. Ensure that they are all straight, and if any one is bent or distorted, renew it. Check the ends of each pushrod. If either end is rough, damaged or

badly worn, the pushrod must be renewed. If it is discovered that one pushrod is worn, examine the corresponding rocker arm and tappet slide (see Section 12) also.

18 Examine the rocker shaft springs for damage and deterioration. It is advisable to renew all the springs as a matter of course.

19 Check the condition of the valve stem caps (where applicable), and renew them if there is any sign of significant wear. Note that if no valve stem caps are fitted, it is permissible to fit caps (the caps must be fitted to all the valves as a set, and are available from Land Rover dealers) to compensate for wear in the valve stems and/or the rocker arm pads.

Refitting

20 Commence refitting by ensuring that all components are clean. Check all oilways for obstructions. Lightly lubricate the tops of the tappet slides with clean engine oil of the correct grade, then refit the pushrods in their original locations. Make sure that the ball-end of each pushrod locates correctly in the tappet slide **(see illustration)**.

21 Where applicable, refit the valve stem caps to the tops of the valves, in their original locations **(see illustration)**.

22 Fit the No 2 rocker pedestal to the rocker shaft, and refit the locating screw and washer.

23 Slide the spacers, rocker arms, springs, and the remaining rocker pedestals onto the shaft, keeping all the components in their original order. Note that the double spacers fit either side of the centre rocker pedestal.

24 With the components reassembled, invert the assembly and engage the valve cover securing studs on the rocker pedestals with the corresponding holes in the valve cover. This will prevent the assembly from falling apart until the assembly is to be refitted.

25 With the rocker shaft reassembled, lubricate the rocker arm contact faces of the pushrods and valve stems.

26 Refit the rocker shaft assembly to the cylinder head. If necessary, loosen the locknuts, and back off the tappet adjuster screws to aid refitting. Ensure that the ball-ends of the tappet adjuster screws locate correctly in the pushrod cups.

27 Refit the cylinder head bolts which retain the rocker pedestals, and tighten progressively to the specified torque.

28 Refit the smaller bolts securing the rocker pedestals to the cylinder head, and tighten to the specified torque.

29 Adjust the valve clearances as described in Chapter 1.

⚠️ *Warning: If the crankshaft is rotated with excessive valve clearances, it is possible for the pushrods to become dislodged and fracture the tappet slides. To prevent the possibility of damage, turn the adjusters to eliminate all clearance from any loose rocker arms before turning the crankshaft to check the valve clearances.*

10.20 Fitting a pushrod

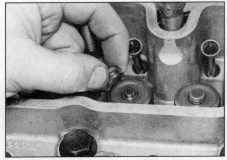

10.21 Fitting a valve stem cap

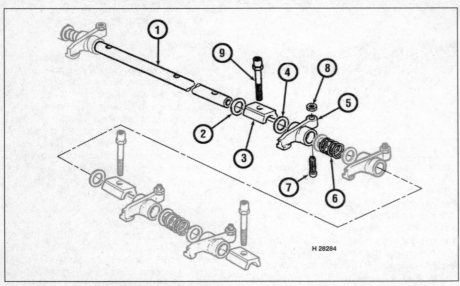

10.35 Valve operating gear components – 200 TDi engine

1	*Rocker shaft*	4	*Spacer*	7	*Tappet adjustment screw*
2	*Spacer*	5	*Rocker arm*	8	*Tappet locknut*
3	*Bearing cap*	6	*Spring*	9	*Rocker shaft securing bolt*

30 On completion, refit the valve cover as described in Section 4.

200 TDi engine

Removal

31 Remove the valve cover as described in Section 4.

32 Slacken the tappet adjuster screw locknuts, and back off the adjuster screws until they are clear of the pushrods.

33 Progressively unscrew the five rocker shaft securing bolts, but do not remove the bolts from the shaft – if the bolts are removed, the rocker assembly will fall apart when removed from the cylinder head.

34 Lift the assembly from the cylinder head.

35 With the rocker shaft removed, withdraw the securing bolt from one end of the shaft (the components will be forced from the shaft by the springs, once the bolt has been removed) **(see illustration)**.

36 Withdraw the spacers, bearing caps, rocker arms, and springs from the shaft. Lay all the components out in order of removal.

Take care not to mix the components up, as they must be refitted to the rocker shaft in their original positions.

HAYNES HINT *To keep the rocker shaft components in order, slide them onto a 'dummy shaft' in order of removal. The 'dummy shaft' can be made from a suitable length of thin bar or rod, which must be longer than the rocker shaft, in order to accommodate the uncompressed springs.*

37 Working progressively along the shaft, withdraw the remaining rocker shaft securing bolts, and slide the remaining components from the shaft, keeping them in order.

38 Proceed as described in paragraphs 8 to 10 inclusive.

Inspection

39 Proceed as described in paragraphs 11 to 19 inclusive.

Refitting

40 Proceed as described in paragraphs 20 and 21, then proceed as follows.

41 Lubricate the rocker shaft, then slide one of the end bearing caps onto the shaft, and refit one of the rocker shaft securing bolts to retain the bearing cap.

42 Slide the spacers, rocker arms, springs and bearing caps onto the shaft, keeping them in their original order. Refit the relevant rocker shaft securing bolt as each bearing cap is fitted, to retain the components on the shaft.

43 With the rocker shaft reassembled, lubricate the rocker arm contact faces of the pushrods and valve stems.

44 Refit the rocker shaft assembly to the cylinder head. If necessary, loosen the locknuts, and back off the tappet adjuster screws to aid refitting. Ensure that the ball ends of the tappet adjuster screws locate correctly in the pushrod cups.

45 Progressively tighten the securing bolts to the specified torque.

46 Proceed as described in paragraphs 29 and 30.

300 TDi engine

Removal

47 Remove the valve cover as described in Section 4.

48 Slacken the tappet adjuster screw locknuts, and back off the adjuster screws until they are clear of the pushrods.

49 Progressively unscrew the three nuts and two bolts securing the rocker shaft to the cylinder head, then lift the assembly from the cylinder head studs **(see illustrations)**. Hold the end pedestals as the assembly is removed, to prevent the components from falling off the rocker shaft. Take care not to dislodge the valve stem caps from the tops of the valves as the rocker gear is removed.

50 With the rocker shaft removed, withdraw the pedestals, spacers, rocker arms and springs from the shaft. Lay all the components out in order of removal. Take care not to mix the components up, as they must be refitted to the rocker shaft in their original positions.

HAYNES HINT *To keep the rocker shaft components in order, slide them onto a 'dummy shaft' in order of removal. The 'dummy shaft' can be made from a suitable length of thin bar or rod, which must be longer than the rocker shaft, in order to accommodate the uncompressed springs.*

51 Proceed as described in paragraphs 8 to 10 inclusive.

Inspection

52 Proceed as described in paragraphs 11 to 19.

10.49a Removing a rocker shaft securing bolt – 300 TDi engine

10.49b Removing the rocker shaft – 300 TDi engine

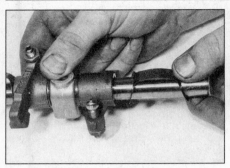

10.54a Refit the spring . . .

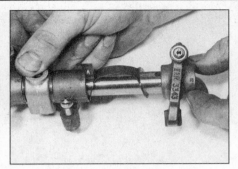

10.54b . . . rocker arm . . .

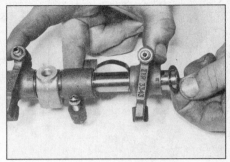

10.54c . . . washer . . .

10.54d . . . and end pedestal to the end of the rocker shaft – 300 TDi engine

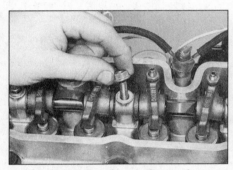

10.57a Refit the rocker shaft securing nuts and bolts . . .

10.57b . . . and tighten to the specified torque, then through the specified angle – 300 TDi engine

Refitting

53 Proceed as described in paragraphs 20 and 21, then proceed as follows.

54 Lubricate the rocker shaft, then slide the components onto the shaft, keeping them in their original order **(see illustrations)**.

55 With the rocker shaft reassembled, lubricate the rocker arm contact faces of the pushrods and the valve stems.

56 Refit the rocker shaft assembly to the cylinder head, ensuring that the three locating studs pass through the shaft and the pedestals. If necessary, loosen the locknuts, and back off the tappet adjuster screws to aid refitting. Ensure that the ball-ends of the tappet adjuster screws locate correctly in the pushrod cups.

57 Refit the securing nuts and bolts, and tighten progressively to the specified torque in the two stages given in the Specifications **(see illustrations)**.

58 Proceed as described in paragraphs 29 and 30.

11 Cylinder head – removal, inspection and refitting

Note: *A new cylinder head gasket must be used on refitting. On 200 TDi and 300 TDi engines, the cylinder head bolts may be re-used a maximum of five times. Unless the history of the cylinder head bolts is certain (make marks to indicate the number of times they have been used), it is advisable to use new bolts when refitting the cylinder head.*

⚠️ **Warning: Access to lift the cylinder head is awkward, due to the width of the engine compartment. It is advisable to enlist the aid of an assistant to help lift the head – do not attempt the job alone.**

Removal

1 Disconnect the battery negative lead.

2 Remove the bonnet as described in Chapter 12.

3 Drain the cooling system as described in Chapter 1.

4 Loosen the hose clips, and disconnect the breather hose(s) from the oil filler cap, valve cover, and/or from the breather on the side of the valve cover, as applicable **(see illustrations)**.

5 Remove the fuel injectors as described in Chapter 4A.

6 Remove the glow plugs as described in Chapter 5.

7 Disconnect the coolant hoses from the thermostat housing and cover **(see illustration)**.

8 Disconnect the wiring from the temperature gauge sender, located in the top of the cylinder

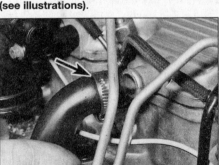

11.4a Disconnect the breather hoses from the valve cover . . .

11.4b . . . and the breather – 300 TDi engine

11.7 Disconnecting the coolant hose from the thermostat housing – 300 TDi engine

11.8 Disconnecting the wiring from the temperature gauge sender – 19J engine

11.12 Unscrew the union bolt (arrowed) and disconnect the oil feed pipe from the cylinder head – 19J engine

head on 10J, 12J and 19J engines, and in the thermostat housing on 200 TDi and 300 TDi engines **(see illustration)**.

9 Remove the inlet manifold, exhaust manifold and, where applicable, the turbocharger, as described in Chapter 4A.

10 On 200 TDi and 300 TDi engines, disconnect the coolant hose connecting the coolant pipe (mounted on the manifold studs) to the water pump, then move the coolant pipe clear of the working area.

11 Where applicable, disconnect the coolant hose from the rear of the cylinder head.

12 On 10J, 12J and 19J engines, unscrew the union bolt and disconnect the oil feed pipe from the rear right-hand side of the cylinder head **(see illustration)**. Recover the sealing washers.

13 Where applicable, unbolt the wiring harness bracket from the cylinder head.

14 Unbolt the transmission breather/wiring harness bracket from the rear of the cylinder head. On engines where the bracket securing bolt also secures the rear engine lifting bracket, refit and tighten the bolt.

15 Remove the valve operating gear as described in Section 10.

16 Where applicable, lift the valve stem caps from the tops of the valves. Keep the caps in order, so that they can be refitted in their original positions.

17 Working in a spiral pattern, progressively loosen and remove the eighteen bolts securing the cylinder head. On 10J, 12J and 19J engines, note that five of the bolts will already

have been removed, in order to remove the valve operating gear (see Section 10).

18 Carefully lift the cylinder head from the cylinder block. If necessary, tap the cylinder head gently with a soft-faced mallet to free it from the block, but **do not** lever at the mating faces. Note that the cylinder head is located on dowels. Lift the cylinder head from the vehicle.

19 Recover the cylinder head gasket, and discard it.

Inspection

20 The mating faces of the cylinder head and block must be perfectly clean before refitting the head. Use a scraper to remove all traces of gasket and carbon, and also clean the tops of the pistons. Take particular care with the aluminium cylinder head, as the soft metal is damaged easily. Also, make sure that debris is not allowed to enter the oil and water channels – this is particularly important for the oil circuit, as carbon could block the oil supply to the camshaft or crankshaft bearings. Using

> **HAYNES HiNT** *To prevent carbon entering the gap between the pistons and bores, smear a little grease in the gap. After cleaning the piston, rotate the crankshaft so that the piston moves down the bore, then wipe out the grease and carbon with a cloth rag.*

adhesive tape and paper, seal the water, oil and bolt holes in the cylinder block. Clean the piston crowns in the same way.

21 Check the block and head for nicks, deep scratches and other damage. If slight, they may be removed carefully with a file. More serious damage may be repaired by machining, but this is a specialist job.

22 If warpage of the cylinder head is suspected, use a straight-edge to check it for distortion. Refer to Part C of this Chapter if necessary.

23 Clean out the bolt holes in the block using a pipe cleaner, or a rag and screwdriver.

> ⚠ *Warning: Make sure that all oil is removed, otherwise there is a possibility of the block being cracked by hydraulic pressure when the bolts are tightened.*

24 Examine the bolt threads and the threads in the cylinder block for damage. If necessary, use the correct-size tap to chase out the threads in the block, and use a die to clean the threads on the bolts.

Gasket selection – 200 TDi and 300 TDi engines

Note: *There is no need to carry out the following procedure on 10J, 12J and 19J engines.*

25 When the pistons are at the top dead centre (TDC) position, they protrude above the top face of the cylinder block. The amount of protrusion determines the thickness of the cylinder head gasket required. The protrusion of all the pistons above the cylinder block must be measured, and the thickness of the gasket to be used is determined by the largest protrusion measured.

26 Turn the crankshaft to bring piston Nos 1 and 4 to just below the TDC position (just below the top face of the cylinder block). Position a dial test indicator (DTI) on the cylinder block, and zero it on the block face. Transfer the probe to the crown of No 1 piston (as close as possible to the centre, avoiding the combustion chamber), then slowly turn the crankshaft back-and-forth past TDC, noting the highest reading produced on the indicator. Record this reading.

27 Repeat this measurement procedure on No 4 piston, then turn the crankshaft half a turn (180°) and repeat the procedure on Nos 2 and 3 pistons **(see illustration)**. Ensure that all measurements are taken along the longitudinal centreline of the crankshaft (this will eliminate errors due to piston slant).

28 If a dial test indicator is not available, piston protrusion may be measured using a straight-edge and feeler blades or vernier calipers. However, these methods are inevitably less accurate, and cannot therefore be recommended **(see illustration)**.

29 Ascertain the greatest piston protrusion measurement, and use this to determine the correct cylinder head gasket from the following table. The gasket identification holes

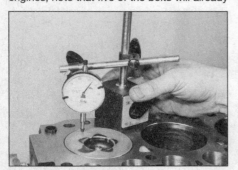

11.27 Measuring piston protrusion using a dial gauge – 300 TDi engine

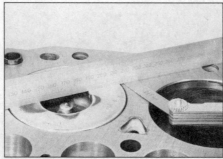

11.28 Measuring piston protrusion using a straight-edge and feeler blades – 300 TDi engine

are located at the rear right-hand (fuel injection pump) side of the gasket (see illustration).

Piston protrusion	Gasket identification
0.5000 to 0.6000 mm	1 hole
0.6100 to 0.7000 mm	2 holes
0.7100 to 0.8000 mm	3 holes

Refitting

30 Ensure that the cylinder head locating dowels are fitted to the cylinder block, then fit the correct gasket the right way round on the cylinder block. On 200 TDi and 300 TDi engines, the identification mark(s) should be positioned at the rear right-hand (fuel injection pump) side of the gasket. The TOP mark should be uppermost, on the fuel injection pump side of the engine (see illustration).

31 Lower the cylinder head onto the block, and position the head over the two dowels in the cylinder block.

32 On 200 TDi and 300 TDi engines, refer to the note at the beginning of this Section; fit new cylinder head bolts, if there is any doubt about the number of times the original bolts have been used.

33 Proceed as follows according to engine type.

10J, 12J and 19J engines

34 Lightly lubricate the cylinder head bolt threads, then loosely fit the bolts, noting that five of the bolts are used to secure the valve operating gear, and cannot be fitted at this stage.

35 Where applicable, refit the valve stem caps to the tops of the valves in their original locations, as noted before removal.

36 Refit the valve operating gear, as described in Section 10, but do not tighten the five cylinder head/valve operating gear securing bolts.

37 Tighten the eighteen cylinder head bolts (including the five used to secure the valve

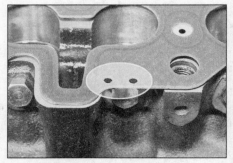

11.29 Cylinder head gasket identification holes – 300 TDi engine

11.30 Cylinder head gasket TOP mark

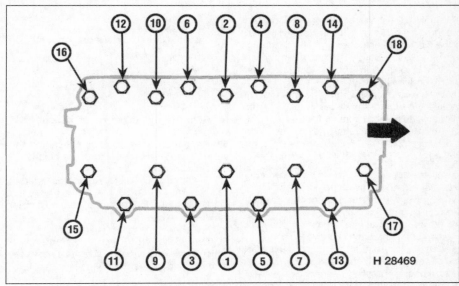

11.37 Cylinder head bolt tightening sequence – 10J, 12J and 19J engines
Arrow points towards timing belt end of engine

operating gear) progressively to the specified torque, in the order shown (see illustration).

38 Proceed to paragraph 43.

200 TDi and 300 TDi engines

39 Lightly lubricate the cylinder head bolt threads, then loosely fit the bolts. Note that there are three different sizes of bolt, and the bolts should be fitted to the locations shown (see illustrations).

11.39a Cylinder head bolt locations and tightening sequence – 200 TDi and 300 TDi engines

M10 x 117 mm bolts at locations 3, 5, 12 and 13
M12 x 140 mm bolts at locations 1, 2, 7, 8, 9, 10, 15, 16, 17 and 18
M12 x 100 mm bolts at locations 4, 6, 11 and 14

11.39b Refit the cylinder head bolts ...

11.40 . . . and tighten to the specified torque, then through the specified angle – 300 TDi engine

40 Tighten the bolts in the order shown in illustration 11.39a, and in the stages given in the Specifications – ie, tighten all bolts in sequence to the Stage 1 torque, then tighten all bolts in sequence to the Stage 2 torque, and so on **(see illustration)**.

41 Where applicable, refit the valve stem caps to the tops of the valves in their original locations, as noted before removal.

42 Refit the valve operating gear as described in Section 10.

All engines

43 Where applicable, unscrew the securing bolt, then refit the transmission breather/wiring harness bracket to the rear of the cylinder head, and tighten the securing bolt.

44 Where applicable, refit the wiring harness bracket, and tighten the securing bolt.

45 On 10J, 12J and 19J engines, reconnect the oil feed pipe to the rear of the cylinder head, using new sealing washers if necessary.

46 Where applicable, reconnect the coolant hose to the rear of the cylinder head.

47 On 200 TDi and 300 TDi engines, reconnect the coolant hose connecting the manifold-mounted coolant pipe to the water pump.

48 Refit the exhaust manifold (and the turbocharger, where applicable), and inlet manifold, as described in Chapter 4A.

49 Reconnect the temperature gauge sender wiring, and reconnect the coolant hoses to the thermostat housing and cover.

50 Refit the glow plugs as described in Chapter 5.

12.2a Cam follower components

1 *Guide locating screw*
2 *Guide*
3 *Roller*
4 *Tappet slide*

51 Refit the fuel injectors as described in Chapter 4A.

52 Reconnect the breather hose(s) to the valve cover, oil filler cap and/or the breather, if not already done.

53 Refill the cooling system as described in Chapter 1.

54 Refit the bonnet as described in Chapter 12.

55 Reconnect the battery negative lead.

56 On completion, start the engine. If difficulty is experienced, bleed the fuel system as described in Chapter 4A.

12 Cam follower components – removal, inspection and refitting

⚠ **Warning: Each cam follower consists of a solid roller, held in position against the camshaft by a slide inside a fixed guide. If the guide is removed before the roller, the roller may fall behind the camshaft and become jammed, or may fall past the camshaft into the crankcase. The following procedure**

12.2b Cam follower guide locating screws (arrowed)

must therefore be followed exactly when removing the cam followers.
Note: *New guide locating screws must be used on refitting.*

Removal

1 Remove the cylinder head as described in Section 11.

2 Starting at the front of the engine, loosen the first cam follower guide locating screw (accessed from the camshaft side of the cylinder block), until the end of the screw rests just below the hole in the inner bore of the guide **(see illustrations)**. Note that on early engines, the screws were secured using locking wire – where applicable, cut away and discard the wire.

3 Using a suitable length of wire with a hooked end, lift out the tappet slide. Note that the FRONT or F mark on the slide should face the timing chain/belt end of the engine **(see illustration)**.

4 Using the same piece of wire, lift out the roller **(see illustration)**. Mark the roller on the side facing the timing chain/belt end of the engine, so that it can be refitted in its original position.

5 Remove the guide locating screw, and lift out the guide **(see illustration)**. Where applicable, recover the washer from under the screw head.

6 Repeat the procedure on the remaining components, and number the components from 1 to 8, so that they can be refitted in their original locations.

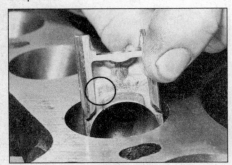

12.3 Lifting out a tappet slide. Note F mark faces timing chain/belt end of engine

12.4 Lifting out a roller

12.5 Lifting out a tappet guide

Inspection

Note: *It is unlikely that individual components will wear significantly, without obvious general wear in all the components. It can be a false economy to renew individual components, and if significant wear is evident, or if the engine is being overhauled after completing a high mileage, it is advisable to renew all the cam follower and valve operating components as a set.*

7 Clean all the components thoroughly, keeping them in order.

8 Examine all the components for wear and damage. Pay particular attention to the rollers.

9 Ensure that the tappet slides move freely in their relevant guides.

10 If there is any sign of significant wear or damage, the relevant components should be renewed.

Refitting

11 Insert the first guide into its original location in the cylinder block, and align the locating screw holes in the block and the guide.

12 Fit a new guide locating screw, but do not allow the end of the screw to protrude into the inner bore of the guide at this stage.

13 Fit the relevant roller, making sure that the mark made before removal faces the timing chain/belt end of the engine. New rollers can be fitted either way round.

14 Before fitting the tappet slide, check that the oilways are clear.

15 Fit the tappet slide with the FRONT or F mark facing the timing chain/belt end of the engine.

16 Tighten the guide locating screw to the specified torque. If the screws were originally secured with locking wire, there is no need to fit locking wire to secure them on refitting, as new bolts will be supplied micro-encapsulated with thread-locking compound.

17 Repeat the procedure for the remaining components, ensuring that all components are refitted in their original locations.

18 Refit the cylinder head as described in Section 11.

13 Sump – removal and refitting

Note: *A new gasket, or suitable sealant (as applicable) will be required on refitting.*

Removal

1 Disconnect the battery negative lead.

2 Drain the engine oil, with reference to Chapter 1 if necessary.

3 To improve access, apply the handbrake, then jack up the front of the vehicle and support securely on axle stands placed under the front axle (see *Jacking and vehicle support*).

4 Loosen the sump securing bolts, then using a sharp knife, break the sealant around the sump flange.

5 Support the sump, then remove the bolts (and washers, where applicable) and the single nut (where applicable). On 200 TDi engines, note the locations of the bolts, as different lengths of bolts are used.

6 Lower the sump from the engine. Where applicable, recover the gasket.

Refitting

7 Clean all traces of gasket (or sealant) and oil from the mating faces of the engine and the sump, taking care not to allow debris to enter the engine.

8 Examine the sump for damage or distortion. Check the condition of the drain plug threads.

9 On engines where the sump is sealed using a gasket, place a new gasket in position on the sump flange.

10 On engines where the sump is sealed using sealant, apply a bead of RTV sealant to the mating face of the sump flange, ensuring that the sealant is applied inboard of the bolt holes. **Do not** apply excess sealant, which may enter the engine when the sump is refitted. Also apply sealant to the groove between the timing belt housing and the cylinder block.

11 Lift the sump into position, then loosely fit the securing bolts (and the washers and nut, where applicable) sufficiently to locate the sump securely on the engine. On 200 TDi engines, ensure that the bolts are refitted to their correct locations, as noted before removal – the three longest bolts fit at the front of the sump.

12 Progressively tighten the fixings to the specified torque.

13 Ensure that the sump drain plug has been refitted and tightened, using a new sealing ring, then lower the vehicle to the ground.

14 Refill the engine with oil as described in Chapter 1.

15 Reconnect the battery negative lead, then start the engine and check for oil leaks.

14 Oil pump and skew gear (all except 300 TDi engine) – removal, inspection and refitting

Oil pump

Note: *A new gasket must be used on refitting.*

Removal

1 Remove the sump as described in Section 13.

2 Where applicable, bend back the locktabs, then loosen the two bolts securing the oil pump to the cylinder block **(see illustration)**. Note that access to the right-hand bolt may require the use of a socket with a universal joint adapter.

3 Remove the bolts and recover the washers, then lower the oil pump from the engine.

4 Recover the gasket.

5 Where possible, withdraw the oil pump driveshaft.

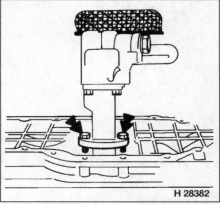

14.2 Oil pump securing bolts (arrowed) – 200 TDi engine

Inspection

6 With the pump removed from the engine, thoroughly clean the external surfaces.

7 Where applicable, unscrew the bolt securing the oil strainer to the support bracket, and recover the washers.

8 Using a suitable screwdriver, bend back the lockwasher, and unscrew the nut securing the strainer pipe to the pump body. Withdraw the strainer, and recover the O-ring if it is loose **(see illustration)**.

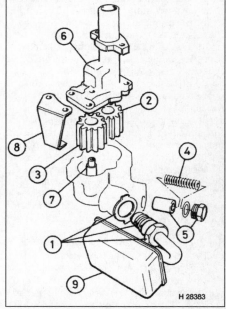

14.8 Oil pump components – 200 TDi engine

1 Lockwasher, O-ring and union nut
2 Driven gear
3 Idler gear
4 Pressure relief valve spring
5 Pressure relief valve plunger and plug
6 Pump cover
7 Idler gear spindle
8 Oil strainer support bracket
9 Oil strainer

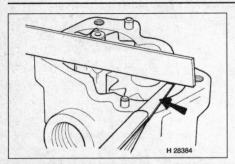

14.14 Checking the oil pump gear endfloat using a feeler blade (arrowed) – 200 TDi engine

9 Unscrew the four securing bolts and washers, and lift off the pump cover. Note that on some engines, two of the bolts also secure the oil strainer support bracket.

10 Lift out the gears, noting their locations, so that they can be refitted in their original positions.

11 Unscrew the oil pressure relief valve plug, and recover the sealing washer.

12 Lift out the relief valve spring and plunger. Also lift out the ball, where applicable.

13 Examine the gears for wear, scoring and pitting, and if there is any evidence of wear or damage, renew the gears. Note that both gears must be renewed as a pair.

14 If the gears appear to be serviceable, check the endfloat as follows. Thoroughly clean the pump body, and refit the gears. Place a straight-edge across the pump body, then using a feeler blade, measure the clearance between the end face of the pump body and the gears (see illustration).

15 Also check the clearance between the gear lobes and the pump body, again using a feeler blade.

16 If either of the measurements is outside the specified limits (see Specifications), it may be possible to renew the gears (gears should always be renewed in pairs – consult a Land Rover dealer for details of availability), otherwise the pump should be renewed.

17 Examine the relief valve plunger for wear or scoring, and check the condition of the spring. Renew the components if there is any sign of wear or damage. If a relief valve ball is fitted, check the ball seat for scoring – the ball seat can be reground as follows:
a) Improvise a tool by soldering a new ball to a length of rod.
b) Apply coarse, then fine grinding paste to the ball, then use the tool to regrind the seat.
c) Clean away all traces of grinding paste.
d) Use a new ball when reassembling the pump.

18 Examine the condition of the idler gear spindle in the pump body. This is unlikely to show wear, but if necessary, the spindle can be renewed as follows. Drive or press the spindle from the pump body, and drive or press the new spindle into position up to the locating shoulder on the spindle.

19 Check the pump cover for signs of wear or scoring, and renew if necessary.

20 Reassemble the pump as follows.

21 Fit the idler gear to the spindle.

22 Fit the driven gear to the pump body, with the plain section of the bore uppermost (facing the pump cover).

23 Fit the pump cover, then refit the securing bolts, ensuring that, where applicable, the oil strainer support bracket is in place on the bolts. Do not fully tighten the bolts at this stage.

24 Hold the pump body so that the pressure relief valve bore is vertical, then fit the relief valve ball (where applicable). Fit the relief valve plunger, solid end first. Fit the spring, then fit the plug using a new sealing washer. Tighten the plug securely.

25 Fill the pump with oil through the strainer pipe orifice in the pump body, then slide the lockwasher over the end of the oil strainer pipe. Fit a new O-ring to the end of the pipe, and engage the pipe with the pump body. Loosely tighten the securing nut.

26 Where applicable, refit and tighten the bolt securing the strainer assembly to the support bracket.

27 Tighten the pump cover bolts.

28 Tighten the strainer pipe nut, and secure with the lockwasher.

Refitting

29 Where applicable, refit the oil pump driveshaft, noting that the longer splined end of the shaft engages with the oil pump.

30 Refit the pump using a new gasket, ensuring that the splines on the oil pump driveshaft engage with the corresponding splined in the driven gear.

31 Refit the securing bolts, ensuring that the washers are in place, and tighten the bolts to the specified torque.

32 Refit the sump as described in Section 13.

Oil pump drive skew gear – 10J engine

Note: *A timing pointer may be required for this operation (see text), and a new timing aperture cover gasket should be used on refitting. A new oil filter adapter gasket will be required on refitting.*

Removal

33 Remove the fuel injection pump as described in Chapter 4A.

34 Unscrew the securing bolts, and withdraw the oil filter adapter assembly from the side of the cylinder block – be prepared for oil spillage. Recover the gasket. Note that, where applicable, there is no need to disconnect the oil cooler pipes from the adapter – move the assembly to one side sufficiently to gain access to the skew gear assembly retaining screw.

35 Remove the retaining screw, then lift out the skew gear assembly (see illustration).

Inspection

36 Thoroughly clean the components.

37 Check the condition of the skew gear teeth, and if there is any sign of wear or damage, renew the gear.

38 If the condition of the skew gear is satisfactory, turn the gear in the bush. If the gear does not turn smoothly, or if there is excessive play between the gear and the bush, the bush should be renewed.

39 On early models, a split bush was fitted, and the bush was retained by a flange on the skew gear – consult a Land Rover dealer for advice if an early split-type bush requires renewal.

40 Later models were fitted with a bush retained by a locknut – proceed as follows to renew the bush:
a) Hold the gear firmly in a vice, taking care not to damage the teeth (wrap a cloth round the gear to protect the teeth).
b) Unscrew the locknut at the base of the gear by turning it clockwise (the gear has a **left-hand thread**). Note that thread-locking compound is used on the nut.
c) Withdraw the thrustwasher, then withdraw the bush from the drivegear.
d) Fit the new bush, ensuring that the retaining screw hole is towards the bottom of the skew gear.
e) Refit the thrustwasher (fit a new washer if there is any sign of wear or scoring).
f) Clean the threads of the locknut, then apply fresh thread-locking compound, and refit the nut. Turn the nut anti-clockwise, and tighten to the specified torque.
g) Check that the gear revolves freely, and that the clearance between the lower end of the bush and the thrustwasher is within the specified limits. If the clearance is outside the specified limits, renew the thrustwasher.

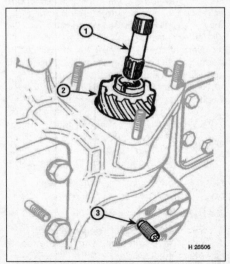

14.35 Oil pump drive skew gear components – 10J engine

1 Fuel injection pump driveshaft
2 Skew gear
3 Retaining screw

14.45 Timing aperture pointer (arrowed) aligned with 13° mark on flywheel – 10J engine

Refitting

41 Remove the valve cover as described in Section 4, to enable the valve rockers to be observed.

42 Unscrew the two securing nuts (recover the washers) securing the timing aperture cover plate to the flywheel housing on the right-hand side of the engine. Lift off the cover plate, and recover the gasket.

43 Look to see if a timing pointer is visible in the aperture. If no pointer is visible, a suitable pointer can be obtained from a Land Rover dealer (part No ERC 2250). Where applicable, fit the timing pointer and secure with the two nuts – note that the pointer arrow should be positioned on the gearbox side of the timing aperture.

44 Using a spanner or socket on the crankshaft pulley bolt, turn the crankshaft clockwise until the both the valves of No 1 cylinder are fully closed.

45 Continue to turn the crankshaft until the 13° mark on the flywheel is aligned with the pointer in the timing aperture **(see illustration)**.

46 If the crankshaft is inadvertently turned beyond the 13° mark, do not turn the crankshaft back – continue to turn in a clockwise direction until the mark is precisely aligned with the pointer.

47 Lubricate the skew gear assembly with fresh engine oil, then insert the assembly into its housing to mesh with the camshaft gear. Due to the angle of the teeth, the gear will turn anti-clockwise as it slides into mesh. The master spline on the skew gear must be positioned at an angle of 20° to the engine crankshaft axis, towards the front of the engine **(see illustration)**. It may take several attempts at fitting to achieve this.

48 Align the screw hole in the bush with the retaining screw hole in the cylinder block, then refit a new bush retaining screw, and recheck the angle of the skew gear master spline.

49 Refit the oil filter adapter assembly, using a new gasket.

50 Refit the fuel injection pump as described in Chapter 4A.

51 On completion, check the engine oil level, with reference to Chapter 1 if necessary.

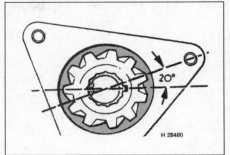

14.47 Fuel injection pump drivegear master spline (arrowed) positioned at 20° to crankshaft axis – 10J engine

Oil pump drive skew gear – 12J and 19J engines

Note: *A new oil filter adapter gasket will be required on refitting.*

Removal

52 Remove the brake vacuum pump as described in Chapter 10.

53 Unscrew the securing bolts, and withdraw the oil filter adapter assembly from the side of the cylinder block – be prepared for oil spillage. Recover the gasket. Note that, where applicable, there is no need to disconnect the oil cooler pipes from the adapter – move the assembly to one side sufficiently to gain access to the skew gear assembly retaining screw.

54 Remove the retaining screw, then lift out the skew gear/drive coupling assembly.

Inspection

55 Proceed as described for 10J engines, in paragraphs 36 to 40 inclusive.

56 If desired, the drive coupling can be separated from the skew gear, using a press.

57 The drive coupling can be dismantled to renew the seals without separating the coupling from the skew gear. Remove the circlips to enable dismantling, and to allow access to the seals **(see illustration)**.

Refitting

58 Lubricate the skew gear assembly with fresh engine oil, then insert the assembly into its housing to mesh with the camshaft gear.

59 Align the screw hole in the bush with the retaining screw hole in the cylinder block, then refit a new bush retaining screw.

60 Tighten the bush retaining screw to the specified torque, then back off one-eighth of a turn.

61 Refit the oil adapter assembly, using a new gasket.

62 Refit the brake vacuum pump as described in Chapter 10.

63 On completion, check the engine oil level, with reference to Chapter 1 if necessary.

Oil pump drive skew gear – 200 TDi engine

Note: *If the skew gear is renewed, the camshaft must also be renewed. This is necessary to preserve the meshing of the skew gear teeth*

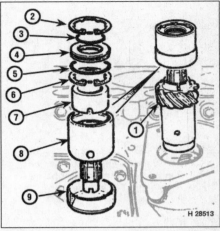

14.57 Oil pump drive skew gear and drive coupling components – 12J and 19J engines

1 *Skew gear*	6 *Circlip*
2 *Circlip*	7 *Collar*
3 *Seal*	8 *Coupling*
4 *Seal collar*	9 *Collar*
5 *Seal*	

with the teeth on the camshaft. New skew gear shaft O-rings will be required on refitting. If the skew gear guide is removed, a new oil filter adapter gasket will be required on refitting.

Removal

64 The skew gear drives the oil pump driveshaft, which also drives the brake vacuum pump.

65 Remove the brake vacuum pump as described in Chapter 10.

66 Make alignment marks between the skew gear flange and the cylinder block, so that the skew gear assembly can be refitted in its original position.

67 Similarly, make alignment marks between the inner face of the skew gear shaft, and the skew gear flange. This is necessary because the skew gear teeth must mesh with the same teeth on the camshaft when the skew gear is refitted.

68 Using a suitable punch or similar tool, tap the skew gear flange round so that the edges overlap the cylinder block **(see illustration)**.

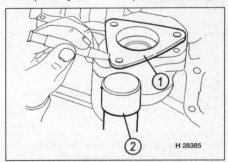

14.68 Tap the skew gear flange (1) round to overlap the cylinder block, then tap upwards using a suitable tool (2) – 200 TDi engine

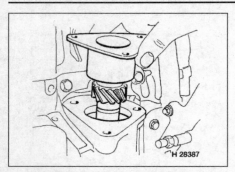

14.69 Withdrawing the skew gear assembly from the cylinder block – 200 TDi engine

14.71 Withdrawing the oil pump driveshaft from the cylinder block – 200 TDi engine

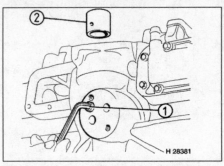

14.72 Unscrew the retaining screw (1) to remove the skew gear guide (2) – 200 TDi engine

69 Carefully tap the skew gear flange upwards until the assembly can be lifted from the cylinder block **(see illustration)**.

70 Remove the O-rings from the inside diameter of the skew gear shaft, and from the outside diameter of the skew gear flange, and discard them.

71 Using a pair of long-nosed pliers, or a suitable length of wire, withdraw the oil pump driveshaft from the cylinder block **(see illustration)**.

72 If desired, the skew gear guide can be removed from the cylinder block as follows:

a) *Unscrew the securing bolts, and withdraw the oil filter adapter assembly from the side of the cylinder block – be prepared for oil spillage. Recover the gasket. Note that there is no need to disconnect the oil cooler pipes from the adapter – move the assembly to one side sufficiently to gain access to the skew gear guide retaining screw.*

b) *Working at the side of the cylinder block, using a suitable Allen key, unscrew the guide retaining screw (see illustration).*

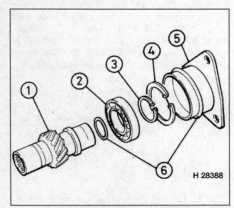

14.76 Oil pump skew gear components – 200 TDi engine

1	Skew gear	4	Bearing retaining
2	Bearing		circlip
3	Skew gear shaft	5	Housing
	circlip	6	O-rings

c) *Using a suitable length of hooked wire, lift the guide from the cylinder block.*

Inspection

73 Thoroughly clean the skew gear and oil pump driveshaft components.

74 Check that the oil pump driveshaft is straight, and check the condition of the splines on the ends of the shaft. If the shaft is bent, or the splines are worn or damaged, the shaft should be renewed. Note that if the splines at the oil pump end of the shaft are damaged or worn, then the condition of the corresponding splines on the oil pump should be checked (remove the oil pump as described previously in this Section).

75 Check the condition of the skew gear teeth, and if there is any sign of wear or damage, renew the assembly (note that in this case, the camshaft must also be renewed – see note at the beginning of this sub-Section).

76 If the condition of the skew gear is satisfactory, turn the gear in the flange to check the condition of the bearing. If the gear does not turn smoothly, or if there is excessive play in the bearing, the bearing should be renewed. To renew the bearing, proceed as follows **(see illustration)**:

a) *Using a suitable pair of circlip pliers, remove the retaining circlip from the skew gear shaft.*

b) *Similarly, remove the bearing retaining circlip from the groove in the skew gear flange.*

c) *Support the skew gear flange, then press the bearing and the skew gear from the flange.*

d) *Support the bearing, then press the skew gear from the bearing.*

e) *Using a tube or socket of suitable diameter on the bearing outer race, press the bearing into the flange, up to the shoulder.*

f) *Refit the bearing retaining circlip.*

g) *Support the bearing inner race using a socket or tube of suitable diameter, then press the skew gear into the bearing.*

h) *Refit the retaining circlip to the skew gear shaft.*

77 Examine the internal surfaces of the skew gear guide for wear or damage, and renew if necessary.

Refitting

78 Where applicable, fit the skew gear guide to the cylinder block, ensuring that the retaining screw hole in the guide aligns with the corresponding hole in the cylinder block. Refit and tighten the guide retaining screw, ensuring that the screw locates correctly in the hole in the guide.

79 Where applicable, refit the oil filter adapter assembly, using a new gasket.

80 Fit the oil pump driveshaft, noting that the longer splined end of the shaft engages with the oil pump.

81 Fit new O-rings to the inside diameter of the skew gear shaft, and to the outside diameter of the flange.

82 Refit the skew gear assembly to the cylinder block, ensuring that the marks made on the inner face of the skew gear shaft and the skew gear flange, and on the skew gear flange and the cylinder block, are aligned. Manipulate the flange and the skew gear as necessary until all the marks are aligned, noting that the skew gear will move as it is engaged with the camshaft.

83 Refit the brake vacuum pump as described in Chapter 10.

84 If the oil filter adapter assembly has been removed, check the engine oil level, with reference to Chapter 1 if necessary.

15 Oil pump and strainer (300 TDi engine) – removal, inspection and refitting

Oil pump

Removal

1 The rotor-type oil pump is driven from the front of the crankshaft, and the rotors are located in the timing belt housing.

2 Remove the timing belt housing as described in Section 17.

3 Working at the rear of the timing belt housing, unscrew the securing screws,

15.3 Removing the oil pump cover plate – 300 TDi engine

15.4a Mark the face of the outer oil pump rotor . . .

15.4b . . . then lift the rotors from the housing – 300 TDi engine

15.6 Oil pressure relief valve plug (arrowed) – 300 TDi engine

and remove the oil pump cover plate (**see illustration**).

4 Mark the face of the outer oil pump rotor so that it can be refitted the same way round, then lift out the oil pump rotors (**see illustrations**).

Inspection

5 At the time of writing, no information was available regarding wear limits for the oil pump rotors. It is recommended that if there is any sign of obvious wear, the rotors are renewed. Always renew the rotors as a pair.

6 Unscrew the oil pressure relief valve plug, using a suitable large-bladed screwdriver, and lift out the spring and plunger (**see illustration**). Note the orientation of the plunger, to ensure correct refitting.

7 Examine the relief valve plunger for wear or

scoring, and check the condition of the spring. Renew the components if there is any sign of wear or damage.

8 Refit the relief valve plunger and spring, ensuring that the plunger is orientated as noted before removal.

9 Coat the threads of the relief valve plug with suitable thread-locking compound, then refit the plug and tighten securely.

Refitting

10 Ensure that the rotors are clean, then lubricate them with clean engine oil, and refit them to the housing. Ensure that the mark made on the outer rotor is visible, indicating that the rotor is orientated correctly.

11 Ensure that the mating faces of the pump cover and the housing are clean, then refit the cover and tighten the screws securely.

Strainer

Note: *A new pick-up pipe O-ring must be used on refitting, and suitable thread-locking compound will be required for the strainer support bracket bolts.*

Removal

12 Remove the sump as described in Section 13.

13 Unscrew the two bolts securing the strainer support bracket to the main bearing cap.

14 Unscrew the bolt securing the oil pick-up pipe to the timing belt housing, then withdraw the strainer. Recover the O-ring from the pick-up pipe (**see illustrations**).

Inspection

15 Check the strainer gauze and the pick-up pipe for obstructions, and clean the assembly thoroughly before refitting.

Refitting

16 Refitting is a reversal of removal, bearing in mind the following points:
 a) *Use a new pick-up pipe O-ring.*
 b) *Coat the threads of the pick-up pipe and strainer support bracket bolts with suitable thread-locking compound, and tighten all fixings to the specified torque (**see illustration**).*
 c) *Refit the sump as described in Section 13.*

16 Oil seals – renewal

Crankshaft front oil seal

10J engine

1 The oil seal is located in the timing chain cover, and the oil seal renewal procedure is described with the timing chain cover removal and refitting procedure in Section 6.

Timing belt cover dust seal

2 The procedure is described with the timing belt cover removal and refitting procedure in Section 6.

15.14a Withdraw the oil strainer . . .

15.14b . . . and recover the O-ring – 300 TDi engine

15.16 Coat the threads of the strainer support bracket bolts with thread-locking compound – 300 TDi engine

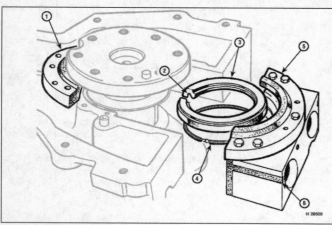

1 Oil seal retainer upper half
2 Split in oil seal
3 Oil seal
4 Oil seal coil spring
5 Oil seal retainer lower half
6 Rear main bearing cap

16.14 Rear crankshaft oil seal components – early 10J engines with 3-bearing crankshaft

Timing belt housing oil seal

3 Remove the crankshaft sprocket, as described in Section 9.

4 Prise out the old oil seal using a small screwdriver, taking care not to damage the surface of the crankshaft.

 HAYNES HiNT *An oil seal can be removed by drilling two small holes diagonally opposite each other, and inserting self-tapping screws in them. A pair of grips can then be used to pull out the oil seal, by pulling on each screw in turn.*

5 Wipe clean the oil seal seating, then dip the new seal in fresh engine oil, and locate it over the crankshaft with its closed side facing outwards. Make sure that the oil seal lip is not damaged as it is located over the crankshaft.

6 Using a tube of suitable diameter, drive the oil seal squarely into the housing until the outer edge of the seal is approximately 0.5 mm below the face of the housing.

7 Refit the crankshaft sprocket as described in Section 9.

Crankshaft rear oil seal
Early 10J engine
with 3-bearing crankshaft

Note: *This is an involved procedure. Read through the Section thoroughly before starting work, and ensure that all the required new components are available.*

8 The oil seal is located in a two-piece retainer, bolted to the rear crankshaft main bearing cap and the cylinder block.

9 Remove the starter motor as described in Chapter 5.

10 Remove the sump and the flywheel, as described in Sections 13 and 19 respectively.

11 Working at the rear of the cylinder block, unscrew the securing bolts, and remove the flywheel housing. Note the locations of any brackets secured by the external housing bolts. Recover the O-ring.

12 Unscrew and remove the rear main bearing cap securing bolts.

13 Withdraw the bearing cap, complete with bearing shell. Tap the cap with a wooden or copper mallet if it is stuck. Note that the sides of the bearing cap are sealed to the cylinder block using plastic or cork seals on each side, which may cause difficulty in removing the cap. If necessary, the cap can be levered from its location, using a suitable bar inserted in the hole in the inside face of the cap – place a suitable piece of wood on the crankshaft web, and lever against the wood.

14 Unbolt the lower half of the oil seal retainer from the bearing cap **(see illustration)**.

15 Working through the cut-out in the crankshaft flange, unscrew the securing bolts and remove the upper half of the oil seal retainer from the rear of the cylinder block. Withdraw the retainer half.

16 Prise the coil spring from the oil seal, and unhook the spring ends. Remove the spring, then pull the oil seal from the crankshaft, noting that the seal is split to enable removal.

17 Thoroughly clean the oil seal mating surfaces of the retainer halves and the oil seal journal on the crankshaft. Similarly, clean the oil seal retainer, cylinder block and bearing cap mating faces.

18 Fit a new oil seal, then refit the bearing cap, using new seals and new bolts, and refit the flywheel housing, as described under *Final refitting* in Chapter 2C, Section 16. Ignore

the references to refitting the crankshaft, remaining bearing caps and checking the crankshaft endfloat.

19 On completion, refit the flywheel and the sump as described in Sections 19 and 13 respectively, and refit the starter motor as described in Chapter 5.

Later 10J engine
with 5-bearing crankshaft,
and 12J, 19J and 200 TDi engines

20 Remove the flywheel as described in Section 19.

21 Proceed as described in paragraphs 4 to 6, bearing in mind the following points:

a) *Wind a length of tape around the crankshaft nose, to prevent damage to the oil seal lips as the seal is fitted over the crankshaft.*

b) *Take care to ensure that the seal enters its housing squarely, and make sure that the seal lip does not fold over.*

c) *Press the seal into position until it rests against the shoulder in the housing.*

22 Refit the flywheel as described in Section 19.

300 TDi engine

Note: *The oil seal is retained in a housing, and the seal and housing must be renewed as an assembly. A new assembly is supplied fitted with a former/seal guide. Do not remove the former/seal guide before fitting the assembly to the engine. If a new assembly is received without a former/seal guide fitted, return it to the supplier. Used formers/seal guides must be discarded. Three M8 studs (or bolts with the heads cut off) will be required when fitting the new seal.*

23 Remove the flywheel as described in Section 19.

24 Unscrew the five securing bolts, and remove the seal/housing assembly from the cylinder block. Recover the gasket, and the housing rubber seal if it is loose.

25 Thoroughly clean the gasket faces of the cylinder block and the new seal/housing assembly.

26 Screw three M8 studs (or bolts with the heads cut off, and slots cut in the top to enable removal) into the cylinder block bolt holes, then fit a new seal housing gasket over the studs **(see illustration)**.

27 Fit a new rubber seal to the rear of the new oil seal housing **(see illustration)**.

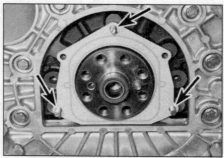

16.26 M8 stud locations (arrowed) for fitting of crankshaft rear oil seal housing – 300 TDi engine

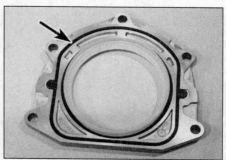

16.27 Fit a new rubber seal (arrowed) to the housing – 300 TDi engine

28 Fit the new assembly, with the former/ seal guide in place, over the studs and the crankshaft flange. The former/seal guide will be ejected as the assembly is fitted (see illustration).

29 Loosely fit the two bolts to the holes not occupied by the studs.

30 Unscrew one of the studs, and loosely refit the bolt in its place. Repeat the procedure for the two remaining studs.

31 Progressively tighten the seal/housing securing bolts to the specified torque.

32 Refit the flywheel as described in Section 19.

Camshaft front oil seal

All except 10J engine

33 Remove the camshaft sprocket as described in Section 9.

34 Proceed as described in paragraphs 4 to 6.

35 Refit the camshaft sprocket as described in Section 9.

17 Timing belt housing gasket (all except 10J engines) – renewal

12J and 19J engines

Removal

1 Remove the fuel injection pump as described in Chapter 4A.

2 Remove the timing belt sprockets and the timing belt tensioner, as described in Section 9.

3 Unscrew the front three sump securing bolts, which screw into the bottom of the timing belt housing.

4 Unscrew the timing belt housing securing bolts, noting their locations, as several different lengths of bolt are used.

5 Withdraw the timing belt housing from the front of the engine. Recover the main gasket and the coolant aperture gasket.

Refitting

6 Thoroughly clean all traces of old gasket from the mating faces of the cylinder block and the timing belt housing.

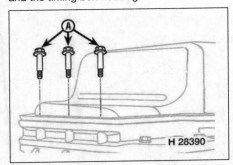

17.17 Unscrew the three bolts (arrowed) securing the sump and ladder frame to the cylinder block – 200 TDi engine

16.28 Fitting the new crankshaft rear oil seal/housing assembly – 300 TDi engine

7 Note that whilst the timing belt housing is removed, it is advisable to renew the oil seals, as described in Section 16.

8 Fit a new main gasket to the cylinder block, using a little grease to hold it in position.

9 Similarly, fit a new gasket to the coolant aperture.

10 Carefully offer the timing belt housing to the cylinder block, taking care not to damage the oil seals as they are passed over the crankshaft and camshaft.

11 Refit the securing bolts to their original locations, as noted before removal, and progressively tighten the bolts to the specified torque.

12 Refit the three front sump securing bolts, and tighten to the specified torque.

13 Refit the timing belt sprockets and the timing belt tensioner, as described in Section 9.

14 Refit the fuel injection pump as described in Chapter 4A.

200 TDi engine

Removal

15 Remove the fuel injection pump as described in Chapter 4A.

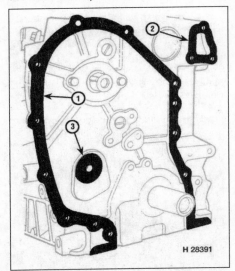

17.19 Timing belt housing main gasket (1), coolant aperture gasket (2) and washer gasket (3) – 200 TDi engine

16 Remove the timing belt sprockets, and the timing belt tensioner, as described in Section 9.

17 Unscrew the three bolts securing the sump and the ladder frame to the timing belt housing (see illustration).

18 Unscrew the five bolts securing the timing belt housing to the cylinder block, noting their locations, as different lengths of bolt are used.

19 Withdraw the timing belt housing from the front of the engine. Recover the main gasket, the coolant aperture gasket, and the gasket washer which fits around the timing belt tensioner pulley bolt hole (see illustration).

Refitting

20 Thoroughly clean all traces of old gasket from the mating faces of the cylinder block and the timing belt housing.

21 Note that whilst the timing belt housing is removed, it is advisable to renew the oil seals, as described in Section 16.

22 Fit a new main gasket to the cylinder block, using a little grease to hold it in position.

23 Similarly, fit new gaskets to the coolant aperture and the timing belt tensioner bolt hole in the cylinder block.

24 Carefully offer the timing belt housing to the cylinder block, taking care not to damage the oil seals as they are passed over the crankshaft and camshaft. Ensure that the housing fits over the locating stud.

25 Refit the five securing bolts to their original locations, as noted before removal, and progressively tighten the bolts to the specified torque (see illustration).

26 Refit the three bolts securing the sump and the ladder frame to the timing belt housing, and tighten to the specified torque.

27 Refit the timing belt tensioner, and the timing belt sprockets, as described in Section 9.

28 Refit the fuel injection pump as described in Chapter 4A.

300 TDi engine

Note: Six M8 studs (or bolts with the heads cut off) will be required when refitting the housing.

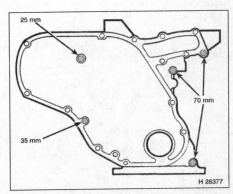

17.25 Timing belt housing securing bolt locations – 200 TDi engine

17.34 Withdrawing the timing belt housing (engine shown inverted) – 300 TDi engine

17.36a Tapping the camshaft oil seal from the timing belt housing

17.36b Fitting a new camshaft oil seal to the timing belt housing using a socket

Removal

29 Remove the fuel injection pump as described in Chapter 4A.

30 Remove the timing belt sprockets as described in Section 9.

31 Remove the sump as described in Section 13.

32 Remove the oil strainer as described in Section 15.

33 Unscrew the ten timing belt housing securing bolts, noting their locations, as several different lengths of bolt are used.

34 Withdraw the timing belt housing from the front of the engine, and recover the gasket **(see illustration)**. Note that the housing locates on two dowels.

Refitting

35 Thoroughly clean the gasket faces of the cylinder block and the timing belt housing.

36 Note that whilst the timing belt housing is removed, it is advisable to renew the oil seals. The seals can be tapped from the housing using a suitable punch, and the new seals can be fitted by tapping into position using a suitable socket or tube **(see illustrations)**.

37 Fit six M8 studs (or bolts with the heads cut off, and slots cut in the top to enable removal) to the bolt holes in the cylinder block, then locate the new gasket over the studs **(see illustration)**.

38 Align the flats on the oil pump driven rotor with the corresponding flats on the crankshaft.

39 Carefully offer the timing belt housing to the cylinder block, taking care not to damage the oil seals as they are passed over the crankshaft and camshaft. Locate the housing on the studs, and the two dowels. If necessary, alter the position of the oil pump rotor using a small screwdriver, to enable it to engage with the crankshaft as the housing is fitted **(see illustration)**.

40 Refit bolts of the correct length to the holes not occupied by the studs, but do not fully tighten them at this stage.

41 Remove one of the studs, and fit the correct length of bolt to the relevant hole. Repeat the procedure for the remaining studs.

42 With all the bolts correctly refitted, progressively tighten the bolts to the specified torque.

43 Refit the oil strainer as described in Section 15.

44 Refit the sump as described in Section 13.

45 Refit the timing belt sprockets as described in Section 9.

46 Refit the fuel injection pump as described in Chapter 4A.

18 Camshaft – removal, inspection and refitting

Note: *On 200 TDi engines, if the camshaft is renewed, the auxiliary drive skew gear must*

also be renewed (see Section 14). This is necessary to preserve the meshing of the skew gear teeth with the teeth on the camshaft.

Removal

1 To provide sufficient clearance to withdraw the camshaft from the front of the engine, remove the radiator as described in Chapter 3.

2 Remove the cylinder head, and the cam follower components, as described in Sections 11 and 12.

3 On all except 300 TDi engines, remove the oil pump drive skew gear assembly as described in Section 14.

4 On all except 10J engines, remove the timing belt housing, as described in Section 17.

5 Before removing the camshaft, check the camshaft endfloat as follows.

6 Mount a dial gauge on the end of the cylinder block, and position the probe to read from the end of the camshaft.

7 Push the camshaft fully into the cylinder block, and zero the dial gauge **(see illustration)**.

8 Pull the camshaft fully towards the front of the engine, and note the reading on the dial gauge.

9 If the reading is outside the specified limits (see *Specifications*), fit a new thrustplate on refitting.

10 Where applicable, bend back the locking tabs, then unscrew the two securing bolts,

17.37 Fitting the timing belt housing gasket. M8 guide stud locations arrowed (engine shown inverted) – 300 TDi engine

17.39 Using a screwdriver to align the oil pump rotor with the flats on the crankshaft (engine shown inverted) – 300 TDi engine

18.7 Measuring the camshaft endfloat – engine shown inverted

18.10 Remove the thrustplate . . .

18.11 . . . and withdraw the camshaft – engine shown inverted

18.13 Examine the camshaft bearings in the cylinder block (arrowed) – engine shown inverted

and remove the camshaft thrustplate, noting which way round it is fitted **(see illustration)**.

11 Carefully withdraw the camshaft from the front of the cylinder block, taking care not to allow the end of the camshaft to drop onto the bearings in the cylinder block as it is removed **(see illustration)**.

Inspection

12 Examine the camshaft bearing surfaces and cam lobes for wear ridges, pitting or scoring. Renew the camshaft if evident.

13 Examine the camshaft bearing surfaces in the cylinder block **(see illustration)**. Deep scoring or other damage means that the bearings must be renewed. To determine the extent of wear, the internal diameter of the bearings can be measured using a suitable internal micrometer. Renewal of the bearings is a specialist job, and should be entrusted to a suitably-equipped specialist with access to line-boring equipment.

Refitting

14 Carefully offer the camshaft into position in the cylinder block, taking care not to damage the bearings or the cam lobes.

15 Refit the camshaft thrustplate, ensuring that it is positioned as noted before removal, then refit the securing bolts (and locking tabs, where applicable), and tighten the securing bolts to the specified torque. Where applicable, bend the locking tabs to secure the bolts.

16 Where applicable, refit the timing belt housing, as described in Section 17.

17 Where applicable, refit the oil pump drive skew gear assembly as described in Section 14.

18 Refit the cam follower components and the cylinder head as described in Sections 12 and 11 respectively.

19 Refit the radiator as described in Chapter 3.

---

19 Flywheel – removal, inspection and refitting

Note: *New flywheel securing bolts must be used on refitting. Two M8 bolts will be required to lift the flywheel from the crankshaft.*

Removal

1 Remove the clutch as described in Chapter 6.

2 Fit two long M8 bolts to two of the clutch cover bolt holes in the flywheel, diametrically opposite each other.

3 Using a suitable length of bar positioned between the two bolts, prevent the crankshaft from turning as the flywheel securing bolts are unscrewed **(see illustration)**. It will be necessary to reposition the M8 bolts and the bar using alternative clutch cover bolt holes in order to reach all of the flywheel securing bolts. Note that the flywheel securing bolts are coated with thread-locking compound, and considerable effort may be required to unscrew them.

4 Remove all the flywheel securing bolts, and where applicable, withdraw the reinforcing plate from the centre of the flywheel.

5 Carefully lift the flywheel from the crankshaft, using the two bolts as 'handles' **(see illustration)**. Note that the flywheel locates on a dowel in the end of the crankshaft.

⚠ **Warning: The flywheel is heavy – take care not to drop it.**

Inspection

6 If the clutch friction disc contact surface of the flywheel is scored, or on close inspection shows signs of small hairline cracks (caused by overheating), it may be possible to have the flywheel surface-ground, provided the overall thickness of the flywheel is not reduced below the minimum limit (see *Specifications*).

19.3 Using a length of bar to counterhold the flywheel as the bolts are unscrewed. M8 bolt locations arrowed – 300 TDi engine

19.5 Lifting the flywheel from the crankshaft

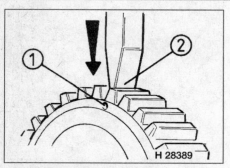

19.10 Removing the ring gear from the flywheel

1 Drill an 8.0 mm hole
2 Split the gear using a cold chisel

Consult a Land Rover dealer or a specialist engine repairer, and if grinding is not possible, renew the flywheel complete.

7 If the teeth on the flywheel starter ring are badly worn, or if some are missing, then it will be necessary to remove the ring gear, and fit a new one.

8 To renew the ring gear, firstly drill an 8.0 mm hole in the side of the ring gear between the roots of any two gear teeth, and the inner diameter of the ring gear. The hole should be just deep enough to weaken the gear – *take great care not to allow the drill to touch the flywheel.*

9 Clamp the flywheel securely in a vice, and cover it with a large cloth to reduce the possibility of personal injury.

 ⚠ Warning: Wear eye protection during the following procedure.

10 Place a cold chisel between the gear teeth above the drilled hole, then split the gear with the chisel. Take great care not to damage the flywheel during this operation., and wear eye protection at all times. Once the ring has been split, it will spread apart, and can be lifted from the flywheel **(see illustration)**.

11 The new ring gear must be heated to between 225 and 250ºC, and unless facilities for heating by oven or flame are available, leave the fitting to a Land Rover dealer or engineering works. The new ring gear must not be overheated during this work, or the temper of the metal will be affected.

12 The ring should be tapped gently down onto its register, and left to cool naturally – the contraction of the metal on cooling will ensure that it is a secure and permanent fit.

Refitting

13 Commence refitting by thoroughly cleaning the mating faces of the flywheel and the crankshaft.

14 If the two M8 'handle' bolts have been removed, refit them to the flywheel.

15 Align the dowel hole in the flywheel with the crankshaft dowel, then lift the flywheel onto the end of the crankshaft.

16 Where applicable, refit the reinforcing plate, then fit new flywheel securing bolts, and tighten them to the specified torque,

preventing the crankshaft from turning as during removal.

17 With all the flywheel bolts tightened, and the two M8 bolts removed, check the flywheel run-out as follows:

a) *Mount a dial test indicator securely on the end face of the flywheel housing.*
b) *Position the probe to read from the flywheel face, at a radius of 114.0 mm from the centre of the crankshaft.*
c) *Turn the crankshaft through one complete revolution, and check that the run-out does not exceed the specified limit.*

18 If the run-out is excessive, remove the flywheel again, and check for damage or dirt between the mating faces of the crankshaft and the flywheel, and the locating dowel. Refit the flywheel, and check the run-out again as described previously. If the problem persists, have the flywheel checked by a suitable engine repair specialist.

19 Refit the clutch as described in Chapter 6.

20 Crankshaft spigot bush – renewal

1 To gain access to the spigot bush, it will be necessary to separate the engine and gearbox. The gearbox can be removed as described in Chapter 7A, but if no work is required on the gearbox, it will prove easier to remove the engine for access, as described in Chapter 2C.

2 Remove the clutch as described in Chapter 6.

3 Using a suitable tap, thread the bore of the bush, located in the end of the crankshaft **(see illustration)**.

4 Screw a suitable bolt into the bush, then use the bolt to pull the bush from the end of the crankshaft using a suitable pair of pliers or grips.

5 Alternatively, the bush can be removed as follows:

a) *Obtain a short length of metal rod, with a diameter which provides a firm sliding fit in the bore of the bush.*
b) *Pack the bore of the bush with grease.*
c) *Insert the metal rod into the bush, and*

20.3 Spigot bush location (arrowed) in end of crankshaft

cover the rod and bush with a cloth or rag (to prevent the possibility of injury due to grease splashes or the ejection of the bush).
d) *Give the rod a sharp tap with a hammer – the grease should force the bush from the crankshaft.*

6 Thoroughly clean the bush location in the end of the crankshaft, and make sure that the new bush is absolutely clean.

7 Tap the bush into position in the end of the crankshaft, using a suitable drift. Take care not to produce any burrs on the edge of the bush. The bush should be fitted flush with the end of the crankshaft.

8 Refit the clutch as described in Chapter 6, then refit the engine as described in Chapter 2C.

21 Engine mountings – removal and refitting

Removal

1 Place a suitable trolley jack with a large interposed block of wood under the engine sump, to just take the weight of the engine. Ensure that the engine is safely supported before proceeding.

2 Working from the relevant side of the engine compartment, where applicable, release the locking tabs, then unscrew the bolts securing the engine mounting bracket to the cylinder block.

3 Working underneath the vehicle, unscrew the nut securing the engine mounting to the chassis bracket **(see illustration)**.

4 Working from the engine compartment, lift the complete engine mounting assembly from the vehicle, taking care not to damage surrounding components in the engine compartment.

5 If desired, the mounting rubber can be renewed by unscrewing the nut securing it to the engine mounting bracket.

Refitting

6 Refitting is a reversal of removal, but tighten all fixings to the specified torque.

21.3 Left-hand engine mounting-to-chassis bracket nut (arrowed)

22.10 Removing the oil cooler thermostat cover – 300 TDi engine

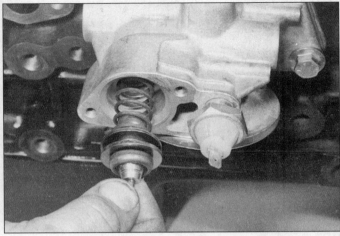

22.11 Lifting out the oil cooler thermostat assembly –
300 TDi engine

22 Engine oil cooler and thermostat – removal and refitting

Oil cooler

Early models with separate oil cooler

1 The oil cooler is located at the front of the vehicle, between the radiator and the front grille panel.

2 Remove the front grille panel as described in Chapter 12.

3 Place a suitable container beneath the oil cooler, then unscrew the unions, and disconnect the oil pipes from the cooler. Allow the oil to drain into the container.

4 Unscrew the nuts from the U-bolts securing the oil cooler frame to the front body tubes, then withdraw the U-bolts, and withdraw the oil cooler.

5 If desired, the oil cooler can be unbolted from the mounting frame.

6 Refitting is a reversal of removal, but ensure that the oil pipe unions are securely tightened. On completion, check the engine oil level, and top-up if necessary.

Later models with oil cooler in radiator

7 The oil cooler is integral with the radiator. Refer to Chapter 3 for removal and refitting details.

Thermostat

Note: *A new thermostat cover O-ring must be used on refitting.*

8 The oil cooler thermostat is located in the oil filter adapter on the right-hand side of the cylinder block.

9 Place a suitable container beneath the oil filter adapter, then disconnect the oil cooler hose union from the thermostat cover. Be prepared for oil spillage, and cover the open end of the hose to prevent further spillage and dirt ingress.

10 Unscrew the two securing bolts, and remove the thermostat cover **(see illustration)**.

11 Lift out the thermostat assembly **(see illustration)**.

12 Refitting is a reversal of removal, but use a new O-ring when refitting the thermostat cover, and on completion check the oil level.

Notes

Chapter 2 Part B:
TD5 engine in-car repair procedures

Contents

	Section number
Camshaft, rocker arms and hydraulic adjusters – removal, inspection and refitting	8
Compression and leakdown tests – description and interpretation	2
Crankshaft pulley – removal and refitting	5
Crankshaft spigot bush – renewal	15
Cylinder head – removal, inspection and refitting	10
Cylinder head cover – removal and refitting	4
Engine mountings – removal and refitting	18
Engine oil, filter and centrifuge rotor renewal	See Chapter 1
Engine oil level check	See Chapter 1
Flywheel – removal, inspection and refitting	14

	Section number
General information	1
Injector rocker shaft – removal refitting	9
Oil cooler – removal and refitting	16
Oil pressure switch – renewal	17
Oil pump/stiffener plate – removal and refitting	12
Oil seals – renewal	13
Sump – removal and refitting	11
Timing chain, sprockets and guides – removal, inspection and refitting	7
Timing chain cover – removal and refitting	6
Top dead centre (TDC) for No 1 piston – locating	3

Degrees of difficulty

Easy, suitable for novice with little experience 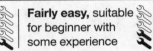	**Fairly easy,** suitable for beginner with some experience	**Fairly difficult,** suitable for competent DIY mechanic	**Difficult,** suitable for experienced DIY mechanic	**Very difficult,** suitable for expert DIY or professional

Specifications

General

Engine type	Five-cylinder, in-line, water-cooled. Double (Duplex) chain-driven camshaft, operating valves via rockers arms and hydraulic clearance adjusters
Bore	84.45 mm
Stroke	88.95 mm
Capacity	2498 cc
Firing order	1-2-4-5-3 (No 1 at timing chain end)
Direction of crankshaft rotation	Clockwise (viewed from timing chain end of engine)
Compression ratio	19.5:1
Maximum power (DIN):	
Upto July '99	95 kW (127 bhp)
From July '99	90 kW (120 bhp)
Maximum torque	315 Nm (232 lbf ft)
Maximum compression pressure difference between cylinders (typical value)	5.0 bars (70 psi)
Maximum engine speed:	
Governed	4850 rpm
Overrun	5460 rpm
Idle speed (not adjustable)	740 ± 50 rpm
Emission standard:	
Engine Serial No prefixes 10P to 14P	EU2
Engine Serial No prefixes 15P to 19P	EU3

Lubrication system

Normal oil pressure:	
At idle speed (cold)	3.0 bar
At 3500 rpm (hot)	1.5 to 3.0 bar
Oil pump type	Eccentric rotor, chain driven from crankshaft
Relief valve opening pressure	4.0 bar
Relief valve spring free length (minimum)	42.00 mm
Pressure switch opening pressure	0.2 to 0.6 bar
Oil pump clearances:	
Outer rotor-to-body	0.295 to 0.375 mm
Inner rotor-to-outer rotor (maximum)	0.13 mm
Outer rotor endfloat	0.038 to 0.075 mm

Camshaft

Drive	Duplex chain
Endfloat	0.16 to 0.60 mm

Torque wrench settings

	Nm	lbf ft
Auxiliary belt tensioner	50	37
Big-end cap bolts*:		
Stage 1	20	15
Stage 2	Angle-tighten a further 80°	
Camshaft carrier bolts	25	18
Camshaft sprocket bolts*	36	27
Centrifugal oil filter housing bolts	25	18
Centrifugal oil filter drain hose bolts	10	7
Crankshaft damper bolts	80	59
Crankshaft pulley bolt*	460	339
Crankshaft rear oil seal housing bolts	10	7
Cylinder head bolts*:		
Stage 1	30	22
Stage 2	65	48
Stage 3	Angle-tighten a further 90°	
Stage 4	Angle-tighten a further 180°	
Stage 5	Angle-tighten a further 45°	
Cylinder head cover bolts	10	7
Cylinder head nut and bolt to engine block (see text)	25	18
EGR valve pipe to cylinder head	25	18
Engine mountings:		
Mounting bracket to cylinder block	48	35
Mounting to chassis	85	63
Mounting to mounting bracket	85	63
Exhaust manifold heat shield:		
M6	10	7
M8	25	18
Flywheel securing bolts*:		
Stage 1	40	30
Stage 2	Angle-tighten a further 90°	
Injector rocker shaft adjusting screw locknut*	16	12
Injector rocker shaft bolts*	32	24
Main bearing cap bolts*:		
Stage 1	33	24
Stage 2	Angle-tighten a further 90°	
Oil cooler bolts	25	18
Oil filter cartridge adapter bolts	25	18
Oil pressure relief valve plug	23	17
Oil pressure warning light switch	15	11
Oil pump cover screws	6	4
Oil pump sprocket bolt	25	18
Oil pump pick up/strainer bolts	10	7
Piston cooling/lubrication jets	8	6
Stiffener plate retaining bolts*	13	10
Sump drain plug	23	17
Sump-to-engine block bolts:		
All except bolts 11, 14, 15 and 18 (see text)	25	18
Bolts 11, 14, 15 and 18 (see text)	28	21
Sump-to-transmission casing bolts	45	33
Timing chain cover bolts	27	20
Timing chain fixed guide bolts:		
Allen screw	25	18
M6	10	7
M10	45	33
Timing chain lubrication jet bolt	10	7
Timing chain tensioner retaining bolt	55	41
Timing chain tensioner blade bolt	25	18
Transmission to engine bolts	50	37
Turbocharger-to-exhaust manifold nuts	30	22
Turbocharger oil feed banjo bolt	25	18

* Do not re-use

1 General information

How to use this Chapter

This Part of Chapter 2 describes the repair procedures which can reasonably be carried out on the engine while it remains in the vehicle. If the engine has been removed from the vehicle and is being dismantled as described in Chapter 2C, any preliminary dismantling procedures can be ignored.

Note that, while it may be *possible* physically to overhaul items such as the piston/connecting rod assemblies while the engine is in the vehicle, this is not recommended. Such tasks are not usually carried out as separate operations, and usually require the execution of several additional procedures (not to mention the cleaning of components and of oilways); for this reason, all such tasks are classed as major overhaul procedures, and are described in Chapter 2C.

Chapter 2C describes the removal of the engine from the vehicle, and the full overhaul procedures which can then be carried out.

Engine description

The TD5 is an new engine from Land Rover, not based on any previous design. The engine is a 5-cylinder single overhead camshaft, 2 valves per cylinder unit, with direct injection, turbocharger and intercooler. The engine block made from cast iron, with an aluminium stiffener plate fitted to its base. The cylinder head and sump are aluminium – no refacing/skimming of the cylinder head is permitted. The cylinders are 'direct' bored into the engine block, then plateau honed – no reboring of the cylinders is possible. Lubrication and cooling of the pistons/gudgeon pins is provided by jets bolted to the base of the cylinder bores.

The single camshaft runs directly in the cylinder head, and is retained by an aluminium camshaft carrier assembly. The valves are operated by roller-rocker arms fitted directly below the camshaft lobes. The roller-rocker arms pivot on hydraulic lash adjusters – no checking or maintenance of the valve clearances is required.

'Unit' fuel injectors are fitted into the cylinder head. With this design, a second set of lobes on the camshaft operate a second set of rocker arms located on a rocker shaft fitted to the camshaft carrier assembly. The rocker arms operate directly on the top of the injectors, forcing the injector pistons down, and highly pressurising (1500 to 1750 bar approx) the fuel within, as the camshaft rotates. When the pressure within the injectors is sufficient to overcome the resistance of the pintle spring, fuel is injected into the combustion chambers. The injectors are fitted with solenoids which control the release of the pressure back into the return system, effectively controlling the injection period. The solenoids are actuated by an ECM (Electronic Control Module), which receives information from the various engine/system sensors.

The camshaft is driven from the crankshaft by a Duplex (Twin-row) timing chain. The chain is tensioned automatically by an hydraulic tensioner assembly. A single row chain from a separate sprocket on the crankshaft drives the eccentric-rotor oil pump, which is integral with the aluminium stiffener plate fitted to the base of the engine block.

The hardened cast iron crankshaft is supported on 6 plain bearing shells, with endfloat controlled by thrustwashers fitted either side of the No 3 main bearing shell.

The connecting rods are attached to the crankshaft by fracture-split big end caps. With this design, the connecting rods are made as one casting, then fractured and split to form the removable big-end cap. This ensures a unique fit between the two components, resulting in greater rigidity and strength. The aluminium pistons have graphite coated skirts to reduce friction, and swirl chambers located in the piston crown. The pistons are attached to the connecting rods by gudgeon pins, which are a push-fit in the connecting rod small-end bores. The gudgeon pins are retained by circlips. The pistons are fitted with three piston rings – two compression rings and an oil control ring.

The coolant pump is located in a casting behind the power steering pump, and is driven by the steering pump, which itself is crankshaft driven via a rubber auxiliary drivebelt.

Operations with engine in place

The following operations can be carried out without having to remove the engine from the vehicle.
a) Removal and refitting of the camshaft/ rocker shaft/hydraulic lash adjusters.
b) Removal and refitting of the cylinder head.
c) Removal and refitting of the timing chain and sprockets.
d) Removal and refitting of the sump.
e) Removal and refitting of the big-end bearings, connecting rods, and pistons*.
f) Removal and refitting of the oil pump/ stiffener plate.
g) Renewal of the engine mountings.
h) Removal and refitting of the flywheel.
Although the operation marked with an asterisk can be carried out with the engine in the vehicle (after removal of the sump), it is preferable for the engine to be removed, in the interests of cleanliness and improved access. For this reason, the procedure is described in Chapter 2C.

2 Compression and leakdown tests – description and interpretation

Compression test

Note: *A compression tester specifically designed for diesel engines must be used for this test.*

1 When engine performance is down, or if misfiring occurs which cannot be attributed to the fuel system, a compression test can provide diagnostic clues as to the engine's condition. If the test is performed regularly, it can give warning of trouble before any other symptoms become apparent.

2 A compression tester specifically intended for diesel engines must be used, because of the higher pressures involved. The tester is connected to an adapter which screws into the glow plug hole. It is unlikely to be worthwhile buying such a tester for occasional use, but it may be possible to borrow or hire one – if not, have the test performed by a garage.

3 Unless specific instructions to the contrary are supplied with the tester, observe the following points:
a) *The battery must be in a good state of charge, the air filter must be clean, and the engine should be at normal operating temperature.*
b) *All the glow plugs should be removed before starting the test.*

4 There is no need to hold the accelerator pedal down during the test, because the diesel engine air inlet is not throttled.

5 The actual compression pressures measured are not so important as the balance between cylinders. Land Rover do not specify compression pressures, but a typical value for the maximum difference between cylinders is given in the Specifications.

6 The cause of poor compression is less easy to establish on a diesel engine than on a petrol one. The effect of introducing oil into the cylinders ('wet' testing) is not conclusive, because there is a risk that the oil will sit in the recess on the piston crown, instead of passing to the rings. However, the following can be used as a rough guide to diagnosis.

7 All cylinders should produce very similar pressures; any difference greater than that specified indicates the existence of a fault. Note that the compression should build-up quickly in a healthy engine; low compression on the first stroke, followed by gradually-increasing pressure on successive strokes, indicates worn piston rings. A low compression reading on the first stroke, which does not build-up during successive strokes, indicates leaking valves or a blown head gasket (a cracked head could also be the cause). Deposits on the undersides of the valve heads can also cause low compression.

8 A low reading from two adjacent cylinders is almost certainly due to the head gasket having blown between them; the presence of coolant in the engine oil will confirm this.

9 If the compression reading is unusually high, the cylinder head surfaces, valves and pistons are probably coated with carbon deposits. If this is the case, the cylinder head should be removed and decarbonised (see Chapter 2C).

Leakdown test

10 A leakdown test measures the rate at which compressed air fed into the cylinder

3.3 The mark on the camshaft sprocket (arrowed) must align between the bronze coloured links on the chain

3.4 Insert a 17/64" diameter drill bit through the hole in the cam carrier (arrowed) into the slot in the camshaft drive flange

3.5a Remove the plug (arrowed) from the transmission bellhousing

is lost. It is an alternative to a compression test, and in many ways it is better, since the escaping air provides easy identification of where pressure loss is occurring (piston rings, valves or head gasket).

11 The equipment needed for leakdown testing is unlikely to be available to the home mechanic. If poor compression is suspected, have the test performed by a suitably-equipped garage.

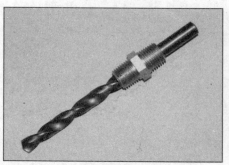

3.5b We used a hydraulic pipe union with a 14 x 1.5 mm thread, and drilled out the centre to accept a 5/16" (8 mm) drill bit

3.5c Screw-in the union and insert the drill bit into the slot in the flywheel perimeter

3 Top dead centre (TDC) for No 1 piston – locating

Note: *Suitable tools will be required to lock the flywheel and the camshaft in position during this operation. The Land Rover special tool available to lock the flywheel is LRT-12-158, and the camshaft tool is LRT-12-058. It is possible to fabricate home-made equivalents, details are given in the text.*

1 Top dead centre (TDC) is the highest point in the cylinder that each piston reaches as the crankshaft turns. Each piston reaches TDC at the end of the compression stoke, and again at the end of the exhaust stroke.

2 Remove the cylinder head cover as described in Section 4.

3 Using a spanner/socket on the crankshaft pulley, rotate the crankshaft until the mark on the camshaft sprocket aligns between

the coloured links on the timing chain **(see illustration)**.

4 Insert LRT-12-058 through the hole in the camshaft carrier and into the camshaft. Note that it may be necessary to turn the crankshaft forwards or backwards a few degrees in order to fully insert the tool. In the absence of the special Land Rover tools, a 17/64" drill bit will suffice **(see illustration)**.

5 With the camshaft locked in position, it should now be possible to insert LRT-12-158 through the bellhousing to lock the flywheel/crankshaft in position **(see illustrations)**. In the absence of the special Land Rover tools, a homemade equivalent may be fabricated using the dimensions given **(see illustration)**.

To improve access, undo the fasteners and move the engine undershield to one side.

6 The engine is now locked at TDC for No 1 cylinder.

4 Cylinder head cover – removal and refitting

Removal

1 Undo the three bolts and remove the acoustic cover from the top of the engine **(see illustrations)**.

2 Release the clip and disconnect the breather hose from the cover **(see illustration)**.

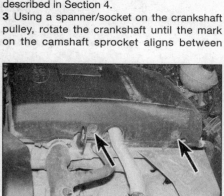

4.1a The acoustic cover is retained by two bolts on the exhaust manifold side (arrowed) . . .

4.1b . . . and one (arrowed) on the intake side

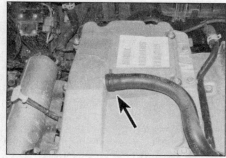

4.2 Release the clip and disconnect the breather hose from the cylinder head cover (arrowed)

4.3a Undo the cylinder head cover bolts

4.3b Check the condition of the sealing washers and spacers

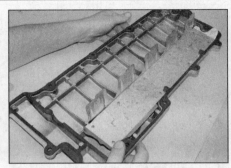

4.6 Fit a new gasket to the cylinder head cover

3 Gradually and evenly undo the 13 bolts, recover the sealing washers and spacers, then remove the cylinder head cover **(see illustration)**. Discard the gasket – a new one must be fitted. Check the condition of the sealing washers and spacers and renew as necessary **(see illustration)**.

Refitting

4 Commence refitting by thoroughly cleaning the gasket faces of the cover and the cylinder head.
5 On engines manufactured before July '99, apply a 3 mm diameter bead of sealant (Land Rover No STC 50550 or equivalent) to the top corners of the semi circular cut-out at the rear of the camshaft carrier.
6 Position the new gasket on the cylinder head cover, then refit the spacers and sealing washers, and tighten the retaining bolts to the specified torque **(see illustration)**.

5.1 Engine undershield front screws (arrowed)

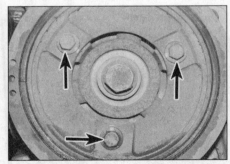

5.4 Undo the 3 bolts (arrowed) securing the damper to the crankshaft pulley

7 Reconnect the breather hose and secure it with the clip.
8 Refit the acoustic cover and tighten the bolts securely.

5 Crankshaft pulley – removal and refitting

Removal

1 Undo the fasteners, and move the engine undershield rearwards **(see illustration)**. **Note:** *If it is required to completely remove the undershield, the front propeller shaft must be disconnected from the from the axle as described in Chapter 8.*
2 Remove the radiator as described in Chapter 3.
3 Use a 15 mm spanner to relieve the tension on the auxiliary drivebelt, then manoeuvre the belt from the pulleys (see Chapter 1).
4 Undo the three bolts and remove the damper from the crankshaft pulley **(see illustration)**.
5 The crankshaft pulley bolt must now be slackened. To prevent the crankshaft from rotating, a special Land Rover tool LRT-51-003, is available which attaches to the bolt holes in the pulley. Alternatively, a home-made tool may be used **(see Tool Tip)**.

To counterhold the crankshaft pulley, use two lengths of steel strip bolted together, and fixed to the crankshaft pulley using two of the damper bolts.

6 With the crankshaft held using the tool previously described, slacken the retaining bolt and slide the pulley from the crankshaft **(see illustration)**. Note that the pulley bolt is extremely tight – an assistant may be required.

Refitting

7 Refitting is a reversal of removal, bearing in mind the following points:
 a) *Tighten the pulley retaining bolt (new) and damper screws to the recommended torque.*
 b) *The damper bolt holes will only align with the pulley holes in one position.*
 c) *Refit and tension the auxiliary drivebelt as described in Chapter 1.*
 d) *Refit the radiator as described in Chapter 3.*
 e) *On completion, refill the cooling system as described in Chapter 1.*

6 Timing chain cover – removal and refitting

Removal

1 Remove the crankshaft pulley as described in Section 5.
2 Remove the cylinder head as described in Section 10.
3 Remove the oil sump as described in Section 11.

5.6 With the pulley held, slacken the centre bolt

6.4 Undo the auxiliary belt tensioner bolt (arrowed)

6.5 Release the clip (arrowed) and disconnect the vacuum pump oil drain hose from the timing chain cover

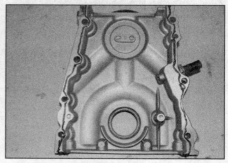

6.9 Apply a bead of sealant to the timing cover

4 Undo the bolt and remove the auxiliary belt tensioner assembly **(see illustration)**.

5 Release the clip and disconnect the vacuum pump drain hose from the timing chain cover **(see illustration)**.

6 Undo the 8 bolts and carefully pull the timing chain cover from place.

Refitting

7 Commence refitting by cleaning all traces of old sealant from the mating faces of the timing chain cover and the cylinder block.

8 It is advisable to fit a new crankshaft front oil seal to the cover as follows:

a) *Prise the old seal from the aperture in the cover using a suitable screwdriver.*

b) *Clean the seal seat in the cover.*

c) *Press a new seal into position using a suitable socket or tube. The seal lips*

7.3 Timing chain fixed guide bolts (arrowed)

7.4 Timing chain tensioner blade bolt (arrowed)

should face the crankshaft. Take care not to damage the seal lips.

9 Apply a thin and even film of sealant (STC-50550 from Land Rover dealers or equivalent) to the timing chain cover **(see illustration)**.

10 Refit the cover to the cylinder block, then refit the securing bolts, and tighten them to the specified torque. **Note:** *The cover must be fitted, and the bolts tightened, within 20 minutes of the sealant being applied.*

11 Reconnect the vacuum pump drain hose and secure the retaining clip.

12 Refit the auxiliary belt tensioner and tighten the bolt to the specified torque.

13 Refit the sump as described in Section 11.

14 Refit the cylinder head as described in Section 10.

15 Refit the crankshaft pulley as described in Section 5.

---

7 Timing chain, sprockets, and guides – removal, inspection and refitting

Removal

1 Remove the timing chain cover as described in Section 6.

2 Withdraw the camshaft sprocket from the timing chain, then manoeuvre the chain over the end of the crankshaft.

3 Undo the two bolts and remove the timing chain fixed guide **(see illustration)**.

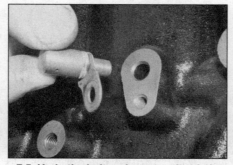

7.5 Undo the bolt and remove the chain lubrication jet

4 Undo the bolt and remove the timing chain tensioner blade **(see illustration)**.

5 If required, undo the bolt and remove the timing chain lubrication jet from the front face of the engine block **(see illustration)**.

6 Undo the bolt and slide the oil pump sprocket, chain and crankshaft sprocket from place **(see illustration)**. If loose, recover the Woodruff (half-moon) key from the crankshaft.

Inspection

7 Examine the timing chain. If there are any obvious signs of wear or damage, renew the chain. Hold the chain horizontally (link plates facing downwards) – if the chain takes on a deeply-bowed appearance, this indicates that the links are worn, and the chain should be renewed.

8 Examine the teeth on the camshaft and crankshaft sprockets.

9 If the teeth are worn or significantly hooked in appearance, the relevant sprocket should be renewed.

Refitting

10 If removed, refit the timing chain lubrication jet to the engine block and tighten the retaining bolt to the specified torque.

11 Ensure the crankshaft is still set to TDC on No 1 cylinder as described in Section 3.

12 Fit the fit the oil pump drive chain around the crankshaft and oil pump sprockets, ensure the Woodruff key is in place on the crankshaft, then side the sprocket/chain over the end of the crankshaft. The locating slot in the inside diameter of the crankshaft sprocket must

7.6 Undo the oil pump sprocket bolt and slide the chain and sprockets from place

align with the Woodruff key, and the flat on the oil pump drive shaft must align with the corresponding flat in the sprocket bore (see illustration).

13 Refit the sprocket to the oil pump, then apply a little thread-locking compound to the sprocket retaining bolt threads and tighten it to the specified torque.

14 Refit the timing chain fixed guide to the engine block and tighten the retaining bolts to the specified torque. Note the are two different torque setting for the two different diameter bolts.

15 Refit the timing chain tensioner blade, and tighten the retaining bolt to the specified torque.

16 Fit the camshaft sprocket into the timing chain, ensuring the timing mark on the sprocket is between the two coloured links (see illustration).

17 Fit the timing chain around the crankshaft sprocket aligning the coloured link of the chain with the timing mark on the sprocket (see illustration 7.16).

18 Refit the timing chain cover as described in Section 6.

8 Camshaft, rocker arms and hydraulic adjusters – removal, inspection and refitting

Removal

1 Remove the cylinder head as described in Section 10.

2 Disconnect the wiring plugs from each of the injectors, and remove the wiring harness from the camshaft carrier. Discard the multiplug O-ring, a new one must be fitted (see illustrations)

3 Slacken the locknuts, and fully undo the injector rocker arms adjusting screws, so that there is maximum clearance between the base of the screws and the top of the injectors (see illustration). Note: *Land Rover recommend that the adjusting screws and locknuts are discarded – new ones must be fitted.*

4 Gradually and evenly slacken and remove the 6 rocker shaft retaining bolts, and lift the

8.3 Slacken the locknuts, then fully unscrew the adjusting screws. Note that the screws will not come up and out through the top of the rocker arms due to the ball at the base of the screw

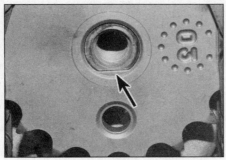

7.12 The flat on the drive sprocket must align with the flat on the oil pump shaft (arrowed)

shaft from position (see illustration). Discard the bolts, new ones must be fitted.

5 Working in the **reverse** of the sequence shown (see illustration 8.19), gradually and evenly slacken and remove the 13 bolts securing the camshaft carrier to the cylinder head.

6 Using a soft-faced hammer, carefully tap the camshaft carrier upwards to release it from the cylinder head. Note that the carrier is located on the cylinder head by two dowels.

7 Lift the camshaft from position. Discard the camshaft rear oil seal – a new one must be fitted.

8 Note their fitted locations, and lift the roller-rocker arms from place. Mark or label them to ensure they are fitted to their original locations (see illustration).

9 Carefully pull the hydraulic adjusters from their locations in the cylinder head, and store

8.2a Depress the clip (arrowed) and pull the wiring plug from each injector

8.4 Injector rocker shaft bolts (front 3 arrowed)

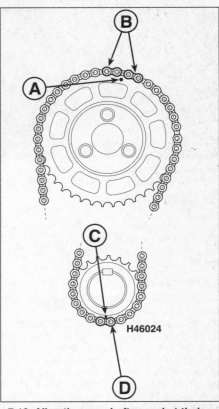

7.16 Align the camshaft sprocket timing mark (A) between the coloured links (B), and the crankshaft sprocket timing mark (C) with the coloured link (D)

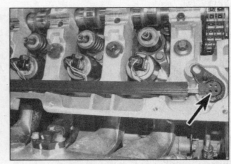

8.2b Pull the harness and plug (arrowed) upwards from the cylinder head

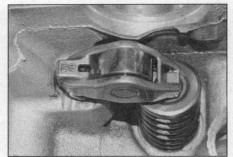

8.8 Lift the roller-rocker arms from place

8.9 Pull the hydraulic adjusters from place, and store them in an upright position

8.13 Attach a DTI gauge to the camshaft carrier, then pull the camshaft forwards and backwards to measure the endfloat

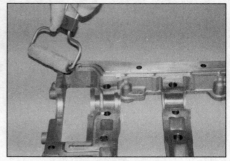

8.17 Use a roller to apply sealant to the camshaft carrier

them in their fitted order to ensure they are refitted to their original locations. It's essential the hydraulic adjusters are stored upright (see illustration).

Inspection

10 Thoroughly clean all components, and check them for obvious signs of wear or damage. Absolute cleanliness is essential – ensure all oil ways and fuel galleries in the cylinder head are free of dirt/debris. Any contamination could cause severe damage to the cylinder head and/or injectors. Check the rollers on the rocker arms are free to rotate with no sign of binding or roughness.

11 Check the hydraulic adjuster bores in the cylinder head for signs of wear or scoring. Check the adjusters themselves for signs of wear or overheating (blueness). Renew as necessary.

12 Check the camshaft lobes and bearing journals for any sign of wear or damage. Check the corresponding bearing surfaces in the cylinder head and the camshaft carrier. As the camshaft carrier and cylinder head are matched, any damage/wear to the carrier means the cylinder head must be renewed, and *vice-versa*. If in doubt, consult an engine reconditioning specialist.

13 Lay the camshaft in position in the camshaft carrier and check the camshaft endfloat in the carrier (see illustration). Have the components inspected by an engine

reconditioning specialist, who should be able to determine which components require renewal.

Refitting

14 Refit the hydraulic adjusters into their original locations in the cylinder head.

15 Refit the roller-rockers arms to their original locations above the hydraulic adjusters and the valve stems.

16 Ensure the bearing surfaces in the cylinder head are clean, then lubricate the surfaces and the camshaft journals with clean engine oil. Carefully lay the camshaft in the cylinder head, with the locking hole at the timing chain end in the vertical position.

17 Using a roller, apply a thin film of sealant (Land Rover STC-4600, STC-611, Hylomar 2000, or equivalent) to the camshaft carrier mating surface. Ensure the sealant does not block any oilways, or contaminate the bearing surfaces (see illustration). Note that the carrier must be refitted, and the bolts tightened within 20 minutes of applying the sealant.

18 Position the carrier over the cylinder head/camshaft, and engage the locating dowels. Refit the bolts and finger-tighten them only at this stage.

19 Progressively tighten the camshaft carrier bolts to the specified torque in sequence (see illustration).

20 Lubricate the lips of the new camshaft

rear seal, and use a socket or tubular spacer to drive the new seal into location at the rear of the cylinder head. Ensure the seal lips face inwards.

21 Locate the injector rocker shaft on the dowels in the camshaft carrier, fit the new bolts and starting from the centre working outwards, tighten them progressively to the specified torque.

22 Fit the new O-ring seal to the injector harness multiplug, then refit the harness and reconnect the wiring plugs to the injectors.

23 Refit the cylinder head as described in Section 10.

24 Prior to fitting the cylinder head cover, rotate the crankshaft clockwise until the injector lobe for No 1 cylinder is at full lift (see illustration).

25 Fit a new adjusting screw to the No 1 injector rocker arm, and tighten the screw, compressing the injector piston, until it is felt to 'bottom out'. Now rotate the screw 1 complete turn anti-clockwise to give the required clearance, then fit and tighten the locknut without allowing the screw to rotate (see illustration). Repeat this procedure on the remaining 4 rocker arms.

26 After completing the adjustment procedure, rotate the crankshaft 2 complete revolutions to ensure that no injectors are 'bottoming out'.

27 Refit the cylinder head cover as described in Section 4.

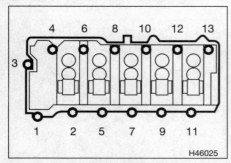

8.19 Camshaft carrier bolt tightening sequence

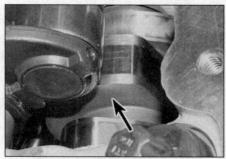

8.24 Rotate the crankshaft clockwise until the injector lobe on the camshaft (arrowed) is in the full lift position

8.25 When the adjuster screw is felt to 'bottom out', rotate it one complete turn anti-clockwise

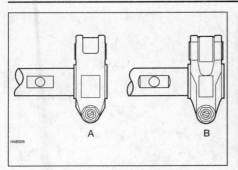

9.7 Injector rocker shaft type A is fitted to engine serial number prefix 10P to 14P, and type B to serial number prefix 15P to 19P

9.8 Ensure the adjusting screws are fully retracted

10.6 Depress the clip (arrowed) and disconnect the airflow meter wiring plug

9 Injector rocker shaft – removal and refitting

Removal

1 Remove the cooling fan as described in Chapter 3.
2 Remove the cylinder head cover as described in Section 4.
3 Slacken the injector rocker arm adjusting screws locknuts, then completely unscrew each of the adjusting screws (**see illustration 8.3**).
4 Rotate the crankshaft clockwise until the timing mark on the camshaft sprocket aligns between the coloured links on the timing chain (**see illustration 7.16**).
5 Insert LRT-12-058 through the hole in the camshaft carrier and into the camshaft (**see illustration 3.4**). Note that it may be necessary to turn the crankshaft forwards or backwards a few degrees in order to fully insert the tool. In the absence of the special Land Rover tools, a 17/64" drill bit will suffice.
6 Gradually and evenly slacken and remove the rocker shaft retaining bolts. Discard the bolts, and the adjusting screws/locknuts – new ones must be fitted. Lift the rocker shaft from place.

Refitting

7 Two different types of rocker shafts may be

fitted. On engines with a serial number prefix 10P to 14P, type A rocker shaft is fitted, and on engine serial number prefix 15P to 19P, type B rocker shaft is fitted (**see illustration**). Note that it is possible to replace type A shafts with type B, but not the other way around.
8 Fit new adjusting screws and locknuts to the rocker arms, but do not tighten the locknuts yet. Ensure the screws are fully retracted (**see illustration**).
9 Locate the rocker shaft assembly on the dowels, then fit the new retaining bolts, and tighten them progressively to the specified torque working from the centre outwards (**see illustration 8.4**).
10 Remove the locking tool from the camshaft carrier/camshaft, then rotate the crankshaft clockwise until the camshaft injector lobe for No 1 injector is at the full lift position (**see illustration 8.24**).
11 Rotate the adjusting screw in No 1 rocker arm clockwise, compressing the injector piston, until it can be felt to 'bottom out'. Now rotate the screw 1 complete turn anti-clockwise to give the required clearance, then fit and tighten the locknut without allowing the screw to rotate (**see illustration 8.25**). Repeat this procedure on the remaining 4 rocker arms.
12 After completing the adjustment procedure, rotate the crankshaft 2 complete revolutions to ensure that no injectors are 'bottoming out'.
13 Refit the cylinder head cover as described in Section 4.

14 Refit the cooling fan as described in Chapter 3.

10 Cylinder head – removal, inspection and refitting

Removal

1 Disconnect the battery negative lead as described in Chapter 5.
2 Disconnect the front propshaft from the axle (see Chapter 8), then undo the bolts and remove the engine undershield.
3 Drain the cooling system as described in Chapter 1.
4 Remove the cylinder head cover as described in Section 4.
5 Remove the cooling fan as described in Chapter 3.
6 Disconnect the wiring plug from the airflow meter, then release the clips and disconnect the meter from the air filter (**see illustration**).
7 Release the clip and disconnect the intake hose from the turbocharger (**see illustration**).
8 Undo the three bolts and remove the heat shield from the top of the exhaust manifold (**see illustration**).
9 Undo the turbocharger oil feed banjo bolt – discard the sealing washers, new ones must be fitted (**see illustration**).
10 Undo the 3 nuts, pull the turbocharger from the exhaust manifold and position it to

10.7 Release the clip and disconnect the turbocharger intake hose

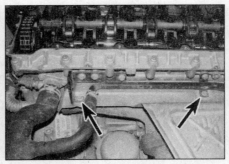

10.8 Remove the exhaust manifold heat shield bolts (top 2 bolts arrowed)

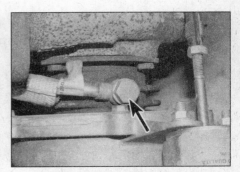

10.9 Turbocharger oil feed banjo bolt (arrowed)

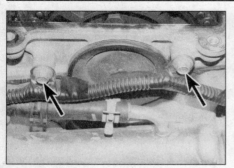

10.11 Wiring loom bolts (arrowed)

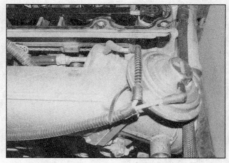

10.14 Disconnect the vacuum hoses from the EGR valve

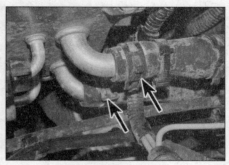

10.16 Release the clips and disconnect the coolant hoses from the cooler (arrowed)

one side. Discard the gasket – a new one must be fitted.

11 Undo the two bolts securing the wiring harness to the front of the camshaft carrier (see illustration).

12 Note their fitted positions, then disconnect the wiring plugs from the injectors, coolant sensor, glow plugs and boost pressure sensor. Check that all electrical connectors/harnesses that will prevent the cylinder heads removal have been disconnected/moved to one side.

13 Disconnect the wiring plug from the MAP (manifold absolute pressure) sensor located on the intake manifold.

14 Note its fitted position/routing, and disconnect the vacuum hose(s) from the EGR valve (see illustration).

15 Release the clip and disconnect the air intake hose from the EGR valve.

16 Release the clips and disconnect the coolant hoses from the fuel cooler (see illustration).

17 Slide off the red plastic cover, then depress the release button and disconnect the fuel hose from the fuel tank to the cooler. Push the black collar towards the hose and disconnect the hose from the cooler. Plug the openings in the cooler and plug the end of the hoses. It is essential that the fuel system is protected from dirt ingress (see illustration).

18 Slide off the green plastic cover, then depress the release button and disconnect the fuel hose from the connector on the cylinder head (see illustration). Again, plug the open

fuel connections to prevent ingress of dirt, etc. Any contamination of the fuel system could wreck the cylinder head/injectors.

19 Undo the four bolts and remove the fuel cooler from the intake manifold.

20 Disconnect the vacuum pump oil union from the cylinder head, and discard the O-ring seal (see illustration).

21 Undo the 2 retaining bolts and disconnect the alternator support bracket from the cylinder head.

Models without an EGR cooler

22 Undo the bolt securing the EGR valve pipe to the cylinder head.

Models with an EGR cooler

23 Release the clips and disconnect the coolant hoses from the EGR cooler, then undo the bolts/nut and detach the cooler from the cylinder head and EGR pipes (see illustrations).

All models

24 Undo the retaining bolt, and remove the oil level dipstick guide tube from right-hand side of the engine block. Discard the tube O-ring seal, a new one must be fitted.

25 Release the clips and disconnect the top hose, and heater hoses from the cylinder head.

26 Undo the nut and bolt securing the cylinder head to the timing chain cover (see illustration).

27 Using a spanner/socket on the crankshaft

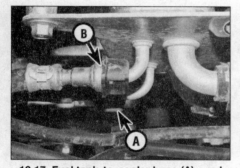

10.17 Fuel tank-to-cooler hose (A) – red collar, and cooler-to-regulator hose (B) – black collar

10.18 Slide off the green collar (see illustration) from the hose at the right-hand rear of the cylinder head

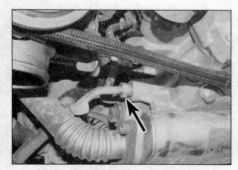

10.20 Undo the vacuum pump oil union (arrowed)

10.23a Using a spring clip release tool on the EGR cooler coolant hoses

10.23b Disconnect the EGR hoses and remove the EGR cooler (arrowed)

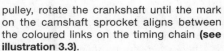

10.26 Undo the nut and bolt (arrowed) securing the cylinder head to the timing cover

10.30 Unscrew the timing chain tensioner

10.31 Undo the Allen screw (arrowed) securing the top of the timing chain fixed guide to the cylinder head

pulley, rotate the crankshaft until the mark on the camshaft sprocket aligns between the coloured links on the timing chain **(see illustration 3.3)**.

28 Insert LRT-12-058 through the hole in the camshaft carrier and into the camshaft **(see illustration 3.4)**. Note that it may be necessary to turn the crankshaft forwards or backwards a few degrees in order to fully insert the tool. In the absence of the special Land Rover tools use a 17/64" drill bit.

29 With the camshaft locked in position, it should now be possible to undo the 13 mm plug and insert LRT-12-158 through the bellhousing to lock the flywheel/crankshaft in position **(see illustration 3.5a)**. In the absence of the special Land Rover tool, a homemade equivalent may be fabricated using the dimensions given **(see illustration 3.5b)**.

30 Undo the timing chain tensioner from the right-hand side of the cylinder head. Discard the sealing washer a new one must be fitted **(see illustration)**.

31 Remove the Allen screw securing the top of the timing chain fixed guide to the cylinder head **(see illustration)**.

32 Carefully lever out the camshaft sprocket access plug from the front of the cylinder head **(see illustration)**. Discard the O-ring seal, a new one must be fitted.

33 Undo the 3 bolts securing the sprocket to the camshaft, and allow the sprocket to rest on the top of the chain guides **(see illustration)**. Discard the sprocket retaining bolts, new ones must be fitted.

34 Working in the **reverse** of the sequence

shown **(see illustration 10.51a)**, gradually slacken and remove the 12 cylinder head bolts, together with their captive washers.

35 With the help of an assistant, carefully lift the cylinder head from the cylinder block. If necessary, tap the cylinder head gently with a soft-faced mallet to free it from the block, but **do not** lever at the mating faces. Note that the cylinder head is located on dowels. Lift the cylinder head from the vehicle.

36 Recover the cylinder head gasket. The thickness of the cylinder head gasket is indicated by a series of holes at the front left hand edge. Take a note of the number or holes before discarding the gasket.

Caution: As the injector nozzles and valves project below the surface of the cylinder head, do not place the head on any work surface without positioning a block at each end to prevent damage.

37 If plastic dowels are fitted to the top of the engine block, discard them – new ones must be fitted **(see illustration)**. Steel ones may be reused.

Inspection

38 The mating faces of the cylinder head and block must be perfectly clean before refitting the head. Use a scraper to remove all traces of gasket and carbon, and also clean the tops of the pistons. Take particular care with the aluminium cylinder head, as the soft metal is damaged easily. Also, make sure that debris is not allowed to enter the oil and water channels – this is particularly important for the oil circuit, as carbon could block the oil supply

to the camshaft or crankshaft bearings. Using adhesive tape and paper, seal the water, oil and bolt holes in the cylinder block. Clean the piston crowns in the same way.

> **HAYNES HiNT** *To prevent carbon entering the gap between the pistons and bores, smear a little grease in the gap. After cleaning the piston, rotate the crankshaft so that the piston moves down the bore, then wipe out the grease and carbon with a cloth rag.*

39 Check the block and head for nicks, deep scratches and other damage. If slight, they may be removed carefully with a file. Note that if the scratches are deep, the head may need to be renewed. Refacing, or skimming of the cylinder head is not permitted. If in doubt have the cylinder head inspected by an engine reconditioning specialist.

40 If warpage of the cylinder head is suspected, use a straight-edge to check it for distortion. Refer to Part C of this Chapter if necessary.

41 Clean out the bolt holes in the block using a pipe cleaner, or a rag and screwdriver.

⚠ *Warning: Make sure that all oil is removed, otherwise there is a possibility of the block being cracked by hydraulic pressure when the bolts are tightened.*

42 Examine the bolt threads and the threads in the cylinder block for damage. If necessary,

10.32 Lever out the rubber plug in front of the camshaft sprocket

10.33 Undo the 3 bolts securing the sprocket to the camshaft

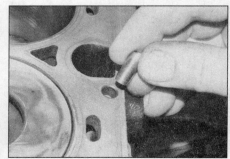

10.37 If plastic dowels are fitted, update them with steel ones

10.45 Measure the piston protrusion using a DTI gauge

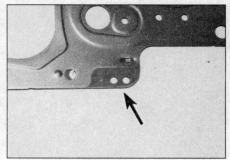

10.47 The holes (arrowed) identify the cylinder head gasket – see text

10.49 Fit the cylinder head gasket with the word TOP uppermost

use the correct-size tap to chase out the threads in the block, and use a die to clean the threads on the bolts.

Gasket selection

Note: *This procedure is only necessary is the pistons, connecting rods or crankshaft have be renewed. If none of these components have been changed, use a new head gasket with the same thickness indicator (number of holes) as the original.*

43 When the pistons are at the top dead centre (TDC) position, they protrude above the top face of the cylinder block. The amount of protrusion determines the thickness of the cylinder head gasket required. The protrusion of all the pistons above the cylinder block must be measured, and the thickness of the gasket to be used is determined by the largest protrusion measured.

44 Turn the crankshaft to bring piston No 1 to just below the TDC position (just below the top face of the cylinder block). Position a dial test indicator (DTI) on the cylinder block, and zero it on the block face. Transfer the probe to the crown of No 1 piston (as close as possible to the centre, avoiding the combustion chamber), then slowly turn the crankshaft back-and-forth past TDC, noting the highest reading produced on the indicator. Record this reading.

45 Repeat this measurement procedure on the remaining pistons **(see illustration)**. Ensure that all measurements are taken along the longitudinal centreline of the crankshaft

(this will eliminate errors due to piston slant).

46 If a dial test indicator is not available, piston protrusion may be measured using a straight-edge and feeler blades or vernier calipers. However, these methods are inevitably less accurate, and cannot therefore be recommended.

47 Ascertain the greatest piston protrusion measurement, and use this to determine the correct cylinder head gasket from the following table. The gasket identification holes are located at the front right-hand side of the gasket **(see illustration)**.

Piston protrusion	Gasket identification
0.351 to 0.500 mm	2 holes
0.501 to 0.570 mm	1 hole
0.571 to 0.650 mm	3 holes

Refitting

48 Clean out the holes in the engine block, then if plastic dowels are fitted, fit the two new steel locating dowels to the gasket face.

49 Fit the correct gasket with the word TOP uppermost on the cylinder block **(see illustration)**.

50 Lower the cylinder head onto the block, and position the head over the two dowels in the engine block.

51 Fit the new cylinder head bolts and washers, then tighten the bolts in the sequence shown to the Stage 1 torque setting, then in sequence to the Stage 2 setting, then angle-tighten them in turn to the Stage 3, 4 and 5 settings as given in the Specifications at the start of this Chapter **(see illustrations)**.

52 Fit the nut and bolt securing the cylinder head to the engine block and tighten them to the specified torque.

53 Check then crankshaft and camshaft locking tools are still in place, then clean the camshaft and sprocket mating faces. **Note:** *If the cylinder head is being refitted with the engine removed from the vehicle, it's impossible to fit the crankshaft locking tool as it fits through the transmission bellhousing. Fit the tool once the engine is refitted.*

54 Check the chain is still correctly positioned on the camshaft sprocket (timing mark between the two coloured links), then position the sprocket on the camshaft. Finger tighten the new sprocket retaining bolts, then undo each one 180°.

55 Apply a little thread-locking compound to the threads, then refit the Allen screw securing the top of the timing chain fixed guide. Tighten the bolt to the specified torque.

56 Position a new sealing washer, then refit the timing chain tensioner to the engine block – tighten the retaining bolt to the specified torque.

57 Now tighten the camshaft sprocket retaining bolts to the specified torque. **Note:** *If the cylinder head is being refitted with the engine removed from the vehicle, do not tighten the camshaft sprocket bolts until the engine is refitted, and the crankshaft locking tool is in place.*

58 Remove the camshaft and crankshaft locking tools.

59 Refit the camshaft sprocket bolts access plug to the cylinder head with a new O-ring seal.

60 The remainder of refitting is a reversal of removal, noting the following points:

a) *Tighten all fasteners to their specified torque where given.*

b) *Refill the cooling system as described in Chapter 1.*

c) *No bleeding of the fuel system should be necessary. Turn the ignition switch to position II, and wait 10 seconds before attempting to start the engine. This should allow sufficient time for the fuel pump to prime the system.*

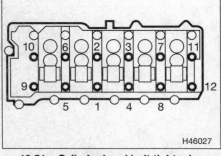

10.51a Cylinder head bolt tightening sequence

H46027

10.51b Use an angle-measuring gauge to correctly tighten the new cylinder head bolts

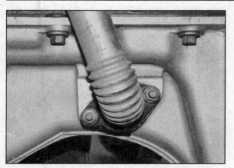

11.5 Centrifugal oil filter drain tube nuts

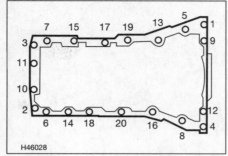

11.6 Sump retaining bolts slackening sequence

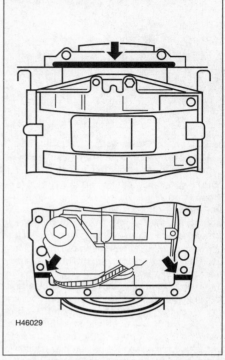

11.10 Apply a bead of sealant to the areas arrowed

11 Sump – removal and refitting

Removal

1 Disconnect the battery negative lead as described in Chapter 5.
2 Remove the front exhaust pipe as described in Chapter 4B.
3 Drain the engine oil as described in Chapter 1.
4 Undo the 4 bolts securing the sump to the transmission casing.
5 Undo the two bolts securing the centrifugal oil filter drain tube to the sump casing **(see illustration)**. Discard the gasket, a new one must be fitted.
6 Working in sequence, gradually and evenly slacken and remove the sump retaining bolts **(see illustration)**.
7 Lower the sump from the engine, and discard the gasket.

Refitting

8 Clean all traces of gasket (or sealant) and oil from the mating faces of the engine and the sump, taking care not to allow debris to enter the engine.
9 Examine the sump for damage or distortion. Check the condition of the drain plug threads.
10 Apply a thin bead of sealant (Land Rover STC 50550 or equivalent) to the underside of the engine block **(see illustration)**.
11 Position the new gasket, lift the sump

into place, then loosely fit the securing bolts sufficiently to locate the sump securely on the engine.
12 Refit the sump-to-transmission casing bolts and tighten them to the specified torque.
13 Refit the sump-to-engine block bolts and tighten them in sequence to the specified torque **(see illustration)**.
14 Using a new gasket, refit the centrifugal oil filter drain hose to the sump casing. Tighten the bolts to the specified torque.
15 The remainder of refitting is a reversal of removal, noting the following points:
  a) *Refit the sump drain plug with a new sealing washer.*
  b) *Refill the engine with new oil as described in Chapter 1.*
  c) *Reconnect the battery negative lead as described in Chapter 5.*

12 Oil pump/stiffener plate – removal, inspection and refitting

Removal

1 Remove the sump as described in Section 11.
2 Undo the bolt securing the oil pump sprocket to the pump driveshaft **(see illustration 7.6)**. Pull the sprocket from the pump.
3 Undo the 3 Torx screws and remove the oil pump pick-up strainer **(see illustration)**.

Discard the O-ring seal, a new one must be fitted.
4 In the **reverse** of the sequence shown **(see illustration 12.20)**, gradually slacken and remove the oil pump/stiffener plate retaining bolts. Discard the bolts, new ones must be fitted.
5 Lower the oil pump/stiffener plate, noting that it is located on dowels. Discard the pump outlet gasket.

Inspection

6 With the pump removed from the engine, thoroughly clean the external surfaces.
7 Undo the 5 screws securing the oil pump cover **(see illustration)**.
8 Using permanent marker pen, make alignment marks between the pump inner

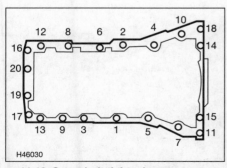

11.13 Sump bolt tightening sequence

12.3 Pick-up pipe Torx screws (arrowed)

12.7 The oil pump cover is secured by 5 Torx screws

12.8 Alignment marks (arrowed) on the inner and outer rotors

12.11a Check the clearance between the outer rotor and body . . .

12.11b . . . and the inner and outer rotor

rotor, outer rotor and pump body **(see illustration)**.

9 Remove the rotors and check all components for signs of wear or damage. If damaged/worn the complete oil pump and stiffener plate must be renewed.

10 Refit the rotors to the pump body, ensuring the marks align.

11 Using feeler gauges, check the clearance between the pump outer rotor and body, and the inner-to-outer rotor clearance. Compare the clearances with those specified at the start of this Chapter. If the clearances are excessive, the complete oil pump and stiffener plate must be renewed **(see illustrations)**.

12 Place a straight-edge along the end of the pump body and use feeler gauges to check the outer rotor endfloat **(see illustration)**. Compare the endfloat with that specified. Again, if the endfloat is excessive, renew the pump and stiffener plate.

13 If the pump is usable, lubricate the rotors with clean engine oil, refit the cover and apply a little thread locking compound and tighten the Torx screws to the specified torque. Rotate the pump shaft to ensure the rotors are free to revolve.

14 Undo the oil pressure relief valve plug, then remove the spring and valve plunger **(see illustrations)**.

15 Clean the spring and valve plunger, then check them for signs of wear, damage or corrosion.

16 Use a ruler to measure the spring free length and compare that dimension with the one specified **(see illustration)**. If any of the relief valve components are damaged or worn, it is possible to renew them separately from the oil pump.

17 Lubricate the pump bore, and refit the relieve valve plunger and spring, then apply a little thread sealing compound to the threads

of the plug and tighten it to the specified torque.

Refitting

18 Clean the mating faces of the stiffener plate and engine block.

19 Fit a new gasket to the pump outlet, and position the oil pump/stiffener plate on the underside of the engine block, ensuring it locates over the two dowels **(see illustration)**.

20 Fit the new stiffener plate retaining bolts and tighten them in sequence to the specified torque **(see illustration)**.

21 Lubricate the new O-ring seal with clean engine oil, then refit the oil pump strainer. Apply a little sealing compound to the retaining screws and tighten them to the specified torque.

22 Refit the drive sprocket to the oil pump shaft, ensuring the flat machined on the shaft

12.12 Check the rotor endfloat with a straight-edge

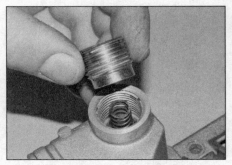

12.14a Unscrew the oil pressure relief valve plug . . .

12.14b . . . then withdraw the spring . . .

12.14c . . . followed by the plunger

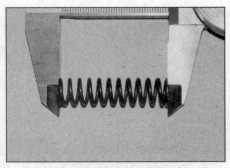

12.16 Measure the spring free length

12.19 Pump outlet gasket

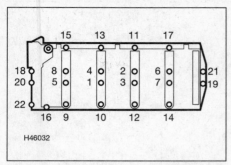

12.20 Stiffener plate retaining bolts tightening sequence

13.2 Lever the oil seal from the timing cover

13.3 Drive the oil seal into place using a socket or tube

aligns with the flat on the sprocket internal diameter **(see illustration 7.12)**.

23 Apply a little thread-locking compound to the threads, then refit the sprocket retaining bolt and tighten it to the specified torque.

24 Refit the sump as described in Section 11.

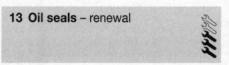

13 Oil seals – renewal

Crankshaft front oil seal

1 Remove the crankshaft pulley as described in Section 5.

2 Note the seal's fitted depth (2.5 mm from the front face of the timing cover), then use a flat-bladed screwdriver to prise the seal from the timing chain cover. Take great care not to mark the crankshaft **(see illustration)**.

3 Ensure the seal bore in the timing chain cover is clean, then drive the new seal into place using a socket or tubular spacer which fits over the end of the crankshaft, and bears only on the outer edge of the seal **(see illustration)**.

4 Refit the crankshaft pulley as described in Section 5.

Crankshaft rear oil seal

5 Remove the flywheel as described in Section 14.

6 Remove the sump as described in Section 11.

13.7 Rear oil seal housing bolts

7 Undo the bolts and prise the oil seal housing from the rear of the engine block **(see illustration)**. Discard the seal and housing, they must be renewed as an assembly.

8 Ensure the seal housing mating face on the engine block is clean, then position the seal/housing and Land Rover tool LRT-12-061 (seal protector – normally supplied with the new seal/housing) over the end of the crankshaft. If the tool is not available, wrap a length of insulating tape around the shoulder of the crankshaft to protect the seal lips as it is installed **(see illustration)**. The seal must be fitted dry.

9 Carefully manoeuvre the new seal and housing over the end of the crankshaft, then remove the seal protector/insulating tape.

10 Refit the housing retaining bolts and tighten them evenly to the specified torque.

11 The remainder of refitting is a reversal of removal.

Camshaft rear oil seal

12 Remove the air cleaner housing as described in Chapter 4B.

13 Undo the bolts and remove the cover from the rear of the cylinder head (where fitted).

14 Note its fitted depth, then using a large, sharp screwdriver (or similar), pierce the centre of the rear camshaft oil seal and lever is from position.

15 Ensure the bore in the camshaft carrier/cylinder head is clean, then lubricate the outer lips of the new seal and drive it into position using a suitable tubular spacer or socket.

16 Refit the cover and air cleaner housing.

13.8 With the inside the seal, fit the assembly over the end of the crankshaft

14 Flywheel – removal, inspection and refitting

Note: *New flywheel securing bolts must be used on refitting.*

Removal

1 Remove the clutch as described in Chapter 6.

2 Undo the 8 bolts and remove the flywheel from the end of the crankshaft. Discard the flywheel bolts, new ones must be fitted. Note the flywheel locates on a dowel.

⚠ **Warning: The flywheel is heavy – take care not to drop it.**

Inspection

3 If the clutch friction disc contact surface of the flywheel is scored, or on close inspection shows signs of small hairline cracks (caused by overheating), it may be possible to have the flywheel surface-ground. Consult a Land Rover dealer or a specialist engine repairer, and if grinding is not possible, renew the flywheel complete.

4 A dual-mass type flywheel is fitted, to insulate the transmission from the torsional and transient vibrations produced by the engine. The flywheel is made up of two halves – a primary and secondary flywheel, with drive between the two transmitted by a torsional damper consisting or four coil springs. A roller bearing is fitted to the centre boss of the primary flywheel, which provides the mounting for the secondary flywheel. This arrangement allows upto 70° of torsional rotation between the two flywheels. No aspect of the dual mass flywheel is serviceable – if faulty it must be renewed.

5 If the teeth on the flywheel starter ring are badly worn, or if some are missing, then it will be necessary to remove the ring gear, and fit a new one.

6 To renew the ring gear, firstly drill a 3.0 mm hole in the side of the ring gear between the roots of any two gear teeth, and the inner diameter of the ring gear. The hole should be just deep enough to weaken the gear – *take great care not to allow the drill to touch the flywheel.*

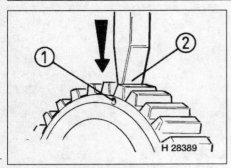

14.8 Removing the ring gear from the flywheel

1 *Drill a 3.0 mm hole*
2 *Split the gear using a cold chisel*

7 Clamp the flywheel securely in a vice, and cover it with a large cloth to reduce the possibility of personal injury.

 Warning: Wear eye protection during the following procedure.

8 Place a cold chisel between the gear teeth above the drilled hole, then split the gear with the chisel. Take great care not to damage the flywheel during this operation, and wear eye protection at all times. Once the ring has been split, it will spread apart, and can be lifted from the flywheel **(see illustration)**.
9 The new ring gear must be heated to 350ºC, and unless facilities for heating by oven or flame are available, leave the fitting to a Land Rover dealer or engineering works. The new ring gear must not be overheated during this work, or the temper of the metal will be affected.
10 The ring should be tapped gently down onto its register, and left to cool naturally – the contraction of the metal on cooling will ensure that it is a secure and permanent fit.

Refitting

11 Commence refitting by thoroughly cleaning the mating faces of the flywheel and the crankshaft.
12 Align the dowel hole in the flywheel with the crankshaft dowel, then lift the flywheel onto the end of the crankshaft **(see illustration)**.
13 Fit the new flywheel bolts, and tighten

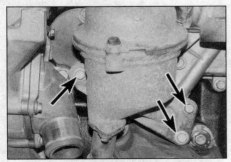

16.6 Centrifugal oil filter housing bolts (arrowed)

14.12 Align the hole in the flywheel with the dowel in the crankshaft (arrowed)

them to the Stage 1 torque setting, then angle-tighten them to the Stage 2 setting, as given in the Specifications.
14 Refit the clutch as described in Chapter 6.

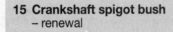

15 Crankshaft spigot bush – renewal

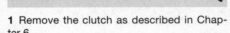

1 Remove the clutch as described in Chapter 6.
2 The bush can be removed as follows:
  a) *Obtain a short length of metal rod, with a diameter which provides a firm sliding fit in the bore of the bush.*
  b) *Pack the bore of the bush with grease.*
  c) *Insert the metal rod into the bush, and cover the rod and bush with a cloth or rag (to prevent the possibility of injury due to grease splashes or the ejection of the bush).*
  d) *Give the rod a sharp tap with a hammer – the grease should force the bush from the crankshaft (see illustration).*
3 Thoroughly clean the bush location in the end of the crankshaft, and make sure that the new bush is absolutely clean.
4 Tap the bush into position in the end of the crankshaft, using a suitable drift. Take care not to produce any burrs on the edge of the bush.
5 Refit the clutch as described in Chapter 6.

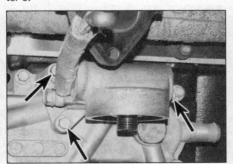

16.10 Oil filter adapter bolts (arrowed)

15.2 Give the rod a sharp tap, and the grease should force the bush out

16 Oil cooler – removal and refitting

Removal

1 Drain the cooling system as described in Chapter 1.
2 Undo the two bolts securing the centrifugal oil filter drain tube to the sump. Discard the gasket.
3 Remove the turbocharger as described in Chapter 4B.
4 On air conditioned models, remove the auxiliary drivebelt as described in Chapter 1, then undo the bolts and move the compressor to one side. There is no need to disconnect the refrigerant hoses.
5 Unscrew the oil filter cartridge from the oil cooler. Be prepared for oil spillage.
6 Undo the 3 retaining bolts and remove the centrifugal oil filter housing from the oil cooler **(see illustration)**. Discard the O-ring seal, a new one must be fitted. Manoeuvre the oil filter from place.
7 Undo the bolts securing the coolant pipe to the rear of the engine.
8 Release the clip and disconnect the coolant hose from the oil cooler.
9 Disconnect the oil pressure switch wiring plug.
10 Undo the three bolts and remove the oil filter cartridge adaptor from the cooler **(see illustration)**.
11 Undo the 7 bolts and remove the oil cooler **(see illustration)**.

16.11 Oil cooler bolts (arrowed)

Refitting

12 Ensure the mating faces of the cooler and engine block are clean. Position a new gasket and refit the oil cooler. Tighten the retaining bolts to the specified torque.

13 Fit the oil cartridge adaptor to the oil cooler with a new gasket, and tighten the bolts to the specified torque.

14 The remainder of refitting is a reversal of removal, noting the following:

a) *Fit a new oil filter cartridge and top-up the engine oil as described in Chapter 1.*

b) *Refill the cooling system as described in Chapter 1.*

c) *Tighten all fasteners to the specified torque where given.*

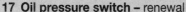

17 Oil pressure switch – renewal

1 Undo the fasteners and remove the plastic cover from the top of the engine.

2 Release the clip and disconnect the breather hose from the cylinder head cover **(see illustration 4.2)**.

3 Release the clips and disconnect the airflow meter from the air filter **(see illustration 10.6)**.

4 Release the clip and disconnect the air intake hose from the turbocharger **(see illustration 10.7)**.

5 Undo the three screws and remove the heat shield from the top of the exhaust manifold.

6 Disconnect the wiring plug from the oil pressure switch, then unscrew the switch from the oil cooler housing **(see illustration)**. Be prepared for oil spillage.

7 Ensure the switch threads are clean then refit it to the oil cooler, and tighten it to the specified torque.

17.6 Oil pressure switch (arrowed)

8 The remainder of refitting is a reversal of removal, remembering to top-up the engine oil as described in Chapter 1.

18 Engine mountings – removal and refitting

Removal

Front left-hand mounting

1 Disconnect the front propshaft from the axle (see Chapter 8), then undo the bolts and move the engine undershield rearwards.

2 Undo the two bolts securing the centrifugal oil filter drain tube to the sump. Discard the gasket.

3 Remove the turbocharger as described in Chapter 4B.

4 On air conditioned models, remove the auxiliary drivebelt as described in Chapter 1, then undo the bolts and move the compressor to one side. There is no need to disconnect the refrigerant hoses.

5 Undo the 3 retaining bolts and remove the centrifugal oil filter housing from the oil cooler **(see illustration 16.6)**. Discard the O-ring seal, a new one must be fitted. Manoeuvre the oil filter from place.

6 Undo the three bolts securing the oil filter cartridge adapter to the oil cooler, and remove it.

7 Suspend the engine using a hoist and lifting chains/straps, or place a workshop jack under the engine sump with a piece of wood on the jack head to protect the sump casing. Take the weight of the engine.

8 Undo the nuts/bolts and remove the mounting. If required, undo the nut and separate the mounting from the bracket.

Front right-hand mounting

9 Undo the fasteners and remove the plastic cover from the top of the engine.

10 Disconnect the battery negative lead as described in Chapter 5.

11 Raise the front of the vehicle and support it securely on axle stands (see *Jacking and vehicle support*).

12 Undo the four retaining bolts and move the fuel cooler to one side.

13 Suspend the engine using a hoist and lifting chains/straps, or place a workshop jack under the engine sump with a piece of wood on the jack head to protect the sump casing. Take the weight of the engine.

14 Undo the nuts/bolts and remove the mounting. If required, undo the nut and separate the mounting from the bracket.

Refitting

15 Refitting is a reversal of removal, but tighten all fixings to the specified torque.

Notes

Chapter 2 Part C:
Engine removal and general overhaul procedures

Contents

Section number

Crankshaft – inspection 13
Crankshaft – refitting 16
Crankshaft – removal 10
Cylinder block/crankcase – cleaning and inspection 11
Cylinder head – dismantling 6
Cylinder head – reassembly 8
Cylinder head and valve components – cleaning and inspection . . . 7
Engine – initial start-up after overhaul 18
Engine – removal and refitting 4

Section number

Engine overhaul – dismantling sequence 5
Engine overhaul – general information 2
Engine overhaul – reassembly sequence 15
Engine removal – methods and precautions 3
General information 1
Main and big-end bearings – inspection 14
Piston/connecting rod assembly – inspection 12
Piston/connecting rod assembly – refitting 17
Piston/connecting rod assembly – removal 9

Degrees of difficulty

Easy, suitable for novice with little experience 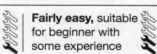	**Fairly easy,** suitable for beginner with some experience	**Fairly difficult,** suitable for competent DIY mechanic	**Difficult,** suitable for experienced DIY mechanic	**Very difficult,** suitable for expert DIY or professional

Specifications

Cylinder head

Maximum permissible distortion of sealing face (typical value):
   Non-TD5 engines . . . . 0.01 mm
   TD5 engines . . . . 0.10 mm
Valve seat angle:
   10J, 12J and 19J engines (intake and exhaust) . . . . 45°
   200 TDi engine:
      Intake . . . . 60°
      Exhaust . . . . 45°
   300 TDi engine:
      Intake . . . . 30°
      Exhaust . . . . 45°
Valve recess in cylinder head:
   200 TDi engine (intake and exhaust) . . . . 0.90 to 1.10 mm
   300 TDi engine:
      Intake . . . . 0.81 to 1.09 mm
      Exhaust . . . . 0.86 to 1.14 mm

Note: *It is not permissible to recut or renew the valve seats on TD5 engines.*

Valves

Valve clearance (intake and exhaust):
10J, 12J and 19J engines	0.25 mm
200 TDi and 300 TDi engines	0.20 mm
TD5	Hydraulic adjusters

Valve stem diameter:
10J, 12J and 19J engines:
Intake	7.912 to 7.899 mm
Exhaust	8.682 to 8.694 mm

200 TDi and 300 TDi engines:
Intake	7.960 to 7.975 mm
Exhaust	7.940 to 7.960 mm

TD5 :
Intake	6.907 to 6.923 mm
Exhaust	6.897 to 6.913 mm
Maximum permissible valve stem play in guide (non-TD5 engines)	0.15 mm

Maximum valve head deflection (TD5 engines – valve head 10 mm out of seat):
Intake valve	0.025 to 0.059 mm
Exhaust valve	0.035 to 0.069 mm

Maximum swirl chamber protrusion:
10J engine	0.025 mm
12J and 19J engines	0.760 mm

Maximum swirl chamber recess:
10J engine	0.050 mm
12J and 19J engines	0.025 mm

Valve springs

Free length:
10J, 12J and 19J engines:
Inner spring	42.67 mm
Outer spring	46.28 mm
300 TDi engine	46.28 mm
TD5 engine	47.00 ± 0.025 mm
Fitted length (200 TDi engine)	40.40 mm

Cylinder block

Cylinder rebore oversizes:
Non-TD5 engines	0.50 mm and 1.01 mm
TD5 engine	No oversizes available

Crankshaft and bearings

Main bearing journal diameter:
10J, and early 12J and 19J engines:
Production standard	63.4870 to 63.5000 mm
Regrind (0.260 mm undersize)*	63.2460 to 63.2333 mm

Later 12J and 19J engines:
Production standard	63.4870 to 63.4750 mm
Regrind (0.260 mm undersize)	63.2460 to 63.2333 mm

200 TDi and 300 TDi engines:
Production standard	63.4750 to 63.4870 mm
Regrind (0.25 mm undersize)	63.2330 to 63.2460 mm

TD5 :
Production standard	62.0000 ± 0.013 mm
No oversizes available	

Big-end bearing journal diameter:
Non-TD5 engines:
Production standard	58.725 to 58.744 mm
Regrind (0.25 mm undersize)*	58.471 to 58.490 mm

TD5 engines:
Production standard	54.00 ± 0.01 mm
No oversizes available	

Crankshaft endfloat:
Non-TD5 engines	0.05 to 0.15 mm
TD5 engines	0.02 to 0.25 mm
Thrustwasher oversizes (all except TD5)	0.0625 mm, 0.1250 mm, 0.2500 mm

*Note: *Crankshaft regrinding not permitted on early 10J engine with 3-bearing crankshaft.*

Piston rings

Ring end gaps:

10J engine:

Top compression	0.350 to 0.500 mm
Middle and lower compression	0.250 to 0.380 mm
Oil control	0.279 to 0.406 mm

12J and 19J engines:

Top compression	0.300 to 0.500 mm
Middle compression	0.250 to 0.450 mm
Oil control	0.300 to 0.600 mm

200 TDi and 300 TDi engines:

Top compression	0.400 to 0.600 mm
Middle compression	0.300 to 0.500 mm
Oil control	0.300 to 0.600 mm

TD5 engine:

Top compression	0.300 to 0.400 mm
Middle compression	0.400 to 0.600 mm
Oil control	0.250 to 0.500 mm

Clearance in piston groove:

10J engine:

Compression (3 rings)	0.060 to 0.110 mm
Oil control	0.038 to 0.064 mm

12J and 19J engines:

Top compression	0.140 to 0.180 mm
Middle compression	0.040 to 0.080 mm
Oil control	0.040 to 0.080 mm

200 TDi and 300 TDi engines:

Top compression	0.167 to 0.232 mm
Middle compression	0.050 to 0.085 mm
Oil control	0.050 to 0.085 mm

TD5 engine:

Top compression	Not available
Middle compression	0.050 to 0.082 mm
Oil control	0.050 to 0.082 mm

Torque wrench settings

Refer to Chapter 2A or 2B Specifications.

---

1 General information

This Part of Chapter 2 includes details of engine removal and refitting, and general overhaul procedures for the cylinder head, cylinder block/crankcase and internal engine components.

The information ranges from advice concerning preparation for an overhaul and the purchase of parts, to detailed step-by-step procedures covering removal, inspection, renovation and refitting of internal engine components.

The following Sections have been compiled based on the assumption that the engine has been removed from the vehicle. For information concerning in-vehicle engine repair, as well as information on the removal and refitting of the external components necessary to facilitate overhaul, refer to Chapters 2A and 2B, and to Section 5 of this Part.

2 Engine overhaul – general information

It is not always easy to determine when, or if, an engine should be completely overhauled, as a number of factors must be considered.

High mileage is not necessarily an indication that an overhaul is needed, while low mileage does not preclude the need for an overhaul. Frequency of servicing is probably the most important consideration. An engine which has had regular and frequent oil and filter changes, as well as other required maintenance, will most likely give many thousands of miles of reliable service. Conversely, a neglected engine may require an overhaul very early in its life.

Excessive oil consumption is an indication that piston rings, valve seals and/or valve guides are in need of attention. Make sure that oil leaks are not responsible before deciding that the rings and/or guides are worn. Perform a cylinder compression check or a leakdown test to determine the extent of the work required.

Check the oil pressure with a gauge fitted in place of the oil pressure sender, and compare it with the Specifications (Chapter 2A or 2B). If it is extremely low, the main and big-end bearings and/or the oil pump are probably worn out.

Loss of power, rough running, knocking or metallic engine noises, excessive valve gear noise and high fuel consumption may also point to the need for an overhaul, especially if they are all present at the same time. If a complete tune-up does not remedy the situation, major mechanical work is the only solution.

An engine overhaul involves restoring the internal parts to the specifications of a new engine. During an overhaul, the pistons and rings are renewed, and the cylinder bores are reconditioned (where possible). New main bearings, connecting rod (big-end) bearings and camshaft bearings are generally fitted, and if necessary/possible, the crankshaft may be reground, to restore the journals. The valves are also serviced as well, since they are usually in less-than-perfect condition at this point. While the engine is being overhauled, other components, such as the starter and alternator, can be overhauled as well. The end result should be a like-new engine that will give many trouble-free miles. **Note:** *Critical cooling system components such as the hoses, drivebelts, thermostat and water pump MUST be renewed when an engine is overhauled. The radiator should be checked carefully, to ensure that it is not clogged or leaking. Also it is a good idea to renew the oil pump whenever the engine is overhauled.*

Before beginning the engine overhaul, read through the entire procedure to familiarise yourself with the scope and requirements of the job. Overhauling an engine is not difficult if you follow all of the instructions carefully, have the necessary tools and equipment, and pay close attention to all specifications; however, it can be time-consuming. Plan on the vehicle being tied up for a minimum of two weeks, especially if parts must be taken to an engineering works for repair or reconditioning. Check on the availability of parts, and make sure that any necessary special tools and equipment are obtained in advance. Most work can be done with typical hand tools, although a number of precision measuring tools are required for inspecting parts to determine if they must be renewed. Often, the engineering works will handle the inspection of parts and offer advice concerning reconditioning and renewal. **Note:** *Always wait until the engine has been completely dismantled, and all components (especially the engine block) have been inspected, before deciding what service and repair operations must be performed by an engineering works. Since the condition of the block will be the major factor to consider when determining whether to overhaul the original engine or buy a reconditioned unit, do not purchase parts or have overhaul work done on other components until the block has been thoroughly inspected. As a general rule, time is the primary cost of an overhaul, so it does not pay to fit worn or substandard parts.*

As a final note, to ensure maximum life and minimum trouble from a reconditioned engine, everything must be assembled with care in a spotlessly-clean environment.

3 Engine removal – methods and precautions

If you have decided that an engine must be removed for overhaul or major repair work, several preliminary steps should be taken.

Locating a suitable place to work is extremely important. Adequate work space, along with storage space for the vehicle, will be needed. If a garage is not available, at the very least a flat, level, clean work surface is required.

Cleaning the engine compartment and engine before beginning the removal procedure will help keep tools clean and organised.

An engine hoist or A-frame will also be necessary. Make sure that the equipment is rated in excess of the weight of the engine. Safety is of primary importance, considering the potential hazards involved in lifting the engine out of the vehicle.

If this is the first time you have removed an engine, an assistant should be available. Advice and aid from someone more experienced would also be helpful. There are many instances when one person cannot simultaneously perform all of the operations required when lifting the engine out of the vehicle.

Plan the operation ahead of time. Arrange for, or obtain, all of the tools and equipment you will need, prior to beginning the job. Some of the equipment necessary to perform engine removal and installation safely and with relative ease are (in addition to an engine hoist) a heavy-duty floor (trolley) jack, complete sets of spanners and sockets as described at the front of this manual, wooden blocks, and plenty of rags and cleaning solvent for mopping-up spilled oil, coolant and fuel. If the hoist must be hired, make sure that you arrange for it in advance, and perform all of the operations possible without it beforehand. This will save you money and time.

Plan for the vehicle to be out of use for quite a while. An engineering works will be required to perform some of the work which the do-it-yourselfer cannot accomplish without special equipment. These places often have a busy schedule, so it would be a good idea to consult them before removing the engine, in order to accurately estimate the amount of time required to rebuild or repair components that may need work.

Always be extremely careful when removing and refitting the engine. Serious injury can result from careless actions. Plan ahead, take your time, and you will find that a job of this nature, although major, can be accomplished successfully.

The engine is most easily removed by separating it from the transmission, and lifting the engine upwards from the engine compartment.

4.9 Disconnect the coolant hoses from the fuel cooler – TD5 engine

4 Engine – removal and refitting

Note: *An engine hoist and suitable lifting tackle will be required for this operation.*

Removal

1 Ensure that the vehicle is parked on level ground, and apply the handbrake. On TD5 models, disconnect the front propshaft from the axle (see Chapter 8), then undo the bolts and remove the engine undershield.
2 Disconnect the battery negative lead (see Chapter 5).
3 Drain the engine oil with reference to Chapter 1.
4 Drain the cooling system as described in Chapter 1.
5 Remove the bonnet as described in Chapter 12.
6 Where applicable, undo the 3 bolts and remove the plastic cover from the top of the engine.

TD5 engines

7 Remove the turbocharger and air cleaner housing as described in Chapter 4B.
8 Remove the starter motor as described in Chapter 5.
9 Release the clips and disconnect the coolant hoses from the fuel cooler and coolant rail **(see illustration)**.
10 Slide off the red plastic collar, depress the release button and disconnect the fuel hose from the fuel cooler. Repeat this procedure on the black collar hose. Plugs the openings to prevent dirt ingress.
11 Disconnect the servo vacuum hose, then undo the four bolts and remove the fuel cooler **(see illustration)**.
12 Release the servo vacuum hose from the retaining clips along its length, then disconnect it from the servo and remove it from the engine compartment.
13 Undo the 3 bolts and remove the power steering pump pulley, then undo the 4 bolts and move the pump to one side without disconnecting the hoses – refer to Chapter 11 if necessary.

4.11 Undo the bolts (upper bolts arrowed) and remove the fuel cooler – TD5 engines

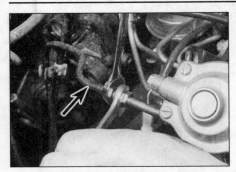

4.22 Disconnecting the fuel return hose (arrowed) from the fuel injection pump

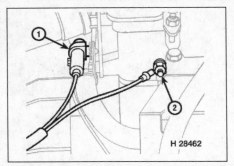

4.26a Main electrical feed (1) and glow plug feed (2) wiring connections – 300 TDi engine

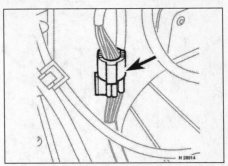

4.26b Main engine wiring harness connector (arrowed) – 300 TDi engine

Non-TD5 engines

14 Loosen the securing clips, and remove the air trunking connecting the air cleaner to the intake manifold or the turbocharger, as applicable.

15 Where applicable, disconnect the engine breather hose(s) from the air cleaner trunking.

16 On 200 TDi and 300 TDi engines, remove the air cleaner and the remaining air trunking, as described in Chapter 4A.

17 If not already done, unscrew the union nuts, and disconnect the engine oil cooler pipes from the oil cooler. Be prepared for oil spillage, and cover the open ends of the oil cooler and pipes, to prevent further oil spillage and dirt ingress. Recover the O-ring seals from the unions.

18 Similarly, disconnect the oil pipes from the oil filter adapter on the cylinder block, and remove the pipes.

19 On models with power steering, place a suitable container beneath the power steering pump to catch escaping fluid, then unscrew the union nut and disconnect the high-pressure fluid hose from the pump. Plug or clamp the open ends of the hose and the pump, to prevent dirt ingress and further fluid loss. Similarly, loosen the hose clip, and disconnect the fluid return hose from the pump.

20 Unscrew and remove the bolt securing the transmission breather pipe/wiring harness bracket to the rear of the cylinder head, then move the pipes/wiring harness to one side, clear of the engine.

21 Disconnect the accelerator cable from the

fuel injection pump or the throttle linkage lever, as applicable, and release the cable from any brackets on the pump and/or engine (refer to Chapter 4A for details if necessary). Move the cable clear of the engine.

22 Unscrew the unions, and disconnect the fuel supply and return pipes from the fuel injection pump **(see illustration)**. It will be necessary to counterhold the union on the pump when disconnecting the return pipe. Be prepared for fuel spillage. Recover the sealing washers from the banjo unions.

 Cover the open ends of the pipes, and plug the openings in the injection pump, to keep dirt out (where applicable, banjo bolts can be refitted to the pump, and covered).

23 Similarly, disconnect the fuel hoses from the fuel lift pump (on the right-hand side of the engine). Again, be prepared for fuel spillage, and cover or plug the open ends of the hoses and the pump.

24 Release the securing clip, and disconnect the vacuum hose from the brake vacuum pump.

25 Disconnect the exhaust front section from the manifold or turbocharger elbow, as applicable, with reference to Chapter 4A.

All engines

26 Disconnect all relevant wiring from the engine ancillary components. Note that on most models, wiring harness connectors

are provided, which eliminates the need to disconnect all the wiring from the individual components – the engine wiring harness can then be removed with the engine. Note the routing of all wiring, to ensure correct refitting. Make a check to ensure that all relevant wiring has been disconnected, to enable the engine to be removed. Undo the bolts/clips and move the harnesses away from the engine **(see illustrations)**.

27 Remove the radiator as described in Chapter 3.

28 On models with 200 TDi, 300 TDi and TD5 engines, loosen the hose clips, and remove the intercooler air trunking from the engine compartment.

29 On models with air conditioning, have the system discharged by a Land Rover dealer, or a suitably-qualified specialist. Once the system has been discharged, unscrew the union bolts, and disconnect the refrigerant pipes from the air conditioning compressor. Note that on TD5 engines, it is possible to unbolt the compressor and move it to one side without disconnecting the refrigerant pipes/discharging the refrigerant.

⚠ **Warning: DO NOT attempt to discharge the system yourself – refer to the precautions given for models with air conditioning in Chapter 3.**

30 Note their fitted positions, then disconnect all vacuum pipes from the engine.

31 Release the clips and disconnect all coolant hoses from the engine **(see illustrations)**.

32 Place a trolley jack under the gearbox, with

4.31a Disconnect the coolant bypass hose . . .

4.31b . . . and release the hose from the clips

4.31c Coolant hoses – TD5 engine

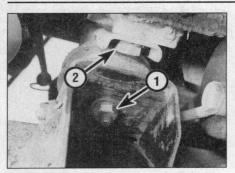

4.37a Left-hand engine mounting-to-chassis nut (1) and lower bracket-to-chassis bolt (2)

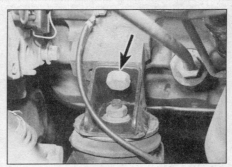

4.37b Left-hand engine mounting bracket upper securing bolt (arrowed)

4.43 Lock two nuts together, and remove the studs (arrowed) each side securing the bonnet slam panel

an interposed block of wood to spread the load. Raise the jack to support the gearbox.
33 Connect a suitable hoist and lifting tackle to the front and rear engine lifting brackets.
34 Raise the hoist sufficiently to just take the weight of the engine.

Non-TD5 engines

35 Working underneath the vehicle, unscrew (but do not remove) all accessible flywheel housing-to-bellhousing nuts.
36 Working at each side of the engine in turn, unscrew the nuts securing the engine mountings to the chassis.
37 Similarly, unscrew the bolts securing the engine mounting brackets to the cylinder block (where applicable, release the locking tabs from the bolts), and withdraw the engine mountings **(see illustrations)**.
38 Lower the engine and transmission, using the hoist and jack, for access to the upper flywheel housing-to-bellhousing nuts.
39 Unscrew and remove the upper flywheel housing-to-bellhousing nuts. Access is difficult, and is easiest from underneath the vehicle, using a suitable socket and extension bar.

 Have an assistant guide the socket onto the nuts from above.

40 Working under the vehicle, remove the remaining flywheel housing-to-bellhousing nuts. Leave the starter motor in position.

TD5 engines

41 Undo the two bolts and remove the plastic acoustic cover from the rear of the engine – where fitted.
42 Undo the bolt and remove the crankshaft position sensor from the right-hand side of the transmission bellhousing. Recover the sensor spacer where fitted.
43 Using two nuts locked together, remove the remaining stud each side securing the bonnet slam panel, then undo the panel support stays lower bolts and move the slam panel to one side **(see illustration)**.
44 Undo the bolts securing the transmission bellhousing to the engine.
45 Undo the nuts securing the left- and

right-hand engine mounting brackets to the mountings.

All engines

46 Carefully raise the hoist, and lift the engine from the gearbox. It will be necessary to pull the engine forwards to disengage the gearbox input shaft from the clutch – take care not to allow the weight of the engine or gearbox to hang on the input shaft. If necessary, alter the position of the jack supporting the gearbox, and the hoist supporting the engine, until the engine is free. Note that on non-TD5 engines, there is sealant between the mating faces of the flywheel housing and the bellhousing.
47 Make a final check to ensure that all hoses, pipes and wires have been disconnected from the engine, and released from any brackets, to facilitate engine removal.
48 With the aid of an assistant, carefully raise the hoist to lift the engine from the vehicle, taking care not to damage surrounding components in the engine compartment.

 Fasten a suitable hose clip around the gearbox input shaft to prevent the release bearing from being inadvertently pushed forwards on the shaft whilst the engine is removed from the vehicle.

Refitting

49 Ensure that the clutch friction disc has been centralised, as described in Chapter 6.
50 Where applicable, remove the hose clip from the gearbox input shaft.
51 On non-TD5 engines, apply jointing compound to the cylinder block mating faces of the gearbox/transmission bellhousing.
52 Apply a little clutch assembly grease to the splines of the gearbox input shaft. Do not apply too much grease, as it may contaminate the clutch.
53 Attach the hoist and lifting tackle to the engine, as during the removal procedure, and lift the engine into position over the vehicle engine compartment.
54 Lower the engine into position, taking care not to damage the surrounding components.
55 Manipulate the engine and gearbox as

necessary to enable the two assemblies to be mated together. Alter the position of the jack supporting the gearbox, and the hoist supporting the engine, until the two assemblies are correctly aligned. Ensure that the weight of the engine or gearbox is not allowed to hang on the gearbox input shaft, and ensure that the gearbox input shaft engages with the splines of the clutch friction disc.

Non-TD5 engines

56 Fit the flywheel housing-to-bellhousing nuts, and tighten them to the specified torque. If necessary, lower the engine/gearbox assembly to gain access to the top nuts, as during removal.
57 Wipe any excess jointing compound from the area around the flywheel housing-to-bellhousing mating faces.
58 Refit and tighten the bolt securing the transmission breather pipe bracket to the rear of the cylinder head.
59 If necessary, raise the engine slightly, then place the engine mountings in position. Refit and tighten the bolts securing the engine mountings to the cylinder block. Where applicable, secure the bolts with the locking tabs.
60 Carefully withdraw the jack and the block of wood used to support the gearbox.
61 Lower the engine, ensuring that the engine mounting studs engage with the corresponding holes in the chassis brackets, then refit the engine mounting washers and nuts, and tighten the nuts to the specified torque.

TD5 engines

62 Refit the transmission-to-engine bolts and tighten them to the specified torque.
63 Ensure the engine mounting brackets locate over the mountings, then refit the nuts and tighten them to the specified torque.

All engines

64 Disconnect the hoist and lifting tackle from the engine lifting brackets.
65 Further refitting is a reversal of removal, bearing in mind the following points:
a) Reconnect all relevant engine harness wiring, and clip the harness into position, ensuring that it is routed as noted before removal.
b) Reconnect the exhaust front section to the

manifold or turbocharger (as applicable), with reference to Chapter 4A or 4B.

c) On TD5 engines, refit the turbocharger as described in Chapter 4B, and the starter motor as in Chapter 5.

d) Reconnect the accelerator cable, and check the cable adjustment as described in Chapter 4A (non-TD5 engines).

e) Where applicable, reconnect the fluid hoses to the power steering pump, using new O-ring seals.

f) Reconnect the oil cooler pipes to the oil filter adapter and the oil cooler, using new O-ring seals (where applicable).

g) Refit the radiator, cooling fan and cowl with reference to Chapter 3.

h) Refit the bonnet with reference to Chapter 12.

i) Where applicable, check the power steering fluid level, and top-up as necessary as described in Chapter 1.

j) Refill the cooling system as described in Chapter 1.

k) Refill the engine with oil as described in Chapter 1.

l) Where applicable, have the system recharged with refrigerant by a Land Rover dealer, or a suitably-equipped specialist.

m) Bleed the fuel system as described in Chapter 4A or 4B.

64 On non-TD5 models fitted with a turbocharger, before starting the engine, the turbocharger **must** be primed with oil as follows. Failure to carry out this procedure may result in serious (and expensive) damage to the turbocharger:

a) Unscrew the oil feed pipe banjo bolt from the top of the turbocharger housing. Recover the two sealing washers, and move the feed pipe away from the oil hole in the housing.

b) Fill the housing with clean engine oil of the correct type and grade, from a freshly-opened sealed container.

c) Reconnect the oil feed pipe, and refit the banjo bolt, ensuring that one sealing washer is positioned on each side of the pipe. Tighten the banjo bolt to the specified torque.

5 Engine overhaul – dismantling sequence

1 It is far easier to dismantle and work on the engine if it is mounted on a portable engine stand. These stands can often be hired from a tool hire shop. Depending on the type of stand used, the flywheel may have to be removed from the engine, to allow the engine stand bolts to be tightened into the end of the cylinder block.

2 If a stand is not available, it is possible to dismantle the engine while supported on blocks on a sturdy workbench, or on the floor. Be extra careful not to tip or drop the engine when working without a stand.

3 Before starting the overhaul procedure, the external engine ancillary components must be removed (this is the case even if a reconditioned engine is to be fitted, in which case, the components from the old engine must be transferred to the reconditioned unit). These components include the following (check with the supplier of a reconditioned unit to see which components are included):

a) Wiring looms (note all connections and routing).
b) Glow plugs.
c) Fuel injectors.
d) Fuel injection pump (except TD5 models).
e) Coolant pump.
f) Alternator.
g) Starter motor.
h) Power steering pump (where applicable).
i) Manifolds and turbocharger (where applicable).
j) Thermostat and housing.
k) Clutch.
l) Oil pressure switch.
m) Temperature gauge sender.
n) Oil filter adapter.
o) Crankcase breather and oil separator components
p) Dipstick and tube
q) Auxiliary component mounting bracket(s)

6 Cylinder head – dismantling

Note: New and reconditioned cylinder heads may be available from the manufacturers, and from engine overhaul specialists. Due to the fact that some specialist tools are required for the dismantling and inspection procedures, and new components may not be readily available, it may be more practical and economical for the home mechanic to purchase a reconditioned head, rather than to dismantle, inspect and recondition the original head. A valve spring compressor tool will be required for this operation.

1 With the cylinder head removed as described in Chapter 2A or 2B, clean away all external dirt, and if desired, remove any ancillaries such as engine lifting brackets,

6.4 Valve spring compressor tool in position on No 8 valve

6.2 Fuel connector block bolts (arrowed) – TD5 engine

thermostat housing, etc, which are still attached to the cylinder head.

2 On TD5 models, remove the camshaft, rocker arms and hydraulic adjusters as described in Chapter 2B, and the injectors as described in Chapter 4B. If required, undo the bolts and remove the fuel connector block from the cylinder head. Discard the gasket and O-rings, new ones must be fitted **(see illustration)**.

3 Where applicable, if not already done, remove the caps from the tops of the valve stems, keeping them in order so that they can be refitted in their original positions. **Note:** Valve stem caps are not fitted to the top of TD5 engine valves.

4 To remove a valve, fit a valve spring compressor tool. Ensure that the arms of the compressor tool are securely positioned on the head of the valve and the spring cap. On non-TD5 engines, as the valves are recessed into the cylinder head, a suitable extension piece may be required for the spring compressor **(see illustration)**.

5 Compress the valve spring to relieve the pressure of the spring cap acting on the collets.

HAYNES HiNT *If the spring cap sticks to the valve stem, support the compressor tool, and give the end a light tap with a soft-faced mallet to help free the spring cap.*

6 Extract the two split collets, then slowly release the compressor tool.

7 Remove the spring cap, spring(s), valve stem oil seal (using long-nosed pliers if necessary) and, on 200 TDi and 300 TDi engines, the spring seat. Withdraw the valve from the cylinder head. Note that 10J, 12J and 19J engines are fitted with double valve springs.

8 Repeat the procedure for the remaining valves, keeping all components in strict order, so that they can be refitted in their original positions, unless all the components are to be renewed. If the components are to be kept and used again, place each valve assembly in a labelled polythene bag or a similar small container. Note that as with cylinder

6.8 Place the valve components in a labelled polythene bag

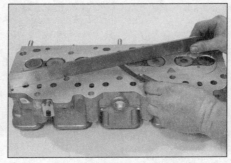

7.6 Checking the cylinder head surface for distortion

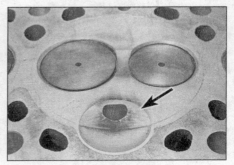

7.9 This swirl chamber shows the initial stages of cracking and burning – 10J, 12J and 19J engines

numbering, the valves are normally numbered from the timing chain/belt end of the engine **(see illustration)**.

7 Cylinder head and valve components – cleaning and inspection

1 Thorough cleaning of the cylinder head and valve components, followed by a detailed inspection, will enable a decision to be made on whether further work is necessary before reassembling the components.

Cleaning

2 Scrape away all traces of old gasket material and sealing compound from the cylinder head surfaces. Take care not to damage the cylinder head surfaces. It is advisable not to use a metal scraper on aluminium heads.
3 Scrape away the carbon from the surface of the cylinder head, then wash the cylinder head thoroughly with paraffin or a suitable solvent.
4 Scrape off any heavy carbon deposits that may have formed on the valves, then use a power-operated wire brush to remove deposits from the valve heads and stems.

Inspection

Note: *Be sure to perform all the following inspection procedures before concluding that the services of a machine shop or engine overhaul specialist are required. Make a list of all items that require attention.*

Cylinder head

5 Inspect the head very carefully for cracks, evidence of coolant leakage, and other damage. If cracks are found, a new cylinder head should be obtained.
6 Use a straight-edge and feeler blade to check that the cylinder head surface is not distorted **(see illustration)**. If the specified distortion limit is exceeded, it may be possible to have the cylinder head resurfaced – consult a Land Rover dealer for further information. **Note:** *Cylinder head refacing/machining is not permissible on TD5 engines.*
7 Examine the valve seats in the cylinder head. If the seats are severely pitted, cracked or burned, then they will need to be recut by

an engine overhaul specialist. If only slight pitting is evident, this can be removed by grinding the valve heads and seats together with coarse then fine grinding paste, as described later in this Section. In extreme cases, it may be possible to have new valve seat inserts fitted, but again this work should be referred to a specialist. **Note:** *Valve seat recutting or renewal is not permissible on TD5 engines.*
8 If the valve guides are worn, indicated by a side-to-side motion of the valve, the guides can be renewed. This work is best carried out by an engine overhaul specialist. To measure the valve stem play in the guide, insert the valve into the relevant guide, with the valve head positioned approximately 10.0 mm from the seat. A square and feeler blade may be used to determine whether the amount of side play of the valve exceeds the specified maximum. If new valve guides have been fitted, repeat the measuring procedure, and if the valve stem play still exceeds the maximum limit, renew the valve. **Note:** *It is not possible to renew the valve guides on TD5 engines.*
9 On 10J, 12J and 19J engines, inspect the fuel injector sleeves and the swirl chambers for burning or cracks **(see illustration)**. Normally, there should be no need to remove the injector sleeves or the swirl chambers from the cylinder head. Small surface cracks in the swirl chambers can be ignored, but if severe cracks are evident, renew the relevant swirl chamber, and carefully inspect the surface of the cylinder head for cracks (see para-

7.12 Checking a swirl chamber protrusion – 10J, 12J and 19J engines

graph 5). Similarly, renew any cracked injector sleeves. Refer to the following sub-Sections for details.
10 On 200 TDi and 300 TDi engines, check the condition of the rocker shaft bearing surfaces in the cylinder head for signs of wear or damage. If evident, the cylinder head must be renewed, as no repair is possible.
11 On TD5 engines, check the camshaft bearing surfaces for wear or damage. If evident, then the cylinder head and camshaft carrier must be renewed, as they are a matched pair.
12 On 10J, 12J and 19J engines, using a dial test indicator, check that the swirl chamber protrusion/recess is within the limits given in the Specifications. Zero the dial test indicator on the gasket surface of the cylinder head, then measure the protrusion or recess of the swirl chamber **(see illustration)**. If the measured figure is outside the specified limits, consult an engine overhaul specialist for advice. It may be possible to bring the swirl chamber protrusion/recess within limits by machining, or it may be necessary to renew components.

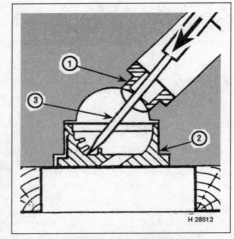

H 28512

7.13 Removing a swirl chamber – 10J, 12J and 19J engines

1 Fuel injector sleeve
2 Swirl chamber
3 Drift

Swirl chamber renewal – 10J, 12J and 19J engines

13 To remove a swirl chamber, pass a thin soft metal drift through the fuel injector bore in the side of the cylinder head, and carefully tap the swirl chamber from its location **(see illustration)**. Take care not to damage the injector sleeve. Recover the roll-pin or peg, as applicable.

14 Thoroughly clean the combustion chamber and the swirl chamber seat in the cylinder head.

15 To fit a swirl chamber, tap the chamber into position in the cylinder head, using a soft-faced mallet, then locate by tapping a new roll-pin or peg into position. If the swirl chamber is loose, it can be retained using a little grease.

16 On completion of refitting, check the swirl chamber protrusion/recess as described in paragraph 12.

Fuel injector sleeve renewal – 10J, 12J and 19J engines

17 To remove an injector sleeve, with the relevant swirl chamber removed, carefully tap the sleeve out towards the injector bore, using a suitable drift.

18 Thoroughly clean the combustion chamber and the injector sleeve seat in the cylinder head.

19 To fit an injector sleeve, smear the sleeve with a little clean engine oil, then place the sleeve into the injector bore, with the hole in the side of the sleeve pointing towards the centre of the cylinder head.

20 Carefully tap the sleeve onto its seat using a soft metal drift, and refit the swirl chamber as described previously.

Valves

Note: *A micrometer will be required for this operation.*

21 Examine the head of each valve for pitting, burning, cracks and general wear, and check the valve stem for scoring and wear ridges. Rotate the valve, and check for any obvious indication that it is bent. Look for pitting and excessive wear on the end of each valve stem. If the valve appears satisfactory at this stage, measure the valve stem diameter at several points, using a micrometer. Any significant difference in the readings obtained indicates wear of the valve stem **(see illustration)**. Should any of these conditions be apparent, the valve(s) must be renewed.

22 If the valves are in satisfactory condition, they should be ground (lapped) onto their respective seats, to ensure a smooth gas-tight seal.

23 Valve grinding is carried out as follows. Place the cylinder head upside down on a bench, with a block of wood at each end to give clearance for the valve stems.

24 Smear a trace of coarse carborundum paste on the seat face in the cylinder head, and press a suction grinding tool onto the relevant valve head. With a semi-rotary action, grind the valve head to its seat, lifting the valve occasionally to redistribute the grinding paste **(see illustration)**. When a dull, matt, even surface is produced on the faces of both the valve seat and the valve, wipe off the paste and repeat the process with fine carborundum paste. A light spring placed under the valve head will greatly ease this operation. When a smooth unbroken ring of light grey matt finish is produced on both the valve and seat faces, the grinding operation is complete. Carefully clean away every trace of grinding paste, taking great care to leave none in the ports or in the valve guides. Clean the valves and valve seats with a paraffin-soaked rag, then with a clean rag, and finally, if an air line is available, blow the valves, valve guides and cylinder head ports clean.

⚠️ **Warning: Wear eye protection when using compressed air.**

25 On 200 TDi and 300 TDi engines, after carrying out the valve grinding operation, the valve recess from the face of the cylinder head must be measured as follows:
  a) *With the cylinder head supported upside down, as during the valve grinding operation, insert the valve into its relevant guide, and push the valve onto its seat.*
  b) *Place a straight-edge across the surface of the cylinder head, so that the straight-edge passes across the centre of the valve.*
  c) *Using a feeler blade, measure the recess of the valve below the surface of the cylinder head. The recess should be* within the specified limits. Repeat the measurement for all the valves.

26 If the valve recess is outside the specified limits, consult an engine overhaul specialist for advice. It may be possible to bring the valve recess within limits by machining, or it may be necessary to renew components.

Valve springs

27 Check that all the valve springs are intact. If any one is broken, all should be renewed.

28 Stand each spring on a flat surface, and check it for squareness. If possible, check the free length of each spring against the value given in the Specifications. If a spring is found to be too short, or damaged in any way, renew all the springs as a set. Springs suffer from fatigue, and it is a good idea to renew them, even if they look serviceable.

Valve stem oil seals

29 All valve stem oil seals should be renewed as a matter of course.

Valve stem caps

30 Certain engines may be fitted with valve stem caps, which are designed to reduce wear between the rocker arms and the valve stems. Where fitted, the caps should be renewed as a matter of course.

8 Cylinder head – reassembly

Note: *A valve spring compressor will be required for this operation. New valve stem oil seals (and, where applicable, new valve stem caps) should be fitted on reassembly.*

1 With all the components cleaned, starting at one end of the cylinder head, fit the valve components as follows. If the original components are being refitted, all components must be refitted in their original positions.

2 On 200 TDi and 300 TDi engines, fit the spring seat to its location in the cylinder head **(see illustration)**.

3 Lubricate the valve stem oil seal with clean engine oil, then fit the oil seal by pushing it into position on the cylinder head or spring seat (as applicable) using a suitable socket

7.21 Measuring a valve stem diameter

7.24 Grinding-in a valve

8.2 Fitting a spring seat

8.3a On TD5 engines, the spring seat is integral with the seal

8.3b Fitting a valve stem oil seal using a socket

8.4 Fitting a valve

(see illustrations). Ensure that the seal engages correctly over the valve guide. Note that on 10J, 12J and 19J engines, the intake and exhaust valve stem seals are different – ensure that the seals are fitted to their correct locations as follows:

	Intake valve seal	Exhaust valve seal
10J engine	Plain exterior	Ridged exterior
12J and 19J engines	Plain exterior	Stepped exterior

4 Insert the appropriate valve into its guide (if new valves are being fitted, insert each valve into the location to which it has been ground), ensuring that the valve stem is well-lubricated with clean engine oil (see illustration). Take care not to damage the valve stem oil seal as the valve is fitted.

8.5a Fitting a valve spring . . .

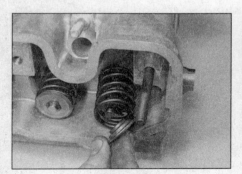

8.5b . . . and a spring cap

5 Fit the valve spring(s) (either way up) and the spring cap (see illustrations). Make sure that the spring cap is correctly located on the top of the spring(s).
6 Fit the spring compressor tool, and compress the valve spring(s) until the spring cap passes beyond the collet groove in the valve stem.
7 Apply a little grease to the collet groove, then fit the split collets into the groove, with the narrow ends nearest the spring (see illustration). The grease should hold them in the groove.
8 Slowly release the compressor tool, ensuring that the collets are not dislodged from the groove. When the compressor is fully released, give the top of the valve assembly a tap with a soft-faced mallet to settle the components.
9 Where applicable, fit a new valve stem cap.
10 Repeat the procedure for the remaining valves, ensuring that if the original components are being used, they are all refitted in their original positions.
11 Where applicable, refit any brackets, etc, which were removed before dismantling the cylinder head.

9 Piston/connecting rod assembly – removal

10J, 12J and 19J engines

1 Before proceeding, the following

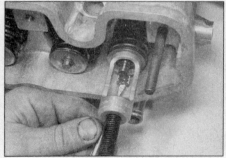

8.7 Fitting a split collet

components must be removed as described in Chapter 2A:
a) Cylinder head.
b) Sump.
c) Oil pump.
2 Rotate the crankshaft so that No 1 big-end cap (nearest the timing chain/belt end of the engine) is at the lowest point of its travel. If the big-end cap and connecting rod are not already numbered, mark them with a centre-punch. Mark both cap and rod to identify the cylinder they operate in, noting that No 1 is nearest the timing chain/belt end of the engine (normally, the connecting rods and caps are already numbered, and the numbers are read from the camshaft side of the engine).
3 Unscrew and remove the big-end bearing cap nuts. Withdraw the cap, complete with bearing shell, from the connecting rod (see illustration). Strike the cap with a wooden or copper mallet if it is stuck.

> **HAYNES HINT** Tape the bearing shell to the cap if it is to be re-used.

4 If only the bearing shells are being attended to, push the connecting rod up and off the crankpin, and remove the upper bearing shell. Again, tape the bearing shell to the rod if it is to be re-used.
5 If desired, push the connecting rod up, and remove the piston and rod assembly from the bore. Note that if there is a pronounced wear ridge at the top of the bore, there is a

9.3 Removing a big-end bearing cap

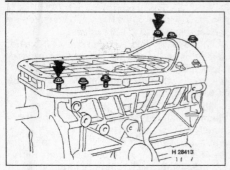

9.8 Unscrew the securing bolts (arrowed) and remove the ladder frame – 200 TDi engine

9.13 Oil strainer securing bolts (arrowed) – 300 TDi engine

9.14 Removing the oil return pipe – 300 TDi engine

risk of damaging the piston as the rings foul the ridge. However, it is reasonable to assume that a rebore and new pistons will be required in any case if the ridge is so pronounced.

6 Repeat the procedure for the remaining piston/connecting rod assemblies. Ensure that the caps and rods are marked before removal, as described previously, and keep all components in order.

200 TDi engine

7 Before proceeding, the following components must be removed as described in Chapter 2A:

a) Cylinder head.
b) Sump.
c) Oil pump.

8 Unscrew and remove the ten bolts securing the ladder frame to the lower face of the cylinder block **(see illustration)**.

9 Gently tap the ladder frame with a soft-faced mallet to break the seal, then withdraw the ladder frame from the cylinder block.

10 Proceed as described in paragraphs 2 to 6 inclusive.

300 TDi engine

11 Before proceeding, the following components must be removed as described in Chapter 2A:

a) Cylinder head.
b) Sump.

12 Unscrew the two bolts securing the oil

strainer support bracket to the main bearing cap.

13 Unscrew the bolt securing the oil pick-up pipe to the timing belt housing, then withdraw the strainer **(see illustration)**. Recover the O-ring from the pick-up pipe.

14 Unscrew the two bolts securing the oil return pipe to the cylinder block **(see illustration)**. Recover the gasket.

15 Proceed as described in paragraphs 2 to 6 inclusive.

TD5 engine

16 Before proceeding, the following components must be removed as described in Chapter 2B:

a) Cylinder head.
b) Oil pump/stiffener plate.

17 Rotate the crankshaft so that No 1 big-end cap (nearest the timing chain end of the engine) is at the lowest point of its travel. If the big-end cap and connecting rod are not already numbered, mark them with a permanent marker. Also make alignment marks between the cap and connecting rod – as these caps are 'split fractured' it is absolutely essential that they are refitted into their original positions **(see illustration)**.

18 Unscrew and remove the big-end bearing cap bolts. Withdraw the cap, complete with bearing shell, from the connecting rod. Strike the cap with a wooden or copper mallet if it is stuck. **Note:** *Land Rover insist that the bearing shells should be renewed whenever the bearing caps are removed.*

19 If only the bearing shells are being attended to, push the connecting rod up and off the crankpin, and remove the upper bearing shell.

20 If desired, push the connecting rod up, and remove the piston and rod assembly from the bore. Note that if there is a pronounced wear ridge at the top of the bore, there is a risk of damaging the piston as the rings foul the ridge. However, it is reasonable to assume that a rebore and new pistons will be required in any case if the ridge is so pronounced.

21 Repeat the procedure for the remaining piston/connecting rod assemblies. Ensure that the caps and rods are marked before removal, as described previously, and keep all components in order.

10 Crankshaft – removal

1 Before proceeding, the following components must be removed:

a) Timing belt housing – all except 10J and TD5 engines (Chapter 2A, Section 17).
b) Flywheel (Chapter 2A or 2B).
c) Piston/connecting rod assemblies (Section 9).
d) Timing chain and rear oil seal – TD5 engines (Chapter 2B).

2 On non-TD5 engines, working at the rear of the cylinder block, unscrew the securing bolts, and remove the flywheel housing **(see illustration)**. Note the locations of any brackets secured by the external housing bolts. Where applicable, recover the gasket or the O-ring.

3 On 300 TDi and TD5 engines, unscrew the securing bolts, and remove the rear crankshaft oil seal housing from the rear of the cylinder block. Discard the housing, and recover the gasket, and the sealing ring if it is loose (where applicable).

4 Before the crankshaft is removed, check the endfloat, using a dial gauge in contact with the end of the crankshaft. Push the crankshaft fully one way, and then zero the gauge. Push the crankshaft fully the other way, and check the endfloat. The result can be compared

9.17 On TD5 engines, the big end caps are 'split fractured'. It's absolutely essential they are refitted to their original positions

10.2 Removing the flywheel housing – 300 TDi engine

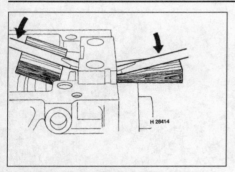

10.8 Using two screwdrivers to lever No 5 main bearing cap from its location. Note location of blocks of wood

10.10 Removing a main bearing shell upper half from the crankcase

with the specified amount, and will give an indication as to whether new thrustwashers are required.

5 If a dial gauge is not available, feeler blades can be used. First push the crankshaft fully towards the flywheel end of the engine. Slip the feeler blade between the web of No 2 (non-TD5 engines) or No 3 (TD5 engines) crankpin and the thrustwasher of the centre main bearing (located in the crankcase).

6 Check the main bearing caps for identification marks, and if none are present, number them so that the numbers can be read from the timing chain/belt end of the engine, using a centre-punch, as was done for the connecting rods and caps. Again note that No 1 cylinder is at the timing chain/belt end of the engine.

7 Unscrew and remove the main bearing cap securing bolts.

8 Withdraw the caps, complete with bearing shells. Tap the caps with a wooden or copper mallet if they are stuck (on non-TD5 engines, the caps locate on dowels). Note that on non-TD5 engines the sides of the rear (flywheel end) bearing cap are sealed to the cylinder block using plastic or cork seals on each side, which may cause difficulty in removing the cap. If necessary, the cap can be levered from its location using a suitable bar inserted in the hole in the inside face of the cap – place a suitable piece of wood on the crankshaft web, and lever against the wood **(see illustration)**. Also note that, on early 10J engines with a 3-bearing crankshaft, the lower half of the

crankshaft rear oil seal retainer is bolted to the rear bearing cap .

9 Carefully lift the crankshaft from the crankcase. On early 10J engines with a 3-bearing crankshaft, remove the oil seal from the rear of the crankshaft, and discard it.

10 Remove the thrustwashers, then remove the bearing shell upper halves from the crankcase **(see illustration)**. Place each shell with its respective bearing cap.

11 Cylinder block/crankcase – cleaning and inspection

Cleaning

1 For complete cleaning, the core plugs should be removed. Drill a small hole in them, then insert a self-tapping screw and pull out the plugs using a pair of grips or a slide-hammer. Also remove all external components, brackets and senders (if not already done), noting their locations. Where applicable, remove the securing bolts, and withdraw the piston oil spray jets from the bottom of the cylinder block (all except 10J engines are fitted with oil spray jets). Also recover the sealing washers, where applicable **(see illustrations)**.

2 Remove all oil gallery plugs, and where applicable, recover the sealing washers. Note that the plugs may be fitted using sealant.

3 Scrape all traces of gasket and sealant from the cylinder block, taking care not to damage

the mating faces of the head and sump (or the ladder frame on 200 TDi engines).

4 Where applicable, also remove all traces of sealant from the mating faces of the cylinder block and the flywheel housing.

5 If the block is extremely dirty, it should be steam-cleaned.

6 After the block has been steam-cleaned, clean all oil holes and oil galleries one more time. Flush all internal passages with warm water until the water runs clear, then dry the block thoroughly and wipe all machined surfaces with a light rust-preventative oil. If you have access to compressed air, use it to speed up the drying process, and to blow out all the oil holes and galleries.

⚠️ *Warning: Wear eye protection when using compressed air.*

7 If the block is not very dirty, you can do an adequate cleaning job with hot soapy water and a stiff brush. Take plenty of time, and do a thorough job. Regardless of the cleaning method used, be sure to clean all oil holes and galleries very thoroughly, dry the block completely, and coat all machined surfaces with light oil.

8 The threaded holes in the block must be clean, to ensure accurate torque wrench readings during reassembly. Run the proper-size tap into each of the holes to remove rust, corrosion, thread sealant or sludge, and to restore damaged threads **(see illustration)**. If possible, use compressed air to clear the holes of debris produced by this operation, noting the warning given in paragraph 6. Now is a good time to clean the threads on the head bolts and the main bearing cap bolts as well.

9 After coating the mating surfaces of the new core plugs with suitable sealant, refit them in the cylinder block. Make sure that they are driven in straight and seated properly, or leakage could result. Special tools are available for this purpose, but a large socket, with an outside diameter that will just slip into the core plug, will work just as well.

10 Refit the oil gallery plugs, using new sealing washers or sealant where applicable.

11 Where applicable, check the oil holes in the piston oil spray jet securing bolts, and the oil holes in the jets themselves for blockage

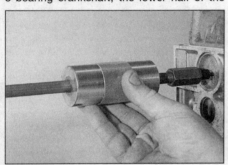

11.1a Using a slide hammer to remove a core plug

11.1b Removing a piston oil spray jet – 300 TDi engine

11.8 Using a tap to clean an cylinder block bolt thread

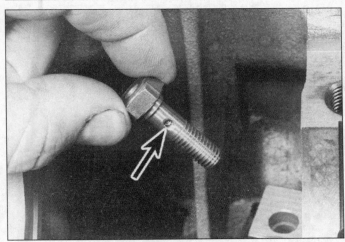

11.11 Check the oil holes (arrowed) in the piston oil jet securing bolts for blockage – 300 TDi engine

12.2 Using a feeler blade to aid removal of a piston ring

(see illustration). Clean if necessary, then refit the jets and tighten the securing bolts. Ensure that the locating pegs on the jets engage with the corresponding holes in the cylinder block. Where applicable, ensure that the larger diameter sealing washer fits under the bolt head.

12 If the engine is not going to be reassembled right away, cover it with a large plastic bag, to keep it clean and prevent it rusting.

13 On 200 TDi engines, thoroughly clean both the cylinder block and sump mating faces of the ladder frame, and remove all traces of old sealant.

Inspection

14 Visually check the block for cracks, rust and corrosion. Look for stripped threads in the threaded holes. If there has been any history of internal water leakage, it may be worthwhile having an engine overhaul specialist check the block with special equipment. If defects are found, have the block repaired, if possible, or renewed.

15 Check the cylinder bores for scuffing and scoring. Normally, bore wear will be evident in the form of a wear ridge at the top of the bore. This ridge marks the limit of piston travel.

16 If in doubt, or there is any sign of wear, have the cylinder bores inspected and measured by an engine reconditioning specialist. If necessary, they will be able to rebore the cylinder block, and supply suitable pistons. **Note:** *On TD5 engines, it is not permissible to rebore the cylinders, consequently no oversize pistons are available. If worn or damaged, the engine block must be renewed.*

17 If the cylinders are in reasonably good condition, then it may only be necessary to renew the piston rings.

18 If this is the case, the bores should be honed, in order to allow the new rings to bed-in correctly and provide the best possible seal. The conventional type of hone has spring-loaded stones, and is used with a power drill. You will also need some paraffin or honing oil

and rags. The hone should be moved up-and-down the cylinder to produce a crosshatch pattern, and plenty of honing oil should be used. Ideally, the crosshatch lines should intersect at approximately a 60° angle. Do not take off more material than is necessary to produce the required finish. If new pistons are being fitted, the piston manufacturers may specify a finish with a different angle, so their instructions should be followed. Do not withdraw the hone from the cylinder while it is still being turned – stop it first. After honing a cylinder, wipe out all traces of the honing oil. If equipment of this type is not available, or if you are not sure whether you are competent to undertake the task yourself, an engine overhaul specialist will carry out the work at a moderate cost.

19 Where applicable, refit all external components and senders in their correct locations, as noted before removal.

20 On 200 TDi engines, check that the ladder frame is not distorted, and is free from burrs and damage to the mating faces, which may cause oil or gas leaks. Renew the ladder frame if it is damaged.

12 Piston/connecting rod assembly – inspection

1 Before the inspection process can begin, the piston/connecting rod assemblies must be cleaned, and the original piston rings removed from the pistons.

2 Carefully expand the old rings over the top of the pistons. The use of two or three old feeler blades will be helpful in preventing the rings dropping into empty grooves (see illustration). Note that the oil control ring has two sections.

3 Scrape away all traces of carbon from the top of the piston. A hand-held wire brush or a piece of fine emery cloth can be used, once the majority of the deposits have been scraped away.

4 Remove the carbon from the ring grooves in the piston by cleaning them using an old ring. Break the ring in half to do this. Be very careful to remove only the carbon deposits; do not remove any metal, nor nick or scratch the sides of the ring grooves. Protect your fingers – piston rings are sharp.

5 Once the deposits have been removed, clean the piston/connecting rod assembly with paraffin or a suitable solvent, and dry thoroughly. Make sure that the oil return holes in the back sides of the ring grooves are clear.

6 If the pistons and cylinder bores are not damaged or worn excessively, and if the cylinder block does not need to be rebored, the original pistons can be re-used. Normal piston wear appears as even vertical wear on the piston thrust surfaces, and slight looseness of the top ring in its groove. New piston rings, however, should always be used when the engine is reassembled.

7 Carefully inspect each piston for cracks around the skirt, at the gudgeon pin bosses, and at the piston ring lands (between the piston ring grooves).

8 Look for scoring and scuffing on the sides of the skirt, holes in the piston crown, and burned areas at the edge of the crown. If the skirt is scored or scuffed, the engine may have been suffering from overheating and/or abnormal combustion, which caused excessively-high operating temperatures. The cooling and lubricating systems should be checked thoroughly. Scorch marks on the sides of the pistons show that blow-by has occurred. A hole in the piston crown, or burned areas at the edge of the piston crown indicates that abnormal combustion has been occurring. If any of the above problems exist, the causes must be investigated and corrected, or the damage will occur again. The causes may include incorrect injection pump timing, or a faulty injector.

9 Corrosion of the piston, in the form of small pits, indicates that coolant is leaking into the

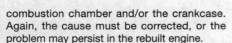

12.12a Prise out the circlip . . .

12.12b . . . and push out the gudgeon pin

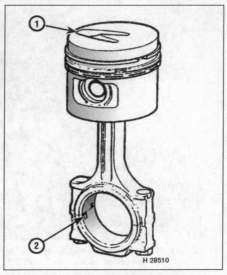

12.14a The arrow-shaped indentation in the piston crown (1) should point towards the camshaft side of the engine, and the bearing shell locating cut-outs (2) should be positioned on the same side as the head of the arrow – 12J and 19J engines

combustion chamber and/or the crankcase. Again, the cause must be corrected, or the problem may persist in the rebuilt engine.

10 If new rings are being fitted to old pistons, measure the piston ring-to-groove clearance by placing a new piston ring in each ring groove, and measuring the clearance with a feeler blade. Check the clearance at three or four places around each groove. If the measured clearance is outside the specified limits, new pistons will be required. If the new ring is excessively tight, the most likely cause is dirt remaining in the groove.

11 Check the fit of the gudgeon pin by twisting the piston and connecting rod in opposite directions. Any noticeable play indicates excessive wear, which must be corrected.

12 To separate a piston from its connecting rod, prise out the circlips and push out the gudgeon pin **(see illustrations)**. Hand pressure is sufficient to remove the pin. Identify the piston and rod, to ensure correct reassembly.

13 The connecting rods themselves should not be in need of renewal, unless seizure or some other major mechanical failure has occurred. Check the alignment of the connecting rods visually – if the rods are not straight, take them to an engine overhaul specialist for a more detailed check.

14 Where applicable, reassemble the pistons and rods. Make sure that the pistons are fitted the right way round, as follows:

a) *10J engines – the head of the arrow-shaped indentation in the piston crown should point towards the camshaft side of the engine, and the connecting rod oil spray hole should be on the same side as the head of the arrow.*

b) *12J and 19J engines – the head of the arrow-shaped indentation in the piston crown should point towards the camshaft side of the engine, and the bearing shell locating cut-outs in the connecting rod and bearing cap should be positioned on the same side as the head of the arrow (see illustration).*

c) *200 TDi and 300 TDi engines – the arrow on the piston crown should point towards the timing belt end of the engine, and the bearing shell locating cut-outs in the connecting rod and bearing cap should be positioned on the camshaft side of the cylinder block (see illustrations).*

d) *TD5 engines – the arrow on the piston crown must be on the same side as the cast boss on the connecting rod.*

15 Oil the gudgeon pins before fitting them. When assembled, the piston should pivot freely on the rod.

16 Before refitting the rings to the pistons, check their end gaps by inserting each of them in their cylinder bores. Use the piston to make sure that they are square. Check that the gaps are within the specified limits **(see illustration)**. Land Rover rings are supplied pregapped; no attempt should be made to adjust the gaps by filing.

17 Once the ring end gaps have been checked, the rings can be fitted to the pistons. **Note:** *Early 10J engines have a fifth piston ring groove located at the bottom of the piston skirt. This groove is provided for the fitment of an additional oil control ring in cases of excessively high oil consumption on high-mileage engines – consult a Land Rover dealer for details of fitting. Normally, a single oil control ring and three compression rings should be fitted to the four ring grooves at the top of the piston skirt.*

18 Fit the piston rings using the same technique as for removal. Fit the bottom (oil control) ring first, and work up. When fitting the oil control ring, first insert the expander, then fit the ring. Where applicable, ensure that the TOP marking on the face of the piston ring faces the piston crown. Also note that, where applicable, the polished chrome compression

12.14b The arrow on the piston crown should point toward the timing belt end of the engine . . .

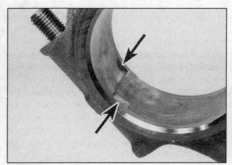

12.14c . . . and the bearing shell locating cut-outs (arrowed) should be on the camshaft side of the cylinder block – 200 TDi and 300 TDi engines

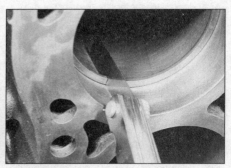

12.16 Measuring a piston ring end gap

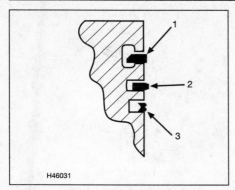

H46031

12.18 Piston ring identification – TD5 engines

1 Top compression ring
2 Middle compression ring
3 Oil control ring

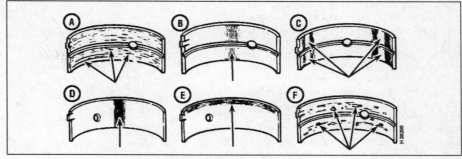

14.2 Typical bearing failures

A Scratched by dirt; dirt embedded into bearing material
B Lack of oil; overlay wiped out
C Improper seating; bright (polished) sections
D Tapered journal; overlay gone from entire surface
E Radius ride
F Fatigue failure; craters or pockets

ring fits in the top piston ring groove – do not mix up the compression rings, as they have different cross-sections. On TD5 engines, identify the top and middle compression rings from their cross-sectional profile **(see illustration)**. Note that the piston ring end gaps must be correctly positioned before refitting the piston/connecting rod assemblies to the engine – see Section 17.

13 Crankshaft – inspection

1 Clean the crankshaft using paraffin or a suitable solvent, and dry it, preferably with compressed air if available. Be sure to clean the oil holes with a pipe cleaner or similar probe, to ensure that they are not obstructed.

⚠ **Warning: Wear eye protection when using compressed air.**

2 Check the main and big-end bearing journals for uneven wear, scoring, pitting and cracking.

3 Big-end bearing wear is accompanied by distinct metallic knocking when the engine is running, particularly noticeable when the engine is pulling from low revs, and some loss of oil pressure.

4 Main bearing wear is accompanied by severe engine vibration and rumble – getting progressively worse as engine revs increase – and again by loss of oil pressure.

5 Check the bearing journal for roughness by running a finger lightly over the bearing surface. Any roughness (which will be accompanied by obvious bearing wear) indicates that the crankshaft requires regrinding.

6 If the crankshaft has been reground, check for burrs around the crankshaft oil holes (the holes are usually chamfered, so burrs should not be a problem, unless regrinding has been carried out carelessly). Remove any burrs with a fine file or scraper, and thoroughly clean the oil holes as described previously.

7 Take the crankshaft to an engine reconditioning specialist for inspection. If the crankshaft journals are worn or damaged, it may be possible to have the crankshaft reground, and new bearing shells supplied. **Note:** It is not possible to regrind the journals on TD5 engines. If damaged or worn, the crankshaft must be renewed.

8 Check the oil seal contact surfaces at each end of the crankshaft for wear and damage. If the seal has worn an excessive groove in the surface of the crankshaft, consult an engine overhaul specialist, who will be able to advise whether a repair is possible or whether a new crankshaft is necessary.

14 Main and big-end bearings – inspection

1 Even though the main and big-end bearings should be renewed during engine overhaul, the old bearings should be retained for close examination, as they may reveal valuable information about the condition of the engine. The bearing shells carry identification marks to denote their size, in the form of a code marked on the back of the shell. If the shells are to be renewed, without carrying out any crankshaft regrinding, the old shells should be taken along when obtaining new shells, to ensure that the correct shells are obtained.

2 Bearing failure occurs because of lack of lubrication, the presence of dirt or other foreign particles, overloading the engine, or corrosion **(see illustration)**. If a bearing fails, the cause must be found and eliminated before the engine is reassembled, to prevent the failure happening again.

3 To examine the bearing shells, remove them from the cylinder block, the main bearing caps, the connecting rods and the big-end bearing caps, and lay them out on a clean surface, in the same order as they were fitted to the engine. This will enable any bearing problems

to be matched with the corresponding crankshaft journal.

4 Dirt and other foreign particles can enter the engine in a variety of ways. Contamination may be left in the engine during assembly, or it may pass through filters or the crankcase ventilation system. Normal engine wear produces small particles of metal, which can eventually cause problems. If particles find their way into the lubrication system, it is likely that they will eventually be carried to the bearings. Whatever the source, these foreign particles often end up embedded in the soft bearing material, and are easily recognised. Large particles will not embed in the bearing, and will score or gouge the bearing and journal. To prevent possible contamination, clean all parts thoroughly and keep everything spotlessly-clean during engine assembly. Once the engine has been installed in the vehicle, ensure that regular engine oil and filter changes are carried out at the recommended intervals.

5 Lack of lubrication (or lubrication breakdown) has a number of interrelated causes. Excessive heat (which thins the oil), overloading (which squeezes the oil from the bearing face) and oil leakage (from excessive bearing clearances, worn oil pump or high engine speeds) all contribute to lubrication breakdown. Blocked oil passages, which may be the result of misaligned oil holes in a bearing shell, will also starve a bearing of oil, and destroy it. When lack of lubrication is the cause of bearing failure, the bearing material is wiped or extruded from the steel backing of the bearing. Temperatures may increase to the point where the steel backing turns blue from overheating.

6 Driving habits can have a definite effect on bearing life. Full-throttle, low-speed operation (labouring the engine) puts very high loads on bearings, which tends to squeeze out the oil film. These loads cause the bearings to flex, which produces fine cracks in the bearing face (fatigue failure). Eventually the bearing

material will loosen in pieces, and tear away from the steel backing. Regular short journeys can lead to corrosion of bearings, because insufficient engine heat is produced to drive off the condensed water and corrosive gases which form inside the engine. These products collect in the engine oil, forming acid and sludge. As the oil is carried to the bearings, the acid attacks and corrodes the bearing material.

7 Incorrect bearing installation during engine assembly will also lead to bearing failure. Tight-fitting bearings leave insufficient bearing lubrication clearance, and will result in oil starvation. Dirt or foreign particles trapped behind a bearing shell results in high spots on the bearing, which can lead to failure.

15 Engine overhaul – reassembly sequence

1 Before reassembly begins, ensure that all new parts have been obtained, and that all necessary tools are available. Read through the entire procedure, to familiarise yourself with the work involved, and to ensure that all items necessary for reassembly of the engine are at hand. In addition to all normal tools and materials, a thread-locking compound will be needed. Note also that certain nuts and bolts must be renewed when reassembling the engine.

2 In order to save time and avoid problems, engine reassembly can be carried out in the following order:
a) Crankshaft.
b) Pistons/connecting rod assemblies.
c) Ladder frame (200 TDi engine only).
d) Flywheel housing and flywheel (flywheel only on TD5 engines).
e) Oil pump (oil pump/stiffener plate on TD5 engines).
f) Timing belt housing (where applicable).
g) Camshaft.
h) Camshaft carrier (TD5 engines).
i) Timing chain/belt.
j) Timing chain cover (TD5 engines).
k) Sump.
l) Cylinder head.
m) Engine external components (use appropriate new gaskets and seals where necessary).

16 Crankshaft – refitting

1 Refit the piston cooling/lubrication jets to the engine block at the base of the cylinder bores (where applicable). Tighten the retaining bolts to the specified torque.

2 Clean the backs of the bearing shells, and the bearing recesses in both the cylinder block and main bearing caps. If new shells are being fitted, ensure that all traces of the protective

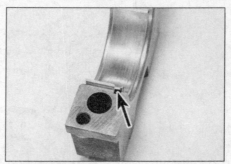

16.3 Ensure that the tag on the bearing shell engages with the cut-out in the cap (arrowed)

grease are cleaned off, using paraffin. **Note:** *Land Rover insist that new shells are fitted whenever the bearing caps are removed.*

Non-TD5 engines

3 Press the bearing shells without oil holes into the caps, ensuring that the tag on the shell engages in the cut-out in the cap **(see illustration)**. Note that the rear bearing shells are wider than the remaining bearing shells.

4 Press the bearing shells with the oil holes/grooves into the recesses in the cylinder block. Note that if the original main bearing shells are being re-used, these must be refitted to their original locations in the block and caps.

5 Using a little grease, stick the thrustwashers to each side of the centre main bearing location in the crankcase. Ensure that the oilway grooves on each thrustwasher face outwards from the bearing location, towards the crankshaft webs **(see illustration)**.

Early 10J engines with 3-bearing crankshaft

6 Before fitting the crankshaft, fit a new crankshaft rear oil seal as follows **(see illustration)**.

7 If not already done, unbolt the upper half

16.5 Fitting the thrustwashers

of the oil seal retainer from the rear of the cylinder block.

8 Loop the new oil seal coil spring around the oil seal journal on the crankshaft, then hook the spring ends together.

9 Open the split in the new oil seal just enough to pass the seal over the crankshaft journal. The seal lips should face in, towards the timing chain of the engine.

10 With the spring ends hooked together, carefully push the spring into the seal recess (in the timing chain side of the oil seal) using a small screwdriver. Position the joint in the spring 90° from the split in the oil seal.

11 Smear a trace of sealing compound on the seal recess of the upper half of the oil seal retainer, then refit the retainer to the cylinder block. Do not fully tighten the bolts at this stage.

12 Lightly grease the outer surface of the oil seal.

TD5 engines

13 Locate the new, grooved bearing shells in their locations in the engine block, and locate the new thrustwashers either side of No 3 main bearing. Ensure the grooves on the thrustwashers face outwards.

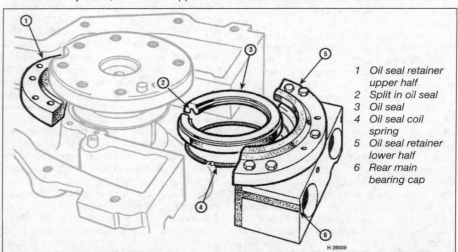

1 Oil seal retainer upper half
2 Split in oil seal
3 Oil seal
4 Oil seal coil spring
5 Oil seal retainer lower half
6 Rear main bearing cap

16.6 Crankshaft rear oil seal components – early 10J engines with 3-bearing crankshaft

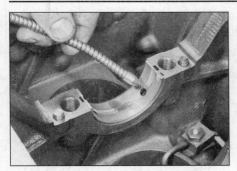

16.14 Lubricate the bearing shells

16.18 Fit the seals to No 5 main bearing cap

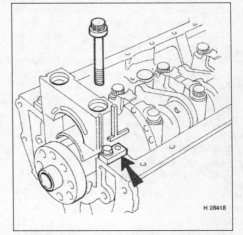

16.20 No 5 main bearing cap seal guide tool (arrowed) in position on cylinder block

All engines

14 Lubricate the bearing surfaces and thrustwashers with clean engine oil (see illustration).

15 Lower the crankshaft into position. On early 10J engines with a 3-bearing crankshaft, position the crankshaft rear oil seal so that the split in the seal is facing vertically towards the top of the engine – as the crankshaft is lowered, make sure that the seal fits into the recess in the upper half of the seal retainer without distorting.

Non-TD5 engines

16 Lubricate the bearing shells, then fit Nos 1 to 4 bearing caps (Nos 1 and 2 bearing caps on early 10J engines with a 3-bearing crankshaft) in their numbered or previously-noted locations. Ensure that the caps locate correctly over the dowels.

17 To prevent the possibility of the rear main bearing cap oil seals becoming trapped between the bearing cap and the crankcase, chamfer the lower inner edge of each seal to between 0.40 and 0.80 mm wide.

18 Smear the seals with clean engine oil, then locate the seals in the bearing cap. Do not trim the seals (see illustration).

19 On early 10J engines with a 3-bearing crankshaft, loosen the bolts securing the lower half of the rear crankshaft oil seal retainer to the rear bearing cap. Smear a trace of sealing compound on the seal recess of the retainer.

20 To prevent damage to the rear main bearing cap oil seals, make up two seal guide

tools. Ensure that the tools are fitted parallel to the edge of the cylinder block, and use two of the sump bolts to secure them. Alternatively, two old feeler blades can be used to protect the seals as the bearing cap is fitted (see illustration).

21 If feeler blades are to be used to protect the seals, lay the feeler blades in position between the cylinder block and the bearing cap. Carefully fit the bearing cap, complete with the bearing shell (see illustration). If feeler blades have been used, withdraw the feeler blades as the bearing cap is pushed into position. If guide tools have been used, remove the tools once the bearing cap is in position. On early 10J engines with a 3-bearing crankshaft, make sure that the crankshaft rear oil seal fits into the recess in the lower half of the seal retainer without distorting.

22 Fit new main bearing cap bolts, noting that

on 300 TDi engines, the bolts with the threaded holes for the oil pick-up pipe should be fitted to No 4 bearing cap, and progressively tighten the bolts to the specified torque, working outwards from the centre bearing cap (see illustrations).

23 Trim the rear main bearing cap seals to approximately 0.80 mm above the face of the cylinder block. Also trim the seals flush with end face of cylinder block (see illustrations).

24 On early 10J engines with a 3-bearing crankshaft, ensure that the rear oil seal is correctly located in the two halves of the rear oil seal retainer, and that the seal is free from

16.21 Feeler blades (arrowed) in position to protect No 5 main bearing cap seals

16.22a Fit the main bearing cap bolts with the threaded holes to No 4 bearing cap

16.22b Tighten the main bearing cap bolts to the specified torque

16.23a Using a 0.80 mm feeler blade and knife to trim the No 5 main bearing cap seals

16.23b Trimming No 5 main bearing cap seal flush with the end face of the cylinder block

distortion. Tighten the oil seal retainer securing bolts by passing a socket through the cut-out in the crankshaft flange. Make sure that the heads of the hexagon bolts are positioned so that they will not foul the flywheel housing sealing ring when it is fitted.

25 Check that the crankshaft is free to turn. Some stiffness is normal if new components have been fitted, but there must be no jamming or tight spots.

26 Refit the flywheel housing as follows, according to engine type.

Early 10J engines with 3-bearing crankshaft

27 Thoroughly clean the O-ring recess in the flywheel housing, then fit a new O-ring to the recess.

28 Refit the housing (use the two locating dowels in the cylinder block to guide the housing into position) and tighten the securing bolts to the specified torque.

Later 10J engines with 5-bearing crankshaft, and 12J and 19J engines

29 Fit a new crankshaft rear oil seal to the flywheel housing, with reference to Chapter 2A.

30 Wind a length of thin tape around the end of the crankshaft flange, to prevent damage to the oil seal lips as the housing is refitted.

31 Proceed as follows, according to whether the flywheel housing is sealed to the cylinder block using an O-ring or sealant.

a) *Flywheel housing sealed using O-ring – proceed as described in paragraphs 39 and 40. Take care not to damage the crankshaft oil seal as the housing is fitted, and remove the protective tape from the crankshaft flange on completion.*

b) *Flywheel housing sealed using sealant – thoroughly clean all traces of old sealant from the mating faces of the housing. Apply a bead of sealant to the face of the flywheel housing, to the dimensions and configuration shown* **(see illustration)**. *Refit the housing (use the two locating dowels in the cylinder block to guide the housing into position) and tighten the securing bolts to the specified torque. Take care not to damage the crankshaft oil seal as the housing is fitted, and remove the protective tape from the crankshaft flange on completion.*

Early 200 TDi engines

32 On early models, the mating faces of the cylinder block and flywheel housing are sealed using a bead of RTV sealant in an annular groove around the oil seal housing. No gasket was fitted in production, but note that a gasket may have been fitted if the housing has been removed previously during service.

33 Thoroughly clean away all traces of old sealant (and gasket, where applicable) before refitting.

34 Fit a new crankshaft rear oil seal to the flywheel housing, with reference to Chapter 2A.

35 When refitting the flywheel housing, fill the groove in the housing with RTV sealant, and use a new gasket (as used on later models, available from a Land Rover dealers) between the mating faces, even if no gasket was originally fitted.

36 Wind a length of tape around the end of the crankshaft, to prevent damage to the crankshaft oil seal as the flywheel housing is fitted. Ensure that the flywheel housing engages with the dowels in the cylinder block.

37 Refit the securing bolts, ensuring that any brackets are in position as noted before removal, and tighten the bolts to the specified torque.

38 Remove the tape from the end of the crankshaft.

Later 200 TDi engines

39 On later models, the mating faces of the cylinder block and flywheel housing are sealed using a gasket.

40 Thoroughly clean away all traces of old gasket before refitting.

41 Fit a new crankshaft rear oil seal to the flywheel housing, with reference to Chapter 2A.

42 Wind a length of tape around the end of the crankshaft, to prevent damage to the crankshaft oil seal as the flywheel housing is fitted, then refit the flywheel housing using a new gasket. Ensure that the flywheel housing engages with the dowels in the cylinder block.

43 Refit the flywheel housing securing bolts, ensuring that any brackets are in position as noted before removal, and tighten the bolts to the specified torque.

44 Remove the tape from the end of the crankshaft.

300 TDi engines

45 On 300 TDi engines, the mating faces of the cylinder block and flywheel housing are sealed using RTV sealant around the periphery of the cylinder block mating face.

46 Thoroughly clean away all traces of old sealant from the cylinder block and flywheel housing before refitting. Also clean the crankshaft rear oil seal housing mating face of the cylinder block.

47 Apply a bead of suitable RTV sealant to the periphery of the cylinder block mating face, then fit the flywheel housing **(see illustration)**. Ensure that the flywheel housing engages with the dowels in the cylinder block.

48 Refit the securing bolts, ensuring that any brackets are in position as noted before removal, and tighten the bolts to the specified torque. Note that the longer, shouldered bolts fit at the top.

49 Clean away any surplus sealant.

50 Fit a new crankshaft rear oil seal assembly as described in Chapter 2A.

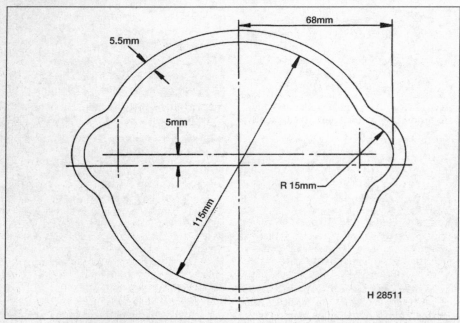

16.31 Flywheel housing sealant bead dimensions – later 10J, 12J and 19J engines

16.47 Apply a bead of RTV sealant to the flywheel housing mating face of the cylinder block – 300 TDi engine

17.1 Tapping a big-end bolt from a connecting rod

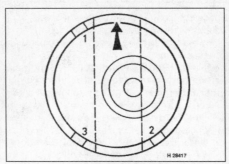

17.4 Piston ring end gap positions (viewed from top of piston)

1 *Top compression ring gap*
2 *Lower compression ring gap*
3 *Oil control ring gap*

17.5a Insert the piston and connecting rod into the cylinder with a piston ring compressor fitted . . .

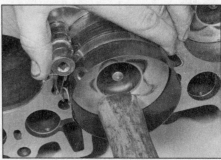

17.5b . . . then drive the piston into the cylinder

TD5 engines

51 Fit the new plain bearing shells into the main bearing caps, then lubricate the crankshaft journals, and refit the bearing caps. Ensure the caps are refitted to their original positions, aligning the previously-made marks.

52 Fit the new main bearing cap bolts, and starting with No 3 cap and working outwards, tighten all of the bolts to the Stage 1 torque setting. Working in the same sequence, tighten the bolts to the Stage 2 angle-tightening setting. **Note:** *Do not lubricate the main bearing cap retaining bolt threads prior to fitting.*

53 Check that the crankshaft is free to rotate, and fit a new rear crankshaft oil seal as described in Chapter 2B.

17 Piston/connecting rod assembly – refitting

Note: *A piston ring compressor tool will be required for this operation. New big-end bolts and nuts must be used on refitting.*

Non-TD5 engines

1 Remove the big-end bolts from the connecting rods (carefully tap them out using a hammer if necessary), and fit new bolts **(see illustration)**. Where applicable, ensure that the eccentrics on the bolt heads locate correctly in the connecting rod recesses.

All engines

2 Clean the backs of the big-end bearing shells and the recesses in the connecting rods and big-end caps. If new shells are being fitted, ensure that all traces of the protective grease are cleaned off, using paraffin. Wipe the shells and connecting rods dry with a lint-free cloth.

3 Press the big-end bearing shells into the connecting rods and caps, in their correct locations if the original shells are to be re-used. Make sure that the locating tabs on the shells are engaged with the cut-outs in the connecting rods and bearing caps. **Note:** *On TD5 engines, 'Sputter' type bearing shells are fitted to the connecting rod. These are easily*

identified as they are darker in colour than the shells fitted into the connecting rod caps. No locating tabs are fitted to TD5 engines.

4 Lubricate No 1 piston and piston rings, and check that the piston ring end gaps are correctly positioned. Position the ring end gaps as follows:

a) *10J, 12J and 19J engines – align the oil control ring gap with the gudgeon pin, on the manifold side of the engine. Arrange the compression rings so that the ring gaps are equidistantly spaced around the piston, but so arranged that no ring gap is positioned on the thrust side of the piston.*

b) *200 TDi and 300 TDi engines – position the oil control ring gap to the manifold side of the piston (the left-hand side when viewed with the arrow on the piston crown pointing forwards). Arrange the gaps of the middle and upper rings 90° either side of the oil control ring gap, but make sure that no gap is positioned on the thrust side of the piston (see illustration).*

c) *TD5 engines – position the ring gaps at 120° to each other, and away from the thrust- (left-hand side) of the piston.*

Note: *Always follow the instructions supplied with the new piston ring sets – different manufacturers may specify different procedures.*

5 Fit a ring compressor to No 1 piston, then insert the piston and connecting rod into No 1 cylinder. On 10J, 12J and 19J engines, the head of the arrow-shaped indentation in the piston crown should point towards the camshaft side of the engine. On 200 TDi and 300 TDi engines, the arrow on the piston crown should point towards the timing belt end of the engine, and the combustion chamber in the piston crown should be on the camshaft side of the engine. On TD5 engines, the arrow on the piston crown should point towards the front of the engine. With No 1 crankpin at its lowest point, drive the piston carefully into the cylinder with the wooden handle of a hammer, at the same time guiding the connecting

onto the crankpin **(see illustrations)**. Take great care not to damage the piston cooling/lubrication jets.

6 Liberally lubricate the crankpin journals and big-end bearing shells. Fit the bearing caps, ensuring the previously-made marks align. Lightly oil the threads, then tighten the new bearing cap nuts/bolts to the specified torque, and turn the crankshaft each time to make sure that it is free before moving on to the next assembly.

10J, 12J and 19J engines

7 Refit the oil pump, the sump and the cylinder head, as described in Chapter 2A.

200 TDi engine

Note: *Since the sealant used to seal the ladder frame to the cylinder block and the sump to the ladder frame cures within 15 minutes, it is important that the ladder frame, oil pump and sump are fitted together without undue delay.*

8 Check that the cylinder block and sump mating faces of the ladder frame are clean.

9 Apply Hylogrip Primer to the mating faces of the cylinder block and the ladder frame. This will clean the surfaces, and speed up curing of the sealant.

10 Apply RTV sealant to the joint between the cylinder block and the flywheel housing at the ladder frame mating face.

11 Apply Hylogrip 2000 to the cylinder block mating face of the ladder frame, then loosely fit the ladder frame to the cylinder block.

12 Fit the bolts securing the ladder frame to

the cylinder block, and the four bolts securing the ladder frame to the flywheel housing, then tighten the bolts to the specified torque.

13 Refit the oil pump, the sump and the cylinder head, as described in Chapter 2A.

300 TDi engine

14 Check the oil strainer gauze, and the pick-up pipe for obstructions, and clean the assembly thoroughly before refitting.

15 Refit the oil return pipe, using a new gasket. Coat the threads of the securing bolts with suitable thread-locking compound, and tighten the bolts to the specified torque.

16 Refit the oil strainer using a new pick-up pipe O-ring. Coat the threads of the securing bolts with suitable thread-locking compound, and tighten the bolts to the specified torque.

17 Refit the sump and the cylinder head, as described in Chapter 2A.

TD5 engine

18 Refit the oil pump/stiffener plate, the sump and the cylinder head, as described in Chapter 2B.

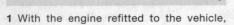

18 Engine –
initial start-up after overhaul

1 With the engine refitted to the vehicle, check the engine oil and coolant levels, and check that the battery is well charged.

2 Prime the fuel system as described in Chapter 4A or 4B.

3 On 19J, 200 TDi and 300 TDi engines, before starting the engine, the turbocharger **must** be primed with oil as follows. Failure to carry out this procedure may result in serious (and expensive) damage to the turbocharger:

 a) *Unscrew the oil feed pipe banjo bolt from the top of the turbocharger housing. Recover the two sealing washers, and move the feed pipe away from the oil hole in the housing.*

 b) *Fill the housing with clean engine oil of the correct type and grade, from a freshly-opened sealed container.*

 c) *Reconnect the oil feed pipe, and refit the banjo bolt, ensuring that one sealing washer is positioned on each side of the pipe. Tighten the banjo bolt to the specified torque.*

4 Prime the remainder of the lubrication circuit by disconnecting the stop solenoid (non-TD5 engines) and cranking the engine on the starter motor in several ten-second bursts, pausing for half a minute or so between each burst. Reconnect the solenoid when satisfied that oil pressure has been established (ensure that the oil pressure

warning light on the facia extinguishes when the engine is cranked).

5 Start the engine using the recommended cold-starting procedure. Additional cranking may be necessary to bleed the fuel system before the engine starts.

6 Once started, keep the engine running at fast tickover. Check that the oil pressure light goes out, then check that there are no leaks of oil, fuel or coolant. Where applicable, check the power steering pipe/hose unions for leakage. Do not be alarmed if there are some odd smells and smoke from parts getting hot and burning off oil deposits.

7 Keep the engine idling until hot coolant is felt circulating through the radiator top hose, indicating that the engine is at normal operating temperature, then stop the engine and allow it to cool.

8 Recheck the oil and coolant levels, and top-up if necessary.

9 Check the fuel injection pump timing and the idle speed as described in Chapter 4A (non-TD5 engines).

10 If new pistons, rings or bearings have been fitted, the engine must be run-in at reduced speeds and loads for the first 500 miles or so. Do not operate the engine at full throttle, or allow it to labour in any gear during this period. It is beneficial to change the engine oil and filter at the end of this period.

Chapter 3
Cooling, heating and ventilation systems

Contents

	Section number
Air conditioning compressor drivebelt – check and renewal	See Chapter 1
Air conditioning system – general information and precautions	10
Air conditioning system components – removal and refitting	11
Air conditioning system refrigerant check	See Chapter 1
Antifreeze mixture	See Chapter 1
Coolant level check	See Chapter 1
Coolant pump – removal and refitting	7
Coolant temperature gauge sender – testing, removal and refitting	6

	Section number
Cooling fan and cowling – removal and refitting	5
Cooling system – draining, flushing and refilling	See Chapter 1
Cooling system hoses – disconnection and renewal	2
General information and precautions	1
Heater/ventilation components – removal and refitting	9
Heating and ventilation system – general information	8
Radiator – removal, inspection and refitting	3
Thermostat – removal, testing and refitting	4

Degrees of difficulty

Easy, suitable for novice with little experience	**Fairly easy,** suitable for beginner with some experience	**Fairly difficult,** suitable for competent DIY mechanic	**Difficult,** suitable for experienced DIY mechanic	**Very difficult,** suitable for expert DIY or professional

Specifications

General

Expansion tank cap opening pressure:
All except TD5 engines	1.0 bar
TD5 engines	1.4 bar

Thermostat

Opening temperatures:
300 TDi engine	88°C
All other engines	82°C

Torque wrench setting

	Nm	lbf ft
Coolant pump nut/bolts:		
Non-TD5 engines	25	18
TD5 engines	10	7
Coolant temperature sensor	20	15

---

1 General information and precautions

General information

The cooling system is of pressurised type, consisting of a belt-driven coolant pump, an aluminium crossflow radiator (incorporating an engine oil cooler), the cooling fan, and a thermostat. On TD5 engines, the coolant pump is attached to, and driven by, the power steering pump, which in turn is driven by the

auxiliary drivebelt. The system functions as follows. Cold coolant from the radiator passes through the hose to the coolant pump, where it is pumped around the cylinder block and head passages. After cooling the cylinder bores, combustion surfaces and valve seats, the coolant reaches the underside of the thermostat, which is initially closed. The coolant passes through the heater, and is returned via the cylinder block to the coolant pump.

When the engine is cold, the coolant circulates only through the cylinder block, cylinder head, expansion tank and heater.

When the coolant reaches a predetermined temperature, the thermostat opens and the coolant passes through to the radiator. As the coolant circulates through the radiator, it is cooled by the inrush of air when the car is in forward motion. Upon reaching the radiator, the coolant is now cooled, and the cycle is repeated.

On all models, except a few early models, the cooling fan is driven via a viscous coupling. The viscous coupling varies the fan speed according to engine temperature. At low temperatures, the coupling provides very little resistance between the fan and pump pulley, so only a slight amount of drive is transmitted to the cooling fan. As the temperature of the coupling increases, so does its internal resistance, therefore increasing drive to the cooling fan.

Refer to Section 10 for information on the air conditioning system.

Precautions

⚠ *Warning: Do not attempt to remove the expansion tank filler cap, nor disturb any part of the cooling system, while the engine is hot, as there is a high risk of scalding. If the expansion tank filler cap must be removed before the engine and radiator have fully cooled (even though this is not recommended) the pressure in the cooling system must first be relieved. Cover the cap with a thick layer of cloth, to avoid scalding, and slowly unscrew the filler cap until a hissing sound can be heard. When the hissing has stopped, indicating that the pressure has reduced, slowly unscrew the filler cap until it can be removed; if more hissing sounds are heard, wait until they have stopped before unscrewing the cap completely. At all times keep well away from the filler cap opening.*

⚠ *Warning: Do not allow antifreeze to come into contact with skin, or with the painted surfaces of the vehicle. Rinse off spills immediately with plenty of water. Never leave antifreeze lying around in an open container, or in a puddle in the driveway or on the garage floor. Children and pets are attracted by its sweet smell, but antifreeze can be fatal if ingested.*

⚠ *Warning: Refer to Section 10 for precautions to be observed when working on models with air conditioning.*

2 Cooling system hoses – disconnection and renewal

Note: *Refer to the warnings given in Section 1 of this Chapter before proceeding.*
1 If the checks described in Chapter 1 reveal a faulty hose, it must be renewed as follows.
2 First drain the cooling system (see Chapter 1). If the coolant is not due for renewal, it may be re-used if it is collected in a clean container.
3 To disconnect a hose, use a screwdriver to slacken the clips, then move them along the hose, clear of the relevant inlet/outlet union. On some models, the clips are released by squeezing together the tangs at the ends of the clips. This can be achieved using pliers/ pipe grips, or using a tool specifically for this purpose **(see illustrations)**. Carefully work the hose free. The hoses can be removed with relative ease when new – on an older vehicle, they may have stuck.
4 If a hose proves stubborn, try to release it by rotating it on its unions before attempting to work it off. Gently prise the end of the hose with a blunt instrument (such as a flat-bladed screwdriver), but do not apply too much force, and take care not to damage the pipe stubs or hoses. Note in particular that the radiator hose unions are fragile; do not use excessive force when attempting to remove the hoses.

 HAYNES HiNT *If all else fails, cut the hose with a sharp knife, then slit it so that it can be peeled off in two pieces. While expensive, this is preferable to buying a new radiator. Check first, however, that a new hose is readily available.*

5 When fitting a hose, first slide the clips onto the hose, then work the hose into position. If clamp-type clips were originally fitted, it is a good idea to update them with screw-type clips when refitting the hose. If the hose is stiff, use a little soapy water as a lubricant, or soften the hose by soaking it in hot water.
6 Work the hose into position, checking that it is correctly routed, then slide each clip along the hose until it passes over the flared end of the relevant inlet/outlet union, before tightening the clips securely.
7 Refill the cooling system with reference to Chapter 1.
8 Check thoroughly for leaks as soon as possible after disturbing any part of the cooling system.

3 Radiator – removal, inspection and refitting

 HAYNES HiNT *If leakage is the reason for wanting to remove the radiator, bear in mind that minor leaks can be often be cured using a radiator sealant, with the radiator in situ.*

Removal

1 If necessary, to improve access, remove the bonnet as described in Chapter 12. On TD5 models, undo the screws and remove the front grille, then remove the 4 screws, 2 bolts and the grille support panel **(see illustration)**. On air conditioned models, undo the 6 screws and remove the grille complete with the surround panel.
2 Drain the cooling system as described in Chapter 1, and proceed as described under the relevant sub-heading.

10J, 12J and 19J engines

3 Slacken the retaining clips, and detach the expansion tank and top and bottom hoses from the radiator.
4 Release the retaining clips, and position the braking system vacuum pump hose clear of the radiator.
5 Where necessary, slacken the union nuts and disconnect the engine oil cooler pipes from the radiator. Be prepared for some oil spillage as the pipes are disconnected; plug the pipe and cooler unions, to minimise oil loss and to prevent dirt entering the lubrication system.
6 Slacken and remove the three nuts and washers securing the cooling fan cowl to the engine. Release the cowl from the mounting bracket, then undo the screws securing the cowl to the radiator. Free the cowl, and manoeuvre it out from the engine compartment.
7 Unscrew the mounting bracket retaining nuts and bolts, then free both mounting brackets from the radiator; recover the upper mounting rubbers.
8 Lift the radiator out from the engine compartment, and recover its lower mounting rubbers.

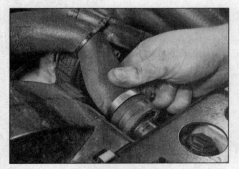

2.3a Disconnecting the radiator top hose

2.3b With spring-type clips, a tool is available to release them

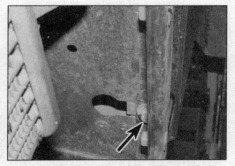

3.1 TD5 grille support panel lower bolt (arrowed)

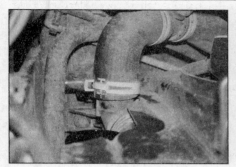

3.19a Radiator bottom hose . . .

3.19b . . . and top hose

3.20 Undo the screws (arrowed) and manoeuvre the lower radiator shroud from position

9 Examine the mounting rubbers for signs of damage or deterioration, and renew if necessary.

200 and 300 TDi engines

10 Remove the cooling fan and cowl as described in Section 5.

11 Slacken the retaining clips, and detach the expansion tank and top and bottom hoses from the radiator.

12 Slacken the union nuts, and disconnect the engine oil cooler pipes from the radiator. Be prepared for some oil spillage as the pipes are disconnected; plug the pipe and cooler unions, to minimise oil loss and to prevent dirt entering the lubrication system.

13 Slacken the retaining clips, and disconnect both hoses from the intercooler.

14 Unscrew the mounting bracket retaining nuts and bolts, then free both mounting brackets from the radiator; recover the upper mounting rubbers.

15 Lift the radiator assembly out from the engine compartment, and recover its lower mounting rubbers.

16 Examine the mounting rubbers for signs of damage or deterioration, and renew if necessary.

TD5 engines

17 Remove the cooling fan as described in Section 5.

18 Release the clip and disconnect the air hoses from the intercooler.

19 Release the clips and disconnect the coolant hoses from the radiator (see illustrations).

20 Undo the screw each side at the top, then manoeuvre the lower radiator shroud upwards and out from the engine compartment (see illustration).

21 Remove the two screws and slacken the two nuts each side securing the bonnet slam panel outer mounting brackets to the inner wings, then lock two nuts together and remove the front bracket mounting studs each side (see illustrations). Pivot the brackets rearwards and remove them.

22 Pivot the top of the radiator rearwards a little, then lift the assembly from position (see illustration). Recover the radiator lower mounting rubbers.

23 Undo the two bolts and securing the intercooler to the radiator. Recover the mounting rubbers.

Refitting

24

Refitting is the reverse of the removal procedure, noting the following points:

a) Ensure that the radiator is correctly engaged with its lower mounting rubbers, then fit the upper mounting brackets and securely tighten the retaining bolts.

b) Securely tighten all hose retaining clips and, where necessary, the oil cooler union nuts.

c) On completion, refill the cooling system as described in Chapter 1.

4 Thermostat – removal, testing and refitting

Removal

1 Drain the cooling system as described in Chapter 1, and proceed as described under the relevant sub-heading.

10J, 12J, 19J and 200 TDi engines

2 Slacken the retaining clip, and disconnect the coolant hose from the thermostat housing.

3 Disconnect the wiring connectors from the housing switch(es), where fitted, then slacken and remove the housing cover retaining bolts.

4 Remove the thermostat housing cover from the engine, and recover the housing gasket.

5 Withdraw the thermostat from its housing.

300 TDi engine

6 Slacken the retaining clip, and disconnect the coolant hose(s) from the thermostat housing.

7 Disconnect the wiring connectors from the switches screwed into the underside of the thermostat cover (where applicable).

8 Slacken and remove the retaining bolts, and

3.21a Release the two screws each side (arrowed) . . .

3.21b . . . then lock two nuts together to unscrew the panel mounting studs each side

3.22 Pivot the radiator rearwards a little, then lift it from place with the intercooler

4.8 On the 300 TDi engine, remove the housing cover, then withdraw the thermostat and recover its sealing ring (arrowed)

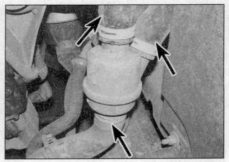

4.11 Disconnect the hoses (arrowed) from the thermostat housing

4.15 On the 300 TDi engine, on refitting ensure that the thermostat is correctly engaged with the housing cut-out (arrowed) so its TOP marking is uppermost

remove the thermostat housing cover from the engine **(see illustration)**.
9 Withdraw the thermostat from its housing, and recover its sealing ring.

TD5 engine

10 Remove the cooling fan as described in Section 5.
11 Release the three clips and disconnect the hoses from the thermostat housing **(see illustration)**. No further dismantling of the thermostat housing is possible.

Testing

12 A rough test of the thermostat may be made by suspending it with a piece of string in a container full of water. Heat the water to bring it to the boil – the thermostat must open by the time the water boils. If not, renew it.
13 If a thermometer is available, the precise opening temperature of the thermostat may be determined, and compared with the figures given in the Specifications. The opening temperature is also marked on the thermostat.
14 A thermostat which fails to close as the water cools must also be renewed.

Refitting

15 Refitting is the reverse of the relevant removal procedure, using a new gasket/sealing ring (as applicable). Make sure that the thermostat is correctly seated in its housing (where applicable) **(see illustration)**. On completion, refill the cooling system as described in Chapter 1.

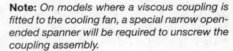

5 Cooling fan and cowling – removal and refitting

Note: *On models where a viscous coupling is fitted to the cooling fan, a special narrow open-ended spanner will be required to unscrew the coupling assembly.*

Removal

10J, 12J and 19J engines

1 Disconnect the battery negative lead, as described in Chapter 5.
2 Slacken and remove the three nuts and washers securing the cowl to the engine (where applicable), then undo the screws securing it to the top of the radiator. Free the cowl, and manoeuvre it out from the engine compartment.
3 On early models where no viscous coupling is fitted, unscrew the four retaining bolts and remove the cooling fan from the engine, complete with the spacer which is fitted between the fan and pump pulley.
4 On models with a viscous coupling, using a suitable open-ended spanner, unscrew the viscous coupling from the coolant pump shaft, and remove it from the engine compartment. **Note:** *The viscous coupling has a left-hand thread – ie, it unscrews clockwise.* If necessary, undo the four retaining bolts and separate the coupling and fan, noting which way around the fan is fitted.

200 and 300 TDi engines

5 Disconnect the battery negative lead, as described in Chapter 5.
6 Drain the cooling system as described in Chapter 1.
7 Slacken the retaining clips, and remove the top hose from the radiator. Also disconnect the top hose from the intercooler, to gain the necessary clearance to withdraw the radiator cowling.
8 Using the special open-ended spanner, unscrew the viscous coupling from the coolant pump/crankshaft **(see illustration)**. **Note:** *The viscous coupling has a left-hand thread – ie, it unscrews clockwise.*
9 Remove the fan and cowling upwards and out from the engine compartment. If necessary, slacken and remove the retaining bolts, and separate the cooling fan from the coupling, noting which way around the fan is fitted.

TD5 engines

10 Disconnect the battery negative lead, as described in Chapter 5.
11 Undo the bolts and remove the plastic cover over the top of the engine.
12 Undo the four screws and remove the cooling fan upper shroud **(see illustration)**.
13 Using the special open-ended spanner, unscrew the viscous coupling from the idler pulley **(see illustration)**. If necessary, use a large screwdriver to counterhold the coupling nut against the pulley bolts. **Note:** *The viscous*

5.8 Using the special open-ended spanner (arrowed) to slacken the viscous coupling

5.12 Cooling fan shroud right-hand bolts (arrowed) – TD5 models

5.13 Use a flat open-ended spanner to slacken the cooling fan coupling (normal right-hand thread on TD5 models)

5.15 Undo the radiator grille screws (3 left-hand side ones arrowed)

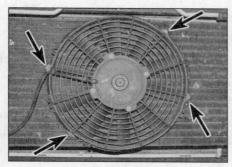

5.16 Condenser cooling fan nuts (arrowed)

6.9 Coolant temperature gauge sender (arrowed) – TD5 engine

coupling has a normal right-hand thread – ie, it unscrews anti-clockwise.

Refitting

14 Refitting is the reverse of removal, making sure that the cooling fan is fitted the correct way around. **Note:** *If the fan is fitted the wrong way around, the efficiency of the cooling system will be significantly reduced.*

Condenser cooling fan

Removal

15 Undo the 6 screws and remove the radiator grille **(see illustration).**
16 Disconnect the wiring plug, then undo the 4 nuts and remove the cooling fan assembly **(see illustration).**

Refitting

17 Refitting is a reversal of removal.

6 Coolant temperature gauge sender – testing, removal and refitting

Testing

Non-TD5 engines

1 The coolant temperature gauge is fed with a stabilised voltage supply from the instrument panel feed (via the ignition switch and a fuse), and its earth is controlled by the sender.
2 The sender is either screwed into the top of the cylinder head (early engines) or into the thermostat housing (later engines). The sender contains a thermistor (an electronic component whose electrical resistance decreases at a predetermined rate as its temperature rises). When the coolant is cold, the sender resistance is high, current flow through the gauge is reduced, and the gauge needle points towards the 'cold' end of the scale. If the sender is faulty, it must be renewed.
3 If the gauge develops a fault, first check the other instruments; if they do not work at all, check the instrument panel electrical feed. If the readings are erratic, there may be a fault in the voltage resistor, which will necessitate renewal of the printed circuit (see Chapter 13). If the fault lies in the temperature gauge alone, check it as follows.

4 If the gauge needle remains at the 'cold' end of the scale, disconnect the sender wire, and earth it to the cylinder head. If the needle then deflects when the ignition is switched on, the sender unit is proved faulty, and should be renewed. If the needle still does not move, remove the instrument panel (Chapter 13) and check the continuity of the wiring between the sender unit and the gauge, and the feed to the gauge unit. If continuity is shown, and the fault still exists, then the gauge is faulty, and the gauge unit should be renewed.
5 If the gauge needle remains at the 'hot' end of the scale, disconnect the sender wire. If the needle then returns to the 'cold' end of the scale when the ignition is switched on, the sender unit is proved faulty, and should be renewed. If the needle still does not move, check the remainder of the circuit as described previously.

TD5 engines

6 The coolant temperature sensor, located in the coolant outlet housing at the front left-hand corner of the cylinder head, provides data to the engine management ECM, which uses the data to adjust the fuelling of the engine, glow plug operation, and control the operation of the temperature gauge/warning system. The sensor is an NTC (Negative Temperature Co-efficient) sensor, meaning that as the temperature rises, the resistance of the sensor decreases. Although no specific values are given by Land Rover, it should be possible to check that the resistance of the sensor changes as the temperature changes using a digital multimeter. Should the sensor fail, a fault code should be stored in the ECM memory by the self-diagnosis system, which can be interrogated using a suitable fault code reader.

Removal

7 Either partially drain the cooling system to just below the level of the sender (as described in Chapter 1), or have ready a suitable plug which can be used to plug the sender aperture whilst it is removed. If a plug is used, take great care not to damage the sender unit threads, and do not use anything which will allow foreign matter to enter the cooling system.
8 Disconnect the battery negative lead, as described in Chapter 5.

9 Disconnect the wiring from the sender, then unscrew the unit from the thermostat housing and recover the sealing washer (where fitted) **(see illustration).**

Refitting

10 If the sender unit was fitted with a sealing washer, fit a new washer. Where no washer was fitted, ensure that the sender threads are clean, and apply a smear of suitable sealant to them. On TD5 engines, renew the sealing ring and apply Loctite 577 to the sensor threads.
11 Refit the sender, tightening it to the specified torque, and reconnect the wiring.
12 Top-up the cooling system as described in Chapter 1.
13 On completion, reconnect the battery negative lead, start the engine and check the operation of the temperature gauge. Also check for coolant leaks.

7 Coolant pump – removal and refitting

Removal – non-TD5 engines

1 Drain the cooling system as described in Chapter 1.
2 Remove the cooling fan as described in Section 5, and proceed as described under the relevant sub-heading.

10J, 12J, 19J and 200 TDi engines

3 Slacken the coolant pump pulley retaining bolts, then remove the auxiliary drivebelt(s) as described in Chapter 1.
4 Unscrew the retaining bolts (where necessary) and remove the drivebelt pulley from the pump, noting which way around it is fitted.
5 Slacken the retaining clips, and disconnect all the coolant hose(s) from the pump.
6 Evenly and progressively slacken and remove the pump retaining nut and/or bolts (as applicable). Note each bolt's correct fitted location, as they are of different lengths.
7 Remove the pump assembly from the engine, and recover the gasket.

300 TDi engine

8 Slacken the bolts securing the pulleys to the coolant pump and power steering pump.

7.12 On the 300 TDi engine, unscrew the retaining bolts . . .

7.13 . . . and remove the coolant pump from the front of the engine

7.18 Centrifugal oil filter housing bolts (arrowed)

9 Remove the auxiliary drivebelt as described in Chapter 1.

10 To improve access, undo the auxiliary drivebelt tensioner retaining nut, then slide the tensioner assembly off its retaining stud. Alternatively, the tensioner can be left in position but this will mean the tensioner arm will have to be lifted to access the lower retaining bolts.

11 Unscrew the retaining bolts and remove both the coolant pump and power steering pump drive pulleys, noting which way around each one is fitted.

12 Evenly and progressively slacken and remove the pump retaining bolts. Note each bolt's correct fitted location, as they are of different lengths (see illustration).

13 Remove the pump assembly from the engine, and recover the gasket (see illustration).

Removal – TD5 engines

14 Drain the cooling system as described in Chapter 1.

15 Raise the front of the vehicle by jacking under the vehicle chassis each side (see *Jacking and vehicle support*), then undo the fasteners and move the engine undershield to the rear. If more access is required, the front propshaft must be disconnected (Chapter 8) to completely remove the undershield.

16 Undo the two bolts securing the centrifugal oil filter drain tube to the sump. Discard the gasket.

17 Remove the turbocharger as described in Chapter 4B. On air conditioned models,

remove the auxiliary drivebelt as described in Chapter 1, then undo the bolts and move the compressor to one side. There is no need to disconnect the refrigerant hoses.

18 Unscrew the oil filter cartridge, then undo the 3 retaining bolts and remove the centrifugal oil filter housing from the oil cooler (see illustration). Discard the O-ring seal, a new one must be fitted. Manoeuvre the oil filter from place.

19 Release the clip and disconnect the coolant hose from the coolant pump cover.

20 Undo the 5 bolts and remove the coolant pump cover. Withdrawn the cover, pump and 3 O-rings from the housing (see illustrations). Discard the O-rings, new ones must be fitted.

Refitting

10J, 12J, 19J and 200 TDi engines

21 Ensure that the pump and cylinder block mating surfaces are clean and dry.

22 Apply a smear of silicone grease to the new pump gasket, and position it on the pump housing.

23 Clean the threads of the long coolant pump retaining bolts (which pass through the housing and screw into the cylinder block), and apply a smear of suitable sealant to each one's threads.

24 Install the coolant pump and refit the retaining bolts (and nut), making sure that each one is installed in its correct position. Tighten all by hand, then working in a diagonal sequence, evenly and progressively tighten them to the specified torque setting.

25 Reconnect the hose(s) to the pump, tightening each retaining clip securely.

26 Refit the drive pulley, making sure that it is the correct way around, then refit the drivebelt as described in Chapter 1. Once the belt is correctly tensioned, securely tighten the pulley retaining bolts.

27 Refit the cooling fan as described in Section 5, then refill the cooling system as described in Chapter 1.

300 TDi engine

28 Ensure that the pump and cylinder block mating surfaces are clean and dry, then fit a new gasket to the housing (see illustration).

29 Install the coolant pump and refit the retaining bolts, making sure that each one is installed in its correct position. Tighten all the bolts by hand, then working in a diagonal sequence, evenly and progressively tighten each one to the specified torque.

30 Refit the drive pulleys to the coolant and power steering pumps, making sure that both are fitted the correct way around.

31 Slide the tensioner assembly onto its stud. Make sure that the tensioner locating pins are correctly engaged with the mounting bracket, then refit the retaining nut and tighten it securely.

32 Refit the auxiliary drivebelt as described in Chapter 1, then securely tighten all the pulley retaining bolts.

33 Refit the cooling fan as described in Section 5, then refill the cooling system as described in Chapter 1.

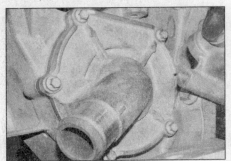

7.20a Undo the coolant pump cover bolts

7.20b Renew the 3 O-rings

7.28 On refitting, ensure that the housing mating surfaces are clean and dry, and fit a new gasket

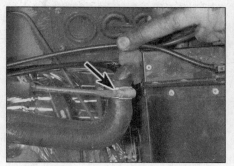

9.3a Slacken the retaining clips . . .

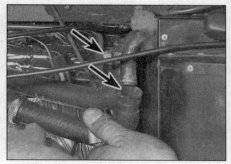

9.3b . . . and disconnect both coolant hoses from the heater unit

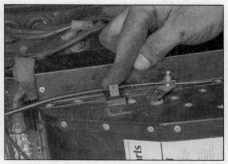

9.4 Release the retaining clips and clamps, and detach both heater control cables

TD5 engine

34 Ensure that the pump and housing mating surfaces are clean and dry, then refit the pump and cover using new O-ring seals. Tighten the cover retaining bolts to the specified torque.

35 Reconnect the hose to the pump cover, and secure it in place with the clip.

36 The remainder of refitting is a reversal of removal, remembering to top-up the cooling system as described in Chapter 1.

8 Heating and ventilation system – general information

1 The heating/ventilation system consists of a multi-speed blower motor, face-level vents in the centre and at each end of the facia, and air ducts to the front footwells.

2 The control unit is located in the facia, and the controls operate flap valves to deflect and mix the air flowing through the various parts of the heating/ventilation system. The flap valves are contained in the air distribution housing, which acts as a central distribution unit, passing air to the various ducts and vents.

3 Cold air enters the system through the grille at the side of the engine compartment.

4 The airflow, which can be boosted by the blower, then flows through the various ducts, according to the settings of the controls. Stale air is expelled through ducts at the rear of the

vehicle. If warm air is required, the cold air is passed through the heater matrix, which is heated by the engine coolant.

5 A recirculation lever enables the outside air supply to be closed off, while the air inside the vehicle is recirculated. This can be useful to prevent unpleasant odours entering from outside the vehicle, but should only be used briefly, as the recirculated air inside the vehicle will soon deteriorate in quality.

9 Heater/ventilation components – removal and refitting

Note: *The following information is only applicable to models which are not fitted with air conditioning. On models with air conditioning, it is not possible to remove any of the heater components without first discharging the air conditioning system (see Section 10). Operations involving the heater components on these models should therefore be entrusted to a Land Rover dealer or specialist.*

Heater unit assembly

1 Disconnect the battery negative terminal, as described in Chapter 5. To improve access, remove the bonnet as described in Chapter 12.

2 Using a suitable hose clamp, clamp the coolant hoses close to the matrix unions, to minimise coolant loss.

3 Slacken the retaining clips, and disconnect the coolant hoses from the heater matrix unions **(see illustrations)**.

4 Noting each cable's correct fitted location, release the outer cable retaining clips, then slacken the inner cable clamps and detach the cables from the heater unit **(see illustration)**.

5 Disconnect the heater unit wiring connector(s), and free the wiring from any necessary retaining clips **(see illustration)**.

6 From inside the vehicle, peel back the carpet from the bulkhead to reveal the heater unit lower retaining bolts.

7 Slacken and remove the lower retaining bolts, then return to the engine compartment and unscrew the upper heater unit retaining bolts **(see illustrations)**.

8 Manoeuvre the heater assembly out of position, and remove it from the vehicle. Recover the seal fitted between the unit and bulkhead. If necessary, undo the retaining screws and remove the inlet grille from the top of the wing, then undo the retaining screws securing the inlet duct to the wing; this will

> **HAYNES HiNT** *Be prepared for some coolant spillage as the heater is removed; wash off any spilt coolant immediately with cold water.*

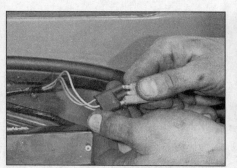

9.5 Disconnect the wiring connector . . .

9.7a . . . then slacken and remove the lower retaining nuts and bolts (arrowed) . . .

9.7b . . . and upper retaining bolts

9.8a To improve clearance, undo the retaining screws and remove the inlet grille . . .

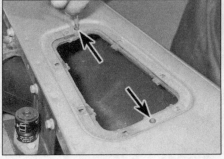

9.8b . . . then undo the two retaining screws and free the inlet duct from the wing

9.8c The heater unit can then be manoeuvred out from the engine compartment

gain extra clearance to manoeuvre the heater unit out of position (see illustrations).

9 Refitting is the reverse of removal, ensuring that an airtight seal is made between the heater unit and bulkhead.

Heater matrix

Note: *A pop-rivet gun and suitable rivets will be required on refitting.*

10 Remove the heater unit assembly as described above.

11 Taking care not to damage the casing, carefully drill out the rivets securing the top cover to the heater unit housing.

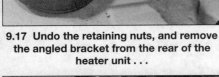

9.17 Undo the retaining nuts, and remove the angled bracket from the rear of the heater unit . . .

12 Lift off the cover and remove the rubber seal, then slide the heater matrix out from the housing. Recover the rubber seal fitted to the outside of the matrix. Examine the seals for signs of damage and deterioration, and renew if necessary.

13 On refitting, fit the seal to the heater matrix, and slide the matrix into the housing.

14 Ensure that the matrix is correctly seated, then check that the housing flap valves operate smoothly without sticking.

15 If all is well, refit the cover, securing it in position with new pop-rivets, then refit the heater unit assembly to the vehicle.

9.19 . . . then lift out the blower motor

Heater blower motor

16 Remove the heater unit assembly as described above.

17 Undo the retaining nuts and remove the angled bracket from the rear of the heater unit (see illustration).

18 Disconnect the wiring connector from the blower motor.

19 Slacken and remove the five retaining nuts and washers, and withdraw the blower motor from the rear of the housing (see illustration).

20 If necessary, release the retaining clip (see illustration), lift off the fan, then undo the retaining nuts and separate the motor and casing.

21 Refitting is the reverse of removal. To ensure an airtight seal is made between the motor and mounting, apply a smear of sealant to its mating surface.

Heater blower motor resistor

Note: *A pop-rivet gun and suitable rivets will be required on refitting.*

22 Remove the heater unit as described above.

23 Carefully drill out the rivets, and remove the resistor from the top of the heater unit (see illustrations).

24 On refitting, ensure that the mating

9.20 Fan is secured to the motor by a circlip (arrowed)

9.23a Drill out the rivets . . .

9.23b . . . then remove the blower motor resistor from the heater unit

9.25 On refitting, secure the resistor in position with new pop-rivets

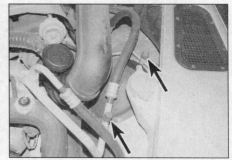

10.1 Air conditioning system high- and low-pressure service points (arrowed)

surfaces are clean and dry, and apply a smear of suitable sealant to the resistor mating surface.

25 Fit the resistor to the heater unit, and secure it in position with new pop-rivets **(see illustration)**.

10 Air conditioning system – general information and precautions

General information

An air conditioning system was offered as an optional extra on some models. It enables the temperature of incoming air to be lowered, and also dehumidifies the air, which makes for rapid demisting and increased comfort.

The cooling side of the system works in the same way as a domestic refrigerator. Refrigerant gas is drawn into a belt-driven compressor, and passes into a condenser mounted in front of the radiator, where it loses heat and becomes liquid. The liquid passes through an expansion valve to an evaporator, where it changes from liquid under high pressure to gas under low pressure. This change is accompanied by a drop in temperature, which cools the evaporator. The refrigerant returns to the compressor, and the cycle begins again.

Air blown through the evaporator passes to the air distribution unit, where it is mixed with hot air blown through the heater matrix, to achieve the desired temperature in the passenger compartment.

The heating side of the system works in the same way as on models without air conditioning (see Section 8).

The operation of the system is controlled electronically by the coolant temperature switches screwed into the thermostat housing, and the pressure switches which are screwed into the compressor high-pressure line. Any problems with the system should be referred to a Land Rover dealer or specialist **(see illustration and Tool tip)**.

Precautions

• When an air conditioning system is fitted, it is necessary to observe special precautions whenever dealing with any part of the system, its associated components and any items

TOOL TIP

Many car accessory shops sell one-shot air conditioning recharge aerosols. These generally contain refrigerant, compressor oil, leak sealer and system conditioner. Some also have a dye to help pinpoint leaks.

 Warning: These products must only be used as directed by the manufacturer, and do not remove the need for regular maintenance.

which necessitate disconnection of the system. If for any reason the system must be disconnected, entrust this task to your Land Rover dealer or a refrigeration engineer.

 Warning: The refrigeration circuit contains a liquid refrigerant under pressure, and it is dangerous to disconnect any part of the system without specialised knowledge and equipment. The refrigerant should only be handled by qualified persons. If it is splashed onto the skin, it can cause frostbite. It is not itself poisonous, but in the presence of a naked flame (including a lighted cigarette) it forms a poisonous gas. Uncontrolled discharging of the refrigerant is dangerous and potentially damaging to the environment.

• Do not operate the air conditioning system if it is known to be short of refrigerant, as this may damage the compressor.

11 Air conditioning system components – removal and refitting

 Warning: Do not attempt to open the refrigerant circuit. Refer to the precautions given in Section 10.

1 The only operation which can be carried out easily without discharging the refrigerant is renewal of the compressor drivebelt, which is covered in Chapter 1. All other operations must be referred to a Land Rover dealer or an air conditioning specialist.

2 If necessary the compressor can be unbolted and moved aside, without disconnecting its flexible hoses, after removing the drivebelt.

Notes

Chapter 4 Part A:
Fuel, exhaust and emissions control systems – non-TD5 engines

Contents

	Section number		Section number
Accelerator cable – removal, refitting and adjustment	3	Fuel system – priming and bleeding	5
Accelerator mechanism checking and lubrication	See Chapter 1	Fuel tank – removal and refitting	7
Accelerator pedal – removal and refitting	4	General information and precautions	1
Air cleaner assembly and ducting – removal and refitting	2	Idle speed – checking and adjustment	10
Air cleaner element renewal	See Chapter 1	Injection timing – checking and adjustment	13
Emissions control systems – general information	21	Injection timing – checking methods and adjustment	12
Emissions control systems – testing and component renewal	22	Intercooler (200 TDi and 300 TDi engine models) –	
Exhaust system – general information and component renewal	20	removal and refitting	18
Fuel filter element renewal	See Chapter 1	Intercooler element cleaning	See Chapter 1
Fuel gauge sender unit – removal and refitting	6	Manifolds – removal and refitting	19
Fuel injection pump – removal and refitting	11	Maximum engine speed – checking and adjustment	9
Fuel injector leak check	See Chapter 1	Turbocharger – description and precautions	15
Fuel injector spray pattern check	See Chapter 1	Turbocharger – examination and overhaul	17
Fuel injectors – testing, removal and refitting	14	Turbocharger – removal and refitting	16
Fuel lift pump – removal and refitting	8	Turbocharger boost pressure check	See Chapter 1
Fuel sedimenter cleaning	See Chapter 1		

Degrees of difficulty

| **Easy,** suitable for novice with little experience | | **Fairly easy,** suitable for beginner with some experience | | **Fairly difficult,** suitable for competent DIY mechanic | | **Difficult,** suitable for experienced DIY mechanic | | **Very difficult,** suitable for expert DIY or professional | |

Specifications

General

System type:

10J engine	Mechanical fuel lift pump, distributor fuel injection pump driven via driveshaft from camshaft, indirect injection
12J engine	Mechanical lift pump, distributor fuel injection pump driven by timing belt, indirect injection
19J engine	Mechanical lift pump, distributor fuel injection pump driven by timing belt, indirect injection. Turbocharger
200 TDi and 300 TDi engines	Mechanical fuel lift pump, distributor fuel injection pump driven by timing belt, direct injection. Turbocharger and intercooler
Firing order	1-3-4-2 (No 1 at timing chain/belt end)

Direction of injection pump rotation:

10J engine	Anti-clockwise (viewed from above)
All except 10J engine	Clockwise (viewed from timing belt end)

Accelerator cable

Freeplay (maximum)	1.57 mm

Injection timing

10J engine	Set using special tool RO605863 – see text
12J and 19J engines	Set using special tool 18G 1458 or dial test indicator and probe – see text
200 TDi and 300 TDi engines	Set using flywheel and pump locking tools – see text

Maximum speed (no-load)

10J engine	4200 rpm
12J and 19J engines	4400 ± 80 rpm
200 TDi engine	4100 to 4260 rpm
300 TDi engine	4600 (+ 40 / -120) rpm

Idle speed

10J and 12J engines	650 ± 20 rpm
19J engine	670 ± 20 rpm
200 TDi engine	790 ± 10 rpm
300 TDi engine	720 ± 20 rpm

Injectors

Type	Pintle
Opening pressure:	
10J and 12J engines	135 bars
19J engine	135 to 140 bars
200 TDi engine:	
Initial	200 bars
Secondary.	280 bars
300 TDi engine:	
Initial	200 bars
Secondary.	300 bars

Turbocharger

Type:	
19J engine	Garrett T2
200 TDi engine	Garrett T25
300 TDi engine	Allied signal
Maximum boost pressure:	
19J engine	0.64 bars
200 TDi engine	0.78 bars
300 TDi engine	0.83 to 1.04 bars
Speed of rotation	Approximately 150 000 rpm

EGR throttle position sensor

Resistance across terminals 1 and 3	1000 to 1050 ohms
Resistance across terminals 1 and 2	850 to 900 ohms

Torque wrench settings

	Nm	lbf ft
Boost pressure pipe-to-fuel injection pump union.	10	7
EGR delivery pipe bolts	25	18
EGR valve securing bolts	25	18
Exhaust manifold securing nuts/bolts:		
19J engine	32	24
200 TDi engine	25	18
300 TDi engine	45	33
Fuel hose-to-fuel filter unions:		
200 TDi engine	15	11
300 TDi engine	33	24
Fuel hose-to-fuel lift pump unions	20	15
Fuel injection pump hub cover plate screws	25	18
Fuel injection pump rear bracket fixings	25	18
Fuel injection pump securing nuts	25	18
Fuel injection pump sprocket nut (12J and 19J engines).	45	33
Fuel injection pump sprocket to hub (200 TDi and 300 TDi engines) . .	25	18
Fuel injector clamp plate nuts (200 and 300 TDi engines)	25	18
Fuel injector pipe unions:		
10J, 12J and 19J engines.	17	13
200 TDi and 300 TDi engines	25	18
Fuel injector securing nuts (10J, 12J and 19J engines)	7	5
Fuel leak-off pipe-to-fuel injection pump union	25	18

Torque wrench settings (continued)

	Nm	lbf ft
Fuel leak-off pipe-to-injector unions	10	7
Fuel lift pump securing bolts	25	18
Fuel supply hose-to-fuel injection pump union:		
200 TDi engine	12	9
300 TDi engine	25	18
Inlet manifold securing nuts/bolts:		
19J engine	35	26
200 TDi and 300 TDi engines	25	18
Turbocharger elbow nuts (19J and 200 TDi engines)	25	18
Turbocharger oil drain pipe-to-cylinder block adapter union	38	28
Turbocharger oil drain pipe-to-turbocharger union:		
19J and 200 TDi engines	40	30
300 TDi engine	25	18
Turbocharger oil feed pipe-to-cylinder block adapter union:		
19J engine	19	14
200 TDi and 300 TDi engines	25	18
Turbocharger oil feed pipe-to-turbocharger union	19	14
Turbocharger-to-manifold bolts (300 TDi engine)	45	33
Turbocharger-to-manifold nuts (19J and 200 TDi engines)	25	18

1 General information and precautions

General information

The fuel system consists of a fuel tank (or twin tanks on certain 110 models), a fuel sedimenter (removes large droplets of water and particles of contamination – not fitted to all models), a fuel filter (incorporating a water separator), a fuel lift pump, a fuel injection pump, injectors and associated components **(see illustration)**. On some models, the fuel is heated as it passes through the filter, by coolant flowing through the filter bowl. A turbocharger is fitted to 19J, 200 TDi and 300 TDi engines, and the turbocharging system operates in conjunction with an intercooler on 200 TDi and 300 TDi engines. The exhaust system is conventional, but on certain 300 TDi engine models, an exhaust gas recirculation (EGR) system and/or an unregulated catalytic converter is/are fitted, to reduce exhaust gas emissions (see Section 21 for further details).

Fuel is drawn from the fuel tank to the fuel injection pump by a camshaft-driven mechanical lift pump. Before reaching the fuel injection pump, the fuel passes through the fuel sedimenter (not fitted to all models) and the fuel filter, where foreign matter and water are removed. Excess fuel lubricates the moving components of the pump, and is then returned to the tank.

The fuel injection pump is driven at half crankshaft speed. On 10J engines, the pump is driven from the camshaft via a driveshaft; on all other engines, the pump is driven by the timing belt. The high pressure required to inject the fuel into the compressed air in the swirl chambers is achieved by a cam plate acting on a piston. The fuel passes through a central rotor with a single outlet drilling which aligns with ports leading to the injector pipes.

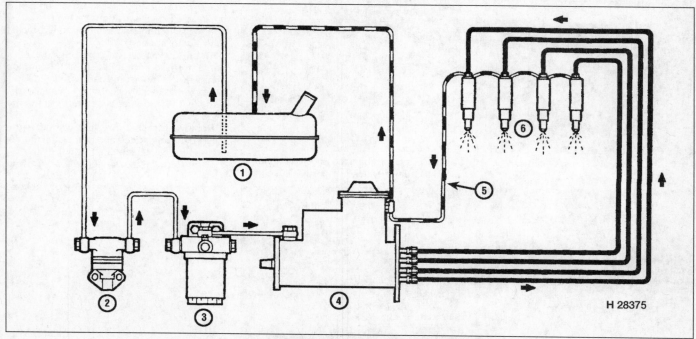

H 28375

1.1 Schematic layout of diesel fuel system

1 Fuel tank
2 Fuel lift pump
3 Fuel filter
4 Fuel injection pump
5 Fuel leak-off return line
6 Fuel injectors

Arrows show direction of fuel flow

Fuel metering is controlled by a centrifugal governor which reacts to accelerator pedal position and engine speed. The governor is linked to a metering valve which increases or decreases the amount of fuel delivered at each pumping stroke. On turbocharged engines, a separate device also increases fuel delivery with increasing turbocharger boost pressure. Basic injection timing is determined when the pump is first fitted to the engine. When the engine is running, the pump timing is varied automatically to suit the prevailing engine speed, by a mechanism which turns the cam plate or ring.

The four fuel injectors produce a homogeneous spray of fuel into the swirl chambers located in the cylinder head. The injectors are calibrated to open and close at critical pressures to provide efficient and even combustion. Each injector needle is lubricated by fuel, which accumulates in the spring chamber, and is channelled to the injection pump return hose by leak-off pipes.

Cold starting is assisted by preheater or 'glow' plugs fitted to each swirl chamber (see Chapter 5 for further details).

A stop solenoid cuts the fuel supply to the injection pump rotor when the ignition is switched off.

Provided that the specified maintenance is carried out, the fuel injection equipment will give long and trouble-free service. The injection pump itself may well outlast the engine. The main potential cause of damage to the injection pump and injectors is dirt or water in the fuel.

Servicing of the injection pump and injectors is very limited for the home mechanic, and

any dismantling or adjustment other than that described in this Chapter must be entrusted to a Land Rover dealer or fuel injection specialist.

Precautions

 Warning: It is necessary to take certain precautions when working on the fuel system components, particularly the fuel injectors. Before carrying out any operations on the fuel system, refer to the precautions given in 'Safety first!' at the beginning of this manual, and to any additional warning notes at the start of the relevant Sections. Absolute cleanliness is essential when working on the fuel system – do not allow dirt to enter when any part of the system is disconnected.

2 Air cleaner assembly and ducting – removal and refitting

10J, 12J and 19J engines

Removal

1 Disconnect all the hoses from the air cleaner canister, noting their locations. If desired, to improve access, the air hoses can be removed completely.
2 Release the securing clips, and lift the complete canister from the base assembly.
3 Unscrew the securing bolts, and remove the base/bracket assembly from the engine compartment.

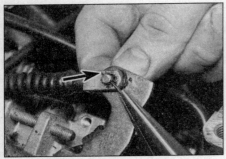

3.2a Remove the split-pin . . .

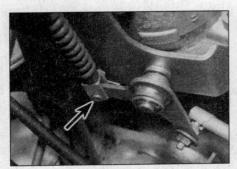

3.2c Throttle cable end fitting (arrowed) at throttle linkage bellcrank – 19J engine

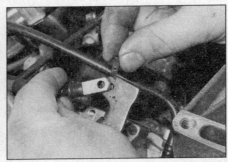

3.2b . . . and withdraw the accelerator clevis pin at the fuel injection pump – 300 TDi engine

3.3 Unclip the cable adjuster ferrule from the bracket on the injection pump – 300 TDi engine

Refitting

4 Refitting is a reversal of removal, but ensure that all hoses are securely reconnected to their correct locations.

200 TDi and 300 TDi engines

Removal

5 Disconnect the air inlet and outlet hoses from the air cleaner casing. If desired, to improve access, the air hoses can be removed completely.
6 Release the two air cleaner retaining clamps.
7 To release the assembly from its mounting bracket, twist the assembly anti-clockwise (viewed from the front of the engine).
8 If desired, the mounting bracket can be unbolted from the body.

Refitting

9 Refitting is a reversal of removal, ensuring that the hoses are securely reconnected.

3 Accelerator cable – removal, refitting and adjustment

Note: *New split-pins should be used to secure the cable end clevis pins on refitting.*

Removal

1 Disconnect the battery negative lead.
2 Working in the engine compartment, remove the split-pin, and withdraw the clevis pin securing the end of the accelerator cable to the accelerator lever on the fuel injection pump, or to the throttle linkage bellcrank, as applicable **(see illustrations)**.
3 Unclip the cable adjuster from its bracket **(see illustration)**.
4 Where applicable, release the accelerator cable from the bracket(s) in the engine compartment, noting the cable routing.
5 Working in the driver's footwell, if necessary, remove the trim panel for access to the pedals.
6 Remove the split-pin, and withdraw the clevis pin securing the end of the cable to the accelerator pedal **(see illustration)**.
7 Where applicable, unscrew the nut and

3.6 Throttle cable-to-throttle pedal clevis pin securing split-pin (arrowed)

3.11 Throttle cable adjuster wheel (arrowed) – 19J engine

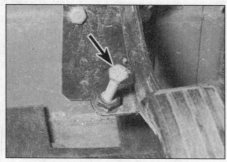

3.15 Throttle pedal stop screw (arrowed)

recover the washers securing the cable outer to the bulkhead. Alternatively, release the cable grommet from the bulkhead.

8 Withdraw the cable through the bulkhead into the engine compartment.

Refitting

9 Refitting is a reversal of removal, bearing in mind the following points:
  a) Ensure that the cable is routed as noted before removal.
  b) Use new split-pins to secure the cable end clevis pins.
  c) On completion, check the cable adjustment, as described in the following paragraphs.

Adjustment

10 Hold the injection pump accelerator lever, or the throttle linkage bellcrank, as applicable, in the fully closed position.

11 Turn the knurled adjuster wheel at the bracket on the fuel injection pump, to eliminate all freeplay from the inner cable (see illustration).

12 Working in the driver's footwell, if not already done, remove the trim panel for access to the pedals.

13 Slacken the locknut on the pedal stop screw.

14 Fully depress the accelerator pedal by hand, until the accelerator lever, or the throttle

linkage bellcrank (as applicable) is in the full-throttle position. Hold the pedal in this position, ensuring that the cable is not under strain.

15 Turn the pedal stop screw until it just touches the bulkhead panel (see illustration).

16 Again, check that the throttle cable is not under strain then, where applicable, tighten the locknut on the pedal stop screw.

17 Refit the footwell trim panel.

4 Accelerator pedal – removal and refitting

Note: A new split-pin should be used to secure the accelerator cable end clevis pin on refitting, and a new pedal pivot rod securing pin should be used.

Removal

1 Working in the driver's footwell, where applicable, remove the trim panel for access to the pedals.

2 Remove the split-pin, and withdraw the clevis pin securing the end of the cable to the accelerator pedal.

3 Unscrew the securing bolts (where applicable, counterhold the nuts in the engine compartment), and withdraw the pedal bracket assembly from the footwell.

4 If desired, the pedal can be removed from the bracket as follows.

5 Tap the securing pin from the pedal pivot rod, using a suitable punch if necessary.

6 Note the location of the pedal return spring.

7 Carefully slide the pivot rod from the pedal bracket and the pedal, noting that the pedal will be pushed free by the return spring. Withdraw the pedal.

Refitting

8 Refitting is a reversal of removal, bearing in mind the following points:
  a) Ensure that the pedal return spring is located as noted before removal.
  b) Where applicable, use a new pedal pivot rod securing pin.
  c) Use a new split-pin to secure the cable end clevis pin.
  d) Where applicable, before refitting the footwell trim panel, check the cable adjustment as described in Section 3.

5 Fuel system – priming and bleeding

Note: Refer to the precautions given in Section 1 before proceeding.

1 After disconnecting part of the fuel supply system (or running out of fuel), it is necessary to prime the system, and bleed off any air which may have entered the system components.

2 All models are fitted with a hand-operated priming lever on the fuel lift pump. Note that if the engine has stopped with the lift pump lever fully raised on its cam, it will not be possible to operate the hand-priming lever – in this case, turn the engine (using a suitable spanner or socket on the crankshaft pulley bolt if necessary), until the lever can be operated.

3 To prime the system on 10J, 12J and 19J engine models, loosen the fuel leak-off pipe union bolt on the top of the fuel filter head. On 200 TDi and 300 TDi engines, loosen the bleed screw, located on the fuel filter head (see illustrations).

5.3a Loosening the fuel leak-off pipe union (arrowed) on the filter head – 19J engine

5.3b Fuel filter head bleed screw (arrowed) – 300 TDi engine

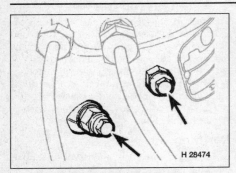

5.6a Fuel injection pump bleed screws (arrowed) – 10J engine

5.6b Fuel injection pump bleed screw (arrowed) – 19J engine

Refitting

7 Refitting is a reversal of removal, but use a new sealing ring and, where applicable, ensure that the lugs on the sender unit engage with the cut-outs in the tank.

Rear-mounted fuel tank

Note: *A new sender unit sealing ring will be required on refitting, and a new fuel tank drain plug sealing ring may be required.*

Removal

8 Disconnect the battery negative lead.
9 Remove the fuel filler cap.
10 Working underneath the vehicle, place a container underneath the fuel tank drain plug in order to catch the escaping fuel, then unscrew the drain plug. Recover the sealing washer.
11 Allow time for all the fuel to drain into the container. Examine the condition of the drain plug sealing washer, and renew if necessary, then refit and tighten the drain plug.
12 Working at the left-hand side of the fuel tank, unscrew the union and disconnect the fuel supply hose from the gauge sender unit.

 HAYNES HINT *Plug or cover the open end of the hose, to prevent dirt ingress and further fuel spillage.*

13 Turn the fuel gauge locking ring anti-clockwise, and remove it (if necessary, tap the locking ring using a soft metal of plastic drift to release it), then withdraw the sender unit, and recover the sealing ring.

Refitting

14 Refitting is a reversal of removal, but use a new sealing ring and, where applicable, ensure that the lugs on the sender unit engage with the cut-outs in the tank.
15 Do not forget to refill the fuel tank on completion.

4 Operate the priming lever until fuel free from air bubbles emerges from the union or bleed screw (as applicable), then retighten the screw. To operate the lever, push the lever down to release it from the catch, then pump the lever up and down.
5 Switch on the ignition (to activate the stop solenoid) and continue operating the priming lever until firm resistance is felt, then pump a few more times.
6 If a large amount of air has entered the fuel injection pump, the pump can be bled by slackening the appropriate bleed screw(s) or union as follows. Place a wad of rag around the bleed screw(s) or union to absorb split fuel.

a) On 10J engines, slacken the two bleed screws on the side of the pump body **(see illustration)**.
b) On 12J and 19J engines, slacken the bleed screw on the top of the pump **(see illustration)**.
c) On 200 TDi and 300 TDi engines, slacken the fuel return pipe union on the pump.

7 Operate the priming lever (with the ignition switched on, to activate the stop solenoid), or crank the engine on the starter motor in 10-second bursts, until fuel free from air bubbles emerges from the fuel bleed screw(s) or union. Tighten the bleed screw(s) or union, and mop-up split fuel.

 Warning: Be prepared to stop the engine if it should fire, to avoid excessive fuel spray and spillage.

8 If air has entered the injector pipes, place wads of rag around the injector pipe unions at the injectors (to absorb spilt fuel), then slacken

the unions. Crank the engine on the starter motor until fuel emerges from the unions, then stop cranking the engine and retighten the unions. Mop-up spilt fuel.

 Warning: Be prepared to stop the engine if it should fire, to avoid excessive fuel spray and spillage.

9 Start the engine with the accelerator pedal fully depressed. Additional cranking may be necessary to finally bleed the system before the engine starts.

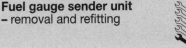

6 Fuel gauge sender unit – removal and refitting

Note: *Refer to the precautions given in Section 1 before proceeding.*

Side-mounted fuel tank

Note: *A new sealing ring will be required on refitting.*

Removal

1 Disconnect the battery negative lead.
2 Remove the right-hand front seat cushion (see Chapter 12).
3 Unscrew the securing bolts, and remove the floor cover panel to expose the fuel tank.
4 Disconnect the wiring from the sender unit **(see illustration)**.
5 Using a suitable soft metal or plastic drift, tap the sender unit locking ring anti-clockwise and remove the locking ring **(see illustration)**.
6 Withdraw the sender unit from the fuel tank, and recover the sealing ring **(see illustration)**.

7 Fuel tank – removal and refitting

Note: *Refer to the precautions given in Section 1 before proceeding.*

6.4 Disconnecting the wiring . . .

6.5 . . . then remove the locking ring . . .

6.6 . . . and remove the fuel gauge sender unit – 90 model

Side-mounted fuel tank

Note: *A new fuel tank drain plug sealing ring may be required on refitting.*

Removal

1 Disconnect the battery negative lead.

2 Remove the fuel filler cap.

3 Working underneath the vehicle, place a container underneath the fuel tank drain plug to catch the escaping fuel, then unscrew the drain plug **(see illustration)**. Recover the sealing washer.

4 Allow time for all the fuel to drain into the container. Examine the condition of the drain plug sealing washer, and renew if necessary. Refit and tighten the drain plug.

5 Remove the right-hand front seat cushion (see Chapter 12).

6 Unscrew the securing bolts, and remove the floor cover panel to expose the fuel tank.

7 Disconnect the wiring plug from the fuel gauge sender unit.

8 Disconnect the fuel supply and return hoses from the pipes on the top of the tank **(see illustration)**. Plug or cover the open ends of the hoses, to prevent dirt ingress.

9 Disconnect the breather pipe from the fuel filler tube.

10 Slacken the hose clip, and disconnect the fuel filler hose from the filler tube.

11 Working at the rear of the tank, unscrew the two tank securing nuts from the captive bolts, and recover the washers **(see illustration)**.

12 Place a jack and interposed block of wood under the rear of the tank, then withdraw the two rear captive bolts/plates.

13 Ensure that the tank is adequately supported then, working at the front of the tank, counterhold the bolt and unscrew the nut securing the tank to the front mounting bracket on the chassis. Recover the washers and spacers, noting their locations to ensure correct refitting **(see illustration)**.

14 Unscrew the three nuts and bolts securing the front mounting bracket to the chassis, and withdraw the bracket.

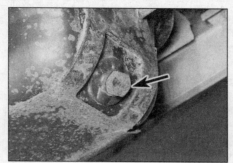

7.3 Fuel tank drain plug (arrowed) – 90 model

15 Lower the front of the tank, at the same time turning it anti-clockwise, then lower the jack, and withdraw the tank from under the vehicle.

16 If desired, the fuel supply and return pipe assemblies can be removed from the tank, after removing the securing screws. Recover the gaskets.

17 Similarly, the fuel gauge sender unit can be removed from the tank. Unscrew the locking ring by turning it anti-clockwise, and recover the sender unit sealing ring.

Refitting

18 Refitting is a reversal of removal, bearing in mind the following points:

a) *Where applicable, refit the fuel gauge sender and the fuel pipe assemblies, using new gaskets and a new sealing ring. Where applicable, note that the lugs on the gauge sender unit must engage with the corresponding cut-outs in the tank.*

b) *If the fuel filler hose has been removed from the tank, refit the hose and loosely refit the lower hose clip before refitting the tank. Position the hose clip so that it can be tightened with the fuel tank in position.*

c) *Ensure that the washers and spacers are correctly positioned on the front tank mounting bolt, as noted during removal.*

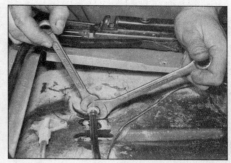

7.8 Disconnect the fuel hoses from the top of the tank – 90 model

d) *Do not fully tighten any of the fixings until the completion of refitting.*

e) *On completion, manipulate the fuel filler hose into position between the tank and filler tube (where applicable), ensuring that it is not twisted or strained, then tighten the upper and lower hose clips.*

Rear-mounted fuel tank

Note: *A new fuel tank drain plug sealing ring may be required on refitting.*

Removal

19 Proceed as described in paragraphs 1 to 4.

20 Disconnect the fuel filler hose from the tank.

21 Disconnect the breather pipe from the fuel filler tube.

22 Working at the left-hand side of the tank, disconnect the wiring plug from the fuel gauge sender unit.

23 Unscrew the union nut, and disconnect the fuel supply hose from the gauge sender unit. Plug or cover the open end of the hose, to prevent dirt ingress.

24 If the vehicle is fitted with a towing ball drop-plate with support bars, the bars must be removed.

25 Where applicable, remove the rear anti-roll bar as described in Chapter 11.

7.11 Unscrew the two fuel tank rear securing nuts (arrowed) – 90 model

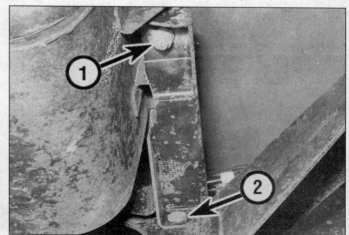

7.13 Fuel tank-to-front mounting bracket nut (1) and lower bracket securing bolt (2) – 90 model

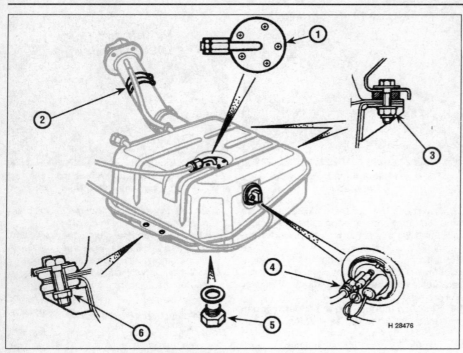

7.27 Fuel tank mounting details – 110 models

1 Fuel return pipe	3 Tank rear mounting nuts	5 Tank drain plug
2 Fuel filler hose	4 Fuel gauge sender unit	6 Tank front mounting nuts

26 To improve access, remove the left-hand lashing eye from the chassis.

27 Place a jack and interposed block of wood under the tank. Unscrew the two tank front mounting nuts, and recover the washers and spacers, noting their locations to ensure correct refitting **(see illustration)**.

28 Similarly, unscrew the tank rear mounting nuts.

29 Carefully lower the tank sufficiently for access to the fuel return hose connection on the top of the tank. Unscrew the union, and disconnect the fuel return hose from the tank. Plug or cover the open end of the hose, to prevent dirt ingress.

30 Continue to lower the tank, and withdraw it from under the vehicle.

31 If desired, the fuel return pipe assembly can be removed from the tank, after removing the securing screws. Recover the gasket.

32 Similarly, the fuel gauge sender unit can be removed from the tank. Unscrew the locking ring by turning it anti-clockwise, and recover the sender unit sealing ring.

Refitting

33 Refitting is a reversal of removal, bearing in mind the following points:

a) Where applicable, refit the fuel gauge sender and the fuel return pipe assembly, using a new gasket and a new sealing ring. Note that the lugs on the gauge sender unit must engage with the corresponding cut-outs in the tank.

b) Ensure that the washers and spacers are correctly positioned on the tank mounting bolts, as noted during removal.

c) Do not fully tighten any of the fixings until the completion of refitting.

8 Fuel lift pump – removal and refitting

Note: Refer to the precautions given in Section 1 before proceeding. New fuel pump gasket(s) (and, where applicable, a new fuel pump housing gasket) will be required on refitting.

Removal

1 The fuel lift pump is mounted on the right-hand side of the cylinder block.

2 Disconnect the battery negative lead.

3 Where applicable, to improve access, remove the air cleaner assembly as described in Section 2.

4 Similarly, where necessary to improve access, unscrew the union nuts, and disconnect the upper two fuel pipes connecting the fuel injectors to the fuel injection pump, from the fuel injectors. Be prepared for fuel spillage, and plug or cover the open ends of the injectors and the pipes, to prevent dirt ingress. Loosen the pipe unions at the fuel injection pump (counterhold the unions on the pump), and manipulate the pipes to allow sufficient access to remove the fuel lift pump.

5 Unscrew the unions (again, counterhold the unions on the pump), and disconnect the fuel supply and feed hoses from the fuel lift pump **(see illustrations)**. Again, plug or cover the open ends of the hoses and pump.

6 Unscrew the two securing nuts or bolts (as applicable), then withdraw the pump and the gasket(s) **(see illustrations)**. Discard the gasket(s), noting that some models may be fitted with a plastic insulating block, sandwiched between two gaskets.

8.5a Disconnecting the fuel pipe unions (arrowed) from the fuel lift pump – 19J engine

8.5b Disconnecting a fuel hose (arrowed) from the fuel lift pump – 300 TDi engine

8.6a Remove the fuel lift pump . . .

8.6b . . . and recover the gasket – 300 TDi engine

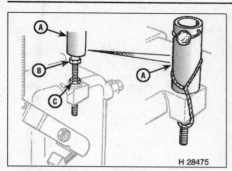

9.3a Maximum speed adjustment screw details – 10J engine

A *Screw cover*
B *Maximum speed adjustment screw*
C *Locknut*

7 On all except 300 TDi engines, if desired, the fuel lift pump housing can be unbolted from the cylinder block – note the locations of any brackets secured by the bolts. Recover the gasket.

Refitting

8 Commence refitting by cleaning all traces of old gasket from the mating faces of the pump and the housing (and the insulating block, where applicable).
9 Similarly, where applicable, clean the mating faces of the fuel pump housing, and refit the housing using a new gasket.
10 Refit the pump, and the insulating block where applicable, using new gasket(s). Ensure that the pump operating lever engages correctly with the camshaft as the pump is refitted.
11 Refit the pump securing bolts or nuts, and tighten them to the specified torque.
12 Reconnect the fuel hoses to the lift pump, and where applicable, reconnect the injector pipes to the injectors. Ensure that all unions are securely tightened. Where applicable, refit the air cleaner assembly.
13 Reconnect the battery negative lead, and start the engine. If difficulty is experienced, bleed the fuel system as described in Section 5.

9 Maximum engine speed – checking and adjustment

Caution: The maximum speed adjustment screw is sealed by the manufacturers at the factory, using paint, or a locking wire and a lead seal. There is no reason why it should require adjustment. Do not disturb the screw if the vehicle is still within the warranty period, otherwise the warranty will be invalidated. This adjustment requires the use of a tachometer – refer to Section 10 for alternative methods.

1 Run the engine to normal operating temperature.
2 Have an assistant fully depress the accelerator pedal, and check that the maximum engine speed is as given in the Specifications. Do not keep the engine at maximum speed for

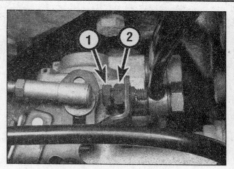

9.3b Maximum speed adjustment screw (1) and locknut (2) – 19J engine

more than two or three seconds.
3 If adjustment is necessary, stop the engine. Loosen the locknut, turn the maximum speed adjustment screw as necessary, and retighten the locknut. Note that the locknut may be sealed using a plastic cover (**see illustrations**).
4 Start the engine, and repeat the procedure in paragraph 2 to check the adjustment.
5 Stop the engine and disconnect the tachometer.

10 Idle speed – checking and adjustment

Note: *The fast idle speed is automatically set by setting the idle speed, and cannot be adjusted independently. Adjustment of the idle speed is permitted in service, but the manufacturers recommend that any other fuel injection pump adjustments are entrusted to authorised agents. For information purposes, details of maximum engine speed adjustment are given in Section 9.*

1 The usual type of tachometer (rev counter), which works from ignition system pulses, cannot be used on diesel engines. If it is not felt that adjusting the idle speed 'by ear' is satisfactory, one of the following alternatives may be used:
a) *Purchase or hire of an appropriate tachometer.*
b) *Delegation of the job to a Land Rover dealer or other specialist.*
c) *Timing light (strobe) operated by a petrol engine running at the desired speed. If*

10.4b Idle speed adjustment screw (1) and locknut (2) – 19J engine

9.3c Maximum speed adjustment screw (1) and locknut cover (2) – 300 TDi engine

the timing light is pointed at a mark on the camshaft or injection pump sprocket, the mark will appear stationary when the two engines are running at the same speed (or multiples of that speed). The sprocket will be rotating at half the crankshaft speed, but this will not affect the adjustment. (In practice, it was found impossible to use this method on the crankshaft pulley, due to the acute viewing angle.)

2 Before making adjustments, warm-up the engine to normal operating temperature. Make sure that the accelerator cable is correctly adjusted (see Section 3).
3 With the accelerator lever resting against the idle stop, check that the engine idles at the specified speed. If necessary, adjust as follows.
4 If adjustment is necessary, loosen the idle speed adjustment screw locknut, and turn the screw as necessary to give the desired engine speed (**see illustrations**). Turn the screw

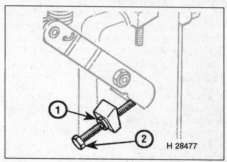

10.4a Idle speed adjustment screw (2) and locknut (1) – 10J engine

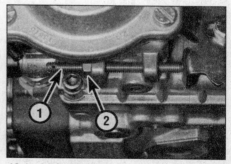

10.4c Idle speed adjustment screw (1) and locknut (2) – 300 TDi engine

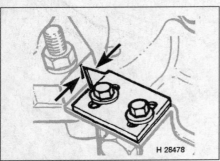

11.7 Mark on pump flange aligned with pump timing pointer (arrowed) – 10J engine

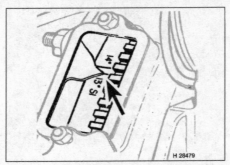

11.12 Timing aperture pointer (arrowed) aligned with 13° mark on flywheel – 10J engine

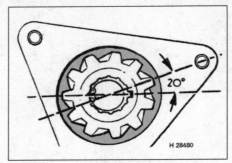

11.14 Fuel injection pump drivegear master spline (arrowed) positioned at 20° to crankshaft axis – 10J engine

clockwise to increase the engine speed, or anti-clockwise to decrease the engine speed.

5 Operate the accelerator lever to increase the engine speed for a few seconds, then recheck the idle speed.

6 When the adjustment is correct, hold the adjustment screw steady as the locknut is tightened.

7 On completion, stop the engine and, where applicable, disconnect the tachometer.

11 Fuel injection pump 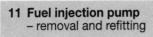 – removal and refitting

10J engines

Note: *Refer to the precautions given in Section 1 before proceeding.*

Note: *Land Rover special tool RO605863 will be required to check the injection pump timing on refitting. A new pump gasket and a new timing aperture cover plate gasket will be required on refitting.*

Removal

1 Disconnect the battery negative lead.

2 To improve access, remove the bonnet as described in Chapter 12.

3 Disconnect the wiring from the stop solenoid.

4 Disconnect the accelerator cable from the pump, with reference to Section 3.

5 Unscrew the unions, and disconnect the fuel supply and return pipes from the pump. Be prepared for fuel spillage. Where applicable, recover the sealing washers from the banjo union. Cover the open ends of the pipes, and plug the openings in the injection pump, to keep dirt out (where applicable, the banjo bolt can be refitted to the pump, and covered).

6 Unscrew the union nuts, and disconnect the injector pipes from the pump, and from the injectors. Remove the pipes, noting their locations to aid refitting. Plug or cover the open ends of the pump, pipes, and injectors, to prevent dirt ingress.

7 Check that there is a clear alignment mark on the pump flange, in line with the pump timing pointer, which is mounted on the

cylinder block side cover plate in front of the pump **(see illustration)**. Make an appropriate mark if necessary.

8 Unscrew the three securing nuts, recover the washers, and withdraw the pump. Recover the gasket.

9 Withdraw the pump driveshaft from the drivegear.

Refitting

10 Unscrew the two securing nuts, and recover the washers securing the timing aperture cover plate to the flywheel housing on the right-hand side of the engine. Lift off the cover plate, and recover the gasket.

11 Look to see if a timing pointer is visible in the aperture. If no pointer is visible, a suitable pointer can be obtained under Land Rover part No ERC 2250. Where applicable, fit the timing pointer and secure with the two nuts – note that the pointer arrow should be positioned on the gearbox side of the timing aperture.

12 Using a socket or spanner on the crankshaft pulley bolt, turn the crankshaft until the 13° mark on the flywheel is aligned with the pointer in the timing aperture **(see illustration)**.

13 If the crankshaft is inadvertently turned beyond the 13° mark, do not turn the crankshaft back, but continue to turn in a

clockwise direction until the mark is precisely aligned with the pointer.

14 Look through the injection pump drivegear aperture, and check that the master spline on the pump drivegear is positioned at an angle of approximately 20° to the engine crankshaft axis **(see illustration)**.

15 It is possible that the master spline may be positioned 180° away from the position described in the previous paragraph, in which case, turn the crankshaft through one complete revolution to bring the master spline to the correct position – again check that the 13° mark on the flywheel is aligned with the timing pointer.

16 Insert special gauge tool RO605863 through the drivegear aperture into the drivegear.

17 Turn the gauge handle firmly clockwise to take up backlash in the timing gears, then hold the gauge in this position.

18 Check that the mark on the edge of the gauge is aligned with the pump timing pointer on the engine. If not, slacken the two bolts securing the pointer, reposition the pointer to align with the gauge mark, then tighten the bolts **(see illustration)**.

19 Remove the gauge, then refit the pump driveshaft, engaging the master spline with the

11.18 Special gauge RO605863 in position in injection pump drivegear aperture – 10J engine

1 Special gauge RO605863   2 Timing mark on gauge flange   3 Timing pointer securing bolts

11.34 Levering the accelerator linkage rod from the fuel injection pump lever – 19J engine

11.36 Disconnecting a fuel injector pipe from the fuel injection pump – 19J engine

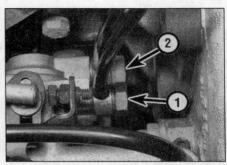

11.38 Disconnect the fuel leak-off pipe (1) and boost pressure pipe (2) from the injection pump – 19J engine

master spline on the drivegear. Note that the longer-splined end of the driveshaft engages with the drivegear.

20 Locate a new pump gasket on the drivegear housing.

21 Turn the injection pump spindle to align the master spline on the spindle with the master spline on the driveshaft, then lower the pump into position. Turn the pump as necessary to align the timing mark on the pump flange with the pump timing pointer on the engine.

22 Refit the washers and the pump securing nuts, then tighten the nuts. Check that the timing mark on the pump flange is still aligned with the pointer on the engine.

23 Refit the injector pipes to their original locations, and tighten the union nuts.

24 Reconnect the fuel supply and return pipes to the pump, and tighten the unions.

25 Reconnect the wiring to the stop solenoid.

26 Reconnect the accelerator cable, and check the cable adjustment with reference to Section 3.

27 Refit the timing aperture cover plate to the flywheel housing, using a new gasket, and tighten the securing nuts.

28 Reconnect the battery negative lead.

29 Bleed the fuel system as described in Section 5, then check the idle speed and maximum speed as described in Sections 10 and 9 respectively.

30 On completion, refit the bonnet with reference to Chapter 12.

12J and 19J engines

Note: *Refer to the precautions given in Section 1 before proceeding.*

Note: *If Land Rover special tool 18G 1457 is available, the pump can be removed without disturbing the timing belt, working through the access hole in the timing belt cover. At the time of writing, no information was available regarding the use of this special tool. The following procedure assumes that the special tool is not available, in which case the timing belt must be removed.*

Note: *A new pump front mounting gasket will be required on refitting.*

Removal

31 To improve access, remove the bonnet as described in Chapter 12.

32 Remove the timing belt, and the fuel injection pump sprocket, as described in Chapter 2A.

33 Disconnect the wiring from the stop solenoid.

34 Using a small screwdriver, carefully lever the accelerator linkage rod from the lever on the fuel injection pump **(see illustration)**.

35 Unscrew the unions, and disconnect the fuel supply and return pipes from the pump. Be prepared for fuel spillage. Where applicable, recover the sealing washers from the banjo union. Cover the open ends of the pipes, and plug the openings in the injection pump, to keep dirt out (where applicable, the banjo bolt can be refitted to the pump, and covered).

36 Unscrew the union nuts, and disconnect the injector pipes from the pump, and from the injectors **(see illustration)**. Remove the pipes, noting their locations to aid refitting. Plug or cover the open ends of the pump, pipes, and injectors, to prevent dirt ingress.

37 Similarly, disconnect the fuel leak-off pipe from the pump.

38 On 19J engines, unscrew the union bolt and disconnect the boost pressure pipe from the pump **(see illustration)**.

39 Unbolt the oil filter adapter assembly from the cylinder block, to allow sufficient clearance to withdraw the pump. Be prepared for oil spillage, and recover the gasket.

40 Make sure that there is an alignment mark on the pump flange, in line with the pump timing pointer (bolted to the rear of the timing belt housing). Make a suitable mark if necessary. If no timing pointer is fitted, simply make alignment marks between the pump flange and the timing belt housing.

41 Unscrew the nut and bolt securing the pump to the rear support bracket.

42 Unscrew the three nuts (and recover the washers) securing the pump to the studs at the rear of the timing belt housing, then withdraw the pump and recover the gasket.

Refitting

43 Commence refitting by thoroughly cleaning the mating faces of the pump flange and the timing belt housing.

44 Place the new gasket in position over the pump mounting studs.

45 Place the pump in position on the mounting studs, ensuring that the gasket is correctly located, and refit the washers and securing nuts. Do not fully tighten the nuts at this stage. Position the pump so that the mark on the pump flange is aligned with the timing pointer or the mark (as applicable) on the timing belt housing.

46 Refit the nut and bolt securing the pump to the rear mounting bracket. Again, do not fully tighten at this stage.

47 Thoroughly clean the mating faces of the oil filter adapter assembly and the cylinder block, then refit the assembly using a new gasket, and tighten the securing bolts.

48 Refit the fuel injection pump sprocket and the timing belt, as described in Chapter 2A.

49 Set up the injection pump timing as described in Section 12.

50 With all pump mountings tightened, refit the injector pipes and tighten the unions.

51 Reconnect the fuel supply and return pipes.

52 Reconnect the fuel leak-off pipe, and where applicable, the boost pressure pipe.

53 Reconnect the accelerator linkage rod to the lever on the pump, then check the accelerator cable adjustment as described in Section 3.

54 Reconnect the wiring to the stop solenoid.

55 On completion, start the engine and check the idle speed and the maximum engine speed, as described in Sections 10 and 9 respectively, then refit the bonnet with reference to Chapter 12.

200 TDi and 300 TDi engines

Note: *Refer to the precautions given in Section 1 before proceeding.*

Note: *To remove the pump without disturbing the timing belt, Land Rover special tool LRT-12-045 will be required to retain the pump sprocket in position. If a suitable tool is not available, remove the timing belt as described in Chapter 2A. A new pump front mounting gasket and a new pump hub cover plate gasket must be used on refitting.*

11.60a Unclip the wiring harness (arrowed) from the bracket on the pump . . .

11.60b . . . then loosen the screw (1) and remove the keeper plate (2) – 300 TDi engine

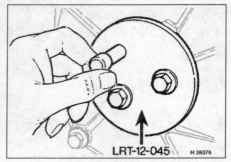

11.63 Special tool LRT-12-045 fitted to retain fuel injection pump sprocket

Removal using tool LRT-12-045

56 Disconnect the battery negative lead.

57 To improve access, remove the bonnet as described in Chapter 12.

58 Turn the crankshaft to bring No 1 piston to TDC on the compression stroke, and fit the tools to lock the crankshaft and injection pump spindle in position, as described in Chapter 2A.

59 With the engine locked in the TDC position, proceed as follows.

60 Loosen the pump locking screw, and remove the keeper plate (located at the front of the pump, behind the timing belt housing). Tighten the locking screw to lock the pump in position **(see illustrations)**.

61 Remove the three pump sprocket-to-hub bolts, and withdraw the sprocket retaining

plate. If necessary, counterhold the injection pump hub using a socket on the hub nut – **do not** rely on the pump spindle locking screw to hold the sprocket in position whilst loosening the pump sprocket-to-hub bolts.

62 Withdraw the pump timing pin.

63 Fit the sprocket retaining tool (LRT-12-045), with an 8.0 mm washer, 1.5 to 2.0 mm thick, under each bolt head, in addition to the washers supplied with the tool. Tighten the two retaining tool bolts, then re-insert the timing pin through the hole provided in the tool plate **(see illustration)**.

64 Disconnect the wiring from the stop solenoid.

65 Disconnect the accelerator cable from the pump, with reference to Section 3.

66 Unscrew the banjo bolt and the union nut,

and disconnect the fuel supply and return pipes from the pump **(see illustrations)**. Be prepared for fuel spillage. Recover the sealing washers from the banjo union. Cover the open ends of the pipes, and plug the openings in the injection pump, to keep dirt out (the banjo bolt can be refitted to the pump, and covered).

67 Similarly, disconnect the boost pressure pipe from the pump.

68 Unscrew the union nuts, and disconnect the injector pipes from the rear of the pump, and from the injectors. Remove the pipes, noting their locations to ensure correct refitting. Plug or cover the open ends of the pump, pipes, and injectors, to prevent dirt ingress.

69 Working at the rear of the pump, counterhold the bolts, and unscrew the two nuts securing the pump to the rear support bracket **(see illustration)**.

70 Unbolt the rear support bracket from the engine, and withdraw the bracket.

71 Unscrew the lower bolt securing the oil filter adapter to the cylinder block (to allow sufficient clearance for the pump to be withdrawn).

72 Unscrew the three nuts securing the pump to the studs at the rear of the timing belt housing, then withdraw the pump and recover the gasket. Where applicable, note the location of any brackets on the studs **(see illustrations)**.

Refitting using tool LRT-12-045

73 Commence refitting by thoroughly

11.66a Disconnecting the fuel supply pipe from the pump

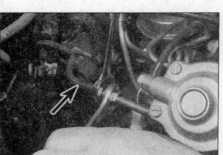

11.66b Counterhold the union on the pump when unscrewing the fuel return pipe (arrowed) union nut

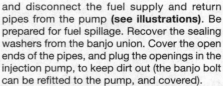

11.69 Unscrew the two nuts and bolts (arrowed) securing the pump to the rear support bracket

11.72a Note the location of any brackets (arrowed) on the timing belt housing studs

11.72b Withdrawing the fuel injection pump

cleaning the mating faces of the pump flange and the timing belt housing.

74 Place the new gasket in position over the pump mounting studs.

75 If a new pump is being fitted, proceed as follows:

a) *Fit the timing pin to the pump. If necessary, rotate the pump spindle to allow the pin to locate fully.*

b) *Slacken the pump locking screw, remove the keeper plate, then tighten the screw to lock the pump.*

c) *Remove the timing pin from the pump.*

76 Place the pump in position on the mounting studs, ensuring that the gasket is correctly located, and tighten the mounting nuts to the specified torque.

77 Refit the pump rear support bracket to the cylinder block, and tighten the securing bolts, then refit and tighten the nuts and bolts securing the pump to the bracket.

78 Refit and tighten the oil filter adapter lower bolt.

79 Refit the injector pipes, and tighten the union nuts.

80 Reconnect the boost pressure pipe to the pump.

81 Reconnect the fuel supply and return pipes to the pump.

82 Reconnect the accelerator cable to the pump, and adjust the cable as described in Section 3.

83 Reconnect the stop solenoid wiring.

84 Unscrew the securing bolts, and remove the injection pump sprocket retaining tool.

85 Refit the sprocket retaining plate, then refit the pump timing pin through the pump hub into the pump body.

86 Refit and tighten the pump sprocket-to-hub bolts.

87 Loosen the pump locking screw, then refit the keeper plate, and tighten the locking screw.

88 Remove the timing pin from the pump, and withdraw the flywheel locking tool centre pin from the slot in the flywheel.

89 Turn the crankshaft through two complete revolutions, then re-engage the flywheel locking tool centre pin with the slot in the flywheel, and check that the pump timing pin can still be inserted easily.

90 If the timing tool cannot be easily inserted into position, proceed as follows.

91 Withdraw the flywheel locking tool centre pin from the slot in the flywheel, then turn the crankshaft as necessary, until the timing pin can be inserted easily into the injection pump.

92 Loosen the pump locking screw, and remove the keeper plate, then tighten the locking screw to lock the pump in position.

93 Loosen the three pump sprocket-to-hub bolts.

94 Turn the crankshaft back to TDC, and engage the flywheel locking tool centre pin with the timing slot in the flywheel.

95 Recheck to ensure that the pump timing pin is an easy sliding fit in the pump.

96 Tighten the pump sprocket-to-hub bolts to the specified torque.

97 Loosen the pump locking screw, then refit the keeper plate, and tighten the locking screw.

98 Remove the timing pin from the pump, and withdraw the flywheel locking tool centre pin from the slot in the flywheel.

99 Refit the blanking plug to the flywheel locking tool aperture (coat the threads of the plug with thread-locking compound before refitting).

100 Refit the injection pump hub cover plate, using a new gasket.

101 Where applicable, refit the air conditioning compressor, and refit the drivebelt as described in Chapter 1.

102 Refit the bonnet as described in Chapter 12.

103 Reconnect the battery negative lead.

104 Start the engine, and check the idle speed and maximum engine speed as described in Sections 10 and 9 respectively.

Removal without tool LRT-12-045

105 Remove the timing belt as described in Chapter 2A.

106 Loosen the pump locking screw, and remove the keeper plate (located at the front of the pump, behind the timing belt housing). Tighten the locking screw to lock the pump spindle in position.

107 Withdraw the pump timing pin from the pump sprocket.

108 Remove the pump sprocket-to-hub securing bolts, then withdraw the sprocket retaining plate and the sprocket.

109 Proceed as described in paragraphs 64 to 72 inclusive.

Refitting without tool LRT-12-045

110 Proceed as described in paragraphs 73 to 83 inclusive.

111 Refit the pump sprocket and retaining plate (noting that the U-shaped slot in the retaining plate should align with the slot in the pump hub), then refit the sprocket-to-hub bolts. Do not fully tighten the bolts at this stage.

112 Refit the pump timing pin through the sprocket into the pump body.

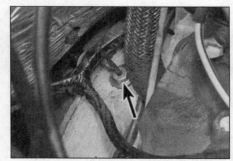

12.5 Improvised flywheel locking tool (arrowed) in position on 19J engine model

113 Loosen the pump locking screw, then refit the keeper plate, and tighten the locking screw.

114 Refit the timing belt as described in Chapter 2A.

115 On completion, start the engine, and check the idle speed and maximum engine speed as described in Sections 10 and 9 respectively.

12 Injection timing – checking methods and adjustment

1 Checking the injection timing is not a routine operation. It is only necessary after the injection pump has been disturbed.

2 Dynamic timing equipment does exist, but it is unlikely to be available to the home mechanic, and there should be no need to carry out dynamic timing. The equipment works by converting pressure pulses in an injector pipe into electrical signals. If such equipment is available, use it in accordance with its maker's instructions.

3 Static timing can be carried out very accurately, provided that the appropriate tools are available.

10J engines

4 The injection pump must be removed to check the timing. The timing procedure is included as part of the pump removal and refitting procedure in Section 11. Note that Land Rover special tool RO605863 will be required.

12J and 19J engines

5 Timing can be carried out very accurately, providing that the appropriate injection pump spindle locking tool (and, where applicable, flywheel locking tool – see Chapter 2A, Section 3) is/are available **(see illustration)**. The Land Rover special tool available to lock the injection pump is 18G 1458. The tool can be improvised by obtaining a spare injection pump timing aperture blanking plug, and accurately drilling a hole through its centre, to accept a 5/32 in twist drill.

200 TDi and 300 TDi engines

6 Timing can be carried out very accurately, providing that the appropriate flywheel and injection pump spindle locking tools are available. The Land Rover special tool available to lock the flywheel is LRT-12-044. The tool can be improvised by obtaining a spare flywheel housing blanking plug, and accurately drilling a hole though its centre, to accept a 3/16 in twist drill. To lock the fuel injection pump sprocket, special tool LRT-12-045 will be required – this tool can be

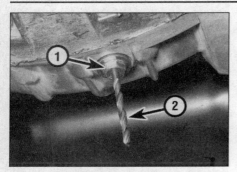

12.6a Improvised flywheel locking tool in position on 300 TDi engine model

1 Blanking plug
2 3/16 in twist drill

improvised using a short length (approximately 50.0 mm) of 9.5 mm diameter round bar **(see illustrations)**.

13 Injection timing – checking and adjustment

Caution: The maximum engine speed and transfer pressure settings, together with timing access plugs, may be sealed by the manufacturers at the factory, using locking wire and seals. Do not disturb the wire or seals if the vehicle is still within the warranty period, otherwise the warranty will be invalidated. Also do not attempt the timing procedure unless suitable tools (see Section 12) are available. Refer to the precautions given in Section 1 of this Chapter before proceeding.

10J engines

1 The injection pump must be removed to check the timing. The timing procedure is included as part of the pump removal and refitting procedure in Section 11. Note that Land Rover special tool RO605863 will be required.

12J and 19J engines

2 Turn the crankshaft to bring No 1 piston to

13.3 Removing the timing aperture blanking plug from the injection pump – 19J engine

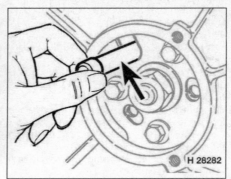

12.6b Injection pump timing pin (arrowed) can be improvised using a length of 9.5 mm diameter bar

TDC as described in Chapter 2A, Section 3.
3 Unscrew the timing aperture blanking plug from the side of the injection pump **(see illustration)**.
4 Insert the timing tool 18G 1458 (or the improvised tool – see Section 12) into the timing aperture, and attempt to screw the tool fully into the pump, so that the centre pin engages with the pump spindle (or insert the twist drill into the hole in the pump spindle), locking the spindle in position – **do not** force the tool. To ensure that the tool centre pin has engaged with the pump spindle, remove the flywheel locking tool (where applicable), then attempt to turn the crankshaft slightly – **do not** force the crankshaft. It will be obvious when the timing tool centre pin engages with the hole in the pump spindle **(see illustration)**.
5 If it is possible to engage the timing tool centre pin with the pump spindle with the crankshaft at TDC, the pump timing is correct, and no adjustment is required. In this case, proceed to paragraph 11.
6 If it is necessary to turn the crankshaft away from the TDC position in order to engage the timing tool centre pin with the pump spindle, withdraw the tool from the pump spindle, then turn the crankshaft in the normal direction of rotation (clockwise) back to TDC – see Chapter 2A, Section 3 (where applicable), engage the flywheel locking tool with the slot in the flywheel). Proceed as follows.

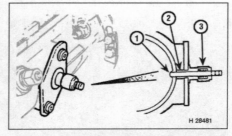

13.4 Timing tool screwed into timing aperture in injection pump – 19J engine

1 Hole in pump spindle
2 Tool centre pin
3 Tool body

a) Unscrew the union nuts securing the injector pipes to the rear of the pump. Counterhold the unions on the pump when unscrewing the nuts. Cover the open unions to keep dirt out.
b) Slacken the rear pump mounting nut and bolt, and the three front pump mounting nuts.
c) Rotate the pump body slightly, until the timing tool centre pin can be engaged with the hole in the pump spindle.
d) Check that the engine timing marks are still aligned (the flywheel timing mark/slot, and camshaft and fuel injection pump sprocket marks should be in alignment with No 1 piston at TDC – see Chapter 2A, Section 3).
e) Tighten the pump mounting nuts and bolt.

7 Check to see if a pump timing pointer is fitted to the rear of the timing belt housing – the pointer was deleted on later models. The pointer is secured by two bolts, and serves as a reference to help preserve the pump timing when removing and refitting the pump.
8 If a pointer is fitted, check to see if there is a corresponding alignment mark on the pump flange.
9 If a mark is present, but it is not aligned with the pointer, loosen the two pointer securing screws, and move the pointer until it aligns with the mark. Tighten the pointer securing screws.
10 If no mark is present on the pump flange, make a suitable mark in the centre of the machined area on the flange. Loosen the two pointer securing screws, align the timing pointer with the mark, and tighten the screws.
11 Withdraw the timing tool from the aperture in the pump, then refit the blanking plug.
12 On engines with timing marks on the flywheel, where applicable remove the timing pointer, then refit the timing aperture cover using a new gasket, and tighten the securing nuts.
13 On engines with a timing slot in the flywheel, remove the timing pin from the flywheel housing, and refit the blanking plug.
14 Refit the timing belt cover as described in Chapter 2A.

200 TDi and 300 TDi engines

Note: *A new injection pump hub cover plate gasket must be used on refitting.*
15 Disconnect the battery negative lead.
16 Turn the crankshaft to bring No 1 piston to TDC, and fit the tools to lock the flywheel and the injection pump sprocket in position, as described in Chapter 2A. If the flywheel and injection pump sprocket can be locked using the tools as described, the injection pump timing is correct.
17 If the flywheel locking tool centre pin cannot be engaged easily with the timing slot in the flywheel, proceed as follows.
18 Withdraw the flywheel locking tool centre pin from the slot in the flywheel, then turn the crankshaft as necessary, until the

timing pin can be inserted easily into the injection pump.

19 Loosen the pump locking screw, and remove the keeper plate (located at the front of the pump, behind the timing belt housing). Tighten the locking screw to lock the pump in position **(see illustration)**.

20 Loosen the three pump sprocket-to-hub bolts.

21 Turn the crankshaft back the small amount to TDC, and engage the flywheel locking tool centre pin with the timing slot in the flywheel.

22 Recheck to ensure that the pump timing pin is an easy sliding fit in the pump.

23 Tighten the pump sprocket-to-hub bolts to the specified torque.

24 Loosen the pump locking screw, then refit the keeper plate, and tighten the locking screw.

25 Remove the timing pin from the pump, and withdraw the flywheel locking tool centre pin from the slot in the flywheel.

26 Turn the crankshaft through two complete revolutions, and check that the flywheel locking tool and the pump timing pin can still be inserted easily at the same time.

27 Withdraw the timing pin and the flywheel locking tool.

28 Refit the blanking plug, or the cover plate bolt, as applicable, to the flywheel locking tool aperture (on models with a blanking plug, coat the threads of the plug with thread-locking compound before refitting).

29 Refit the injection pump hub cover plate, using a new gasket.

30 Where applicable, refit the air conditioning compressor, and refit the drivebelt as described in Chapter 1.

---

14 Fuel injectors – testing, removal and refitting

⚠️ **Warning: Exercise extreme caution when working on the fuel injectors. Never expose the hands, or any part of the body, to injector spray, as the high working pressure can cause the fuel to penetrate the skin, with possibly fatal results. You are strongly advised to have any work which involves testing the injectors under pressure carried out by a Land Rover dealer or fuel injection specialist. Refer to the precautions given in Section 1 of this Chapter before proceeding.**

Testing

1 Injectors do deteriorate with prolonged use, and it is reasonable to expect them to need reconditioning or renewal after 60 000 miles or so. Accurate testing, overhaul and calibration of the injectors must be left to a specialist. A defective injector which is causing knocking or smoking can be located without dismantling as follows.

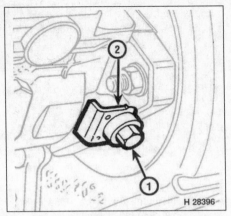

13.19 Pump locking screw (1) and keeper plate (2)

2 Run the engine at a fast idle. Slacken each injector union in turn, placing rag around the union to catch spilt fuel, and being careful not to expose the skin to any spray. When the union on the defective injector is slackened, the knocking or smoking will stop.

Removal

3 Disconnect the battery negative lead.

4 Where applicable, remove the oil filler cap, and unclip the plastic cover from the top of the valve cover.

5 Carefully clean around the relevant injector and injector pipe union nuts.

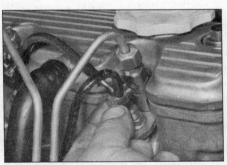

14.6 Disconnecting the leak-off pipes – 300 TDi engine

14.9a Unscrew the securing nuts . . .

6 Unscrew the banjo bolt, and disconnect the leak-off pipe(s) from the injector. On models with a rigid leak-off pipe connected to all the injectors, disconnect the pipe from all four injectors, and remove it. Recover the sealing washers. Plug or cover the openings in the injectors, to keep dirt out (the banjo bolts can be refitted, and covered) **(see illustration)**.

7 Unscrew the union nut securing the injector pipe to the fuel injector **(see illustration)**. Cover the open ends of the injector and the pipe, using small plastic bags, or fingers cut from discarded (but clean) rubber gloves.

8 Counterhold the union on the pump, and slacken the union nut securing the relevant injector pipe to the injection pump. On some models, it may be necessary to completely remove the pipe, but on most models, the pipe can be moved sufficiently to allow injector removal. If the pipe is removed, again cover the openings in the pipe and the pump.

9 On 10J, 12J, and 19J engines, unscrew the two nuts (recover the washers) securing the injector to the studs on the cylinder head. Carefully lift the injector from the cylinder head, and recover the two washers from the base of the injector, or from the recesses in the cylinder head, as applicable **(see illustrations)**.

10 On 200 TDi and 300 TDi engines, unscrew the nut securing the injector clamp plate to the cylinder head. Withdraw the clamp plate and the injector from the cylinder head,

14.7 Disconnecting the injector pipe from a fuel injector – 300 TDi engine

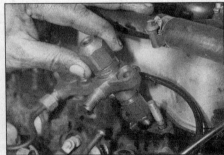

14.9b . . . and withdraw the fuel injector – 19J engine

14.10a Unscrew the securing nut . . .

14.10b . . . then withdraw the clamp plate . . .

14.10c . . . and the injector – 300 TDi engine

then recover the copper washer from the injector location in the cylinder head **(see illustrations)**.

11 Take care not to drop the injectors, nor allow the needles at their tips to become damaged. The injectors are precision-made to fine limits, and must not be handled roughly. In particular, do not mount them in a bench vice.

Refitting

12 On 10J, 12J and 19J engines, fit a new steel sealing washer to the cylinder head, with the raised corrugation uppermost.
13 On 200 TDi and 300 TDi engines, fit a new copper washer to the cylinder head, with the concave side towards the injector.
14 Fit the injector to the cylinder head. On 10J, 12J and 19J engines, the hole for the injector pipe union should face away from the cylinder head. On 200 TDi engines, the hole for the leak-off pipe union should face towards the rear of the engine. On 300 TDi engines, the hole for the leak-off pipe union should face away from the cylinder head.
15 Refit the two securing nuts and washers, or the clamp plate and the securing nut, as applicable, then tighten the nut(s) to the specified torque.
16 Reconnect the injector pipe to the injector, and tighten the union nut. Similarly (where

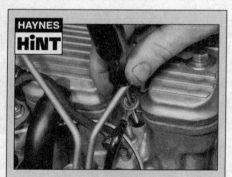

The washer can be guided into position by sliding it down the shaft of a screwdriver positioned over the injector hole in the cylinder head.

applicable) reconnect the pipe to the injection pump, and tighten the union nut.
17 Reconnect the leak-off pipe to the injector(s), and tighten the banjo bolt(s). Note that there are two copper washers on the union, and one washer should be fitted each side of the pipe banjo.
18 Reconnect the battery negative lead, then start the engine. If difficulty is experienced, bleed the fuel system as described in Section 5.

15 Turbocharger – description and precautions

Description

1 A turbocharger is fitted to 19J, 200 TDi and 300 TDi engines. It increases engine efficiency by raising the pressure in the inlet manifold above atmospheric pressure. Instead of the air simply being sucked into the cylinders, it is forced in. Additional fuel is supplied by the injection pump, in proportion to the increased amount of air.
2 Energy for the operation of the turbocharger comes from the exhaust gas. The gas flows through a specially-shaped housing (the turbine housing) and in so doing, spins the turbine wheel. The turbine wheel is attached to a shaft, at the end of which is another vaned wheel, known as the compressor wheel. The compressor wheel spins in its own housing, and compresses the inducted air on the way to the inlet manifold.
3 On 200 TDi and 300 TDi engines, the compressed air passes through an intercooler, between the turbocharger and the inlet manifold. The intercooler is an air-to-air heat exchanger, mounted at the front of the vehicle, next to the radiator, and supplied with air through the front grille. The purpose of the intercooler is to remove from the inducted air some of the heat gained in being compressed. Because cooler air is denser, removal of this heat further increases engine efficiency.
4 Boost pressure (the pressure in the inlet manifold) is limited by a wastegate, which diverts the exhaust gas away from the turbine

wheel in response to a pressure-sensitive actuator.
5 The turbo shaft is pressure-lubricated by an oil feed pipe from the main oil gallery. The shaft 'floats' on a cushion of oil. A drain pipe returns the oil to the sump.

Precautions

⚠️ *Warning:*
• The turbocharger operates at extremely high speeds and temperatures. Certain precautions must be observed to avoid premature failure of the turbo, or injury to the operator.
• Do not operate the turbo with any parts exposed. Foreign objects falling onto the rotating vanes could cause excessive damage and (if ejected) personal injury.
• Do not race the engine immediately after start-up, especially if it is cold. Give the oil a few seconds to circulate.
• Always allow the engine to return to idle speed before switching it off – do not blip the throttle and switch off, as this will leave the turbo spinning without lubrication.
• Allow the engine to idle for several minutes before switching off after a high-speed run.
• Observe the recommended intervals for oil and filter changing, and use a reputable oil of the specified quality. Neglect of oil changing, or use of inferior oil, can cause carbon formation on the turbo shaft, and subsequent failure.

16 Turbocharger – removal and refitting

19J engine

Note: *New turbocharger-to-manifold and exhaust elbow-to-turbocharger gaskets should be used on refitting.*

Removal

1 Disconnect the battery negative lead.
2 To improve access, remove the bonnet as described in Chapter 12.
3 Slacken the clamps, and remove the air

16.4 Removing the turbocharger heat shield – 19J engine

trunking connecting the air cleaner to the turbocharger.

4 Unscrew the securing nuts and bolts, and remove the turbocharger heat shield **(see illustration)**.

5 Disconnect the exhaust front section from the turbocharger elbow, with reference to Section 20.

6 Slacken the clamps, and remove the air trunking connecting the turbocharger to the inlet manifold.

7 Disconnect the boost pressure pipe from the turbocharger wastegate actuator.

8 Unscrew the union nut, and disconnect the oil feed pipe from the top of the turbocharger. Be prepared for oil spillage, and plug or cover the open ends of the pipe and the turbocharger, to prevent dirt ingress.

9 Slacken the clamp, and disconnect the flexible hose from the turbocharger oil return pipe. Again, be prepared for oil spillage, and plug or cover the open ends of the pipe and hose.

10 Unscrew the five nuts and washers securing the exhaust elbow to the turbocharger, then withdraw the elbow and recover the gasket.

11 Prise back the lockwasher tabs, then unscrew the four nuts securing the turbocharger to the exhaust manifold. Withdraw the turbocharger, and recover the gasket.

Refitting

12 Refitting is a reversal of removal, bearing in mind the following points:

a) Refit the turbocharger to the manifold using a new gasket (the raised bead side of the gasket should be uppermost). Tighten the securing nuts to the specified torque, then secure by bending up the lockwasher tabs.

b) Use a new gasket when refitting the exhaust elbow.

c) Ensure that the oil pipes are securely reconnected.

d) Reconnect the exhaust front section to the turbocharger elbow, with reference to Section 20.

13 Before starting the engine, the turbocharger **must** be primed with oil as follows. Failure to

carry out this procedure may result in serious (and expensive) damage to the turbocharger:

a) Unscrew the oil feed pipe union from the top of the turbocharger housing. Move the feed pipe away from the oil hole in the housing.

b) Fill the housing with clean engine oil of the correct type and grade, from a freshly-opened sealed container.

c) Reconnect the oil feed pipe, and tighten the union nut.

200 TDi engine

Note: A new gasket will be required when refitting the turbocharger.

Removal

14 Disconnect the battery negative lead.

15 To improve access, remove the bonnet as described in Chapter 12.

16 Unscrew the securing nuts and bolts, and remove the turbocharger heat shield.

17 Disconnect the exhaust front section from the turbocharger elbow, with reference to Section 20.

18 Release the exhaust front section from the support bracket on the cylinder block.

19 Unscrew the five securing nuts, and remove the exhaust elbow from the turbocharger. Recover the gasket.

20 Loosen the securing clips, and disconnect the air trunking from the turbocharger. If desired, to improve access, remove the air trunking.

21 Disconnect the boost pressure pipe from the T-piece at the turbocharger.

22 Slacken the turbocharger oil feed pipe clamp bolt.

23 Unscrew the union nut, and disconnect the oil feed pipe from the top of the turbocharger. Be prepared for oil spillage, and plug or cover the open ends of the pipe and the turbocharger, to prevent dirt ingress.

24 Slacken the clamp, and disconnect the flexible hose from the turbocharger oil return pipe. Again, be prepared for oil spillage, and plug or cover the open ends of the pipe and hose.

25 Unscrew the four securing nuts, and withdraw the turbocharger from the exhaust manifold. Recover the gasket.

Refitting

26 Refitting is a reversal of removal, bearing in mind the following points:

a) Refit the turbocharger to the manifold using a new gasket, and tighten the securing nuts to the specified torque.

b) Use a new gasket when refitting the exhaust elbow.

c) Ensure that the oil pipes are securely reconnected.

d) Reconnect the exhaust front section to the turbocharger elbow, with reference to Section 20.

27 Before starting the engine, the

turbocharger **must** be primed with oil as described in paragraph 13. Failure to carry out this procedure may result in serious (and expensive) damage to the turbocharger.

300 TDi engine

28 On 300 TDi engines, the turbocharger is integral with the exhaust manifold. Although the turbocharger and manifold can be separated once the manifold assembly has been removed, at the time of writing, it is unclear whether the turbocharger can be renewed independently of the manifold – check with a Land Rover dealer for details.

29 Removal and refitting of the turbocharger is described as part of the exhaust manifold removal and refitting procedure in Section 19.

17 Turbocharger – examination and overhaul

1 With the turbocharger removed, inspect the housing for cracks or other visible damage.

2 Spin the turbine or the compressor wheel, to verify that the shaft is intact, and to feel for excessive shake or roughness. Some play is normal, since in use the shaft is 'floating' on a film of oil. Check that the wheel vanes are undamaged.

3 The wastegate actuator is a separate unit, and can be renewed independently of the turbocharger. Testing of the wastegate actuator (boost pressure check) is described in Chapter 1.

4 If the exhaust or inlet passages are oil-contaminated, the turbo shaft oil seals have probably failed. (On the inlet side, this will also have contaminated the intercooler, which if necessary should be flushed with a suitable solvent.)

5 Check the oil feed and return pipes for contamination or blockage, and clean if necessary.

6 No DIY repair of the turbocharger is possible. A new unit may be available on an exchange basis.

18 Intercooler (200 TDi and 300 TDi engine models) – removal and refitting

200 TDi engine models

Removal

1 Disconnect the battery negative lead.

2 Remove the viscous cooling fan and coupling, and the fan cowl, as described in Chapter 3.

3 Loosen the clips securing the two hoses

to the intercooler, and carefully pull the hoses from the intercooler stubs (see illustration).

4 Remove the four bolts (two bolts on each side) securing the two radiator mounting brackets to the front body panel. Withdraw the brackets.

5 Remove the four bolts (two at each side) securing the radiator top cover, and withdraw the cover.

6 Lift the intercooler upwards from the support frame (see illustration).

Refitting

7 Before refitting, check the condition of the intercooler locating lug grommets in the lower body panel and the radiator top cover, and renew if necessary. Also check the condition of the foam insulating pad, and ensure that it is securely attached to the intercooler.

8 Refitting is a reversal of removal, ensuring that the hose sleeves are securely reconnected. Refit the viscous cooling fan and coupling as described in Chapter 3.

300 TDi engine models

9 The procedure is as described previously for the 200 TDi engine models, but instead of removing the viscous cooling fan and coupling, and the fan shroud, simply remove the two nuts securing the top of the cooling fan cowl to the radiator top cover.

19 Manifolds –
removal and refitting

10J and 12J engines

Note: *A new gasket may be required on refitting.*

Inlet manifold

1 Disconnect the battery negative lead.
2 Disconnect the air trunking from the manifold.
3 Where applicable, disconnect the breather hose from the manifold.
4 Unscrew the six securing nuts, recover the clamp plates, then withdraw the inlet manifold from the cylinder head.
5 Refitting is a reversal of removal, bearing in mind the following points:
   a) Check the condition of the manifold gasket, and renew if necessary (in which case, the exhaust manifold will have to be removed) – if the original gasket has deteriorated, clean all traces of old gasket from the mating faces of the cylinder head and manifold before fitting a new gasket.
   b) Tighten the manifold securing nuts securely.

Exhaust manifold

6 Remove the inlet manifold as described previously.
7 Disconnect the exhaust front section from the manifold as described in Section 20.

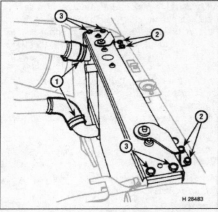

18.3 Intercooler fixings – 200 TDi engine models

1 Hose clips
2 Radiator mounting bracket bolts
3 Radiator top cover bolts

8 Unscrew the remaining three securing nuts, recover the clamp plates, and withdraw the manifold. Recover the gasket.

9 Refitting is a reversal of removal, bearing in mind the following points:
   a) Thoroughly clean the mating faces of the manifolds and the cylinder head, and refit the manifolds using a new gasket.
   b) Tighten the manifold nuts securely.

19J engines

Note: *A new gasket will be required on refitting.*

Inlet manifold

10 To remove the inlet manifold, the exhaust manifold must be removed first. Refer to the following paragraphs for details.

Exhaust manifold

11 Remove the turbocharger as described in Section 16.
12 Unscrew the securing nuts and bolts, recover the clamp plates, then withdraw the exhaust manifold.
13 Unscrew the two through-bolts, and withdraw the inlet manifold from the cylinder head. Recover the gasket.
14 Refitting is a reversal of removal, bearing in mind the following points:
   a) Thoroughly clean the mating faces of the manifolds and the cylinder head, and refit the manifolds using a new gasket.
   b) Tighten the manifold nuts and bolts to the specified torque.
   c) Refit the turbocharger as described in Section 16.

200 TDi engines

Note: *A new gasket will be required on refitting.*

Inlet manifold

15 To remove the inlet manifold, the exhaust manifold must be removed first. Refer to the following paragraphs for details.

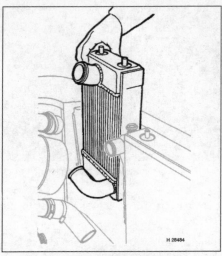

18.6 Lifting out the intercooler – 200 TDi engine

Exhaust manifold

16 Remove the turbocharger as described in Section 16.
17 Unscrew the two nuts (and recover the washers) securing the coolant pipe to the top manifold studs, and lift the pipe clear of the studs.
18 Unscrew the securing nuts, and recover the washers, then lift the manifold from the cylinder head. Recover the gasket.
19 Unscrew the two bolts and two nuts, and withdraw the inlet manifold. Recover the gasket (see illustration).
20 Refitting is a reversal of removal, bearing in mind the following points:
   a) Thoroughly clean the mating faces of the manifolds and the cylinder head, and refit the manifolds using a new gasket.
   b) Tighten the manifold nuts and bolts to the specified torque.
   c) Refit the turbocharger as described in Section 16.

300 TDi engines

Inlet manifold

Note: *A new gasket may be required on refitting.*

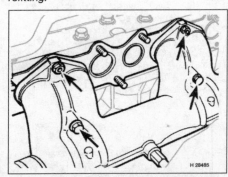

19.19 Inlet manifold securing nuts and bolts (arrowed) – 200 TDi engine

19.23 Remove the bolts and nuts (arrowed) . . .

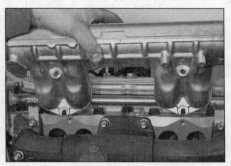

19.24 . . . and withdraw the inlet manifold – 300 TDi engine

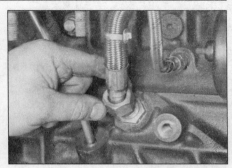

19.31 Disconnecting the turbocharger oil return hose union from the cylinder block – 300 TDi engine

21 Disconnect the battery negative lead.

22 Slacken the clamps, and remove the air trunking connecting the intercooler to the inlet manifold.

23 Unscrew the two inlet manifold lower securing nuts, located below the exhaust manifold **(see illustration)**.

24 Unscrew the inlet manifold upper securing bolts, and withdraw the manifold upwards **(see illustration)**.

25 Refitting is a reversal of removal, bearing in mind the following points:

  a) *Check the condition of the manifold gasket, and renew if necessary (in which case, the exhaust manifold will have to be removed) – if the original gasket has deteriorated, clean all traces of old gasket from the mating faces of the cylinder head and manifold before fitting a new gasket.*

  b) *Tighten the manifold fixings to the specified torque.*

Exhaust manifold

Note: *If the turbocharger is removed from the manifold, a new turbocharger-to-manifold gasket, and a new wastegate pushrod clip, will be required. On 300 TDi engines, the turbocharger is integral with the exhaust manifold. Although the turbocharger and manifold can be separated once the manifold assembly has been removed, at the time of writing, it is unclear whether the turbocharger can be renewed independently of the manifold – check with a Land Rover dealer for details. A new manifold gasket should be used on refitting (a single gasket is used for both the inlet and exhaust manifolds).*

26 Remove the inlet manifold, as described previously in this Section.

27 Loosen the securing clips, and remove the air cleaner-to-turbocharger inlet trunking, and the turbocharger outlet-to-intercooler trunking. Note the breather hose connected to the inlet trunking.

28 On models with EGR (see Section 22), unscrew the two securing bolts and disconnect the EGR delivery pipe from the intercooler-to-inlet manifold trunking.

29 Where applicable, disconnect the wiring plug from the EGR valve.

30 Disconnect the exhaust front section from the turbocharger, with reference to Section 20.

31 Place a suitable container beneath the engine to catch escaping oil, then unscrew the union nuts, and disconnect the turbocharger oil feed and return hoses from the cylinder block (counterhold the unions on the cylinder block) **(see illustration)**. Plug the open ends of the hoses and at the cylinder block, to prevent dirt ingress.

32 Disconnect the turbocharger boost pressure pipe from the turbocharger **(see illustration)**.

33 Unscrew the two manifold nuts securing the coolant pipe to the top manifold studs, and lift the pipe clear of the studs **(see illustration)**.

34 Unscrew the remaining manifold securing nuts, then lift the complete manifold/turbocharger assembly from the cylinder head. Recover the gasket.

35 It is possible that some of the manifold

studs may be unscrewed from the cylinder head when the manifold securing nuts are unscrewed. In this event, the studs should be screwed back into the cylinder head once the manifolds have been removed, using two manifold nuts locked together.

36 If the turbocharger is to be removed from the manifold, refer to the note at the beginning of this sub-Section before proceeding.

37 To remove the turbocharger from the manifold, prise off the clip securing the operating lever to the wastegate pushrod, then remove the four bolts and the two clamp plates securing the turbocharger **(see illustrations)**.

38 Withdraw the turbocharger, and recover the gasket.

39 If the turbocharger has been removed from the manifold, thoroughly clean the mating faces of the turbocharger and the

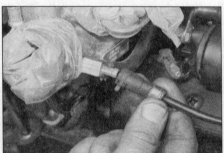

19.32 Disconnecting the boost pressure pipe from the turbocharger – 300 TDi engine

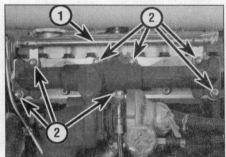

19.33 Coolant pipe (1) and exhaust manifold securing nuts (2) – 300 TDi engine

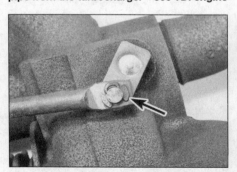

19.37a Turbocharger wastegate pushrod securing clip (arrowed) – 300 TDi engine

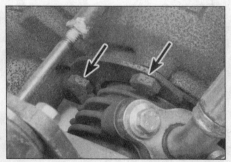

19.37b Two of the turbocharger securing bolts (arrowed) – 300 TDi engine

manifold, then refit the turbocharger using a new gasket.

40 Reconnect the operating lever to the wastegate pushrod, using a new clip.

41 Check the condition of the manifold gasket, and renew if necessary – if the original gasket has deteriorated, clean all traces of old gasket from the mating faces of the cylinder head and manifold before fitting a new gasket.

42 Fit the gasket and the manifold, and refit the coolant pipe to the top manifold studs. Refit the securing nuts and washers, and tighten the nuts progressively to the specified torque.

43 Reconnect the turbocharger boost pressure pipe.

44 Reconnect the turbocharger oil pipes, and securely tighten the union nuts.

45 Reconnect the exhaust front section to the turbocharger, with reference to Section 20.

46 Where applicable, reconnect the EGR valve wiring plug.

47 Refit the air trunking, and reconnect the breather hose to the inlet trunking.

48 On models with EGR, reconnect the EGR delivery pipe to the intercooler-to-inlet manifold trunking, and tighten the securing bolts.

49 Refit the inlet manifold as described previously in this Section.

50 Before starting the engine, the turbocharger **must** be primed with oil as follows. Failure to carry out this procedure may result in serious (and expensive) damage to the turbocharger:

a) *Unscrew the oil feed pipe banjo bolt from the top of the turbocharger housing. Recover the two sealing washers, and move the feed pipe away from the oil hole in the housing.*

b) *Fill the housing with clean engine oil of the correct type and grade, from a freshly-opened sealed container.*

c) *Reconnect the oil feed pipe, and refit the banjo bolt, ensuring that one sealing washer is positioned on each side of the pipe. Tighten the banjo bolt to the specified torque.*

20 Exhaust system – general information and component renewal

General information

1 The exhaust system consists of a number of separate sections, the sections varying in detail depending on model. Each exhaust section can be renewed individually, leaving the remaining section(s) in place.

2 On certain 300 TDi engine models a catalytic converter is located in the exhaust front section.

Component renewal

3 To remove the system or part of the system, first jack up the front or rear of the vehicle, as

applicable, and support it securely on axle stands (see *Jacking and vehicle support*).

Exhaust front section

Note: *Suitable jointing compound may be required on refitting, and a new gasket and/or sealing ring may be required.*

4 Where applicable, unbolt the heat shield for access to the exhaust front section-to-manifold joint.

5 Unscrew the three exhaust-to-manifold nuts, or loosen the clamp nut and bolt, and slide the clamp from the exhaust-to-manifold joint, as applicable.

6 Where applicable, unbolt the exhaust mounting brackets from the cylinder block and/or the chassis, then release the mounting rubbers and brackets from the exhaust pipe.

7 Unscrew the nuts (counterhold the bolts where necessary) securing the exhaust front section to the intermediate section, and release the flanged joint.

8 Lower the front end of the exhaust from the manifold, and where applicable, recover the gasket. Where applicable, also recover the exhaust front section-to-intermediate section gasket.

9 Carefully manipulate the exhaust front section out from under the vehicle.

10 Refitting is a reversal of removal, bearing in mind the following points:

a) *Where applicable, check the condition of the exhaust mounting rubbers, and renew if necessary.*

b) *Where applicable, use a new exhaust-to-manifold gasket. On models with a clamped joint, apply a little exhaust jointing compound to the joint before fitting.*

c) *Where applicable, check the condition of the exhaust front section-to-intermediate section sealing ring, and renew if necessary.*

d) *Do not fully tighten the mountings and clamp nuts and bolts until the completion of refitting.*

Exhaust intermediate and rear sections

11 A number of different configurations of system may be used, depending on model.

12 Generally, it should be possible to remove each individual component, leaving the remaining components in place. In some cases, it may be necessary to release the surrounding exhaust components from their mountings, in order to allow sufficient movement to withdraw the desired component.

13 Various types of mountings and clamp fixings may be encountered, and removal should be self-evident. Note the positions of any washers and spacers, so that they can be refitted in their original locations.

14 Always renew gaskets and sealing rings if they show signs of deterioration. Similarly, renew mounting rubbers and clamp bolts/U-bolts, etc, if they shown signs of damage or corrosion.

15 Where necessary, apply exhaust jointing compound to seal flanged joints where no gasket or sealing ring is used.

16 When refitting, do not fully tighten mounting and clamp fixings until the components have been manipulated into their final positions. Similarly, ensure that the components are not under strain before tightening the fixings.

21 Emissions control systems – general information

1 Certain engines are equipped with systems designed to reduce the emissions of harmful by-products of the combustion process into the atmosphere.

2 The following systems may be fitted according to model.

Crankcase emissions control

3 A crankcase ventilation system is fitted to all models.

4 Oil fumes and piston blow-by gases (combustion gases which have passed by the piston rings) are drawn from the crankcase through an oil separator, through the main oil separator, into the air inlet tract. The gases are then drawn into the engine together with fresh air/fuel mixture. Condensed oil vapour is returned from the main oil separator to the engine sump.

Exhaust emissions control

5 This system is fitted to certain models with the 300 TDi engine.

6 To minimise the level of exhaust gas pollutants released into the atmosphere a catalytic converter is fitted, located in the exhaust system.

7 The catalytic converter consists of a canister containing a fine mesh impregnated with a catalyst material, over which the exhaust gases pass. The catalyst speeds up the oxidation of harmful carbon monoxide, unburnt hydrocarbons and soot, effectively reducing the quantity of harmful products reaching the atmosphere.

Exhaust gas recirculation system

8 This system is fitted to certain models with the 300 TDi engine.

9 The system is designed to recirculate small quantities of exhaust gas into the inlet tract, and therefore into the combustion process. This process reduces the level of oxides of nitrogen present in the final exhaust gas which is released into the atmosphere, and also lowers the combustion temperature.

10 The volume of exhaust gas recirculated is controlled by vacuum, via a solenoid valve. The solenoid valve is controlled by a fuel injection pump-mounted sensor.

11 A vacuum-operated recirculation valve is fitted to the exhaust manifold, to regulate the quantity of exhaust gas recirculated. The valve is operated by the vacuum supplied via the solenoid valve.

12 Between idle speed and a predetermined engine load, power is supplied to the solenoid valve, which allows the recirculation valve to open. Under full-load conditions, the exhaust gas recirculation is cut off. Additional control is provided by the engine temperature sensor, which cuts off the vacuum supply until the coolant temperature reaches 40°C, preventing the recirculation valve from opening during the engine warm-up period.

22 Emissions control systems – testing and component renewal

Crankcase emissions control

Testing

1 If the system is thought to be faulty, first, check that the hoses are unobstructed. On high-mileage vehicles, particularly those regularly used for short journeys, a jelly-like deposit may be evident inside the system hoses and oil separator. If excessive deposits are present, the relevant component(s) should be removed and cleaned.

2 Periodically inspect the system components for security and damage, and renew them as necessary. Note that damaged or loose hoses can cause various engine running problems (erratic idle speed, stalling, etc) which can be difficult to trace.

Component renewal

3 Renewal procedures for the hoses and oil separator are self-evident.

Exhaust emissions control

Testing

4 The system can only be tested accurately using a suitable exhaust gas analyser (suitable for use with diesel engines).

Component renewal

5 The catalytic converter is integral with the exhaust system front section.

6 Removal and refitting are described in Section 20.

EGR system

EGR valve testing

7 Testing of the EGR valve should be entrusted to a Land Rover dealer or specialist.

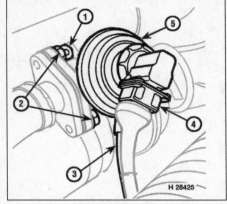

22.9 EGR valve location

1 Valve securing bolts
2 EGR delivery pipe securing bolts
3 Vacuum hose
4 Wiring plug
5 Valve

EGR valve removal

Note: *New EGR valve-to-manifold, and delivery pipe-to-EGR valve gaskets must be used on refitting.*

8 Disconnect the battery negative lead, then where applicable, disconnect the wiring plug from the valve.

9 Disconnect the vacuum hose from the valve **(see illustration)**.

10 Unscrew the two bolts securing the valve to the exhaust manifold.

11 Remove the two securing bolts, and disconnect the EGR delivery pipe from the valve.

12 Withdraw the valve, and recover the gaskets.

EGR valve refitting

13 Refitting is a reversal of removal, but use new gaskets when refitting the valve and reconnecting the delivery pipe.

Coolant temperature sensor

Testing

14 The system uses the coolant temperature gauge sender unit. Details of removal and refitting are given in Chapter 3.

Removal and refitting

15 Refer to the coolant temperature gauge sender unit procedure in Chapter 3.

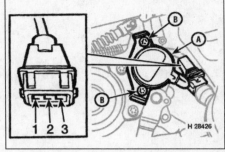

22.18 EGR throttle position sensor location – note plug terminal numbers (inset)

A Sensor
B Securing screws

Throttle position sensor

Testing

16 Start the engine, and run it until normal operating temperature is reached.

17 Stop the engine, and disconnect the throttle position sensor wiring plug.

18 Connect an ohmmeter across pins 1 and 3 of the wiring plug. The reading on the ohmmeter should be as given in the Specifications **(see illustration)**.

19 Reconnect the ohmmeter between pins 1 and 2 of the wiring plug. Again, the reading should be as specified.

20 If the readings are not as specified, loosen the two sensor retaining screws, and rotate the sensor to achieve the correct readings. Tighten the retaining screws when the readings are correct.

21 If the correct readings cannot be obtained by rotating the sensor, the sensor is faulty and should be renewed.

22 Reconnect the wiring plug on completion.

Removal

23 This sensor is located on the fuel injection pump.

24 Disconnect the battery negative lead, then disconnect the wiring plug from the sensor.

25 Unscrew the two securing screws, and withdraw the sensor.

Refitting

26 Refitting is a reversal of removal, but before tightening the securing screws, adjust the position of the sensor as described previously in this Section (*Testing*).

Notes

Chapter 4 Part B:
Fuel, exhaust and emissions control systems – TD5 engines

Contents

Section number

Accelerator pedal – removal and refitting. 3
Air cleaner assembly and ducting – removal and refitting 2
Air cleaner element renewal . . . . See Chapter 1
Emissions control systems – general information 17
Emissions control systems – testing and component renewal 18
Engine management electronic components –
    removal and refitting 10
Exhaust system – general information and component renewal 16
Fuel cooler – removal and refitting. 4
Fuel filter element renewal . . . . See Chapter 1
Fuel gauge sender unit – removal and refitting 6
Fuel injectors – testing, removal and refitting. 8

Section number

Fuel pressure regulator/connector block – removal and refitting . . . 9
Fuel sedimenter cleaning . . . . See Chapter 1
Fuel system – priming and bleeding. 5
Fuel tank – removal and refitting 7
General information and precautions. 1
Intercooler – removal and refitting. 14
Intercooler element cleaning . . . . See Chapter 1
Manifolds – removal and refitting. 15
Turbocharger – description and precautions 11
Turbocharger – examination and overhaul 13
Turbocharger – removal and refitting 12

Degrees of difficulty

Easy, suitable for novice with little experience 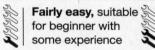	**Fairly easy,** suitable for beginner with some experience	**Fairly difficult,** suitable for competent DIY mechanic	**Difficult,** suitable for experienced DIY mechanic	**Very difficult,** suitable for expert DIY or professional

Specifications

General

System type . . . .   Direct injection, with unit injectors, two-stage tank mounted lift pump, fuel cooler and regulator. Injector timing controlled by ECM (Electronic Control Module)

Firing order . . . .   1-2-4-5-3 (No 1 at timing chain end)

Maximum engine speed (not adjustable):

    Governed . . . .   4850 rpm

    Overrun. . . . .   5460 rpm

Idle speed (not adjustable) . . . .   740 ± 50 rpm

Emission standard:

    Engine Serial No prefixes 10P to 14P EU2

    Engine Serial No prefixes 15P to 19P EU3

Injection timing

All TD5 engines . . . .   ECM controlled (not adjustable)

Injectors

Type . . . .   Lucas EV1 Unit injectors, solenoid controlled

Maximum pressure. . . . .   1750 bar

Turbocharger

Type . . . .   Garrett GT20

Maximum boost pressure. . . . .   Not available

Torque wrench settings

	Nm	lbf ft
Accelerator pedal retaining bolts	25	18
Alternator support bracket	45	33
Crankshaft speed and position sensor bolt	10	7
EGR delivery pipe bolts	10	7
EGR valve securing bolts	10	7
Exhaust front pipe to turbocharger	30	22
Exhaust manifold securing nuts	25	18
Fuel cooler bolts		
Upper bolts	18	13
Lower bolts	25	18
Fuel injector clamp bolt	32	24
Fuel pressure regulator housing bolts	25	18
Fuel temperature sensor	13	10
Intake manifold securing nuts/bolts	25	18
Manifold absolute pressure/Intake air temperature sensor bolts	10	7
Turbocharger oil drain pipe to turbocharger	10	7
Turbocharger oil feed pipe banjo bolt	25	18
Turbocharger to manifold	30	22

1 General information and precautions

General information

The fuel system consists of a moulded fuel tank containing a two-stage fuel lift pump combined with a level sender unit, a fuel filter with sedimenter/water sensor, a pressure regulator, five unit injectors, and a fuel cooler for the fuel returning to the tank **(see illustration)**. A turbocharger, intercooler and EGR system (Exhaust Gas Recirculation) is fitted to all models.

The engine management ECM (Electronic Control Module) energises a relay which causes the low pressure side (0.75 bar) of the pump to draw fuel through a coarse filter and into the main fuel filter. A proportion of the low-pressure fuel passes through a restrictor to the jet pump in the swirl pot at the base of the pump, to keep the fuel there circulating. The high-pressure stage (4.0 bar) of the pump draws fuel from the main filter and feeds it to the pressure regulator at the rear of the cylinder head. The regulator maintains fuel at this pressure, with the excess being passed to the fuel cooler on the intake manifold. The pressurised fuel passes through channels in the cylinder head to feed the five injectors. Any fuel not used by the injectors passes through further channels in the cylinder head back to the regulator, on to the fuel cooler, then through the filter before passing to the fuel tank. The fuel cooler is essential, as the hot fuel from the cylinder head may otherwise cause damage to the moulded fuel tank.

The TD5 engine is not equipped with a fuel injection pump. Instead the fuel from the tank-mounted pump is fed to the injectors through channels in the cylinder head, where it is then compressed to very high pressure (up to 1700 bar) by a piston arrangement on the

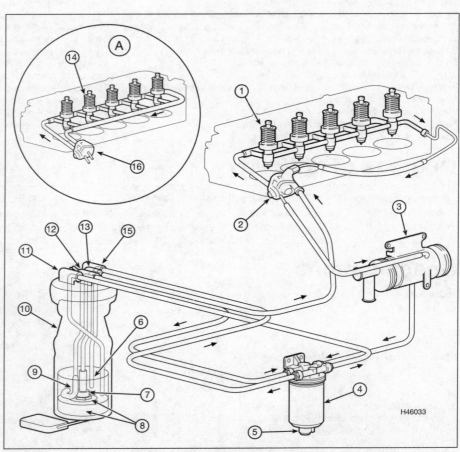

1.1 Fuel system – TD5 models

1 Unit injectors	8 Filters	13 High pressure feed
2 Fuel pressure regulator	9 Jet pump	connection
3 Fuel cooler	10 Fuel pump and level	14 Unit injectors
4 Fuel filter	gauge sender unit	15 Air bleed connection
5 Water sensor	11 Low pressure return	16 Fuel pressure regulator
6 Pump high pressure	connection	
stage	12 Low pressure feed	A = Models with EU2
7 Pump low pressure stage	connection	emission standard

H46033

2.1 Slacken the clip (arrowed) and disconnect the intake hose from the air filter housing

2.2 Release the clips and detach the airflow meter

2.4 Air filter housing mounting grommets

top of each injector. The piston is operated by a rocker arm which in turn is operated by a second set of lobes on the camshaft. This arrangement results in high engine power and torque output, with reduced exhaust emissions and noise. As the camshaft rotates, the lobes begin to lift the injector rocker arms, the injector pistons begin to depress, compressing the fuel within the injectors. When the pressure of the fuel inside the injector reaches 1500 or 1700 bar (depending on emission standard) the pintle spring at the base of the injectors is overcome and the pintle is forced off its seat, allowing the highly pressurised fuel to inject into the combustion chamber. The injection period is controlled by the engine management ECM, energising a solenoid on the injector, which opens a port and allows the pressurised fuel to flow through another channel in the cylinder head, onto the pressure regulator and fuel cooler. When the pressure within the injector collapses, the spring forces the pintle back down, terminating the injection of fuel. The length of the injection period is determined by the ECM based on data concerning engine speed, intake manifold pressure, ambient air pressure, accelerator pedal position/rate of change, coolant temperature, fuel temperature, and airflow volume into the intake manifold.

No accelerator cable is fitted to TD5 models. Instead, a position sensor is attached to the accelerator pedal, which informs the engine management ECM of the pedal position and rate of change.

A turbocharger is fitted to the exhaust manifold

on all TD5 models, which uses the energy from the exhaust gases to spin a turbine on a shaft. The other end of the shaft is attached to another turbine which, when spinning, pressurises the air entering the intake manifold. This results in much improved engine torque and power output, whilst at the same time reducing fuel consumption and noise generation. The intake air leaving the turbocharger passes through an intercooler mounted in front of the coolant radiator. This cools the intake air, increasing its density, which further enhances the efficiency of the combustion process.

In order to reduce harmful emissions from the engine, an EGR (Exhaust Gas Recirculation) system and a crankcase emission control system are fitted. The EGR system allows a controlled amount of the exhaust gases to combine with the fresh air entering the intake system. This reduces the combustion temperature by slowing the fuel-burn rate, which results in lower NO_2 emissions. The flow of exhaust gases into the intake manifold is controlled by the engine management ECM via solenoid valves which control the flow of vacuum to a diaphragm attached to the EGR valve. The crankcase emission control system allows vapour and gases from the crankcase to pass through an oil separator plate in the cylinder head cover, then through a breather hose into the intake ducting, to be burnt during the combustion process. A depression limiting valve is fitted to the end of the breather hose, which limits the depression in the crankcase as the engine speed increases.

Precautions

⚠️ **Warning: It is necessary to take certain precautions when working on the fuel system components,** particularly the fuel injectors. Before carrying out any operations on the fuel system, refer to the precautions given in 'Safety first!' at the beginning of this manual, and to any additional warning notes at the start of the relevant Sections. Absolute cleanliness is essential when working on the fuel system – do not allow dirt to enter when any part of the system is disconnected.

2 Air cleaner assembly and ducting – removal and refitting

Removal

1 Slacken the clip and disconnect the intake hose from the filter housing **(see illustration)**.
2 Release the two clips and position the airflow sensor to one side **(see illustration)**. Recover the O-ring seal.
3 Undo the two screws and pull the AAP (Ambient Air Pressure) sensor from the housing cover. Recover the O-ring seal **(see illustration 10.22)**. There is no needed to disconnect the wiring plug.
4 Pull the air cleaner assembly upwards, release it from the three mounting grommets **(see illustration)**.

Refitting

5 Refitting is a reversal of removal, but inspect the O-ring seals for damage/wear, and renew as necessary.

3 Accelerator pedal – removal and refitting

Removal

1 Working in the driver's footwell, where applicable, remove the trim panel for access to the pedals.
2 Undo the two bolts/nuts and manoeuvre the accelerator pedal assembly from position **(see illustrations)**.

3.2a Accelerator pedal mounting bolts ...

3.2b ... the nuts for the bolts are on the engine compartment bulkhead, below the servo (arrowed)

4.4 Disconnect the coolant hoses from the fuel cooler

3 Disconnect the accelerator pedal position sensor wiring plug as the pedal is withdrawn. Note that the position sensor is integral with the pedal assembly and no attempt should be made to disassemble it.

Refitting

4 Refitting is a reversal of removal, tightening the retaining bolts to the specified torque.

4 Fuel cooler –
removal and refitting

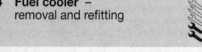

Note: *Refer to the precautions given in Section 1 of this Chapter before proceeding.*

Removal

1 Undo the bolts and remove the plastic cover from the top of the engine.
2 Disconnect the battery negative lead as described in Chapter 5.

6.2 Unscrew the plastic retaining collar

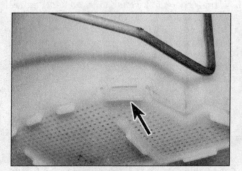

6.4a Release the retaining clips (arrowed) . . .

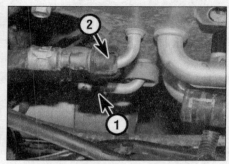

4.5 Disconnect the fuel hose from the tank (1) by pulling off the red cover, and depressing the coupling release button. The hose to the regulator (2) is disconnected by pushing the black collar towards the hose

3 Drain the cooling system as described in Chapter 1.
4 Release the clips, then note their fitted locations and disconnect the coolant hoses from the cooler **(see illustration)**.
5 Disconnect the two fuel hoses from the cooler **(see illustration)**. Be prepared for fuel spillage. Plug all fuel cooler/hose openings, it is essential that the fuel system is not contaminated by dirt, etc.
6 Release the vacuum pipe clip, undo the four bolts and remove the cooler from the intake manifold.

Refitting

7 Position the fuel cooler on the intake manifold, then apply a little locking compound to the threads, and tighten the retaining bolts to the specified torque.

6.3 Carefully lift the sender/pump unit from the fuel tank

6.4b . . . and slide the filter from the unit

8 Ensure the connections are clean, then reconnect the fuel hoses to the cooler.
9 Reconnect the coolant hoses to the cooler, and secure them with the retaining clips.
10 The remainder of refitting is a reversal of removal, remembering to refill the cooling system as described in Chapter 1.

5 Fuel system –
priming and bleeding

Note: *Refer to the precautions given in Section 1 before proceeding.*
Note: *There should be no need to bleed/purge the system after renewing the fuel filter or pump assembly.*

1 If the vehicle runs out of fuel, or fails to start due to air in the system, it is necessary to purge the air from the system as follows:
2 Switch off the ignition and wait for 15 seconds.
3 Turn the ignition switch to position II, and wait for 3 minutes.
4 Repeat the procedures in paragraphs 2 and 3, six times. This allows the fuel system to purge any air from the cylinder head fuel channels.
5 Fully depress the accelerator pedal, and turn the ignition switch to the start position whilst holding the pedal down. Note that this procedure is controlled by the engine management ECM, and should not be performed on a vehicle that has not run out of fuel/become starved of fuel, as it can lead to flooding the engine with unburnt fuel.

 Warning: Do not crank the engine for more than 20 seconds at a time. Allow the starter motor/battery to rest for a few minutes.

6 The ECM will cancel the purging operation as soon the engine speed exceeds 600 rpm, the driver lifts the accelerator pedal to less than 90% of its travel, or the ignition switch is released from the 'start' position.

6 Fuel gauge sender unit
– removal and refitting

Note: *Refer to the precautions given in Section 1 before proceeding.*

Removal

1 Remove the fuel tank as described in Section 7.
2 Unscrew the sender unit plastic retaining collar using a pair of large, crossed-screwdrivers, or improvise a tool **(see illustration)**.
3 Withdraw the sender unit from the fuel tank, and discard the sealing ring **(see illustration)**. An new sealing ring must be fitted. At the time of writing, it would appear that the sender unit is not available separately from the pump.
4 Press the 3 retaining clips to the outside and slide off the filter from the base of the unit **(see illustrations)**. No further dismantling is recommended.

6.6 The lug on the sender unit (arrowed) must engage with the cut-out in the tank

7.5a Undo the fuel tank support bolts at the front (arrowed) . . .

7.5b . . . and at the rear (arrowed)

Refitting

5 Remove all debris from the filter, then slide it back into position, until the clips engage.
6 Refitting is a reversal of removal, but use a new sealing ring and, where applicable, ensure that the lugs on the sender unit engage with the cut-outs in the tank **(see illustration)**.

7 Fuel tank – removal and refitting

Note: *Refer to the precautions given in Section 1 before proceeding.*

Removal

1 As no drain plug is fitted to the base of the moulded tank, this procedure is best performed when the tank is almost empty. If this is not possible, use a syphoning device to remove as much fuel from the tank as possible.
2 Raise the rear of the vehicle and support it securely on axle stands (see *Jacking and vehicle support*).
3 On vehicles fitted with a rear tow bar, undo the two nuts and bolts, then remove the two tow bar support bars from the underside of the vehicle.
4 Position a workshop jack under the fuel tank, with a length of wood on the jack head to prevent any damage to the tank. Take the weight of the tank.

7.9 Squeeze together the sides of the sender/pump unit wiring plug to release the clips (arrowed)

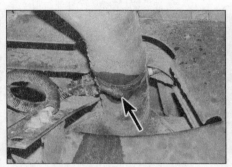

7.6a Disconnect the filler hose from the tank (arrowed) . . .

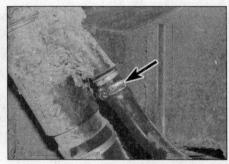

7.6b . . . and the vent hose from the filler neck (arrowed)

5 Undo the two bolts securing the front of the fuel tank support to the chassis member, and the two nuts securing it to the rear chassis member **(see illustrations)**.
6 Release the clips and disconnect the filler hose from the filler neck and tank, then disconnect the vent hose from the neck **(see illustrations)**.
7 Disconnect the tank vent hose from the clips on the left-hand rear chassis member.
8 Lower the front of the fuel tank a little, and remove the support plate. The help of an assistant is recommended.
9 Squeeze together the locking tabs and disconnect the wiring plug from the pump connection on the top of the tank **(see illustration)**.
10 Note their fitted positions, squeeze

7.10 The fuel tank connections are colour-coded: white, green, blue, black from the left-hand to the right-hand side of the vehicle

together the sides of the collars and disconnect the 4 hoses from the pump cover on the top of the tank **(see illustration)**.
11 With assistance, lower and remove the fuel tank, feeding the right-hand vent hose through the chassis opening as the tank is lowered.

Refitting

12 Refitting is a reversal of removal.

8 Fuel injectors – testing, removal and refitting

⚠️ **Warning: Exercise extreme caution when working on the fuel injectors. Never expose the hands, or any part of the body, to injector spray, as the high working pressure can cause the fuel to penetrate the skin, with possibly fatal results. You are strongly advised to have any work which involves testing the injectors under pressure carried out by a Land Rover dealer or fuel injection specialist. Refer to the precautions given in Section 1 of this Chapter before proceeding.**

Testing

1 Injectors do deteriorate with prolonged use, and it is reasonable to expect them to need reconditioning or renewal after 100 000 miles or so. Accurate testing, overhaul and calibration of the injectors must be left to a specialist.

8.3a Slide off the green plastic cover, and pull the collar towards the hose (arrowed) to disconnect it from the connector block/regulator . . .

8.3b . . . and pull the black collar towards the hose to disconnect it from the cooler (arrowed)

8.4 Depress the clip (arrowed) and disconnect the wiring plugs from the injectors

Removal

Note: *If new injectors are to be fitted, the engine management ECM must be reprogrammed before use. This can only be carried out using Land Rover dedicated test equipment. Entrust this task to a Land Rover dealer or suitably-equipped specialist.*

2 Remove the injector rocker shaft as described in Chapter 2B.

3 Carefully clean around the area, then disconnect the fuel feed and return connections to the pressure regulator at the rear of the cylinder head, and the black-collared hose from the fuel cooler to drain the cylinder head of fuel **(see illustrations)**. Be prepared for fuel spillage. Immediately plug or cover the openings to prevent dirt ingress.

4 Press in the wire clips, and disconnect the injector wiring plugs **(see illustration)**.

5 Undo the bolt securing each injector clamp to the cylinder head **(see illustration)**. Recover the clamps.

6 In order to remove the injectors, they must be pulled straight upwards sharply. Land Rover special tool LRT-12-154/1 is intended for this task, and may be available from Land Rover dealers. This is a slide hammer which engages in the sides of the injector. A generic slide hammer, available from good automotive tool shops, will do the same job. Hook the end of the slide hammer under injector body (not the solenoid body), and pull the injector out using a few gentle taps **(see illustrations)**. **Note:** *In order to remove some of the injectors, it will*

be necessary to rotate the crankshaft to align the camshaft lobes for access. If the injectors are to be re-used, store them in their fitted order, so they can be refitted to their original positions.

7 With the injectors removed, rotate the crankshaft to TDC for each cylinder in turn, and use a syringe to remove any fuel from the crown in the top of the pistons.

8 Carefully remove the sealing washer and O-ring seal from each injector. No further dismantling of the injectors is recommended. If the injectors are not to be refitted for some time, cover the holes in the cylinder head to prevent dirt ingress.

Refitting

9 Prior to refitting the injectors, the O-ring and sealing washer on each injector must be renewed. Due to the high injection pressures, it is essential that the O-rings are fitted without being twisted **(see illustration)**.

10 With the O-ring and sealing washer, position the clamp on the injector and fit it into the cylinder head, ensuring it locates on its dowel **(see illustration)**. Tighten the clamp bolt to the specified torque. Repeat this procedure on the remaining injectors.

11 The remainder of refitting is a reversal of removal, noting that if new injectors have been fitted, the engine management ECM may need to be programmed using Land Rover's dedicated test equipment.

8.5 Undo the injector clamp bolt (arrowed)

8.6a Hook the slide hammer hook under the injector body, not the solenoid . . .

8.6b . . . and pull the injector from the head

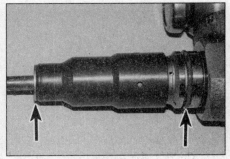

8.9 Renew the sealing washer and O-ring seal (arrowed). The seal must be installed without twisting it

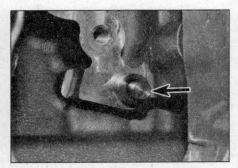

8.10 The injector clamp must located over the dowel (arrowed)

9.3 Pull back the black collar to disconnect the hose from the regulator body (arrowed)

9.6 Withdraw the O-ring and pull the gauze filter from the cylinder head

9.7 The regulator is retained by a circlip

9 Fuel pressure regulator/ connector block – removal and refitting

Note: *Refer to the precautions given in Section 1 of this Chapter before proceeding.*

Removal

1 Disconnect the battery negative lead, as described in Chapter 5.
2 Undo the bolts and remove the plastic cover from the top of the engine.
3 Disconnect the fuel hoses/pipe from the regulator/connector block (see illustration). Be prepared for fuel spillage, and plug/cover all fuel openings to prevent dirt ingress. Note that on EU3 emission standard models, it is

necessary to undo the union and pull the pipe from the regulator – discard the O-ring, a new one must be fitted.
4 Disconnect the fuel temperature sensor wiring plug.
5 Undo the 3 retaining bolts, and remove the regulator/connector block.
6 Note that a small gauze filter is fitted in to the fuel channel in the cylinder head (see illustration). If required, pull the filter from the channel, and discard the O-ring – a new one must be fitted.
7 Although it is possible to remove the circlip and withdraw the regulator from the connector block, at the time or writing, the regulator and O-rings were not available as separate parts, and must be renewed as an assembly with the connector block (see illustration).

Refitting

8 Ensure the regulator/connector block and cylinder head mating surfaces are clean.
9 Where removed, refit the filter into the cylinder head channel, and fit a new O-ring.
10 Using a new gasket, position the pressure regulator/connector block and tighten the bolts to the specified torque.
11 Reconnect the hoses to the regulator/ connector block. Where applicable, reconnect the return pipe to the regulator with a new O-ring and tighten the union securely.
12 The remainder of refitting is a reversal of removal.

10 Engine management electronic components – removal and refitting

ECM (Electronic Control Module)

1 Disconnect the battery negative lead, as described in Chapter 5, then wait at least 10 minutes for any residual electrical energy in the ECM to dissipate.
2 The ECM is located under the front driver's seat cushion. Remove the cushion with reference to Chapter 12 if necessary.
3 Release the clip and remove the access panel (see illustration).
4 Undo the 3 bolts and lift the ECM from position. Release the catches and disconnect the 2 multiplugs from the ECM (see illustrations).
5 Refitting is a reversal of removal.

Fuel temperature sensor

6 Undo the 3 bolts and remove the plastic cover from the top of the engine.
7 Disconnect the battery negative lead as described in Chapter 5.
8 The sensor is fitted to the fuel pressure regulator located at the right-hand rear of the cylinder head. Disconnect the sensor wiring plug (see illustration).
9 Thoroughly clean the area around the sensor, then unscrew it from the regulator. Discard the sealing washer, a new one must be fitted. Plug the open fuel port to prevent dirt ingress.

10.3 Release the clip and remove the ECM access panel

10.4a ECM retaining bolts (arrowed)

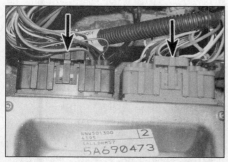

10.4b Depress the clips (arrowed) and disconnect the wiring plugs

10.8 Fuel temperature sensor (arrowed)

10.11 Inertia fuel cut-off switch

10.14 Mass airflow sensor (arrowed)

10.19 Manifold Absolute Pressure/Intake Air Temperature sensor (MAP/IAT)

10 Refitting is a reversal of removal, remembering to fit a new sealing washer and tighten it to the specified torque.

Inertia fuel cut-off switch

11 The inertial fuel cut-off switch is located on the engine compartment bulkhead. In the event of a collision, the switch cuts electrical power to the fuel pump **(see illustration)**.
12 Disconnect the switch wiring plug, Undo the two retaining screws and remove the switch.
13 Refitting is a reversal of removal. To reset the switch, depress the top of the switch.

Mass airflow sensor

14 The sensor is fitted into the air filter housing intake hose **(see illustration)**.
15 Disconnect the wiring plug from the sensor. Slacken the clip and disconnect intake hose from the sensor.
16 Release the 2 clips and detach the sensor from the air cleaner cover.
17 Refitting is a reversal of removal.

Manifold absolute pressure/ intake air temperature sensor

18 Undo the bolts and remove the plastic cover from the top of the engine.
19 The sensor is fitted into the intake manifold. Disconnect the sensor wiring plug **(see illustration)**.
20 Undo the two retaining bolts and remove the sensor from the intake manifold. Discard the O-ring seal, a new one must be fitted.
21 Refitting is a reversal of removal. Tighten the retaining bolts to the specified torque.

Ambient air pressure sensor

22 The AAP sensor is fitted to the side of the air cleaner cover **(see illustration)**.
23 Disconnect the sensor wiring plug. Undo the two screws and remove the sensor. Discard the O-ring, a new one must be fitted.
24 Refitting is a reversal of removal. Tighten the retaining screws securely.

Accelerator pedal position sensor

25 The accelerator pedal position sensor is integral with the accelerator pedal. Refer to Section 3.

Fuel filter water sensor

26 Refer to Fuel filter renewal in Chapter 1.

Crankshaft speed and position sensor

27 The crankshaft speed and position sensor is located on the right-hand side of the transmission bellhousing, with the tip of the sensor adjacent to the circumference of the flywheel. The outer circumference of the flywheel is divided into 36 segments. 31 of the segments have drilled holes, whilst the remaining 5 do not. These undrilled segments corresponds to TDC on each of the five cylinders. As each undrilled segment passes the sensor tip, the magnetic field produced by the sensor is cut. The ECM measures this fluctuation in the magnetic field as an AC voltage. From the level of the voltage and the

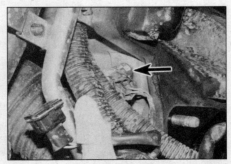

10.28 The crankshaft speed and position sensor is buried under a mound of wiring and pipes on the right-hand side of the transmission bellhousing (arrowed)

position of the voltage peaks, the ECM can determine crankshaft position and speed.
28 Disconnect the sensor wiring plug **(see illustration)**.
29 Undo the retaining bolt and remove the sensor. Discard the O-ring seal, a new one must be fitted. Recover the spacer (if fitted).
30 Ensure the mating faces or the sensor and bellhousing are clean.
31 Refit the spacer (where applicable), then refit the sensor with a new O-ring seal. Tighten the retaining bolt to the specified torque.
32 Reconnect the sensor wiring plug.

Coolant temperature sensor

33 Refer to Chapter 3.

11 Turbocharger – description and precautions

Description

1 The turbocharger increases engine efficiency by raising the pressure in the intake manifold above atmospheric pressure. Instead of the air simply being sucked into the cylinders, it is forced in. Additional fuel is supplied by the injectors, in proportion to the increased amount of air.
2 Energy for the operation of the turbocharger comes from the exhaust gas. The gas flows through a specially-shaped housing (the turbine housing) and in so doing, spins the turbine wheel. The turbine wheel is attached to a shaft, at the end of which is another vaned wheel, known as the compressor wheel. The compressor wheel spins in its own housing, and compresses the inducted air on the way to the intake manifold.
3 The compressed air passes through an intercooler, between the turbocharger and the intake manifold. The intercooler is an air-to-air heat exchanger, mounted at the front of the vehicle, next to the radiator, and supplied with air through the front grille. The purpose of the intercooler is to remove some of the heat gained in being compressed from the inducted air. Because cooler air is denser, removal of this heat further increases engine efficiency.
4 Boost pressure (the pressure in the intake manifold) is limited by a wastegate, which

10.22 Ambient Air Pressure sensor (AAP)

diverts the exhaust gas away from the turbine wheel. The position of the wastegate is controlled by a vacuum valve, which in turn is controlled by the engine management ECM.

5 The turbo shaft is pressure-lubricated by an oil feed pipe from the main oil gallery. The shaft 'floats' on a cushion of oil. A drain pipe returns the oil to the sump.

Precautions

⚠️ **Warning:**
• **The turbocharger operates at extremely high speeds and temperatures. Certain precautions must be observed to avoid premature failure of the turbo, or injury to the operator.**
• **Do not operate the turbo with any parts exposed. Foreign objects falling onto the rotating vanes could cause excessive damage and (if ejected) personal injury.**
• **Do not race the engine immediately after start-up, especially if it is cold. Give the oil approximately 15 seconds to circulate.**
• **Always allow the engine to return to idle speed before switching it off – do not blip the throttle and switch off, as this will leave the turbo spinning without lubrication.**
• **Allow the engine to idle for several minutes before switching off after a high-speed run.**
• **Observe the recommended intervals for oil and filter changing, and use a reputable oil of the specified quality. Neglect of oil**

changing, or use of inferior oil, can cause carbon formation on the turbo shaft, and subsequent failure.

12 Turbocharger – removal and refitting

Removal

1 Disconnect the battery negative lead, as described in Chapter 5.
2 Undo the 3 bolts and remove the plastic cover from the top of the engine.
3 Release the clip and disconnect the engine breather hose from the cylinder head cover.
4 Release the clips and detach the airflow sensor from the air cleaner cover. Disconnect the wiring plug as the sensor is withdrawn.
5 Slacken the clip and disconnect the air intake hose from the turbocharger **(see illustration)**.
6 Undo the 3 bolts and remove the heat shield from above the exhaust manifold.
7 Release the clip and disconnect the vacuum hose from the turbocharger wastegate control diaphragm.
8 Slacken the clip and disconnect the outlet hose from the turbocharger **(see illustration)**.
9 Undo the oil feed banjo bolt and discard the sealing washers **(see illustration)**.

10 Undo the 3 nuts and detach the exhaust front pipe from the turbocharger. Discard the gasket, a new one must be fitted.
11 Slacken and remove the 3 nuts securing the turbocharger to the exhaust manifold **(see illustration)**.
12 Undo the union securing the turbocharger drain pipe to the engine block.
13 Withdraw the turbocharger from the exhaust manifold. Discard the gasket.
14 If required, undo the 2 bolts and detach the drain pipe from the turbocharger. Discard the gasket

Refitting

15 Refitting is a reversal of removal, bearing in mind the following points:
a) Refit the turbocharger to the manifold using a new gasket, and tighten the securing nuts to the specified torque.
b) Tighten the drain tube union securely.
c) Ensure that the oil fed pipe banjo bolt is tightened to the specified torque.
d) Reconnect the exhaust front section to the turbocharger elbow.

13 Turbocharger – examination and overhaul

1 With the turbocharger removed, inspect the housing for cracks or other visible damage.
2 Spin the turbine or the compressor wheel, to verify that the shaft is intact, and to feel for excessive shake or roughness. Some play is normal, since in use the shaft is 'floating' on a film of oil. Check that the wheel vanes are undamaged.
3 The wastegate actuator would appear not to be available as a separate unit. If faulty, the complete turbocharger must be renewed.
4 If the exhaust or intake passages are oil-contaminated, the turbo shaft oil seals have probably failed. (On the intake side, this will also have contaminated the intercooler, which if necessary should be flushed with a suitable solvent.)

12.5 Slacken the clip and disconnect the intake hose from the turbocharger (arrowed)

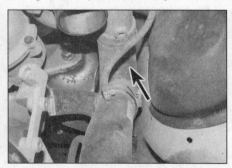

12.8 Turbocharger outlet pipe (arrowed)

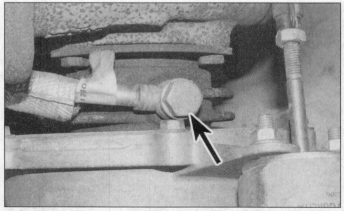

12.9 Undo the banjo bolt (arrowed) and disconnect the oil feed pipe

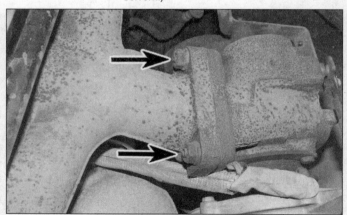

12.11 Turbocharger-to-manifold upper nuts (arrowed)

14.2 Intercooler mounting bolts (arrowed)

15.8 Fuel injector harness multiplug (arrowed)

15.10 The intake manifold is secured by 2 nuts and 8 bolts

5 Check the oil feed and return pipes for contamination or blockage, and clean if necessary.

6 No DIY repair of the turbocharger is possible. A new unit may be available on an exchange basis.

14 Intercooler – removal and refitting

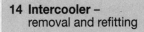

Removal

1 Remove the radiator as described in Chapter 3.

2 Undo the two bolts and detach the intercooler from the radiator **(see illustration)**. Recover the two nuts from the radiator side brackets. and the rubber mountings from the intercooler.

3 Loosen the clips securing the hose to the intercooler, and carefully pull the hose from the intercooler stub.

Refitting

4 Refitting is a reversal of removal, ensuring that the hose sleeves are securely reconnected.

15 Manifolds – removal and refitting

Intake manifold

Removal

1 Disconnect the battery negative lead, as described in Chapter 5.

2 Undo the 3 bolts and remove the plastic cover from the top of the engine.

3 Undo the bolts and remove the cooling fan upper shroud.

4 Disconnect the MAP sensor, and glow plug wiring connectors.

5 Undo the 4 bolts and detach the EGR valve from the manifold **(see illustration 18.12)**. Discard the gasket.

6 Undo the 4 bolts securing the fuel cooler to the intake manifold.

7 Slacken and remove the two bolts, and remove the alternator support bracket.

8 Disconnect the fuel injector harness multiplug **(see illustration)**.

9 Undo the retaining bolt, then pull the oil level dipstick and guide tube upwards from position. Discard the O-ring seal, a new one must be fitted.

10 The manifold is secured to the cylinder head by 2 nuts and 8 bolts **(see illustration)**. Undo the nuts and bolts.

11 Detach the wiring harness from its retaining clips, and remove the manifold. Discard the gasket.

Refitting

12 Refitting is a reversal of removal, bearing in mind the following points:

a) *Renew the manifold gasket – clean all traces of old gasket from the mating faces of the cylinder head and manifold before fitting a new gasket.*

b) *Tighten all fasteners to their specified torque (where given)*

Exhaust manifold

Removal

13 Remove the turbocharger as described in Section 12.

14 On models with air conditioning, remove the auxiliary drivebelt (Chapter 1), then undo the bolts and move the compressor to one side, without disconnecting the refrigerant hoses.

15 Undo the 2 bolts securing the EGR pipe to the exhaust manifold **(see illustration)**.

16 Undo the 10 nuts and remove the exhaust manifold **(see illustration)**. Discard the gasket.

15.15 EGR pipe-to-exhaust manifold Allen bolts (arrowed)

Refitting

17 Refitting is a reversal of removal, bearing in mind the following points:

a) *Thoroughly clean the mating faces of the manifold and the cylinder head, and refit the manifold using a new gasket.*

b) *Tighten all fasteners to their specified torque (where given).*

c) *Refit the EGR pipe to the manifold using a new gasket.*

16 Exhaust system – general information and component renewal

General information

1 The exhaust system consists of a number of separate sections, the sections varying in detail depending on model. Each exhaust section can be renewed individually, leaving the remaining section(s) in place.

Component renewal

2 To remove the system or part of the system, first jack up the front or rear of the vehicle, as applicable, and support it securely on axle stands (see *Jacking and vehicle support*).

Exhaust front section

3 Undo the bolts and remove the plastic cover from the top of the engine.

4 Release the clip and disconnect the breather hose from the cylinder head cover.

5 Disconnect the wiring plug, then release the

15.16 The exhaust manifold is secured by 10 nuts

clip and disconnect the airflow sensor from the air cleaner cover.

6 Slacken the clip and disconnect the air intake hose from the turbocharger.

7 Undo the bolts and remove the heat shield from the top of the exhaust manifold.

8 Undo the 3 nuts and detach the exhaust front pipe from the turbocharger.

9 Disconnect the front propshaft from the axle as described in Chapter 8, then undo the bolts and remove the engine undershield.

10 Undo the nuts and detach the front pipe from the intermediate section.

11 Release the front exhaust pipe from the rubber mounting and remove it from the vehicle.

12 Refitting is a reversal of removal, bearing in mind the following points:

  a) *Where applicable, check the condition of the exhaust mounting rubbers, and renew if necessary.*

  b) *Where applicable, use a new exhaust-to-manifold gasket. On models with a clamped joint, apply a little exhaust jointing compound to the joint before fitting.*

  c) *Where applicable, check the condition of the exhaust front section-to-intermediate section sealing ring, and renew if necessary.*

  d) *Do not fully tighten the mountings and clamp nuts and bolts until the completion of refitting.*

Exhaust intermediate and rear sections

13 A number of different configurations of system may be used, depending on model.

14 Generally, it should be possible to remove each individual component, leaving the remaining components in place. In some cases, it may be necessary to release the surrounding exhaust components from their mountings, in order to allow sufficient movement to withdraw the desired component.

15 Various types of mountings and clamp fixings may be encountered, and removal should be self-evident. Note the positions of any washers and spacers, so that they can be refitted in their original locations.

16 Always renew gaskets and sealing rings if they show signs of deterioration. Similarly, renew mounting rubbers and clamp bolts/U-bolts, etc, if they shown signs of damage or corrosion.

17 Where necessary, apply exhaust jointing compound to seal flanged joints where no gasket or sealing ring is used.

18 When refitting, do not fully tighten mounting and clamp fixings until the components have been manipulated into their final positions. Similarly, ensure that the components are not under strain before tightening the fixings.

17 Emissions control systems – general information

1 The following systems are fitted, and are designed to reduce the emissions of harmful by-products of the combustion process into the atmosphere.

Crankcase emissions control

2 Oil fumes and piston blow-by gases (combustion gases which have passed by the piston rings) are drawn from the crankcase/cylinder head cover through an oil separator, into the air intake tract. The gases are then drawn into the engine together with fresh air/fuel mixture. Condensed oil vapour is returned from the main oil separator to the engine sump.

Exhaust gas recirculation

3 The system is designed to recirculate small quantities of exhaust gas into the intake tract, and therefore into the combustion process. This process reduces the level of oxides of nitrogen present in the final exhaust gas which is released into the atmosphere, and also lowers the combustion temperature.

4 The volume of exhaust gas recirculated is controlled by vacuum, via a solenoid valve. The solenoid valve is controlled by the engine management ECM.

5 A vacuum-operated recirculation valve is fitted to the exhaust manifold, to regulate the quantity of exhaust gas recirculated. The valve is operated by the vacuum supplied via the solenoid valve.

6 Between idle speed and a predetermined engine load, power is supplied to the solenoid

valve, which allows the recirculation valve to open. Under full-load conditions, the exhaust gas recirculation is cut off. Additional control is provided by the engine temperature sensor, which cuts off the vacuum supply until the coolant temperature reaches 40°C, preventing the recirculation valve from opening during the engine warm-up period.

18 Emissions control systems – testing and component renewal

Crankcase emissions control

Testing

1 If the system is thought to be faulty, firstly, check that the hoses are unobstructed. On high-mileage vehicles, particularly those regularly used for short journeys, a jelly-like deposit may be evident inside the system hoses and oil separator. If excessive deposits are present, the relevant component(s) should be removed and cleaned.

2 Periodically inspect the system components for security and damage, and renew them as necessary. Note that damaged or loose hoses can cause various engine running problems (erratic idle speed, stalling, etc) which can be difficult to trace.

Component renewal

3 Renewal procedures for the hoses and oil separator are self-evident.

Exhaust emissions control

Testing

4 The system can only be tested accurately using a suitable exhaust gas analyser (suitable for use with diesel engines).

Component renewal

5 The catalytic converter is integral with the exhaust system front section.

6 Removal and refitting are described in Section 16.

EGR system

EGR valve testing

7 Testing of the EGR valve should be entrusted to a Land Rover dealer or suitably-equipped specialist.

EGR valve removal

8 Disconnect the battery negative lead, as described in Chapter 5.

9 Undo the 3 bolts and remove the plastic cover from the top of the engine.

10 Disconnect the vacuum hose(s) from the EGR valve **(see illustration)**.

11 Slacken the clip and disconnect the air intake hose from the EGR valve.

12 Undo the 4 bolts and detach the EGR valve from the intake manifold **(see illustration)**. Discard the gasket.

13 Remove the 2 bolts and release the EGR valve clip from the cylinder head.

18.10 Disconnect the vacuum hoses from the EGR valve (arrowed)

18.12 EGR valve mounting bolts (arrowed)

14 Release the 2 Allen screws and detach the EGR pipe from the exhaust manifold **(see illustration 15.16).**

EGR valve refitting

15 Refitting is a reversal of removal, but use new gaskets when refitting the valve and reconnecting the delivery pipe.

EGR modulator valve

16 Two different types of modulator are fitted: Type 1 has a single modulator, and Type 2 has two modulators. On both systems, the modulator valves are mounted on a plate on the right-hand side of the engine compartment **(see illustrations).**

17 Removal and refitting of the valve(s) should be self-evident, but note the fitted locations of the vacuum hoses prior to removal.

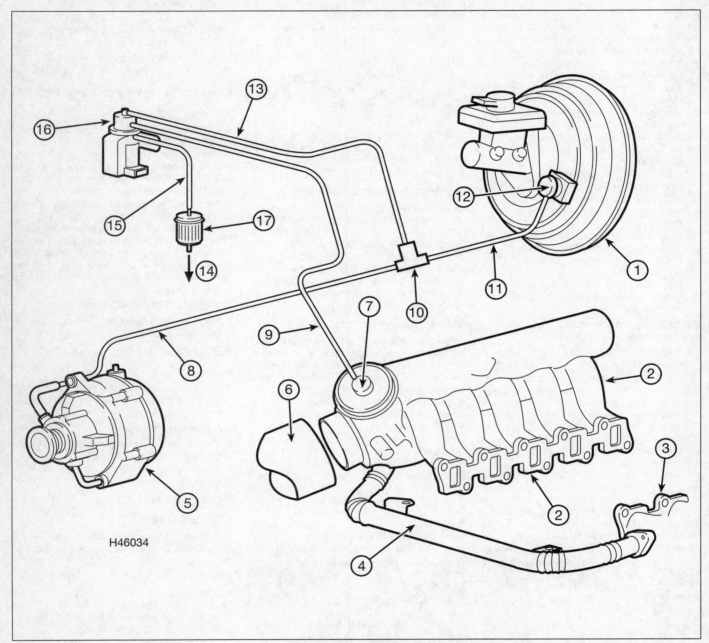

H46034

18.16a Type 1 EGR system

1 Brake servo	8 Hose to vacuum pump	14 To atmosphere
2 Intake manifold	9 Vacuum hose to EGR valve suction port (blue)	15 Vent hose – EGR modulator-to-in line filter (green)
3 Exhaust manifold	10 T-piece	16 EGR modulator
4 EGR pipe	11 Vacuum hose to brake servo	17 In-line filter
5 Vacuum pump/alternator assembly	12 Non-return valve	
6 Intake hose from intercooler	13 Vacuum hose (light brown)	
7 EGR valve assembly		

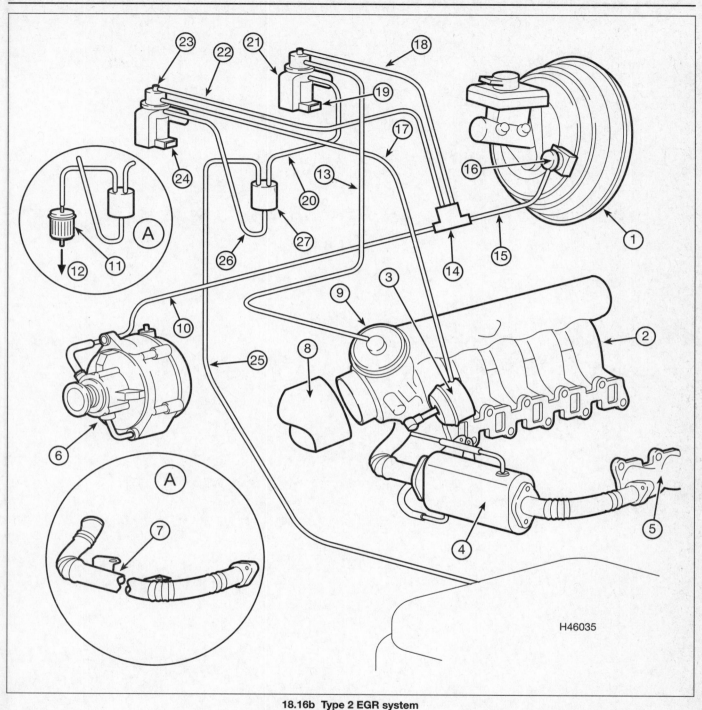

18.16b Type 2 EGR system

1   Brake servo
2   Intake manifold
3   ILT valve
4   EGR cooler – EU3 models
5   Exhaust manifold
6   Alternator/vacuum pump assembly
7   EGR pipe – EU2 models
8   Air intake hose from the intercooler
9   EGR valve
10 Vacuum hose to pump
11 In-line filter

12 To atmosphere
13 Vacuum hose to EGR valve suction port
    (blue)
14 T-piece
15 Vacuum hose to brake servo
16 Non-return valve
17 Vacuum hose to ILT valve suction port
    (blue)
18 EGR modulator vacuum hose (brown)
19 EGR modulator electrical
    connection

20 Vent hose – EGR modulator to
    in-line filter (green)
21 EGR valve modulator
22 ILT modulator vacuum hose (brown)
23 ILT valve modulator
24 ILT modulator wiring connector (green)
25 Vent hose to air cleaner
26 Vent hose – ILT valve modulator to in-line
    filter (green)
27 3-way connector
A = pre-EU3 emission standard

Notes

Chapter 5
Engine electrical systems

Contents

Section number

Alternator – removal and refitting 6
Alternator brushes – inspection and renewal 7
Auxiliary drivebelt checking and renewal . . . . See Chapter 1
Battery – removal and refitting 4
Battery – testing and charging 3
Battery check . . . . See Chapter 1
Charging system – testing 5
Electrical fault finding – general information 2
Electrical system check . . . . See Chapter 1
General information and precautions 1

Section number

Glow plugs – removal, inspection and refitting 14
Ignition switch – removal and refitting 11
Oil pressure warning light switch – removal and refitting 12
Preheating system – description and testing 13
Preheating system relay/timer unit – removal and refitting 15
Starter motor – brush renewal 10
Starter motor – removal and refitting 9
Starting system – testing 8
Stop solenoid – description, removal and refitting 16

Degrees of difficulty

Easy, suitable for novice with little experience	**Fairly easy,** suitable for beginner with some experience	**Fairly difficult,** suitable for competent DIY mechanic	**Difficult,** suitable for experienced DIY mechanic	**Very difficult,** suitable for expert DIY or professional

Specifications

General
Electrical system type . . . .   12 volt, negative-earth

Battery
Type . . . .   Lead-acid, low-maintenance or maintenance-free

Alternator
Type . . . .   Lucas A115, A127 or A133, Marelli (300 TDi engine), or Nippon Denso 120 A (TD5 engine)
Regulated voltage . . . .   13.6 to 14.4 volts at 3000 engine rpm
Minimum brush length:
   Lucas alternators . . . .   5.0 mm
   Marelli alternators . . . .   No information available
   Nippon Denso . . . .   No information available

Starter motor
Make and type . . . .   Lucas or Paris-Rhone, or Bosch (TD5 engine) reduction gear

Torque wrench settings

	Nm	lbf ft
Non-TD5 engines		
Alternator mounting bolts and nut	25	18
Glow plug wiring nuts	2	1
Glow plugs	23	17
Starter motor mounting bolts and nut	45	33
TD5 engines		
Alternator mounting bolt	45	33
Alternator support bracket	25	18
Auxiliary drivebelt tensioner bolt	50	37
Glow plugs	16	12
Starter motor nuts/bolts	27	20
Vacuum pump bolts	10	7
Vacuum pump oil feed pipe bolt	10	7

1 General information and precautions

The engine electrical system includes all charging, starting and preheating components, and the engine oil pressure sensor. Because of their engine-related functions, these components are covered separately from the body electrical devices such as the lights, instruments, etc (which are covered in Chapter 13).

The electrical system is of the 12 volt, negative-earth type.

The battery is of the low-maintenance or maintenance-free type, and is charged by the alternator, which is belt-driven from a crankshaft-mounted pulley.

The starter motor is of the pre-engaged reduction gear type, incorporating an integral solenoid. On starting, the solenoid moves the drive pinion into engagement with the flywheel ring gear before the starter motor is energised. Once the engine has started, a one-way clutch prevents the motor armature being driven by the engine until the pinion disengages from the flywheel. The motor is fitted with a reduction gear mechanism, in order to achieve the high torque necessary to turn the engine against the high compression pressures encountered in a diesel engine.

Precautions

Further details of the various systems are given in the relevant Sections of this Chapter. While some repair procedures are given, the usual course of action is to renew the component concerned. The owner whose interest extends beyond mere component renewal should obtain a copy of the *Automotive Electrical & Electronic Systems Manual*, available from the publishers of this manual.

It is necessary to take extra care when working on the electrical system, to avoid damage to semi-conductor devices (diodes and transistors), and to avoid the risk of personal injury. In addition to the precautions given in *Safety first!* at the beginning of this manual, observe the following when working on the system:

• *Always remove rings, watches, etc, before working on the electrical system.* Even with the battery disconnected, capacitive discharge could occur if a component's live terminal is earthed through a metal object. This could cause a shock or nasty burn.

• *Do not reverse the battery connections.* Components such as the alternator, preheating electronic control unit, or any other components having semi-conductor circuitry could be irreparably damaged.

• If the engine is being started using jump leads and a slave battery, connect the batteries *positive-to-positive* and *negative-to-negative* (see *Jump starting*). This also applies when connecting a battery charger.

• Never disconnect the battery terminals, the alternator, any electrical wiring or any test instruments, when the engine is running.

• Do not allow the engine to turn the alternator when the alternator is not connected.

• Never 'test' for alternator output by 'flashing' the output lead to earth.

• Never use an ohmmeter of the type incorporating a hand-cranked generator for circuit or continuity testing.

• Always ensure that the battery negative lead is disconnected when working on the electrical system.

• Before using electric-arc welding equipment on the car, disconnect the battery, alternator and components such as the preheating electronic control unit, ABS electronic control unit, etc, to protect them from the risk of damage.

• The radio/cassette unit fitted as standard equipment by Land Rover may have a built-in security code, to deter thieves. If the power source to the unit is cut, the anti-theft system will activate. Even if the power source is immediately reconnected, the radio/cassette unit will not function until the correct security code has been entered. Therefore, if you do not know the correct security code for the radio/cassette unit, do not disconnect the battery negative terminal of the battery, nor remove the radio/cassette unit from the vehicle. Refer to the manufacturer's handbook supplied with the vehicle for details of how to enter the security code.

2 Electrical fault finding – general information

Refer to Chapter 13.

3 Battery – testing and charging

Note: *Refer to the precautions given in 'Safety first!' and in Section 1 of this Chapter before proceeding.*

Testing

Standard and low-maintenance battery

1 If the vehicle covers a small annual mileage, it is worthwhile checking the specific gravity of the electrolyte every three months to determine the state of charge of the battery. Use a hydrometer to make the check and compare the results with the following table. Note that the specific gravity readings assume an electrolyte temperature of 15°C; for every 10°C below 15°C subtract 0.007. For every 10°C above 15°C add 0.007.

	Above 25°C	Below 25°C
Fully-charged	1.210 to 1.230	1.270 to 1.290
70% charged	1.170 to 1.190	1.230 to 1.250
Discharged	1.050 to 1.070	1.110 to 1.130

2 If the battery condition is suspect, first check the specific gravity of electrolyte in each cell. A variation of 0.040 or more between any cells indicates loss of electrolyte or deterioration of the internal plates.

3 If the specific gravity variation is 0.040 or more, the battery should be renewed. If the cell variation is satisfactory but the battery is discharged, it should be charged as described later in this Section.

Maintenance-free battery

4 In cases where a 'sealed for life' maintenance-free battery is fitted, topping-up and testing of the electrolyte in each cell is not possible. The condition of the battery can therefore only be tested using a battery condition indicator or a voltmeter.

5 Certain models may be fitted with a maintenance-free battery, with a built-in charge condition indicator. The indicator is located in the top of the battery casing, and indicates the condition of the battery from its colour. If the indicator shows green, then the battery is in a good state of charge. If the indicator shows black, then the battery requires charging, as described later in this Section. If the indicator shows blue, then the electrolyte level in the battery is too low to allow further use, and the battery should be renewed.

Caution: Do not attempt to charge, load or jump start a battery when the indicator shows clear/yellow.

All battery types

6 If testing the battery using a voltmeter, connect the voltmeter across the battery. The test is only accurate if the battery has not been subjected to any kind of charge for the previous six hours. If this is not the case, switch on the headlights for 30 seconds, then wait four to five minutes before testing the battery after switching off the headlights. All other electrical circuits must be switched off, so check that the doors or tailgate are fully shut when making the test.

7 If the voltage reading is less than 12.2 volts, then the battery is discharged, whilst a reading of 12.2 to 12.4 volts indicates a partially discharged condition.

8 If the battery is to be charged, remove it from the vehicle (Section 4) and charge it as described later in this Section.

Charging

Note: *The following is intended as a guide only. Always refer to the manufacturer's recommendations (often printed on a label attached to the battery) before charging a battery.*

Standard and low-maintenance battery

9 Charge the battery at a rate of 3.5 to 4 amps and continue to charge the battery at this rate until no further rise in specific gravity is noted over a four hour period.

10 Alternatively, a trickle charger charging at the rate of 1.5 amps can safely be used overnight.

11 Specially rapid 'boost' charges which are

claimed to restore the power of the battery in 1 to 2 hours are not recommended, as they can cause serious damage to the battery plates through overheating.

12 While charging the battery, note that the temperature of the electrolyte should never exceed 38°C.

Maintenance-free battery

13 This battery type takes considerably longer to fully recharge than the standard type, the time taken being dependent on the extent of discharge, but it can take anything up to three days.

14 A constant voltage type charger is required to be set, when connected, to 13.9 to 14.9 volts with a charger current below 25 amps. Using this method, the battery should be usable within three hours, giving a voltage reading of 12.5 volts, but this is for a partially-discharged battery and, as mentioned, full charging can take considerably longer.

15 If the battery is to be charged from a fully-discharged state (condition reading less than 12.2 volts), have it recharged by your Land Rover dealer or local automotive electrician, as the charge rate is higher and constant supervision during charging is necessary.

4 Battery – removal and refitting

Note: *Refer to the precautions given in 'Safety first!' and in Section 1 of this Chapter before proceeding.*

Removal

Non-TD5 models

1 The battery is located in a compartment under the left-hand front seat.

2 Remove the left-hand front seat cushion (see Chapter 12).

3 Release the securing clip, and lift the cover panel from the battery compartment **(see illustration)**.

4 Loosen the clamp nut and bolt, and disconnect the battery negative lead.

5 Similarly, disconnect the battery positive lead.

6 Unscrew the nuts securing the battery clamp in position. Recover the washers **(see illustration)**.

7 Lift off the clamp bracket, then lift out the battery.

8 Clean the battery terminal posts, clamps, tray and battery casing.

TD5 models

9 The battery is located under the passenger's seat.

10 Remove the passenger's seat cushion, and where applicable, lift the rubber insulation material to expose the battery cover and clip.

11 Release the clip and remove the battery cover **(see illustration)**.

12 In order to prevent the anti-theft alarm from sounding and the vehicle being immobilised, turn the ignition switch to position II, then to position 0, remove the ignition key and disconnect the battery negative lead within 15 seconds **(see illustration)**.

13 Slacken the nut and disconnect the battery positive lead clamp **(see illustration)**, followed by the positive lead clamp.

14 Slacken the nuts and move the battery clamp to one side **(see illustration)**.

15 Lift the battery from position.

Refitting

16 Refitting is a reversal of removal, but always connect the positive terminal clamp first and the negative terminal clamp last. After connecting the battery terminals, it's a good idea to apply a layer of petroleum jelly to the terminals to prevent corrosion.

5 Charging system – testing

Note: *Refer to the warnings given in 'Safety first!' and in Section 1 of this Chapter before proceeding.*

1 If the ignition (no-charge) warning light fails to illuminate when the ignition is switched on, first check the security of the alternator wiring connections. If satisfactory, check that the warning light bulb has not blown, and that the bulbholder is secure in its location in the instrument panel. If the light still fails to illuminate, check the continuity of the warning light feed wire from the alternator to the bulbholder. If all is satisfactory, the alternator is at fault, and should be renewed, or taken to an auto-electrician for testing and repair.

2 If the ignition warning light illuminates when the engine is running, stop the engine and check that the drivebelt is correctly tensioned

4.3 Releasing the battery cover panel securing clip

4.6 Unscrewing a battery clamp securing nut (arrowed)

4.11 Release the battery cover clip and slide the cover forward

4.12 Turn the ignition switch to position II

4.13 Slacken the bolt and disconnect the positive lead clamp

4.14 Battery clamp nuts (arrowed)

(Chapter 1) and that the alternator connections are secure. If all is so far satisfactory, check the alternator brushes and slip-rings (see Section 7). If the fault persists, the alternator should be renewed, or taken to an auto-electrician for testing and repair.

3 If the alternator output is suspect even though the warning light functions correctly, the regulated voltage may be checked as follows.

4 Connect a voltmeter across the battery terminals, and start the engine.

5 Increase the engine speed until the voltmeter reading remains steady; as a rough guide, the reading should be between 13.6 and 14.4 volts.

6 Switch on as many electrical accessories (headlights, heater blower, cigarette lighter, etc) as possible, and check that the alternator maintains the regulated voltage between 13.6 and 14.4 volts. It may be necessary to increase engine speed slightly.

7 If the regulated voltage is not as stated, the fault may be due to worn brushes, weak brush springs, a faulty voltage regulator, a faulty diode, a severed phase winding, or worn or damaged slip-rings. The brushes and slip-rings may be checked (see Section 7), but if the fault persists, the alternator should be renewed, or taken to an auto-electrician for testing and repair.

6 Alternator – removal and refitting

Note: *Refer to the precautions given in 'Safety first!' and in Section 1 of this Chapter before proceeding.*

10J, 12J, 19J and 200 TDi engines
Removal

1 Disconnect the battery negative lead.

2 Where necessary to improve access, remove the air cleaner assembly as described in Chapter 4A, and the cooling fan and cowl as described in Chapter 3.

3 On 200 TDi engine models, to improve access, slacken the securing clips, and remove the hoses connecting the intercooler to the inlet manifold and the turbocharger.

4 Disconnect the wiring from the rear of the alternator.

5 Slacken the alternator adjuster bracket pivot bolt.

6 Remove the bolt securing the alternator to the adjuster bracket, and recover the washers **(see illustration)**.

7 Loosen the two bolts (and nuts, where applicable) securing the alternator to the mounting bracket **(see illustration)**. Where necessary, counterhold the nuts as the bolts are loosened.

8 Pivot the alternator sufficiently to release the drivebelt from the alternator pulley.

9 Remove the two bolts (and nuts, where applicable) securing the alternator to the mounting bracket, and withdraw the alternator.

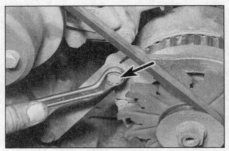

6.6 Unscrewing the bolt securing the alternator to the adjuster bracket – 19J engine

Refitting

10 Refitting is a reversal of removal, but tension the drivebelt as described in Chapter 1.

300 TDi engines
Removal

11 Disconnect the battery negative lead.

12 Remove the auxiliary drivebelt as described in Chapter 1.

13 Where applicable, unscrew the three securing nuts and withdraw the heat shield from the rear of the alternator, to expose the wiring connections.

14 Disconnect the electrical leads from the rear of the alternator **(see illustration)**.

15 Remove the lower alternator securing bolt. Where applicable, recover the washers, noting their locations **(see illustration)**.

16 Working at the top of the alternator, counterhold the through-bolt, and unscrew the nut. Again recover the washers, noting their locations.

6.14 Disconnect the wiring (arrowed) from the rear of the alternator

6.18 Removing the alternator through-bolt – 300 TDi engine

6.7 Unscrewing an alternator securing bolt (arrowed) – 19J engine

17 Where applicable, withdraw the heat shield from the rear of the through-bolt.

18 Remove the through-bolt, and withdraw the alternator from the engine **(see illustration)**.

Refitting

19 Refitting is a reversal of removal, but refit and tighten the auxiliary drivebelt as described in Chapter 1.

TD5 engines
Removal

20 Disconnect the battery negative lead as described in Section 4.

21 Remove the auxiliary drivebelt as described in Chapter 1.

22 Prise up the rubber boot, undo the nut and disconnect the lead from the alternator **(see illustration)**, then disconnect the wiring plug from the rear of the alternator.

6.15 Removing the lower alternator securing bolt – 300 TDi engine

6.22 Prise up the rubber boot and disconnect the wiring

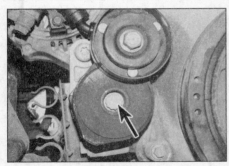

6.23 Undo the drivebelt tensioner retaining bolt (arrowed)

6.25 Release the oil drain hose clip

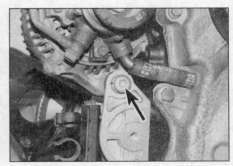

6.27 Undo the alternator lower mounting bolt

23 Undo the bolt, and remove the auxiliary drivebelt tensioner pulley assembly **(see illustration)**.

24 Remove the bolt securing the support bracket to the top of the alternator.

25 Release the clip securing the oil drain hose to the vacuum pump **(see illustration)**.

26 Slacken the union bolt and disconnect the vacuum pump oil feed pipe. Discard the sealing washers, new ones must be fitted.

27 Undo the alternator lower mounting Torx bolt and remove the alternator, disconnecting the vacuum pump oil drain hose as the alternator is withdrawn **(see illustration)**. Take great care not to damage the radiator cooling fins as the unit is withdrawn.

28 If necessary, undo the 4 bolts and detach the vacuum pump from the alternator **(see illustration)**.

Refitting

29 Refitting is a reversal of removal, but tighten all fasteners to there specified torque (where given).

---

7   Alternator brushes
       – inspection and renewal

Lucas A115 and A133 alternators

1 For improved access, remove the alternator as described in Section 6.

2 Disconnect the wiring plug, then remove the securing screw and withdraw the interference

6.28 Vacuum pump mounting bolts (arrowed)

suppression capacitor from the rear cover **(see illustration)**.

3 Extract the two securing screws, and remove the alternator rear cover.

4 Make a careful note of the fitted positions of the regulator wires, then disconnect the wires from the diode pack and the brush box.

5 Remove the regulator securing screws, and withdraw the regulator. Note that the regulator securing screw also holds one of the brush mounting plates in position.

6 Remove the two securing screws, and withdraw the brush box. Remove the securing screws, and lift the brushes from the brush box.

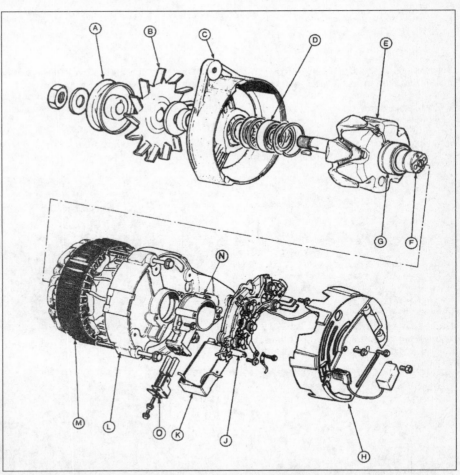

7.2 Exploded view of Lucas A115 and A133-type alternators

A Pulley	F Slip-ring	L Slip-ring end
B Fan	G Bearing	housing
C Drive end housing	H End cover	M Stator
D Bearing	J Diode pack	N Brush box
E Rotor	K Regulator	O Brushes

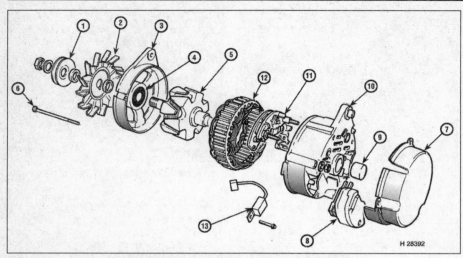

7.12 Exploded view of Lucas A127-type alternator

1 Pulley	6 Through-bolt	10 Slip-ring end housing
2 Fan	7 End cover	11 Diode pack
3 Drive end housing	8 Voltage regulator/brush	12 Stator
4 Bearing	holder	13 Suppressor
5 Rotor	9 Bearing	

7 If the length of either brush is less than the minimum given in the Specifications, renew both brushes.

8 Wipe the slip-rings clean with a fuel-moistened cloth. If the rings are very dirty, use fine glass paper to clean them, then wipe with the cloth.

9 Refitting is a reversal of removal, but make sure that the brushes move freely in their holders.

10 Where applicable, refit the alternator as described in Section 6.

Lucas A127 alternator

11 For improved access, remove the alternator as described in Section 6.

12 If necessary, unscrew the suppressor securing nut from the through-bolt, then disconnect the wiring and withdraw the suppressor for access to the voltage regulator/brush box assembly **(see illustration)**.

13 Remove the three screws securing the voltage regulator/brush box assembly to the rear of the alternator.

14 Tip the outside edge of the assembly upwards, and withdraw it from its location. Disconnect the wiring plug, and withdraw the assembly from the alternator.

15 If the length of either brush is less than the minimum given in the Specifications, the complete regulator/brush box assembly must be renewed.

16 Before refitting, wipe the alternator slip-rings clean with a fuel-moistened cloth. If the rings are very dirty, use fine glasspaper to clean them, then wipe with the cloth.

17 Refitting is a reversal of removal, but make sure that the brushes move freely in their holders.

18 Where applicable, refit the alternator as described in Section 6.

Marelli alternator

Note: *Check on the availability of new brushes before proceeding.*

19 With the alternator removed as described in Section 6, unscrew the three studs from the rear of the alternator, noting that the suppressor is secured by one of the studs **(see illustration)**.

20 Unscrew the nut and recover the washer securing the wiring terminal to the rear of the alternator, then remove the terminal **(see illustrations)**. Note that the suppressor wiring is connected to the terminal.

21 Withdraw the alternator rear cover **(see illustration)**.

22 To remove a brush, remove the screw securing the brush wiring terminal to the top of the brush plate, then withdraw the wiring, spring and brush as an assembly **(see illustration)**.

23 Refitting is a reversal of removal, but make sure that the brushes move freely in their holders, and make sure that the suppressor

7.19 Unscrew the studs from the rear of the alternator – Marelli alternator

7.20a Unscrew the nut . . .

7.20b . . . and remove the wiring terminal – Marelli alternator

7.21 Withdrawing the alternator rear cover – Marelli alternator

7.22 Removing an alternator brush – Marelli alternator

When fitting a brush, use a small screwdriver to push the brush into position in the brush holder as the wiring terminal is lined up with the securing screw.

is positioned as noted before removal (see Haynes hint).

Denso alternator

24 It would appear that, at the time of writing, no spare parts are available for the Denso alternator. Check with a Land Rover dealer or automotive electrical specialist concerning exchange/repaired units.

8 Starting system – testing

Note: Refer to the precautions given in 'Safety first!' and in Section 1 of this Chapter before proceeding.

1 If the starter motor fails to operate when the ignition key is turned to the appropriate position, the possible causes are as follows:

a) The battery is faulty.

b) The electrical connections between the switch, solenoid, battery and starter motor are somewhere failing to pass the necessary current from the battery through the starter to earth.

c) The solenoid is faulty.

d) The starter motor is mechanically or electrically defective.

e) The starter motor solenoid relay is faulty (TD5 models only).

2 To check the battery, switch on the headlights. If they dim after a few seconds, this indicates that the battery is discharged – recharge (see Section 3) or renew the battery. If the headlights glow brightly, operate the starter switch and observe the lights. If they dim, then this indicates that current is reaching the starter motor, therefore the fault must lie in the starter motor. If the lights continue to glow brightly (and no clicking sound can be heard from the starter motor solenoid), this indicates that there is a fault in the circuit or solenoid – see the following paragraphs. If the starter motor turns slowly when operated, but the battery is in good condition, then this indicates either that the starter motor is faulty, or there is considerable resistance somewhere in the circuit.

3 If a fault in the circuit is suspected, disconnect the battery leads, the starter/solenoid wiring and the engine/transmission earth strap(s). Thoroughly clean the connections, and reconnect the leads and wiring. Use a voltmeter or test light to check that full battery voltage is available at the battery positive lead connection to the solenoid. Smear petroleum jelly around the battery terminals to prevent corrosion – corroded connections are among the most frequent causes of electrical system faults.

4 If the battery and all connections are in good condition, check the circuit by disconnecting the wire from the solenoid blade terminal. Connect a voltmeter or test light between the wire end and a good earth (such as the battery negative terminal), and check that the wire is live when the ignition switch is turned to the 'start' position. If it is, then the circuit is sound – if not, there is a fault in the ignition/starter switch or wiring.

5 The solenoid contacts can be checked by connecting a voltmeter or test light between the battery positive feed connection on the starter side of the solenoid, and earth. When the ignition switch is turned to the 'start' position, there should be a reading or lighted bulb, as applicable. If there is no reading or lighted bulb, the solenoid is faulty and should be renewed.

6 If the circuit and solenoid are proved sound, the fault must lie in the starter motor. The starter motor can be checked by a Land Rover dealer or an automotive electrical specialist. A specialist may be able to overhaul the unit at a cost significantly less than that of a new or exchange starter motor.

7 TD5 vehicles from 2002 model year are fitted with a starter solenoid relay in the fusebox in front of the gear lever (see illustration). The solenoid should be heard to 'click' when the key is turned to the start position. If it doesn't, and the wiring seems OK, the relay may be faulty.

9 Starter motor – removal and refitting

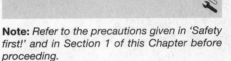

Note: Refer to the precautions given in 'Safety first!' and in Section 1 of this Chapter before proceeding.

Removal

Non-TD5 engines

1 The starter motor is located on the left-hand side of the engine, and access is most easily obtained from above.

2 Disconnect the battery negative lead.

3 Where applicable, to improve access, unbolt the exhaust heat shield from the exhaust manifold.

4 On 200 TDi engines, where applicable, unscrew the three securing bolts, and remove the starter motor heat shield (see illustration).

5 Disconnect the wiring from the rear of the starter motor, and where applicable, release the securing clip.

6 Where applicable, unbolt the earth lead from the starter motor, or the cylinder block. Note that on certain engines, the earth lead is

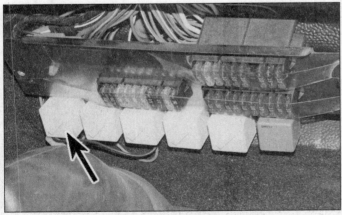

8.7 TD5 starter solenoid (arrowed)

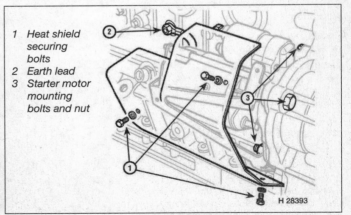

1 Heat shield securing bolts
2 Earth lead
3 Starter motor mounting bolts and nut

9.4 Starter motor mounting details – 200 TDi engine

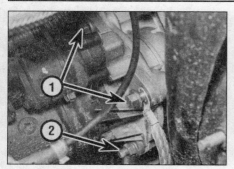

9.7a Starter motor securing bolts (1) and nut (2) – 300 TDi engine

9.7b Removing the starter motor – 19J engine

9.10 Starter motor connections – TD5 engine

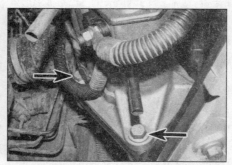

9.11 Starter motor mounting lower bolts (arrowed) – TD5 engine

secured by one of the starter motor mounting bolts or nuts.

7 Unscrew the securing bolt(s), and the nut(s) (there are three starter motor-to-flywheel housing mounting points), and withdraw the starter motor, complete with the heat shield bracket, where applicable **(see illustrations)**.

TD5 engines

8 Disconnect the battery negative lead as described in Section 4.
9 Disconnect the front propshaft from the axle as described in Chapter 8, then undo the bolts and move the engine undershield to one side.
10 Disconnect the electrical connections from the starter motor **(see illustration)**.
11 Undo the nuts/bolts, and detach the starter from the transmission bellhousing **(see illustration)**.

Refitting

12 Refitting is a reversal of removal, but where applicable, ensure that the earth lead is in place on the appropriate starter motor mounting nut or bolt. Tighten the fasteners to their specified torque, where given.

10 Starter motor – brush renewal

Starter motor brush renewal is considered to be beyond the scope of the DIY mechanic, and the task should be entrusted to a Land Rover dealer, or an automotive electrical specialist.

11 Ignition switch – removal and refitting

The ignition switch is integral with the steering column lock, and can be removed as described in Chapter 11.

12 Oil pressure warning light switch – removal and refitting

Removal

Non-TD5 engines

Note: *A new sealing ring may be required on refitting.*
1 The oil pressure warning light switch is

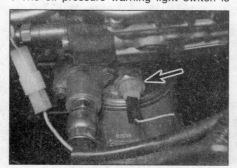

12.1 Oil pressure warning light switch (arrowed) – 300 TDi engine

located in the oil filter adapter at the right-hand side of the cylinder block **(see illustration)**.
2 Disconnect the battery negative lead, then release the wiring connector from the switch.
3 Carefully unscrew the switch, and withdraw it from the oil filter adapter. Be prepared for some oil spillage.
4 Recover the sealing ring, where applicable.

TD5 engines

5 Undo the fasteners and remove the plastic cover from the top of the engine.
6 Release the clip and disconnect the breather hose from the cylinder head cover.
7 Release the clips and disconnect the airflow meter from the air filter.
8 Release the clip and disconnect the air intake hose from the turbocharger.
9 Undo the three screws and remove the heat shield from the top of the exhaust manifold.
10 Disconnect the wiring plug from the oil pressure switch, then unscrew the switch from the oil cooler housing **(see illustration)**. Be prepared for oil spillage.

Refitting

11 Refitting is a reversal of removal, but clean the threads of the switch before screwing it into the oil filter adapter, and where applicable, use a new sealing ring.

13 Preheating system – description and testing

Description

Non-TD5 engines

1 Each swirl chamber (10J, 12J and 19J engines) or combustion chamber (200 TDi and 300 TDi engines) has a heater plug (commonly called a glow plug). The plugs are electrically-operated. On all models except those with 200 TDi and 300 TDi engines, the electrical supply to the plugs is controlled manually by the driver, by turning the ignition key to position II. On models with 200 TDi and 300 TDi engines, the electrical supply to the plugs is controlled by a relay/timer unit.
2 On those models with 200 TDi and 300 TDi engines, the glow plugs also provide a 'post-heating' function, whereby the glow plugs

12.10 Oil pressure warning light switch (arrowed) – TD5 engine

remain switched on for a period after the engine has started. The length of time for which the glow plugs are switched on is dependent on underbonnet temperature, which is monitored by a temperature sensor located in the relay/timer unit. The electrical supply to the glow plugs will be interrupted by:

a) *Opening of the 'no-load' switch – a microswitch located on the fuel injection pump, which operates when the accelerator is depressed.*

b) *The signal from the underbonnet temperature sensor when the temperature reaches a predetermined level.*

3 A warning light in the instrument panel tells the driver that preheating is taking place. On all models except those with 200 TDi and 300 TDi engines, the warning light will illuminate when the ignition key is in position II, and will not extinguish until the driver turns the ignition key to an alternative position. On models with 200 TDi and 300 TDi engines, when the light goes out, the engine is ready to be started – the voltage supply to the glow plugs may continue for several seconds after the light goes out. If no attempt is made to start, the timer then cuts off the supply, in order to avoid draining the battery and overheating the glow plugs.

TD5 engines

4 Heater (glow) plugs are only fitted to 4 of the 5 cylinders on this engine – Nos 1, 2, 3 and 4. The plugs are electrically-operated, and controlled by the engine management ECM. Using information supplied from engine coolant temperature sensors the ECM energises the plugs for a brief period before starting to aid combustion, and a brief period after starting – to reduce the warm-up period and improve exhaust emissions.

Testing

Note: *Refer to the precautions given in 'Safety first!' and in Section 1 of this Chapter before proceeding.*

10J, 12J and 19J engines

Note: *Early models were fitted with glow plugs which were wired to the supply cable in series. Later models had the plugs wired in parallel. If any one plug fails on an engine with series-wired plugs, the supply to ALL plugs will be interrupted. Testing of series-wired plugs **must not** be done by applying 12 volts to them directly, or they will burn out.*

5 To test the supply to the plugs, connect a 12 volt test light (approximately 5 watts) between the glow plug supply cable and earth (engine or vehicle metal). Make sure that the live connection is kept well clear of the engine and bodywork.

6 Have an assistant switch on the ignition (position II) and check that voltage is applied to the glow plugs.

7 If there is no supply, the wiring or associated fuse is at fault.

8 To locate a defective glow plug, first refer to the note at the beginning of this sub-Section, then disconnect the wiring from the plugs, and test each plug individually by connecting a 12 volt battery to the plug in series with a 12 volt (approximately 5 watt) test bulb. If the light comes on, the plug is working.

200 TDi and 300 TDi engines

9 If the system malfunctions, testing is ultimately by substitution of known good units, but some preliminary checks may be made as follows.

10 Connect a voltmeter or 12 volt test light between the glow plug supply cable and earth (engine or vehicle metal). Make sure that the live connection is kept clear of the engine and bodywork.

11 Have an assistant switch on the ignition (position II) and check that voltage is applied to the glow plugs. Note the time for which the warning light is lit, and the total time for which voltage is applied before the system cuts out. Switch off the ignition.

12 At an underbonnet temperature of 20°C, typical times noted should be 5 or 6 seconds for warning light operation, followed by a further 4 to 5 seconds supply after the light goes out (provided that the starter motor is not operated). Warning light time will increase with lower temperatures, and decrease with higher temperatures.

13 If there is no supply at all, the relay or associated wiring is at fault.

14 To locate a defective glow plug, disconnect the main supply cable and the interconnecting wire or strap from the top of the glow plugs. Be careful not to drop the nuts and washers.

15 Use a continuity tester, or a 12 volt test light connected to the battery positive terminal, to check for continuity between each glow plug terminal and earth. The resistance of a glow plug in good condition is very low (less than 1 ohm), so if the test light does not come on, or the continuity tester shows a high resistance, the glow plug is certainly defective.

16 If an ammeter is available, the current draw of each glow plug can be checked. After an initial surge of around 15 to 20 amps, each plug should draw around 10 amps. Any plug which draws much more or less than this is probably defective.

17 As a final check, the glow plugs can be removed and inspected as described in Section 14.

TD5 engines

18 Remove the glow plugs as described in Section 14.

19 With battery voltage applied, the tip of the plug should start to glow within 5 seconds. If the tip fails to glow first, renew it.

14 Glow plugs – removal, inspection and refitting

Caution: If the preheating system has just been energised, or if the engine has been running, the glow plugs may be extremely hot.

Removal

Non-TD5 engines

Note: *Refer to the precautions given in 'Safety first!' and in Section 1 of this Chapter before proceeding. Where applicable, a new crankcase ventilation valve O-ring will be required on refitting – see text.*

1 Disconnect the battery negative lead.

2 If the No 1 cylinder (timing belt end) glow plug is to be removed on 300 TDi engine models with air conditioning, proceed as follows:

a) *Remove the air conditioning compressor drivebelt, as described in Chapter 1.*

b) *Remove the four securing bolts, and move the compressor to one side, to provide access to the glow plug. **DO NOT** disconnect the refrigerant lines from the compressor (see Chapter 3).*

3 If the No 3 cylinder glow plug is to be removed on 300 TDi engine models, remove the securing bolt, and withdraw the crankcase ventilation system valve from the valve cover. Move the valve to one side for access to the glow plug.

4 Unscrew the nut from the relevant glow plug terminal, and recover the washer **(see illustration)**.

5 Disconnect the wiring, noting the routing if all the glow plugs are to be removed.

6 Unscrew the glow plug, and remove it from the cylinder head **(see illustrations)**.

TD5 engines

7 Undo the 3 bolts and remove the plastic cover from the top of the engine.

8 Disconnect the battery negative lead as described in Section 4.

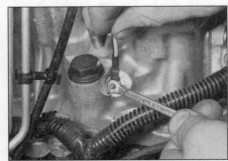

14.4 Unscrewing a glow plug wiring nut – 300 TDi engine

14.6a Removing a glow plug – 300 TDi engine

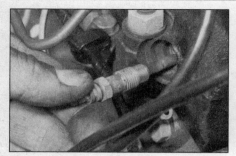

14.6b Removing a glow plug – 19J engine

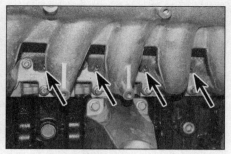

14.9 The glow plugs (arrowed) are accessible through the intake manifold – TD5 engine

14.10 Slacken and remove the glow plug – TD5 engine

9 Pull the wiring connector from each glow plug (see illustration).
10 Slacken and remove the glow plugs (see illustration).

Inspection

11 Inspect the glow plugs for physical damage. Burnt or eroded glow plug tips can be caused by a bad injector spray pattern. Have the injectors checked if this sort of damage is found.
12 If the glow plugs are in good physical condition, check them electrically using a 12 volt test light or continuity tester as described in Section 13 (not TD5 models).
13 The glow plugs can be energised by applying 12 volts to them, to verify that they heat up evenly and in the required time. Observe the following precautions:

a) *Support the glow plug by clamping it carefully in a vice or self-locking pliers. Remember – it will become red-hot.*
b) *Make sure that the power supply or test lead incorporates a fuse or overload trip, to protect against damage from a short-circuit.*
c) *After testing, allow the glow plug to cool for several minutes before attempting to handle it.*

14 A glow plug in good condition will start to glow red at the tip after drawing current for 5 seconds or so. Any plug which takes much longer to start glowing, or which starts glowing in the middle instead of at the tip, is defective.

Refitting

15 Refitting is a reversal of removal, bearing in mind the following points:

a) *Apply a smear of copper-based anti-seize compound to the plug threads, and tighten the glow plugs to the specified torque. Do not overtighten, as this can damage the glow plug element.*
b) *Ensure that the glow plug wiring is routed as noted before removal. On 10J, 12J and 19J engines, ensure that the wiring to each plug is routed vertically downwards, to shield the wiring against heat from the cylinder head.*
c) *Where applicable, use a new O-ring, lubricated with clean engine oil, when refitting the crankcase ventilation valve.*
d) *Where applicable, refit and tighten the air conditioning compressor drivebelt as described in Chapter 1.*

15 Preheating system relay/timer unit – removal and refitting

Note: *Refer to the precautions given in 'Safety first!' and in Section 1 of this Chapter before proceeding.*

Removal

1 The relay/timer unit is located on the engine compartment bulkhead.
2 Disconnect the battery negative lead.
3 Disconnect the wiring plug from the relay/timer unit.
4 Unscrew the bolt, or the nut and bolt, as applicable, and withdraw the unit.

Refitting

5 Refitting is a reversal of removal.

16 Stop solenoid – description, removal and refitting

Note: *A stop solenoid is not fitted to TD5 engines.*

Description

1 The stop solenoid is located at the rear of the fuel injection pump. Its purpose is to cut the fuel supply when the ignition is switched off. If an open-circuit occurs in the solenoid or supply wiring, it will be impossible to start the engine, as the fuel will not reach the injectors. The same applies if the solenoid plunger jams in the 'stop' position. If the solenoid jams in the

16.4a Disconnecting the wiring from the stop solenoid – 19J engine

'run' position, the engine will not stop when the ignition is switched off. In an emergency, the engine can be stalled by letting the clutch out abruptly with top gear selected.
2 If the solenoid has failed and the engine will not run, a temporary repair may be made by removing the solenoid as described in the following paragraphs. Refit the solenoid body, without the plunger and spring. Tape up the wire, so that it cannot touch earth. The engine can now be started as usual, but it will be necessary to use the manual stop lever on the fuel injection pump (or to stall the engine in gear) to stop it.

Removal

Caution : Be careful not to allow dirt into the injection pump during this procedure. A new sealing washer or O-ring must be used on refitting.
Note: *Refer to the precautions given in 'Safety first!' and in Section 1 of this Chapter before proceeding.*
3 Disconnect the battery negative lead.
4 Withdraw the rubber boot (where applicable), then unscrew the terminal nut and disconnect the wire from the top of the solenoid (see illustrations).
5 Carefully clean around the solenoid, then unscrew and withdraw the solenoid, and recover the sealing washer or O-ring (as applicable). Recover the solenoid plunger and spring if they remain in the pump. Operate the hand-priming lever on the fuel lift pump as the solenoid is removed, to flush away any dirt.

Refitting

6 Refitting is a reversal of removal, using a new sealing washer or O-ring.

16.4b Stop solenoid location (arrowed) in rear of injection pump – 300 TDi engine

Chapter 6
Clutch

Contents

Section number

Clutch assembly – removal, inspection and refitting 2
Clutch fluid level check . . . . See Chapter 1
Clutch pedal – removal, refitting and adjustment. 7
Clutch release mechanism – removal, inspection and refitting 3

Section number

General information 1
Hydraulic slave cylinder – removal, overhaul and refitting. 4
Hydraulic system – bleeding 6
Master cylinder – removal, overhaul and refitting 5

Degrees of difficulty

Easy, suitable for novice with little experience		**Fairly easy,** suitable for beginner with some experience		**Fairly difficult,** suitable for competent DIY mechanic		**Difficult,** suitable for experienced DIY mechanic		**Very difficult,** suitable for expert DIY or professional	

Specifications

General
Clutch type. . . . . Single dry plate, diaphragm spring, hydraulically-operated
Adjustment. . . . . Automatic
Hydraulic fluid type. . . . . See *Lubricants and fluids*

Clutch friction disc
Diameter:
   Early 10J and 12J engines . . . . 242.1 mm
   Later 10J and 12J engines, and 19J, 200 TDi and 300 TDi engines . 235.0 mm
   TD5 engines . . . . 267.0 mm

Clutch pedal adjustment (non-TD5 engines only)
Pedal height . . . . 140.0 mm
Master cylinder pushrod-to-piston freeplay. . . . . 1.5 mm
Pedal free movement at pedal rubber . . . . 6.0 mm

Torque wrench settings

	Nm	lbf ft
Clutch cover bolts	34	25
Clutch cover nuts (TD5 engines)	25	18
Clutch slave cylinder bolts.	25	18
Hydraulic fluid pipe and hose unions.	15	11

1 General information

All models are fitted with a single dry plate clutch, which consists of five main components – friction disc, pressure plate, diaphragm spring, cover, and release bearing.

The friction disc is free to slide along the splines of the gearbox input shaft, and is held in position between the flywheel and the pressure plate by the pressure exerted on the pressure plate by the diaphragm spring. Friction lining material is riveted to both sides of the friction disc, and on non-TD5 models, spring cushioning between the friction linings and the hub absorbs transmission shocks, and helps to ensure a smooth take-up of power as the clutch is engaged. TD5 models are equipped with a dual mass flywheel which incorporates torsional damping to absorb transmission shocks.

The diaphragm spring is mounted on pins, and is held in place in the cover by annular fulcrum rings.

The release bearing is located on a guide sleeve at the front of the gearbox. The bearing is free to slide on the sleeve, under the action of the release arm which pivots inside the clutch bellhousing.

The release mechanism is operated by the clutch pedal, using hydraulic pressure. The pedal acts on the hydraulic master cylinder pushrod, and a slave cylinder, mounted on the gearbox bellhousing, operates the clutch release lever via a pushrod.

When the clutch pedal is depressed, the release arm pushes the release bearing forwards, to bear against the centre of the diaphragm spring, thus pushing the centre of the diaphragm spring inwards. The diaphragm spring acts against the fulcrum rings in the cover; as the centre of the spring is pushed in, the outside of the spring is pushed out, so allowing the pressure plate to move backwards away from the friction disc.

When the clutch pedal is released, the diaphragm spring forces the pressure plate into contact with the friction linings on the friction disc, and simultaneously pushes the

2.4 Withdrawing the clutch cover and friction disc

friction disc forwards on its splines, forcing it against the flywheel. The friction disc is now firmly sandwiched between the pressure plate and the flywheel, and drive is taken up.

The clutch is self-adjusting. As wear takes place on the friction disc over a period of time, the pressure plate automatically moves closer to the friction disc to compensate.

2 Clutch assembly – removal, inspection and refitting

⚠️ **Warning: Dust created by clutch wear and deposited on the clutch components may contain asbestos, which is a health hazard. DO NOT blow it out with compressed air, nor inhale any of it. DO NOT use petrol (or petroleum-based solvents) to clean off the dust. Brake system cleaner or methylated spirit should be used to flush the dust into a suitable receptacle. After the clutch components are wiped clean with rags, dispose of the contaminated rags and cleaner in a sealed, marked container.**

Removal

1 Remove the gearbox, as described in Chapter 7A, or the engine, as described in Chapter 2C. Note that if no other work is to be carried out on the gearbox, it is far simpler to remove the engine.

2 If the original clutch is to be refitted, make alignment marks between the clutch cover and the flywheel, so that the clutch can be refitted in its original position.

3 Progressively unscrew the bolts or nuts (TD5 engines only) securing the clutch cover to the flywheel, and recover the washers. Do not disturb the three bolts located in the side of the clutch cover (non-TD5 engines only).

4 Withdraw the clutch cover from the flywheel. Be prepared to catch the clutch friction disc, which may drop out of the cover as it is withdrawn, and note which way round the friction disc is fitted **(see illustration)**. The greater projecting side of the hub faces the flywheel.

2.10 FW SIDE mark on clutch friction disc

Inspection

5 With the clutch assembly removed, clean off all traces of dust using a dry cloth. Although most friction discs now have asbestos-free linings, some do not, and it is wise to take suitable precautions; *asbestos dust is harmful, and must not be inhaled.*

6 Examine the linings of the friction disc for wear or loose rivets, and for distortion, cracks, broken torsion springs (where applicable) and worn splines. The surface of the friction linings may be highly glazed, but, as long as the friction material pattern can be clearly seen, this is satisfactory. If there is any sign of oil contamination, indicated by a continuous, or patchy, shiny black discolouration, the disc must be renewed. The source of the contamination must be traced and rectified before fitting new clutch components; typically, a leaking crankshaft rear oil seal or gearbox input shaft oil seal – or both – will be to blame (renewal procedures are given in the appropriate part of Chapter 2 and Chapter 7A). The disc must also be renewed if the lining thickness has worn down to, or just above, the level of the rivet heads.

7 Check the machined faces of the flywheel and pressure plate. If either is grooved, or heavily scored, renewal is necessary. The pressure plate must also be renewed if any cracks are apparent, or if the diaphragm spring is damaged or its pressure suspect.

8 With the clutch removed, it is advisable to check the condition of the release bearing, as described in Section 3. It is considered good practice to renew the release bearing as a matter of course, whenever new clutch components are fitted, given the amount of work required to gain access to the clutch.

Refitting

9 It is important to ensure that no oil or grease gets onto the friction disc linings, or the pressure plate and flywheel faces. It is advisable to refit the clutch assembly with clean hands, and to wipe down the pressure plate and flywheel faces with a clean rag before assembly begins.

10 Apply a smear of clutch assembly grease to the splines of the friction disc hub, then offer the disc to the flywheel, with the greater projecting side of the hub facing the flywheel (most friction discs will have a Flywheel side or FW SIDE marking, which should face the flywheel) **(see illustration)**. Hold the friction disc against the flywheel while the cover/pressure plate assembly is offered into position.

11 Fit the clutch cover assembly, where applicable aligning the marks on the flywheel and clutch cover. Refit the securing bolts/nuts and washers, and tighten them finger-tight, so that the friction disc is gripped,

2.11 The pressure plate assembly locates on dowels (arrowed)

Using a clutch alignment tool . . .

. . . to centre the friction disc

If a suitable clutch alignment tool can be obtained, this will eliminate all the guesswork, and obviate the need for visual alignment.

but can still be moved. Note that the pressure plate assembly locates on dowels **(see illustration)**.

12 The friction disc must now be centralised, so that when the engine and gearbox are mated, the gearbox input shaft splines will pass through the splines in the friction disc hub.

13 Centralisation can be carried out by inserting a round bar or a long screwdriver through the hole in the centre of the friction disc, so that the end of the bar rests in the spigot bearing in the centre of the crankshaft. Where possible, use a blunt instrument, but if a screwdriver is used, wrap tape around the blade, to prevent damage to the bearing surface. Moving the bar sideways or up-and-down as necessary, move the friction disc in whichever direction is necessary to achieve centralisation. With the bar removed, view the friction disc hub in relation to the hole in the centre of the crankshaft and the circle created by the ends of the diaphragm spring fingers. When the hub appears exactly in the centre, all is correct. Alternatively, use a clutch plate alignment tool **(see Haynes hint)**.

14 Tighten the cover retaining bolts/nuts gradually in a diagonal sequence, to the specified torque. Remove the alignment tool.

15 Refit the gearbox or engine, as applicable, as described in Chapter 7A or Chapter 2C respectively.

3 Clutch release mechanism
– removal, inspection and refitting

Release bearing

Removal

1 Remove the gearbox, described in Chapter 7A, or the engine, as described in Chapter 2C. Note that if no other work is to be carried out on the gearbox, it is far simpler to remove the engine.

2 Where applicable, remove the clip securing the release bearing assembly to the release

lever. Note that the clip is used to hold the bearing in position when mating the engine and gearbox in production – the clip may fall out or become dislodged with no adverse effects.

3 Slide the bearing assembly from the guide sleeve **(see illustration)**.

4 On certain models, the bearing is attached to a separate retaining sleeve, and if the bearing is to be renewed, it must be pressed from the sleeve. Note that on TD5 models, the bearing is not available separately from the bearing carrier.

Inspection

5 Spin the release bearing, and check it for excessive roughness. Hold the outer race, and attempt to move it laterally against the inner race. If any excessive movement or roughness is evident, renew the bearing. If a new clutch has been fitted, it is wise to renew the release bearing as a matter of course.

Refitting

6 On models with a separate bearing retaining sleeve, if a new bearing is to be fitted, press the new bearing onto the retaining sleeve. Note that the domed face of the bearing must face away from the sleeve (the domed face acts on the clutch pressure plate).

7 Lightly smear the outer faces of the release bearing guide sleeve with clutch assembly grease.

8 Slide the bearing assembly onto the guide sleeve, ensuring that the guide slippers on the release arm engage with the release bearing collar.

9 Where applicable, refit the clip securing the release bearing assembly to the release lever.

10 Refit the gearbox or engine, as applicable, as described in Chapter 7A or Chapter 2C respectively.

Release lever

Removal

11 Remove the release bearing, as described previously in this Section, and the slave cylinder, as described in Section 4 (note that if the gearbox is in position in the vehicle, there is no need to disconnect the hydraulic fluid pipe from the slave cylinder – move the slave cylinder to one side, leaving the pipe connected).

12 Unclip the slave cylinder pushrod from the end of the release lever, and withdraw the pushrod through the bellhousing **(see illustration)**.

13 Where applicable, remove the securing screw (and washer), and prise off the clip securing the release lever to the pivot post.

3.3 Sliding the clutch release bearing from the guide sleeve – R380 type gearbox shown

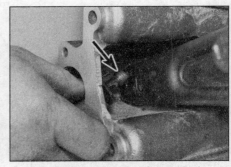

3.12 Withdrawing the slave cylinder pushrod from the bellhousing – R380 type gearbox shown

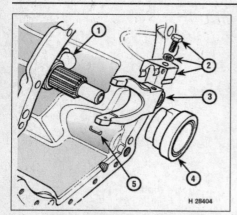

3.13 Clutch release components – early models

1 Release lever pivot post
2 Release lever securing clip, screw and washer
3 Release lever
4 Release bearing
5 Release bearing securing clip

Note that the clip locates behind the washer on the pivot post **(see illustration)**.

14 On models where there is no screw securing the release lever clip, pull the release lever out, and slide it towards the release bearing guide sleeve to release the clip from the pivot post.

15 Withdraw the release lever from the bellhousing, and where applicable, recover the release bearing guide slippers **(see illustrations)**.

Refitting

16 Where applicable, ensure that the release bearing guide slippers are in position on the release lever.

17 Apply a little high melting-point grease to the contact faces of the pivot post and the release lever **(see illustration)**.

18 Manipulate the release lever into position

3.15a Withdraw the release lever . . .

on the pivot post, and engage the securing clip. Where applicable, ensure that the securing clip locates behind the washer on the pivot post.

19 Where applicable, refit the securing screw and washer to the release lever securing clip.

20 Refit the slave cylinder pushrod to the end of the release arm, ensuring that the securing clip is engaged.

21 Refit the release bearing as described previously in this Section, and the slave cylinder as described in Section 4.

4 Hydraulic slave cylinder – removal, overhaul and refitting

⚠️ **Warning: Hydraulic fluid is poisonous; wash off immediately and thoroughly in the case of skin contact, and seek immediate medical advice if any fluid is swallowed or gets into the eyes. Certain types of hydraulic fluid are inflammable, and may ignite when allowed into contact with hot components. When servicing any hydraulic system, it is safest to assume that the fluid IS inflammable, and to take precautions against the risk of fire as though it is petrol that is being handled. Finally, it is hygroscopic (it absorbs moisture from the air)**

3.15b . . . and recover the release bearing guide slippers. Note release bearing securing clip (arrowed) – R380 type gearbox shown

– old fluid may be contaminated, and unfit for further use. When topping-up or renewing the fluid, always use the recommended type, and ensure that it comes from a freshly-opened sealed container.
Caution: Hydraulic fluid is an effective paint stripper, and will attack plastics; if any is spilt, it should be washed off immediately, using copious quantities of fresh water
Note: *Suitable jointing compound may be required to coat the mating faces of the slave cylinder mounting plate on refitting.*

Removal

1 Unscrew the union nut, and disconnect the hydraulic fluid pipe from the end of the slave cylinder **(see illustration)**. Plug or cover the open ends of the pipe and the slave cylinder, to prevent dirt ingress and fluid loss. If desired, to improve access, the pipe can be removed completely, in which case, plug or cover the open end of the flexible hose-to-pipe union.

2 Unscrew the two securing bolts, and withdraw the slave cylinder and the mounting plate from the gearbox bellhousing. Note that one of the bolts also secures the fluid pipe mounting bracket – move the assembly to one side, taking care not to strain the hydraulic

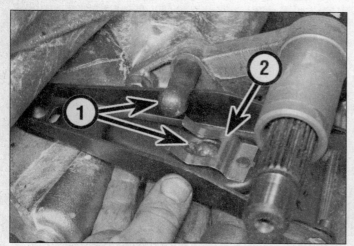

3.17 Apply high melting-point grease to the contact faces (1). Note release lever securing clip (2) – R380 type gearbox shown

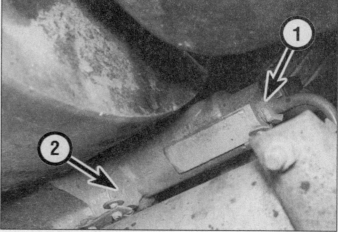

4.1 Slave cylinder fluid pipe union (1) and one of the slave cylinder securing bolts (2) – LT77 type gearbox shown

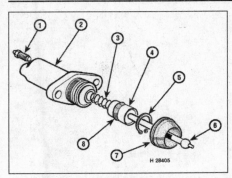

4.6 Slave cylinder components

1 Bleed nipple	5 Circlip
2 Slave cylinder	6 Pushrod
3 Spring	7 Dust seal
4 Piston	8 Piston seal

hose. Recover the slave cylinder pushrod if it is loose.

3 Both sides of the mounting plate may coated with jointing compound – if necessary, carefully separate the components, taking care not to damage the mating faces or the dust cover.

Overhaul

Note: *Before dismantling the slave cylinder, check on the availability of spares, and ensure that the appropriate overhaul kit is obtained. Suitable rubber grease will be required to pack the dust cover on refitting.*

4 With the slave cylinder removed as described previously in this Section, thoroughly clean the exterior of the assembly, then proceed as follows.

5 If not already done, withdraw the dust cover and the pushrod from the end of the cylinder.

6 Where applicable, using a suitable pair of circlip pliers, remove the piston retaining circlip from the cylinder bore **(see illustration)**. Note that not all cylinders are fitted with a piston retaining circlip.

7 Extract the piston and seal assembly from the cylinder bore. If necessary, tap the cylinder body on a clean wooden surface to dislodge the components – alternatively, apply low pressure air (such as from a tyre foot-pump) to the fluid inlet to eject the components.

8 Prise the seal from the groove in the piston.

9 Withdraw the spring from the cylinder bore.

10 Unscrew the bleed screw from the rear of the cylinder.

11 Clean all the components thoroughly, using clean fresh hydraulic fluid, and dry them using a clean, lint-free cloth. Check that the fluid inlet port is free from obstructions.

12 Examine the cylinder bore, which must be free from corrosion, scoring and ridges. Similarly, examine the piston. If either the cylinder bore or the piston show signs of damage or wear, the complete assembly must be renewed.

13 Refit the bleed screw to the cylinder. Take care not to overtighten the screw.

14 Lubricate the new seal, the piston and the cylinder bore with clean, fresh hydraulic fluid.

15 Fit the seal to the groove in the piston, noting that the larger diameter of the seal should face towards the rear (fluid inlet end) of the cylinder.

16 Push the spring and piston assembly to the cylinder bore (using a wooden dowel if necessary), ensuring that the piston seal does not fold back. Note that the smaller diameter of the piston should seat against the spring.

17 Where applicable, secure the piston assembly with the circlip.

18 Fill the dust cover with suitable rubber grease, then fit the dust cover to the groove in the end of the cylinder.

19 Where applicable, feed the pushrod through the dust cover, ensuring that the pushrod engages with the piston.

20 Refit the assembly, as described in the following paragraphs.

Refitting

21 If the mounting plate was originally fitted using sealant, commence refitting by cleaning all traces of sealant from the mating faces of the mounting plate, slave cylinder and bellhousing. Coat both sides of the mounting plate with suitable jointing compound.

22 Fit the mounting plate to the slave cylinder. Where applicable, also fit the dust cover, ensuring that it engages with the groove in the slave cylinder.

23 Manipulate the slave cylinder into position in the bellhousing, and feed the pushrod through the slave cylinder dust cover, ensuring that the pushrod engages with the slave cylinder piston.

24 Ensure that the fluid pipe mounting bracket is in position, then refit and tighten the slave cylinder securing bolts.

25 Reconnect the fluid pipe to the slave cylinder, and tighten the union nut.

26 Refill the clutch hydraulic fluid reservoir, and bleed the hydraulic system as described in Section 6.

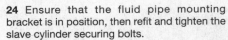

5 Master cylinder – removal, overhaul and refitting

 Warning: *Refer to the warning at the beginning of Section 4 before proceeding.*

Right-hand-drive vehicles

Note: *Suitable sealant or a new gasket (as applicable) will be required to seal the pedal box to the bulkhead on refitting, and a new pedal box cover gasket will be required.*

Removal

1 Disconnect the battery negative lead.

2 To improve access, remove the bonnet as described in Chapter 12.

3 Drain the clutch hydraulic system. Follow the procedure described in Section 6 for bleeding the hydraulic system, but do not top-up the fluid reservoir. Pump the clutch pedal until all the hydraulic fluid has been expelled from the bleed screw.

4 Unscrew the union nut, and disconnect the hydraulic fluid pipe from the master cylinder **(see illustration)**. Plug the open ends of the pipe and master cylinder, to prevent dirt ingress.

5 Working in the driver's footwell, release the securing clips and remove the trim panel for access to the pedals.

6 On models where the clutch pedal return spring is located between the pedal and an anchor plate on the bulkhead, carefully unhook the return spring from the anchor plate **(see illustration)**. On later models, the return spring is located on the pedal pivot shaft.

7 Unscrew the six bolts securing the clutch pedal box to the bulkhead. Where applicable, note that one of the pedal box securing bolts also secures the pedal return spring anchor plate – note the location of the anchor plate, to ensure correct refitting **(see illustration)**.

5.4 Unscrewing the master cylinder fluid pipe union nut (arrowed)

5.6 Disconnecting the clutch pedal return spring from the anchor plate (arrowed)

5.7 Clutch pedal box securing bolts (arrowed). Note the location of the return spring anchor plate (A)

5.9 Unclip the accelerator cable (arrowed) from the pedal box bracket

5.10 Withdrawing the clutch pedal box from the engine compartment

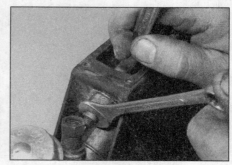

5.12 Unscrewing a clutch master cylinder securing nut

5.13 Unscrew the nut and washer (arrowed) from the end of the master cylinder pushrod

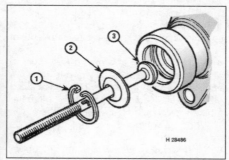

5.17 Withdraw the circlip (1), washer (2) and pushrod (3) from the master cylinder bore

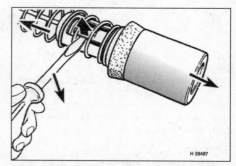

5.19 Release the spring seat locking tab (arrowed), then withdraw the piston

8 Unclip the rubber from the pedal.

9 Where applicable, unclip the accelerator cable from the bracket on the pedal box, and move the cable to one side **(see illustration)**.

10 Working in the engine compartment, withdraw the pedal box/master cylinder assembly from the bulkhead, and manipulate the assembly from the engine compartment. The pedal box may be sealed to the bulkhead using sealant or a gasket – where applicable, recover the gasket. It will be necessary to turn the pedal box in order to allow the pedal to pass through the aperture in the bulkhead **(see illustration)**.

11 Remove the securing screws, and lift the top cover from the pedal box. Recover the gasket.

12 Unscrew the two nuts and bolts securing the master cylinder to the pedal box **(see illustration)**.

13 Unscrew the nut and recover the washer from the end of the master cylinder pushrod, then withdraw the master cylinder from the pedal box **(see illustration)**. Recover the mounting plate, and recover the remaining washer from the end of the pushrod.

Overhaul

Note: *Before dismantling the master cylinder, check on the availability of spares, and ensure that the appropriate overhaul kit is obtained. Suitable rubber grease will be required to lubricate the new seals refitting.*

14 With the master cylinder removed as described previously in this Section,

thoroughly clean the exterior of the assembly, then proceed as follows.

15 Where applicable, prise the dust cover from the end of the cylinder then, if desired, unscrew the locknuts from the end of the pushrod.

16 Depress the pushrod into the cylinder, then using a suitable pair of circlip pliers, extract the pushrod retaining circlip from the cylinder bore.

17 Withdraw the pushrod, circlip and washer **(see illustration)**.

18 Withdraw the piston assembly and spring. If necessary, tap the cylinder body on a clean wooden surface to dislodge the components. Alternatively, apply low pressure air (such as from a tyre foot pump) to the fluid inlet to eject the components.

19 Using a small screwdriver, release the

spring seat locking tab from the slot in the piston, then withdraw the piston **(see illustration)**.

20 Prise the seal from the piston.

21 Compress the spring, and manipulate the valve stem to align with the larger diameter of the keyhole slot in the spring seat.

22 Withdraw the spring and the spring seat **(see illustration)**.

23 Withdraw the valve spacer and the spring washer from the valve stem.

24 Prise the seal from the end of the valve.

25 Clean all the components thoroughly, using clean fresh hydraulic fluid, and dry them using a clean, lint-free cloth. Check that the fluid port is free from obstructions.

26 Examine the cylinder bore, which must be free from corrosion, scoring and ridges. Similarly, examine the piston. If either the

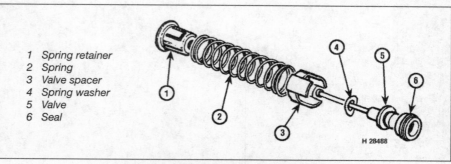

1 Spring retainer
2 Spring
3 Valve spacer
4 Spring washer
5 Valve
6 Seal

5.22 Clutch master cylinder components

cylinder bore or the piston show signs of damage or wear, the complete assembly must be renewed.

27 Clean the fluid reservoir cap, and check that the vent hole in the cap is free from obstructions.

28 Smear the new seals with a little rubber grease, then lubricate the remaining components with clean hydraulic fluid.

29 Fit the valve seal, flat side first, onto the end of the valve.

30 Fit the spring washer, domed side first, over the valve stem.

31 Fit the valve spacer, legs first, over the valve stem.

32 Fit the spring over the valve stem, then fit the spring seat.

33 Compress the spring until the valve stem can be engaged with the keyhole slot in the spring seat. Manipulate the valve stem as necessary to lock it in position in the spring seat.

34 Fit the new seal to the piston, small diameter first.

35 Push the piston into the spring seat until the spring seat locking tab engages with the slot in the piston.

36 Slide the piston assembly, valve end first, into the cylinder.

37 Fit the pushrod, complete with the washer and circlip, to the cylinder, ensuring that the end of the pushrod engages with the piston. Push the assembly into position until the circlip engages in the slot in the cylinder bore.

38 Where applicable, refit the locknuts to the end of the pushrod, and refit the dust cover to the end of the cylinder.

39 Operate the pushrod several times to check for free movement of the piston.

Refitting

40 Where applicable, clean all traces of old sealant from the mating faces of the pedal box and the bulkhead.

41 Ensure that the adjuster nut, locknut and washer have been refitted to the end of the master cylinder pushrod.

42 Fit the master cylinder mounting plate to the pedal box, then manipulate the master cylinder into position, feeding the pushrod through the pedal trunnion. Loosely fit the washer and nut to the end of the pushrod.

43 Secure the master cylinder to the pedal box with the two nuts and bolts.

44 If the pedal box was originally sealed to the bulkhead with sealant, apply fresh sealant to the bulkhead mating face of the pedal box. Alternatively, place a new gasket in position.

45 Refit the pedal box, then refit and tighten the securing bolts. Where applicable, ensure that the pedal return spring anchor plate is in position on the relevant bolt.

46 Where applicable, reconnect the return spring to the anchor plate.

47 Where applicable, refit the accelerator cable to the clip on the brake pedal box.

48 Refit the rubber to the pedal.

49 Check and if necessary adjust the pedal height, as described in Section 7.

50 Where applicable, clean all traces of old gasket from the pedal box top cover, then refit the cover using a new gasket, and tighten the securing bolts.

51 Refit the footwell trim panel.

52 Reconnect the fluid pipe to the master cylinder.

53 Refill the reservoir with fluid of the recommended type (see *Lubricants and fluids*), then bleed the hydraulic system as described in Section 6.

54 Refit the bonnet as described in Chapter 12.

55 Reconnect the battery negative lead.

Left-hand-drive models

Note: *Suitable sealant or a new gasket (as applicable) will be required to seal the clutch and brake pedal boxes to the bulkhead on refitting, and a new clutch pedal box cover gasket will be required.*

Removal

56 Disconnect the battery negative lead.

57 Remove the bonnet as described in Chapter 12.

58 Working in the engine compartment, where applicable, release the bracket securing the three-way hydraulic pipe union to the brake servo.

59 Remove the two nuts securing the brake master cylinder to the servo, then carefully move the master cylinder forwards from the servo, taking care not to strain the hydraulic pipes. If necessary, release the pipes from the securing clips to allow sufficient movement of the master cylinder.

60 Disconnect the vacuum hose from the brake servo.

61 Disconnect the two brake light wiring connectors, located in the engine compartment, between the clutch master cylinder and the brake servo.

62 Working in the driver's footwell, remove the trim panel for access to the pedals.

63 Carefully unhook the two return springs from the brake pedal, and the single return spring from the clutch pedal.

64 Working in the footwell, unscrew the six bolts securing the brake pedal box to the bulkhead, then withdraw the brake pedal box/servo assembly into the engine compartment sufficiently to allow access for removal of the clutch pedal box/master cylinder assembly. The pedal box may be sealed to the bulkhead using sealant or a gasket – where applicable, recover the gasket.

65 Proceed as described previously for right-hand-drive models in paragraphs 7 to 13 inclusive.

Overhaul

66 The procedure is as described previously for right-hand-drive models.

Refitting

67 Proceed as described previously for right-

hand-drive models in paragraphs 40 to 50 inclusive.

68 Reconnect the fluid pipe to the clutch master cylinder.

69 If the brake pedal box was originally sealed to the bulkhead with sealant, apply fresh sealant to the bulkhead mating face of the pedal box. Alternatively, place a new gasket in position.

70 Refit the brake pedal box, and tighten the securing bolts.

71 Reconnect the brake pedal return springs to the pedal.

72 Refit the footwell trim panel.

73 Refit the brake master cylinder to the servo, and tighten the securing nuts.

74 Reconnect the brake light wiring connectors.

75 Reconnect the brake servo vacuum hose.

76 Where applicable, refit the three-way hydraulic pipe union to the brake servo.

77 Refill the clutch fluid reservoir with fluid of the recommended type (see *Lubricants, fluids and capacities*), then bleed the hydraulic system as described in Section 6.

78 Refit the bonnet as described in Chapter 12.

79 Reconnect the battery negative lead.

6   Hydraulic system – bleeding

⚠️ *Warning: Hydraulic fluid is poisonous; wash off immediately and thoroughly in the case of skin contact, and seek immediate medical advice if any fluid is swallowed or gets into the eyes. Certain types of hydraulic fluid are inflammable, and may ignite when allowed into contact with hot components; when servicing any hydraulic system, it is safest to assume that the fluid is inflammable, and to take precautions against the risk of fire as though it is petrol that is being handled. Hydraulic fluid is also an effective paint stripper, and will attack plastics; if any is spilt, it should be washed off immediately, using copious quantities of fresh water. Finally, it is hygroscopic (it absorbs moisture from the air) – old fluid may be contaminated and unfit for further use. When topping-up or renewing the fluid, always use the recommended type, and ensure that it comes from a freshly-opened sealed container.*

General

1 The correct operation of any hydraulic system is only possible after removing all air from the components and circuit; and this is achieved by bleeding the system.

2 During the bleeding procedure, add only clean, unused hydraulic fluid of the recommended type; never re-use fluid that has already been bled from the system. Ensure that sufficient fluid is available before starting work.

3 If there is any possibility of incorrect fluid being already in the system, the hydraulic components and circuit must be flushed completely with uncontaminated, correct fluid, and new seals should be fitted throughout the system.

4 If hydraulic fluid has been lost from the system, or air has entered because of a leak, ensure that the fault is cured before proceeding further.

Bleeding procedure

5 Unscrew the master cylinder reservoir cap, and top the master cylinder reservoir up to the MAX level line; refit the cap loosely, and remember to maintain the fluid level at least above the MIN level line throughout the procedure, otherwise there is a risk of further air entering the system.

6 There is a number of one-man, do-it-yourself brake/clutch bleeding kits currently available from motor accessory shops. It is recommended that one of these kits is used whenever possible, as they greatly simplify the bleeding operation, and also reduce the risk of expelled air and fluid being drawn back into the system. If such a kit is not available, the basic (two-man) method must be used, which is described in detail below.

7 If a kit is to be used, prepare the vehicle as described previously, and follow the kit manufacturer's instructions, as the procedure may vary slightly according to the type being used; generally, they are as outlined below in the relevant sub-Section.

Bleeding

Basic (two-man) method

8 Clean the area around the bleed screw at the rear of the clutch slave cylinder (located on the gearbox bellhousing). Where applicable, remove the dust cover from the bleed screw **(see illustration)**. Note that on certain models, it may be necessary to remove the exhaust heat shield for access to the slave cylinder.

9 Collect a clean glass jar, a suitable length of plastic or rubber tubing which is a tight fit over the bleed screw, and a ring spanner to fit the screw. The help of an assistant will also be required.

10 Fit a suitable spanner and tube to the screw, place the other end of the tube in the jar, and pour in sufficient fluid to cover the end of the tube.

6.8 Clutch slave cylinder bleed screw (arrowed) – LT77 type gearbox shown

11 Ensure that the master cylinder reservoir fluid level is maintained at least above the MIN level line throughout the procedure.

12 Unscrew the bleed screw (approximately one turn).

13 Have the assistant fully depress the clutch pedal, then hold the pedal depressed. When the flow of fluid into the jar stops, tighten the bleed screw again, have the assistant release the pedal slowly, and recheck the reservoir fluid level.

14 Repeat the steps given in paragraphs 12 and 13 until the fluid emerging from the bleed screw is free from air bubbles. If the master cylinder has been drained and refilled, allow approximately five seconds between cycles for the master cylinder passages to refill.

15 When no more air bubbles appear, tighten the bleed screw securely, remove the tube and spanner, and refit the dust cap (where applicable). Do not overtighten the bleed screw.

16 On completion, recheck the fluid level in the reservoir, and top-up if necessary.

17 Discard any hydraulic fluid that has been bled from the system; it will not be fit for re-use.

Using a one-way valve kit

18 As their name implies, these kits consist of a length of tubing with a one-way valve fitted, to prevent expelled air and fluid being drawn back into the system; some kits include a translucent container, which can be positioned so that the air bubbles can be more easily seen flowing from the end of the tube.

19 The kit is connected to the bleed screw, which is then opened. The user returns to the

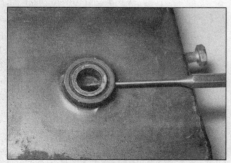

7.4 Driving out the clutch pedal pivot shaft retaining pin

7.12 Withdrawing the cover from the clutch pedal box

driver's seat, depresses the clutch pedal with a smooth, steady stroke, and slowly releases it; this is repeated until the expelled fluid is clear of air bubbles.

20 Note that these kits simplify work so much that it is easy to forget the master cylinder reservoir fluid level; ensure that this is maintained at least above the MIN level line at all times.

---

7 Clutch pedal – removal, refitting and adjustment

Early models with return spring between pedal and bulkhead

Note: *A new pedal box cover gasket should be used on refitting. Where applicable, a new pedal pivot shaft retaining pin should be used on refitting.*

Removal

1 Remove the pedal box assembly, as described for the master cylinder removal procedure in Section 5.

2 Remove the securing screws, and lift the top cover from the pedal box. Recover the gasket.

3 Unscrew the nut from the end of the master cylinder pushrod, and recover the washer.

4 Working at the side of the pedal box, unscrew the pedal pivot pin securing screw, and recover the washer. Alternatively, drive out the pivot shaft retaining pin using a suitable punch, as applicable **(see illustration)**.

5 Slide the pivot pin from the pedal box, then withdraw the pedal, manipulating the pedal trunnion from the master cylinder pushrod.

Refitting

6 If desired, the pedal pivot bushes in the pedal box can be renewed. Pull the old bushes from the pedal box, and press the new bushes into position.

7 Lightly grease the pedal pivot bushes.

8 Manipulate the pedal into position in the pedal box, engaging the pedal trunnion with the master cylinder pushrod.

9 Slide the pedal pivot pin into position in the pedal box, and through the pedal. Secure with the screw, ensuring that the washer is in place (or fit a new pivot shaft retaining pin, as applicable).

10 Refit the pedal box assembly, as described in Section 5.

11 If not already done, check the pedal adjustment as described in the following paragraphs.

Adjustment

Note: *A new pedal box cover gasket should be used on refitting.*

12 Working in the engine compartment, if not already done, remove the securing screws, and withdraw the cover from the clutch pedal box **(see illustration)**. Recover the gasket.

13 Slacken the master cylinder pushrod

locknuts, to allow free movement of the pushrod through the pedal trunnion **(see illustration)**.

14 Slacken the adjustment screw locknut **(see illustration)**.

15 Measure the distance between the floor of the footwell (without a mat in place) to the lower edge of the clutch pedal rubber. The distance should be as specified (see *Specifications*).

16 If adjustment is necessary, turn the adjustment screw clockwise to reduce the pedal height, or anti-clockwise to increase the pedal height. When the height is correct, tighten the adjustment screw locknut.

17 The master cylinder pushrod must now be adjusted, to give the specified freeplay between the pushrod and the master cylinder piston. Adjust the position of the three locknuts on the pushrod as necessary to give the specified freeplay, then tighten the locknuts.

18 Check that the free movement of the pedal, measured at the pedal rubber, is as specified.

7.13 Slacken the master cylinder pushrod locknuts (arrowed)

If not, re-adjust the pushrod locknuts to give the specified free movement.

19 On completion of adjustment, refit the pedal box cover using a new gasket.

Later models

Note: *On models from 2002, the return spring is located as on Early models.*

7.14 Clutch pedal adjustment screw (1) and locknut (2)

20 The procedure is as described previously for earlier models, but note that the pedal return spring is located on the pedal pivot shaft, and the ends of the return spring locate in bushes in the pedal box. Take care not to allow the spring to fly out during dismantling, and ensure that the spring is correctly located on the pivot shaft on reassembly.

Notes

Chapter 7 Part A:
Manual gearbox

Contents

	Section number		Section number
Diff lock and low detect switches – removal and refitting	6	Manual gearbox oil renewal	See Chapter 1
General information	1	Manual gearbox overhaul – general information	4
Manual gearbox – removal and refitting	3	Reversing light switch – testing, removal and refitting	2
Manual gearbox oil level check	See Chapter 1	Vehicle speed sensor – removal and refitting	5

Degrees of difficulty

Easy, suitable for novice with little experience	**Fairly easy,** suitable for beginner with some experience	**Fairly difficult,** suitable for competent DIY mechanic	**Difficult,** suitable for experienced DIY mechanic	**Very difficult,** suitable for expert DIY or professional

Specifications

General

Gearbox type:

Models with 10J, 12J or 19J engines	LT 77 type gearbox, with five forward speeds and reverse
Models with 200 TDi engine	LT 77S type gearbox, with five forward speeds and reverse
Models with 300 TDi or TD5 engines	R380 type gearbox, with five forward speeds and reverse

Torque wrench settings

	Nm	lbf ft
Clutch slave cylinder-to-bellhousing bolts	25	18
Gearbox bellhousing-to-engine flywheel housing bolts and nuts	45	33
Transfer gearbox-to-main gearbox bolts	45	33

1 General information

A five-speed gearbox is fitted to all models.

Drive from the clutch is picked up by the input shaft, which runs in parallel with the layshaft and the mainshaft. The input shaft runs on the same axis as the mainshaft, and a bearing between the two shafts allows the shafts to rotate independently. A fixed gear at the rear of the input shaft drives the layshaft. The input shaft and mainshaft gears are in constant mesh, and selection of gears is by sliding synchromesh hubs, which lock the appropriate mainshaft gear to the mainshaft. The direct-drive fourth gear is obtained by locking the input shaft to the mainshaft.

Reverse gear is obtained by sliding an idler gear into mesh with two straight-cut gears on the mainshaft (the 1st/2nd gear synchro sleeve) and the layshaft.

All the forward gear teeth are helically-cut, to reduce noise and to improve wear characteristics.

The mainshaft provides drive to the transfer gearbox, which is described in Part B of this Chapter.

Gear selection is by means of a floor-mounted gearchange lever, acting directly on the gearchange rail in the gearbox.

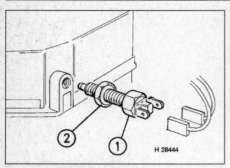

2.1 Reversing light switch (1) and locknut (2) – LT77 and LT77S type gearboxes

2.16 Reversing light switch location (arrowed) – R380 type gearbox

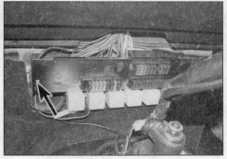

2.19 Undo the screws (left-hand one arrowed), remove the fuse/relay panel, and recover the spacers

2 Reversing light switch – testing, removal and refitting

LT 77 and LT 77S gearboxes

Testing

1 The reversing light switch is located in the rear of the main gearbox selector housing, and is accessible from under the vehicle **(see illustration)**.
2 Disconnect the battery negative lead, and disconnect the wiring from the switch.
3 Connect a continuity tester or an ohmmeter across the switch terminals. There should be no continuity (infinite resistance) between the switch terminals.
4 Engage reverse gear. There should now be continuity (close to zero resistance) between the terminals.
5 If the above readings are not as expected, try cleaning the switch terminals. If the readings are still not as expected, it is likely that the switch is faulty.

Removal

6 Disconnect the battery negative lead.

7 Disconnect the wires from the terminals on the switch.
8 Loosen the switch locknut, then unscrew the switch from the selector housing.

Refitting

9 Select reverse gear.
10 Loosely screw the switch into position in the selector housing (ensure that the locknut is fitted to the switch).
11 Connect a 12 volt supply to one of the switch terminals, and connect a test light between the remaining terminal and earth.
12 Screw the switch into the selector housing until the test light illuminates, then screw the switch into the housing a further half-turn.
13 Tighten the locknut, ensuring that the switch does not move.
14 Disconnect the test light, and reconnect the wiring to the switch.
15 Reconnect the battery negative lead.

R380 gearbox

Testing

16 The switch is located in the left-hand side of the main gearbox casing **(see illustration)**.
17 Testing is as described in paragraphs 2 to 5.

Removal

Note: *A new sealing ring may be required on refitting.*
18 Unscrew the two gear lever knobs, and remove the carpet from the gearbox tunnel.
19 Remove the cover, then undo the two screws and remove the fuse/relay panel from in front of the gear levers. Recover the spacers where fitted **(see illustration). Note:** *On the 2004 model we examined, we found it necessary to unclip the fuse holders and relays from the panel to allow enough room to remove the gearbox tunnel cover.*
20 Prise up and remove the gear lever gaiters, followed by the insulation pad surrounding the gear levers.
21 Move aside the bulkhead carpet from the left- and right-hand side of the gearbox tunnel.
22 Undo the retaining screws, and remove the gearbox tunnel cover **(see illustration)**.
23 Disconnect the reverse switch wiring plug, then unscrew it from the transmission **(see illustration)**. Discard the sealing washer, a new one must be fitted.

Refitting

24 Refitting is a reversal of removal, but use a new sealing ring.

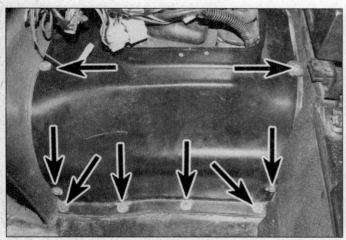

2.22 The gearbox tunnel cover is retained by 13 screws (left-hand ones arrowed)

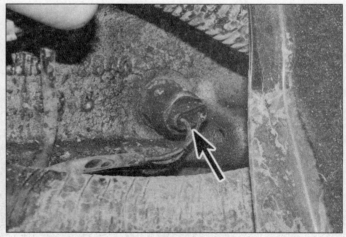

2.23 Unscrew the reversing light switch (arrowed)

3.4 Removing a fusebox lid securing screws (arrowed)

3.5 Lifting the carpet panel from the transmission tunnel

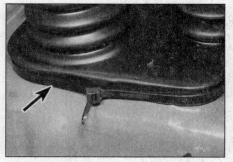

3.6a Release the cable-tie (arrowed) . . .

3 Manual gearbox – removal and refitting

Note: *Although the following procedure is not difficult, the transmission assembly (the main gearbox is removed complete with the transfer gearbox) is heavy, and awkward to handle. Read through the procedure to familiarise yourself with the steps before proceeding. The help of an assistant will prove invaluable during this operation.*

3.6b . . . and withdraw the gear lever gaiter

3.7 Unscrew the locknut . . .

Removal

1 Disconnect the battery negative lead as described in Chapter 5.

2 Jack up the vehicle, and support securely on axle stands placed under the axle tubes (see *Jacking and vehicle support*). Note that the vehicle must be raised to give enough clearance for the transmission assembly to be removed from under the vehicle.

3 Unscrew the main gearbox and transfer gearbox selector lever knobs.

4 Remove the securing screws and withdraw the fusebox lid **(see illustration)**.

5 Lift the carpet panel from the transmission tunnel **(see illustration)**.

6 Release the securing cable-tie (where applicable), and withdraw gear lever gaiter **(see illustrations)**. Remove the insulation surrounding the gear levers.

7 Unscrew the locknut and washer securing the upper section of the main gear

selector lever to the lower lever section **(see illustration)**.

8 Make alignment marks between the lever sections, then pull the upper selector lever from the splined lower lever section **(see illustration)**.

9 Move the transfer gear selector lever to the Low range position.

10 Remove the centre front seat cushion (see Chapter 12), then remove the securing screws and withdraw the central floor cover panel **(see illustrations)**.

11 Remove the securing screws, and withdraw the transmission tunnel cover panel **(see illustration 2.22)**.

LT77 and LT77S gearboxes

12 Remove the bonnet as described in Chapter 12.

13 Where applicable, release the heater coolant pipes from the clamp on the top of the engine, to prevent the heater pipes from fouling the bulkhead as the engine is tilted.

14 Release the transmission breather pipes, the speedometer cable, and the starter motor wiring harness from the clips at the rear of the engine.

15 Disconnect the speedometer cable from the rear of the transfer gearbox, with reference to Chapter 13 if necessary.

All gearboxes

16 Remove the cooling fan cowl, as described in Chapter 3.

17 Working under the vehicle, remove the propeller shafts, as described in Chapter 8 (it is only strictly necessary to disconnect the propeller shafts from the transfer gearbox, but it is recommended that the shafts are removed completely, to provide additional working space).

18 Remove the exhaust intermediate section as described in Chapter 4A or 4B.

19 On models with R380 gearboxes, remove the starter motor as described in Chapter 5.

3.8 . . . and withdraw the upper gear selector lever

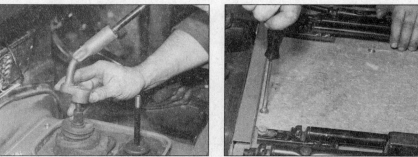

3.10a Remove the securing screws . . .

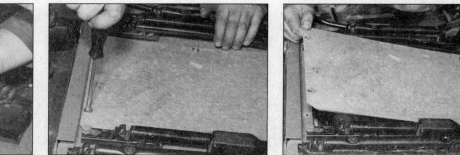

3.10b . . . and withdraw the central floor cover panel

3.23 Disconnecting the wiring from the reversing light switch – LT77 type gearbox

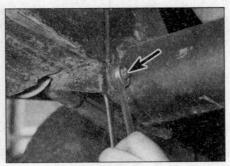

3.24 Unscrewing a chassis crossmember securing nut and bolt

20 Disconnect the handbrake cable from the linkage and bracket on the side of the transmission, as described in Chapter 10.

21 Unscrew the two securing bolts, and withdraw the slave cylinder and the mounting plate from the gearbox bellhousing. Note that one of the bolts also secures the fluid pipe mounting bracket. Move the assembly to one side, taking care not to strain the hydraulic hose. Recover the slave cylinder pushrod if it is loose.

22 If work is to be carried out on the main gearbox and/or transfer gearbox, drain the oil from the main gearbox and/or the transfer gearbox, with reference to Chapter 1 if necessary. Move the slave cylinder clear of the bellhousing, but take care not to strain the hydraulic fluid pipe.

23 Disconnect all electrical wiring connectors from the main gearbox and the transfer gearbox, noting their locations **(see illustration)**. Release the wiring from any clips on the main gearbox/transfer gearbox casing, noting its routing.

24 On non-TD5 models, working under the vehicle, unscrew the four nuts and bolts on each side securing the crossmember to the chassis **(see illustration)**. Withdraw the crossmember. If necessary, spread the chassis members using a suitable large jack and spacers to enable the crossmember to be removed.

25 The main gearbox/transfer gearbox assembly must now be supported. This is most easily and safely accomplished using an engine crane as follows:

a) *Working through the hole in the transmission tunnel, unscrew one of the top securing bolts from the power take-off cover at the rear of the transfer gearbox.*

Make up a lifting bracket, and bolt it to the transfer gearbox using the previously-removed bolt (see illustration).

b) *Pass a lifting strap or chain around the main gearbox casing. Pass the ends of the strap/chain up through the hole in the transmission tunnel (see illustration).*

c) *Attach a second lifting strap/chain to the lifting bracket on the transfer gearbox, and again pass the end of the strap/chain up through the transmission tunnel (see illustration).*

d) *Open one of the front doors, and secure the door in the fully open position using a length of string.*

e) *Pass the engine lifting crane in through the front door aperture, and position the lifting hook over the transmission tunnel aperture. Attach the previously-fitted lifting straps to the crane (see illustration). Take care not to damage the interior trim when positioning the lifting gear.*

f) *Raise the crane sufficiently to just take the weight of the transmission assembly.*

26 Ensure that the transmission assembly is adequately supported before proceeding.

27 Working under the vehicle, unscrew the nuts securing the transmission mounting rubbers to the mounting brackets **(see illustration)**.

28 Unscrew the nuts and bolts securing the transmission mounting brackets to the chassis, then withdraw the two transmission mounting brackets **(see illustration)**.

3.25a Lifting bracket in place on top power take-off cover bolt – transfer gearbox removed for clarity

3.25b Pass a lifting strap around the main gearbox casing

3.25c Attach a lifting chain to the lifting bracket on the transfer gearbox

3.25d Attach the lifting tackle to an engine hoist

3.27 Unscrew the nuts securing the mounting rubbers to the transmission mounting brackets

3.28 Unscrew the nuts and bolts securing the transmission mounting brackets to the chassis

29 Lower the transmission assembly slightly, using the engine crane, to gain access to the upper engine flywheel housing-to-gearbox bellhousing nuts.

LT77 and LT77S gearboxes

30 Unscrew and remove the upper flywheel housing-to-gearbox bellhousing nuts.

31 Progressively unscrew the lower flywheel housing-to-gearbox bellhousing nuts. Note that the transmission assembly may move backwards from the engine once the nuts are removed – be prepared for this, and do not allow the assembly to swing uncontrolled.

32 If necessary, carefully tap around the flywheel housing-to-bellhousing joint to break the sealant, then slide the transmission assembly back from the engine, taking care not to strain the gearbox input shaft. Note that the engine/transmission assembly must be tilted sufficiently to allow the transfer gearbox selector lever to pass through the hole in the transmission tunnel.

R380 gearboxes

33 Working underneath the vehicle and in the engine compartment as necessary, remove the nuts/bolts securing the gearbox bellhousing to the engine.

All gearboxes

34 Position a trolley jack and a large block of wood under the transmission assembly (the wood should be suitably shaped to support the transmission when it is lowered). Lower the engine crane, to position the transmission assembly on the trolley jack and support block.

35 Disconnect the lifting straps/chains from the transmission assembly and the engine crane, then carefully slide the transmission assembly out from under the vehicle, using the trolley jack. Take care when moving the transmission, and do not attempt to lift the assembly without suitable lifting tackle – the assembly is very heavy.

36 If desired, the transfer gearbox can be separated from the main gearbox as described in Part B of this Chapter.

Refitting

37 Where applicable, refit the transfer gearbox to the main gearbox, as described in Part B of this Chapter. Ensure that the Low range is selected in the transfer gearbox.

38 Thoroughly clean the mating faces of the engine flywheel housing and the gearbox bellhousing (where applicable).

39 Apply sealing compound to the gearbox bellhousing mating face of the engine flywheel housing (where applicable).

40 Position the transmission assembly under the vehicle using the trolley jack and support block, then fit the lifting straps/chains to the transmission (as during removal). Pass the lifting straps/chains up through the transmission tunnel, and connect them to the engine crane.

41 Using the crane, lift the transmission assembly into position, then slide the bellhousing onto the flywheel housing studs/ engine block dowels. Ensure that the wiring harness and connectors, and the breather pipes, are not trapped as the transmission is moved into position. Note that it will be necessary to tilt the rear of the engine down to align the engine and gearbox (the engine can easily be tilted on its mountings, if an assistant pushes the assembly from above). Push the gearbox bellhousing onto the studs/dowels sufficiently to refit the nuts to the studs.

42 Manipulate the engine and gearbox as necessary, to align the gearbox input shaft splines with the splines in the clutch friction disc hub (it may be necessary to turn the crankshaft using a spanner or socket on the pulley bolt). Once the input shaft is engaged with the clutch, progressively tighten the engine-to-gearbox nuts/bolts, to draw the gearbox bellhousing flush against the flywheel housing/engine block.

43 With the engine-to-gearbox nuts/bolts tightened, wipe any surplus sealing compound from the flywheel housing/bellhousing/engine block mating face.

44 Using the crane, raise the transmission assembly sufficiently to enable the transmission mounting brackets to be fitted, then fit the brackets, and tighten all the fixings.

45 The remainder of the refitting procedure is a reversal of removal, bearing in mind the following points:

a) *Ensure that all wiring is routed correctly, and that all plugs are reconnected to their correct locations.*

b) *Reconnect the handbrake cable to the linkage, and check the cable adjustment, as described in Chapter 1.*

c) *Refit the propeller shafts with reference to Chapter 8.*

d) *Refit the exhaust intermediate section with reference to Chapter 4A or 4B.*

e) *When refitting the upper section of the main gear selector lever, ensure that the marks made on the upper and lower lever sections are aligned.*

f) *Where applicable, on completion, refill the main gearbox and transfer gearbox with oil of the correct type, as described in Chapter 1.*

4 Manual gearbox overhaul – general information

Overhauling a gearbox is a difficult and involved job for the DIY home mechanic. In addition to dismantling and reassembling many small parts, clearances must be precisely measured and, if necessary, changed by selecting shims and spacers. Gearbox internal components are also often difficult to obtain, and in many instances, extremely expensive. Because of this, if the gearbox develops a fault or becomes noisy, the best course of action is to have the unit overhauled by a specialist repairer, or to obtain an exchange reconditioned unit.

Nevertheless, it is not impossible for the more experienced mechanic to overhaul a gearbox, provided the special tools are available and the job is done in a deliberate step-by-step manner so that nothing is overlooked.

The tools necessary for an overhaul include internal and external circlip pliers, bearing pullers, a slide-hammer, a set of pin punches, a dial test indicator, and possibly a hydraulic press. In addition, a large, sturdy workbench and a vice will be required.

During dismantling of the gearbox, make careful notes of how each component is fitted, to make reassembly easier and more accurate.

Before dismantling the gearbox, it will help if you have some idea of which area is malfunctioning. Certain problems can be closely related to specific areas in the gearbox, which can make component examination and renewal easier. Refer to the *Fault finding* Section at the end of this manual for more information.

5 Vehicle speed sensor – removal and refitting

1 Vehicles from 1999 model year are fitted with a vehicle speed sensor, fitted to the rear of the transfer box, adjacent to the output shaft.

2 Disconnect the wiring plug from the sensor.

3 Undo the retaining bolt and pull the sensor from the casing **(see illustration)**. Discard the sealing ring, a new one must be fitted.

4 Fit the new sealing ring, and position the sensor in the casing. Tighten the retaining bolt securely, and reconnect the wiring plug.

6 Diff lock and low detect switches – removal and refitting

Note: *A new sealing ring may be required on refitting.*

Removal

1 Unscrew the two gear lever knobs, and remove the carpet from the gearbox tunnel.

5.3 The vehicle speed sensor is located on the rear of the transfer box (arrowed)

6.6a Low detect switch (arrowed)

6.6b Diff lock switch (arrowed)

2 Remove the cover, then undo the two screws and remove the fuse/relay panel from in front of the gear levers. Recover the spacers where fitted **(see illustration 2.19)**. **Note:** *On the 2004 model we examined, we found it necessary to unclip the fuse holders and relays from the panel to allow enough room to remove the gearbox tunnel cover.*

3 Prise up and remove the gear lever gaiters, followed by the insulation pad surrounding the gear levers.

4 Move aside the bulkhead carpet from the left- and right-hand side of the gearbox tunnel.

5 Undo the retaining screws, and remove the gearbox tunnel cover **(see illustration 2.22)**.

6 Disconnect the diff lock or low detect switches wiring plug, then unscrew it from the transmission **(see illustrations)**. Discard the sealing washer, a new one must be fitted.

Refitting

7 Refitting is a reversal of removal, but use a new sealing washer.

Chapter 7 Part B:
Transfer gearbox

Contents

	Section number		Section number
General information	1	Transfer gearbox oil renewal	See Chapter 1
Transfer gearbox – removal and refitting	2	Transfer gearbox overhaul – general information	3
Transfer gearbox oil level check	See Chapter 1	Transfer gearbox rear oil seal – renewal	4

Degrees of difficulty

Easy, suitable for novice with little experience	**Fairly easy,** suitable for beginner with some experience	**Fairly difficult,** suitable for competent DIY mechanic	**Difficult,** suitable for experienced DIY mechanic	**Very difficult,** suitable for expert DIY or professional

Specifications

General

Transfer gearbox type:

Models with 10J and 12J engines	LT230R
Models with 19J, 200 TDi and 300 TDi engines	LT230T
Models with TD5 engines	LT230TE

Torque wrench setting

	Nm	lbf ft
Rear output flange nut*	140	103
Transfer gearbox-to-main gearbox bolts and nuts	45	33

* Do not re-use

1 General information

The transfer gearbox is mounted in-line with the main gearbox. The transfer gearbox is a two-speed ratio-reducing gearbox, and provides drive to the front and rear axles via the propeller shafts.

Permanent four-wheel-drive is provided, and the unit incorporates a differential assembly, to allow for any difference in the rotational speed of the front and rear wheels (and a resulting difference in speed between the front and rear propeller shafts). This centre differential (the axles also incorporate differentials to allow for

the difference in rotational speed between left- and right-hand wheels on the same axle) can be locked by mechanical means to provide increased traction in particularly slippery conditions.

Selection of the High/Low ranges, and of the differential lock, is made using a selector lever mounted behind the main gear lever.

A shiftlock/neutral switch is fitted to models in certain territories, and is used as a safety device to ensure that the handbrake is effective when parking. The shiftlock/neutral switch prevents accidental disengagement of the transfer gears when the ignition is switched off. Additionally, an audible alarm is provided, which alerts the driver to move the gear selector lever to the High or Low position when parking.

2 Transfer gearbox – removal and refitting

General

1 The transfer gearbox is most easily removed complete with the main gearbox as an assembly. This procedure is described in Part A of this Chapter.

LT230R gearbox
Removal

2 To separate the transfer gearbox from the main gearbox, proceed as follows.

3 Position the transmission assembly securely

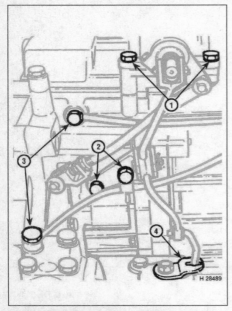

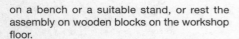

2.4 LT230R transfer gearbox selector linkage and breather pipe layout

1 Transfer gearchange housing securing bolts
2 Gear linkage pivot bracket bolts
3 Breather pipe unions
4 Differential lock lever

on a bench or a suitable stand, or rest the assembly on wooden blocks on the workshop floor.

4 Unscrew the four bolts securing the transfer gearchange housing to the main gearchange housing (see illustration).

5 Unscrew the two bolts securing the gear linkage pivot bracket to the extension housing.

6 Unscrew the union bolts, recover the sealing washers, and disconnect the breather pipes from the gearbox casing.

7 Remove the split-pin, spring clip, or locknut, as applicable, securing the differential lock connecting rod to the lever on the transfer gearbox, and disconnect the rod from the lever. Where applicable, recover the washers.

8 Ensure that the main gearbox and the transfer gearbox are adequately supported, then unscrew the two nuts and the four bolts securing the transfer gearbox to the main gearbox extension housing. Slide the transfer gearbox from the main gearbox.

Refitting

9 Refitting is a reversal of removal, bearing in mind the following points:
  a)) Thoroughly clean the mating faces of the transfer gearbox and the main gearbox.
  b) Ensure that the upper locating dowel is fitted to the gearbox casing before mating the transfer gearbox and main gearbox together.
  c) Note that the longer transfer gearchange

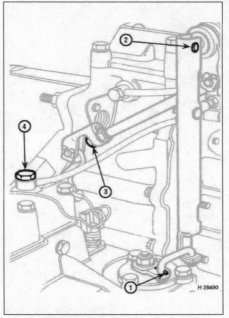

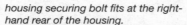

2.12a Early LT230T transfer gearbox selector linkage and breather pipe layout

1 Differential lock lever
2 Operating arm-to-selector shaft clevis pin
3 Selector rod lower locknut
4 Breather pipe union

housing securing bolt fits at the right-hand rear of the housing.
  d) Where applicable, use a new split-pin or locking nut to secure the differential lock connecting rod to the lever on the transfer gearbox.
  e) Refit the complete transmission assembly as described in Chapter 7A.

LT230T and LT230TE gearbox

Removal

10 To separate the transfer gearbox from the main gearbox, proceed as follows.

11 Position the transmission assembly securely on a bench or a suitable stand, or rest the assembly on wooden blocks on the workshop floor.

2.12c Disconnect the differential lock connecting rod (1) from the lever (2) – later LT230TE transfer gearbox

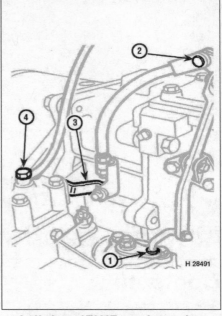

2.12b Later LT230T transfer gearbox selector linkage and breather pipe layout

1 Differential lock lever
2 Operating arm-to-selector shaft clevis pin
3 Transfer gear selector lever
4 Breather pipe union

12 Remove the split-pin, spring clip, or locknut, as applicable, securing the differential lock connecting rod to the lever on the transfer gearbox, and disconnect the rod from the lever (see illustrations). Where applicable, recover the washers.

13 Remove the spring clip, and withdraw the clevis pin securing the operating arm to the transfer gear selector shaft.

14 On early models, move the transfer gear selector lever upwards, to gain access to the transfer gearbox-to-main gearbox nut.

15 On later models, unscrew the transfer gear selector rod lower locknut, and withdraw the rod from the yoke (see illustration).

16 Unscrew the union bolt, and disconnect the breather pipe from the top of the transfer

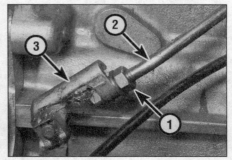

2.15 Unscrew the locknut (1) and withdraw the rod (2) from the yoke (3) – later LT230T transfer gearbox

gearbox casing **(see illustration)**. Recover the sealing washers.

17 Ensure that the main gearbox and the transfer gearbox are adequately supported, then unscrew the two nuts and the four bolts securing the transfer gearbox to the main gearbox extension housing **(see illustration)**. Slide the transfer gearbox from the main gearbox.

Refitting

18 Refitting is a reversal of removal, bearing in mind the following points:
 a) *Thoroughly clean the mating faces of the transfer gearbox and the main gearbox.*
 b) *Ensure that the upper locating dowel is fitted to the gearbox casing before mating the transfer gearbox and main gearbox together.*
 c) *On later models, as the two assemblies are mated together, engage the transfer gear selector rod with the yoke.*
 d) *Where applicable, use a new split-pin or locking nut to secure the differential lock connecting rod to the lever on the transfer gearbox.*
 e) *Refit the complete transmission assembly as described in Chapter 7A.*

2.16 Breather pipe union bolt (arrowed) – later LT230T transfer gearbox

2.17 Three of the transfer gearbox-to-main gearbox bolts and nuts (arrowed) – later LT230T transfer gearbox

3 Transfer gearbox overhaul – general information

Overhauling a transfer gearbox is a difficult and involved job for the DIY home mechanic. In addition to dismantling and reassembling many small parts, clearances must be precisely measured and, if necessary, changed by selecting shims and spacers. Gearbox internal components are also often difficult to obtain, and in many instances, extremely expensive. Because of this, if the gearbox develops a fault or becomes noisy, the best course of action is to have the unit overhauled by a specialist repairer, or to obtain an exchange reconditioned unit.

Nevertheless, it is not impossible for the more experienced mechanic to overhaul a gearbox, provided the special tools are available and the job is done in a deliberate step-by-step manner so that nothing is overlooked.

The tools necessary for an overhaul include internal and external circlip pliers, bearing pullers, a slide-hammer, a set of pin punches, a dial test indicator, and possibly a hydraulic press. In addition, a large, sturdy workbench and a vice will be required. Certain Land Rover special tools will be required for work on the differential assembly.

During dismantling of the gearbox, make careful notes of how each component is fitted, to make reassembly easier and more accurate.

Before dismantling the gearbox, it will help if you have some idea of which area is malfunctioning. Certain problems can be closely related to specific areas in the gearbox, which can make component examination and renewal easier. Refer to the *Fault finding* Section at the end of this manual for more information.

4 Transfer gearbox rear oil seal – renewal

1 Remove the handbrake drum as described in Chapter 10.

2 Prevent the output flange from rotating using a lever bar, then undo the retaining nut. Discard the nut, steel and felt washers – new ones must be fitted.

3 Use a three-legged puller to remove the output flange.

4 Note its fitted depth, then use a flat-bladed screwdriver to carefully prise out the oil seal.

5 Ensure the seal recess is clean and dry, then use a large tubular spacer to drive the new seal home. The seal must be fitted dry.

6 Refit the drive flange, then the new felt and steel washer.

7 Using the same method as during removal, restrain the drive flange, and tighten the new nut to the specified torque.

8 Refit the brake drum as described in Chapter 10, then top-up the transfer gearbox oil level as described in Chapter 1.

Chapter 8
Propeller shafts

Contents

Section number

Front propeller shaft rubber gaiter – renewal 4
General information 1
Propeller shaft – inspection and overhaul 3

Section number

Propeller shaft – removal and refitting 2
Propeller shaft coupling bolt check . . . . See Chapter 1
Propeller shaft joint lubrication. . . . . See Chapter 1

Degrees of difficulty

Easy, suitable for novice with little experience	**Fairly easy,** suitable for beginner with some experience	**Fairly difficult,** suitable for competent DIY mechanic	**Difficult,** suitable for experienced DIY mechanic	**Very difficult,** suitable for expert DIY or professional

Specifications

General
Propeller shaft type . . . . Tubular, splined joint
End joints . . . . Hookes non-constant velocity joints, with needle-roller bearings

Torque wrench setting	Nm	lbf ft
Propeller shaft securing nuts and bolts	47	35

1 General information

The drive is transmitted from the transfer gearbox to the front and rear axle differentials by two tubular propeller shafts.

The propeller shafts are fitted with non-constant velocity universal joints at each end, which run in needle-roller bearings. The universal joints cater for the varying angle between the axle and the transmission, caused by suspension movement.

To allow for the fore-and-aft movement between the axles and transmission, a sliding, splined joint is incorporated in each propeller shaft. On certain models, a rubber gaiter is fitted to protect the front propeller shaft sliding joint.

Grease nipples are fitted to the universal joints, and the universal joints and sliding joints should periodically be lubricated in accordance with the maintenance schedule given in Chapter 1.

2 Propeller shaft – removal and refitting

Front propeller shaft

Removal

1 Jack up the vehicle, and support securely on axle stands positioned under the axles, as described in *Jacking and vehicle support* at the rear of this manual. Undo the fasteners and lower the engine undershield.

2 If the original propeller shaft is to be refitted, make alignment marks between the front propeller shaft flange and the differential flange.

3 Counterhold the bolts, and unscrew the nuts securing the front of the propeller shaft to the differential flange.

4 Again, if the original propeller shaft is to be refitted, make alignment marks between the rear propeller shaft flange and the transfer gearbox flange **(see illustration)**.

5 Unscrew the nuts (again, where applicable, counterhold the bolts) securing the rear of the propeller shaft to the transfer gearbox flange.

6 Remove the bolts from the front shaft flange, then compress the propeller shaft sliding joint until the rear of the shaft can be withdrawn from the bolts or studs (as applicable) on the transfer gearbox flange.

7 Withdraw the propeller shaft from under the vehicle.

2.4 Making alignment marks between the rear propeller shaft flange and the transfer gearbox flange

2.10 Make alignment marks between the propeller shaft flange and the handbrake drum

2.13 Counterhold the bolts, and unscrew the nuts securing the propeller shaft to the rear differential flange

2.14 Withdraw the front of the propeller shaft from the studs on the brake drum

Refitting

8 Refitting is a reversal of removal, bearing in mind the following points:
a) *Ensure that the propeller shaft is refitted with the sliding joint towards the front of the vehicle (nearest the front axle).*
b) *If the original propeller shaft is being refitted, align the marks made on the differential flange, transfer gearbox flange, and the propeller shaft flanges before removal.*
c) *Tighten the securing nuts and bolts to the specified torque.*

Rear propeller shaft

Removal

9 Proceed as described in paragraph 1.
10 If the original propeller shaft is to be refitted, make alignment marks between the front propeller shaft flange and the handbrake drum at the transfer gearbox **(see illustration)**.
11 Unscrew the nuts securing the front of the propeller shaft to the handbrake drum.
12 Again, if the original propeller shaft is to be refitted, make alignment marks between the rear propeller shaft flange and the rear differential flange.
13 Counterhold the bolts, and unscrew the nuts securing the rear of the propeller shaft to the rear differential flange **(see illustration)**.
14 Withdraw the flange bolts, then compress the propeller shaft sliding joint until the front of the propeller shaft can be withdrawn from the studs on the brake drum **(see illustration)**.
15 Withdraw the propeller shaft from under the vehicle.

Refitting

16 Refitting is a reversal of removal, bearing in mind the following points:
a) *Ensure that the propeller shaft is refitted with the sliding joint towards the front of the vehicle (nearest the transfer gearbox).*
b) *If the original propeller shaft is being refitted, align the marks made on the handbrake drum, rear differential flange, and the propeller shaft flanges before removal.*
c) *Tighten the securing nuts and bolts to the specified torque.*

3 Propeller shaft – inspection and overhaul

Inspection

1 Wear in the universal joint needle-roller bearings is characterised by vibration in the transmission, 'clonks' on taking up the drive, and in extreme cases unpleasant metallic noises as the bearings break up (lack of lubrication).
2 To test the universal joints for wear with the propeller shaft in place, apply the handbrake, and chock the wheels.
3 Working under the vehicle, apply leverage between the yokes using a large screwdriver or a flat metal bar. Wear is indicated by movement between the shaft yoke and the coupling flange yoke. Check all the universal joints in this way.
4 To check the splined sleeve on the front of both shafts, attempt to push the shafts

from side-to-side, and look for any excessive movement between the sleeve and the shaft. A further check can be made by gripping the shaft and sleeve, and turning them in opposite directions, again looking for excessive movement. As a rough guide, if *any* movement can be seen, the splines are worn, and the shaft assembly should be renewed.
5 If a universal joint is worn, a new joint must be obtained and fitted as described later in this Section.
6 If the sliding joint is excessively worn, the complete shaft assembly must be renewed.

Overhaul

Dismantling

7 With the propeller shaft removed as described in Section 2, proceed as follows.
8 Where applicable, release the clips securing the rubber gaiter over the sliding joint, and slide the gaiter towards the rear of the shaft **(see illustration)**.
9 Check that alignment marks are visible

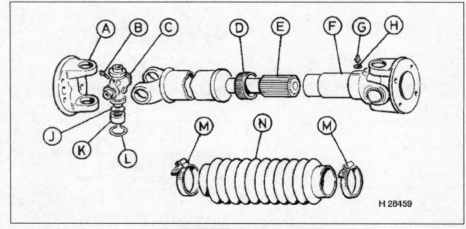

3.8 Propeller shaft components

A Yoke	G Grease nipple for splined joint	L Bearing retaining circlip
B Grease nipple for universal joint	H Washer	M Gaiter clips (front shaft only)
C Spider	J Seal	N Sliding joint gaiter (front shaft only)
D Dust cap	K Needle-roller bearing assembly	
E Splined shaft		
F Splined sleeve		

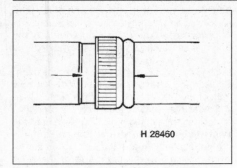

3.9 Alignment marks on two halves of propeller shaft

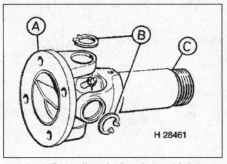

3.14 Propeller shaft universal joint

A *Coupling flange*
B *Circlips*
C *Shaft*

3.15 Tapping the uppermost bearing cup

on the two halves of the shaft (normally two stamped arrows) **(see illustration)**. If no marks can be found, scribe a line along the two halves of the shaft, to ensure that the two halves are reassembled in exactly the same position. This is vital, to ensure that the correct universal joint alignment and shaft balance is maintained.

10 Unscrew the dust cap, and withdraw the front section of the shaft from the splined end of the rear section.

11 Working on one of the universal joints, note the position of the grease nipple on the spider, in relation to the adjacent shaft yoke and coupling flange yoke (make alignment marks on the yokes). This is vital to ensure correct reassembly, and to ensure that the shaft balance is maintained.

12 Clean away all traces of dirt and grease from the circlips located on the ends of the joint spiders, and from the grease nipple.

13 Unscrew the grease nipple.

14 Using a suitable pair of circlip pliers, remove the four joint circlips **(see illustration)**. If a circlip proves difficult to remove, as a last resort, place a drift on the bearing cup, in the centre of the circlip, and tap the top of the bearing cup to ease the pressure on the circlip.

15 Support the end of the shaft in a vice, with the yoke in a vertical plane. Using a hammer and a suitable drift, tap the uppermost bearing cup until the bottom bearing cup protrudes from the yoke **(see illustration)**.

16 Remove the shaft from the vice, then securely grip the protruding bearing cup in the

vice jaws. Turn the shaft from side-to-side, at the same time lifting the shaft until the bearing cup comes free.

17 Refit the shaft to the vice, with the exposed spider uppermost. Tap the spider with the hammer and drift until the lower bearing cup protrudes, then remove the cup as described previously.

18 The coupling flange and the spider can now be removed from the shaft, and the remaining two bearing cups can be removed as described previously.

19 Where applicable, repeat the operations described in paragraphs 11 to 18 to remove the remaining joint from the shaft.

Inspection

20 With the universal joint dismantled, carefully examine the needle-rollers, bearing cups and spider for wear, scoring and pitting of the surface finish. If any wear is detected, the joint must be renewed **(see illustration)**.

21 Where applicable, unscrew the sliding joint grease nipple, and thoroughly clean the nipple and its hole.

22 Where applicable, examine the condition of the sliding joint rubber gaiter, and renew if necessary.

23 Temporarily fit the front section of the shaft to the rear section, ensuring that the alignment marks are correctly positioned. Grip the front section of the shaft in a vice, and check for wear in the sliding joint splines, as described in paragraph 4.

Reassembly

24 If a new joint is being fitted, remove the bearing cups from the new spider. Check that all the needle-rollers are present, and correctly positioned in the bearing cups.

25 Ensure that the bearing cups are one-third full of fresh grease (multi-purpose lithium-based grease – see *Lubricants and fluids* at the front of this manual).

26 Fit the new spider, complete with seals, into the coupling flange yoke. Make sure that the grease nipple hole is aligned with the mark on the yoke made during dismantling, and note that the grease nipple hole must face away from the coupling flange.

27 Partially insert one of the bearing cups into the yoke, and enter the spider trunnion into the bearing cup, taking care not to dislodge the needle-rollers **(see illustration)**.

28 Similarly, insert a bearing cup into the opposite yoke.

29 Using the vice, carefully press both bearing cups into place, ensuring that the spider trunnions do not dislodge any of the needle-rollers.

30 Using a suitable tube or socket of a slightly smaller diameter than the bearing cups, press each cup into its respective yoke, until the top of the cup just reaches the lower land of the circlip groove. **Do not** press the cups below this point, as damage may be caused to the cups and seals.

31 Fit the new circlips to retain the bearing cups **(see illustration)**.

32 Engage the spider with the yokes on the relevant propeller shaft section, then partially

3.20 Universal joint bearing components

3.27 Press the cups into place using a vice and socket

3.31 Fit new circlips to retain the bearing cups

fit both bearing cups to the yokes, taking care not to dislodge any of the needle-rollers.

33 Press the bearing cups into position, and fit the new circlips, as described in paragraphs 29 to 31.

34 Screw the grease nipple into position in the joint spider.

35 Where applicable, repeat the operations described in paragraphs 24 to 34 to fit the remaining joint to the shaft.

36 Where applicable, screw the sliding joint grease nipple into position.

37 Smear the sliding joint splines on the end of the rear section of the shaft with grease, then slide the rear section of the shaft into the front section, ensuring that the marks made during dismantling are aligned. **Note:** *Do not pack grease into the open end of the shaft front section, as this may prevent the shaft from being pushed fully home.*

38 Screw the sliding joint dust cap into position.

39 Where applicable, slide the rubber gaiter over the sliding joint, and secure in position with the two clips. If screw-type clips are used, fit the clips with the screws 180° apart, to help maintain the balance of the shaft.

40 Refit the propeller shaft, as described in Section 2, then lubricate the joints using a grease gun applied to the grease nipples (see Chapter 1).

4 Front propeller shaft rubber gaiter – renewal

1 Remove the propeller shaft as described in Section 2.

2 Loosen the two gaiter securing clips, and slide the gaiter towards the rear of the shaft.

3 Check that alignment marks are visible on the two halves of the shaft (normally two stamped arrows). If no marks can be found, scribe a line along the two halves of the shaft, to ensure that the two halves are reassembled in exactly the same position. This is vital, to ensure that the correct universal joint alignment and shaft balance is maintained.

4 Unscrew the dust cap, and withdraw the front section of the shaft from the splined end of the rear section.

5 Slide the gaiter and the clips from the shaft.

6 Clean the shaft splines, then slide the new gaiter onto the rear section of the shaft.

7 Smear the shaft splines with fresh grease, and slide the rear section of the shaft onto the front section, ensuring that the marks made during dismantling are aligned. **Note:** *Do not pack grease into the open end of the shaft front section, as this may prevent the shaft from being pushed fully home.*

8 Screw the sliding joint dust cap into position.

9 Slide the rubber gaiter over the sliding joint, and secure in position with the two clips. If screw-type clips are used, fit the clips with the screws 180° apart, to help maintain the balance of the shaft.

10 Refit the propeller shaft as described in Section 2.

Chapter 9
Front and rear axles

Contents

Section number

Axle differential overhaul – general information 13
Front axle – removal and refitting 7
Front axle halfshaft – removal, inspection and refitting 2
Front axle oil level check . . . . See Chapter 1
Front axle oil renewal . . . . See Chapter 1
Front axle swivel pin housing assembly – removal, overhaul and
  refitting 6
Front hub assembly – removal and refitting 3
Front hub bearing – renewal 4

Section number

Front stub axle – removal and refitting 5
General information 1
Rear axle – removal and refitting 12
Rear axle halfshaft – removal, inspection and refitting 8
Rear axle oil level check . . . . See Chapter 1
Rear axle oil renewal . . . . See Chapter 1
Rear hub assembly – removal and refitting 9
Rear hub bearing – renewal 10
Rear stub axle – removal and refitting 11

Degrees of difficulty

Easy, suitable for novice with little experience 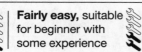	**Fairly easy,** suitable for beginner with some experience	**Fairly difficult,** suitable for competent DIY mechanic	**Difficult,** suitable for experienced DIY mechanic	**Very difficult,** suitable for expert DIY or professional

Specifications

Type
Front . . . . Spiral bevel, with enclosed CV joints and fully-floating halfshafts
Rear . . . . Spiral bevel, with fully-floating halfshafts
Differential ratio (front and rear) 3.54:1

Adjustment data
Hub endfloat (front and rear – up to 1999 model year only) . . . . 0.05 to 0.10 mm
Front halfshaft endfloat (up to 1999 model year only) . . . . 0.12 to 0.25 mm
Front swivel pin housing bearing preload . . . . See text

Torque wrench settings

	Nm	lbf ft
Driving member retaining bolts	65	48
Halfshaft flange retaining bolts	65	48
Hub locknut:		
Vehicles up to 1999 model year	65	48
Vehicles from 1999 model year (staked nut)*	210	155
Rear axle upper link balljoint nut	176	130
Roadwheel nuts:		
Steel wheels	108	80
Alloy wheels	130	96
Heavy duty wheel	170	125
Stub axle bolts	65	48
Swivel pin assembly-to-axle bolts	72	53
Swivel pin housing oil seal retaining plate bolts	10	7
Swivel pin retaining bolts:		
Upper pin bolts	65	48
Lower pin bolts	25	18

* Do not re-use

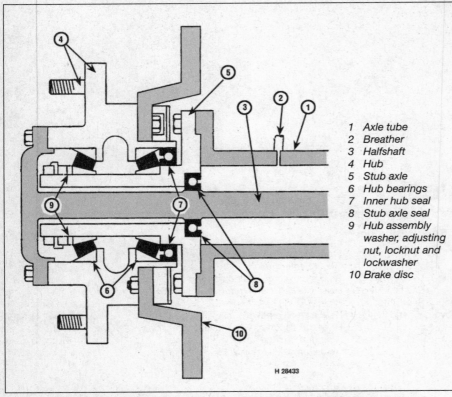

1 Axle tube
2 Breather
3 Halfshaft
4 Hub
5 Stub axle
6 Hub bearings
7 Inner hub seal
8 Stub axle seal
9 Hub assembly
washer, adjusting
nut, locknut and
lockwasher
10 Brake disc

1.1 Cross-sectional view of rear axle hub and associated components

1 General information

Both the front and rear axles are of a similar design, comprising a one-piece steel casing, which houses the differential assembly and two driveshafts (halfshafts). The rear shafts are of solid steel construction, the inner ends of which are splined into the differential assembly, while the outer ends are attached to the hubs **(see illustration)**.

To enable the front wheels to turn from lock-to-lock while being driven, the front halfshafts incorporate a CV joint on their outer ends. The CV joint runs inside an oil-filled swivel pin housing, the swivel pins being located in tapered roller bearings **(see illustration)**.

Refer to Chapter 11 for details of axle attachment and suspension details.

2 Front axle halfshaft
– removal, inspection and refitting

Removal

1 Apply the handbrake, then jack up the front of the vehicle and support it on axle stands positioned underneath the chassis (see *Jacking and vehicle support*). Remove the relevant front roadwheel.

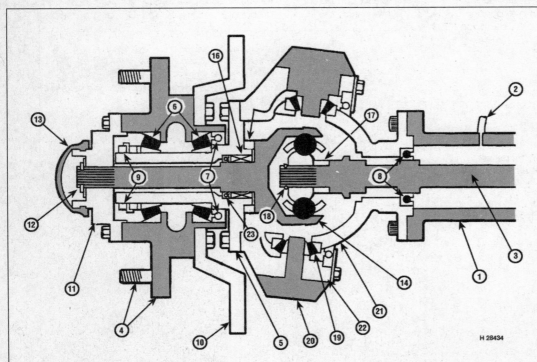

1 Axle tube
2 Breather
3 Inner halfshaft section
4 Hub
5 Stub axle
6 Hub bearings
7 Inner hub seal
8 Circlip
9 Hub assembly washer,
adjusting nut, locknut and
lockwasher
10 Brake disc
11 Driving member
12 Shim and circlip
13 Hub cap
14 Outer halfshaft section
16 Needle roller bearing
17 Spacer
18 Circlip
19 Swivel pin bearing
20 Swivel pin
21 Swivel ball
22 Swivel pin housing
23 Seal

1.2 Cross-sectional view of front axle hub and associated components – later model (early model similar)

2 Remove the stub axle as described in Section 5.

3 Pull the halfshaft assembly out from the axle **(see illustration)**.

4 Clamp the inner section of the shaft in a vice with soft jaws then, using a soft-faced mallet, tap the constant velocity joint off the end of the inner shaft.

5 Remove the circlip from the end of the inner shaft, and slide off the spacer. Discard the circlip – a new one must be used on refitting.

Inspection

6 Thoroughly clean all components using paraffin, or a suitable solvent, and dry thoroughly. Carry out a visual inspection as follows.

7 Inspect the halfshaft inner sections for signs of wear or damage, paying particular attention to its splines. Check the bush for signs of wear or damage, and renew worn components as necessary. Note that the constant velocity joint circlip must be renewed whenever it is disturbed.

8 Move the constant velocity joint inner member from side-to-side, to expose each ball in turn at the top of its track. Examine the balls for cracks, flat spots or signs of surface pitting.

9 Inspect the ball tracks on the inner and outer members. If the tracks have widened, the balls will no longer be a tight fit. At the same time, check the ball cage windows for wear or cracking between the windows.

10 If the constant velocity joint assembly shows signs of wear or damage, it must be renewed.

Refitting

11 Slide the spacer onto the inner shaft, then fit a new circlip, making sure that it is correctly located in the shaft groove.

12 Locate the constant velocity joint on inner shaft splines, and tap it onto the driveshaft until the circlip engages in its groove. Make sure that the joint is securely retained by the circlip.

13 Insert the halfshaft inner section into the axle, aligning its splines with those of the differential sunwheel.

14 Check the halfshaft inner section is correctly located, then refit the stub axle as described in Section 5.

---

3   Front hub assembly
   – removal and refitting

Note: *The following information applies only to the standard hub assembly. For information on freewheeling hubs, refer to your Land Rover dealer.*

Removal

1 Apply the handbrake, then jack up the front of the vehicle and support it on axle stands positioned underneath the chassis (see

2.3 Removing the halfshaft assembly – later models

3.3 Slide the brake caliper assembly off the disc

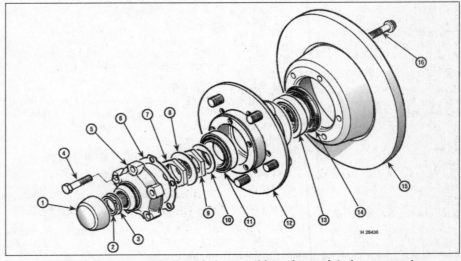

3.4 Exploded view of the front hub assembly and associated components

1 Dust cap	*7 Locknut (models up to 1999 model year only)*	*10 Spacer*
2 Circlip		*11 Outer bearing and race*
3 Shim	*8 Lockwasher (models up to 1999 model year only)*	*12 Hub*
4 Bolt		*13 Inner bearing and race*
5 Driving member	*9 Adjusting nut (models up to 1999 model year only)*	*14 Seal*
6 Gasket		*15 Brake disc*
		16 Bolt

Jacking and vehicle support). Remove the relevant front roadwheel.

2 Clamp the flexible brake hose, then undo the union nut and disconnect the brake pipe from the caliper.

3 Slacken and remove the two retaining bolts securing the brake caliper in position.

Slide the caliper assembly off the disc **(see illustration)**.

4 Lever off the dust cap from the centre of the hub assembly **(see illustration)**.

5 Using circlip pliers, remove the circlip from the end of the halfshaft, then slide off the thrustwasher(s) **(see illustrations)**.

3.5a Remove the circlip from the end of the halfshaft . . .

3.5b . . . and recover the thrustwasher(s)

3.6 Removing the hub driving member

3.7 Using a hammer and suitable chisel, bend back the lockwasher from the locknut flat

3.10 Knock back the staking and unscrew the hub nut

6 Slacken and remove the five retaining bolts, then slide the driving member off the end of the halfshaft **(see illustration)**. Remove the member gasket and discard it, a new gasket must be used on refitting.

Models up to 1999 model year

7 Using a hammer and suitable chisel, bend back the lockwasher tab from the hub locknut flat **(see illustration)**.

8 Slacken and remove the hub locknut, and slide off the lockwasher. Discard the lockwasher – a new one must be used on refitting.

9 Unscrew the hub adjusting nut, then slide off the spacer, noting which way around it is fitted.

Models from 1999 model year

10 Knock back the staking, then undo the hub nut – 52 mm socket required **(see illustration)**. Discard the nut, a new one must be fitted.

11 Remove the washer.

All models

12 Slide the hub assembly off the stub axle, taking care not to allow the outer bearing to fall out of position **(see illustration)**.

Refitting

13 Prior to refitting, remove all traces of locking compound from the hub assembly threads, ideally by running a tap of the correct size and pitch down them.

Models up to 1999 model year

14 Apply a smear of lithium-based grease to the lips of the hub oil seals.

15 Carefully slide the hub assembly onto the stub axle, taking care not to damage the oil seal lips.

16 Ensure that the outer bearing is correctly fitted, then slide the spacer onto the stub axle, ensuring that it is fitted the correct way around **(see illustration)**.

17 Fit the hub adjusting nut, tightening it by hand only **(see illustration)**.

18 If a new hub/bearing has been fitted, tighten the hub adjusting nut whilst rotating the hub to settle the bearings in position. Tighten the nut until all free play is removed from the bearings, then slacken it by a quarter of a turn; this will settle the bearings in position.

19 Attach a dial test indicator to the hub assembly, positioning it so that its pointer is in contact with the end of the stub axle **(see illustration)**. Move the hub assembly in-and-out, and measure the hub endfloat. The hub endfloat should be within the range given in the Specifications. If necessary, rotate the adjusting nut as required until the endfloat is within the specified range (set the endfloat as close as possible to the minimum endfloat setting, to allow for wear in use).

20 When the endfloat is correctly set, slide a new lockwasher onto the stub axle, then fit the locknut **(see illustrations)**.

3.12 Removing the front hub assembly

3.16 Fit the spacer . . .

3.17 . . . then screw on the hub adjusting nut

3.19 Tighten the hub adjusting nut as described, then check the hub endfloat

3.20a Once the endfloat is correctly set, fit a new lockwasher . . .

3.20b . . . and screw on the locknut

3.23a Tighten the locknut to the specified torque, then bend one side of the lockwasher inwards so it contacts one of the adjusting nut flats . . .

3.23b . . . then bend the opposite side outwards so that it contacts one of the locknut flats

3.24 Fit the inner and outer bearings to the hub

3.25 The new seal should have a fitted depth of approximately 4 mm

3.26a Fit the spacer . . .

3.26b . . . followed by the outer bearing

21 Tighten the hub locknut to the specified torque setting, whilst holding the adjusting nut stationary with a large open-ended spanner.
22 Recheck the hub endfloat, to ensure that the adjusting nut has not moved as the locknut is tightened. If necessary, loosen the locknut and repeat the adjustment procedure.
23 Once the locknut is tightened and the hub endfloat is correct, secure the adjusting nut and locknut in position with the lockwasher. Bend one side of the washer down so it contacts one of the adjusting nut flats, and bend the opposite side of the washer up so that it contacts one of the locknut flats **(see illustrations)**.

Models from 1999 model year

24 Fit the inner and outer bearing cups to the hub, then pack the inner bearing with grease and fit it to the hub **(see illustration)**.
25 Fit the new seal so that it bears against the shoulder in the hub. This should correspond to a fitted depth of 4 mm **(see illustration)**.
26 Pack the outer bearing with grease, then fit spacer Part no TOF100000 (purple colour code) and outer bearing to the hub assembly **(see illustrations)**.
27 Fit the hub assembly, taking care not to damage the seal lips on the stub axle threads.
28 Fit the washer and new hub nut, then tighten it to 30 Nm only at this stage.

29 Rotate the hub, pushing and pulling it at the same time to settle the bearings, then tighten the nut to the full specified torque.
30 Attach a dial test indicator to the hub assembly, positioning it so that its pointer is in contact with the face of the nut **(see illustration)**. Move the hub assembly in-and-out, and measure the hub endfloat. Compare the measurement obtained with that shown in the table to determine the correct spacer size **(see illustration)**. If no endfloat is present, proceed to paragraph 33.
31 With the correct sized spacer obtained, undo the nut, remove the washer, and fit the new spacer.
32 Remove the DTI gauge.

3.30a Measure the hub endfloat

End float (mm)	Colour code	Spacer size (mm)
0.000	Purple	15.5
0.025	Yellow	15.4
0.050	Yellow	15.4
0.075	Yellow	15.4
0.100	Red	15.3
0.125	Red	15.3
0.150	Red	15.3
0.175	Blue	15.2
0.200	Blue	15.2
0.225	Blue	15.2
0.250	Blue	15.2
0.275	Green	15.1
0.300	Green	15.1
0.325	Green	15.1
0.350	Green	15.1
0.375	Black	15.0
0.400	Black	15.0
0.425	Black	15.0
0.450	Black	15.0
0.475	White	14.9
0.500	White	14.9
0.525	White	14.9
0.550	White	14.9

H46036

3.30b Front hub spacer selection table

3.33a Fit the washer . . .

3.33b . . . then stake the nut to the stub axle

3.34 Ensure that the mating surfaces are clean and dry, and fit a new driving member gasket to the hub

3.36 Prior to installation, apply locking compound to the driving member retaining bolt threads

3.38 Checking halfshaft endfloat

3.39 Refit the dust cap to the hub

33 Fit the washer, tighten the nut, and use a punch to 'stake' the nut (see illustrations).

All models

34 Ensure that the hub and driving member mating surfaces are clean and dry, and fit a new gasket (see illustration).
35 Slide the driving member into position.
36 Clean the threads of each driving member retaining bolt, and apply a drop of fresh locking compound to each one. Install the bolts, and tighten them to the specified torque setting (see illustration).
37 Slide the thrustwasher(s) onto the halfshaft, and secure it in position with the circlip. Ensure that the circlip is correctly located in the halfshaft groove.

Models up to 1999 model year

38 Screw a suitable bolt into the threaded end of the halfshaft, then attach a dial test indicator to the hub assembly, positioning it so that its pointer is in contact with the end of the bolt (see illustration). Move the halfshaft in-and-out, using the bolt, and measure the endfloat. The halfshaft endfloat should be within the range given in the Specifications. To adjust the endfloat, remove the circlip, and slide off the thrustwasher. Calculate the required thickness of shim needed, and obtain

HAYNES HiNT Set the endfloat as close as possible to the minimum endfloat setting, to allow for wear in use.

it from your Land Rover dealer. Fit the shim, and secure it in position with the circlip.

All models

39 Once the halfshaft endfloat is correctly set (where applicable), unscrew the bolt (where applicable) and refit the dust cap to the hub assembly (see illustration).
40 Slide the brake caliper assembly back into position, ensuring that its pads pass either side of the disc. Refit the caliper retaining bolts, tighten them to the specified torque setting (see Chapter 10).
41 Reconnect the metal brake pipe to the caliper, remove the hose clamp, then bleed the relevant caliper as described in Chapter 10.
42 Refit the roadwheel, then lower the vehicle to the ground and tighten the wheel nuts to the specified torque setting.

4.3 Lever the oil seal out from the hub using a large flat-bladed screwdriver

4 Front hub bearing – renewal

Note: A press may be required to dismantle and rebuild the assembly, if the bearing outer races are a tight fit in the hub. If such a tool is not available, a large bench vice and suitable spacers (such as very large sockets) will serve as an adequate substitute.

1 Remove the hub assembly as described in Section 3.
2 Remove the brake disc as described in Chapter 10.
3 Note its fitted depth, then using a large flat-bladed screwdriver, lever out the inner oil seal from the hub assembly (see illustration).
4 Remove the outer and inner bearing inner races from the hub assembly.
5 Support the hub securely on blocks or in a vice, then using a hammer and suitable punch, carefully tap the inner and outer bearing outer races out from the hub assembly.
6 Thoroughly clean the hub bore, removing all traces of dirt and grease, and polish away any burrs or raised edges which might hinder reassembly. Check both for cracks or any other signs of wear or damage, and renew them if necessary. Examine the stub axle for signs of wear or damage and renew, if necessary (see Section 5). Renew both bearings and oil seal(s) as a matter of course.

4.9 Pack the hub bearings with a suitable multi-purpose lithium-based grease

5.7 On later models, inspect the bearing, oil seal and thrust ring fitted to the rear of the stub axle for signs of wear or damage

5.12 Fit a new gasket (arrowed), then slide the stub axle into position

7 On reassembly, apply a light film of oil to the inner bearing outer race and hub bore, to aid installation.

8 Securely support the hub, and locate the inner bearing outer race in the hub. Press the race fully into position, ensuring that it enters the hub squarely, using a suitable tubular spacer which bears only on the bearing outer race.

9 Pack the bearing inner race with a multi-purpose lithium-based grease. Work the grease well into the bearing race, apply a smear to the outer race surface, then fit the inner race to the hub assembly (see illustration).

10 Install the new inner oil seal, making sure that its sealing lip is facing inwards. Press the seal into position, ensuring that it enters the hub squarely, to the same depth as noted on removal.

11 Turn the hub over, and fit the outer bearing as described in paragraphs 7 to 9.

12 Refit the brake disc as described in Chapter 10.

13 Install the hub assembly as described in Section 3.

5 Front stub axle – removal and refitting

Removal

1 Remove the hub assembly as described in Section 3.

2 If not already done, drain the swivel pin housing oil as described in Chapter 1.

3 Make alignment marks between the stub axle and housing, then slacken and remove the six retaining bolts and washers.

4 Lift off the mudshield (where fitted), then remove the stub axle from the swivel pin housing and recover the gasket. Discard the gasket – a new one must be used on refitting.

5 Inspect the stub axle for signs of wear or damage, and renew if necessary.

6 On early models, check the bush fitted to the rear of the stub axle for signs of wear or damage. If renewal is necessary, it is recommended that the task is entrusted to a Land Rover dealer.

7 On later models, check the needle-roller bearing and oil seal arrangement fitted to the inside of the stub axle, and the thrust ring fitted to the rear of the axle flange, for signs of wear or damage (see illustration). If renewal is necessary, the task should be entrusted to a Land Rover dealer.

Refitting

8 Prior to refitting, remove all traces of locking compound from the swivel housing threads, ideally by running a tap of the correct size and pitch down them.

9 Ensure that the halfshaft is correctly engaged with the differential splines.

10 Make sure that the stub axle and swivel pin housing mating surfaces are clean and dry, then fit a new gasket to the swivel housing.

11 Apply a smear of oil to the stub axle bush/ bearing and seal (as applicable).

12 Slide the stub axle into position, aligning the marks made prior to removal (see illustration).

13 Refit the mudshield to the stub axle (where applicable) (see illustration).

14 Clean the threads of the retaining bolts, and apply a drop of fresh locking compound to them. Install the bolts and washers, and tighten them to the specified torque setting (see illustrations).

15 Refit the hub assembly as described in Section 3.

6 Front axle swivel pin housing assembly – removal, overhaul and refitting

Removal

1 Remove the halfshaft as described in Section 2.

2 Withdraw the split-pin, then unscrew the nut securing the track rod to the swivel pin housing. Using a universal balljoint separator, free the track rod from the hub.

3 Where necessary, also free the drag link from the swivel pin housing as described in paragraph 2.

4 Slacken and remove the bolts and washers securing the swivel housing assembly to the axle, and remove it from the vehicle (see

5.13 Refit the mudshield . . .

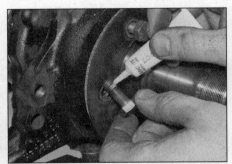

5.14a . . . then apply locking compound to the threads of the stub axle retaining bolts . . .

5.14b . . . and tighten them to the specified torque

6.4a Slacken and remove the swivel pin housing retaining bolts . . .

6.4b . . . then lift off the housing assembly and recover the gasket (arrowed)

illustrations). Recover the gasket and discard it – a new one must be used on refitting.

Overhaul

Note: *Refer to 'Vehicle identification numbers' at the end of this book for information on VIN numbers.*

**Early models –
up to VIN LA930455 (90 models)
or LA930434 (110 models)**

5 Remove all traces of grease and dirt from the outside of the swivel housing assembly **(see illustration)**.

6 Undo the retaining bolts and washers, and remove the retaining plate and oil seal from the rear of the swivel housing, noting which way around the seal is fitted **(see illustration)**.

7 Undo the brake disc mudshield retaining bracket bolt and nut, and remove the shield **(see illustration)**.

8 Bend back the locking tabs (where necessary), then slacken and remove the two bolts securing the lower swivel pin to the housing. Remove the brake disc mudshield bracket **(see illustration)**.

9 Ease the lower swivel pin out of position, and recover the gasket.

10 Undo the retaining bolts and washers, ease the upper swivel pin from the housing, and recover its shims.

11 Free the swivel ball from the housing. Recover the lower swivel pin bearing, and the thrustwashers and bearing from the upper pin bush. Support the swivel ball, and tap the bearing race and bush out of position with a hammer and suitable punch.

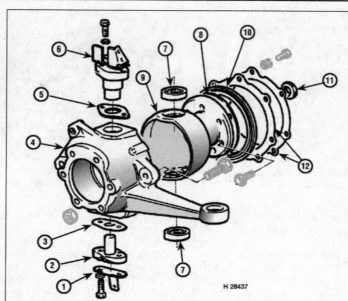

1 Mudshield bracket
2 Lower swivel pin
3 Gasket
4 Swivel pin housing
5 Gasket
6 Upper swivel pin and brake hose bracket
7 Swivel pin bearing and race
8 Shim
9 Swivel ball
10 Oil seal
11 Oil seal
12 Retaining plate and gasket

H 28437

**6.5 Exploded view of the swivel pin housing components – later models
(early models similar)**

12 Check all components, paying particular attention to the contact surfaces of the swivel ball and swivel pins. Check that each bearing rotates smoothly, without any sign of roughness – renew worn components as necessary. Renew the oil seals and gaskets as a matter of course.

13 Obtain the necessary components from your Land Rover dealer. Prior to reassembly, remove all traces of locking compound from the swivel housing threads, ideally by running a tap of the correct size and pitch down them **(see illustration)**.

14 Remove the oil seal from the rear of the swivel ball, noting which way around it is fitted. Fit the new oil seal to the rear of the

6.6 Remove the retaining plate from the rear of the swivel housing, and recover the oil seal

6.7 Removing the brake disc mudshield

6.8 Remove the lower swivel pin retaining bolts, and recover the mudshield bracket, noting which way around it is fitted

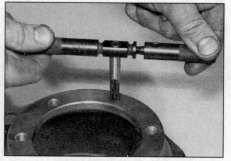

6.13 Prior to reassembly, remove all traces of old locking compound from the housing threads

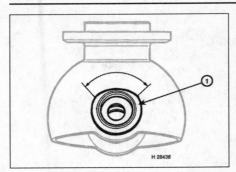

6.16 On early models, ensure that the relieved lip of the upper swivel pin bush (1) is positioned as shown when fitting the bush to the swivel ball

6.20 Insert the lower swivel pin and gasket . . .

6.21 . . . then fit the upper swivel pin and shim assembly

swivel ball, making sure that its sealing lip is facing away from the ball. Press the seal squarely into the housing, until it is flush with the housing face.

15 Fit the new lower swivel pin bearing race to the swivel ball, tapping it squarely into position with a suitable tubular drift which bears only on the outer edge of the race.

16 Fit the new upper swivel pin bush to the swivel ball, ensuring that the relieved lip of the bush is facing towards the rear of the ball **(see illustration)**.

17 Lubricate the bearings with the specified oil (see Chapter 1). Insert the bearing and thrustwashers into the upper pin bush, and fit the bearing to the lower race.

18 Reassemble the swivel ball with the housing, making sure that the bearings remain correctly seated.

19 Apply a smear of suitable sealant to either side of the lower swivel pin gasket, and fit the gasket to the pin.

20 Install the lower swivel pin with its lug outermost, then fit the mudshield bracket and refit the retaining bolts, tightening them loosely only at this stage **(see illustration)**.

21 Fit the upper swivel pin and shim(s) to the top of the swivel housing, and install the

retaining bolts, tightening them loosely only at this stage **(see illustration)**.

22 With both pins in position, remove the lower pin retaining bolts, and clean their threads. Apply a drop of fresh locking compound to the bolt threads, then refit them and tighten them to the specified torque setting **(see illustration)**. Secure the bolts in position by bending down the locking tabs (where fitted).

23 Tighten the top swivel pin bolts to the specified torque setting.

24 It is now necessary to check the swivel pin bearing preload setting. Secure retain the swivel ball axle flange, and attach a spring balance to the swivel housing track rod balljoint hole. Use the spring balance to move the swivel housing back-and-forth, whilst noting the force necessary to do this **(see illustration)**. If the bearing preload is correct, a weight (force) of approximately 3.6 to 4.5 kg (36 to 45 N) will be required to turn the housing. The preload is adjusted by varying the thickness of the shim(s) fitted beneath the upper swivel pin. If the preload is too high (more force then specified required to turn housing), thicker shim(s) will be needed; if the preload is too low (less force than specified required to turn the housing), thinner shim(s) will be required. Remove the upper swivel pin, measure the thickness of the shims fitted,

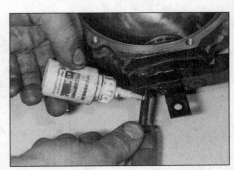

6.22 Apply locking compound to the lower swivel pin retaining bolts, and tighten them to the specified torque setting

and obtain the relevant new shims from your Land Rover dealer. Refit the swivel pin and shim(s), and tighten the retaining bolts to the specified torque. Repeat the above procedure as necessary until the preload is correctly set.

25 Once the swivel housing bearing preload is correctly adjusted, apply a smear of lithium-based grease to the lip of the swivel housing oil seal. Apply a smear of oil to the outer edge seal to aid installation then, making sure that its sealing lip is facing inwards, fit the seal to the swivel housing. Ensure that it enters the housing squarely **(see illustration)**.

6.24 Checking swivel pin bearing preload (see text)

6.25 Fit a new oil seal to the rear of the swivel pin housing, making sure that it is fitted the correct way around

6.29a On later models, separate the swivel ball and housing, and recover the bearings

6.29b Tap the bearing outer races out of position using a hammer and suitable punch

6.31 Install the new bearing outer races using a suitable tubular drift which bears only on the hard outer edge of the race

26 Ensure that the housing and retaining plate mating surfaces are clean and dry, and refit the plate to the housing. Refit the plate retaining bolts, tightening them to the specified torque setting.

27 Refit the mudshield to the housing, and securely tighten its retaining nut and bolt.

Later models – from VIN LA930456 (90 models) or LA930435 (110 models)

28 Carry out the operations described above in paragraphs 5 to 10.

29 Free the swivel ball from the housing, and recover the swivel pin bearings. Support the swivel ball, and tap the bearing races out of position with a hammer and suitable punch **(see illustrations)**.

30 Carry out the operations described above in paragraphs 12 to 14.

31 Fit the new swivel pin bearing races to the swivel ball, tapping them squarely into position with a suitable tubular drift which bears only on the outer edge of the race **(see illustration)**.

32 Lubricate the bearings with the specified oil (see Chapter 1), and seat them in the races **(see illustration)**.

33 Reassemble the swivel ball with the housing, making sure that the bearings remain correctly seated.

34 Carry out the operations described above in paragraphs 19 to 27.

Refitting

35 Ensure that the swivel ball and axle mating surfaces are clean and dry, and remove all traces of locking compound from the axle threads, ideally by running a tap of the correct size and pitch down them.

36 Fit a new gasket, and locate the swivel pin housing assembly on the axle **(see illustration)**.

37 Apply a drop of locking compound to the thread of each retaining bolt, then refit the bolts and washers, tightening them evenly and progressively to the specified torque setting.

38 Engage the track rod balljoint with the swivel pin housing, and refit its retaining nut. Tighten the nut to the specified torque setting

6.32 Lubricate the bearings with the specified oil, and seat them in their races

6.36 Ensure that the axle mating surface is clean and dry, and fit a new swivel pin housing gasket

(see Chapter 11), and secure it in position with a new split-pin.

39 Where necessary, reconnect the drag link to the swivel pin housing as described in paragraph 38.

40 Refit the halfshaft as described in Section 2.

41 On completion, check and if necessary adjust the steering lock stops as described in Chapter 11.

7 Front axle – removal and refitting

⚠ **Warning: This procedure requires at least two people, ideally three, to be carried out safely.**

Removal

1 Apply the handbrake, then jack up the front of the vehicle and support it on axle stands positioned underneath the chassis (see *Jacking and vehicle support*). Remove both front roadwheels.

2 Undo the (upper swivel pin) bolts securing the brake hose retaining bracket to the swivel housing. Position the bracket clear of the housing, then refit the bolts to prevent oil leakage. Repeat the procedure on the opposite side.

3 Slacken and remove the two retaining bolts securing the brake caliper in position. Slide the caliper assembly off the disc and, using a

piece of wire or string, tie the caliper to the front suspension coil spring, to avoid placing any strain on the hydraulic brake hose. Repeat the procedure on the opposite side.

4 Disconnect the propeller shaft from the front differential as described in Chapter 8.

5 Position a hydraulic jack beneath the front axle assembly, then raise the jack until it is supporting the axle weight.

6 Carry out the following procedures as described in Chapter 11:

a) *Remove both radius arms.*
b) *Remove the Panhard rod.*
c) *Remove the track rod.*
d) *Disconnect the drag link from the swivel pin housing.*
e) *Disconnect the anti-roll bar connecting links from the axle (where fitted).*
f) *Remove the nuts securing the shock absorbers to the axle.*

7 With an assistant supporting either end of the axle, carefully lower the axle away from the vehicle, making sure that all the relevant components have been disconnected.

8 Remove the axle from underneath the vehicle, and recover the front coil springs.

Refitting

9 On refitting, position the axle assembly on the jack.

10 With the aid of two assistants, carefully raise the axle assembly into position, whilst aligning the front coil springs with their upper and lower spring seats.

11 With the axle raised and both coil springs

8.3 Removing a rear axle halfshaft

8.7 Fit a new gasket to the hub assembly . . .

8.8 . . . then refit the halfshaft, and tighten its retaining bolts to the specified torque

correctly seated, carry out the following procedures as described in Chapter 11:

a) *Refit the nuts securing the shock absorbers to the axle.*
b) *Connect the anti-roll bar connecting links to the axle (where applicable).*
c) *Connect the drag link from the swivel pin housing.*
d) *Refit the track rod.*
e) *Refit the Panhard rod.*
f) *Refit both radius arms.*

12 Slide the brake caliper assembly back into position, ensuring that its pads pass either side of the disc. Refit the caliper retaining bolts, and tighten them to the specified torque setting (see Chapter 10). Repeat the procedure on the opposite side.

13 Clean the upper swivel pin retaining bolts, and apply a drop of locking compound to each one's threads. Position the brake hose bracket on top of the swivel pin, then refit the retaining bolts and tighten them to the specified torque setting. Repeat the procedure on the opposite side.

14 Reconnect the propeller shaft to the axle as described in Chapter 8.

15 Refit the front roadwheels, then lower the vehicle to the ground and tighten the wheel nuts to the specified torque setting.

16 Rock the vehicle to settle all disturbed suspension components in position, then go around and tighten all the relevant suspension fasteners which need to be tightened with the vehicle resting on its wheels.

8 Rear axle halfshaft – removal, inspection and refitting

Removal

1 Chock the front wheels, then jack up the rear of the vehicle and support it on axle stands positioned underneath the chassis (see *Jacking and vehicle support*). Remove the relevant rear roadwheel.

2 Drain the differential housing oil as described in Chapter 1, or be prepared for some oil spillage as the shaft is removed.

3 Slacken and remove the five bolts and washers securing the halfshaft to the centre

of the hub, and withdraw the shaft from the centre of the hub assembly **(see illustration)**. Recover the gasket from the halfshaft flange, and discard it.

4 On models with a two-piece halfshaft assembly, if necessary, remove the dust cap from the end of the shaft, remove the circlip, and separate the shaft and driving member.

Inspection

5 Inspect the halfshaft splines and hub flange for signs of wear or damage, and renew if necessary.

Refitting

6 Where necessary, engage the halfshaft with the driving member, and secure it in position with the circlip. Ensure that the circlip is correctly seated in the shaft groove, and refit the dust cap.

7 Ensure that the halfshaft and hub mating surfaces are clean and dry, and fit a new gasket **(see illustration)**.

8 Slide the halfshaft carefully into position, and refit its retaining bolts and washers, tightening them to the specified torque setting **(see illustration)**

9 Refit the roadwheel, then lower the vehicle to the ground and tighten the wheel nuts to the specified torque.

10 If necessary, top-up/refill the differential housing with oil as described in Chapter 1.

9 Rear hub assembly – removal and refitting

Note: *The following information applies only to the standard hub assembly. For information on freewheeling hubs, refer to your Land Rover dealer.*

Removal

1 Remove the halfshaft as described in Section 8 **(see illustration)**.

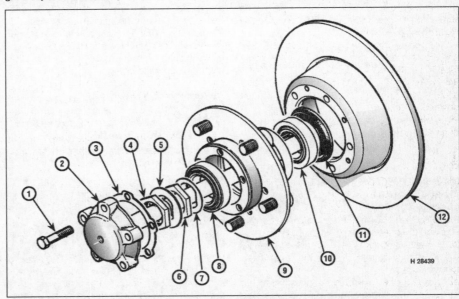

9.1 Exploded view of the rear hub and associated components

1 Retaining bolt
2 Halfshaft
3 Gasket
4 Locknut
5 Lockwasher
6 Adjusting nut
7 Spacer
8 Outer bearing and race
9 Hub
10 Inner bearing and race
11 Seal
12 Brake disc

H 28439

9.3a Slide the brake caliper assembly off the disc . . .

9.3b . . . and tie it to the coil spring, to prevent the brake pipe being strained

9.4 Bend back the lockwasher from the locknut flat using a suitable chisel

2 On models with rear drum brakes, remove the brake drum as described in Chapter 10.

3 On models with rear disc brakes, release the retaining clips securing the rear brake pipe to the axle. Slacken and remove the two retaining bolts securing the brake caliper in position. Slide the caliper assembly off the disc and, using a piece of wire or string, tie the caliper to the suspension coil spring, to avoid placing any strain on the hydraulic brake pipe **(see illustrations)**. Note: *Do not bend the pipe any more than is absolutely necessary.*

Vehicles up to 1999 model year

4 Using a hammer and suitable chisel, bend back the lockwasher tab from the hub locknut flat **(see illustration)**.

5 Slacken and remove the hub locknut, and slide off the lockwasher. Discard the lockwasher – a new one must be used on refitting.

6 Unscrew the hub adjusting nut, then slide off the washer/spacer, noting which way around it is fitted.

Vehicles from 1999 model year

7 Knock back the staking, then undo the hub nut **(see illustration 3.10)**. Discard the nut, a new one must be fitted.

8 Remove the washer.

All models

9 Slide the hub assembly off the stub axle, complete with bearings.

Refitting

10 Apply a smear of lithium-based grease to the lips of the hub oil seal(s).

Vehicles up to 1999 model year

11 Carefully slide the hub assembly onto the stub axle, taking care not to damage the oil seal lips **(see illustration)**.

12 Slide the washer/spacer onto the stub axle, ensuring that it is fitted the correct way around **(see illustration)**.

13 Fit the hub adjusting nut, tightening it by hand only **(see illustration)**.

14 If a new hub/bearing has been installed, tighten the hub adjusting nut whilst rotating the hub to settle the bearings in position. Tighten the nut until all free play is removed from the bearings, then slacken it by a quarter of a turn; this will settle the bearings in position.

15 On all models, attach a dial test indicator to the hub assembly, positioning it so that its pointer is in contact with the end of the stub axle. Move the hub assembly in-and-out, and measure the hub endfloat. The hub endfloat should be within the range given in the Specifications. If necessary, rotate the adjusting nut as required until the endfloat is within the specified range.

> **HAYNES HiNT** *Set the endfloat as close as possible to the minimum endfloat setting, to allow for wear in use.*

16 When the endfloat is correctly set, slide a new lockwasher onto the stub axle, then fit the locknut.

17 Tighten the hub locknut to the specified torque setting, whilst holding the adjusting nut stationary with a large open-ended spanner.

18 Recheck the hub endfloat, to ensure that the adjusting nut has not moved as the locknut is tightened. If necessary, loosen the locknut and repeat the adjustment procedure.

19 Once the locknut is tightened and the hub endfloat is correct, secure the adjusting nut and locknut in position with the lockwasher. Bend one side of the washer down so it contacts one of the adjusting nut flats, and bend the opposite side of the washer up so it contacts one of the locknut flats.

Vehicles from 1999 model year

20 Fit the hub assembly, taking care not to damage the seal lips on the stub axle threads. It's essential that spacer Part no TOF100000 (purple colour code) is fitted between the inner bearings, to establish the correct spacer to eliminate endfloat.

21 Fit a new washer and hub nut, then tighten it to 30 Nm only at this stage.

22 Rotate the hub, pushing and pulling it at the same time to settle the bearings, then tighten the nut to the full specified torque.

23 Attach a dial test indicator to the hub assembly, positioning it so that its pointer is in contact with the end of the stub axle (see

9.11 Slide the rear hub assembly into position . . .

9.12 . . . then refit the spacer . . .

9.13 . . . and screw on the hub adjusting nut

illustration). Move the hub assembly in-and-out, and measure the hub endfloat. Compare the measurement obtained with that shown in the table to determine the correct spacer size (see illustration 3.30b). If no endfloat is present, proceed to paragraph 25.

24 With the correct sized spacer obtained, undo the nut, remove the washer, and fit the new spacer.

25 Remove the DTI gauge.

26 Fit the washer, tighten the nut, and use a chisel to 'stake' the nut (see illustration 3.33b).

All models

27 On models with rear disc brakes, slide the brake caliper assembly back into position, ensuring that its pads pass either side of the disc. Refit the caliper retaining bolts, and tighten them to the specified torque setting (see Chapter 10). Secure the brake pipe back in position with all the necessary retaining clips.

28 On models with rear drum brakes, refit the brake drum as described in Chapter 10.

29 On all models, refit the halfshaft as described in Section 8.

10 Rear hub bearing – renewal

Note: A press may be required to dismantle and rebuild the assembly, if the bearing outer races are a tight fit in the hub. If such a tool is not available, a large bench vice and suitable spacers (such as large sockets) will serve as an adequate substitute.

1 Remove the hub assembly as described in Section 9.

2 On models with rear disc brakes, remove the brake disc as described in Chapter 10.

3 Note the correct fitted depth of the seal(s) in the hub. Using a large flat-bladed screwdriver, lever the outer and/or inner oil seal(s) out from the hub assembly (as applicable).

4 Remove the outer and inner bearing inner races from the hub assembly. **Note:** On vehicles from 1999 model year (with staked hub nut), remove the spacer from between the two bearing races.

5 Support the hub securely on blocks or in a vice. Using a hammer and suitable punch, carefully tap the inner and outer bearing outer races out from the hub assembly.

6 Thoroughly clean the hub bore, removing all traces of dirt and grease, and polish away any burrs or raised edges which might hinder reassembly. Check both for cracks or any other signs of wear or damage, and renew them if necessary. Examine the stub axle for signs of wear or damage, and renew if necessary (see Section 11). Renew both bearings and oil seal(s) as a matter of course.

7 On reassembly, apply a light film of oil to the inner bearing outer race and hub bore, to aid installation.

8 Securely support the hub, and locate the

9.23 Measure the endfloat with a DTI gauge

inner bearing outer race in the hub. Press the race fully into position, ensuring that it enters the hub squarely, using a suitable tubular spacer which bears only on the bearing outer race.

9 Pack the bearing inner race with a multi-purpose lithium-based grease. Work the grease well into the bearing race, apply a smear to the outer race surface, then fit the inner race to the hub assembly.

10 Install the new inner oil seal, making sure that its sealing lip is facing inwards. Press the seal into position, ensuring that it enters the hub squarely, until it is positioned at the same depth as the original was noted prior to removal.

11 Turn the hub over, and fit the outer bearing (and, where necessary, oil seal) as described in paragraphs 7 to 10. **Note:** On vehicles from 1999 model year, fit spacer Part no TOF100000 (purple colour code) before fitting the outer, inner bearing race.

12 On models with rear disc brakes, refit the brake disc as described in Chapter 10.

13 Install the hub assembly as described in Section 9.

11 Rear stub axle – removal and refitting

Note: New stub axle retaining bolt nuts will be required on refitting.

Removal

Models with rear drum brakes

1 Remove the rear hub assembly as described in Section 9.

2 To minimise fluid loss, remove the master cylinder reservoir cap, then tighten it down onto a piece of polythene to obtain an airtight seal. Alternatively, use a brake hose clamp, a G-clamp or a similar tool to clamp the flexible hose at the nearest convenient point to the wheel cylinder.

3 Wipe away all traces of dirt around the brake pipe union at the rear of the wheel cylinder, and unscrew the union nut. Carefully ease the pipe out of the wheel cylinder, and plug or tape over its end to prevent dirt entry. Wipe off any spilt fluid immediately.

11.10 Rear stub axle retaining bolts (arrowed)

4 If not already done, drain the differential housing oil as described in Chapter 1.

5 Slacken and remove the six stub axle retaining bolts and nuts. Lift off the retaining plate, and remove the brake plate assembly from the stub axle.

6 Make alignment marks between the stub axle and axle, then remove the stub axle and recover the gasket. Discard the gasket – a new one must be used on refitting.

7 Inspect the stub axle for signs of wear or damage, and renew if necessary.

Models with rear disc brakes

8 Remove the rear hub assembly as described in Section 9.

9 If not already done, drain the differential housing oil as described in Chapter 1.

10 Make alignment marks between the stub axle and axle, then slacken and remove the six retaining bolts and nuts (see illustration).

11 Lift off the mudshield, then remove the stub axle from the axle and recover the gasket. Discard the gasket – a new one must be used on refitting.

12 Inspect the stub axle for signs of wear or damage, and renew if necessary.

13 Check the oil seal fitted to the rear of the stub axle for signs of wear or damage. If renewal is necessary, lever out the old seal, noting which way around it is fitted. Apply a smear of grease to the new seal lip, to aid installation. Fit the new seal to the axle, making sure that its sealing lip is facing away from the stub axle. Press it into position using a suitable tubular spacer which bears only on the outer edge of the seal. Ensure that the seal squarely enters the stub axle, and is positioned flush with the axle end.

Refitting

Models with rear drum brakes

14 Make sure that the stub axle and axle mating surfaces are clean and dry, then fit a new gasket to the axle.

15 Ensure that the brake backplate, retaining plate and stub axle mating surfaces are clean and dry, then apply a smear of suitable sealant to the rear of the retaining plate.

16 Slide the stub axle into position, aligning the marks made prior to removal, then refit the brake backplate assembly. Ensure that the

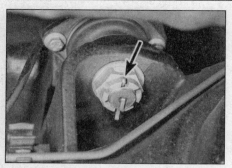

12.6 Withdraw the split-pin, then slacken and remove the nut securing the upper link balljoint to the rear axle

brake backplate and stub axle are correctly engaged, then refit the retaining ring.

17 Refit the stub axle retaining bolts and fit the new nuts, tightening them to the specified torque setting.

18 Reconnect the brake pipe to the wheel cylinder, and tighten its union nut to the specified torque setting (see Chapter 10). Remove the polythene/brake hose clamp (where fitted).

19 Refit the hub assembly as described in Section 9.

20 On completion, bleed the brake hydraulic system as described in Chapter 10. Providing suitable precautions were taken to minimise loss of fluid, it should only be necessary to bleed the relevant rear brake.

Models with rear disc brakes

21 Make sure that the stub axle and axle mating surfaces are clean and dry, then fit a new gasket to the axle.

22 Slide the stub axle into position, aligning the marks made prior to removal, and refit the mudshield to the stub axle.

23 Fit the retaining bolts and new nuts, and tighten them to the specified torque setting.

24 Refit the hub assembly as described in Section 9.

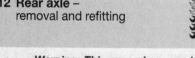

12 Rear axle –
removal and refitting

⚠️ *Warning: This procedure requires at least two people, ideally three, to be carried out safely.*

Removal

1 Chock the front wheels, then jack up the rear of the vehicle and support it on axle

stands positioned underneath the chassis (see *Jacking and vehicle support*). Remove both rear roadwheels.

2 Unscrew the master cylinder fluid reservoir cap, then tighten the cap down onto a piece of polythene, to minimise fluid loss. Trace the brake pipes back from the wheel cylinders/ calipers to their union piece situated on top of the axle. Slacken the union nut(s) and disconnect the pipe(s). Remove the retaining clips, and release the pipes from the axle/ vehicle body.

> **HAYNES HINT** *Plug the hydraulic pipe end(s) to minimise fluid loss and to prevent the entry of dirt into the hydraulic system.*

3 Disconnect the propeller shaft from the rear differential as described in Chapter 8.

4 Position a hydraulic jack beneath the rear axle assembly, then raise the jack until it is supporting the axle weight.

5 Carry out the following procedures as described in Chapter 11:
   a) *Disconnect the lower links from the axle.*
   b) *Disconnect the shock absorbers from the axle.*
   c) *Disconnect the anti-roll bar connecting links from the axle (where applicable).*

6 Withdraw the split-pin, then slacken and remove the nut securing the upper link balljoint to the top of the axle **(see illustration)**.

7 With an assistant supporting either end of the axle, carefully lower the axle away from the vehicle, making sure that all the relevant components have been disconnected.

8 Remove the axle from underneath the vehicle, and recover the spring seats from the tops of the front coil springs.

Refitting

9 On refitting, position the axle assembly on the jack, and refit the spring seats to the coil springs.

10 With the aid of two assistants, carefully raise the axle assembly into position, whilst aligning the front coil springs with their upper seats and the upper link balljoint with the axle.

11 With the axle raised and both coil springs correctly seated, refit the balljoint retaining nut, and tighten it to the specified torque setting. Secure the nut in position with a new split-pin.

12 Carry out the following procedures as described in Chapter 11:
   a) *Connect the anti-roll bar connecting links to the axle (where applicable).*
   b) *Connect the shock absorbers to the axle.*
   c) *Connect the lower links to the axle.*

13 Reconnect the propeller shaft to the differential as described in Chapter 8.

14 Referring to Chapter 10, reconnect the brake pipe(s) to the axle, tightening them to the specified torque setting, then bleed the complete hydraulic braking system.

15 Refit the roadwheels, then lower the vehicle to the ground and tighten the wheel nuts to the specified torque setting.

16 Rock the vehicle to settle all disturbed suspension components in position, then tighten the lower link pivot bolts to the specified torque (See Chapter 11).

13 Axle differential overhaul
– general information

Overhauling a differential unit is a difficult and involved job for the DIY home mechanic. In addition to dismantling and reassembling many small parts, clearances must be precisely measured and, if necessary, changed by selecting shims and spacers. Components are also often difficult to obtain, and in many instances, extremely expensive. Because of this, if the differential develops a fault or becomes noisy, the best course of action is to have the unit overhauled by a specialist repairer, or to obtain an exchange reconditioned unit.

Nevertheless, it is not impossible for the more experienced mechanic to overhaul the differential, provided the special tools are available and the job is done in a deliberate step-by-step manner so that nothing is overlooked.

The tools necessary for an overhaul include internal and external circlip pliers, bearing pullers, a slide hammer, a set of pin punches, a dial test indicator, and possibly a hydraulic press. In addition, a large, sturdy workbench and a vice will be required.

During dismantling, make careful notes of how each component is fitted, to make reassembly easier and accurate.

Before dismantling, it will help if you have some idea what area is malfunctioning. Refer to *Fault finding* at the end of this manual for more information.

Chapter 10
Braking system

Contents

	Section number
Anti-lock braking system (ABS) – general information	23
Anti-lock braking system (ABS) components – removal and refitting	24
Brake pedal – removal and refitting	14
Front brake caliper – removal, overhaul and refitting	10
Front brake disc – inspection, removal and refitting	7
Front brake pad wear check	See Chapter 1
Front brake pads – renewal	4
General information	1
Handbrake cable – removal and refitting	19
Handbrake lever – removal and refitting	18
Handbrake shoes – renewal	17
Hydraulic fluid level check	See Chapter 1
Hydraulic fluid renewal	See Chapter 1
Hydraulic pipes and hoses – renewal	3

	Section number
Hydraulic system – bleeding	2
Master cylinder – removal, overhaul and refitting	13
Rear brake caliper – removal, overhaul and refitting	11
Rear brake disc – inspection, removal and refitting	8
Rear brake drum – removal, inspection and refitting	9
Rear brake pad wear check	See Chapter 1
Rear brake pads – renewal	5
Rear brake pressure-regulating valve – testing, removal and refitting	20
Rear brake shoes – renewal	6
Rear wheel cylinder – removal, overhaul and refitting	12
Stop-light switch – removal, refitting and adjustment	21
Vacuum pump – removal and refitting	22
Vacuum servo unit – testing, removal and refitting	15
Vacuum servo unit check valve – removal, testing and refitting	16

Degrees of difficulty

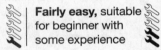

Easy, suitable for novice with little experience	**Fairly easy,** suitable for beginner with some experience	**Fairly difficult,** suitable for competent DIY mechanic	**Difficult,** suitable for experienced DIY mechanic	**Very difficult,** suitable for expert DIY or professional

Specifications

Front brakes

Type	Disc, with opposed-piston caliper
Disc diameter	300 mm
Disc thickness:	
Non-ventilated disc	14.1 mm
Ventilated disc	24.0 mm
Maximum wear (per side)	1.0 mm
Maximum disc run-out	0.15 mm
Brake pad friction material minimum thickness	3.0 mm

Rear drum brakes

Type	Single leading-shoe drum
Drum diameter	280 mm
Maximum drum ovality	N/A
Brake shoe friction material minimum thickness	1.5 mm

Rear disc brakes

Type	Disc, with opposed-piston caliper
Disc diameter	290 mm
Disc thickness:	
90 models	12.5 mm
110/130 models	14.1 mm
Maximum wear (per side):	
90 models	0.38 mm
110/130 models	1.0 mm
Maximum disc run-out	0.15 mm
Brake pad friction material minimum thickness	3.0 mm

Torque wrench settings

	Nm	lbf ft
Brake caliper mounting bolts (front and rear)	82	61
Brake disc bolts (front and rear)	72	53
Brake pipe union nut	13	10
Handbrake backplate bolts	25	18
Master cylinder mounting nuts	14	10
Rear wheel cylinder nuts	11	8
Roadwheel nuts:		
Steel wheels	108	80
Alloy wheels	130	96
Heavy duty wheel	170	125
Vacuum servo unit mounting nuts	14	10
Vacuum pump to alternator (TD5 engine)	10	7

1 General information

The braking system is of the servo-assisted, dual-circuit hydraulic type, operating from a tandem master cylinder. The primary circuit operates the rear brake cylinders/calipers (as applicable), and the secondary circuit operates the front brake calipers. Under normal circumstances, both circuits operate in unison. However, in the event of hydraulic failure in one circuit, braking force will still be available for at least two wheels.

As with all diesel engines, since there is insufficient vacuum in the inlet manifold to operate the braking system servo unit, a vacuum pump is fitted to the engine to provide the required vacuum.

Early models (up to 1993) were fitted with front disc brakes and rear drum brakes; later models (1993 onwards) have disc brakes all round as standard.

The disc brakes are actuated by opposed-piston type calipers, which ensure that equal pressure is applied to each disc pad. The rear drum brakes (where fitted) incorporate leading and trailing shoes which are actuated by twin-piston wheel cylinders.

On all models, the handbrake is in the form of a drum brake assembly mounted onto the rear of the transfer box. When the handbrake is applied, it locks the rear axle by preventing propeller shaft rotation.

Note: *When servicing any part of the system, work carefully and methodically; also observe scrupulous cleanliness when overhauling any part of the hydraulic system. Always renew components (in axle sets, where applicable) if in doubt about their condition, and use only genuine Land Rover parts, or at least those of known good quality. Note the warnings given in 'Safety first!' and at relevant points in this Chapter concerning the dangers of asbestos dust and hydraulic fluid.*

2 Hydraulic system – bleeding

Note: *Hydraulic fluid is poisonous; wash off immediately and thoroughly in the case of skin contact, and seek immediate medical advice if any fluid is swallowed or gets into the eyes. Certain types of hydraulic fluid are inflammable, and may ignite when allowed into contact with hot components; when servicing any hydraulic system, it is safest to assume that the fluid IS inflammable, and to take precautions against the risk of fire as though it is petrol that is being handled. Finally, it is hygroscopic (it absorbs moisture from the air) – old fluid may be contaminated, and unfit for further use. When topping-up or renewing the fluid, always use the recommended type, and ensure that it comes from a freshly-opened sealed container.*

Caution: Hydraulic fluid is also an effective paint stripper, and will attack plastics; if any is spilt, it should be washed off immediately, using copious quantities of fresh water.

General

1 The correct operation of any hydraulic system is only possible after removing all air from the components and circuit; this is achieved by bleeding the system.

2 During the bleeding procedure, add only clean, unused hydraulic fluid of the recommended type; never re-use fluid that has already been bled from the system. Ensure that sufficient fluid is available before starting work.

3 If there is any possibility of incorrect fluid being already in the system, the brake components and circuit must be flushed completely with uncontaminated, correct fluid, and new seals should be fitted to the various components.

4 If hydraulic fluid has been lost from the system, or air has entered because of a leak, ensure that the fault is cured before proceeding further.

5 Park the vehicle on level ground, switch off the engine and select first or reverse gear, then chock the wheels and release the handbrake.

6 Check that all pipes and hoses are secure, unions tight, and bleed screws closed. Clean any dirt from around the bleed screws.

7 Unscrew the master cylinder reservoir cap, and top the master cylinder reservoir up to the MAX level line; refit the cap loosely. Remember to maintain the fluid level at least above the MIN level line throughout the procedure,

or there is a risk of further air entering the system.

8 There is a number of one-man, do-it-yourself brake bleeding kits currently available from motor accessory shops. It is recommended that one of these kits is used whenever possible, as they greatly simplify the bleeding operation, and also reduce the risk of expelled air and fluid being drawn back into the system. If such a kit is not available, the basic (two-man) method must be used, which is described in detail below.

9 If a kit is to be used, prepare the vehicle as described previously, and follow the kit manufacturer's instructions, as the procedure may vary slightly according to the type being used; generally, they are as outlined below in the relevant sub-Section.

10 Whichever method is used, the same sequence must be followed (paragraphs 11 and 12) to ensure the removal of all air from the system.

Bleeding sequence

11 If the system has been only partially disconnected, and suitable precautions were taken to minimise fluid loss, it should be necessary only to bleed that part of the system (ie, the primary or secondary circuit).

12 If the complete system is to be bled, then it should be done working in the following sequence:

  a) Left-hand rear brake.
  b) Right-hand rear brake.
  c) Right-hand front brake.
  d) Left-hand front brake.

Bleeding

Basic (two-man) method

13 Collect a clean glass jar, a suitable length of plastic or rubber tubing which is a tight fit over the bleed screw, and a ring spanner to fit the screw. The help of an assistant will also be required.

14 Remove the dust cap from the first screw in the sequence. Fit the spanner and tube to the screw, place the other end of the tube in the jar, and pour in sufficient fluid to cover the end of the tube.

15 Ensure that the master cylinder reservoir fluid level is maintained at least above the MIN level line throughout the procedure.

16 Have the assistant fully depress the brake

pedal several times to build-up pressure, then maintain it on the final stroke.

17 While pedal pressure is maintained, unscrew the bleed screw (approximately one turn), and allow the compressed fluid and air to flow into the jar. The assistant should maintain pedal pressure, following it down to the floor if necessary, and should not release it until instructed to do so. When the flow stops, tighten the bleed screw again, then the pedal can be released slowly. Recheck the reservoir fluid level.

18 Repeat the steps given in paragraphs 16 and 17 until the fluid emerging from the bleed screw is free from air bubbles. If the master cylinder has been drained and refilled, and air is being bled from the first screw in the sequence, allow approximately five seconds between cycles for the master cylinder passages to refill.

19 When no more air bubbles appear, tighten the bleed screw securely, remove the tube and spanner, and refit the dust cap. Do not overtighten the bleed screw.

20 Repeat the procedure on the remaining screws in the sequence, until all air is removed from the system and the brake pedal feels firm again.

Using a one-way valve kit

21 As their name implies, these kits consist of a length of tubing with a one-way valve fitted, to prevent expelled air and fluid being drawn back into the system; some kits include a translucent container, which can be positioned so that the air bubbles can be more easily seen flowing from the end of the tube **(see illustration)**.

22 The kit is connected to the bleed screw, which is then opened. The user returns to the driver's seat, depresses the brake pedal with a smooth, steady stroke, and slowly releases it; this is repeated until the expelled fluid is clear of air bubbles.

23 These kits simplify work so much that it is easy to forget the master cylinder reservoir fluid level; ensure that this is maintained at least above the MIN level line at all times.

Using a pressure-bleeding kit

Note: *Ensure that the pressure in the reservoir does not exceed 4.5 bars (60 psi approx).*

24 These kits are usually operated by the reservoir of pressurised air contained in the spare tyre, although note that it will probably be necessary to reduce the pressure to a lower limit than normal; refer to the instructions supplied with the kit.

25 By connecting a pressurised, fluid-filled container to the master cylinder reservoir, bleeding can be carried out simply by opening each screw in turn (in the specified sequence), and allowing the fluid to flow out until no more air bubbles can be seen in the expelled fluid.

26 This method has the advantage that the large reservoir of fluid provides an additional safeguard against air being drawn into the system during bleeding.

27 Pressure bleeding is particularly effective when bleeding 'difficult' systems, or when bleeding the complete system at the time of routine fluid renewal.

All methods

28 When bleeding is complete, and firm pedal feel is restored, wash off any spilt fluid, tighten the bleed screws securely, and refit their dust caps.

29 Check the hydraulic fluid level, and top-up if necessary (*Weekly checks*).

30 Discard any hydraulic fluid that has been bled from the system; it will not be fit for re-use.

31 Check the feel of the brake pedal. If it feels at all spongy, air must still be present in the system, and further bleeding is required. Failure to bleed satisfactorily after a reasonable repetition of the bleeding procedure may be due to worn master cylinder seals.

3 Hydraulic pipes and hoses – renewal

Note: *Before starting work, refer to the note at the beginning of Section 2 concerning the dangers of hydraulic fluid.*

1 If any pipe or hose is to be renewed, to minimise fluid loss, remove the master cylinder reservoir cap, then tighten it down onto a piece of polythene to obtain an airtight seal. Alternatively, flexible hoses can be sealed, if required, using a proprietary brake hose clamp, while metal brake pipe unions can be plugged (if care is taken not to allow dirt into the system)

or capped immediately they are disconnected. Place a wad of rag under any union that is to be disconnected, to catch any spilt fluid.

2 If a flexible hose is to be disconnected, unscrew the brake pipe union nut before removing the spring clip which secures the hose to its mounting bracket (where fitted).

3 To unscrew the union nuts, it is preferable to obtain a proper brake pipe spanner of the correct size; these are available from most large motor accessory shops **(see illustration)**. Failing this, a close-fitting open-ended spanner will be required, though if the nuts are tight or corroded, their flats may be rounded-off if the spanner slips. In such a case, a self-locking wrench is often the only way to unscrew a stubborn union, but it follows that the pipe and the damaged nuts must be renewed on reassembly. Always clean a union and surrounding area before disconnecting it.

> **HAYNES HINT**
> *If disconnecting a component with more than one union, make a careful note of the connections before disturbing any of them.*

4 If a brake pipe is to be renewed, it can be obtained, cut to length and with the union nuts and end flares in place, from Land Rover dealers. All that is then necessary is to bend it to shape, following the line of the original, before fitting it to the car. Alternatively, most motor accessory shops can make up brake pipes from kits, but this requires very careful measurement of the original, to ensure that the replacement is of the correct length. The safest answer is usually to take the original to the shop as a pattern.

5 On refitting, do not overtighten the union nuts. It is not necessary to exercise brute force to obtain a sound joint.

6 Ensure that the pipes and hoses are correctly routed with no kinks, and that they are secured in the clips or brackets provided. After fitting, remove the polythene from the reservoir (or the hose clamps/plugs, if used) and bleed the hydraulic system as described in Section 2. Wash off any spilt fluid, and check carefully for fluid leaks.

4 Front brake pads – renewal

> ⚠ *Warning: Renew BOTH sets of front brake pads at the same time – NEVER renew the pads on only one wheel, as uneven braking may result. Note that the dust created by wear of the pads may contain asbestos, which is a health hazard. Never blow it out with compressed air, and don't inhale any of it. An approved filtering mask should be worn when working on the brakes. DO NOT use petroleum-based solvents to clean brake parts – use brake cleaner or methylated spirit only.*

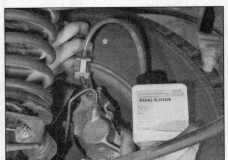

2.21 Bleeding a rear brake caliper using a one-way valve kit

3.3 Using a brake pipe spanner to slacken and union nut

4.5a On later models, remove the split-pins . . .

4.5b . . . then withdraw the pad retaining pins and recover the anti-rattle springs (arrowed)

4.6 Lift the brake pads out from the caliper

1 Apply the handbrake, then jack up the front of the vehicle and support it on axle stands. Remove both front roadwheels.

2 There are three possible types of pad retaining pin which may be used:
 a) Pads retained by large split-pins, and plate-type anti-rattle springs fitted.
 b) Pads secured in position with pins and R-clips, and wire-type anti-rattle springs used.
 c) Pad retaining pins are secured in position by a split-pin, with coil-type anti-rattle springs fitted over the pins.

Identify the type of retaining pin used, and proceed as follows.

3 On models with the first type of retaining pin, noting the correct fitted locations of the pad anti-rattle springs, straighten the ends of the pad retaining split-pins, and withdraw them from the caliper. Recover the springs from the top of the caliper, noting which way around they are fitted.

4 On models with the second type of retaining pin, remove the R-clips/split-pins (as applicable) from the inner end of each retaining pin. Noting the correct fitted positions of the anti-rattle springs, withdraw the retaining pins, and recover the spring from the top of each pad.

5 On models with the third type of retaining pin, using a pair of pliers, remove the R-clip/split-pin (as applicable) from the inner end of each pad retaining pin. Carefully withdraw the pad retaining pins, recovering the anti-rattle springs as they are released (see illustrations).

6 On all models, withdraw the pads from caliper (see illustration). Note the location of any brake pad shims fitted.

7 Brush the dirt and dust from the caliper, but take care not to inhale it. Carefully remove any rust from the edge of the brake disc.

8 First measure the thickness of each brake pad's friction material (see illustration). If either pad is worn at any point to the specified minimum thickness or less, all four pads must be renewed. Also, the pads should be renewed if any are fouled with oil or grease; there is no satisfactory way of degreasing friction material, once contaminated. If any of the brake pads are worn unevenly or fouled with oil or grease, trace and rectify the cause before reassembly. The pad retaining pins and anti-rattle springs should be also renewed if the pads are to be renewed. New brake pads, pins and springs are available from Land Rover dealers.

9 If the brake pads are still serviceable, carefully clean them using a clean, fine wire brush or similar, paying particular attention to the sides and back of the metal backing. Clean out the grooves in the friction material, and pick out any large embedded particles of dirt or debris. Carefully clean the pad locations in the caliper body/mounting bracket.

10 Prior to fitting the pads, brush the dust and dirt from the caliper pistons, but do not inhale it, as it is a health hazard. Inspect the dust seal around the piston for damage, and the piston for evidence of fluid leaks, corrosion or damage. If attention to any of these

components is necessary, refer to Section 10.

11 If new brake pads are to be fitted, the caliper pistons must be pushed back into the caliper, to make room for them. Either use a G-clamp or similar tool, or use suitable pieces of wood as levers. Provided that the master cylinder reservoir has not been overfilled with hydraulic fluid, there should be no spillage, but keep a careful watch on the fluid level while retracting the piston. If the fluid level rises above the MAX level line at any time, the surplus should be syphoned off, or ejected via a plastic tube connected to the bleed screw (see Section 2). Note: Do not syphon the fluid by mouth, as it is poisonous; use a syringe or an old poultry baster.

12 Apply a thin smear of high-temperature brake grease or anti-seize compound to the sides and back of each pad's metal backing, and to those surfaces of the caliper body which bear on the pads. Do not allow the lubricant to foul the friction material.

13 Locate the pads in the caliper, ensuring that the friction material of each pad is against the brake disc. Note: The friction material on new pads may have a chamfered edge. The pads must be fitted with this chamfer on the leading edge, ie, this edge is the first part of the pad that the disc encounters in the normal direction of rotation (see illustration).

14 On models with the first type of pad retaining pin, position the anti-rattle springs on top of the pads, ensuring that they are fitted the correct way around. Insert the new retaining pins into the caliper, making sure each pin is correctly engaged with its anti-rattle spring, and secure them in position by bending over their ends.

15 On models with the second type of retaining pin, locate the anti-rattle springs with the brake pads, making sure that the spring ends are on the inside of the pad. Slide the retaining pins into position, making sure they pass through the pad holes and over the spring ends, and secure them in position with the R-clips or new split-pins (as applicable).

16 On models with the third type of retaining pin, fit the anti-rattle springs between the pads, then insert the pad retaining pins. Make sure each pin passes through its anti-rattle spring and both pads. Secure each retaining

4.8 Measuring brake pad friction material thickness

4.13 New pads may have a chamfered edge which must be fitted at the leading edge

Arrow shows normal direction of rotation

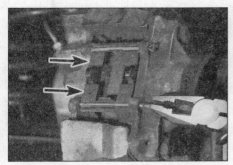

5.1a Withdraw the pad retaining split-pins, then remove the anti-rattle springs (arrowed) . . .

5.1b . . . and lift out the pads

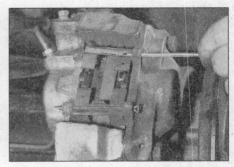

5.1c On refitting, ensure that the anti-rattle springs are correctly seated, and engage with the retaining split-pins as they are inserted

pin in position with an R-clip or new split-pin (as applicable).

17 On all models, depress the brake pedal repeatedly, until the pads are pressed into firm contact with the brake disc and normal (non-assisted) pedal pressure is restored.

18 Repeat the above procedure on the remaining front brake caliper.

19 Refit the roadwheels, then lower the vehicle to the ground and tighten the roadwheel nuts to the specified torque setting.

20 Check the hydraulic fluid level as described in *Weekly checks*.

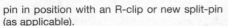

5 Rear brake pads – renewal

⚠️ *Warning: Renew BOTH sets of rear brake pads at the same time – NEVER renew the pads on only one wheel, as uneven braking may result. Note that the dust created by wear of the pads may contain asbestos, which is a health hazard. Never blow it out with compressed air, and don't inhale any of it. An approved filtering mask should be worn when working on the brakes. DO NOT use petroleum-based solvents to clean brake parts – use brake cleaner or methylated spirit only.*

1 The rear brake caliper is similar to the front brake caliper. Pad renewal can be carried out as described in Section 4 **(see illustrations)**. Note that on some models, shims will be fitted to the rear of the brake pad(s) (as applicable). Where this is so, note their correct fitted locations on removal, and ensure that they are correctly positioned on refitting **(see illustration)**.

6 Rear brake shoes – renewal

⚠️ *Warning: Brake shoes must be renewed on BOTH rear wheels at the same time – NEVER renew the shoes on only one wheel, as uneven braking may result. Also, the dust created by wear of the shoes may contain*

5.1d On vehicles from 2002 models year, coil type anti-rattle springs are fitted between the pads

asbestos, which is a health hazard. Never blow it out with compressed air, and don't inhale any of it. An approved filtering mask should be worn when working on the brakes. DO NOT use petroleum-based solvents to clean brake parts – use brake cleaner or methylated spirit only.

1 Remove the brake drum as described in Section 9.

2 Working carefully and taking the necessary precautions, remove all traces of brake dust from the brake drum, backplate and shoes.

3 Measure the thickness of the friction material of each brake shoe at several points. If the friction material thickness, or the depth from the friction material surface to any of the of rivet heads, is less than that specified, **all four** shoes must be renewed as a set. Also,

6.6a Where necessary, undo the two bolts . . .

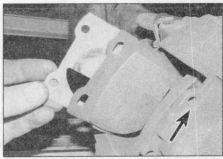

5.1e On some models, shims are fitted to the rear to the rear of the brake pads

Arrow shows normal direction of rotation

the shoes should be renewed if any are fouled with oil or grease; there is no satisfactory way of degreasing friction material, once contaminated.

4 If any of the brake shoes are worn unevenly or fouled with oil or grease, trace and rectify the cause before reassembly. If the shoes are to be renewed, proceed as described below. If all is well, refit the drums as described in Section 9.

5 Note the location and orientation of all components before dismantling, as an aid to reassembly.

6 Where necessary, bend down the locktabs, then undo the retaining bolts and remove the retaining plate and lockwasher from the shoe lower pivot point **(see illustrations)**.

7 Ease the lower ends of the shoes out from the pivot, then free the upper ends from the

6.6b . . . and remove the lockwasher and retaining plate from the shoe lower pivot point

6.8 Disconnect the return springs, and ease the assembly away from the backplate

6.9 Whilst the shoes are removed, wrap an elastic band around the wheel cylinder to prevent the pistons being accidentally expelled

6.17 Where necessary, securely tighten the retaining plate bolts, and secure them in position by bending up the lockwasher tabs against the bolt head flats

wheel cylinder, and remove the shoes and return springs from the backplate.

8 With the assembly on a bench, remove the return springs, noting their correct fitted locations, and separate the brake shoes **(see illustration)**.

9 Do not depress the brake pedal until the brakes are reassembled. As a precaution, wrap a strong elastic band around the wheel cylinder pistons to retain them **(see illustration)**.

10 Although linings are available separately (without shoes), renewal of the shoes complete with linings is to be preferred, unless the necessary skills and equipment are available to fit new linings to the old shoes.

11 Examine the return springs. If they are distorted, or if they have seen extensive service, renewal is advisable. Weak springs may cause the brakes to bind. Peel back the rubber protective caps, and check the wheel cylinder for fluid leaks or other damage. Also check that both cylinder pistons are free to move easily. Refer to Section 12, if necessary, for information on wheel cylinder overhaul.

12 Check that the shoe adjuster(s) rotates easily. If the adjuster(s) is/are damaged, a new backplate assembly will be required (see Chapter 9, Section 11).

13 Prior to installation, clean the backplate and apply a thin smear of high-temperature brake grease or anti-seize compound to all those surfaces of the backplate which bear on the shoes, particularly the wheel cylinder pistons and lower pivot point. Do not allow the lubricant to foul the friction material.

14 Assemble the new shoes and return springs, making sure that the return springs are fitted the correct way around.

15 Set both brake shoe adjusters to the minimum position, and remove the rubber band from the wheel cylinder.

16 Manoeuvre the shoes and springs into position, locating their upper ends with the piston slots, then ease the shoes onto the lower pivot point.

17 Where necessary, refit the retaining plate to the lower pivot point, and fit a new locking plate. Securely tighten the retaining bolts, and secure them in position by bending up the locking plate tabs against the bolt head flats **(see illustration)**.

18 Check that the shoes and springs are correctly located, then check the operation of the adjuster(s). Make sure that the shoe(s) move out smoothly and return easily under return spring pressure.

19 Refit the brake drum as described in Section 9.

20 Repeat the operation on the remaining brake.

21 On completion, check the hydraulic fluid level as described in *Weekly checks*.

---

7 Front brake disc – inspection, removal and refitting

Note: *Before starting work, refer to the note at the beginning of Section 4 concerning the dangers of asbestos dust.*

Inspection

Note: *If either disc requires renewal, BOTH should be renewed at the same time, to ensure even and consistent braking.*

1 Firmly apply the handbrake, then jack up the front of the car and support it on axle stands. Remove the appropriate front roadwheel.

2 Slowly rotate the brake disc so that the full area of both sides can be checked; remove the brake pads if better access is required to the inner surface. Light scoring is normal in the area swept by the brake pads, but if heavy scoring is found, the disc must be renewed.

3 It is normal to find a lip of rust and brake

7.3 Measuring brake disc thickness using a micrometer

dust around the disc's perimeter; this can be scraped off if required. If, however, a lip has formed due to excessive wear of the brake pad swept area, the disc's thickness must be measured using a micrometer **(see illustration)**. Take measurements at several places around the disc, at the inside and outside of the pad swept area. If any disc is found to be excessively worn, it may be possible to have it refinished, otherwise it will have to be renewed.

4 If the disc is thought to be warped, it can be checked for run-out as follows. Use a dial gauge mounted on any convenient fixed point, while the disc is slowly rotated, or use feeler blades to measure (at several points all around the disc) the clearance between the disc and a fixed point such as the brake caliper. If the measurements obtained indicate a run-out at the specified maximum or beyond, the disc is excessively warped and must be renewed; however, it is worth checking first that the axle hub bearing is in good condition (Chapter 9).

5 Check the disc for cracks, especially around the wheel studs, and for any other wear or damage.

Removal

6 Remove the front hub assembly as described in Chapter 9.

7 Using chalk or paint, make alignment marks between the disc and hub.

8 Slacken and remove the bolts securing the brake disc to the hub assembly, and separate the two components **(see illustration)**.

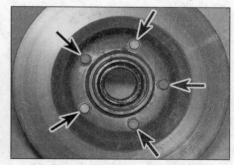

7.8 Front brake disc retaining bolts (arrowed)

Refitting

9 Refitting is the reverse of the removal procedure, noting the following points:
a) *Ensure that the mating surfaces of the disc and hub are clean and flat.*
b) *If a new disc has been fitted, use a suitable solvent to wipe any preservative coating from the disc before refitting the caliper.*
c) *Remove all traces of old locking compound from the brake disc holes in the hub assembly, ideally by running a tap of the correct size and pitch through them.*
d) *Fit the disc to the hub, aligning (if applicable) the marks made prior to removal.*
e) *Apply a suitable locking compound to the threads of the disc retaining bolts, then fit the bolts and tighten them to the specified torque setting.*
f) *Refit the roadwheel, lower the vehicle to the ground and tighten the roadwheel nuts to the specified torque. On completion, repeatedly depress the brake pedal until normal (non-assisted) pedal pressure returns.*

---

8 Rear brake disc – inspection, removal and refitting

Note: *Before starting work, refer to the note at the beginning of Section 5 concerning the dangers of asbestos dust.*

Inspection

1 Refer to Section 7.

Removal

2 Remove the rear hub assembly as described in Chapter 9. Using chalk or paint, make alignment marks between the disc and hub.
3 Slacken and remove the bolts securing the disc to the hub assembly, and separate the two.

Refitting

4 Refitting is the reverse of the removal procedure, noting the following points:
a) *Ensure that the mating surfaces of the disc and hub are clean and flat.*
b) *If a new disc has been fitted, use a suitable solvent to wipe any preservative coating from the disc before refitting the caliper.*
c) *Remove all traces of old locking compound from the brake disc holes in the hub assembly, ideally by running a tap of the correct size and pitch through them.*
d) *Fit the disc to the hub, aligning (if applicable) the marks made prior to removal.*
e) *Apply a suitable locking compound to the threads of the disc retaining bolts,*

then fit the bolts and tighten them to the specified torque setting.
f) *Refit the roadwheel, lower the vehicle to the ground and tighten the roadwheel nuts to the specified torque. On completion, repeatedly depress the brake pedal until normal (non-assisted) pedal pressure returns.*

---

9 Rear brake drum – removal, inspection and refitting

Note: *Before starting work, refer to the note at the beginning of Section 6 concerning the dangers of asbestos dust.*

Removal

1 Chock the front wheels, then jack up the rear of the vehicle and support it on axle stands. Remove the appropriate rear wheel.
2 Rotate each shoe adjuster on the backplate to position the shoes clear of the drum.
3 Undo the retaining screw(s), and remove the drum from the axle. If necessary, tap the drum with a soft-faced mallet to free it from the hub mating surface. If the hub still proves difficult to remove, screw a suitable bolt into the threaded hole in the drum, and use the bolt to push the drum off the hub flange **(see illustrations)**.

Inspection

Note: *If either drum requires renewal, BOTH should be renewed at the same time, to ensure even and consistent braking.*

4 Working carefully, remove all traces of brake dust from the drum, but *avoid inhaling the dust, as it is a health hazard.*
5 Scrub clean the outside of the drum, and check it for obvious signs of wear or damage such as cracks around the roadwheel stud holes; renew the drum if necessary, bearing in mind the note at the start of this sub-Section.
6 Examine carefully the inside of the drum. Light scoring of the friction surface is normal, but if heavy scoring is found, the drum must be renewed. It is usual to find a lip on the drum's inboard edge which consists of a mixture of rust and brake dust; this should be scraped away, to leave a smooth surface which can be

polished with fine (120- to 150-grade) emery paper. If, however, the lip is due to the friction surface being recessed by excessive wear, then the drum must be renewed.
7 If the drum is thought to be excessively worn, or oval, its internal diameter must be measured at several points using an internal micrometer. Take measurements in pairs, the second at right-angles to the first, and compare the two to check for signs of ovality. Since the manufacturer does not quote a specified maximum diameter for the brake drum, it will be necessary to seek the advice of your Land Rover dealer. It may be possible to have the drum refinished by skimming or grinding; if this is not possible, the drums on both sides must be renewed. Note that if the drum is to be skimmed, **both** drums must be refinished, to maintain consistent braking performance on both sides.

Refitting

8 If a new brake drum is to be installed, use a suitable solvent to remove any preservative coating that may have been applied to its interior.
9 Ensure that the hub and disc mating surfaces are clean and dry, and make sure that each shoe adjuster is fully retracted.
10 Slide the drum into position, making sure that it is correctly located on the hub flange. Refit the retaining screw(s), and tighten securely.
11 With the drum in position, rotate the leading shoe adjuster until the shoe is forced against the surface of the brake drum. From this point, back the adjuster off slightly, until it is felt to have travelled through two notches of the adjuster snail cam.
12 Check the brake drum rotates freely and, where necessary, repeat the operation on the trailing shoe adjuster.
13 When the adjuster(s) correctly set, depress the brake pedal repeatedly until normal (non-assisted) pedal pressure is restored.
14 Check that the brake drum still rotates easily, then refit the roadwheel.
15 Lower the vehicle to the ground, and tighten the wheel nuts to the specified torque setting.

9.3a Removing a drum retaining screw

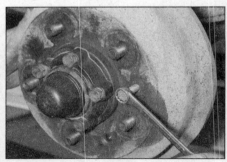

9.3b If necessary, the drum can be released from the hub by screwing a suitable bolt into the threaded hole provided

10 Front brake caliper –
removal, overhaul and refitting

Note: *Before starting work, refer to the note at the beginning of Section 2 concerning the dangers of hydraulic fluid, and to the warning at the beginning of Section 4 concerning the dangers of asbestos dust.*

Removal

1 Apply the handbrake, then jack up the front of the vehicle and support it on axle stands. Remove the appropriate roadwheel.
2 Remove the brake pads as described in Section 4.
3 To minimise fluid loss, remove the master cylinder reservoir cap, then tighten it down onto a piece of polythene to obtain an airtight seal. Alternatively, use a brake hose clamp, a G-clamp or a similar tool to clamp the flexible hose at the nearest convenient point to the caliper.

4 Clean the area around the caliper brake hose union nut. Undo the union nut, and disconnect the brake pipe from the caliper. Plug the hose end and caliper hole, to minimise fluid loss and to prevent the ingress of dirt into the hydraulic system.
5 Slacken and remove the two retaining bolts, and remove the caliper assembly from the vehicle.

Overhaul

Note: *Prior to dismantling the caliper, check the availability of spares from your Land Rover dealer; on some models, it may prove difficult to obtain caliper components.*
6 With the caliper on the bench, wipe away all traces of dust and dirt, but *avoid inhaling the dust, as it is a health hazard* **(see illustration)**.
7 Push both the pistons on one side of the caliper fully into the caliper bore and retain them in position with a suitable G-clamp.
8 Withdraw both the partially-ejected pistons from the opposite side of the caliper body. The pistons can be withdrawn by hand, if loose. If one or both of the pistons are not

loose enough to be withdrawn by hand, they can be pushed out by applying compressed air to the (relevant) brake hose union hole. Only low pressure should be required, such as is generated by a foot pump. **Note:** *Ensure that both pistons are expelled from the caliper at the same time.*
9 Extract both pistons from the caliper. Mark identification marks between the caliper and bore, to ensure that each piston is refitted to its original bore.
10 Using a small screwdriver, carefully remove the wiper seal retainer from the caliper, taking great care not to mark the bore. Repeating the procedure, remove the wiper seal and piston (fluid) seal in the same way.
11 Thoroughly clean all components, using only methylated spirit, isopropyl alcohol or clean hydraulic fluid as a cleaning medium. Never use mineral-based solvents such as petrol or paraffin, as they will attack the hydraulic system's rubber components. Dry the components immediately, using compressed air or a clean, lint-free cloth. Use compressed air to blow clear the fluid passages.

⚠ *Warning: Wear eye protection when using compressed air.*

12 Check all components, and renew any that are worn or damaged. Check particularly the cylinder bores and pistons; these should be renewed if they are scratched, worn or corroded in any way.
13 If the assembly is fit for further use, obtain the necessary components from your Land Rover dealer or specialist. Renew the caliper seals and retainers as a matter of course; these should never be re-used.
14 On reassembly, ensure that all components are absolutely clean and dry.
15 Soak the pistons and the new piston (fluid) seals in clean hydraulic fluid. Smear clean fluid on the cylinder bore surface.
16 Fit the new piston (fluid) seals, using fingers only (no tools) to manipulate them into the cylinder bore grooves.
17 Ensure that the piston (fluid) seals are correctly located, then fit the new wiper seals in the same way.
18 Make sure that each wiper seal is correctly seated, then install the new wiper seal retainers in the caliper body, ensuring that both are fitted the correct way around.
19 Fit each piston using a twisting motion, ensuring that they enter the caliper bore squarely. If the original pistons are being re-used, use the marks made on removal to ensure that they are refitted to the correct bores.
20 Remove the G-clamp from the caliper, and repeat the operations described in paragraphs 7 to 19 on the remaining two pistons in the caliper.

Refitting

21 Refit the caliper assembly to the vehicle, apply a little thread locking compound and tighten its retaining bolts to the specified torque setting.

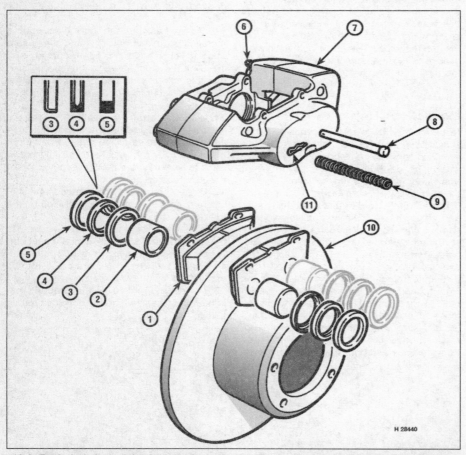

10.6 Exploded view of the front brake caliper and associated components. Inset shows cross-section of each seal – later models shown (early models similar)

1 *Brake pad*	5 *Fluid seal*	9 *Anti-rattle spring*
2 *Piston*	6 *Bleed screw*	10 *Brake disc*
3 *Wiper seal retainer*	7 *Caliper*	11 *R-clip*
4 *Wiper seal*	8 *Pad retaining pin*	

22 Refit the brake pipe to the caliper, tightening the union nut to the specified torque setting.

23 Refit the brake pads as described in Section 4.

24 Remove the brake hose clamp or polythene, where fitted, and bleed the hydraulic system as described in Section 2. Note that, providing the precautions described were taken to minimise brake fluid loss, it should only be necessary to bleed the relevant front brake.

25 Refit the roadwheel, then lower the vehicle to the ground and tighten the roadwheel nuts to the specified torque.

11 Rear brake caliper –
removal, overhaul and refitting

Note: *Before starting work, refer to the note at the beginning of Section 2 concerning the dangers of hydraulic fluid, and to the warning at the beginning of Section 5 concerning the dangers of asbestos dust.*

Removal

1 Chock the front wheels, then jack up the rear of the vehicle and support on axle stands. Remove the relevant rear wheel.

2 Remove the brake pads as described in Section 5.

3 To minimise fluid loss, remove the master cylinder reservoir cap, then tighten it down onto a piece of polythene to obtain an airtight seal. Alternatively, use a brake hose clamp, a G-clamp or a similar tool to clamp the flexible hose at the nearest convenient point to the brake caliper.

4 Wipe away all traces of dirt around the brake pipe union on the caliper, then undo the union nut and disconnect the brake pipe from the caliper. Plug the hose end and caliper hole, to minimise fluid loss and to prevent the ingress of dirt into the hydraulic system.

5 Slacken the two bolts securing the caliper assembly in position. Lift the caliper assembly away from the disc, and remove it from the vehicle.

Overhaul

Note: *Prior to dismantling the caliper, check the availability of spares from your Land Rover dealer or specialist; on some models, it may prove difficult to obtain caliper components.*

6 With the caliper on the bench, wipe away all traces of dust and dirt, but *avoid inhaling the dust, as it is a health hazard* (**see illustration**).

7 Push the piston on one side of the caliper fully into the caliper bore, and retain it in position with a suitable G-clamp.

8 Withdraw the partially ejected piston from the opposite side of the caliper body. The piston can be withdrawn by hand, if loose, or can be pushed out by applying compressed air to the brake hose union hole. Only low pressure should be required, such as is generated by a foot pump.

9 Using a small screwdriver, carefully remove the wiper seal retainer from the caliper, taking great care not to mark the bore. Repeating the procedure, remove the wiper seal and piston (fluid) seal in the same way.

10 Thoroughly clean all components, using only methylated spirit, isopropyl alcohol or clean hydraulic fluid as a cleaning medium. Never use mineral-based solvents such as petrol or paraffin, as they will attack the hydraulic system's rubber components. Dry the components immediately, using compressed air or a clean, lint-free cloth. Use compressed air to blow clear the fluid passages.

⚠ *Warning: Wear eye protection when using compressed air.*

11 Check all components, and renew any that are worn or damaged. Check particularly the cylinder bore and piston; these should be renewed if they are scratched, worn or corroded in any way.

12 If the assembly is fit for further use, obtain the necessary components from your Land Rover dealer or specialist. Renew the caliper seals and retainers as a matter of course; these should never be re-used.

13 On reassembly, ensure that all components are absolutely clean and dry.

14 Soak the piston and new piston (fluid) seal in clean hydraulic fluid. Smear clean fluid on the cylinder bore surface.

15 Fit the new piston (fluid) seal, using fingers only (no tools) to manipulate it into the cylinder bore groove.

16 Ensure that the piston (fluid) seal is correctly located, then fit the new wiper seal in the same way.

17 Make sure that the wiper seal is correctly seated, then install the new wiper seal retainer in the caliper body, ensuring that it is fitted the correct way around.

18 Fit the piston using a twisting motion, ensuring that it enters the caliper bore squarely.

19 Remove the G-clamp from the caliper, and repeat the operations described in paragraphs 7 to 18 on the remaining caliper piston.

Refitting

20 Refit the caliper assembly to the vehicle, and tighten its retaining bolts to the specified torque setting.

21 Refit the brake pipe to the caliper, and tighten its union nut to the specified torque setting.

22 Refit the brake pads as described in Section 5.

23 Remove the brake hose clamp or

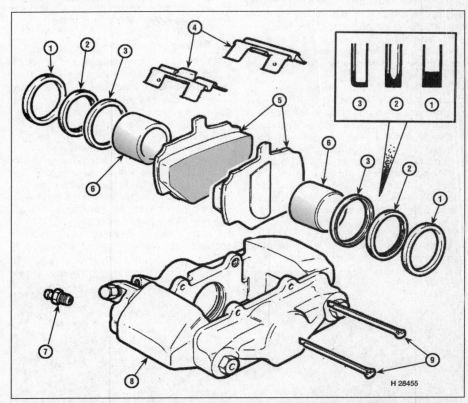

11.6 Exploded view of the rear brake caliper and associated components. Inset shows cross-section of each seal

1 Fluid seal	4 Anti-rattle springs	7 Bleed screw
2 Wiper seal	5 Brake pads	8 Caliper
3 Wiper seal retainer	6 Piston	9 Pad retaining pins

polythene, as applicable, and bleed the hydraulic system as described in Section 2. Providing the precautions described were taken to minimise brake fluid loss, it should only be necessary to bleed the relevant rear brake.

24 Refit the roadwheel, then lower the vehicle to the ground and tighten the roadwheel nuts to the specified torque.

12 Rear wheel cylinder – removal, overhaul and refitting

Note: *Before starting work, refer to the note at the beginning of Section 2 concerning the dangers of hydraulic fluid, and to the warning at the beginning of Section 6 concerning the dangers of asbestos dust.*

Removal

1 Remove the brake drum as described in Section 9.

2 Using pliers, carefully unhook the upper brake shoe return spring, and remove it from both brake shoes. Pull the upper ends of the shoes away from the wheel cylinder, to disengage them from the pistons.

3 To minimise fluid loss, remove the master cylinder reservoir cap, then tighten it down onto a piece of polythene to obtain an airtight seal. Alternatively, use a brake hose clamp, a G-clamp or a similar tool to clamp the flexible hose at the nearest convenient point to the wheel cylinder.

4 Wipe away all traces of dirt around the brake pipe union at the rear of the wheel cylinder, and unscrew the union nut. Carefully ease the pipe out of the wheel cylinder, and plug or tape over its end to prevent dirt entry. Wipe off any spilt fluid immediately.

5 Unscrew the two wheel cylinder retaining nuts and washers from the rear of the backplate. Remove the cylinder, taking great care not to allow surplus hydraulic fluid to contaminate the brake shoe linings.

Overhaul

6 Brush the dirt and dust from the wheel cylinder, but take care not to inhale it.

7 Pull the rubber dust seals from the ends of the cylinder body.

8 The pistons will normally be ejected by the pressure of the coil spring, but if they are not, tap the end of the cylinder body on a piece of wood, or apply low air pressure (eg, from a foot pump) to the hydraulic fluid union hole to eject the pistons from their bores.

9 Recover the seals from each piston, noting which way around they are fitted.

10 Inspect the surfaces of the pistons and their bores in the cylinder body for scoring, or evidence of metal-to-metal contact. If evident, renew the complete wheel cylinder assembly.

11 If the pistons and bores are in good condition, discard the seals and obtain a repair kit, which will contain all the necessary renewable items.

12 Lubricate the piston seals with clean brake fluid, and fit them onto the pistons. Use finger pressure only to install the seals, and make sure that they are fitted the correct way around **(see illustration)**.

13 Dip the pistons in clean brake fluid, and insert them into the cylinder bores, not forgetting to fit the spring in between them **(see illustrations)**.

14 Fit the dust seals, making sure that they are correctly located in their grooves on both the pistons and cylinder, then check that the pistons can move freely in their bores.

Refitting

15 Ensure that the backplate and wheel cylinder mating surfaces are clean, then spread the brake shoes and manoeuvre the wheel cylinder into position.

16 Engage the brake pipe, and screw in the union nut two or three turns to ensure that the thread has started.

17 Refit the wheel cylinder washers and retaining nuts, and tighten them to the specified torque setting. Now tighten the brake pipe union nut to the specified torque.

18 Remove the clamp from the flexible brake hose, or the polythene from the master cylinder reservoir (as applicable).

19 Ensure that the brake shoes are correctly located in the cylinder pistons, then carefully refit the brake shoe upper return spring,

using a screwdriver to stretch the spring into position.

20 Refit the brake drum as described in Section 9.

21 Bleed the brake hydraulic system as described in Section 2. Providing suitable precautions were taken to minimise loss of fluid, it should only be necessary to bleed the relevant rear brake.

13 Master cylinder – removal, overhaul and refitting

Note: *Before starting work, refer to the warning at the beginning of Section 2 concerning the dangers of hydraulic fluid.*

Removal

1 Disconnect the wiring connector from the brake fluid level sender unit. Remove the master cylinder reservoir cap, and syphon the hydraulic fluid from the reservoir. **Note:** *Do not syphon the fluid by mouth, as it is poisonous; use a syringe or an old poultry baster.* Alternatively, open any convenient bleed screw in the system, and gently pump the brake pedal to expel the fluid through a plastic tube connected to the screw (see Section 2).

2 Wipe clean the area around the brake pipe unions on the side of the master cylinder, and place absorbent rags beneath the pipe unions to catch any surplus fluid. Make a note of the correct fitted positions of the unions, then unscrew the union nuts and carefully withdraw the pipes. Wash off any spilt fluid immediately with cold water. Plug or tape over the pipe ends and master cylinder orifices, to minimise the loss of brake fluid and to prevent the entry of dirt into the system.

3 Slacken and remove the two nuts and washers securing the master cylinder to the vacuum servo unit. Withdraw the master cylinder assembly from the engine compartment, and recover the O-ring from the rear of the cylinder.

Overhaul

Note: *Refer to 'Vehicle identification numbers' section at the end of this book for information on VIN numbers.*

12.12 Carefully ease the seals onto the piston, making sure they are fitted the correct way around

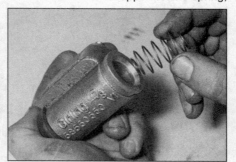

12.13a Fit the first piston assembly to the cylinder, then install the spring . . .

12.13b . . . and fit the second piston assembly

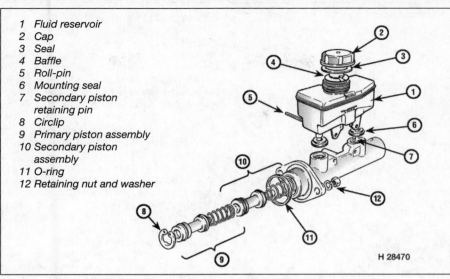

1 Fluid reservoir
2 Cap
3 Seal
4 Baffle
5 Roll-pin
6 Mounting seal
7 Secondary piston
   retaining pin
8 Circlip
9 Primary piston assembly
10 Secondary piston
   assembly
11 O-ring
12 Retaining nut and washer

13.4 Exploded view of the master cylinder – early models

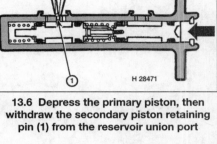

13.6 Depress the primary piston, then withdraw the secondary piston retaining pin (1) from the reservoir union port

Note: *Prior to dismantling the master cylinder, check the availability of spares from your Land Rover dealer or specialist.*

Early models – up to VIN HA701009 (90 models) or HA901220 (110 models)

4 Remove all traces of dirt from the exterior of the assembly, then tap out the roll-pins securing the reservoir in position **(see illustration)**.

5 Ease the reservoir out from the master cylinder, and recover the two mounting seals from the cylinder ports.

6 Secure the master cylinder in a vice with soft jaws. Using a suitable wooden dowel, depress the master cylinder primary piston then, using a pair of pointed-nose pliers, withdraw the secondary piston retaining pin from the front master cylinder reservoir union port **(see illustration)**.

7 Depress the primary piston again and, using circlip pliers, remove the circlip from the rear of the master cylinder body.

8 Gently release the primary piston, and withdraw the piston assembly from the master cylinder.

9 Tap the master cylinder body on a clean wooden surface, and withdraw the secondary piston and spring assembly, noting each component's correct fitted location.

10 Thoroughly clean all components, using only methylated spirit, isopropyl alcohol or clean hydraulic fluid as a cleaning medium. Never use mineral-based solvents such as petrol or paraffin, as they will attack the hydraulic system's rubber components. Dry the components immediately, using compressed air or a clean, lint-free cloth.

11 Check all components, and renew any that are worn or damaged. Check particularly the cylinder bore and pistons; the complete assembly should be renewed if these are scratched, worn or corroded. If there is any doubt about the condition of the assembly or of any of its components, renew it. Check that the body's fluid passages are clear.

12 If the assembly is fit for further use, obtain a repair kit from your Land Rover dealer. The kit consists of the primary piston assembly, all seals and springs, as well as a rear housing. Renew all seals disturbed on dismantling, and the rear housing, as a matter of course; these should never be re-used.

13 Prior to reassembly, soak the piston assemblies and all new seals in clean hydraulic fluid. Smear clean fluid into the cylinder bore.

14 Taking great care not to damage the piston, unscrew the retaining screw, and remove the spring and spring seat from the primary piston **(see illustration)**. Note each component's correct fitted location, then slide off the seal retainer and remove the inner seal and washer from the piston. Using a small flat-bladed screwdriver, carefully remove the outer seal from the rear of the piston. Manoeuvre the new outer seal carefully into the piston groove, then fit the new washer, inner seal and retainer to the piston. Make sure that both seals are fitted the correct way around, then fit the new spring and spring seat, tighten the spring retaining bolt to 3 Nm. **Note:** *Do not overtighten the bolt.*

15 Using a small flat-bladed screwdriver, remove the seal retainer from the inner end of the secondary piston, and slide off the inner piston seal and washer **(see illustration)**. Remove the outer seal, taking great care not to mark the piston. Carefully manipulate the new outer seal into position on the piston, making sure that it is the correct way around. Fit the washer and inner seal, again making sure that it is the correct way around, and secure it in position with the seal retainer.

16 Locate the spring on the end of the secondary piston assembly, and insert the assembly into the master cylinder body. Insert the piston assembly using a twisting motion, ensuring that the piston seals do not become trapped as they enter the cylinder.

17 Fit the new primary piston assembly as described above.

18 With both piston assemblies in position, depress the primary piston, and install the circlip. Make sure that the circlip is correctly located in the master cylinder groove, then release the piston.

19 Depress the piston again, and refit the secondary piston retaining pin to the front reservoir union port.

20 Ensure that the retaining pin is correctly

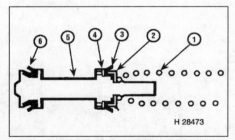

13.14 Primary piston components – early models

1 Spring retainer
2 Spring
3 Seal retainer
4 Inner seal
5 Washer
6 Spring retainer screw
7 Outer seal

13.15 Secondary piston components – early models

1 Spring
2 Seal retainer
3 Inner seal
4 Washer
5 Piston
6 Outer seal

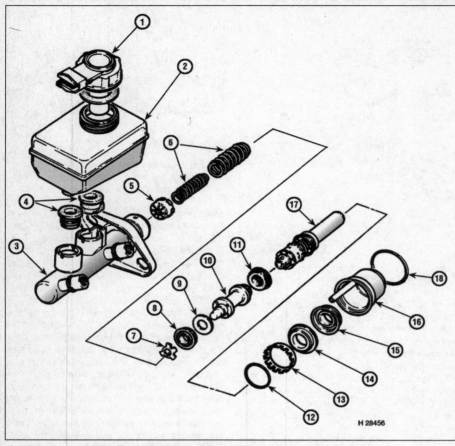

13.21 Exploded view of the master cylinder – later models

1 Cap (incorporating fluid level sender unit)	7 Seal retainer	14 Guide ring
	8 Seal	15 Vacuum seal
2 Fluid reservoir	9 Washer	16 Rear housing cover
3 Master cylinder	10 Secondary piston	17 Primary piston
4 Mounting seals	11 Seal	assembly
5 Swirl tube	12 O-ring seal	18 O-ring
6 Springs	13 Retaining ring	

located, then fit the new reservoir seals to the master cylinder. Engage the reservoir with the master cylinder, and secure it in position with both roll-pins. Remove the baffle plate and seal from the reservoir cap, and fit the new ones supplied in the repair kit.

Later models – from VIN HA701010 (90 models) or HA901221 (110 models)

21 Carefully ease the reservoir out from the master cylinder body, and recover the two mounting seals from the master cylinder ports, noting each seal's correct fitted location **(see illustration)**.
22 Carefully grip the master cylinder body in a vice with soft jaws. Using a suitable pair of grips, ease the rear housing cover out from the cylinder. The housing should come away complete with the vacuum seal.
23 Carefully remove the retaining ring from the master cylinder, along with its O-ring.
24 Ease the guide ring out from the rear of the master cylinder. **Note:** *The guide is not*

supplied with the repair kit, and will have to be re-used, so take care not to damage it.
25 Withdraw the primary piston assembly from the cylinder.
26 Noting the order of removal and the direction of fitting of each component, tap the body on a clean wooden surface, and withdraw the secondary piston assembly,

springs and swirl tube from the master cylinder. Note which way around the swirl tube is fitted.
27 Thoroughly clean all components, using only methylated spirit, isopropyl alcohol or clean hydraulic fluid as a cleaning medium. Never use mineral-based solvents such as petrol or paraffin, as they will attack the hydraulic system's rubber components. Dry the components immediately, using compressed air or a clean, lint-free cloth.
28 Check all components, and renew any that are worn or damaged. Check particularly the cylinder bores and pistons; the complete assembly should be renewed if these are scratched, worn or corroded. If there is any doubt about the condition of the assembly or of any of its components, renew it. Check that the body's fluid passages are clear.
29 If the assembly is fit for further use, obtain a repair kit from your Land Rover dealer or specialist. The kit consists of the primary piston assembly, all seals and springs, as well as a rear housing. Renew all seals disturbed on dismantling, and the rear housing, as a matter of course; these should never be re-used.
30 Prior to reassembly, soak the piston assemblies and all new seals in clean hydraulic fluid. Smear clean fluid into the cylinder bore.
31 Using a small flat-bladed screwdriver, remove the seal retainer from the inner end of the secondary piston, and slide off the inner piston seal and washer. Remove the outer seal, taking great care not to mark the piston. Carefully manipulate the new outer seal into position on the piston, making sure that it is the correct way around. Fit the washer and inner seal, again making sure that it is correct way around, and secure it in position with the seal retainer **(see illustration)**.
32 Fit the new swirl tube to the master cylinder bore, ensuring that it is fitted the correct way around.
33 Locate both springs on the end of the secondary piston assembly, and insert the assembly into the master cylinder body. Insert the piston assembly using a twisting motion, ensuring that the piston seals do not become trapped as they enter the cylinder.
34 Fit the new primary piston assembly as described above.

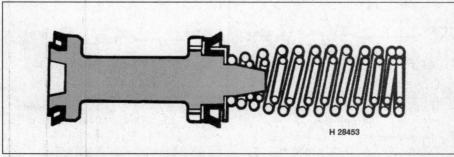

13.31 Assemble the secondary piston and associated components as shown, noting that the inner and outer seals are different

14.3 Disconnect the wiring from the stop-light switch, which is mounted onto the rear of the brake pedal bracket

14.5a Slacken and remove the six retaining bolts (one hidden behind pedal) . . .

14.5b . . . then manoeuvre the pedal box assembly out through the engine compartment

35 With both piston assemblies in position, refit the guide ring to the end of the cylinder bore.

36 Fit the smaller O-ring to the groove on the master cylinder body.

37 Fit the new vacuum seal to the new rear housing, making sure that its sealing lip is correctly positioned (facing the towards the primary piston).

38 Fit the new retaining ring to the rear of the master cylinder body, so that its teeth are in contact with the cylinder body.

39 Carefully ease the rear housing assembly into position on the master cylinder, and press it fully into the cylinder body. Fit the larger O-ring to the outside of the housing.

Refitting

40 Inspect the master cylinder O-ring for signs of damage or deterioration and, if necessary, renew it.

41 Remove all traces of dirt from the master cylinder and servo unit mating surfaces, then fit the master cylinder, ensuring that the servo unit pushrod enters the master cylinder bore centrally. Refit the master cylinder washers and mounting nuts, and tighten them to the specified torque.

42 Wipe clean the brake pipe unions, then refit them to the master cylinder ports and tighten them to the specified torque setting.

43 Refill the master cylinder reservoir with new fluid, and bleed the complete hydraulic system as described in Section 2.

14 Brake pedal –
removal and refitting

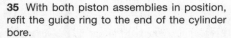

Removal

1 Disconnect the battery negative terminal, as described in Chapter 5.

2 Slacken and remove the retaining nuts and washers securing the master cylinder to the servo unit. Disengage the master cylinder from the servo, and position it clear, taking great care not to place any excess strain on the brake pipes. Recover the O-ring from the rear of the master cylinder.

3 Disconnect the wiring from the stop-light switch (see illustration).

4 From within the vehicle, undo the retaining

screws and remove the trim panel from around the pedals, to reveal the pedal box retaining bolts.

5 Unscrew the six retaining bolts, then return to the engine compartment and lift out the pedal box assembly. Recover the rubber seal fitted between the box and bulkhead (see illustrations).

6 With the assembly on the bench, carefully unhook the return springs from the base of the brake pedal (see illustration).

7 Prise out the rubber sealing grommets, then remove the split-pin and washer, and withdraw the clevis pin securing the pedal to the servo unit pushrod (see illustrations).

8 Using a hammer and punch, tap out the roll-pin securing the pedal pivot shaft in position, then slide out the shaft and remove the pedal (see illustrations).

14.6 Unhook the pedal return springs using a pair of pliers

14.7a Remove the rubber grommets from the pedal box . . .

14.7b . . . then remove the split-pin and washer, and withdraw the clevis pin and washer securing the servo unit to the pedal

14.8a Tap out the roll-pin . . .

14.8b . . . then withdraw the pivot shaft and remove the pedal from its mounting box

14.9 Inspect the pedal pivot bushes for signs of wear or damage, and renew if necessary

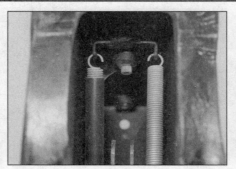

14.11 Prior to refitting, ensure that the return springs are correctly engaged with the holes in the mounting box

14.13 Align the servo unit pushrod with the pedal, then refit the clevis pin and washers, and secure in position with a new split-pin

9 Inspect the pedal pivot bushes and shaft for signs of wear, and renew if necessary **(see illustration)**.

Refitting

10 Press the pivot bushes into the pedal bore.

11 Apply a smear of multi-purpose grease to the bushes, and fit the return springs to the pedal mounting box **(see illustration)**.

12 Manoeuvre the pedal assembly into position, ensuring that it is correctly engaged with the servo pushrod, and insert the pivot shaft. Secure the pivot shaft in position with the roll-pin.

13 Align the pedal hole with the pushrod end, and insert the clevis pin. Refit the washer, and secure the pin in position with a new split-pin **(see illustration)**. Refit the sealing grommets to the box.

14 Refit the seal to the bulkhead, then manoeuvre the pedal box assembly into position.

15 Refit the pedal box retaining bolts, tighten them securely, then refit the pedal trim panel.

16 Return to the engine compartment, and reconnect the wiring connectors to the stop-light switch.

17 Ensure that the seal is in position, and refit the master cylinder to the servo unit. Fit the washers and retaining nuts, tightening them to the specified torque.

18 Reconnect the battery, and check the operation of the brake pedal and stop-light switch.

---

15 Vacuum servo unit – testing, removal and refitting

Testing

1 To test the operation of the servo unit, with the engine switched off, depress the footbrake several times to exhaust the vacuum. Keeping the pedal depressed, start the engine. As the engine starts, there should be a noticeable 'give' in the brake pedal as the vacuum builds-up. Allow the engine to run for at least two minutes, then switch it off. If the brake pedal is now depressed it should feel normal, but further applications should result in the pedal feeling firmer, with the pedal stroke decreasing with each application.

2 If the servo does not operate as described, first inspect the servo unit check valve as described in Section 16.

3 If the servo unit still fails to operate satisfactorily, the fault lies within the unit itself. On early models, it is possible to overhaul the unit but this is a task which should be entrusted to a Land Rover dealer. On later models, repairs to the unit are not possible, and if faulty the servo unit must be renewed.

Removal

4 Disconnect the battery negative terminal, as described in Chapter 5.

5 Slacken and remove the retaining nuts and washers securing the master cylinder to the servo unit **(see illustration)**. Disengage the master cylinder from the servo, and position it clear, taking great care not to place any excess strain on the brake pipes. Recover the O-ring from the rear of the master cylinder.

6 Release the retaining clip (where fitted), and disconnect the vacuum hose from the servo unit check valve **(see illustration)**.

7 Prise out the rubber sealing grommets from the brake pedal mounting box.

8 Working through the mounting box aperture, remove the split-pin and washer, and withdraw the clevis pin securing the pedal to the servo unit pushrod.

9 Slacken and remove the four nuts and washers securing the servo unit to the pedal mounting bracket, and lift the servo unit out of position.

10 Recover the rubber seal which is fitted between the servo unit and bracket. Examine the seal for signs of damage or deterioration, and renew if necessary.

Refitting

11 Apply a smear of grease to the pushrod fork, fit the rubber seal to the rear of the servo unit, and manoeuvre the assembly into position.

12 Ensure that the servo unit pushrod is correctly engaged with the brake pedal, then refit the washers and mounting nuts, and tighten them to the specified torque setting.

13 Align the pedal hole with the pushrod end, and insert the clevis pin. Refit the washer, and secure the pin in position with a new split-pin. Refit the sealing grommets to the box.

14 Reconnect the vacuum hose to the servo unit check valve.

15 Ensure that the seal is in position, then refit the master cylinder, tightening its retaining nuts to the specified torque.

15.5 Slacken and remove the retaining nuts and washers, and free the master cylinder from the front of the servo unit

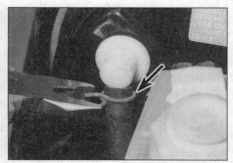

15.6 Release the retaining clip, and disconnect the vacuum hose from the servo unit check valve

16 Vacuum servo unit check valve – removal, testing and refitting

Removal

1 Slacken the retaining clip (where fitted), and disconnect the vacuum hose from the servo unit check valve.
2 Withdraw the valve from its rubber sealing grommet, using a pulling and twisting motion. Remove the grommet from the servo **(see illustration)**.

Testing

3 Examine the check valve for signs of damage, and renew if necessary. The valve may be tested by blowing through it in both directions. Air should flow through the valve in one direction only – when blown through from the servo unit end of the valve. Renew the valve if this is not the case.
4 Examine the rubber sealing grommet and flexible vacuum hose for signs of damage or deterioration, and renew as necessary.

Refitting

5 Fit the sealing grommet into position in the servo unit.
6 Carefully ease the check valve into position, taking great care not to displace or damage the grommet. Reconnect the vacuum hose to the valve and, where necessary, securely tighten its retaining clip.
7 On completion, start the engine, and check the check valve-to-servo unit connection for signs of air leaks.

17 Handbrake shoes – renewal

Note: There are two types of handbrake assembly fitted. To distinguish which type is fitted, examine the rear of the handbrake assembly. On early models, the brake assembly is operated by a cable attached to a rod operating linkage which is mounted onto the transfer box. On later models, the brake assembly is operated directly by cable.

1 Chock the front wheels, then jack up the rear of the vehicle and support on axle stands.
2 Working as described in Chapter 8, disconnect the propeller shaft from the rear of the transfer box, and position the shaft clear of the handbrake assembly.
3 Apply the handbrake, then slacken and remove the handbrake drum retaining screw(s) **(see illustration)**.
4 Release the handbrake, and remove the brake drum from the rear of the transfer box. It may be difficult to remove the drum, due to the brake shoes binding on the inner circumference of the drum. If the brake shoes are binding, first check that the handbrake is fully released then, referring to Chapter 1 for

16.2 Withdraw the check valve from the servo unit, and recover the rubber grommet (arrowed)

further information, fully slacken the handbrake cable adjuster nut to obtain maximum freeplay in the cable, and rotate the adjuster bolt anti-clockwise so that the shoes are retracted clear of the drum. The brake drum should then slide easily off the transfer box.
5 With the drum removed, inspect the shoes for signs of wear or damage. If the friction material of either shoe has worn down to, or close to, the rivets, the shoes must be renewed. The shoes should also be renewed if any are fouled with oil; there is no satisfactory way of degreasing friction material, once contaminated. If there are traces of oil on the shoes, the transfer box output shaft seal should be renewed before new handbrake

17.3 Removing the handbrake drum retaining screw

shoes are fitted (see Chapter 7B). Proceed as described under the relevant sub-heading.

Rod-actuated brakes

6 To remove the shoes, note the correct fitted locations of the shoes and springs, then carefully unhook the shoes from the expander and adjuster assemblies **(see illustration)**. Remove the shoes and return spring assembly from the backplate, and separate the components.
7 Whilst the shoes are removed, take the opportunity to inspect the expander and adjuster assemblies as follows.
8 Operate the expander drawlink, and check that both plungers are free to move easily in

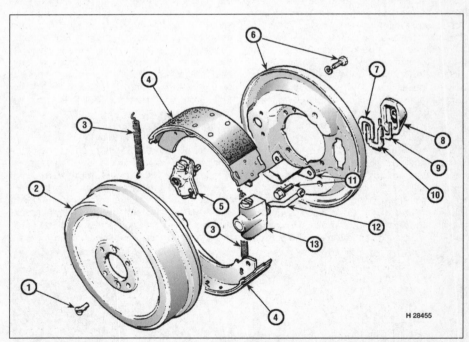

17.6 Exploded view of the handbrake assembly components – early models (with rod-actuated brake assembly)

1 Retaining screw	6 Backplate and retaining bolt	10 Packing plate
2 Drum	7 Spring plate	11 Oil catcher and retaining bolt (where fitted)
3 Return springs	8 Rubber cover	12 Drawlink
4 Shoe	9 Retaining clip	13 Expander assembly
5 Adjuster assembly		

the expander body. If necessary, withdraw both the plungers and their rollers from the expander body, and remove all traces of corrosion from them. Apply a smear of high-temperature grease to both rollers and the plungers, and refit them to the expander assembly. If this does not cure the problem, the expander assembly must be renewed as follows. Withdraw the split-pin and clevis pin securing the drawlink to the actuating mechanism, then undo the four bolts and remove the backplate assembly and oil catcher (where fitted) from the rear of the transfer box. Peel back the rubber cover from the rear of the expander, then slide out the horseshoe-type retaining clip and recover the spring plate and packing plate, noting their correct fitted locations. Withdraw the expander assembly from the backplate. Install the new expander, securing it in position with the spring plate, packing plate and retaining clip, then fit the rubber cover to the rear of the assembly. Refit the oil catcher (where fitted) and backplate assembly to the transfer box, and tighten its retaining bolts. Apply a smear of grease to the clevis pin, then align the drawlink with the operating rod and slide in the pin, securing it in position with a new split-pin.

9 Rotate the adjuster bolt, and check that both the adjuster plungers are free to move easily. If necessary, withdraw both the plungers from the adjuster, and unscrew the adjuster bolt. Remove all traces of corrosion from them, and apply a smear of high-temperature grease to both the plungers and adjuster bolt threads. Screw the adjuster bolt into position, and refit the plungers. If this does not cure the problem, the adjuster assembly must be renewed. To renew the adjuster, undo the two retaining bolts and washers, and remove it from the backplate. Install the new adjuster assembly, and securely tighten the retaining bolts.

10 With both adjuster and expander assemblies operating correctly, apply a smear of high melting-point grease to the contact areas of the new shoes and backplate. Take care to ensure that the grease does not contaminate the friction material.

11 Position the handbrake shoes so that the fully-lined end of the lower shoe is next to the expander assembly, and the fully-lined end of the upper shoe is next to the adjuster

assembly. Engage the new return springs with the shoes, then install the shoes and springs as an assembly.

12 Make sure that each shoe is correctly located on the adjuster plunger slots, then refit the brake drum. Refit the brake drum retaining screws, and tighten them securely.

13 Adjust the cable as described in Chapter 1, then check the operation of the handbrake.

14 If all is well, reconnect the propeller shaft to the transfer box as described in Chapter 8.

Cable-actuated brakes

15 Note the correct fitted locations of all components then, using a suitable pair of pliers, unhook the return springs and remove them from the brake shoes.

16 Using a pair of pliers, remove the left-hand shoe retainer spring cup by depressing and turning it through 90°. With the cup removed, lift off the spring and withdraw the retainer pin from the rear of the backplate.

17 Remove the left-hand shoe, and recover the strut which is fitted between the shoe upper ends, noting which way around it is fitted.

18 Remove the right-hand shoe spring cup, spring and retainer pin as described in paragraph 16, then detach the shoe from the handbrake cable and remove it from the vehicle.

19 If the new handbrake shoes are supplied without the operating lever already fitted to the right-hand shoe, it will be necessary to transfer the old one over from the original shoe. Remove the spring clip, then withdraw the pivot pin and recover the spring washers, noting their correct fitted positions. Inspect the pivot pin and spring clip for signs of wear or damage, and renew if necessary. Apply a smear of high melting-point grease to the pin, then fit the operating lever to the new shoe, and insert the pin and spring washers, securing them in position with the spring clip.

20 Whilst the shoes are removed, rotate the adjuster bolt, and check that both the adjuster plungers are free to move easily. If necessary, withdraw both the plungers from the adjuster, and unscrew the adjuster bolt and tapered nut. Remove all traces of corrosion from them, and apply a smear of high-temperature grease to both the plungers and adjuster bolt threads. Screw the adjuster bolt and tapered

nut into position, and refit the plungers. If this does not cure the problem, renew the adjuster assembly components.

21 With the adjuster assembly operating correctly, apply a smear of high melting-point grease to the contact areas of the new shoes and backplate. Take care to ensure that the grease does not contaminate the friction material.

22 Engage the right-hand shoe with the handbrake cable, and locate the shoe on the backplate. Install the shoe retainer pin and spring, and secure it in position with the spring cup.

23 Refit the strut to the upper end of the right-hand shoe, making sure that it is the correct way up.

24 Hook the lower return spring onto the right-hand shoe, then engage the left-hand shoe with the return spring. Locate the left-hand shoe on the backplate, engaging it with the adjuster plunger slot and strut, and secure it in position with its retainer pin, spring and spring cup.

25 Check that all components are correctly positioned, then refit the upper return spring.

26 Refit the brake drum to the transfer box, tightening its retaining screws securely.

27 Adjust the handbrake as described in Chapter 1 then, if all is well, reconnect the propeller shaft to the transfer box as described in Chapter 8.

18 Handbrake lever – removal and refitting

Removal

1 Remove the screws/fasteners securing the handbrake lever gaiter in position, and slide the gaiter off the lever **(see illustrations)**.

2 Remove the split-pin and washer, and withdraw the clevis pin securing the handbrake cable to the lever.

3 Slacken and remove the lever retaining nuts/bolts, and remove the handbrake lever from the vehicle.

Refitting

4 Refit the handbrake lever, making sure that it is correctly engaged with the cable. Refit the retaining nuts/bolts, and tighten them securely.

5 Apply a smear of multi-purpose grease to the clevis pin, then align the cable with the lever, and insert the pin. Refit the washer, and secure the pin in position with a new split-pin.

6 Refit the gaiter over the lever, and secure it in position with its screws/fasteners.

7 Adjust the handbrake cable as described in Chapter 1.

19 Handbrake cable – removal and refitting

Note: *Refer to the note at the start of Section 17, and identify the type of handbrake fitted before proceeding.*

18.1a Undo the retaining screw . . .

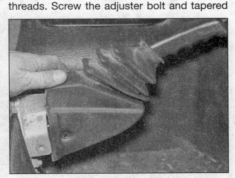

18.1b . . . and remove the gaiter from the handbrake lever

19.3 Remove the split-pin (arrowed), and remove the clevis pin securing the handbrake cable to the lever

Removal

1 Chock the front wheels, then jack up the rear of the vehicle and support on axle stands.
2 Release the screws/fasteners securing the handbrake lever gaiter in position, and slide the gaiter off the lever.
3 Remove the split-pin and washer, and withdraw the clevis pin securing the handbrake cable to the lever **(see illustration)**. If necessary, to improve access, unclip the seat cushion, then undo the retaining screws and remove the access panel from beneath the front seat(s). Proceed as described under the relevant sub-heading.

Rod-actuated brakes

4 From underneath the vehicle, work back along the cable, freeing it from any relevant retaining clips and ties whilst noting its correct routing.
5 Remove the split-pin and washer, then withdraw the clevis pin securing the handbrake inner cable to the rod linkage on the rear of the handbrake assembly.
6 Slacken the cable locknut and adjuster nut, then free the cable from its mounting bracket on the transfer box.
7 Unscrew the front end of the cable from the rear of the handbrake lever mounting plate, withdraw the cable from underneath the vehicle, and recover its washer.

Cable-actuated brakes

8 From underneath the vehicle, free the cable from the handbrake lever mounting plate, then work back along the cable, freeing it from any relevant retaining clips and ties whilst noting its correct routing.
9 Referring to Section 17, remove the upper and lower return springs, then remove the spring cup, spring and retainer pin, and remove the right-hand handbrake shoe. Note that the left-hand shoe and strut can be left in position on the backplate.
10 Free the handbrake cable from the rear of the backplate, and withdraw it from underneath the vehicle.

Refitting

Rod-actuated brakes

11 Refit the washer to the front end of the cable, and screw the cable into the rear of the

handbrake lever mounting plate, tightening it securely.
12 Work along the cable, routing it correctly and securing it in position with all the relevant clips and ties, and engage the lower end of the cable with its mounting bracket. Tighten the adjuster nut and locknut by hand only.
13 Apply a smear of grease to the clevis pin. Align the inner cable with the rod linkage, then insert the clevis pin and washer, and secure it in position with a new split-pin.
14 From inside the vehicle, apply a smear of grease to the clevis pin, then align the cable with the lever, and insert the pin. Refit the washer, and secure the pin in position with a new split-pin.
15 Refit the gaiter over the lever, and secure it in position with its screws/fasteners. Where necessary, refit the access cover and seat cushion.
16 Adjust the handbrake cable as described in Chapter 1.

Cable-actuated brakes

17 Apply a smear of high melting-point grease to the cable lower end fitting, then insert the cable through the rear of the backplate.
18 Refit the right-hand brake shoe as described in Section 17, and refit the brake drum.
19 Work along the cable, routing it correctly and securing it in position with all the relevant clips and ties. Feed it up through the handbrake lever mounting plate, and secure it in position.
20 From inside the vehicle, apply a smear of grease to the clevis pin, then align the cable with the lever, and insert the pin. Refit the washer, and secure the pin in position with a new split-pin.
21 Refit the gaiter over the lever, and secure it in position with its screws/fasteners. Where necessary, refit the access cover and seat cushion.
22 Adjust the handbrake cable as described in Chapter 1.

20 Rear brake pressure-regulating valve – testing, removal and refitting

Testing

1 On most models, a pressure-regulating valve is incorporated in the hydraulic braking circuit, to regulate the pressure applied to the rear brakes, and reduce the risk of the rear wheels locking under heavy braking. The valve is situated on either the left- or right-hand side of the engine compartment, mounted onto the wing valance. **Note:** *A pressure regulating valve is not fitted to models equipped with ABS.*
2 Depending on specification, the valve may incorporate a switch, connected to a warning light in the instrument panel. This warning light should illuminate temporarily as the starter is actuated, and then go out. If the light illuminates at any time when the vehicle is

being used, a fault in the valve/braking system is present. The vehicle should be taken immediately to a Land Rover dealer.
3 Specialist equipment is required to check the performance of the valve, and therefore if the valve is thought to be faulty, the vehicle should be taken to a suitably-equipped Land Rover dealer for testing. Repairs are not possible and, if faulty, the valve must be renewed.

Removal

Note: *Before starting work, refer to the note at the beginning of Section 2 concerning the dangers of hydraulic fluid.*
4 Disconnect the sender unit wiring connector, and unscrew the master cylinder reservoir filler cap. Place a piece of polythene over the filler neck, and securely refit the cap (taking care not to damage the sender unit). This will minimise brake fluid loss during subsequent operations. As an added precaution, place absorbent rags beneath the pressure-regulating valve brake pipe unions.
5 Disconnect the wiring connector from the valve switch (where fitted).
6 Wipe clean the area around the brake pipe unions on the pressure-regulating valve, then make a note of how the pipes are arranged, to use as a reference on refitting. Unscrew the union nuts, and carefully withdraw the pipes. Wash off any spilt fluid immediately with cold water.

> **HAYNES HiNT** *Plug or tape over the pipe ends and valve orifices, to minimise the loss of brake fluid and to prevent the entry of dirt into the system.*

7 Slacken the retaining bolt(s), and remove the valve from the engine compartment. Note that on some models, there is a spacer fitted behind the valve – take care not to lose this as the retaining bolt is withdrawn.

Refitting

8 Refit the pressure-regulating valve, positioning the spacer (where fitted) between the valve and body, and securely tighten its mounting bolt.
9 Wipe the brake pipe unions clean and refit them to the valve, using the notes made prior to removal to ensure that they are correctly positioned. Tighten the union nuts to the specified torque.
10 Reconnect the wiring connector to the valve warning light switch (where fitted).
11 Remove the polythene from the master cylinder reservoir filler neck, and bleed the complete hydraulic system as described in Section 2.

21 Stop-light switch – removal, refitting and adjustment

Removal

1 The stop-light switch is located on the rear of the pedal mounting box.

2 Disconnect the wiring connector(s) from the stop-light switch.

3 Slacken the switch locknut, and unscrew the switch from the mounting box.

Refitting and adjustment

4 Refitting is a reversal of removal, adjusting the switch as follows.

5 The switch should be positioned so that the stop-lights are illuminated after the brake pedal has travelled approximately 5 mm. Adjust the position of the switch as required until the stop-lights are functioning correctly, then securely tighten its locknut.

22 Vacuum pump – removal and refitting

Removal

10J engine

1 The vacuum pump is mounted onto the side of the cylinder block, and is belt-driven.

2 Slacken the retaining clips and disconnect the vacuum hoses from the top of the pump, noting their correct fitted locations.

3 Loosen the pump pulley retaining bolts, then slacken the pump adjuster strap bolt and the pump lower mounting bolt to release the drivebelt tension, and slip the belt off the pump pulley.

4 Unscrew the retaining bolts, and remove the pulley from the front of the vacuum pump.

5 Slacken and remove the two bolts and washers securing the adjuster strap to the top of the pump.

6 Unscrew the nut and washer, then withdraw the lower mounting bolt and remove the vacuum pump from the engine.

12J, 19J and 200 TDi engines

7 The vacuum pump is mounted onto the right-hand side of the cylinder block.

8 Disconnect the battery negative terminal, then release the retaining clip and disconnect the vacuum hose from the top of pump.

9 Make alignment marks between the pump and cylinder block, then undo the three bolts and washers, and withdraw the pump from the engine. **Note:** *Take great care not to disturb the drivegear assembly in the cylinder block.*

10 Recover the gasket, and discard it.

300 TDi engine

11 The vacuum pump is mounted onto the right-hand side of the cylinder block.

12 Position No 1 cylinder at TDC as described in Chapter 2A (this will release tension from the pump operating plunger). Disconnect the battery negative terminal.

13 To improve access to the pump, slacken and remove the retaining bolt, and position the air cleaner mounting bracket clear of the pump.

14 Slacken and remove the pump retaining bolts and washers, noting the correct fitted location of the wiring bracket.

15 Remove the pump from the side of the block. Recover the gasket, and discard it.

TD5 engine

Note: *At the time of writing, it was unclear whether the vacuum pump is available separately from the alternator – check with a Land Rover dealer or specialist.*

16 Remove the alternator as described in Chapter 5.

17 Undo the 4 bolts and detach the vacuum pump from the alternator **(see illustration)**.

Refitting

10J engine

18 Fit the pump and insert the lower mounting bolt, tightening its nut by hand only.

19 Align the pump with the adjuster strap, and refit its mounting bolts, tightening them both securely.

20 Refit the pulley to the pump, then refit its mounting bolts and engage the drivebelt with the pulley.

21 Position the pump so that the drivebelt tension is such that there is approximately 12 mm of movement in the belt, measured at the centre point of the belt top run, under firm thumb pressure. When the pump is correctly positioned, securely tighten its lower mounting bolt and the adjuster strap bolt.

22 Reconnect the vacuum hoses to the pump, and securely tighten their retaining clips.

23 On completion, unscrew the level plug from the rear of the vacuum pump, and check that the oil level is up to the base of the level

plug hole. If necessary, top-up the pump using SAE 15/50W motor oil. Allow excess oil to drain out of the pump, then refit the level plug, tightening it securely.

12J, 19J and 200 TDi engines

24 Ensure that the pump and drivegear mating surfaces are clean and dry, and position the new gasket on the drivegear.

25 Using the marks made prior to removal, refit the pump to the cylinder block, aligning its driveshaft so that it is correctly engaged with the drivegear.

26 Refit the pump retaining bolts, and tighten them securely.

27 Reconnect the vacuum hose to the pump, and (where necessary) securely tighten its retaining clip.

300 TDi engine

28 Ensure that the pump and cylinder block mating surfaces are clean and dry.

29 Offer up a new gasket, and refit the pump to the cylinder block **(see illustrations)**.

30 Refit the pump retaining bolts (not forgetting to fit the wiring bracket to the relevant bolt), and tighten them securely.

31 Reconnect the vacuum hose to the pump, and (where applicable) securely tighten its retaining clip.

32 Where necessary, locate the air cleaner mounting bracket in position, and securely tighten its retaining bolt.

TD5 engine

33 Ensure that the alternator and vacuum pump mating faces are clean and dry.

34 Refit the pump to the alternator, and tighten the bolts to the specified torque.

35 Refit the alternator as described in Chapter 5.

23 Anti-lock braking system (ABS) – general information

1 ABS is available on models from 1998. The system comprises a hydraulic block (modulator) which contains the hydraulic solenoid valves and the electrically-driven return pump, the four roadwheel sensors (one fitted to each wheel), and the electronic

22.17 Undo the 4 bolts (arrowed) and detach the vacuum pump from the alternator

22.29a On 300 TDi engines, ensure that the mating surfaces are clean and dry, then fit a new gasket to the cylinder block . . .

22.29b . . . and refit the braking system vacuum pump

control unit (ECU). The purpose of the system is to prevent the wheel(s) locking during heavy braking. This is achieved by automatic release of the brake on the relevant wheel, followed by re-application of the brake.

2 The solenoids are controlled by the ECU, which itself receives signals from the four wheel sensors (one fitted on each hub), which monitor the speed of rotation of each wheel. By comparing these signals, the ECU can determine the speed at which the vehicle is travelling. It can then use this speed to determine when a wheel is decelerating at an abnormal rate, compared to the speed of the vehicle, and therefore predicts when a wheel is about to lock. During normal operation, the system functions in the same way as a non-ABS braking system.

3 If the ECU senses that a wheel is about to lock, it operates the relevant solenoid valve in the hydraulic unit, which then isolates the brake caliper on the wheel which is about to lock from the master cylinder, effectively sealing-in the hydraulic pressure.

4 If the speed of rotation of the wheel continues to decrease at an abnormal rate, the ECU switches on the electrically-driven return pump operates, and pumps the hydraulic fluid back into the master cylinder, releasing pressure on the brake caliper so that the brake is released. Once the speed of rotation of the wheel returns to an acceptable rate, the pump stops; the solenoid valve opens, allowing the hydraulic master cylinder pressure to return to the caliper, which then re-applies the brake. This cycle can be carried out at up to 10 times a second.

5 The action of the solenoid valves and return pump creates pulses in the hydraulic circuit. When the ABS system is functioning, these pulses can be felt through the brake pedal.

6 The operation of the ABS system is entirely dependent on electrical signals. To prevent the system responding to any inaccurate signals, a built-in safety circuit monitors all signals received by the ECU. If an inaccurate signal or low battery voltage is detected, the ABS system is automatically shut down, and the warning light on the instrument panel is illuminated, to inform the driver that the ABS system is not operational. Normal braking should still be available, however.

7 If a fault does develop in the ABS system, the vehicle must be taken to a Land Rover dealer or specialist for fault diagnosis and repair.

24 Anti-lock braking system (ABS) components – removal and refitting

Hydraulic unit

1 It is not possible for the home mechanic to remove the hydraulic unit. If the hydraulic unions are disconnected from the unit, air will enter the high-pressure hydraulic system linking the master cylinder and hydraulic unit. Bleeding of the high-pressure system can only be safely carried out by a Land Rover dealer or specialist who has access to the service tester. Hydraulic unit removal and refitting should therefore be entrusted to a Land Rover dealer or specialist.

Electronic control unit (ECU)

Removal

2 Disconnect the battery negative terminal as described in Chapter 5.

3 Remove the driver's seat base.

4 Release the clip and remove the ECU cover plate.

5 Lift the ECU wiring connector locking clip, and carefully disconnect the wiring connectors from the ABS ECU and the engine management ECM. The ABS ECU is the one at the rear.

6 Release the seat base carpet for access to the mounting plate that the ECU and ECM are secured to.

7 Slacken and remove the 2 Torx screws at the front edge, and the nut at the rear edge securing the ECU mounting bracket, and remove it from the car.

8 Undo the 3 nuts securing the ABS ECU to the mounting plate.

Refitting

9 Refitting is a reversal of the removal procedure, ensuring the ECU and ECM wiring connectors are correctly and securely reconnected.

Front wheel sensor

Removal

10 Chock the rear wheels, then firmly apply the handbrake, jack up the front of the vehicle and support on axle stands. Remove the appropriate front roadwheel. Trace the wiring back from the sensor to the connector. Unplug the connector, and release the wiring harness clips.

11 Carefully prise the sensor from the front hub.

Refitting

12 Prior to refitting, ensure the sensor and mounting hole are clean, then apply a thin coat of multi-purpose grease to the sensor body. **Note:** *If the sensor is being renewed, the kit from Land Rover includes a bush and a quantity of grease.*

13 Carefully fit the sensor to the hub.

14 Ensure that the sensor wiring is correctly routed and retained by all the necessary clips, and reconnect it to its wiring connector.

15 Refit the roadwheel, then lower the vehicle to the ground and tighten the roadwheel bolts to the specified torque.

Rear wheel sensor

Removal

16 Chock the front wheels, then jack up the rear of the vehicle and support it on axle stands. Remove both roadwheels.

17 Undo the 3 retaining bolts and remove the brake backplates from both sides.

18 Trace the wiring harness back from both sensors, releasing the retaining clips, then unplug the harness connector.

19 Carefully prise both sensors from the hubs, and remove them.

Refitting

20 Prior to refitting, ensure the sensors and mounting holes are clean, then apply a thin coat of multi-purpose grease to the sensor bodies. **Note:** *If the sensors are being renewed, the kit from Land Rover includes bushes and a quantity of grease.*

21 Carefully fit the sensors to the hubs.

22 Ensure that the sensors' wiring is correctly routed and retained by all the necessary clips, and reconnect it to its wiring connector.

23 Refit the roadwheel, then lower the vehicle to the ground and tighten the roadwheel bolts to the specified torque.

Notes

Chapter 11
Suspension and steering

Contents

Section number

Drag link – removal and refitting. 29
Drag link balljoint/end fitting – removal and refitting 30
Front anti-roll bar – removal and refitting 6
Front anti-roll bar connecting link – removal, inspection and refitting 7
Front coil spring – removal and refitting. 3
Front shock absorber – removal, testing and refitting 2
Front suspension and steering check . . . . See Chapter 1
Front suspension Panhard rod – removal, inspection and refitting . . 4
Front suspension radius arm – removal, inspection and refitting. . . . 5
General information 1
Ignition switch/steering column lock – removal and refitting 19
Power steering fluid level check. . . . . See Chapter 1
Power steering pump – removal and refitting 26
Power steering pump drivebelt check, adjustment and
 renewal . . . . See Chapter 1
Power steering system – bleeding 27
Rear anti-roll bar – removal and refitting 15
Rear anti-roll bar connecting link – removal, inspection and refitting 16
Rear coil spring – removal and refitting 10
Rear shock absorber – removal, testing and refitting 9
Rear suspension lower link – removal, inspection and refitting 11

Section number

Rear suspension lower link mounting – renewal 12
Rear suspension self-levelling unit – inspection,
 removal and refitting. 17
Rear suspension upper link – removal, inspection and refitting. 13
Rear suspension upper link balljoint – removal and refitting 14
Steering – adjustment 23
Steering box – removal, inspection and refitting 24
Steering box drop arm – removal and refitting. 25
Steering column – removal, inspection and refitting 20
Steering column intermediate shaft – removal, inspection
 and refitting. 21
Steering column universal joint – removal, inspection and
 refitting 22
Steering damper – removal and refitting 28
Steering wheel – removal and refitting. 18
Suspension bump stop – inspection, removal and refitting. 8
Track rod – removal and refitting 31
Track rod balljoint – removal and refitting 32
Wheel alignment and steering angles – general information 33
Wheel and tyre maintenance and tyre pressure
 checks . . . . See Weekly checks

Degrees of difficulty

Easy, suitable for novice with little experience	**Fairly easy,** suitable for beginner with some experience	**Fairly difficult,** suitable for competent DIY mechanic	**Difficult,** suitable for experienced DIY mechanic	**Very difficult,** suitable for expert DIY or professional

Specifications

Front suspension

Type . . . . Axle with coil springs and shock absorbers. Axle movement controlled by radius arms and Panhard rod, with an anti-roll bar fitted to some models

Rear suspension

Type . . . . Axle with coil springs and shock absorbers. Axle movement controlled by upper and lower links, with an anti-roll bar being fitted on some models

Steering

Type . . . . Steering box (power-assisted on some models) with drag link and track rod arrangement. Steering damper fitted to drag link

Front wheel alignment and steering angles

Note: *All measurements should be taken with the vehicle unladen, with approximately five gallons of fuel in the tank.*

Camber angle. . . . . -10' ± 45'
Castor angle. . . . . 3° ± 45'
Swivel pin inclination . . . . 7°
Toe setting:
 Models up to 1998 . . . . 0° 0' to 0° 16' toe-out (0 to 2.0 mm toe-out)
 Models from 1998. . . . . -0° 10' ± 10' toe-out

Roadwheels

Type . . . . Pressed-steel or alloy

Tyres

Size:

90 models...	6.00 x 16, 7.50 x 16, 205R16 or 7.50R16 (depending on model)
110 models..	7.50 x 16 or 7.50R16 (depending on model)
130 models..	7.50R16
Pressures	*See Weekly checks*

Torque wrench settings

	Nm	lbf ft
Front suspension		
Anti-roll bar:		
Connecting link balljoint nuts...............................	40	30
Mounting clamp bolts..	30	22
Pivot bolt nuts..	68	50
Panhard rod:		
Models up to 2002 model year:		
Mounting bracket bolts..................................	123	91
Pivot bolts...	88	65
Models from 2002 model	230	170
Radius arm:		
Pivot bolts..	197	145
Retaining nut	176	130
Rear suspension		
Anti-roll bar:		
Connecting link balljoint nuts...............................	40	30
Mounting clamp bolts..	24	18
Pivot bolt nuts..	68	50
Lower link:		
Front nut..	176	130
Pivot bolt	176	130
Shock absorber:		
Mounting bracket nuts and bolts...........................	64	47
Upper mounting nut	82	61
Lower mounting nut	75	55
Upper link:		
Mounting bracket bolts	47	35
Balljoint bracket bolts.......................................	176	130
Pivot bolt	176	130
Upper link balljoint nut	176	130
Steering		
Drag link:		
Balljoint/end fitting nuts	40	30
Clamp bolts	14	10
Drop arm retaining nut	176	130
Power steering pump:		
Feed pipe union nut	20	15
Mounting bolts..	25	18
Pulley retaining bolts:		
Non-TD5 engines	10	7
TD5 engines	25	18
Steering box:		
Mounting bolts..	81	60
Tie-bar bolts/nuts..	81	60
Steering pipe union nuts:		
14 mm thread...	15	11
16 mm thread...	20	15
Steering wheel nut:		
Early (pre-1992) models.....................................	25	18
Later (1992-on) models	30	22
Track rod:		
Balljoint nuts...	40	30
Clamp bolts	14	10
Universal joint clamp bolts.....................................	25	18
Roadwheels		
Roadwheel nuts:		
Steel wheels..	108	80
Alloy wheels	130	96
Heavy duty wheel...	170	125

1 General information

The front and rear suspension are of live beam axle type, with coil springs and shock absorbers.

On the front suspension, axle movement is controlled by two radius arms and a Panhard rod. On some models, an anti-roll bar is also fitted. The anti roll bar is rubber-mounted onto the vehicle body, and is connected to the axle at each end by a balljointed connecting link **(see illustrations).**

On the rear suspension, axle movement is controlled by the upper and lower links. The upper link is connected to the top of the axle via a balljoint **(see illustration overleaf).** On some models, an anti-roll bar is also fitted. Self-levelling suspension was offered as an option on some models. The system consists of a gas-filled unit which is fitted between the chassis and upper link balljoint bracket.

The steering column is linked to the steering box by an intermediate shaft and two universal joints. The lower universal joint is secured to the steering box pinion by a clamp bolt.

The steering box is mounted onto the chassis. The steering box is connected to one of the swivel pin housing assemblies by a drag link, which has a balljoint at each end, and the swivel pin housing assemblies are linked by means of a track rod which also has a balljoint at each end. All balljoint ends are threaded to facilitate adjustment.

Power-assisted steering was fitted to

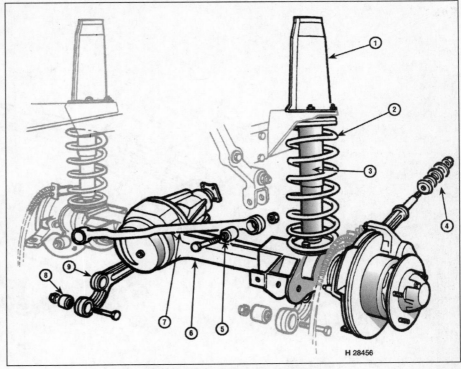

1.2a Front suspension components

1	Shock absorber mounting	4	Mounting bush	7	Panhard rod
2	Coil spring	5	Mounting bush	8	Mounting bush
3	Shock absorber	6	Front axle	9	Radius arm

some models. The hydraulic steering system is powered by a belt-driven pump which is driven off the crankshaft pulley.

Note: Many of the suspension and steering components are secured in position with self-locking nuts. Whenever a self-locking nut is disturbed, it must be discarded and a new nut fitted.

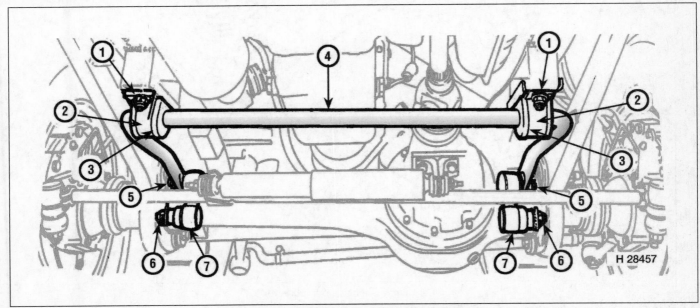

1.2b Front suspension anti-roll bar components

1	Clamp nut	3	Mounting rubber	5	Retaining nut	7	Connecting link
2	Mounting clamp	4	Anti-roll bar	6	Retaining nut		

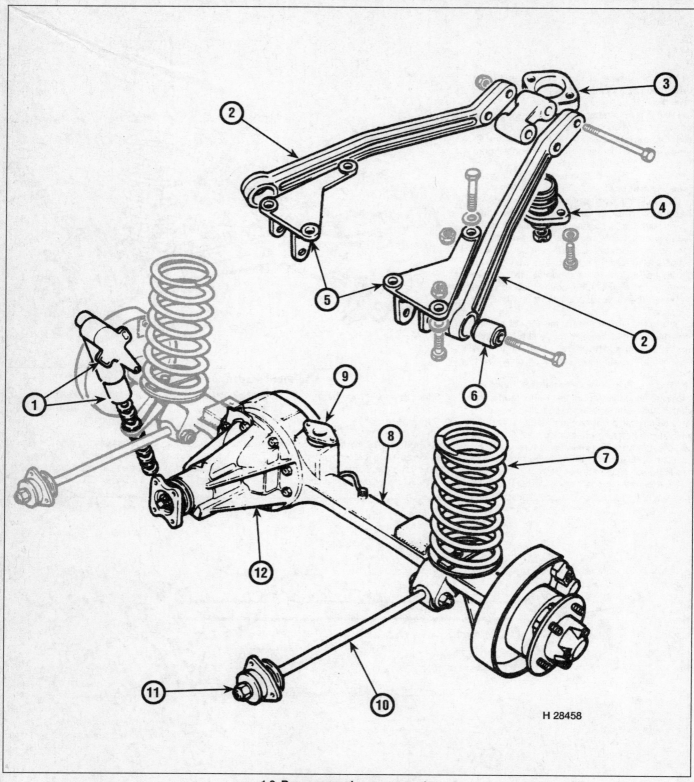

1.3 Rear suspension components

1 Shock absorber and mounting bracket
2 Upper link
3 Upper link mounting bracket
4 Upper link balljoint

5 Upper link mounting bracket
6 Mounting bush
7 Coil spring
8 Rear axle

9 Balljoint mounting plate
10 Lower link
11 Rubber mounting
12 Differential housing

2.3a Slacken and remove the shock absorber lower mounting nut (arrowed) . . .

2.3b . . . and slide off the washer and mounting rubber arrangement

2.5 Slacken and remove the four shock absorber mounting nuts and washers

2 Front shock absorber
– removal, testing and refitting

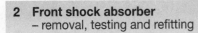

Note: *New shock absorber mounting nuts will be required on refitting (see Note in Section 1).*

Removal

1 Apply the handbrake, then jack up the front of the vehicle and support it on axle stands positioned underneath the chassis (see *Jacking and vehicle support*). Remove both front roadwheels.

2 Position a hydraulic jack beneath the front axle assembly, then raise the jack until it is supporting the axle weight.

3 Slacken and remove the shock absorber lower mounting nut, and recover the outer washer and rubber mounting arrangement, noting each component's correct fitted position **(see illustrations). Note:** *The washers are different, and must not be interchanged.*

4 From within the engine compartment, undo the retaining screws and remove the access cover from inside the wing.

5 Undo the four nuts and washers securing the shock absorber upper mounting bracket to the vehicle body **(see illustration)**.

6 Lift the shock absorber and upper mounting assembly upwards and out of position. As the shock absorber is removed, recover the inner washer and mounting rubber arrangement from its lower end – refer to the Note in paragraph 3 **(see illustration)**.

2.6 Lift out the shock absorber, and recover the second washer and mounting rubber arrangement from the its lower end

7 With the assembly on a bench, unscrew the upper mounting nut, and lift off the outer washer and mounting rubber arrangement – refer to the Note in paragraph 3 **(see illustration)**.

8 Separate the shock absorber and mounting, and recover the inner washer and mounting rubber arrangement from the upper end of the shock absorber – refer to the Note in paragraph 3.

Testing

9 Examine the shock absorber for signs of fluid leakage or damage. Test the operation of the strut, while holding it in an upright position, by moving the piston through a full stroke, and then through short strokes of 50 to 100 mm. In both cases, the resistance felt should be smooth and continuous. If the resistance is jerky, or uneven, or if there is any visible sign of wear or damage to the strut, renewal is necessary. Renew the complete unit if any damage or excessive wear is evident.

10 Inspect the mounting rubber for signs of damage or deterioration, and renew if necessary.

Refitting

11 Refitting is a reversal of the removal procedure, noting the following points:

a) Ensure that all washer and rubber mounting arrangement components are positioned correctly. The flat (seating) washer should be fitted so that its flat face abuts the upper mounting bracket/axle (as applicable), and the slightly-cupped

2.7 Shock absorber upper mounting nut

washer should be fitted with its concave side towards the rubber mounting **(see illustration)**.

b) Fit **new** shock absorber mounting nuts, and tighten them to the securely.

3 Front coil spring –
removal and refitting

Note: *A suitable tool to hold the coil spring in compression must be obtained. Adjustable coil spring compressors are readily available, and are essential for this operation.*

Removal

1 Remove the relevant shock absorber assembly as described in Section 2. Note that it is not necessary to separate the shock absorber from the upper mounting bracket.

2 Fit the spring compressors to the coil spring, and compress the spring slightly to relieve the spring tension from its seats.

3 Carefully lower the axle, until it is possible to withdraw the coil spring. Whilst lowering the axle, keep a careful watch on the brake pipes and hoses, to ensure that no excess strain is being placed on them.

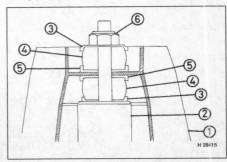

H 28415

2.11 On refitting, ensure that the shock absorber mounting rubbers and washers are correctly positioned (upper mounting shown)

1 Shock absorber mounting
2 Shock absorber
3 Cupped washer
4 Mounting rubber
5 Flat (seating) washer
6 Mounting nut

3.4a Remove the front suspension coil spring . . .

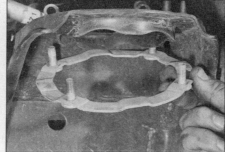

3.4b . . . and recover the upper spring seat

3.5 Lower spring seat is secured to the axle by two bolts (arrowed)

4 Remove the coil spring, noting which way around it is fitted, and recover the upper spring seat **(see illustrations)**.

5 Slacken and remove the retaining bolts and washers, and remove the lower spring seat from the axle **(see illustration)**.

6 Inspect the spring closely for signs of damage, such as cracking, and check the spring seats for signs of wear or damage. Renew worn components as necessary.

Refitting

7 Refit the lower spring seat to the axle, and securely tighten its retaining bolt.

8 Fit the upper spring seat to the body, and secure it in position by temporarily fitting one of the strut nuts.

9 Install the coil spring, then carefully raise the axle into position, making sure that the upper spring seat studs remain correctly aligned with the body holes.

10 Refit the shock absorber as described in Section 2, then carefully remove the spring compressors.

4 Front suspension Panhard rod – removal, inspection and refitting

Note: *New pivot bolt nuts will be required on refitting (see Note in Section 1).*

Removal

1 To improve access, jack up the front of

the vehicle and support it on axle stands positioned underneath the chassis (see *Jacking and vehicle support*).

2 Slacken and remove the nuts and pivot bolts securing the Panhard rod to the chassis and axle, and remove the rod from underneath the vehicle **(see illustration)**.

3 If necessary, slacken and remove the retaining nuts and bolts, and remove the Panhard rod mounting bracket from the chassis.

Inspection

4 Inspect the rod bar and mounting bracket for signs of damage, paying particular attention to the areas around the mounting bushes. Check the pivot bolt shanks for signs of wear, and renew if necessary.

5 Examine the Panhard rod mounting bushes for signs of wear and damage. If renewal is necessary, a hydraulic press and suitable spacers will be required, to press the bush out of position and install the new one. Press the old bush out, and install the new bush using a suitable tubular spacer which bears only on the hard outer edge of the bush, not the bush rubber.

Refitting

6 Where removed, refit the mounting bracket to the chassis, and insert its retaining bolts and nuts, tightening them to the specified torque setting.

7 Offer up the Panhard rod, and insert both

pivot bolts. Fit the new nuts to the pivot bolts, tightening them loosely only.

8 Lower the vehicle to the ground. With the vehicle resting on its wheels, tighten both pivot bolt nuts to the specified torque setting.

5 Front suspension radius arm – removal, inspection and refitting

Note: *New radius arm upper and lower pivot bolt nuts will be required on refitting (see Note in Section 1).*

Removal

1 Apply the handbrake, then jack up the front of the vehicle and support it on axle stands positioned underneath the chassis (see *Jacking and vehicle support*). Remove the relevant front roadwheel.

2 Position a hydraulic jack beneath the front axle assembly, then raise the jack until it is supporting the axle weight.

3 Unscrew the nut securing the radius arm to the chassis, and remove the washer and outer mounting bush **(see illustrations)**.

4 Remove the split-pin, then slacken and remove the nut and washer securing the steering gear track rod balljoint to the swivel pin housing. Release the balljoint tapered shank using a universal balljoint separator.

5 Slacken and remove the nuts and bolts securing the radius arm to the axle, and

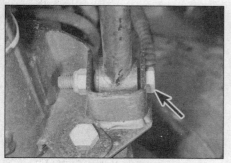

4.2 Panhard rod-to-axle pivot bolt (arrowed)

5.3a Slacken and remove the nut and washer securing the radius arm to the chassis . . .

5.3b . . . then slide off the outer mounting bush

remove the arm from underneath the vehicle **(see illustration)**.

6 With the arm removed, slide off the inner mounting bush and washer from its upper end.

Inspection

7 Inspect the arm for signs of damage, paying particular attention to the threaded end of the arm, and the areas around the mounting bushes. Check the pivot bolt shanks for signs of wear, and renew if necessary.

8 Inspect the upper mounting bushes for signs of damage or deterioration, and renew if necessary.

9 Examine the radius arm lower mounting bushes for signs of wear and damage. If renewal is necessary, a hydraulic press and suitable spacers will be required, to press the bush out of position and install the new one. Press the old bush out, and install the new bush using a suitable tubular spacer which bears only on the hard outer edge of the bush, not the bush rubber.

Refitting

10 Fitted the washer and inner mounting bush to the threaded end of the radius arm.

11 Manoeuvre the arm assembly into position, and insert the pivot bolts. Fit the new nuts to the pivot bolts, tightening them loosely only at this stage.

12 Reconnect the track rod balljoint to the swivel pin housing assembly, tightening its retaining nut to the specified torque setting. Secure the nut in position with a new split-pin.

13 Slide the outer mounting bush and washer onto the threaded end of the arm, and fit the new retaining nut, tightening it to the specified torque setting.

14 Refit the wheel, then lower the vehicle to the ground and tighten the wheel nuts to the specified torque.

15 With the vehicle resting on its wheels, tighten both radius arm pivot bolt nuts to the specified torque setting.

6 Front anti-roll bar – removal and refitting

Note: *New anti-roll bar mounting clamp and connecting link nuts will be required on refitting (see Note in Section 1).*

Removal

1 Apply the handbrake, then jack up the front of the vehicle and support it on axle stands positioned underneath the chassis (see *Jacking and vehicle support*).

2 Position a hydraulic jack beneath the front axle assembly, then raise the jack until it is supporting the axle weight.

3 Prior to removal, mark the position of each mounting clamp rubber on the anti-roll bar.

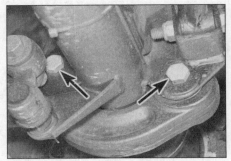

5.5 Unscrew the radius arm to axle bolts (arrowed) and remove the arm from underneath the vehicle

4 Slacken and remove the nuts, and withdraw the bolts and washers securing each end of the anti-roll bar to the connecting links.

5 Unscrew the nuts and washers securing the mounting clamps to the vehicle body. Remove bolts and mounting clamps, and lower the anti-roll bar out from underneath the vehicle **(see illustration)**.

6 Remove the mounting rubbers from the anti-roll bar, and inspect them for signs of damage. Renew both rubbers if they are damaged or show signs of deterioration.

Refitting

7 Fit the mounting rubbers to the anti-roll bar, positioning them so that their splits will be facing towards the axle once the bar is installed.

8 Align both rubbers with the marks made prior to removal, and manoeuvre the anti-roll bar into position.

9 Ensure that the flat side of each rubber is against the vehicle body, then refit the mounting clamps. Insert the bolts and fit the washers and new nuts, tightening them loosely only at this stage.

10 Align the anti-roll bar ends with the connecting links, and insert the pivot bolts and washers. Fit the new retaining nuts to the bolts, and tighten them loosely only.

11 Lower the vehicle to the ground. With the vehicle resting on its wheels, tighten the mounting clamp and pivot bolt nuts to the specified torque.

7.4a Release the balljoint shank with a balljoint separator . . .

6.5 Front anti-roll bar mounting clamp. Note which way the mounting rubber split is facing

7 Front anti-roll bar connecting link – removal, inspection and refitting

Note: *New connecting link pivot bolt nuts will be required on refitting (see Note in Section 1).*

Removal

1 Apply the handbrake, then jack up the front of the vehicle and support it on axle stands positioned underneath the chassis (see *Jacking and vehicle support*). Remove the relevant front roadwheel.

2 Position a hydraulic jack beneath the front axle assembly, then raise the jack until it is supporting the axle weight.

3 Slacken and remove the nut, then withdraw the pivot bolt and washer securing the connecting link to the anti-roll bar.

4 Remove the split-pin, and undo the nut and washer securing the connecting link balljoint to the axle assembly. Release the balljoint tapered shank using a universal balljoint separator, and remove the connecting link from the vehicle **(see illustrations)**.

Inspection

5 Check that the link balljoint moves freely, without any sign of roughness. Also check that the balljoint gaiter shows no sign of deterioration, and is free from cracks and splits. If any sign of wear or damage is found, the complete link must be renewed.

7.4b . . . and remove the connecting link from underneath the vehicle

7.7 Offer up the connecting link, and insert its pivot bolt and washer

7.8a Locate the balljoint in the axle, and refit its retaining nut and washer

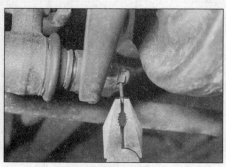

7.8b Tighten the nut to the specified torque, and secure it in position with a new split-pin

6 Examine the upper mounting bushes for signs of wear and damage, and renew if necessary. A hydraulic press and suitable spacers may be required, to press the bushes out of position and install the new ones.

Refitting

7 Fit the connecting link assembly, and insert its pivot bolt and washer **(see illustration)**.
8 Locate the balljoint shank in the axle, and refit its washer and nut. Tighten the nut to the specified torque setting, and secure it in position with a new split-pin **(see illustrations)**.
9 Fit a new nut to the pivot bolt, tighten it to the specified torque setting, then lower the vehicle to ground.

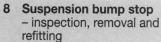

8 Suspension bump stop
– inspection, removal and refitting

Inspection

1 The bump stops are mounted onto the chassis, directly above the axle assembly **(see illustration)**. Inspect each bump stop rubber for signs of damage or deterioration, and renew if necessary.

Removal

2 Slacken and remove the nuts, washers and bolts securing the bump stop in position, and remove it from the chassis.

Refitting

3 Fit the bolts to the slots in the chassis, then offer up the bump stop, ensuring it is correctly located in the chassis slot. Refit the washers and nuts to the retaining bolts, and tighten them securely.

9 Rear shock absorber
– removal, testing and refitting

Removal

1 Chock the front wheels, then jack up the rear of the vehicle and support it on axle stands positioned underneath the chassis (see *Jacking and vehicle support*). Remove the relevant rear roadwheel.
2 Position a hydraulic jack beneath the rear axle assembly, then raise the jack until it is supporting the axle weight.
3 Slacken and remove the nut and outer washer from the shock absorber upper mounting **(see illustration)**.
4 Unscrew the nut from the lower mounting, and slide off the outer mounting rubber and its washers, noting their correct fitted positions **(see illustration)**. Free the shock absorber from the axle, and recover the second mounting rubber and washer arrangement from its lower end.
5 Remove the shock absorber from the vehicle, and recover the inner washer from its upper mounting.

6 If necessary, slacken and remove the retaining nuts and bolts, and remove the upper mounting bracket from the chassis.

Testing

7 Examine the shock absorber for signs of fluid leakage or damage. Test the operation of the strut, while holding it in an upright position, by moving the piston through a full stroke, and then through short strokes of 50 to 100 mm. In both cases, the resistance felt should be smooth and continuous. If the resistance is jerky, or uneven, or if there is any visible sign of wear or damage to the strut, renewal is necessary. Renew the complete unit if any damage or excessive wear is evident.
8 Inspect the upper mounting bush and the lower mounting rubbers for signs of damage or deterioration, and renew as necessary.

Refitting

9 Where removed, refit the upper mounting bracket to the chassis, and insert its retaining bolts and nuts, tightening them securely.
10 Fit the inner washer, then locate the shock absorber on the upper mounting bracket.
11 Fit the first mounting rubber and washer arrangement to the lower end of the shock absorber, positioning a washer on each side of the rubber. Engage the shock absorber with the axle, then fit the second rubber mounting and washer arrangement, followed by the retaining nut.
12 Refit the outer washer and upper retaining nut, then tighten both retaining nuts to the specified torque setting.

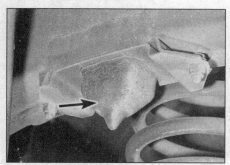

8.1 Bump stops are mounted onto the vehicle underbody (arrowed), directly above each end of the axle

9.3 Slacken and remove the shock absorber upper mounting nut and washer . . .

9.4 . . . then unscrew the lower mounting nut, and recover the washers and mounting rubber

10 Rear coil spring – removal and refitting

Note: *A suitable tool to hold the coil spring in compression must be obtained. Adjustable coil spring compressors are readily available, and are essential for this operation. Any attempt to dismantle the strut without such a tool is likely to result in damage or personal injury.*

Removal

1 Chock the front wheels, then jack up the rear of the vehicle and support it on axle stands positioned underneath the chassis (see *Jacking and vehicle support*). Remove the relevant rear roadwheel.

2 Position a hydraulic jack beneath the rear axle assembly, then raise the jack until it is supporting the axle weight.

3 Slacken and remove the nut and outer washer from the shock absorber upper mounting, and disengage the shock absorber from its mounting bracket.

4 Fit the spring compressor, and compress the coil spring.

5 Carefully lower the axle, until the upper end of the spring is released from its seat. Whilst lowering the axle, keep a careful watch on the brake pipes and hoses, to ensure that no strain is being placed on them.

6 Recover the upper spring seat, slacken and remove the retaining bolts and washers, then remove the retaining plate securing the spring to the axle. Withdraw the coil spring, and lift off the lower spring seat from the axle.

7 Inspect the spring closely for signs of damage, such as cracking, and check the spring seats for signs of wear or damage. Renew worn components as necessary.

Refitting

8 If a new spring is being installed, slowly release the old spring, then transfer the spring compressor from the old spring to the new one.

9 Refit the lower spring seat to the axle, then manoeuvre the coil spring into position.

10 Ensure that the spring is correctly seated, then refit the retaining plate to the axle, and securely tighten its retaining bolts.

11 Fit the upper spring seat to the top of the coil spring.

12 Align the upper spring seat with the chassis, then carefully raise the axle assembly with the jack.

13 Locate the shock absorber on its upper mounting, then refit the outer washer and retaining nut, tightening it to the specified torque setting.

14 Carefully release the spring compressor, ensuring that the spring remains correctly seated.

15 Remove the jack from underneath the axle, and lower the vehicle to the ground.

11 Rear suspension lower link – removal, inspection and refitting

Note: *New a new lower link pivot bolt nut and front mounting nut will be required on refitting (see Note in Section 1). If the rubber mounting is to be removed, new mounting bolt nuts will also be required.*

11.2 Remove the pivot bolt securing the lower link to the axle . . .

Removal

1 Chock the front wheels, then jack up the rear of the vehicle and support it on axle stands positioned underneath the rear axle (see *Jacking and vehicle support*). Remove the relevant rear roadwheel.

2 Slacken and remove the nut, then withdraw the pivot bolt securing the lower link to the axle **(see illustration)**.

3 Slacken and remove the lower link front retaining nut and washer, then manoeuvre the link out from underneath the vehicle **(see illustrations)**.

4 If necessary, undo the three nuts and bolts securing the rubber mounting in position, and remove it from the chassis **(see illustration)**.

Inspection

5 Inspect the link for signs of damage, paying particular attention to its threaded end, and the area around its mounting bush. Check the pivot bolt shanks for signs of wear, and renew if necessary.

6 Examine the lower link mounting bush for signs of wear and damage. If renewal is necessary, a hydraulic press and suitable spacers will be required, to press the bush out of position and install the new one. Press the old bush out, and install the new bush using a suitable tubular spacer which bears only on

11.3a . . . then unscrew the front retaining nut and washer . . .

11.3b . . . and manoeuvre the lower link out from underneath the vehicle

11.4 The lower link mounting is secured to the chassis by three bolts

11.12a With the vehicle standing on its wheels, tighten the lower link pivot bolt . . .

11.12b . . . and front retaining nut to the specified torque

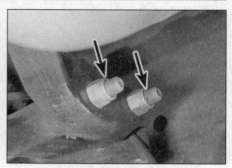

13.4 Upper link-to-balljoint bracket retaining bolts (arrowed)

the hard outer edge of the bush, not the bush rubber.

7 Inspect the rubber mounting for signs of damage or deterioration, and renew if necessary.

Refitting

8 Where necessary, fit the rubber mounting to the chassis, and insert its mounting bolts. Fit new nuts to the bolts, and tighten them securely.

9 Manoeuvre the link into position, and insert the pivot bolt.

10 Refit the washer to the threaded end of the link, then fit the new nuts to both the link and pivot bolt. Tighten each nut loosely only at this stage.

11 Refit the roadwheel, then lower the vehicle to the ground and tighten the wheel nuts to the specified torque.

12 With the vehicle resting on its wheels, tighten both the lower link front nut and pivot bolt nut to the specified torque setting **(see illustrations)**.

12 Rear suspension lower link mounting – renewal

To renew the rubber mounting, the lower link must be removed. Refer to Section 11 for removal and refitting details.

13 Rear suspension upper link – removal, inspection and refitting

Note: *New upper link pivot bolt and mounting bracket retaining bolt nuts will be required on refitting (see Note in Section 1).*

Removal

1 Chock the front wheels, then jack up the rear of the vehicle and support it on axle stands positioned underneath the chassis (see *Jacking and vehicle support*).

2 Position a hydraulic jack beneath the rear axle assembly, then raise the jack until it is supporting the axle weight.

3 Slacken and remove the nuts and bolts securing the upper link mounting bracket to the chassis.

4 Slacken and remove the nuts securing the upper links to the balljoint bracket on the top of the axle **(see illustration)**. Withdraw both retaining bolts, and remove the relevant upper link and mounting bracket assembly from underneath the vehicle.

5 If necessary, undo the nut, withdraw the pivot bolt, and separate the link from its mounting bracket.

Inspection

6 Inspect the link for signs of damage, paying particular attention to the area around its mounting bush. Check the pivot bolt shanks for signs of wear, and renew if necessary.

7 Examine the upper link mounting bush for signs of wear and damage. If renewal is necessary, a hydraulic press and suitable spacers will be required, to press the bush out of position and install the new one. Press the old bush out, and install the new bush using a suitable tubular spacer which bears only on the hard outer edge of the bush, not the bush rubber.

8 Inspect the mounting bracket for signs of damage, and renew if necessary.

Refitting

9 Reassemble the upper link and mounting bracket, and insert the pivot bolts. Fit a new nut to the bolt, tightening it loosely only at this stage.

10 Manoeuvre the link and bracket assembly into position, and insert the bolts securing them to the balljoint bracket and second upper link. Fit the new nuts to the bolts, and tighten them to the specified torque setting.

11 Insert the mounting bracket-to-chassis bolts, then fit the new nuts and tighten them to the specified torque setting.

12 Lower the vehicle to the ground and, with the vehicle resting on its wheels, tighten the upper pivot bolt nut to the specified torque setting.

14 Rear suspension upper link balljoint – removal and refitting

Removal

1 Remove both rear suspension upper links as described in Section 13.

2 Withdraw the split-pin, then slacken and remove the nut securing the balljoint to the top of the rear axle.

3 Remove the balljoint and upper link bracket assembly from the top of the axle, then slacken and remove the two retaining bolts and washers, and separate the two components.

4 Check that the lower arm balljoint moves freely, without any sign of roughness. Also check that the balljoint gaiter shows no sign of deterioration, and is free from cracks and splits. If necessary, renew the balljoint.

Refitting

5 Refit the upper link bracket to the balljoint, and securely tighten its retaining bolts.

6 Locate the balljoint shank in its bracket on top of the axle, and refit its retaining nut. Tighten the balljoint nut to the specified torque setting, and secure it in position with a new split-pin.

7 Refit the rear suspension upper links as described in Section 13.

15 Rear anti-roll bar – removal and refitting

Note: *New anti-roll bar mounting clamp and connecting link nuts will be required on refitting (see Note in Section 1).*

Removal

1 Chock the front wheels, then jack up the rear of the vehicle and support it on axle stands positioned underneath the chassis (see *Jacking and vehicle support*).

2 Position a hydraulic jack beneath the axle assembly, then raise the jack until it is supporting the axle weight.

3 Prior to removal, mark the position of each mounting clamp rubber on the anti-roll bar.

4 Slacken and remove the nuts, and withdraw the bolts and washers securing each end of the anti-roll bar to the connecting links. If they are loose, remove the mounting rubbers from the connecting link.

5 Unscrew the nuts/bolts and washers securing the mounting clamps to the vehicle body. Remove the bolts and mounting clamps,

15.5 Rear anti-roll bar mounting clamp assembly

16.3a Slacken and remove the nut . . .

16.3b . . . then withdraw the pivot bolt and washer securing the anti-roll bar to the connecting link

and lower the anti-roll bar out from underneath the vehicle **(see illustration)**.

6 Remove the mounting rubbers from the anti-roll bar, and inspect them for signs of damage. Renew both rubbers if they are damaged or show signs of deterioration.

Refitting

7 Fit the mounting rubbers to the anti-roll bar, aligning them with the marks made prior to removal.

8 Manoeuvre the anti-roll bar into position, ensuring that the flat side of each mounting rubber is against the vehicle body, then refit the mounting clamps. Insert the bolts and fit the washers and new nuts, tightening them loosely only at this stage.

9 Ensure that the mounting rubbers are in position, and align the anti-roll bar ends with the connecting links. Insert the pivot bolts and washers, then fit the new retaining nuts and tighten them loosely.

10 Lower the vehicle to the ground and, with it resting on its wheels, tighten the mounting clamp and pivot bolt nuts to the specified torque.

16 Rear anti-roll bar connecting link – removal, inspection and refitting

Note: *New connecting link pivot bolt nuts will be required on refitting (see Note in Section 1).*

Removal

1 Chock the front wheels, then jack up the rear of the vehicle and support it on axle stands positioned underneath the chassis (see *Jacking and vehicle support*).

2 Position a hydraulic jack beneath the axle assembly, then raise the jack until it is supporting the axle weight.

3 Slacken and remove the nut, then withdraw the pivot bolt and washer securing the connecting link to the anti-roll bar. If they are loose, remove the mounting rubbers from the connecting link **(see illustrations)**.

4 Remove the split-pin, and undo the nut and washer securing the connecting link balljoint to the axle assembly. Release the balljoint tapered shank using a universal balljoint separator, and remove the connecting link from the vehicle **(see illustrations)**.

16.3c If they are loose, remove the mounting rubbers from the connecting link

Inspection

5 Check that the link balljoint moves freely, without any sign of roughness. Also check that the balljoint gaiter shows no sign of deterioration, and is free from cracks and splits. If any sign of wear or damage is found, the complete link must be renewed.

6 Examine the link mounting bushes for signs of wear and damage. If renewal is necessary, a hydraulic press and suitable spacers may be required, to press the bushes out of position and install the new ones.

Refitting

7 Locate the balljoint shank in the axle, and refit its washer and nut. Tighten the nut to the specified torque setting, and secure it in position with a new split-pin **(see illustration)**.

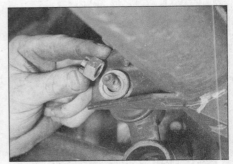

16.4a Slacken and remove the nut and washer . . .

16.4b . . . then use a universal balljoint separator . . .

16.4c . . . to free the connecting link from the axle

16.7 Tighten the balljoint nut to the specified torque setting, and secure it in position with a new split-pin

8 Ensure that the mounting rubbers are correctly fitted, and insert the pivot bolt and washer.

9 Fit a new nut to the pivot bolt, tighten it to the specified torque setting, then lower the vehicle to ground.

17 Rear suspension self-levelling unit – removal, inspection and refitting

Note: *New upper bracket retaining nuts will be required on refitting (see Note in Section 1).*

Removal

1 Chock the front wheels, then jack up the rear of the vehicle and support it on axle stands positioned underneath the chassis (see *Jacking and vehicle support*).

2 Slacken and remove the two bolts and nuts securing the reservoir support bracket in position.

3 Slacken and remove the four nuts and bolts securing the self-levelling unit upper mounting bracket to the chassis.

4 Release the circlip, and free the gaiter from the lower balljoint.

5 Using a suitable open-ended spanner, unscrew the self-levelling unit lower balljoint from the upper link balljoint bracket, and manoeuvre the assembly out from underneath the vehicle. **Note:** *Do not attempt to separate the reservoir from the unit.*

Inspection

6 Inspect the self-levelling unit balljoint gaiters for signs of damage or deterioration. Check that both the upper and lower balljoints pivot smoothly, without any sign of roughness or free play. Renew damaged components as necessary.

7 If renewal is necessary, unscrew the relevant balljoint from the self-levelling unit, and remove the gaiter. The upper balljoint can also be unscrewed from its mounting bracket, if required. Fit the new gaiter, and clean the threads of the balljoints and levelling unit. Apply a few drops of locking compound to the balljoint shank threads, and screw them into the levelling unit, tightening them securely. Ensure that the upper balljoint gaiter is correctly seated, and secure it in position with its circlips.

Refitting

8 Manoeuvre the assembly into position, and screw the lower balljoint into the upper link balljoint bracket.

9 Securely tighten the balljoint, then align the upper bracket with the chassis, and insert its retaining bolts. Fit the new nuts to the bolts, and tighten them securely.

10 Ensure that the lower balljoint is securely tightened, and seat the lower gaiter in its grooves. Secure the gaiter in position with its circlips.

11 Refit the reservoir support bracket retaining bolts, tighten them securely, then lower the vehicle to the ground.

18.2a On early models, undo the retaining screw (arrowed) . . .

18.4 Slacken and remove the steering wheel retaining nut, recover the washer, and remove the wheel . . .

18.2b . . . and remove the trim cover from the centre of the steering wheel

18.5 . . . if it is a tight fit, a suitable puller will be required to draw the wheel off the column splines

18 Steering wheel – removal and refitting

Removal

1 Set the front wheels in the straight-ahead position, and release the steering lock by inserting the ignition key.

2 On early models, undo the retaining screw(s) and remove the trim cover from the centre of the steering wheel **(see illustrations)**.

3 On vehicles up to 1999 model year, carefully prise the badge out from the centre of the wheel, to reveal the retaining nut. On vehicles from 1999 model year, the steering wheel centre trim cover simply pulls from place.

4 Slacken and remove the steering wheel retaining nut and washer **(see illustration)**.

5 Make alignment marks between the steering wheel and steering column shaft, then pull the wheel off the column. If the wheel is a tight fit on the column splines, it will be necessary to draw the wheel off using a suitable puller which screws into the threaded holes in the wheel. A suitable home-made puller can be fabricated from a strip of steel and two suitable size bolts **(see illustration)**.

Refitting

6 Prior to refitting, inspect the indicator cancelling cam (which is fitted to the base of the wheel) for signs of damage, and renew if necessary.

7 Ensure that the indicator switch is in the central (off) position, and locate the wheel on the column splines, aligning the marks made on removal. As the wheel is fitted, make sure that the cancelling cam lugs engage correctly with the cancelling ring slots.

8 Refit the washer and retaining nut, and tighten it to the specified torque setting.

9 On early models, refit the trim cover, securely tightening its retaining screw(s).

10 On later models, clip the badge into the centre of the wheel.

19 Ignition switch/steering column lock – removal and refitting

Note: *If the lock assembly is to be removed, new shear-bolts will be required on refitting.*

Removal

1 Remove the instrument panel as described in Chapter 13.

2 Undo the retaining screws from the steering column shrouds, then unclip the shrouds and remove them from the steering column.

3 If necessary, remove the steering wheel as described in Section 18 to improve access.

Lock assembly

4 Noting their correct fitted locations,

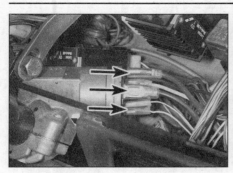

19.4 Disconnect the wiring connectors from the rear of the lock assembly, noting each one's correct fitted location

disconnect the wiring connectors from the rear of the lock assembly **(see illustration)**.

5 Using a hammer and suitable chisel, tap the head of each shear-bolt around anti-clockwise until each bolt is loose enough to be unscrewed by hand. If this proves difficult, it will be necessary to carefully drill the head off each bolt, taking great care not to damage the lock clamp.

6 Unscrew both shear-bolts and remove the retaining clamp, collecting the washers which are fitted between the clamp and lock assembly. Remove the lock assembly from the steering column.

Ignition switch wiring block

7 Noting their correct fitted locations, disconnect the wiring connectors from the rear of the lock assembly.

8 Slacken and remove the wiring block retaining screw(s), and withdraw the wiring block from the end of the switch assembly.

Refitting

Lock assembly

9 Refit the lock assembly retaining clamp, making sure that its lug is correctly located in the steering column hole.

10 Manoeuvre the lock assembly onto the column, positioning the washers between the lock and retaining clamp. Fit the new shear-bolts, tightening them loosely at this stage **(see illustration)**.

11 Reconnect the switch wiring, ensuring it is correctly routed. Reconnect the battery, then

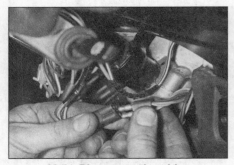

20.5a Disconnect the wiring connectors . . .

19.10 On refitting, fit the washer between the lock and clamp, and screw in the new shear-bolts

check the operation of the ignition switch and steering column lock. If all is well, tighten each lock assembly bolt until its head shears off.

12 Manoeuvre the steering column shrouds into position, and clip them securely together. Refit the shroud retaining screws, and tighten them securely.

13 Refit the instrument panel as described in Chapter 13.

Ignition switch wiring block

14 Fit the wiring block to the rear of the column lock, making sure that it is correctly seated, and secure it in position with its retaining screw(s).

15 Reconnect the switch wiring, ensuring that it is correctly routed. Reconnect the battery, then check the operation of the ignition switch.

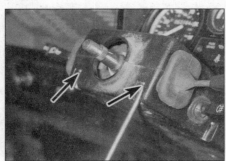

20.4a Undo the retaining screws . . .

20.5b . . . then slacken the clamp bolt, and slide the combination switch assembly off the column

16 Manoeuvre the steering column shrouds into position, and clip them securely together. Refit the shroud retaining screws, and tighten them securely.

17 Refit the instrument panel as described in Chapter 13.

20 Steering column – removal, inspection and refitting

Note: *A new universal joint clamp bolt nut will be required on refitting (see Note in Section 1).*

Removal

1 Remove the steering wheel as described in Section 18.

2 Remove the steering column lock assembly as described in Section 19.

3 Remove the instrument panel as described in Chapter 13.

4 Undo the retaining screws, then unclip the steering column upper and lower shrouds and remove them from the vehicle **(see illustrations)**.

5 Trace the wiring back from the combination switches, and disconnect their wiring connectors. Slacken the switch assembly clamp bolt, then slide the switch assembly off the top of the steering column **(see illustrations)**.

6 Slacken and remove the nut and bolt securing the upper end of the steering column to its tie-bar **(see illustration)**.

7 From within the vehicle, undo the retaining

20.4b . . . and remove the shrouds from the steering column

20.6 Slacken and remove bolt (arrowed) securing the upper end of the column to its tie-bar

20.12 Remove the clamp bolt securing the column to the universal joint . . .

20.13 . . . then slacken and remove the column lower mounting bolts (arrowed) and nuts

20.14a Slacken and remove the four bolts (arrowed) . . .

screws and remove the trim from around the pedals, to reveal the pedal box retaining bolts.

8 From within the engine compartment, slacken and remove the two nuts and washers securing the braking system master cylinder to the servo unit. Carefully disengage the master cylinder; position it clear of the servo unit, taking great care not to place any excess strain on the brake pipes. Recover the seal from the rear of the master cylinder.

9 Slacken the retaining clip (where fitted) and disconnect the vacuum hose from the servo unit.

10 From inside of the vehicle, undo the six brake pedal mounting box retaining bolts. Return to the engine compartment, and disconnect the wiring connectors from the

stop-light switch. Manoeuvre the pedal box upwards and out of position, and recover the seal fitted between the box and bulkhead.

11 Using paint or a similar, make alignment marks between the steering column and universal joint.

12 Slacken and remove the nut and clamp bolt securing the universal joint to the steering column (see illustration).

13 Unscrew the two bolts and nuts securing the column lower mounting to its mounting bracket (see illustration).

14 Slacken and remove the bolts securing the top half of the column upper mounting clamp in position. Undo the two clamp bolts and remove both halves of the clamp, complete with its rubber seal (see illustrations).

15 Undo the two bolts securing the upper

mounting bracket in position, then manoeuvre the column and bracket assembly out from the vehicle (see illustrations). Recover the bracket seal from the bulkhead. **Note:** *If the ventilation housing obscures the bulkhead hole, it will be necessary to remove the facia assembly to allow the column to be withdrawn. See Chapter 12 for facia removal details.*

Inspection

16 Examine the steering column and mountings for signs of damage and deformation, and check the steering shaft for signs of freeplay in the column bushes. If there are signs of damage or play, the column must be renewed since, at the time of writing, it appears no spare parts are available for the column. Refer to your Land Rover dealer or specialist for the latest information.

17 Examine the upper mounting bracket and clamp rubber seals, and renew them if they show signs of damage or deterioration.

Refitting

18 Ensure that the mounting bracket seal is in position, and manoeuvre the column assembly into position.

19 Align the marks made prior to removal, and engage the steering column shaft with the universal joint splines (see illustration).

20 Fit the upper mounting bracket retaining bolts, tightening them lightly only.

20.14b . . . then remove both halves of the column upper mounting clamp . . .

20.14c . . . and recover the rubber seal from the steering column

20.15a Unscrew the two bolts (arrowed) securing the upper mounting bracket in position . . .

20.15b . . . and manoeuvre the column assembly out of position

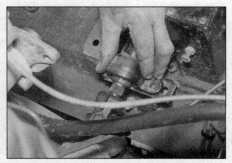

20.19 On refitting, engage the steering column with the universal joint prior to refitting its mounting bolts

21 Fit the rubber seal to the column, then refit the upper mounting clamp, tightening its bolts by hand only.

22 Refit the column lower mounting bolts and nuts, and tighten them by hand.

23 From inside the vehicle, refit the bolt securing the upper end of the column to the tie-bar, and tighten it securely.

24 Working in the engine compartment, tighten the upper mounting bracket bolts, followed by the mounting clamp bolts, and then the lower bracket retaining bolts. Ensure that all bolts are securely tightened.

25 The remainder of refitting is a direct reversal of the removal procedure, ensuring that all bolts are tightened securely.

21 Steering column intermediate shaft – removal, inspection and refitting

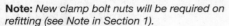

Note: *New clamp bolt nuts will be required on refitting (see Note in Section 1).*

Removal

1 Set the front wheels in the straight-ahead position.

2 Using paint or a similar, make alignment marks between the intermediate shaft and the upper and lower universal joints.

3 Slacken and remove the nuts and clamp bolts securing the intermediate shaft to the universal joints.

4 Disengage the shaft from both universal joints, and remove it from the vehicle.

Inspection

5 Inspect the intermediate shaft collapsible joint for signs of wear or damage and, if necessary, renew the shaft assembly.

Refitting

6 Aligning the marks made on removal, engage the shaft with the upper and lower universal joints.

7 Make sure that the shaft is correctly seated, then insert both its clamp bolts. Fit a new nut to each clamp bolt, and tighten them both securely.

22 Steering column universal joint – removal, inspection and refitting

Note: *New clamp bolt nuts will be required on refitting (see Note in Section 1).*

Removal

1 Set the front wheels in the straight-ahead position.

2 Using paint or a similar, make alignment marks between the universal joint and intermediate shaft, and the steering column/steering box pinion (as applicable).

3 Slacken and remove the nuts and clamp bolts securing the universal joint in position,

then disengage it from the splines and remove it from the vehicle.

Inspection

4 Inspect the universal joint for signs of roughness in its bearings, and for ease of movement. If it is damaged in any way, the joint must be renewed.

Refitting

5 Aligning the marks made on removal, engage the universal joint with the intermediate shaft splines and steering column/steering box pinion (as applicable).

6 Make sure that the joint is correctly seated, then insert both its clamp bolts. Fit a new nut to each clamp bolt, and tighten them both securely.

23 Steering – adjustment

1 If at any time it is noted that the steering action has become stiff or sloppy, the vehicle should be taken to a Land Rover dealer or specialist for the steering components to be checked. Adjustments of the steering components and steering box are possible, but specialist knowledge and equipment are needed. Therefore, this task must be entrusted to a Land Rover dealer.

2 The only adjustment which can easily be carried out by the home mechanic is steering lock stop adjustment. Once the wheel alignment is known to be correct (see Section 33), turn the steering onto full left-hand lock, and measure the clearance between the left-hand front tyre wall and the radius arm. This should be 54 mm on models with 750 x 16 tyres, and 51 mm on all other models. **Note:** *On models where gaiters are fitted to the swivel pin housings, set the clearance to 56 mm, regardless of the tyre size.* If adjustment is necessary, slacken the stop bolt locknut, and rotate the bolt as required. Once the clearance is correctly set, securely tighten the locknut. Turn the steering onto full right-hand lock, and then repeat the adjustment on the right-hand side.

24.5 Using a balljoint separator to release the drag link balljoint from the steering box drop arm

24 Steering box – removal, inspection and refitting

Note: *New tie-bar mounting bolt nuts, and a new clamp bolt nut, will be required on refitting (see Note in Section 1).*

Removal

1 Apply the handbrake, then jack up the front of the vehicle and support it on axle stands positioned underneath the chassis (see *Jacking and vehicle support*).

2 Position the front wheels in the straight-ahead position.

3 On models with power-assisted steering, using brake hose clamps, clamp both the supply and return hoses near the power steering fluid reservoir, to minimise fluid loss. Clean the area around the steering box hose unions, then make identification marks between on each pipe to ensure that they are correctly positioned on reassembly. Unscrew the feed and return pipe union nuts from the steering box; be prepared for fluid spillage, and position a suitable container beneath the pipes whilst unscrewing the union nuts. Once both pipes have been disconnected, plug the pipe ends and steering box orifices, to prevent excessive fluid leakage and to keep dirt out of the hydraulic system.

4 On all models, withdraw the split-pin, then unscrew the nut securing the drag link to the steering box drop arm.

5 Using a universal balljoint separator, free the drag link from the drop arm **(see illustration)**.

6 Using paint or a similar, make an alignment mark between the universal joint and steering box pinion.

7 Slacken and remove the nut and clamp bolt securing the universal joint to the steering box pinion.

8 Loosen the nut securing the steering box tie-bar to its mounting. Slacken and remove the remove the nuts, washers and bolts securing the tie-bar to the steering box, and position the tie-bar clear of the box **(see illustration)**.

9 Unscrew the mounting bolts, and remove the steering box assembly from the vehicle.

24.8 Steering box tie-bar retaining nut locations (arrowed)

24.15a Refit the balljoint retaining nut . . .

24.15b . . . then tighten it to the specified torque, and secure it in position with a new split-pin

necessary retaining clips. Remove the clamp from the steering hoses.

17 Lower the vehicle to the ground. On power-assisted steering models, bleed the hydraulic system as described in Section 27.

Inspection

10 Inspect the steering box assembly for signs of wear or damage. If overhaul of the steering box assembly is necessary, the task must be entrusted to a Land Rover dealer.

Refitting

11 Manoeuvre the steering box into position, and engage it with the universal joint splines, aligning the marks made prior to removal.

12 Position the steering box assembly on the chassis, making sure that it is locating lug is correctly engaged, then fit the mounting bolts and tighten them to the specified torque setting.

13 Insert the clamp bolt securing the universal joint to the steering box. Fit a new nut to the clamp bolt, and tighten the bolt to the specified torque.

14 Align the tie-bar with the box, and insert the retaining bolts and washers. Fit new nuts to the bolts, tighten them to the specified torque setting, then tighten the tie-bar-to-mounting nut to the specified torque setting.

15 Connect the drag link to the drop arm, and refit its retaining nut. Tighten the nut to the specified torque setting, and secure it in position with a new split-pin **(see illustrations)**.

16 On models with power-assisted steering, wipe clean the feed and return pipe unions, and refit them to their respective unions on the steering box. Tighten the union nuts to the specified torque setting, and ensure that the pipes are securely retained by all the

25 Steering box drop arm
– removal and refitting

Note: *A new retaining nut lockwasher will be required on refitting.*

Removal

1 Apply the handbrake, then jack up the front of the vehicle and support it on axle stands positioned underneath the chassis (see *Jacking and vehicle support*).

2 Position the front wheels in the straight-ahead position.

3 Withdraw the split-pin, then unscrew the nut securing the drag link to the steering box drop arm.

4 Using a universal balljoint separator, free the drag link from the drop arm.

5 Bend down the lockwasher tab, then slacken and remove the drop arm retaining nut and lockwasher **(see illustrations)**.

6 Make alignment marks between the drop arm and steering box shaft.

7 A suitable legged puller will now be required to draw the arm off the box shaft. Locate the legs of the puller behind the arm, and carefully draw it off the steering box shaft **(see illustration)**.

8 Once the arm is loose, remove the puller, then lower the drop arm away from the steering box.

9 Check that the link balljoint moves freely, without any sign of roughness. Also check that the balljoint gaiter shows no sign of deterioration, and is free from cracks and splits. If any sign of wear or damage is found, the drop arm assembly should be renewed (or overhauled). Overhaul of the balljoint components requires the use of several special service tools, and should be entrusted to a Land Rover dealer or specialist.

Refitting

10 Align the marks made prior to removal, and locate the drop arm on the steering box shaft splines.

11 Fit the new lockwasher to the shaft, and refit the retaining nut. Tighten the nut to the specified torque setting, then secure it in position by bending down the tab of the lockwasher so that it contacts one of the nut flats **(see illustration)**.

12 Connect the drag link to the drop arm, and refit its retaining nut. Tighten the nut to the specified torque setting, and secure it in position with a new split-pin.

13 Lower the vehicle to the ground, and reconnect the battery.

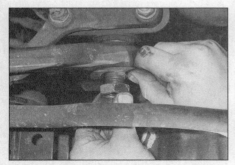

25.5a Unscrew the drop arm retaining nut . . .

25.5b . . . and recover the lockwasher

25.7 Using a two legged-puller to draw the drop arm off the steering box

25.11 Tighten the drop arm retaining nut to the specified torque, and secure it in position by bending down the lockwasher against one of its flats (arrowed)

26.8 Power steering pump mounting bolts (TD5 engine)

26 Power steering pump – removal and refitting

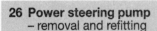

Removal

1 Apply the handbrake, then jack up the front of the vehicle and support it on axle stands positioned underneath the chassis (see *Jacking and vehicle support*).

2 On 300 TDi and TD5 engines, remove the cooling fan and viscous coupling as described in Chapter 3.

3 On all engines, loosen the bolts securing the drivebelt pulley to the power steering pump.

4 Remove the auxiliary drivebelt as described in Chapter 1, then remove the retaining bolts and withdraw the power steering pump pulley, noting which way around it is fitted.

5 Using brake hose clamps, clamp both the supply and return hoses near the power steering fluid reservoir. This will minimise fluid loss during subsequent operations.

6 On non-TD5 engines, release the fasteners and remove the undershield from beneath the engine.

7 Slacken the retaining clip, and disconnect the fluid supply hose from the pump. Slacken the union nut, and disconnect the feed pipe from the pump; be prepared for some fluid spillage as the pipe and hose are disconnected. Plug the hose/pipe end and pump unions, to minimise fluid loss and to prevent the entry of dirt into the system.

8 Slacken and remove the power steering pump mounting bolts, and remove the pump from the engine **(see illustration)**.

9 Overhaul of the pump is not possible; if the pump is worn or damaged, it must be renewed.

Refitting

10 Manoeuvre the pump into position, then refit its mounting bolts and tighten them to the specified torque setting where given. On TD5 models, ensure the drive lugs on the rear of the pump engage correctly with the coolant pump drive lugs **(see illustration)**

11 Reconnect the feed pipe to the pump, and tighten its union nut to the specified torque.

26.10 The power steering pump drive lugs (arrowed) must engage with the coolant pump drive lugs (TD5 models only)

12 Reconnect the supply hose, and securely tighten its retaining clip.

13 Refit the pulley to the pump, making sure it is the correct way around, and install the mounting bolts.

14 Refit and tension the auxiliary drivebelt as described in Chapter 1, then tighten the pulley retaining bolts to the specified torque setting.

15 On 300 TDi and TD5 engines, refit the viscous coupling and cooling fan as described in Chapter 3.

16 Where applicable, install the engine undershield, then lower the vehicle to the ground.

17 Bleed the hydraulic system as described in Section 27.

27 Power steering system – bleeding

1 With the engine stopped, top-up the fluid reservoir to the maximum mark with the specified type of fluid.

2 Have an assistant start the engine, whilst you keep watch on the fluid level. Be prepared to add more fluid as the engine starts, since the fluid level is likely to drop quickly.

3 Once the fluid level has stabilised, warm the engine up to normal operating temperature. Ensure that the front wheels are in the straight-ahead position, then turn the engine off.

4 Check that the power steering fluid level is still up to the maximum mark, topping-up if necessary.

5 Start the engine and allow it idle. During the following procedure, the engine must remain at idle speed, and the steering must not be turned.

6 Slowly slacken the bleed screw, which is situated on the top of the power steering box assembly. Ensuring that the fluid level in the reservoir remains at the maximum level, allow fluid to seep from the screw until a steady flow of fluid which is free from air bubbles is seen to be emerging. Once this is so, securely tighten the bleed screw, and mop-up all traces of fluid from the top of the steering box.

7 Turn the steering onto full left-hand lock,

holding it there for a few seconds, and then onto full right-hand lock; check all steering hose/pipe unions for signs of leakage. **Note:** *Do not hold the steering at full lock for more than 10 seconds at a time, otherwise the hydraulic system may become damaged.*

8 Once all air is removed from the system, stop the engine, and check the fluid level as described in Chapter 1.

28 Steering damper – removal and refitting

Note: *A new pivot bolt nut will be required on refitting (see Note in Section 1).*

Removal

1 Apply the handbrake, then jack up the front of the vehicle and support it on axle stands positioned underneath the chassis (see *Jacking and vehicle support*).

2 Slacken and unscrew the locknut and retaining nut securing the damper to its mounting bracket. Slide off the outer washer, rubber mounting and mounting seat arrangement, noting each component's correct fitted location. Free the damper from the bracket, and recover the inner washer rubber mounting and mounting seat arrangement from the damper.

3 Slacken and remove the nut and washer, then withdraw the pivot bolt securing the damper to the drag link.

4 Remove the steering damper from underneath the vehicle.

5 Inspect the damper assembly for signs of wear or damage, and renew if necessary. Inspect the rubber mountings for signs of damage and deterioration, and renew if necessary.

Refitting

6 Refitting is the reverse of removal, ensuring that the mounting rubber components are correctly positioned **(see illustration)**. Fit a new nut to the pivot bolt, and tighten it securely. Tighten the retaining nut, and secure it in position by securely tightening the locknut.

28.6 Ensure that the steering damper-to-chassis mounting rubbers and washers are correctly arranged on each side of the mounting bracket

29 Drag link – removal and refitting

Note: *A new steering damper pivot bolt nut will be required on refitting (see Note in Section 1).*

Removal

1 Apply the handbrake, then jack up the front of the vehicle and support it on axle stands positioned underneath the chassis (see *Jacking and vehicle support*).
2 Position the front wheels in the straight-ahead position.
3 Slacken and remove the nut and washer, then withdraw the pivot bolt securing the steering damper to the drag link.
4 Withdraw the split-pin, then unscrew the nut securing the drag link to the steering box drop arm. Using a universal balljoint separator, free the drag link from the drop arm.
5 Repeat paragraph 4, and free the drag link from the swivel pin housing assembly. Remove the drag link from underneath the vehicle. If necessary, remove the roadwheel to improve access to the balljoint nut.
6 Check that the link balljoint moves freely, without any sign of roughness. Also check that the balljoint gaiter shows no sign of deterioration, and is free from cracks and splits. If any sign of wear or damage is found, the balljoint must be renewed (see Section 30). If the drag link itself is damaged it must be renewed; do not attempt to straighten it.

Refitting

7 Offer up the drag link, and engage it with the swivel pin housing and steering box drop arm. Refit the retaining nuts, and tighten them to the specified torque setting. Secure each nut in position with a new split-pin.
8 Engage the steering damper with the drag link, and insert its pivot bolt. Fit a new nut to the pivot bolt, and tighten it to the specified torque setting.
9 Refit the roadwheel (where removed), then lower the vehicle to the ground and reconnect the battery negative terminal. Where necessary, tighten the roadwheel nuts to the specified torque setting.
10 Road test the vehicle, and check that the steering wheel is centralised when the vehicle is driven straight-ahead. If the steering wheel is more than 5° out of position, adjustment should be made by removing the wheel and repositioning it on the column splines. If the wheel is less than 5° out of alignment, adjustment can be made by altering the drag link length as follows.
11 Apply the handbrake, then raise the front of the vehicle, and detach the outer balljoint from the swivel pin housing assembly as described above. Slacken the balljoint clamp

bolt, and adjust the drag link length by screwing the balljoint in or out (as applicable). On right-hand drive models, if the steering wheel was found to be slightly right of centre, shorten the drag link length; if it was found to be slightly left of centre, extend the drag link length. On left-hand drive models, if the steering wheel was found to be slightly right of centre, extend the drag link length; if it was found to be slightly left of centre, shorten the drag link length. Once the drag link length is correct, refit the balljoint to the swivel pin housing, and tighten its retaining nut to the specified torque setting. Secure the nut in position with a new split-pin, then tighten the drag link clamp bolt to the specified torque. Refit the roadwheel, then lower the vehicle to the ground and tighten the wheel nuts to the specified torque. Road test the vehicle and, if necessary, repeat the adjustment procedure.

30 Drag link balljoint/end fitting – removal and refitting

Removal

1 Remove the drag link as described in Section 29.
2 Using a straight-edge and a scriber, or similar, mark the relationship of the balljoint/end fitting to the drag link. Also note the correct fitted relationship between the end fitting and balljoint.
3 Slacken the clamp bolt(s) then counting the **exact** number of turns necessary to do so, unscrew the balljoint/end fitting from the drag link end.
4 Carefully clean the balljoint/end fitting and the drag link threads. Renew the balljoint if its movement is sloppy or if it is too stiff, if it is excessively worn, or if it is damaged in any way; carefully check the stud taper and threads. If the balljoint gaiter is damaged, the complete balljoint assembly must be renewed; it is not possible to obtain the gaiter separately.

Refitting

5 Screw the balljoint/end fitting into the drag link by the exact number of turns noted on removal, and tighten the clamp bolt(s) to the specified torque. This should line up the balljoint in relation to the end fitting, and should set the track rod to its original length.
6 Check that the balljoint and end fitting are correctly positioned in relation to each other, then tighten the drag link clamp bolt to the specified torque setting.
7 Refit the drag link as described in Section 29, and check that the steering wheel is centralised.

31 Track rod – removal and refitting

Removal

1 Apply the handbrake, then jack up the front of the vehicle and support it on axle stands positioned underneath the chassis (see *Jacking and vehicle support*).
2 Position the front wheels in the straight-ahead position.
3 Withdraw the split-pin, then unscrew the nut securing the track rod to the left-hand swivel pin housing. Using a universal balljoint separator, free the track rod from the swivel pin housing.
4 Repeat paragraph 3, and free the track rod from the right-hand swivel pin housing assembly. Remove the track rod from underneath the vehicle.
5 Check that the track rod balljoints move freely, without any sign of roughness. Also check that the balljoint gaiters show no sign of deterioration, and are free from cracks and splits. If any sign of wear or damage is found, the balljoint(s) must be renewed (see Section 32). If the track rod itself is damaged, it must be renewed; do not attempt to straighten it.

Refitting

6 Offer up the track rod, and engage it with the swivel pin housings. Refit the retaining nuts, and tighten them to the specified torque setting. Secure each nut in position with a new split-pin.
7 Check the front wheel alignment as described in Section 33.

32 Track rod balljoint – removal and refitting

Removal

1 Remove the track rod as described in Section 31.
2 Using a straight-edge and a scriber, or similar, mark the relationship of the balljoint to the track rod.
3 Slacken the clamp bolt(s) then counting the **exact** number of turns necessary to do so, unscrew the balljoint from the track rod end.
4 Carefully clean the balljoint and the track rod threads. Renew the balljoint if its movement is sloppy or if it is too stiff, if it is excessively worn, or if it is damaged in any way; carefully check the stud taper and threads. If the balljoint gaiter is damaged, the complete balljoint assembly must be renewed; it is not possible to obtain the gaiter separately.

Refitting

5 Screw the balljoint into the track rod by the exact number of turns noted on removal, and tighten the clamp bolt(s) to the specified torque. This should set the track rod to its original length.

6 Ensure that both balljoints are correctly aligned, then tighten the clamp bolt(s) to the specified torque setting.

7 Refit the track rod as described in Section 31.

8 Prior to using the vehicle, check the front wheel alignment as described in Section 33.

33 Wheel alignment and steering angles – general information

1 Accurate front wheel alignment is essential for precise steering and handling, and for even tyre wear. Before carrying out any checking or adjusting operations, make sure that the tyres are correctly inflated, that all steering and suspension joints and linkages are in sound condition, and that the wheels are not buckled or distorted, particularly around the rims. It will also be necessary to have the vehicle positioned on flat, level ground, with enough space to push the car backwards and forwards through about half its length.

2 Front wheel alignment consists of four factors **(see illustration)**:

Camber is the angle at which the roadwheels are set from the vertical, when viewed from the front or rear of the vehicle. 'Positive' camber is the angle (in degrees) that the wheels are tilted outwards at the top from the vertical.

Castor is the angle between the steering axis and a vertical line when viewed from each side of the vehicle. 'Positive' castor is indicated when the steering axis is inclined towards the rear of the vehicle at its upper end.

Steering axis inclination is the angle, when viewed from the front or rear of the vehicle, between the vertical and an imaginary line drawn between the upper and lower front suspension strut mountings.

Toe setting is the amount by which the distance between the front inside edges of the roadwheels differs from that between the rear inside edges, when measured at hub height. If

the distance between the front edges is less than at the rear, the wheels are said to 'toe-in'. If it is greater than at the rear, the wheels are said to 'toe-out'.

3 Camber, castor and steering axis inclination are set during manufacture, and are not adjustable. Unless the vehicle has suffered accident damage, or there is gross wear in the suspension mountings or joints, it can be assumed that these settings are correct. If for any reason it is believed that they are not correct, the task of checking them should be left to a Land Rover dealer, who will have the necessary special equipment needed to measure the small angles involved.

4 It is, however, within the scope of the home mechanic to check and adjust the front wheel toe setting. To do this, a tracking gauge must first be obtained. Two types of gauge are available, and can be obtained from motor accessory shops. The first type measures the distance between the front and rear inside edges of the roadwheels, as previously described, with the vehicle stationary. The second type, known as a `scuff plate', measures the actual position of the contact surface of the tyre, in relation to the road surface, with the vehicle in motion. This is achieved by pushing or driving the front tyre over a plate, which then moves slightly according to the scuff of the tyre, and shows this movement on a scale. Both types have their advantages and disadvantages, but either can give satisfactory results if used correctly and carefully.

5 Many tyre specialists will also check toe settings free, or for a nominal charge.

6 Make sure that the steering is in the straight-ahead position when making measurements. If adjustment is necessary, apply the handbrake then jack up the front of the vehicle and support it securely on axle stands. Slacken the track rod balljoint clamp bolts then rotate the track rod to alter the length of the rod (as necessary); shortening the track rod will reduce toe-in/increase toe-out.

7 When the setting is correct, tighten both the clamp bolts to the specified torque setting.

8 Recheck the toe setting and, if necessary, repeat the adjustment procedure.

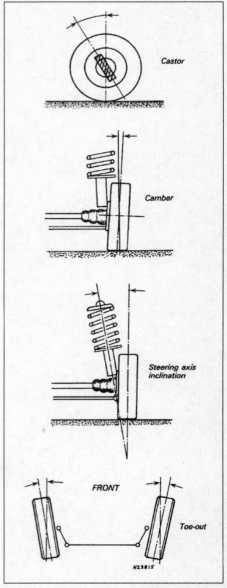

33.2 Wheel alignment and steering angle measurements

Notes

Chapter 12
Bodywork and fittings

Contents

Section number

Body exterior fittings – removal and refitting 19
Bonnet – removal, refitting and adjustment 8
Bonnet lock – removal and refitting 10
Bonnet release cable – removal and refitting 9
Door – removal, refitting and adjustment 11
Door handle and lock components – removal and refitting 13
Door inner trim panel – removal and refitting 12
Door window glass and regulator – removal and refitting 14
Exterior mirror – removal and refitting 17
Facia panel assembly – removal and refitting 24
Front bumper – removal and refitting 6
General information 1
Interior trim – removal and refitting 22

Section number

Maintenance – bodywork and underframe. 2
Maintenance – upholstery and carpets 3
Major body damage – repair 5
Minor body damage – repair 4
Rear bumper – removal and refitting 7
Seat belt components – removal and refitting 21
Seats – removal and refitting 20
Storage box and centre console – removal and refitting 23
Tailgate – removal and refitting. 15
Tailgate lock assembly – removal and refitting. 16
Underbody and general body check . . . . See Chapter 1
Windscreen, tailgate and fixed windows – general information. 18

Degrees of difficulty

| **Easy,** suitable for novice with little experience | ⚒ | **Fairly easy,** suitable for beginner with some experience | ⚒ | **Fairly difficult,** suitable for competent DIY mechanic | ⚒ | **Difficult,** suitable for experienced DIY mechanic | ⚒ | **Very difficult,** suitable for expert DIY or professional | ⚒ |

Specifications

Torque wrench setting	Nm	lbf ft
Seat belt mounting nuts and bolts.	32	24

1 General information

The bodyshell and associated panels consist of a mixture of both pressed-steel and aluminium alloy sections. Most components are welded together, but some use is made of structural adhesives; the front wings are bolted on.

Extensive use is made of plastic materials, mainly on the interior but also in exterior components. Plastic components such as wheel arch liners are fitted to the underside of the vehicle, to improve the body's resistance to corrosion.

2 Maintenance – bodywork and underframe

The general condition of a vehicle's bodywork is the one thing that significantly affects its value. Maintenance is easy, but needs to be regular. Neglect, particularly after minor damage, can lead quickly to further deterioration and costly repair bills. It is important also to keep watch on those parts of the vehicle not immediately visible, for instance the underside, inside all the wheel arches, and the lower part of the engine compartment.

The basic maintenance routine for the bodywork is washing – preferably with a lot of water, from a hose. This will remove all the loose solids which may have stuck to the vehicle. It is important to flush these off in such a way as to prevent grit from scratching the finish. The wheel arches and underframe need washing in the same way, to remove any accumulated mud, which will retain moisture and tend to encourage rust. Paradoxically enough, the best time to clean the underframe and wheel arches is in wet weather, when the mud is thoroughly wet and soft. In very wet weather, the underframe is usually cleaned of large accumulations automatically, and this is a good time for inspection.

Periodically, except on vehicles with a wax-based underbody protective coating, it is a good idea to have the whole of the underframe of the vehicle steam-cleaned, engine compartment included, so that a thorough inspection can be carried out to see what minor repairs and renovations are necessary. Steam-cleaning is available at many garages, and is necessary for the removal of the accumulation of oily grime, which sometimes is allowed to become thick in certain areas. If steam-cleaning facilities are not available, there are some excellent grease solvents available which are brush-applied; the dirt can then be simply hosed off. Note that these methods should not be used on vehicles with wax-based underbody protective coating, or the coating will be removed. Such vehicles should be inspected annually, preferably just prior to Winter, when the underbody should be washed down, and any damage to the wax coating repaired. Ideally, a completely fresh coat should be applied. It would also be worth considering the use of such wax-based protection for injection into door panels, sills, box sections, etc, as an additional safeguard against rust damage, where such protection is not provided by the vehicle manufacturer.

After washing paintwork, wipe off with a chamois leather to give an unspotted clear finish. A coat of clear protective wax polish will give added protection against chemical pollutants in the air. If the paintwork sheen has dulled or oxidised, use a cleaner/polisher combination to restore the brilliance of the shine. This requires a little effort, but such dulling is usually caused because regular washing has been neglected. Care needs to be taken with metallic paintwork, as special non-abrasive cleaner/polisher is required to avoid damage to the finish. Always check that the door and ventilator opening drain holes and pipes are completely clear, so that water can be drained out. Brightwork should be treated in the same way as paintwork. Windscreens and windows can be kept clear of the smeary film which often appears, by the use of proprietary glass cleaner. Never use any form of wax or other body or chromium polish on glass.

3 Maintenance – upholstery and carpets

Mats and carpets should be brushed or vacuum-cleaned regularly, to keep them free of grit. If they are badly stained, remove them from the vehicle for scrubbing or sponging, and make quite sure they are dry before refitting. Seats and interior trim panels can be kept clean by wiping with a damp cloth. If they do become stained (which can be more apparent on light-coloured upholstery), use a little liquid detergent and a soft nail brush to scour the grime out of the grain of the material. Do not forget to keep the headlining clean in the same way as the upholstery. When using liquid cleaners inside the vehicle, do not over-wet the surfaces being cleaned. Excessive damp could get into the seams and padded interior, causing stains, offensive odours or even rot.

HAYNES HINT *If the inside of the vehicle gets wet accidentally, it is worthwhile taking some trouble to dry it out properly, particularly where carpets are involved. Do not leave oil or electric heaters inside the vehicle for this purpose.*

4 Minor body damage – repair

Minor scratches

If the scratch is very superficial, and does not penetrate to the metal of the bodywork, repair is very simple. Lightly rub the area of the scratch with a paintwork renovator, or a very fine cutting paste, to remove loose paint from the scratch and to clear the surrounding bodywork of wax polish. Rinse the area with clean water.

Apply touch-up paint to the scratch using a thin paintbrush; continue to apply thin layers of paint until the surface of the paint in the scratch is level with the surrounding paintwork. Allow the new paint at least two weeks to harden, then blend it into the surrounding paintwork by rubbing the paintwork in the scratch area with a paintwork renovator or a very fine cutting pastepaste. Finally, apply wax polish.

Where the scratch has penetrated right through to the metal of the bodywork, a different repair technique is required. Remove any loose paint, etc from the bottom of the scratch with a penknife. Using a rubber or nylon applicator, fill the scratch with bodystopper paste. Before the stopper-paste in the scratch hardens, wrap a piece of smooth cotton rag around the top of a finger. Dip the finger in cellulose thinners, and then quickly sweep it across the surface of the stopper-paste in the scratch; this will ensure that the surface of the stopper-paste is lightly hollowed. The scratch can now be painted over as described earlier in this Section.

Dents

The alloy body panels on the Land Rover are easier to work on than steel, and minor dents or creases can be beaten out fairly easily. However, if the damaged area is quite large, prolonged hammering will cause the metal to harden; to avoid the possibility of cracking, it must be softened or 'annealed'. This can be done easily with a gas blowlamp, but great care is required to avoid actually melting the metal. The blowlamp must always be kept moving in a circular pattern, whilst being held a respectable distance from the metal.

One method of checking when the alloy is hot enough is to rub down the surface to be annealed, and then apply a thin film of oil over it. The blowlamp should be played over the rear side of the oiled surface, until the oil evaporates and the surface is dry. Turn off the blowlamp, and allow the metal to cool naturally; the treated areas will now be softened, and it will be possible to work it with a hammer or mallet. After panel-beating, the damaged section should be rubbed down and painted as described later in this Section.

When deep denting of the vehicle's bodywork has taken place, the first task is to pull the dent out until the affected bodywork almost attains its original shape. There is little point in trying to restore the original shape completely, as the metal in the damaged area will have stretched on impact, and cannot be reshaped to its original contour. It is better to bring the level of the dent up to a point which is about 3 mm below the level of the surrounding bodywork. In cases where the dent is very shallow anyway, it is not worth trying to pull it out at all.

If the underside of the dent is accessible, it can be hammered out gently from behind using the method described earlier.

Should the dent be in a section of the

bodywork which has a double skin, or some other factor making it inaccessible from behind, a different technique is called for. Drill several small holes through the metal inside the dent area, particularly in the deeper sections. Then screw long self-tapping screws into the holes just sufficiently for them to gain a good purchase in the metal. Now the dent can be pulled out by pulling on the protruding heads of the screws with a pair of pliers.

The next stage of the repair is the removal of the paint from the damaged area, and from an inch or so of the surrounding 'sound' bodywork.

Note: *On no account should coarse abrasives be used on aluminium panels in order to remove paint. The use of a wire brush or abrasive on a power drill for example, will cause deep scoring of the metal and in extreme cases, penetrate the thickness of the relatively soft aluminium alloy.*

Removal of paint is best achieved by applying paint remover to the area, allowing it to act on the paintwork for the specified time, and then removing the softened paint with a wood or nylon scraper. This method may have to be repeated in order to remove all traces of paint. A good method of removing small stubborn traces of paint is to rub the area with a nylon scouring pad soaked in thinners or paint remover. **Note:** *If it is necessary to use this method, always wear rubber gloves to protect the hands from burns from the paint remover. It is also advisable to wear eye protection, as any paint remover that gets into the eyes will cause severe inflammation, or worse.*

Finally, remove all traces of paint and remover by washing the area with plenty of clean fresh water.

To complete the preparations for filling, score the surface of the bare metal with a screwdriver or the tang of a file, or alternatively, drill small holes in the affected area. This will provide a really good 'key' for the filler paste.

To complete the repair, see the Section on filling and respraying.

Holes or gashes

Remove all the paint from the affected area, and from an inch or so of the surrounding 'sound' bodywork, using the method described in the previous Section. With the paint removed, you will be able to gauge the severity of the damage, and therefore decide whether to replace the whole panel (if this is possible) or to repair the affected area. It is often quicker and more satisfactory to fit a new panel than to attempt to repair large areas of damage.

Remove all fittings from the affected area, except those which will act as a guide to the original shape of the damaged bodywork (eg, headlight shells, etc). Then, using tin snips or a hacksaw blade, remove all loose metal and other metal badly affected by damage. Hammer the edges of the hole inwards, in order to create a slight depression for the filler paste.

Before filling can take place, it will be necessary to block the hole in some way. This can be achieved by the use of zinc gauze or aluminium tape.

Zinc gauze is probably the best material to use for a large hole. Cut a piece to the approximate size and shape of the hole to be filled, then position it in the hole so that its edges are below the level of the surrounding bodywork. It can be retained in position by several blobs of filler paste around its periphery.

Aluminium tape should be used for small or very narrow holes. Pull a piece off the roll and trim it to the approximate size and shape required, then pull off the backing paper (if used) and stick the tape over the hole; it can be overlapped if the thickness of one piece is insufficient. Burnish down the edges of the tape with the handle of a screwdriver or similar, to ensure that the tape is securely attached to the metal underneath.

Filling and respraying

Before using this Section, see the Section on dent, deep scratch, hole and gash repairs.

Many types of bodyfiller are available, but generally speaking, those proprietary kits which contain a tin of filler paste and a tube of resin hardener are best for this type of repair. A wide, flexible plastic or nylon applicator will be found invaluable for imparting a smooth and well-contoured finish to the surface of the filler.

Mix up a little filler on a clean piece of card or board. Use the hardener sparingly (follow the maker's instructions on the packet) otherwise the filler will set rapidly.

Using the applicator, apply the filler paste to the prepared area; draw the applicator across the surface of the filler to achieve the correct contour, and to level the filler surfaces. As soon as a contour that approximates the correct one is achieved, stop working the paste; if you carry on too long, the paste will become sticky and begin to 'pick-up' on the applicator. Continue to add thin layers of filler paste at twenty-minute intervals until the level of the filler is just 'proud' of the surrounding bodywork.

Once the filler has hardened, excess can be removed using a metal plane or file. From then on, progressively finer grades of abrasive paper should be used, starting with a 40-grade production paper, and finishing with a 400-grade wet-or-dry paper. Always wrap the abrasive paper around a flat rubber, cork, or wooden block, otherwise the surface of the filler will not be completely flat. During the smoothing of the filler surface, the wet-or-dry paper should be periodically rinsed in water. This will ensure that a very fine smooth finish is imparted to the filler at the final stage.

At this stage, the 'dent' should be surrounded by a ring of bare metal, which in turn should be encircled by the finely 'feathered' edge of the good paintwork. Rinse and repair with clean water, until all the dust produced by the rubbing-down operation is gone.

Spray the whole area with a light coat of grey primer, this will show up any imperfections in the surface of the filler. If at all possible, it is recommended that an etch-primer is used on untreated alloy surfaces, otherwise the primer may not be keyed sufficiently, and may subsequently flake off. Repair imperfections with fresh filler paste or bodystopper and once more, smooth the surface with abrasive paper. Repeat the spray-and-repair procedures until you are satisfied that the surface of the filler, and the feathered edge of the paintwork, is perfect. Clean the repair area with clean water, and allow it to dry fully.

 If bodystopper is used, it can be mixed with cellulose thinners, to form a really thin paste which is ideal for filling small holes.

The repair area is now ready for spraying. Paint spraying must be carried out in a warm, dry, windless and dust-free atmosphere. This condition can be created artificially if you have access to a large indoor working area, but if you are forced to work in the open, you will have to pick your day very carefully. If you are working indoors, dousing the floor in the work area with water will 'lay' the dust which would otherwise be in the atmosphere. If the repair is confined to one body panel, mask off the surrounding panels; this will help to minimise the effects of a slight mis-match in paint colours. Bodywork fittings will also need to be masked off. Use genuine masking tape and several thickness of newspaper for the masking operation.

Before commencing to spray, agitate the aerosol can thoroughly, then spray a test area (an old tin, or similar) until the technique is mastered. Cover the repair area with a thick coat of primer; the thickness should be built up using several thin layers of paint, rather than one thick one. Using 400-grade wet-or-dry paper, rub down the surface of the primer until it is really smooth. Whilst doing this, the work area should be thoroughly doused with water, and the wet-or-dry paper periodically rinsed in water. Allow to dry before spraying on more paint.

Spray on the top coat, again building up the thickness by using several thin layers of paint. Start spraying at the top of the repair area and then, using a side-to-side motion, work downwards until the whole repair area and about 50 mm of the surrounding original paintwork is covered. Remove all masking material 10 to 15 minutes after spraying on the final coat of paint.

Allow the new paint at least two weeks to harden, then, using a paintwork renovator or a very fine cutting paste, blend the edges of the paint into the existing paintwork. Finally, apply wax polish.

Plastic components

With the use of more and more plastic body components by the vehicle manufacturers (eg bumpers. spoilers, and in some cases major body panels), rectification of more serious damage to such items has become a matter of either entrusting repair work to a specialist in this field, or renewing complete components. Repair of such damage by the DIY owner is not really feasible, owing to the cost of the equipment and materials required for effecting such repairs. The basic technique involves making a groove along the line of the crack in the plastic, using a rotary burr in a power drill. The damaged part is then welded back together, using a hot-air gun to heat up and fuse a plastic filler rod into the groove. Any excess plastic is then removed, and the area rubbed down to a smooth finish. It is important that a filler rod of the correct plastic is used, as body components can be made of a variety of different types (eg, polycarbonate, ABS, polypropylene).

Damage of a less serious nature (abrasions, minor cracks etc) can be repaired by the DIY owner using a two-part epoxy filler repair material. Once mixed in equal proportions, or applied directly from the tube, this is used in similar fashion to the bodywork filler used on metal panels. The filler is usually cured in twenty to thirty minutes, ready for sanding and painting.

If the owner is renewing a complete component himself, or if he has repaired it with epoxy filler, he will be left with the problem of finding a suitable paint for finishing which is compatible with the type of plastic used. At one time, the use of a universal paint was not possible, owing to the complex range of plastics encountered in body component applications. Standard paints, generally speaking, will not bond to plastic or rubber satisfactorily. However, it is now possible to obtain a plastic body parts finishing kit which consists of a pre-primer treatment, a primer and coloured top coat. Full instructions are normally supplied with a kit, but basically, the method of use is to first apply the pre-primer to the component concerned, and allow it to dry for up to 30 minutes. Then the primer is applied, and left to dry for about an hour before finally applying the special-coloured top coat. The result is a correctly-coloured component, where the paint will flex with the plastic or rubber, a property that standard paint does not normally possess.

5 Major body damage – repair

Where serious damage has occurred, or large areas need renewal due to neglect, it means that complete new panels will need welding-in, and this is best left to professionals. If the damage is due to impact, it will also be necessary to check completely the alignment of the bodyshell, and this can only be carried out accurately by a Land Rover dealer, using special jigs. If the body is left misaligned, it is primarily dangerous, as the car will not handle properly; secondly, uneven stresses will be imposed on the steering, suspension and possibly transmission, causing abnormal wear, or complete failure, particularly to such items as the tyres.

6 Front bumper – removal and refitting

Removal

1 Slacken and remove the four mounting bolts from the top of the bumper, and recover the nut retaining plates from under the bumper **(see illustration)**. On models with air conditioning, undo the 6 screws and remove the radiator grille (see illustration).
2 Remove the bumper from the vehicle.

Refitting

3 Refitting is the reverse of removal, ensuring that the mounting bolts are securely tightened.

7 Rear bumper – removal and refitting

Removal

1 If necessary to improve access, chock the front wheels, then jack up the rear of the vehicle and support it on axle stands.
2 Support the bumper, then slacken and remove the nuts and bolts securing bumper to the chassis. Manoeuvre the bumper away from the vehicle.

Refitting

3 Refitting is the reverse of removal.

8 Bonnet – removal, refitting and adjustment

Removal

1 Where necessary, remove the spare wheel from the bonnet.
2 On models with a scissor-type bonnet prop, open the bonnet, and get an assistant to support it. Remove the circlip, and withdraw the clevis pin securing the prop to the bonnet.
3 On all models, with the aid of an assistant, lift the bonnet to the upright position, then unhook the bonnet and remove it from the vehicle. Recover the bush from each bonnet pivot, and store them with the bonnet for safe-keeping.
4 Inspect the bonnet hinges for signs of wear or damage; the hinges are bolted in position, and can easily be renewed.

Refitting and adjustment

5 Refitting is the reverse of removal, ensuring that the bushes are in position on the bonnet pivots.
6 Close the bonnet, and check for alignment with the adjacent panels. If necessary, slacken the bonnet bolts and realign the bonnet to suit. The bonnet height is adjusted by rotating the striker on the front edge of the bonnet. Once the bonnet is correctly aligned, securely tighten the bolts.
7 Once the bonnet is correctly aligned, check that the bonnet fastens and releases in a satisfactory manner. If necessary, adjust the release cable described in Section 10.

9 Bonnet release cable – removal and refitting

Removal

1 Remove the bonnet lock assembly as described in Section 10.
2 Work back along the cable, releasing it from all the relevant retaining clips and ties, whilst noting its correct routing. Release the rubber sealing grommets from the body, and slide them off the end of the cable. Tie a piece of string to the cable end – this can then be used to draw the cable back into position.
3 From inside the vehicle, unscrew the retaining nut securing the bonnet release handle to its mounting bracket.
4 Withdraw the lever and cable assembly from inside the vehicle. Once the cable end appears, untie the string and leave it in position in the vehicle – the string can then be used to draw the new cable back into position.

Refitting

5 Tie the string to the end of the cable, and use the string to draw the bonnet release cable through from inside the vehicle into the engine compartment. Once the cable is through, untie the string, and slide on both the rubber sealing grommets. Seat the handle in its mounting bracket, and securely tighten the retaining nut.
6 Ensure that the cable is correctly routed

and retained by all the relevant clips and ties, then seat the cable grommets in the vehicle body.
7 Refit the bonnet lock assembly as described in Section 10.

10 Bonnet lock – removal and refitting

Removal

1 Undo the retaining screws, and remove the radiator grille from the front of the vehicle.
2 Using a suitable marker pen, draw around the outline of the bonnet lock top plate and adjusting plates. These marks can then be used as a guide on refitting.
3 Undo the single bolt and remove both the bonnet adjusting plates, noting their correct fitted locations.
4 Undo the two retaining bolts, and lift the top plate away from the bonnet crossmember.
5 Free the lock assembly and mounting plate from the underside of the bonnet crossmember, and detach the lock assembly from its return spring.
6 Slacken the release cable clamp, then detach the cable and remove the lock and mounting plate from the vehicle.

Refitting

7 Refitting is the reverse of the removal procedure, using the alignment marks made prior to removal. Prior to refitting the radiator grille, check the operation of the release mechanism. Adjustment of the cable can be made by either slackening the clamp and adjusting the inner cable or, alternatively, by releasing the outer cable retaining clip and repositioning the clip on the cable (as applicable).

11 Door – removal, refitting and adjustment

Front door removal

1 Remove the split-pin and washer, then

6.1a Undo the four mounting bolts and remove the bumper

6.1b On air conditioned models, undo the 6 screws (3 left-hand ones arrowed) and remove the radiator grille

11.1 Remove the split-pin, and withdraw the clevis pin from the check link

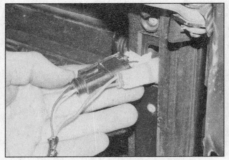

11.2 On models with electric front windows, pull the gaiter from the A-pillar and disconnect the door wiring loom plugs

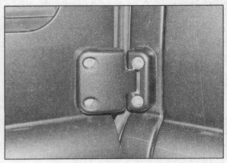

11.7 4 bolts secure the door hinges to the body

withdraw the clevis pin securing the check link to the door **(see illustration)**.

2 Where necessary, remove the door inner trim panel to gain access to hinge retaining nuts (Section 12). On vehicles with electric front windows and/or central locking, pull the rubber loom covering from the A-pillar and disconnect the door loom wiring plugs **(see illustration)**.

3 Have an assistant support the weight of the door, then slacken and remove the four nuts and bolts securing the hinges to the door. Remove the door from the vehicle, and recover the nylon spacers which are fitted between the hinge and door.

4 Examine the hinges for signs of wear or damage. If renewal is necessary, mark the outline of the original hinge on the pillar, then slacken and remove the retaining bolts and remove the hinge. Recover the special retaining nuts, and remove the hinge seal. Fit the seal and new hinge, and refit the retaining bolts. Align the hinge with the marks made prior to removal, and securely tighten the retaining bolts.

Rear door removal

5 Unscrew the retaining nut, then free the check link from its pivot, recovering the washer which is fitted on each side of the link.

Vehicles up to 1999 model year

6 Have an assistant support the weight of the door, then slacken and remove the four nuts and bolts securing the hinges to the door. Remove the door from the vehicle, and recover the nylon spacers which are fitted between the hinge and door.

Vehicles from 1999 model year

7 Have an assistant support the weight of the door, then slacken and remove the 4 bolts securing the door hinges to the body. Remove the door **(see illustration)**.

All vehicles

8 Examine the hinges for signs of damage. If necessary, they can be renewed as described in paragraph 4.

Front door refitting

9 Ensure that the nylon spacers are in position on the rear of the hinge then, with the aid of an assistant, offer up the door.

10 Refit the hinge retaining nuts and bolts, tighten them loosely at this stage.

11 Apply a smear of grease to the clevis pin, then align the check link with its bracket, and insert the pin. Refit the washer, and secure the pin in position with a new split-pin.

12 Close the door, and check that it is correctly aligned with the surrounding body panels. Adjust the door position on the hinges, then securely tighten the four hinge retaining bolts.

13 Refit the inner trim panel (where removed).

Rear door refitting

Vehicles up to 1999 model year

14 Refit the door as described above in paragraphs 9 and 10.

15 Locate the check link on its stud, positioning a washer on each side of the strap, and refit the retaining nut. Tighten the

retaining nut lightly only, so that the check link is free to pivot easily.

16 Close the door, and check that it is correctly aligned with the surrounding body panels. Adjust the door position on the hinges, then securely tighten the four hinge retaining bolts.

Vehicles from 1999 model year

17 Position the door, and refit the hinge-to-body bolts, tighten them loosely at this stage.

18 Refit the check link and tighten the retaining nut.

19 Close the door and check that it aligns correctly with the surrounding body panels. Securely tighten the hinge-to-body bolts.

Adjustment

20 Some vertical adjustment of the doors can be achieved by slackening the hinge retaining bolts and repositioning the hinge/door.

---

12 Door inner trim panel
 – removal and refitting

Removal

1 Unclip the access covers from the armrest/grab handle, then undo the two retaining screws and remove it from the door **(see illustration)**.

2 Lift the inner door lock handle, and carefully prise the trim cap out from the handle surround. Undo the retaining screw, and remove the handle surround from the door panel **(see illustrations)**.

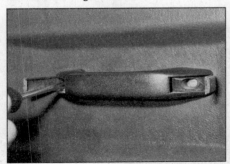

12.1 Open up the access cover, and undo the two armrest handle retaining screws

12.2a Undo the retaining screw . . .

12.2b . . . and unclip the handle surround from the trim panel

12.3 Remove the trim cap, then undo the retaining screw and remove the regulator handle from the door

12.4 Unclip the lock button surround from the trim panel

12.5a Unclip the trim panel, and remove it from the door

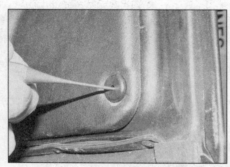

12.5b Push in the centre pins and prise out the expanding studs (where fitted)

3 On models with manual windows, carefully prise the trim cap out from the centre of the regulator handle, then slacken and remove the retaining screw and washer **(see illustration)**. On some models, no centre screw is fitted to the regulator handle. On these vehicles, thread a length of rag behind the handle, and using a sawing motion, release the clip. Remove the handle from the regulator, and recover the handle surround.

4 On all models, slide up the inner lock button surround from the trim panel **(see illustration)**.

5 Remove the trim clips from the corners of the panel (where fitted), then release the door trim panel studs by carefully levering between the panel and door with a suitable flat-bladed screwdriver. Work around the outside of the panel, and when all the studs are released, slide the panel upwards and away from the door **(see illustration)**. Where fitted, push in the centre pins and prise out the expanding studs **(see illustration)**.

Refitting

6 Refitting is a reverse of the removal procedure. Prior to refitting, examine the panel retaining clips for signs of damage, and renew any broken clips.

13 Door handle and lock components – removal and refitting

Removal

1 Remove the inner trim panel as described in Section 12.

2 Peel the polythene weathershield away from the door to gain access to the door lock components, then proceed as described under the relevant sub-heading.

Front door interior handle

3 Release the retaining clip, and release the handle link rod from the lock assembly.

4 Slacken and remove the retaining screws, and remove the handle and link rod assembly from the door **(see illustration)**.

Front door exterior handle

5 Ensure that the window is in the fully-raised position, then securely tape the window glass to its frame, to prevent the window dropping when the mounting panel is removed.

6 Release the retaining clip, and disconnect the interior handle link rod from the lock assembly.

7 Using a suitable marker pen, mark the outline of each regulator retaining bolt on the mounting panel, then slacken and remove the four retaining bolts **(see illustration)**.

8 Slacken and remove the bolts securing the regulator mounting panel to the door **(see illustration)**.

9 Free the regulator arm from its guide on the base of the mounting panel, and remove the mounting panel from the door **(see illustration)**.

10 Release the retaining clips, and disconnect

13.4 Undo the retaining screws, and remove the interior handle from the door

13.7 Slacken and remove the four bolts securing the regulator to the mounting plate . . .

13.8 . . . then undo the retaining bolts (arrowed) . . .

13.9 . . . and remove the mounting plate from the door

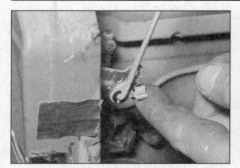

13.10 Release the retaining clips, and detach the link rods from the handle

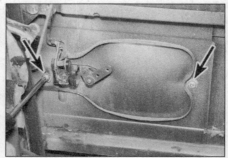

13.11a Undo the two retaining screws (arrowed) . . .

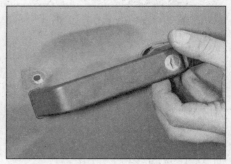

13.11b . . . and remove the exterior handle from the door

the handle and lock cylinder link rods from the lock assembly **(see illustration)**.

11 Slacken and remove the two retaining screws, and remove the exterior handle from the door. Recover the rubber seals fitted to the rear of the handle **(see illustrations)**.

Front lock cylinder

12 Remove the exterior handle as described above.

13 Insert the key into the lock cylinder, then undo the retaining screw and washer from rear of the mounting plate **(see illustration)**. Lift off the link rod bracket and spring, noting their correct fitted locations, and withdraw the lock cylinder and retaining sleeve from the handle.

Front door lock

14 Remove the exterior handle as described above.

15 Slacken and remove the screw(s) securing the lower end of the window glass rear guide rail to the door **(see illustration)**.

16 Undo the three retaining screws (Torx screws on later models), then carefully, taking great care not to damage it, ease the guide rail away from the door and manoeuvre the lock assembly out of position **(see illustrations)**.

Front door interior lock button

17 Release the retaining clip, and detach the lock button link rod from the lock assembly.

18 Undo the two retaining screws, and remove the lock button from the door **(see illustration)**.

Rear interior door handle

19 Release the retaining clip, and release the handle link rod from the lock assembly.

20 Slacken and remove the retaining screws, and remove the handle and link rod assembly from the door.

Rear exterior door handle

21 Release the retaining clip, and detach the link rod from the handle.

22 Undo the two retaining screws, and remove the handle from the door. Recover the rubber seals fitted to the rear of the handle.

Rear door lock

23 Release the retaining clips, and detach the link rods from the lock assembly.

24 Release the retaining clip, and detach

13.13 Undo the retaining screw, and remove the link rod bracket from the rear of the lock cylinder

the link rod from the rear of the exterior door handle.

25 Undo the three retaining screws, and remove the lock assembly from the door.

Rear door interior lock button

26 Release the retaining clip, and detach the lock button link rod from the lock assembly.

27 Undo the two retaining screws, and remove the lock button from the door.

Refitting

28 Refitting is the reverse of the removal sequence, noting the following points:

a) *If a lock cylinder has been removed, on refitting, ensure that the spring and link rod bracket are correctly positioned, and are securely held by the screw. Check*

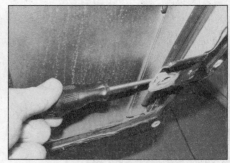

13.15 Undo the screw(s) securing the glass rear guide rail

13.16a Undo the three retaining screws . . .

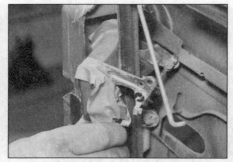

13.16b . . . and manoeuvre the lock assembly out from behind the window guide rail

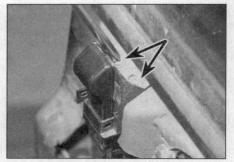

13.18 Interior lock button is secured to the door by two screws (arrowed)

13.28 On refitting, ensure that all link rods are securely retained by their clips

14.4a Remove the outer . . .

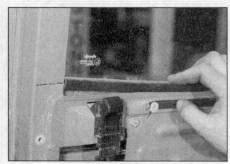

14.4b . . . and inner sealing strips from the top edge of the door

the operation of the lock cylinder before refitting the handle to the door.
b) Ensure that all link rods are securely held in position by their retaining clips **(see illustration)**.
c) Apply grease to all lock and link rod pivot points.
d) On the front door, if the regulator mounting panel has been removed, check the window movement and, if necessary, adjust the regulator as described in Section 14.
e) Before installing the relevant trim panel, thoroughly check the operation of all the door lock handles.

14.5a Slacken the screws and remove the window guide rails from the door

14.5b Window front guide rubber screw (arrowed) – models from 2002

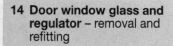

14 Door window glass and regulator – removal and refitting

Removal

1 Remove the door inner trim panel as described in Section 12.
2 Peel the polythene weathershield away from the door to gain access to the door lock components. Proceed as described under the relevant sub-heading.

Front door window glass

3 Remove the regulator assembly as described below.
4 Carefully prise both the window glass inner and outer sealing strips out from the top edge of the door **(see illustrations)**.
5 On vehicles up to 2002 model year, slacken and remove the two screws securing the base of the rear of the window guide to the door, and the single screw securing the front of the guide to the door **(see illustration)**. On vehicles from 2002 model year, undo the single screw securing the front window guide rubber to the door frame **(see illustration)**.
6 Remove the tape from the window glass, then carefully lower the glass down into the door. Free the glass from its guides, and manoeuvre it out from the door **(see illustration)**.

Rear door window glass – vehicles up to 2002 model year

7 Remove the regulator assembly as described below.
8 Release the retaining clip, and detach the lock button link rod from the lock assembly. Undo the two retaining screws, and remove the lock button from the door.
9 Release the retaining clips, and detach the interior handle and lock button link rods from the lock assembly.
10 Unscrew the retaining bolts, and remove the regulator mounting panel from the door, complete with the lock button linkage and interior handle.
11 Undo the retaining screw, and remove the water channel from inside the door.
12 Slacken and remove the two retaining bolts, and free the check link from inside the

door. Note that it may be necessary to bend the end stop to enable the link to be freed from the door.
13 Slacken and remove the four retaining screws (two at the front and two at the rear) securing the window guide rails to the door.
14 Carefully prise both the window glass inner and outer sealing strips out from the top edge of the door.
15 Remove the tape from the window glass, then carefully lower the glass down into the door. Free the glass from its guides, and manoeuvre it out from the door.

Rear door window glass – vehicles from 2002 model year

16 Lower the window and undo the two bolts securing the regulator arm guide to the window clamps **(see illustration)**.

14.6 Manoeuvre the window glass out from the rear of the door

14.16 Undo the two regulator arm guide bolts (arrowed)

14.18 Detach the solenoid link rod clip

14.20 Detach the link rod from the lock button

14.22 Undo the 4 bolts and 2 nuts (arrowed) and remove the mounting panel

14.23 Remove the check link torsion bar and plate

14.25a Undo the front . . .

14.25b . . . and rear window guide rail screws

17 Raise the window and secure it in place with adhesive tape.
18 Release the clip and detach the lock solenoid link rod **(see illustration)**.
19 Release the clip and detach the interior handle link rod from the latch mechanism.
20 Release the clip and disconnect the link rod from the lock button **(see illustration)**.
21 Unclip the wiring harness from the mounting panel, and disconnect the lock solenoid wiring plug.
22 Undo the 4 bolts and 2 nuts, then remove the mounting panel **(see illustration)**.
23 Undo the two nuts and remove the door check link torsion bar and plate **(see**

illustration), then undo the nut and detach the check link.
24 Prise up and remove the inner and outer door waist rubber seals.
25 Undo the screw securing the front window guide rail, and the screw securing the rear window guide rail **(see illustrations)**.
26 Lower the window and manoeuvre it from the door.

Front door window regulator

27 Ensure that the window is fully raised, then securely tape the window glass to its frame, to prevent the window dropping when the regulator is removed.
28 Release the retaining clip, and disconnect

the interior handle link rod from the lock assembly. Where applicable, disconnect the link rod from the lock solenoid **(see illustration)**.
29 On vehicles with manual windows, using a suitable marker pen, mark the outline of each regulator retaining bolt on the mounting plate. On vehicles with electric windows, pull the rubber loom conduit from the pillar and disconnect the door loom wiring plugs **(see illustration 11.2)**.
30 Slacken and remove the bolts securing the regulator mounting panel to the door, then remove it complete with the regulator.
31 Undo the retaining bolts, and remove the regulator from the door mounting panel **(see illustration)**.

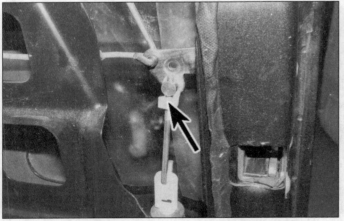

14.28 Disconnect the lock solenoid link rod (arrowed)

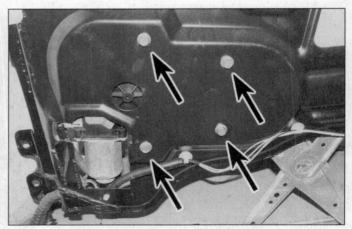

14.31 Window regulator bolts (arrowed)

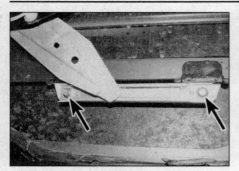

14.34 Undo the 2 bolts (arrowed) securing the regulator clamps

14.35 The regulator assembly is secured by 4 bolts

15.2a Trace the tailgate wiring back to its connectors, and disconnect it from the main wiring loom

Rear door window regulator – vehicles up to 1999 model year

32 Ensure that the window is fully raised, then securely tape the window glass to its frame, to prevent the window dropping when the regulator is removed.

33 Slacken and remove the four retaining bolts, then release the regulator arm from its window glass guide and manoeuvre it out from the door panel. It may be necessary to lower the window glass slightly, to disengage the regulator arm from the guide.

Rear door window regulator – vehicles from 1999 model year

34 Fully lower the window, then undo the two bolts securing the regulator arm guide to the window **(see illustration)**. Raise the window and use adhesive tape to secure it in position.

35 Undo the 4 bolts retaining bolts and manoeuvre the regulator downwards from the door **(see illustration)**.

Refitting

36 Refitting is the reverse of the removal procedure, noting the following points:

 a) *On the front door, align the regulator bolts with the marks made prior to removal (where applicable), and tighten them lightly. Refit the regulator handle, then wind up the window, checking that the glass moves easily, and seats squarely in the frame. If necessary, adjust the window position by altering the position of the regulator until window operation*

is satisfactory, then securely tighten the regulator retaining bolts.

 b) *Refit the weathershield, making sure it is securely stuck to the door, then refit the trim panel as described in Section 12.*

15 Tailgate – removal and refitting

Removal

1 Disconnect the battery negative terminal and (see Chapter 5), where necessary, remove the spare wheel from the tailgate.

2 Trace the wiring back from the tailgate harness to its wiring connectors, and disconnect them from the main wiring loom. It may be necessary to undo the retaining screws and remove the cover panel from inside the vehicle to gain access to the wiring connectors **(see illustration)**. On later models, prise out the rubber grommet, pull out the loom and disconnect the wiring plugs **(see illustration)**.

3 Remove the split-pin and washer, then withdraw the clevis pin securing the tailgate check link to the body **(see illustration)**. On later models, the check link is secured by a single bolt **(see illustration)**.

4 Remove the trim caps (where fitted) from the rear of the tailgate hinge bolts, to reveal the nuts.

5 Using a suitable marker pen, make

alignment marks between the tailgate and hinges.

6 Have an assistant support the tailgate, then slacken and remove the nuts, bolts and washers (as applicable) securing the tailgate to its hinges, and remove the tailgate assembly from the vehicle.

7 Examine the tailgate hinges for signs of wear or damage. If renewal is necessary, first mark the outline of the hinge on the body, then undo the retaining bolts and remove the hinge. Fit the new hinges, and align them with the marks made prior to removal before securely tighten their retaining bolts.

Refitting

8 Refitting is the reverse of removal. Locate the tailgate on its hinges, and refit the retaining bolts, washers and nuts (as applicable), tightening them by hand only. Align the marks made prior to removal, then securely tighten the hinge retaining bolts. Reconnect the check link, then close the tailgate and check for alignment with the surrounding body panels. Slight adjustments can be made by loosening the hinge bolts and repositioning the tailgate.

16 Tailgate lock assembly – removal and refitting

Removal

Vehicles up to 2002 model year

1 Disconnect the battery negative terminal.

15.2b On later models, prise out the grommet to access the loom plugs

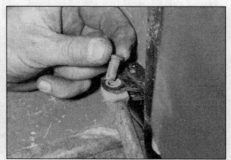

15.3a Remove the split-pin and clevis pin securing the tailgate check link to the body

15.3b The link is secured by a bolt on later models

16.2 Undo the two retaining screws, and remove the tailgate grab handle

16.3a Undo the retaining screws, and remove the wiper motor cover . . .

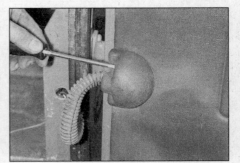

16.3b . . . and wiring harness cover from the tailgate

2 Undo the two retaining screws, and remove the grab handle from the tailgate **(see illustration)**.

3 Undo the retaining screws, and remove the wiper motor and wiring harness covers from the tailgate trim panel **(see illustrations)**.

4 Undo the retaining screws, release the clips, and remove the inner trim panel from the tailgate **(see illustration)**. If the check link passes through the trim panel, it will be necessary to remove the split-pin and clevis pin in order to allow the panel to be removed.

5 Undo the retaining screw(s) and remove the trim cover from the lock **(see illustration)**.

6 Peel the polythene weathershield (where fitted) away from the tailgate to gain access to the lock assembly.

7 Slacken and remove the lock upper retaining screws, and recover the retaining plate from outside the tailgate **(see illustrations)**.

8 Unscrew the lock lower retaining nuts, and remove the lower stud retaining plate from the tailgate.

9 Remove the lock assembly, and recover the rubber seal which is fitted between the lock and tailgate **(see illustration)**.

10 To remove the lock cylinder, fit the key, then insert a small punch in through the hole in the lock assembly to depress the cylinder plunger **(see illustration)**. The cylinder can then be withdrawn from the lock assembly.

Vehicles from 2002 model year

11 Undo the Torx retaining screws, and remove the grab handle.

12 Prise out the plastic panel from the tailgate latch handle recess **(see illustration)**.

13 Using a flat-bladed tool, carefully release

16.4 Undo the retaining screws, and unclip the trim panel from the tailgate

16.5 Undo the retaining screws and remove the lock trim cover

16.7a Slacken and remove the lock retaining screws and nuts (arrowed) . . .

16.7b . . . and recover the retaining plates from the outside of the tailgate

16.9 Remove the lock assembly from the tailgate, and recover the rubber seal

16.10 To remove the lock cylinder, insert the key, then depress the cylinder plunger with a suitable punch or screwdriver

16.12 Prise out the plastic panel

16.13 Release the tailgate panel clips

16.14 Tailgate lock retaining nuts (arrowed)

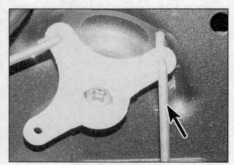

16.15 Central locking link rod (arrowed)

the 9 clips securing the panel to the tailgate **(see illustration)**.

14 Undo the 4 retaining nuts and partially withdrawn the lock assembly from the tailgate **(see illustration)**. Recover the gasket.

15 Disconnect the central locking link rod, and remove the lock assembly **(see illustration)**.

16 To remove the lock cylinder, proceed as described in Paragraph 10.

Refitting

17 Refitting is the reverse of the removal procedure, noting the following:

a) *On vehicles up to 2002 model year, ensure that the retaining plate and tailgate surfaces are clean and dry, and apply a smear of sealant to each plate prior to fitting.*

b) *Ensure that the lock gasket is in good condition – don't forget to fit it between the lock and tailgate.*

c) *If required, the position of the striker plate can be adjusted by slackening the retaining bolts.*

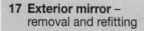

17 Exterior mirror – removal and refitting

Removal

1 Undo the retaining screw, and remove the balljoint clamp from the base of the mirror. Lift the mirror assembly off its mounting bracket **(see illustrations)**.

2 To remove the mounting bracket, first remove the front door as described in Section 11. Undo the retaining screws, and remove the mirror mounting bracket from the door hinge.

Refitting

3 Refitting is the reverse of removal. Position the mirror correctly, then securely tighten its balljoint clamp screw.

18 Windscreen, tailgate and fixed windows – general information

These areas of glass are secured by the tight fit of the weatherstrip in the body aperture, and are bonded in position with a

special adhesive. The removal and refitting of these areas of fixed glass is difficult, messy and time-consuming task which is beyond the scope of the home mechanic. It is difficult, unless one has plenty of practice, to obtain a secure, waterproof fit. Furthermore, the task carries a high risk of breakage; this applies especially to the laminated glass windscreen. In view of this, owners are strongly advised to have this sort of work carried out by one of the many specialist windscreen fitters.

19 Body exterior fittings – removal and refitting

Wheel arch liners and body under panels

1 The various plastic covers fitted to the underside of the vehicle are secured in position by a mixture of screws, nuts and retaining clips, and removal will be fairly obvious on inspection. Work methodically around the panel, removing its retaining screws and releasing its retaining clips until the panel is free and can be removed from the underside of the vehicle. Most clips used on the vehicle, with the exception of some of the trim fasteners, are simply prised out of position. These special clips are released by pressing out their centre pins and then removing the outer section of the clip; new clips will be required on refitting if the centre pins are not recovered.

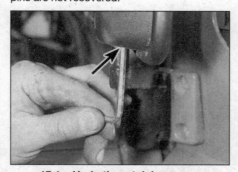

17.1a Undo the retaining screw (arrowed) . . .

2 On refitting, renew any retaining clips that may have been broken on removal, and ensure that the panel is securely retained by all the relevant clips, nuts and screws.

Body trim strips and badges

3 Most of the various body trim strips and badges are held in position with a special adhesive tape. Removal requires the trim/badge to be heated, to soften the adhesive, and then cut away from the surface. Due to the high risk of damage to the vehicle's paintwork during this operation, it is recommended that this task should be entrusted to a Land Rover dealer.

20 Seats – removal and refitting

Note: *Due to the large amount of seating options available, it is not possible to give detailed instructions on how to remove each individual type of seat. Using the text as a guide; removal details will be self-evident on inspection.*

Removal

Front seats

1 Unclip/lift up the seat cushion, and remove it from the vehicle. Undo the retaining screws, and remove the access panel (where fitted) situated beneath the seat.

2 Slide the seat fully rearwards, then slacken and remove the front bolts (and nuts) securing the seat to the floor.

17.1b . . . then free the balljoint clamp and remove the mirror from its mounting bracket

21.1 Remove the trim cover from the upper mounting to reveal the mounting bolt

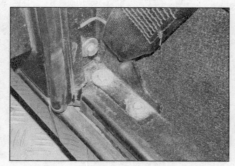

21.3 The seat belt bracket is secured by 3 bolts

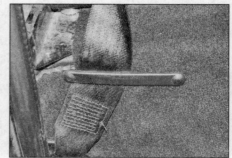

21.4 Remove the two studs and the belt retaining clip

3 Slide the seat fully forwards, undo the rear bolts (and nuts) securing the seat to the floor, then remove the seat from the vehicle. Where applicable, disconnect the seat heating wiring plugs.

Rear seat

4 Slacken and remove the bolts securing the seat mounting brackets and/or hinges to the floor, and remove the assembly from the vehicle.

Luggage compartment seats

5 On models with individual seats, slacken and remove the retaining bolts securing the seat hinges to the vehicle. Undo the seat back mounting bolts, and remove the seat from the vehicle.

6 On models with bench-type seats, unclip the seat cushion, and remove it from the vehicle. Slacken and remove the bolts securing the seat assembly in position, and remove it from the vehicle.

Refitting

7 Refitting is a reverse of the relevant removal procedure.

21 Seat belt components – removal and refitting

Front seat side belt removal

1 Unclip the trim cover from the seat belt upper mounting point, then unscrew the retaining bolt and free the belt from its mounting **(see illustration)**. Recover the flanged spacer and washers which are fitted to the rear of the belt anchorage, noting their correct fitted locations.

Vehicles up to 1999 model year

2 Where necessary, slacken and remove the seat belt lower mounting point bolt, and recover the washers and spacer fitted between the belt and floor. **Note:** *On some models, the seat belt lower mounting point is on the inertia reel.*

Vehicles from 1999 model year

3 Undo the 3 bolts securing the belt bracket to the seat base **(see illustration)**. Note that one some models, the seat belt is attached to the inertia reel bracket **(see illustration 21.5b)**.

4 Remove the 2 studs and the seat belt retaining clip **(see illustration)**.

All models

5 Unscrew the retaining nuts/bolts (as applicable) securing the inertia reel in position, and remove the seat belt from the vehicle **(see illustrations)**. On some models, it may be necessary to remove the pillar trim panel to gain access to the inertia reel (see Section 22).

Front seat belt stalks and centre belt removal

6 Prise off the trim cap, then slacken and

remove the mounting bolt(s). Remove the stalk/belt (as applicable), and recover the washers and spacer, noting their correct fitted location.

Rear seat side belt removal

7 Unclip the trim cover from the seat belt upper mounting point, then unscrew the retaining bolt, and free the belt from its mounting. Recover the flanged spacer and washers which are fitted to the rear of the belt anchorage, noting their correct fitted locations.

Models up to 1999 model year

8 On models where no inertia reel is fitted to the belt, slacken and remove the lower seat belt mounting bolt and washer, and remove the belt from the vehicle.

9 Where the belt incorporates an inertia reel, remove the trim cap from the lower mounting bolt, then unscrew the bolt and recover the flanged spacer and washers which are fitted to the rear of the belt anchorage, noting their correct fitted locations. Slacken and remove the inertia reel retaining bolt and washer, and remove the belt from the vehicle.

Models from 1999 model year

10 Prise out the seat belt guide, then unclip the upper seat belt anchor bolt cap and undo the bolt **(see illustration)**.

11 Carefully prise away the C-pillar trim panel

21.5a Undo the two retaining nuts, and remove the inertia reel from the floor

21.5b One some models, the seat belt is attached to the inertia reel bracket

21.10 Rear seat belt upper anchor bolt

21.11a Prise out the clip . . .

21.11b . . . and prise away the C-pillar trim panel

proper forked type of tool) is to use a large flat-bladed screwdriver. Note in many cases that an adjacent sealing strip must be prised back to release a panel.

4 When removing a panel, **never** use excessive force, or the panel may be damaged; always check carefully that all fasteners have been removed or released before attempting to withdraw a panel.

5 Refitting is the reverse of the removal procedure; secure the fasteners by pressing them firmly into place, and ensure that all disturbed components are correctly secured, to prevent rattles.

sufficiently to access the inertia reel securing bolt **(see illustrations)**.

12 Unclip the cover and undo the seat belt lower retaining bolt.

13 Pull the seat belt through the pillar trim panel, then undo the bolts and remove the inertia reel securing bolt.

Rear seat belt buckles and centre belt removal

14 Free the seat belt/buckle (as applicable) from the rear seat, then prise off the trim cap (where fitted) and unbolt its mounting from the floor.

Refitting

15 Refitting is a reversal of the removal procedure, ensuring that all the mounting bolts are tightened to the specified torque, where given.

22 Interior trim – removal and refitting

1 The interior trim panels are secured using either screws or various types of trim fasteners, usually studs or clips.

2 Check that there are no other panels overlapping the one to be removed; usually there is a sequence to be followed that will become obvious on close inspection.

3 Remove all obvious fasteners, such as screws. If the panel will not come free, it is held by hidden clips or fasteners. These are usually situated around the edge of the panel, and can be prised up to release them. Note, however, that they can break quite easily, so have new ones available. The best way of releasing such clips (in the absence of a

23 Storage box and centre console – removal and refitting

Storage box removal

Models up to 1999 model year

1 Open up the storage box lid to gain access to the retaining screws.

2 Slacken and remove the retaining screws (and nuts), and remove the storage box from in between the front seats.

Models from 1999 model year

3 Open the storage box lid, prise up the plastic caps (where fitted) and remove the two retaining screws **(see illustration)**.

4 Prise up the front flap/remove the cupholders, and remove the two bolts at the front of the storage box **(see illustrations)**.

5 Remove the box.

Centre console removal

6 Disconnect the battery negative lead as described in Chapter 5.

7 Remove the radio/cassette player and instrument panel as described in Chapter 13.

8 Undo the 3 retaining screws, and release the heater control from the facia **(see illustration)**.

9 Carefully prise off the Land Rover decal from the passenger end of the facia, then undo the two screws and remove the grab handle **(see illustration)**.

23.3 Undo the retaining screws (arrowed)

23.4a Lift out the cupholders . . .

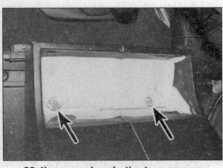

23.4b . . . and undo the two screws (arrowed)

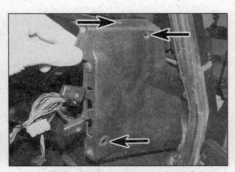

23.8 Undo the heater control retaining screws (arrowed)

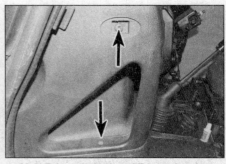

23.9 Prise off the Land Rover decal to access the grab handle screws (arrowed)

23.10 Each demister vent is retained by 2 screws

23.11a The 'crash pad' is retained by 3 screws on the top edge (left-hand and middle screw arrowed) . . .

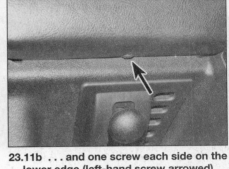

23.11b . . . and one screw each side on the lower edge (left-hand screw arrowed)

10 Undo the 4 screws and remove the demister vents **(see illustration)**.

11 Undo the 5 retaining screws and remove the 'crash pad' from the upper facia **(see illustrations)**.

12 Slacken and remove the 5 retaining screws, and pull the centre console rearwards. Note their fitted positions, and disconnect the console wiring plugs as it is withdrawn **(see illustrations)**.

Refitting

13 Refitting is the reverse of removal.

23.12a Centre console upper screws (arrowed) . . .

23.12b . . . and lower retaining screws

24 Facia panel assembly
– removal and refitting

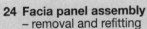

HAYNES HiNT *Label each wiring connector as it is disconnected from its relevant component. The labels will prove useful on refitting, when routing the wiring and feeding the wiring through the facia apertures.*

Note: *On models with air conditioning, if it is intended to remove the lower half of the facia,* have the refrigerant circuit discharged by a suitable equipped specialist, as the evaporator assembly must be removed.

Removal

1 Disconnect the battery negative terminal, as described in Chapter 5.

2 Remove the steering wheel as described in Chapter 11.

Models with air conditioning

3 Undo the bolts and disconnect the refrigerant pipe unions at the engine compartment bulkhead **(see illustration)**. Discard the O-ring seals, new ones must be fitted. Plug the openings to prevent contamination.

4 Undo the two screws at each end of the air conditioning ducting in the cabin, and remove the ducting complete with evaporator, etc. Disconnect the evaporator drain tube and any wiring connections as the ducting is removed **(see illustration)**.

Models up to 1999 model year

5 Remove the instrument panel, facia switch panel, and steering column combination switches, as described in Chapter 13. Where applicable, also remove the radio/cassette player.

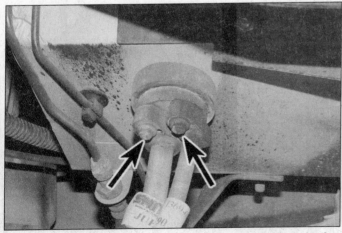

24.3 Undo the bolts (arrowed) and disconnect the refrigerant pipe unions

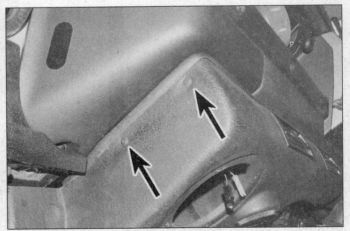

24.4 Undo the two screws (left-hand ones arrowed) at each end securing the air conditioning ducting

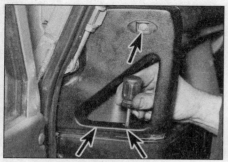

24.7a Undo the three retaining screws (arrowed) . . .

24.7b . . . and remove the grab handle from the left-hand end of the facia

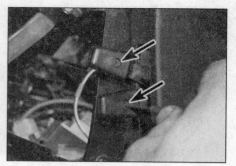

24.9a Undo the retaining screws (arrowed), and remove the knobs from the heater control levers

24.9b Undo the two retaining screws (arrowed), then free the trim cover from the facia

24.9c Undo the screws securing the cover to the lever assembly, and recover the spacers

24.10a Slacken the inner cable clamp screw . . .

24.10b . . . then loosen the outer cable clamp screw (arrowed), and remove the control lever assembly from the facia

6 Unscrew the two fasteners and remove the fusebox cover from the facia.

7 Prise out the badge from the top of the grab handle which is fitted to the left-hand end of the facia. Undo the three retaining screws, then lift the handle upwards to disengage it and remove it from the facia (see illustrations).

8 Undo the three retaining screws, and remove the lower cover panel from the left-hand end of the facia.

9 Undo the two screws, and remove the knobs from the heater and ventilation control levers. Undo the retaining screws, and free the cover/heater control lever assembly from the right-hand end of the facia. Undo the two screws, then lift the cover away from the heater and ventilation controls. Recover the spacers fitted between the cover and control levers (see illustrations).

10 Noting each cable's correct fitted location, release the cables and remove the heater and ventilation controls. Noting the correct routing of the ventilation housing cable, free the cable from any relevant retaining clips, so that it is free to be removed with the lower facia assembly (see illustrations).

11 Slacken and remove the retaining screws, and remove the top panel and vent covers from the facia (see illustrations).

12 Undo the retaining screws, and remove the trim rail from the front of the facia storage compartment.

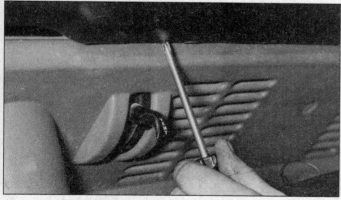

24.11a Undo the retaining screws situated along the front edge . . .

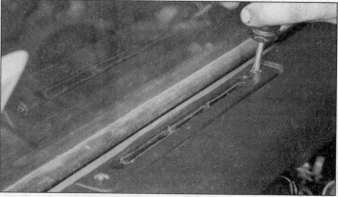

24.11b . . . and the upper edge, and remove the vent covers and top panel from the facia

24.13a Slacken the retaining screws and remove the nuts . . .

24.13b . . . then undo the two rear screws . . .

24.13c . . . and lift off the wiring cover

13 Slacken and remove the two retaining screws and nuts, and withdraw the switch panel from the centre of the facia. Undo the two rear retaining screws, and lift the switch panel wiring cover out from the storage compartment. Disconnect the wiring from the panel, and remove it from the facia **(see illustrations)**.

14 Prise out the retaining clips, then undo the retaining screws (where fitted) and remove the vent cover panel from the rear of the facia storage compartment. Lift off the duct trim cover, and remove the duct **(see illustrations)**.

15 Lift out the facia storage compartment insert **(see illustration)**.

16 Undo the retaining screws, and remove the outlet ducts from the base of the facia **(see illustration)**.

17 Working along the upper and lower edges

24.13d Withdraw the switch panel from the facia, and disconnect its wiring connectors

of the lower facia housing, slacken and remove all of its retaining screws **(see illustration)**. Also undo the two screws situated on the edge of the storage compartment.

18 Check that all the retaining screws have

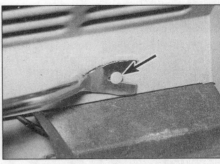

24.14a Prise out the retaining clips (note the use of a forked tool) . . .

been removed, then carefully ease the lower facia assembly away from the bulkhead, and remove it from the vehicle **(see illustration)**. Recover the foam seals from the ventilation housing inlets.

24.14b . . . then remove the vent cover panel from the facia

24.14c Disconnect the duct, and remove it from the lower facia assembly

24.15 Remove the insert from the facia storage compartment

24.16 Undo the retaining screws (arrowed) and remove the outlet ducts

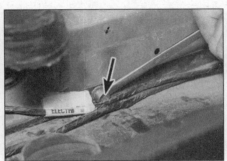

24.17 Undo the retaining screws (arrowed) . . .

24.18 . . . and withdraw the lower facia assembly out from the vehicle

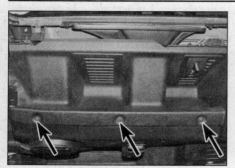

24.40 Undo the 7 screws (3 left-hand side ones arrowed) and remove the panel

24.43 The passenger's side lower facia panel end cap is retained by 3 screws (arrowed)

24.45 Release the demister tubes from the facia panel

Models from 1999 to 2002 model year

19 Undo the 7 retaining screws, and remove the upper and lower steering column shrouds.
20 Remove the instrument cluster as described in Chapter 13.
21 Undo the 3 retaining screws and move the heater control assembly to one side.
22 Prise out the heated rear window, rear foglight and hazard warning switches from the facia, then label and disconnect the switch wiring plugs.
23 Prise off the locking rings, then undo the screws and remove the front speakers. Disconnect the speaker wiring plugs as they are withdrawn.
24 Carefully prise the 'Land Rover' decal from the passenger end of the facia, then undo the two retaining screws, and remove the grab handle.
25 Undo the two screws each side, and remove the demister vents from the 'crash pad'.
26 Undo the 3 screws and remove the 'crash pad' from the top of the facia.
27 Remove the radio/cassette player as described in Chapter 13.
28 Undo the two screws and remove the facia switch panel. Label and disconnect the switch wiring plugs as it is withdrawn.
29 Remove the fusebox cover.
30 Undo the two screws and remove the footwell vent from the each side.

31 Undo the bolt each side securing the door check strap covers. Remove the covers.
32 Undo the 3 screws, and remove the wiper motor cover.
33 The finisher rail is secured to the lower facia panel by 3 screws. Remove the screws followed by the rail.
34 Release the 7 clips securing the upper facia trim to the bulkhead, then fold back the trim over the fresh air vent operating levers, and remove it.
35 Release the demister hose from the parcel shelf, and undo the 18 screws and remove the parcel shelf.
36 Undo the 7 screws securing the bottom edge of the lower facia panel to the bulkhead.
37 Undo the 2 bolts securing the upper edge of the lower facia and, with assistance, manoeuvre it from the vehicle.

Models from 2002 model year

38 Undo the 7 retaining screws, and remove the upper and lower steering column shrouds.
39 Remove the centre console as described in Section 23.
40 Unscrew the air vent control knobs, then undo the 7 screws and remove the panel from the upper facia **(see illustration)**.
41 Remove the front speakers as described in Chapter 13.
42 Undo the screw each side and remove the door check strap covers.

43 Undo the 3 screws and remove the lower facia panel end cap from the passenger's side **(see illustration)**.
44 Slacken the clamp screw and disconnect the air distribution cable from the control lever.
45 Release the demister tubes from the facia panel **(see illustration)**.
46 Undo the two screws and remove the fusebox cover from in front of the gear lever.
47 The facia panel is secured by 7 screws. Undo these fasteners, and with the help of an assistant, manoeuvre the facia from the vehicle.

Refitting

48 Refitting is a reversal of the removal procedure, noting the following points:
a) *Fit the foam seals to the inlets, then manoeuvre the facia into position. Using the labels stuck on during removal, ensure that the wiring is correctly routed, and fed through the relevant facia apertures. Take great care not to trap the wiring as the facia is installed.*
b) *Make sure that the facia is correctly located, then refit all its retaining screws and tighten them securely.*
c) *On completion, reconnect the battery and check that all the electrical components and switches function correctly.*

Chapter 13
Body electrical systems

Contents

Section number

Battery – removal and refitting . . . . See Chapter 5
Battery check and maintenance. . . . . See *Weekly checks*
Bulbs (exterior lights) – renewal 5
Bulbs (interior lights) – renewal. 6
Central locking components – general information, removal and
    refitting 23
Cigarette lighter – removal and refitting 13
Clock – removal and refitting 11
Dim-dip lighting system (UK models only) – general information . . . 22
Electrical fault finding – general information 2
Exterior light units – removal and refitting 7
Fuses and relays – general information 3
General information and precautions. 1
Headlight beam alignment – general information. 8
Headlight washer system components – removal and refitting 20
Horn – removal and refitting. 14
Ignition switch – removal and refitting . . . . See Chapter 11

Section number

Instrument panel – removal and refitting 9
Instrument panel components – removal and refitting. 10
Lights-on warning system – general information. 12
Radio/cassette player and speakers – removal and refitting 21
Reversing light switch – removal and refitting . . . . See Chapter 7A
Speedometer drive cable – removal and refitting. 15
Stop-light switch – removal and refitting . . . . See Chapter 10
Switches – removal and refitting 4
Tailgate wiper motor – removal and refitting 18
Windscreen wiper motor and cable – removal and refitting. 17
Windscreen/headlight washer system check and
    adjustment . . . . *Weekly checks*
Windscreen/tailgate washer system components –
    removal and refitting. 19
Windscreen/tailgate wiper blade check and
    renewal. . . . . *Weekly checks*
Wiper arm – removal and refitting 16

Degrees of difficulty

Easy, suitable for novice with little experience	**Fairly easy,** suitable for beginner with some experience	**Fairly difficult,** suitable for competent DIY mechanic	**Difficult,** suitable for experienced DIY mechanic	**Very difficult,** suitable for expert DIY or professional

Specifications

System type	12 volt, negative-earth

Bulbs	**Wattage**
Direction indicator side repeater	4
Direction indicator	21
Headlight:	
Sealed-beam unit	75/50
Quartz halogen light unit	60/55
High-level stop-light	21
Instrument panel lights:	
Ignition/no-charge warning light.	2
All other warning/illumination lights	1.2
Interior lights.	10
Number plate light	4
Rear foglight.	21
Reversing light	21
Sidelight	5
Stop/tail light	21/5

1 General information and precautions

⚠️ **Warning: Before carrying out any work on the electrical system, read through the precautions given in 'Safety first!' at the beginning of this manual, and in Chapter 5.**

The electrical system is of the 12 volt negative-earth type. Power for the lights and all electrical accessories is supplied by a lead-acid type battery, which is charged by the engine-driven alternator.

This Chapter covers repair and service procedures for the various electrical components not associated with engine. Information on the battery, alternator and starter motor can be found in Chapter 5.

It should be noted that, prior to working on any component in the electrical system, the battery negative terminal should first be disconnected, to prevent the possibility of electrical short-circuits and/or fires.

2 Electrical fault finding – general information

Note: Refer to the precautions given in 'Safety first!' and in Section 1 of this Chapter before starting work. The following tests relate to testing of the main electrical circuits, and should not be used to test delicate electronic circuits, particularly where an electronic control module is used.

General

1 A typical electrical circuit consists of an electrical component, any switches, relays, motors, fuses, fusible links or circuit breakers related to that component, and the wiring and connectors which link the component to both the battery and the chassis. To help to pinpoint a problem in an electrical circuit, wiring diagrams are included at the end of this Chapter.

2 Before attempting to diagnose an electrical fault, first study the appropriate wiring diagram, to obtain a complete understanding of the components included in the particular circuit concerned. The possible sources of a fault can be narrowed down by noting if other components related to the circuit are operating properly. If several components or circuits fail at one time, the problem is likely to be related to a shared fuse or earth connection.

3 Electrical problems usually stem from simple causes, such as loose or corroded connections, a faulty earth connection, a blown fuse, a melted fusible link, or a faulty relay (refer to Section 3 for details of testing relays). Visually inspect the condition of all fuses, wires and connections in a problem circuit before testing the components. Use the wiring diagrams to determine which terminal

connections will need to be checked in order to pinpoint the trouble spot.

4 The basic tools required for electrical fault finding include a circuit tester or voltmeter (a 12 volt bulb with a set of test leads can also be used for certain tests); a self-powered test light (sometimes known as a continuity tester); an ohmmeter (to measure resistance); a battery and set of test leads; and a jumper wire, preferably with a circuit breaker or fuse incorporated, which can be used to bypass suspect wires or electrical components. Before attempting to locate a problem with test instruments, use the wiring diagrams to determine where to make the connections.

5 To find the source of an intermittent wiring fault (usually due to a poor or dirty connection, or damaged wiring insulation), a 'wiggle' test can be performed on the wiring. This involves wiggling the wiring by hand to see if the fault occurs as the wiring is moved. It should be possible to narrow down the source of the fault to a particular section of wiring. This method of testing can be used in conjunction with any of the tests described in the following sub-Sections.

6 Apart from problems due to poor connections, two basic types of fault can occur in an electrical circuit – open-circuit, or short-circuit.

7 Open-circuit faults are caused by a break somewhere in the circuit, which prevents current from flowing. An open-circuit fault will prevent a component from working, but will not cause the relevant circuit fuse to blow.

8 Short-circuit faults are caused by a 'short' somewhere in the circuit, which allows the current flowing in the circuit to 'escape' along an alternative route, usually to earth. Short-circuit faults are normally caused by a breakdown in wiring insulation, which allows a feed wire to touch either another wire, or an earthed component such as the bodyshell. A short-circuit fault will normally cause the relevant circuit fuse to blow.

Finding an open-circuit

9 To check for an open-circuit, connect one lead of a circuit tester or voltmeter to either the negative battery terminal or a known good earth.

10 Connect the other lead to a connector in the circuit being tested, preferably nearest to the battery or fuse.

11 Switch on the circuit, bearing in mind that some circuits are live only when the ignition switch is moved to a particular position.

12 If voltage is present (indicated either by the tester bulb lighting or a voltmeter reading, as applicable), this means that the section of the circuit between the relevant connector and the battery is problem-free.

13 Continue to check the remainder of the circuit in the same fashion.

14 When a point is reached at which no voltage is present, the problem must lie between that point and the previous test point with voltage. Most problems can be traced to a broken, corroded or loose connection.

Finding a short-circuit

15 To check for a short-circuit, first disconnect the load(s) from the circuit (loads are the components which draw current from a circuit, such as bulbs, motors, heating elements, etc).

16 Remove the relevant fuse from the circuit, and connect a circuit tester or voltmeter to the fuse connections.

17 Switch on the circuit, bearing in mind that some circuits are live only when the ignition switch is moved to a particular position.

18 If voltage is present (indicated either by the tester bulb lighting or a voltmeter reading, as applicable), this means that there is a short-circuit.

19 If no voltage is present, but the fuse still blows with the load(s) connected, this indicates an internal fault in the load(s).

Finding an earth fault

20 The battery negative terminal is connected to 'earth' – the metal of the engine/transmission and the car body – and most systems are wired so that they only receive a positive feed, the current returning via the metal of the car body. This means that the component mounting and the body form part of that circuit. Loose or corroded mountings can therefore cause a range of electrical faults, ranging from total failure of a circuit, to a puzzling partial fault. In particular, lights may shine dimly (especially when another circuit sharing the same earth point is in operation), motors (eg, wiper motors or the radiator cooling fan motor) may run slowly, and the operation of one circuit may have an apparently-unrelated effect on another. Note that on many vehicles, earth straps are used between certain components, such as the engine/transmission and the body, usually where there is no metal-to-metal contact between components due to flexible rubber mountings, etc.

21 To check whether a component is properly earthed, disconnect the battery and connect one lead of an ohmmeter to a known good earth point. Connect the other lead to the wire or earth connection being tested. The resistance reading should be zero; if not, check the connection as follows.

22 If an earth connection is thought to be faulty, dismantle the connection and clean back to bare metal both the bodyshell and the wire terminal or the component earth connection mating surface. Be careful to remove all traces of dirt and corrosion, then use a knife to trim away any paint, so that a clean metal-to-metal joint is made. On reassembly, tighten the joint fasteners securely; if a wire terminal is being refitted, use serrated washers between the terminal and the bodyshell to ensure a clean and secure connection. When the connection is remade, prevent the onset of corrosion in the future by applying a coat of petroleum jelly or silicone-based grease. Alternatively, spray on (at regular intervals) a proprietary ignition sealer, or a water-dispersant lubricant.

3.2a Unscrew the two retaining screws and remove the cover . . .

3.2b . . . to gain access to the fusebox

3.2c Release the clip and slide the panel forwards to access the additional fusebox is located under the driver's seat (2002 model year onwards)

3 Fuses and relays – general information

Fuses

1 The fuses are located behind the small panel in the centre of the facia, and on vehicles from 2002 model year, under the driver's seat.
2 To gain access to the fusebox, unscrew the retaining screws and remove the panel situated directly in front of the gearchange/selector lever, or remove the passenger's seat cushion and open the fusebox lid **(see illustrations)**.
3 A label identifying each fuse should be attached to the cover panel **(see illustration)**.
4 To remove a fuse, first switch off the circuit

concerned (or the ignition), then pull the fuse out of its terminals. The wire within the fuse is clearly visible; if the fuse is blown, it will be broken or melted.
5 Always renew a fuse with one of an identical rating; never use one with a different rating from the original, nor substitute anything else. Never renew a fuse more than once without tracing the source of the trouble. The rating is stamped on top of the fuse; they are also colour-coded for easy recognition.
6 If a new fuse blows immediately, find the cause before renewing it again; a short to earth as a result of faulty insulation is most likely cause. Where more than one circuit is protected, try to isolate the defect by switching on each circuit in turn (if possible) until it blows again. Always carry a supply of spare fuses/fusible links of each relevant

rating on the vehicle – a spare of each fuse rating should be clipped into the base of the fusebox.

Relays

7 The majority of relays are mounted onto the rear of the fusebox, the exceptions to this being the heated rear window relay, the voltage switching relay and the low fuel relay, which are located behind the instrument panel **(see illustrations)**. On models with twin fuel tanks, the fuel tank and fuel pump changeover relays are located on the right-hand side of the engine compartment, as is the split charging facility relay (where fitted). Note that on vehicles from 2002 model year, the hazard flasher unit, headlamps relay, window lift relay, starter motor relay, and heated front screen timing relay may also be fitted behind the instrument panel **(see illustration)**, whilst the heated front screen power relay, air conditioning relay, glow plug relay, main relay, fuel pump relay and ABS relay, are located under the front seat cushion adjacent to the engine management ECM **(see illustration)**.
8 If a circuit or system controlled by a relay develops a fault and the relay is suspect, operate the system; if the relay is functioning, it should be possible to hear it click as it is energised. If this is the case, the fault lies with the components or wiring of the system. If

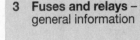

3.3 A fuse identification sticker is attached to the rear of the fusebox cover

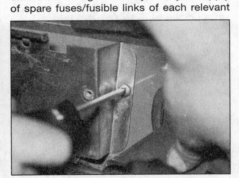

3.7a To gain access to the relays fitted to the rear of the fusebox, undo the retaining screws . . .

3.7d Other relays are located under the driver's side front seat cushion

1 *Fuel pump relay*
2 *Main relay*
3 *Glow plug relay*

3.7b . . . then ease the fusebox away from the bulkhead and turn it around

3.7c On vehicles from 2002 model year, additional relays are mounted behind the instrument panel

the relay is not being energised, then either the relay is not receiving a main supply or a switching voltage, or the relay itself is faulty. Testing is by the substitution of a known good unit, but be careful; while some relays are identical in appearance and in operation, others look similar but perform different functions.

9 To renew a relay, first ensure that the ignition switch is off. The relay can then simply be pulled out from the socket, and the new relay pressed in.

4.3 Removing the rear foglight switch

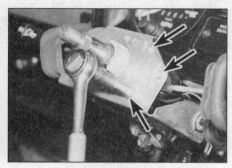
4.4a To remove the right-hand combination switch assembly, undo the retaining screws (arrowed) . . .

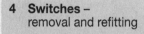
4 Switches – removal and refitting

Note: Disconnect the battery negative lead before removing any switch, and reconnect the lead after refitting the switch (see Chapter 5).

Ignition switch/ steering column lock

1 Refer to Chapter 11.

Steering column switches

2 Undo the steering column shroud retaining screws, unclip the shroud halves, and remove both the upper and lower shrouds from the steering column.

3 To remove the lighting switch or the rear foglight switch, slacken the retaining nut, then slide the switch out from the mounting bracket and disconnect its wiring connector **(see illustration)**.

4 To remove the right-hand combination (windscreen wiper/washer) switch assembly, first remove the steering wheel (see Chapter 11). Undo the retaining screws and remove the switch, disconnecting its wiring connector as it becomes accessible **(see illustrations)**.

5 To remove the left-hand combination (direction indicator/horn/lighting) switch, carry out the operations described in paragraph 4. Disconnect the wiring connectors from the switch, then slacken the clamp screw, and slide the switch and mounting bracket assembly off the steering column.

6 Refitting is a reversal of the relevant removal procedure.

4.4b . . . then free the switch from the mounting bracket and disconnect its wiring connector

Facia switches

Vehicles up to 2002 model year

7 Undo the two retaining screws, and ease the switch panel out from the facia **(see illustrations)**.

8 Disconnect the wiring connector from the rear of the relevant switch, then depress the retaining clips, and slide the switch out from the panel **(see illustration)**.

9 Refitting is the reverse of removal.

Vehicles from 2002 model year

10 Remove the radio/cassette player as described in Section 21.

11 Reach through the radio/cassette player aperture, and push the switch from the facia

4.7a Undo the retaining screws . . .

(see illustration). Disconnect the switch wiring plug as it is withdrawn.

12 Refitting is a reversal of removal.

Tailgate wiper switch

13 Slacken and remove the two retaining screws and nuts, then free the small switch panel from the facia.

14 Pull off the control knob, then unscrew the nut and washer and remove the wiper switch from the rear of the panel.

15 Disconnect the wiring connector, and remove the switch from the vehicle.

16 Refitting is the reverse of removal.

Heater blower motor switch

17 Remove the instrument panel as described in Section 9.

18 Release the retaining clip, then detach the control cable from the switch/control lever assembly.

4.7b . . . and withdraw the switch panel from the facia

4.8 Disconnect the wiring connector from the relevant switch, then depress the retaining clips and slide the switch out from the panel

4.11 Push the switch from the facia

19 Disconnect the wiring connectors, noting their correct fitted locations, then undo the retaining screws and remove the switch assembly from the facia (see illustrations).
20 Refitting is the reverse of removal. Prior to refitting the instrument panel, check the operation of the ventilation control lever; if necessary, adjust the cable by releasing the retaining clip and repositioning the outer cable.

Headlight-levelling switch

21 Remove the centre console as described in Chapter 12.
22 Pull the knob from the switch, then undo the nut and remove the switch (see illustration).
23 Refitting is a reversal of removal.

Handbrake warning switch

24 Undo the screws/remove the clips and remove the gaiter from the handbrake lever.
25 Unplug the connectors from the switch.
26 Undo the two retaining screws and remove the switch (see illustration).
27 Refitting is a reversal of removal, tightening the handbrake lever bolts securely.

5 Bulbs (exterior lights) – renewal

General

1 Whenever a bulb is renewed, note the following points:
 a) *Remember that if the light has just been in use, the bulb may be extremely hot.*
 b) *Always check the bulb contacts and holder, ensuring that there is clean metal-to-metal contact between the bulb and its live(s) and earth. Clean off any corrosion or dirt before fitting a new bulb.*
 c) *Wherever bayonet-type bulbs are fitted ensure that the live contact(s) bear firmly against the bulb contact.*
 d) *Always ensure that the new bulb is of the correct rating, and that it is completely clean before fitting it; this applies particularly to halogen headlight bulbs (see below).*

Headlight

Early (pre-1987) models

2 Undo the retaining screws, and free the headlight surround panel from the front of the vehicle.
3 Slacken and remove the retaining screws, and lift the rim from the headlight unit.
4 Withdraw the light unit, disconnecting it from its wiring connector as it becomes accessible (see illustration).
5 Where possible (sealed-beam units are fitted on some models), remove the rubber cover, then release the retaining clip and withdraw the bulb from the rear of the unit (see illustrations). When handling the new bulb,

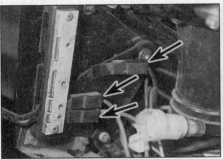

4.19a To remove the blower motor switch, disconnect the wiring connectors (arrowed) and free the heater control cable . . .

4.19b . . . then undo the two retaining screws and remove the switch from the facia

4.22 Pull the headlight-levelling switch knob from the facia, then undo the retaining nut

4.26 Undo the switch retaining screws (arrowed)

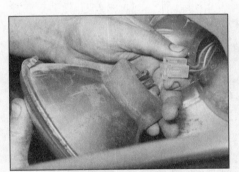

5.4 Withdraw the headlight unit, disconnecting its wiring connector as it becomes accessible

5.5a Where halogen light units are fitted, remove the rubber cover . . .

5.5b . . . then release the retaining clip . . .

5.5c . . . and withdraw the bulb. Do not touch the new bulb's glass with your fingers

5.10a Undo the two retaining screws . . .

5.10b . . . and free the sidelight and indicator light units from the surround panel

5.17 Undo the screws (arrowed) and remove the headlight surround panel

use a tissue or clean cloth to avoid touching the glass with the fingers; moisture and grease from the skin can cause blackening and rapid failure of this type of bulb. Install the new bulb, ensuring that its locating tabs are correctly located in the light cut-outs, and secure it in position with the retaining clip.

 HAYNES HiNT *If the headlight bulb glass is accidentally touched, wipe it clean using methylated spirit.*

6 Offer up the light unit, and reconnect its wiring connector.
7 Refit the rim, and secure it in position with its retaining screws.
8 Refit the surround panel, and secure it in position with its retaining screws.

1987 to 1999 models

9 Undo the retaining screws and washers, and remove the direction indicator and sidelight lenses. Recover the rubber seal from each lens, and renew it if it is damaged.
10 Slacken and remove the retaining screws and washers, and free the direction indicator and sidelight units from the surround panel **(see illustrations)**.
11 Undo the two retaining screws, and withdraw the surround panel sufficiently to gain access to the headlight unit.
12 Carry out the procedures described above in paragraphs 3 to 7.
13 Refit the surround panel, and securely tighten its retaining screws.
14 Locate the sidelight and direction indicator light units in the panel, and secure them in position with their retaining screws and washers.

15 Ensure that the seals are in position, then refit the lenses and secure them in position with their retaining screws and washers. Do not overtighten the screws, as the lenses are easily cracked.

1999 onwards models

16 Undo the retaining screws and remove the sidelight and direction indicator light units. Disconnect the wiring plugs as the units are removed.
17 Undo the two screws and remove the headlight surround panel **(see illustration)**.
18 Undo the screw at the 3 o'clock position, then twist the headlight and rim clockwise, remove the headlight assembly from the shell **(see illustration)**. Disconnect the wiring plugs as the unit is removed.
19 Peel off the rubber boot, then spread apart the retaining clip and remove the bulb **(see illustrations)**.
20 Refitting is a reversal of removal.

Direction indicator, sidelight, reversing light and rear light

Note: *Later-model lights can also be fitted to early models.*

Early (pre-1994) models

21 Undo the two retaining screws and washers, and remove the lens. Recover the lens seal; it must be renewed if it is damaged **(see illustration)**.
22 Twist the bulb anti-clockwise, and withdraw it from the light unit **(see illustration)**.
23 Fit the new bulb, then refit the lens and seal, and secure them in position with

5.18 Undo the screw (arrowed) and twist the headlight and rim clockwise

5.19a Peel off the rubber boot . . .

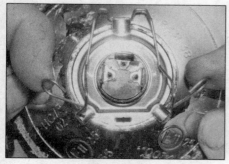

5.19b . . . and spread apart the bulb retaining clip

5.21 Undo the retaining screws and remove the lens . . .

5.22 . . . then twist the bulb anti-clockwise, and remove it from the light unit

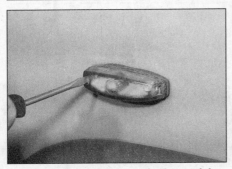

5.27a On early models, undo the retaining screw . . .

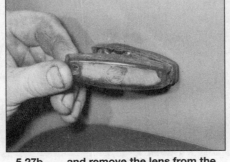

5.27b . . . and remove the lens from the direction indicator side repeater light

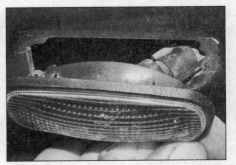

5.30 Push the repeater lens forward, and pull the rear end from the wing

5.33 Undo the retaining screw, and remove the cover from the rear number plate light unit

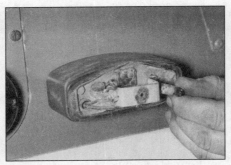

5.34 Twist the relevant bulb anti-clockwise, and remove it from the light unit

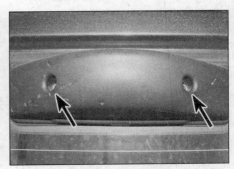

5.36 The high-level brake light cover is retained by 2 screws (arrowed)

the retaining screws and washers. Do not overtighten the screws, as the lens is easily cracked.

Later (1994 onwards) models

24 Undo the two retaining screws and withdraw the light unit.
25 Twist the bulbholder anti-clockwise to free it from the rear of the lens unit. Twist the bulb anti-clockwise, and remove it from the bulbholder.
26 Fit the new bulb, then refit the bulbholder to the rear of the lens unit. Refit the light unit, and secure it in position with the retaining screws. Do not overtighten the screws, as the lens is easily cracked.

Direction indicator side repeater

Early models

27 Undo the screw, and remove the lens from the light unit **(see illustrations)**.
28 Twist the bulb anti-clockwise, and remove it from the light unit. Inspect the lens seal for signs of damage, and renew it if necessary.
29 Ensure that the seal is in position, then fit the new bulb. Refit the lens, and secure it in position with the retaining screw. Do not overtighten the screw, as the lens is easily cracked.

Later models

30 Carefully push the lens firmly forward, and withdraw the rear end of the unit from the wing **(see illustration)**. Turn the bulbholder anti-clockwise to release it, and remove it from the lens unit.

31 The bulb is of the capless (push-fit) type, and can be removed by simply pulling it out of the bulbholder.
32 Refitting is a reverse of the removal procedure.

Rear number plate light

33 Undo the retaining screw, and remove the light unit cover **(see illustration)**. Recover the seal, renewing it if it is damaged.
34 Twist the relevant bulb anti-clockwise, and withdraw it from the light unit **(see illustration)**.
35 Fit the new bulb, then refit the cover and seal, and secure them in position with the retaining screw.

High-level brake light

36 Undo the 2 screws and remove the

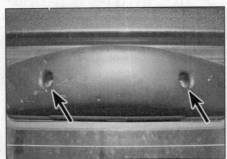

6.2 On some models, the lens simply unclips from place

cover from the rear of the light unit **(see illustration)**.
37 Rotate the bulbholder anti-clockwise and pull it from the light unit.
38 Twist the bulbholder anti-clockwise and remove it.
39 Refitting is a reversal of removal.

6 Bulbs (interior lights) – renewal

General

1 Refer to Section 5, paragraph 1.

Courtesy light

2 Undo the retaining screw (where fitted), then carefully unclip the lens from the light unit, using a small flat-bladed screwdriver **(see illustration)**.
3 Twist the bulb anti-clockwise and withdraw it from the light unit, or simply free the bulb from its contacts and remove it from the vehicle (as applicable).
4 Fit the new bulb, ensuring that it is securely held by its contacts, then refit the lens and (where necessary) secure it in position with the retaining screw.

Instrument panel illumination

5 Remove the instrument panel as described in Section 9.
6 Twist the relevant bulbholder anti-clockwise, and withdraw it from the rear of the panel

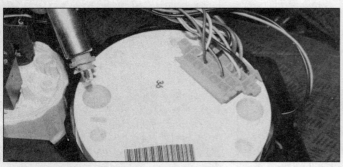

6.6 Twist the bulbholder anti-clockwise from the rear of the instrument panel

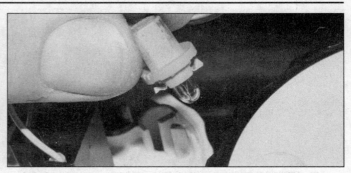

6.7 On some models, the bulb is integral with the bulbholder

(see illustration). We used an 11/32 inch deep socket to undo the bulbholder from the speedometer, as the bulbholders are deeply recessed.

7 On some models, the bulbs are of the capless (push-fit) type, and can be removed by simply pulling them out of the bulbholder. On others, the bulb is integral with holder (see illustration). Note that the warning lights on models after 2002 are illuminated by non-renewable LEDs (Light Emitting Diodes).

8 Refit the bulbholder to the rear of the instrument panel, then refit the instrument panel as described in Section 9.

Warning lights

9 Undo the two retaining screws, and remove the warning light panel from the front of the instrument panel. Disconnect the wiring connectors, and remove the panel. Note that the warning lights on models after 2002, are illuminated by non-renewable LEDs (Light Emitting Diodes).

10 Twist the relevant bulbholder anti-clockwise, and withdraw it from the rear of the panel.

11 The bulbs are of the capless (push-fit) type, and can be removed by simply pulling them out of the bulbholder.

12 Refit the bulbholder, then reconnect the wiring connectors and refit the warning panel, securing it in position with the retaining screws.

Facia-mounted clock and gauge illumination

13 Slacken and remove the two retaining

7.9 Undo the screws (arrowed) and remove the rear light unit

screws and nuts, then free the small panel from the centre of the facia.

14 Twist the relevant bulbholder anti-clockwise, and withdraw it from the rear of the clock/gauge.

15 The bulbs are of the capless (push-fit) type, and can be removed by simply pulling them out of the bulbholder.

16 Refit the bulbholder then refit the panel, securely tightening its retaining screws and nuts.

7 Exterior light units – removal and refitting

Headlight

1 Remove the headlight unit as described in Section 5.

Models up to 1999

2 Undo the four retaining screws, and release the shell from the wing. Disconnect the wiring connectors, and remove the headlight shell from the vehicle.

3 If necessary, release the headlight aim screws and the spring, and separate the headlight rim seating from the shell.

Models from 1999

4 Undo the 3 screws securing the retaining rim to the headlight, and recover the metal clips.

All models

5 Refitting is the reverse of removal. On completion, check the headlight beam alignment using the information given in Section 8.

Direction indicator, sidelight and rear lights

Note: Later-model lights can also be fitted to early models.

Early (pre-1994) models

6 Undo the two retaining screws and washers, and remove the lens. Recover the lens seal; it must be renewed if it is damaged.

7 Slacken and remove the screws securing the light unit in position. Withdraw the unit, disconnect its wiring connector, and remove it from the vehicle. If there is not enough wiring

to allow the connector to be withdrawn, it will be necessary to disconnect the connector prior to withdrawing the light unit. For the front light units, remove any items (such as the air cleaner) to gain access to the rear of the light, and disconnect the connector. For the rear lights, undo the retaining screws and remove the access cover from inside the vehicle, then disconnect the wiring connector.

8 Refitting is the reverse of removal, ensuring that the light unit drain hole cut-out is at the bottom. Refit the lens, taking care not to overtighten its retaining screws, as the lenses are easily cracked.

Later (1994 onwards) models

9 Undo the retaining screws and withdraw the light unit (see illustration).

10 Disconnect the wiring connector, and remove the light unit from the vehicle. Inspect the light unit seal for signs of damage or deterioration, and renew if necessary.

11 On refitting, reconnect the wiring connector, and secure the light unit in position with the retaining screws. Do not overtighten the screws, as the lens is easily cracked.

Direction indicator side repeater

Early models

12 Reach in behind the wing, and slacken and remove the light unit retaining nuts and washers. Where necessary, remove any ancillary components (such as the air cleaner) as described in the relevant Chapters of this manual, to gain access to the rear of the light.

13 Withdraw the light unit from the wing, disconnecting its wiring connectors as they become accessible. Examine the light unit seal, renewing it if it shows signs of damage or deterioration.

14 On refitting, ensure that the light seal is in position, then reconnect the wiring connectors. Make sure that the earth lead is correctly located on one of the light studs, and seat the light unit in the wing. Refit the lens, taking care not to overtighten the screws as the lens is easily cracked.

Later models

15 Firmly push the lens forward, and carefully pull the rear end of the light unit out and withdraw the unit from the wing,

8.1 Headlamp vertical (1) and horizontal adjustment screws (2) – later models

disconnecting its wiring connectors as they become accessible. Examine the light unit seal, renewing it if it shows signs of damage or deterioration.

16 On refitting, ensure that the seal is in position, and reconnect the wiring connectors. Clip the light unit into position in the wing.

Rear foglight and reversing light

17 Reaching behind the light, release the wiring and disconnect its wiring connectors.
18 Slacken and remove the retaining nuts and washers, and remove the light unit from the vehicle.
19 Refitting is the reverse of removal, ensuring that the wiring is retained by the necessary clips.

Rear number plate light

20 Undo the retaining screw and remove the

9.2 Undo the retaining screws (right-hand screws arrowed) . . .

9.3b . . . disconnecting the speedometer cable and wiring connectors as they become accessible

light unit cover. Recover the seal, renewing it if it is damaged.
21 Twist the bulbs anti-clockwise, and remove them from the light unit.
22 Remove the trim cover to gain access to the rear of the light unit, and disconnect its wiring connectors.
23 Undo the two retaining screws and nuts, and remove the light unit from the vehicle. Inspect the seal, renewing it if it is damaged.
24 Refitting is the reverse of removal.

8 Headlight beam alignment – general information

Accurate adjustment of the headlight beam is only possible using optical beam-setting equipment, and this work should therefore be carried out by a Land Rover dealer or suitably-equipped workshop.

For reference, the headlights can be adjusted using the screws located in the headlight rim **(see illustration)**.

9 Instrument panel – removal and refitting

Removal

1 Disconnect the battery negative terminal, as described in Chapter 5.

9.3a . . . then withdraw the instrument panel from the facia . . .

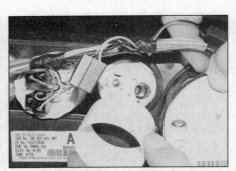

10.3 Slacken the clamping rings to remove the instrument

2 Undo the four retaining screws securing the instrument panel assembly in position **(see illustration)**.
3 Move the panel forwards until access can be gained to the panel wiring connectors. Disconnect each wiring connector, noting its correct fitted location. To avoid confusion on refitting, label each connector as it is disconnected **(see illustrations)**.
4 Disconnect the speedometer cable (where applicable) from the rear of the instrument panel, then carefully manoeuvre the instrument panel out of position.

Refitting

5 Ease the instrument panel into position, and reconnect the speedometer cable (where applicable).
6 Reconnect the panel wiring connectors, making sure that each one is connected to its original location, and seat the panel in position.
7 Securely tighten the retaining screws, and reconnect the battery.

10 Instrument panel components – removal and refitting

Removal

1 Remove the instrument panel as described in Section 9.
2 Free the bulbholder from the rear of the relevant instrument then, making a note of each connector's correct fitted location, disconnect the relevant wiring connectors.
3 Slacken the retaining nut(s) or clamping rings (as applicable) and remove the relevant instrument from the panel **(see illustration)**.

Refitting

4 Refitting is the reverse of removal, ensuring that the instrument wiring is correctly reconnected.

11 Clock – removal and refitting

Removal

Facia-mounted clock

1 Undo the two retaining screws and nuts, and withdraw the panel from the centre of the facia.
2 Disconnect the wiring connectors, then release the clock and remove it from the vehicle.

Instrument panel clock

3 Refer to Section 10.

Refitting

4 Refitting is the reverse of removal.

13.2 Withdraw the switch panel from the centre of the facia, and disconnect the cigarette lighter wiring

12 Lights-on warning system – general information

Some vehicles covered in this manual have a lights-on warning system. The purpose of the system is to inform the driver that the lights have been left on after the ignition switch has been turned off; the buzzer will sound when a door is opened. The system consists of a buzzer relay unit which is linked to the driver's door courtesy light switch.

13 Cigarette lighter – removal and refitting

Removal

1 Disconnect the battery negative terminal as described in Chapter 5.

Vehicles up to 2002 model year

2 Slacken and remove the two retaining screws and nuts, then free the small panel from the centre of the facia. Disconnect the wiring from the rear of the lighter **(see illustration)**, then depress the retaining tangs and push the lighter out from the centre panel.

Vehicles from 2002 model year

3 Remove the centre console as described in Chapter 12.

4 Release the clip and remove the lighter body from the console.

Refitting

5 Refitting is the reverse of removal.

14 Horn – removal and refitting

Removal

1 Undo the retaining screws, and remove the radiator grille from the front of the vehicle **(see illustration)**. **Note:** *To remove the left-hand horn on vehicles from 2002 model year, remove the headlight unit as described in Section 5.*

2 Disconnect the wiring connectors from the relevant horn.

3 Slacken and remove the retaining nut/bolts, then remove the horn from the vehicle **(see illustrations)**.

Refitting

4 Refitting is the reverse of removal.

15 Speedometer drive cable – removal and refitting

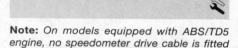

Note: *On models equipped with ABS/TD5 engine, no speedometer drive cable is fitted – an electronic speedometer is fitted.*

Removal

1 Firmly apply the handbrake, then jack up the front of the vehicle and support it on axle stands.

2 Detach the lower end of the speedometer cable from its drive on the transfer box.

3 Remove the instrument panel as described in Section 9. Tie a piece string to the upper end of the cable – this can then be used to draw the cable back into position.

4 From within the engine compartment, free the speedometer cable from any relevant retaining clips and ties, noting its correct routing.

5 Release the cable grommet from the engine compartment bulkhead, and withdraw the cable forwards and out through the bulkhead. Once the cable is free, untie the string, leaving it in position in the vehicle; the string can then be used to draw the new cable back into position.

Refitting

6 Tie the end of the string to the end of the cable, then use the string to draw the speedometer cable through from the engine compartment and into position. Once the cable is through, untie the string.

7 Ensure that the cable is correctly routed and retained by all the relevant clips and ties, then seat the outer cable grommet in the engine compartment bulkhead.

8 Reconnect the lower end of the cable to its drive, ensuring that it is securely reconnected, then lower the vehicle to the ground.

9 Refit the instrument panel as described in Section 9.

16 Wiper arm – removal and refitting

Removal

1 Operate the wiper motor, then switch it off so that the wiper arm returns to the at rest ('parked') position.

2 Stick a piece of masking tape to the glass along the edge of the wiper blade, to use as an alignment aid on refitting. If the tailgate wiper arm is being removed, remove the spare wheel.

Vehicles up to 2002 model year

3 To remove a windscreen wiper arm, simply lift up the arm and, using a suitable flat-bladed screwdriver, carefully lever it off the spindle splines.

Vehicles from 2002 model year

4 Lift up the spindle cover, and undo the

14.1 Undo the retaining screws, and remove the radiator grille from the front of the vehicle

14.3a Disconnect the wiring connector (arrowed), then undo the retaining bolts and remove the horn from the vehicle

14.3b Undo the bolt (arrowed) and remove the horn (vehicles from 2002 model year)

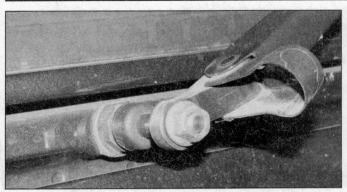

16.4 Lift up the cover and undo the spindle nut (vehicles from 2002 model year)

16.5 Lift up the trim cap, then undo the retaining nut and remove the tailgate wiper arm

spindle nut **(see illustration)**. Lift the blade from the glass and pull the wiper arm from the spindle.

All vehicles

5 To remove the tailgate wiper arm, lift up/remove (as applicable) the wiper arm spindle nut cover, then slacken and remove the spindle nut **(see illustration)**. Lift the blade off the glass, and pull the wiper arm off its spindle. If necessary, the arm can be levered off the spindle using a suitable flat-bladed screwdriver. On models where the spare wheel is mounted onto the tailgate, it will be necessary to remove the wheel to gain access to the wiper arm.

Refitting

6 Ensure that the wiper arm and spindle splines are clean and dry. Locate the wiper arm on the spindle, aligning the wiper blade with the tape fitted on removal.

Vehicles up to 2002 model year

7 When refitting the windscreen wiper arms, push the arm fully onto the spindle, and check that it is securely retained by its clip.

Vehicles from 2002 model year

8 Refit the arm, aligning the blade with the tape fitted on removal. Tighten the spindle nut securely.

All vehicles

9 On the tailgate wiper arm, refit and securely tighten the spindle nut, and clip the nut cover

back in position. Where necessary, refit the spare wheel to the tailgate.

---

17 Windscreen wiper motor and cable – removal and refitting

Removal

1 Disconnect the battery negative terminal as described in Chapter 5.
2 Remove both windscreen wiper arms as described in Section 16.

Vehicles up to 2002 model year

3 Prise out the badge from the top of the grab handle which is fitted to the left-hand end of the facia. Undo the three retaining screws, then lift the handle upwards to disengage it and remove it from the facia **(see illustrations)**.
4 Undo the three retaining screws, then remove the lower cover panel from the left-hand end of the facia, to gain access to the wiper motor **(see illustration)**.
5 Disconnect the motor wiring connector, and free the earth lead from the wiper motor upper mounting point (where necessary) **(see illustration)**.
6 Peel back the rubber sleeve, to gain access to the large nut securing the wiper motor cable to the motor. Unscrew the nut so that the motor is free to be removed from the outer cable **(see illustration)**.

17.3a Prise out the badge from the facia left-hand grab handle . . .

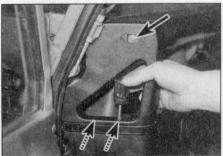

17.3b . . . then undo the three retaining screws (arrowed) and remove the grab handle

17.4 Undo the retaining screws, and remove the lower cover panel from the left-hand end of the facia

17.5 Disconnect the wiring connector from the wiper motor

17.6 Lift up the rubber cover, and unscrew the nut (arrowed) securing the cable to the motor

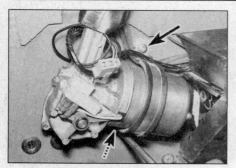

17.7a Undo the retaining screws . . .

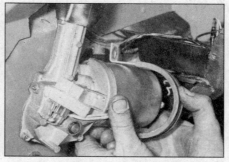

17.7b . . . then remove the mounting clamp and rubber, and remove the motor assembly from the vehicle

17.9a To remove the cable, undo the retaining screws . . .

7 Slacken and remove the two retaining screws and mounting clamp, and recover the mounting rubber(s) from the motor. Take care not to lose the earth lead connector from the upper mounting screw (see illustrations).

8 Remove the motor and cable assembly from the vehicle.

9 To remove the cable, undo the retaining screws and remove the cover from the rear of the wiper motor. Remove the circlip, then free the cable from the motor linkage and remove it (see illustrations).

10 If the outer cable/drive box assembly needs to be renewed, it will be necessary to remove the facia assembly as described in Chapter 12.

Vehicles from 2002 model year

11 Remove the centre console as described in Chapter 12.

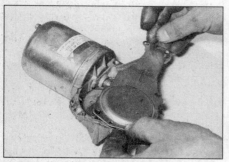

17.9b . . . and remove the cover from the rear of the motor

12 Undo the fresh air vent control knobs.
13 Undo the 7 retaining screws and remove the facia upper panel. Recover the captive nut plate (see illustration).
14 Move the cover to one side, then slacken the motor drive tube nut (see illustration).
15 Undo the 2 retaining screws, and remove the motor mounting strap.
16 Disconnect the motor wiring plug, then undo the drive tube nut and remove the motor complete with rack (see illustration). Recover the motor mounting pad.

Refitting

Vehicles up to 2002 model year

17 Where removed, refit the cable to the motor. Ensure that the cable is securely retained by the circlip (see illustration), then

17.13 Undo the screws (3 left-hand side ones arrowed) and remove the facia upper panel

refit the motor cover and securely tighten its retaining screws.

18 Offer up the motor and cable. Feed the cable into position, noting that it may be necessary to have an assistant rotate the wiper arm spindles to allow the cable to engage with them.

19 Once the cable is fully engaged, screw the large nut onto the motor.

20 Fit the mounting rubber(s) and clamp around the motor, then refit the retaining screws, not forgetting the earth lead connector, and tighten them securely.

21 Securely tighten the cable retaining nut, and seat the rubber cover over it.

22 Reconnect the motor wiring connector, then reconnect the earth lead to its mounting point.

23 Refit the lower cover panel to the facia, and securely tighten its retaining screws.

24 Refit the grab handle, making sure that its locating pins are correctly located, and securely tighten its retaining screws. Press the badge back into the side of the handle.

Vehicles from 2002 model year

25 Apply a little grease to the motor drive rack, and then feed the rack into the drive tube. Only finger-tighten the drive tube nut at this stage.

26 Ensure the mounting pad is correctly positioned, then refit the motor and secure it in place with the retaining strap. Securely tighten the strap screws.

27 Tighten the drive tube nut securely, and reposition the nut cover.

17.14 Slacken the motor drive tube nut (arrowed)

17.16 Remove the motor complete with rack

17.17 Refit the cable to the motor, and secure it in position with the circlip

18.3 Unscrew the nut, and remove the washer and rubber seal from the tailgate wiper motor spindle

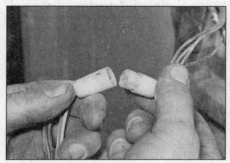

18.7a Disconnect the wiring connector . . .

18.7b . . . then undo the retaining bolt(s) . . .

18.7c . . . and remove the wiper motor from the tailgate

18.9 Release the clips and remove the tailgate trim panel

18.10 Undo the wiper motor/lock solenoid retaining bolt (arrowed)

28 The remainder of refitting is a reversal of removal.

All vehicles

29 Refit the windscreen wiper arms, then reconnect the battery and check the operation of the motor.

18 Tailgate wiper motor – removal and refitting

Removal

1 Remove the spare wheel (where necessary).
2 Remove the wiper arm as described in Section 16.
3 Unscrew the large nut from the wiper spindle, and recover the washer and rubber seal (see illustration).
4 Undo the retaining screws and remove the grab handle from the tailgate.

Vehicles up to 2002 model year

5 Undo the retaining screws, and remove the wiper motor and wiring harness covers from the tailgate trim panel.
6 Undo the retaining screws and remove the inner trim panel from the tailgate.
7 Disconnect the wiring connector, undo the retaining bolts and washers, and remove the wiper motor from the tailgate. Recover the spindle spacer which is fitted inside the tailgate (see illustrations).

Vehicles from 2002 model year

8 Prise out the plastic panel from the tailgate latch handle recess.
9 Using a flat-bladed tool, carefully release the 9 clips securing the panel to the tailgate (see illustration).
10 Undo the bolt securing the door locking solenoid to the tailgate, then manoeuvre the wiper motor from the tailgate (see illustration). Disconnect the wiring plug as the motor is withdrawn.

Refitting

11 Refitting is a reversal of removal.

19 Windscreen/tailgate washer system components – removal and refitting

Note: On models with headlight washers, an additional reservoir may also be fitted in the left-hand rear corner of the engine compartment.

Washer system reservoir

Vehicles up to 1999 model year

1 To remove the main reservoir, undo the retaining nuts and screws, and free the reservoir from the wheel arch panel. Withdraw the reservoir from underneath the wing, then slacken the retaining clips (where fitted) and disconnect the hoses from the washers pump(s). Mark each hose for identification purposes, to avoid the possibility of reconnecting the hoses incorrectly on refitting. Disconnect the pump wiring connector(s), and remove the reservoir from the vehicle.
2 To remove the secondary reservoir (where fitted), disconnect the wiring connector and washer hose from the pump, then unclip the reservoir and remove it from the vehicle.
3 Refitting is the reverse of removal.

Vehicles from 1999 model year

4 Remove the left-hand headlight as described in Section 5.
5 Undo the screws and remove the heater intake grille from the left-hand wing.
6 Undo the 2 screws securing the heater intake ducting to the wing, and the 2 bolts securing the ducting retaining bracket (see illustrations). Manoeuvre the ducting from under the wing.

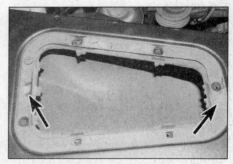

19.6a Undo the ducting retaining screws in the grille recess (arrowed) . . .

19.6b . . . and the bracket screws (arrowed)

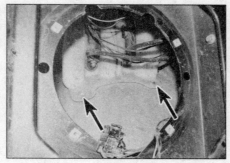

19.8a Washer reservoir screws at the front (arrowed) . . .

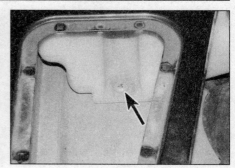

19.8b . . . and at the rear (arrowed)

7 Undo the 4 screws, release the clips and manoeuvre the left-hand wheel arch liner to gain access to the nuts on the underside of the reservoir retaining screws.

8 Undo the 3 screws and remove the reservoir from the inner wing **(see illustration)**. Disconnect the hoses from the washers pump(s). Mark each hose for identification purposes, to avoid the possibility of reconnecting the hoses incorrectly on refitting. Disconnect the pump wiring connector(s), and remove the reservoir from the vehicle.

9 Refitting is a reversal of removal.

Washer pump

Vehicles up to 1999 model year

10 Remove the washer reservoir as described above.

11 Tip out the contents of the reservoir, then

carefully ease the pump out from the reservoir and recover its sealing grommet.

12 Refitting is the reverse of removal, using a new sealing grommet if the original one shows signs of damage or deterioration.

Vehicles from 1999 model year

13 Remove the left-hand headlight as described in Section 5, then undo the screws and remove the headlight shell from the wing.

14 Note their fitted positions, and disconnect the wiring plug and washer hose from the pump **(see illustration)**.

15 Pull the pump from the sealing grommet on the reservoir. Be prepared for fluid spillage.

16 Refitting is a reversal of removal.

Non-return valves

17 A non-return valve is fitted to both the windscreen and tailgate washer hoses.

18 To remove the valve, trace the hose back from the relevant pump to the valve, then disconnect the hoses and remove the valve from the vehicle.

19 On refitting, ensure that the valve is fitted the correct way around.

Windscreen washer jet

20 To gain access to the rear of the jet, undo the retaining screws and remove the top panel from the facia. Note that it may be necessary to slacken the grab handle (left-hand end) and heater control cover (right-hand end) screws in order to allow the panel to be removed the from the facia.

21 Disconnect the washer hose from the jet, then unscrew the retaining nut and washer, and remove the jet from the front of the vehicle.

22 On refitting, refit the washer and retaining nut, tightening it securely then reconnect the washer hose. Check the operation of the jet. If necessary, adjust the nozzle using a pin, aiming the spray to a point slightly above the centre of the swept area.

Tailgate washer jet

Vehicles up to 1999 model year

23 Disconnect the washer hose from the jet, then unscrew the retaining nut and washer, and remove the jet from the rear of the vehicle.

24 On refitting, securely tighten the retaining nut, then reconnect the washer hose. Check the operation of the jet and, If necessary, adjust the nozzle using a pin, aiming the spray to a point slightly above the centre of the swept area.

Vehicle from 1999 model year

25 Carefully prise off the rear window surround trims on both sides **(see illustration)**.

26 Prise open the caps and undo the screws and remove both rear grab handles.

27 Release the 4 studs and remove the trim panel above the rear door **(see illustration)**.

28 Disconnect the hose from the washer jet. Be prepared for fluid spillage.

29 Undo the retaining nut and remove the washer jet **(see illustration)**.

30 On refitting, securely tighten the retaining nut, then reconnect the washer hose. Check

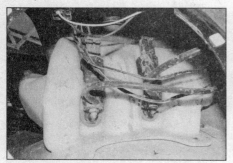

19.14 Disconnect the wiring plug(s) and washer hose(s) from the pump(s)

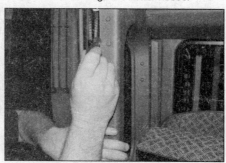

19.25 Carefully prise off the window surround trims each side

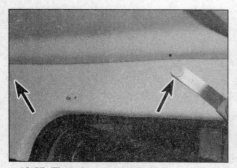

19.27 The trim panel above the tailgate is secured by 4 studs (2 right-hand ones arrowed)

19.29 Undo the jet retaining nut (arrowed)

21.4 Insert the Allen key into the holes, rotate then anti-clockwise a few turns, and pull the radio/cassette player from place

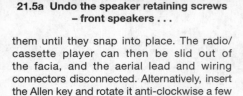

21.5a Undo the speaker retaining screws – front speakers . . .

21.5b . . . and rear speakers

the operation of the jet and, If necessary, adjust the nozzle using a pin, aiming the spray to a point slightly above the centre of the swept area.

20 Headlight washer system components – removal and refitting

Washer reservoir and pump

1 Refer to Section 19.

Washer jet

2 If necessary to improve access, chock the rear wheels then jack up the front of the vehicle and support it on axle stands.
3 Slacken the retaining clip, and detach the washer hose from the rear of the relevant washer jet.
4 Unscrew the retaining nut, and remove the washer jet from the bumper.
5 Refitting is the reverse of removal.

21 Radio/cassette player and speakers – removal and refitting

Note: *The following removal and refitting procedure is for the radio/cassette units and speakers which Land Rover fit as an optional extra. Removal and refitting procedures of non-standard units may differ slightly.*

Removal

Radio/cassette player

1 Most of the radio/cassette players fitted by Land Rover have DIN standard fixings. Two special tools, obtainable from most car accessory shops, are required for removal. Alternatively, suitable tools can be fabricated from 3 mm diameter wire, such as welding rod. Some 'low-line' models are fitted with units released using 2.5 mm Allen keys.
2 Disconnect the battery negative lead as described in Chapter 5.
3 Unclip the small access covers (where fitted) from either side of the radio/cassette unit, to reveal the fixing holes.
4 Insert the tools into the holes, and push

them until they snap into place. The radio/cassette player can then be slid out of the facia, and the aerial lead and wiring connectors disconnected. Alternatively, insert the Allen key and rotate it anti-clockwise a few turns to release the clips **(see illustration)**.

Speakers

5 Undo the retaining screws then withdraw the speaker, disconnecting its wiring connectors as they become accessible **(see illustrations)**.

Refitting

Radio/cassette player

6 To refit the radio/cassette player, reconnect the aerial lead and wiring connectors, then push the unit into the facia until the retaining lugs snap into place.
7 Refit the access covers and reconnect the battery.

Speakers

8 Refitting is the reverse of removal.

22 Dim-dip lighting system (UK models only) – general information

To comply with UK regulations, a dim-dip lighting system is fitted to most UK models until approximately 1995 model year. The system comprises of a control unit which is situated behind the instrument panel.

The system is supplied with current from the sidelight circuit, and energised by a feed

from the ignition switch. When energised, the dim-dip unit allows battery voltage to pass through a resistor to the headlight dipped-beam circuits; this lights the headlights with approximately one-sixth of their normal power, so that the car cannot be driven using sidelights alone.

23 Central locking components – general information, removal and refitting

General information

1 A central door locking function is standard on all vehicles from 2002 model year. The system operates on the front and rear passenger doors, and on Station Wagon and County Station Wagon models it also operates on the rear tailgate.

Electronic control unit

2 The central door locking function is controlled by the anti-theft system control unit, which is located behind the instrument cluster. The control unit is also responsible for the operation of the interior lights.

Removal

Front door lock solenoid

3 Remove the door inner trim panel and weathershield as described in Chapter 12.
4 Unclip the lock solenoid link rod from the door lock **(see illustration)**.
5 Undo the 2 screws and remove the solenoid form the mounting panel **(see illustration)**.

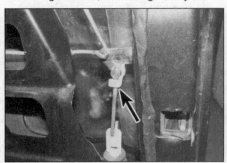

23.4 Unclip the link rod from the door lock . . .

23.5 . . . then undo the solenoid screws (arrowed)

23.9 Undo the 3 bolts at the rear of the mounting panel (arrowed)

23.10 Door lock solenoid retaining bolts (arrowed)

Disconnect the solenoid wiring plug as it is withdrawn.

Rear door lock solenoid

6 Remove the door inner trim panel as described in Chapter 12.

7 Unclip the lock solenoid link rod.

8 Unclip the interior release handle link rod from the lock mechanism.

9 Undo the 3 bolts at the rear of the mounting panel **(see illustration)**. Slacken the remaining nuts and bolts, then pull the mounting panel away from the door sufficiently to gain access to the lock solenoid.

10 Disconnect the solenoid wiring plug, then undo the 2 retaining bolts, and manoeuvre the solenoid from position **(see illustration)**. Disconnect the solenoid link rod as it is withdrawn.

Tailgate lock solenoid

11 Undo the retaining screws and remove the grab handle from the tailgate.

12 Prise out the plastic panel from the tailgate latch handle recess.

13 Using a flat-bladed tool, carefully release the 9 clips securing the panel to the tailgate **(see illustration 18.9)**.

14 Disconnect solenoid wiring plug, then undo the screw and bolt securing the solenoid to the tailgate **(see illustration 18.10)**.

15 Disconnect the solenoid link rod as the solenoid is withdrawn.

16 If required, undo the two screws and separate the solenoid from the mounting bracket.

Refitting

17 Refitting is a reversal of removal.

Wiring diagram colour code

B	Black	P	Purple
G	Green	R	Red
K	Pink	S	Slate
L	Light	U	Blue
N	Brown	W	White
O	Orange	Y	Yellow

The last letter indicates the tracer colour

Note: *Page limitations have forced the use of a representative sample of wiring diagrams.*

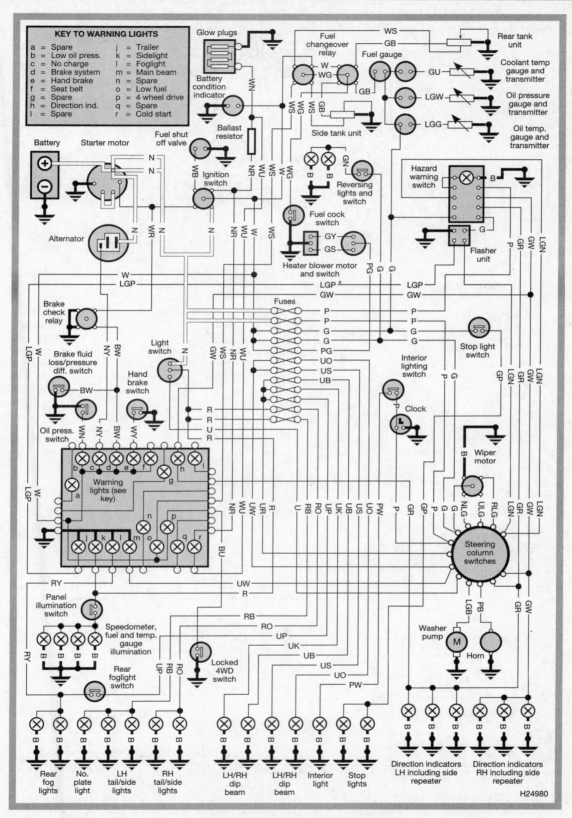

Diagram 1 : 10J engine models up to 1984

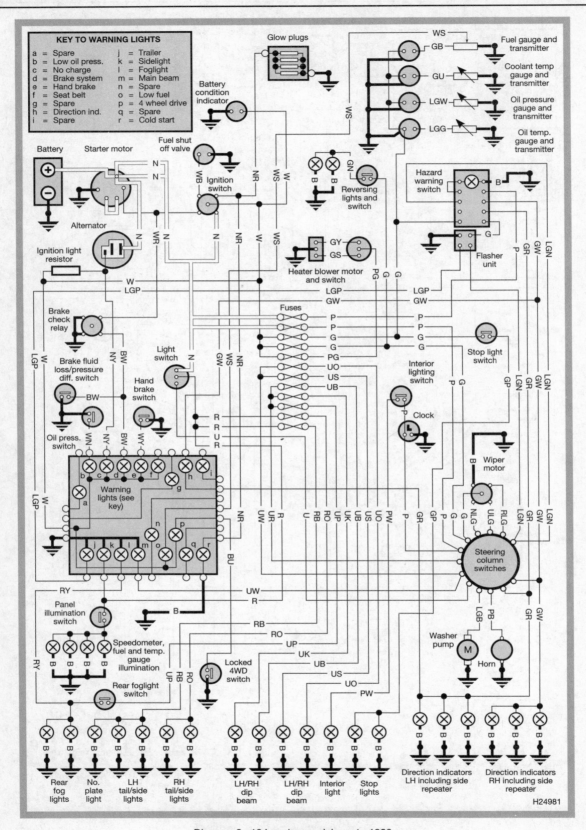

Diagram 2 : 12J engine models up to 1986

H24981

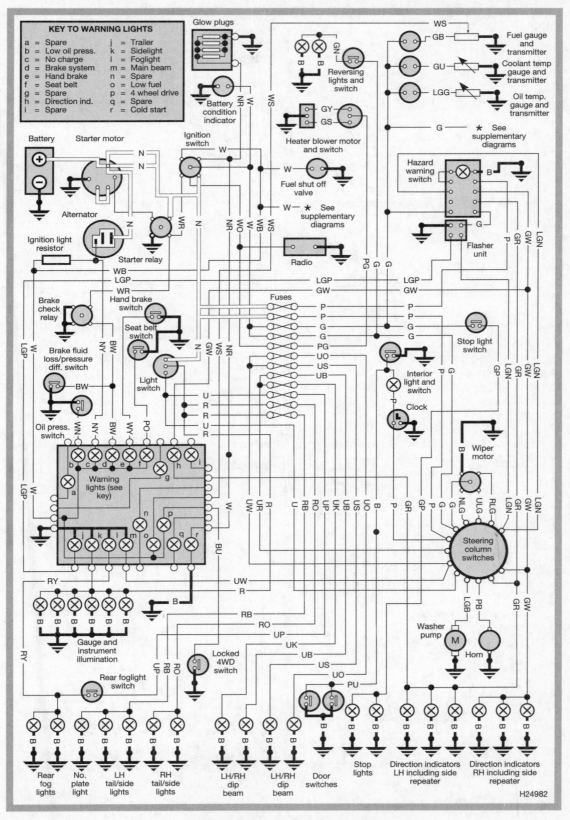

Diagram 3 : Main diagram - all models from 1986-91

H24982

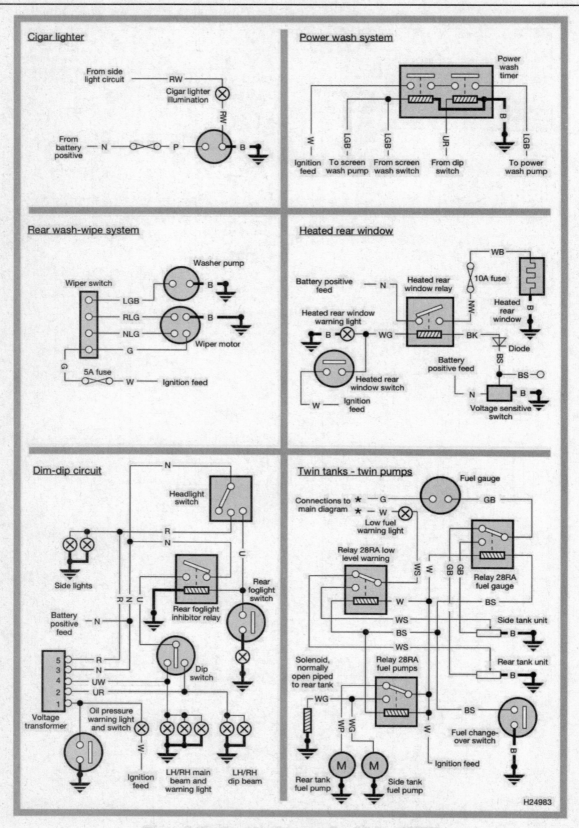

Diagram 4 : Supplementary diagrams - all models from 1986-91

H24983

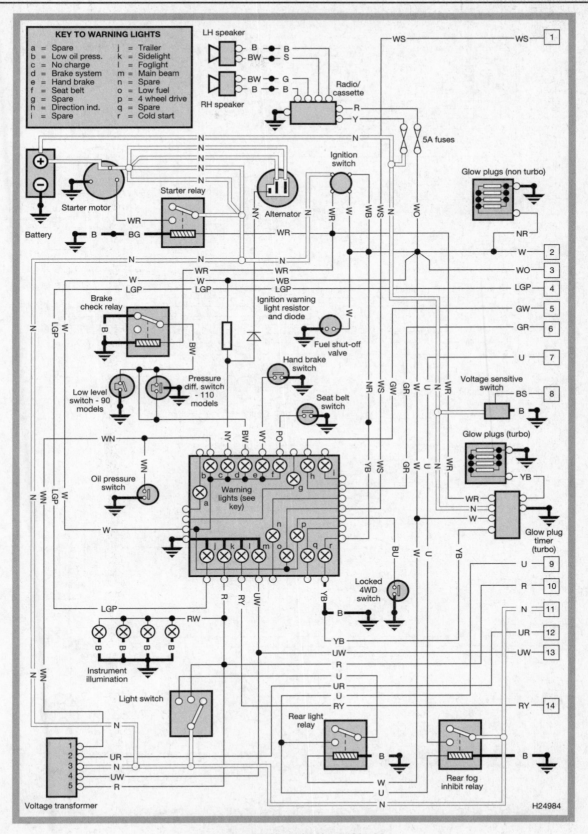

Diagram 5 : All models from 1991-96

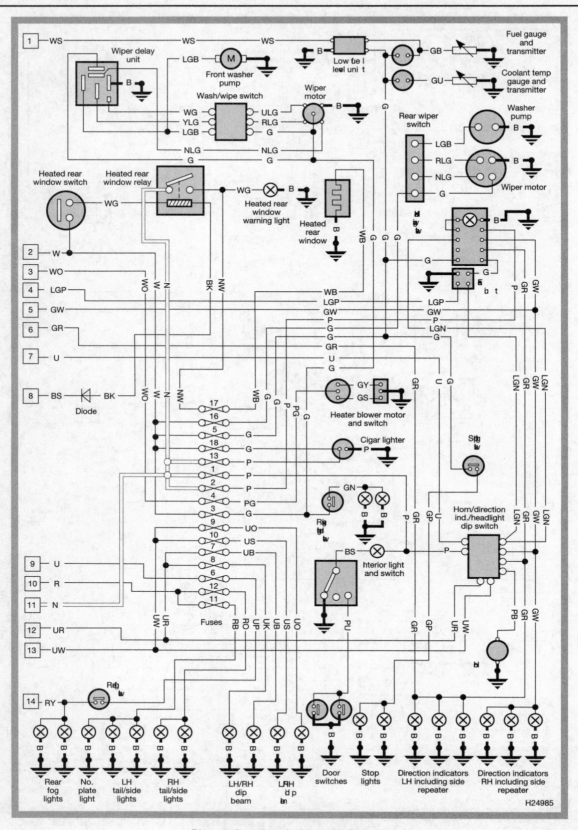

Diagram 5 continued : All models from 1991-96

LAND ROVER DEFENDER 2002 on wiring diagrams

Diagram 1

Key to symbols

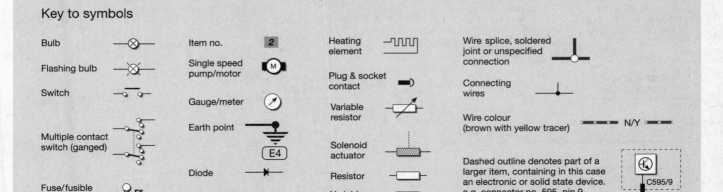

Bulb	⊗
Flashing bulb	⊗
Switch	
Multiple contact switch (ganged)	
Fuse/fusible link and current rating	**F5** 30A
Item no.	**2**
Single speed pump/motor	Ⓜ
Gauge/meter	
Earth point	E4
Diode	
Light emitting diode (LED)	
Heating element	
Plug & socket contact	
Variable resistor	
Solenoid actuator	
Resistor	
Variable resistor	

Wire splice, soldered joint or unspecified connection

Connecting wires

Wire colour (brown with yellow tracer) — N/Y

Dashed outline denotes part of a larger item, containing in this case an electronic or solid state device. e.g. connector no. 595, pin 9.

C595/9

Under seat fusebox 5

Fuse	Rating	Circuit protected
FL1	100A	TD5 - FL2, FL3 & FL4, F1, F2 & F3 of the under seat fusebox, F36 of the satellite fusebox, glowplug relay
FL1	100A	300TDi - FL2, FL3 & FL4, F1, F2 & F3 of the under seat fusebox, glowplug relay
FL2	60A	F28, F29, F30, F31 & F32 of the satellite fusebox
FL3	60A	Seat heater/electric window relay
FL4	30A	ABS return pump relay
FL5	60A	Ignition switch, starter motor relay
FL6	30A	Lighting switch
F1	30A	TD5 - ABS ECU
F1	30A	300TDi - not used
F2	20A	Accessory socket
F3	30A	Column switch
F4	20A	TD5 - Fuel pump relay
F4	20A	300TDi - not used
F5	30A	TD5 - main relay, inertia switch, glow plug relay
F5	30A	300TDi - not used
F6	15A	BBUS, alarm relay, alarm ECU
F7	20A	Alarm ECU

R1 R2 R3 R4 R5   R6

F7
F6
F5
F4
F3
F2
F1

FL1 FL2 FL3 FL4 FL5 FL6

R1	A/C relay
R2	A/C relay
R3	Glow plug relay
R4	Main relay
R5	Fuel pump relay
R6	ABS return pump relay

Key to circuits

Diagram 1	Key to symbols, fuses
Diagram 2	Starting & charging, preheating, horn & cigar lighter
Diagram 3	Engine management (TD5)
Diagram 4	Engine cooling fan (300TDi), diagnostic socket & ABS
Diagram 5	Instrument cluster
Diagram 6	Stop, reversing, side, tail & number plate lights, headlights (without dim/dip) & trailer socket
Diagram 7	Headlights (with dim/dip), direction indicators & hazard warning lights, rear foglights
Diagram 8	Headlight levelling, interior lighting, clock & accessory socket, heater blower & heated seats
Diagram 9	Heated front screen & rear window, wash/wipe
Diagram 10	Audio system, central locking, electric windows

Passenger fusebox 6

Fuse	Rating	Circuit protected
F8	10A	Alarm ECU, BBUS
F9	15A	Front wiper
F10	10A	Rear wiper
F11	10A	TD5 - ABS ECU
F11	10A	300TDi - not used
F12	10A	TD5 - engine management ECU
F12	10A	300 TDi - speed transducer
F13	10A	Stop lights
F14	10A	Reversing lights, glow plug control unit (300TDi), heated front screen timer relay, heated rear window
F15	5A	Headlight relay, dim/dip relay, A/C compressor clutch relay, cooling fan relay, rear foglight relay, instrument cluster, A/C unit, seat heater/electric window relay
F16	20A	Heater blower motor, cigar lighter
F17	5A	Radio/cassette player
F18	10A	RH side/tail light, interior illumination
F19	10A	LH side/tail light, trailer socket
F20	10A	Dim/dip relay, headlight levelling, switch illumination
F21	10A	Hazard warning lights
F22	10A	RH headlight dipped beam
F23	10A	LH headlight dipped beam
F24	10A	RH headlight main beam
F25	10A	LH headlight main beam
F26	10A	Rear foglight ECU
F27	10A	Horn, column switch

Satellite fusebox 34

Fuse	Rating	Circuit protected
F28	30A	Heater blower relay
F29	20A	Cooling fan relay
F30	5A	Audio system, diag. socket, instrument cluster, clock, interior light
F31	15A	Hazard warning lights
F32	20A	Heated rear window relay
F33	20A	TD5 - heated seat switches
F33	20A	300TDi - not used
F34	20A	RH front window switch
F35	20A	LH front window switch
F36	30A	TD5 - heated front screen relay
F36	20A	300TDi - not used

F17 F16 F15 F14 F13 F12 F11 F10 F9 F8
F27 F26 F25 F24 F23 F22 F21 F20 F19 F18
F35 F34 F33 F32 F31 F30 F29 F28

R7 R8 R9 R10 R11 R12

R7	Heated screen relay
R8	Starter relay
R9	Heated rear window relay
R10	Headlight relay
R11	Alarm relay
R12	Seat heater/electric window relay

H33547

Wire colours

B	Black	**P**	Purple
G	Green	**R**	Red
K	Pink	**S**	Slate
Lg	Light green	**U**	Blue
N	Brown	**W**	White
O	Orange	**Y**	Yellow

Key to items

1 Battery
2 Starter motor
3 Alternator
4 Ignition switch
5 Under seat fusebox
6 Passenger fusebox
7 Starter relay
8 Immobilsation control unit
9 Glow plug control unit
10 Glow plugs
11 Horn
12 Column switch
   a = horn switch
13 Cigar lighter

Diagram 2

H33547

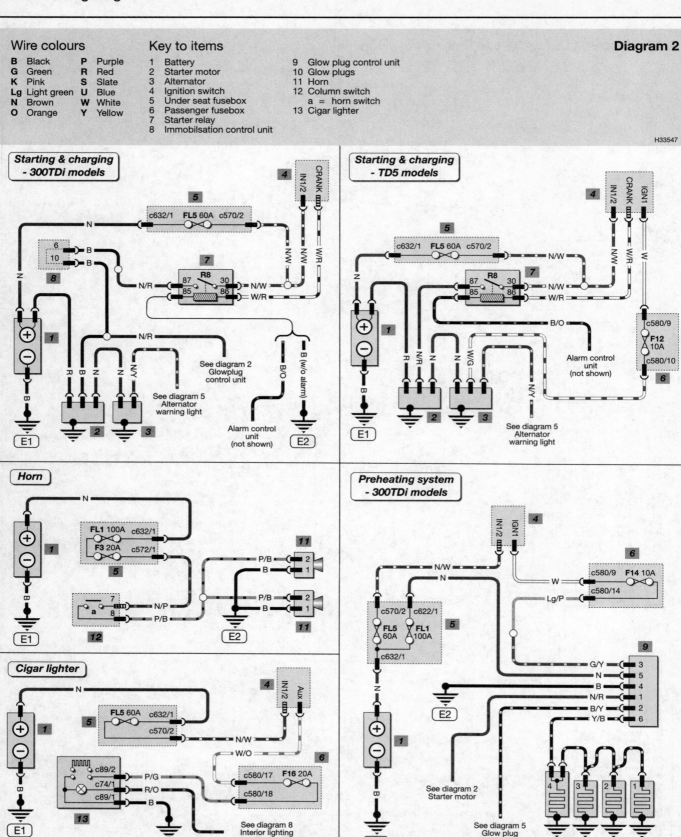

Starting & charging - 300TDi models

Starting & charging - TD5 models

Horn

Preheating system - 300TDi models

Cigar lighter

Wire colours

B	Black	**P**	Purple
G	Green	**R**	Red
K	Pink	**S**	Slate
Lg	Light green	**U**	Blue
N	Brown	**W**	White
O	Orange	**Y**	Yellow

Key to items

1 Battery
4 Ignition switch
5 Under seat fusebox
6 Passenger fusebox
10 Glow plugs
15 Engine management control unit
16 Glow plug relay
17 Inertia switch
18 Main relay
19 Fuel pump relay
20 Fuel pump/gauge sender unit
21 Fuse holder
22 EGR valve
23 MAF sensor
24 Fuel injectors
25 Transmission switch (hi/lo)
26 Inlet air temp. sensor
27 MAP sensor
28 Ambient air temp. sensor
29 Throttle position switch
30 Crank position sensor
31 Fuel rail temp. switch
32 Coolant temp. sensor
33 EGR inlet valve
34 Satellite fusebox
35 Engine cooling fan relay
36 Engine cooling fan

Diagram 3

H33549

Engine management - TD5 models

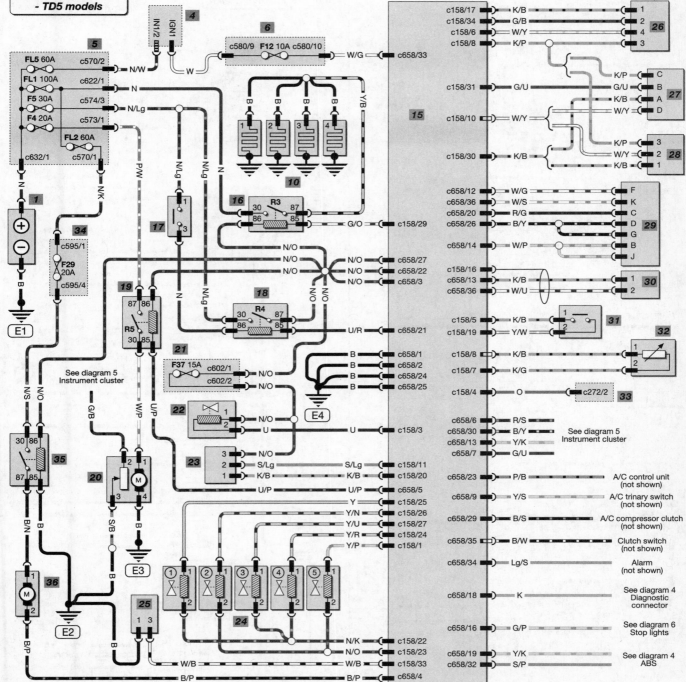

Wire colours

B	Black	P	Purple
G	Green	R	Red
K	Pink	S	Slate
Lg	Light green	U	Blue
N	Brown	W	White
O	Orange	Y	Yellow

Key to items

1 Battery
4 Ignition switch
5 Under seat fusebox
6 Passenger fusebox
34 Satellite fusebox
35 Engine cooling fan relay
38 Cooling fan switch
39 Diagnostic socket

40 ABS control unit
41 Return pump relay
42 Return pump
43 Modulator
44 LH front wheel sensor
45 LH rear wheel sensor
46 RH front wheel sensor
47 RH rear wheel sensor

Diagram 4

H33550

Engine cooling fan - 300TDi models

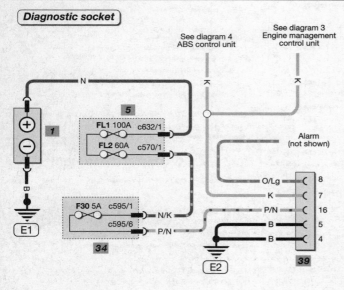

Diagnostic socket

Anti-lock braking system

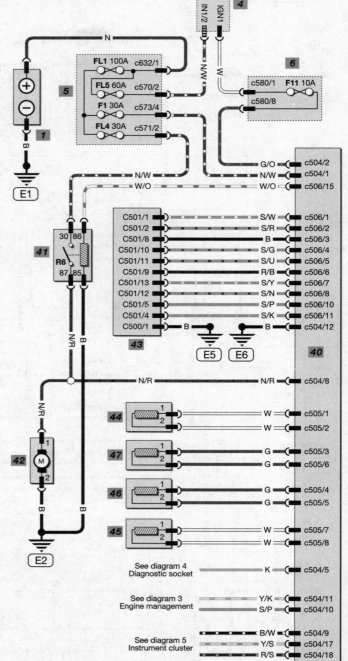

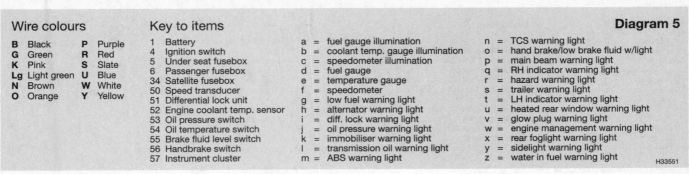

Wire colours

B	Black	P	Purple
G	Green	R	Red
K	Pink	S	Slate
Lg	Light green	U	Blue
N	Brown	W	White
O	Orange	Y	Yellow

Key to items

1 Battery
4 Ignition switch
5 Under seat fusebox
6 Passenger fusebox
34 Satellite fusebox
50 Speed transducer
51 Differential lock unit
52 Engine coolant temp. sensor
53 Oil pressure switch
54 Oil temperature switch
55 Brake fluid level switch
56 Handbrake switch
57 Instrument cluster

a = fuel gauge illumination
b = coolant temp. gauge illumination
c = speedometer illumination
d = fuel gauge
e = temperature gauge
f = speedometer
g = low fuel warning light
h = alternator warning light
i = diff. lock warning light
j = oil pressure warning light
k = immobiliser warning light
l = transmission oil warning light
m = ABS warning light

n = TCS warning light
o = hand brake/low brake fluid w/light
p = main beam warning light
q = RH indicator warning light
r = hazard warning light
s = trailer warning light
t = LH indicator warning light
u = heated rear window warning light
v = glow plug warning light
w = engine management warning light
x = rear foglight warning light
y = sidelight warning light
z = water in fuel warning light

Diagram 5

H33551

Instrument cluster

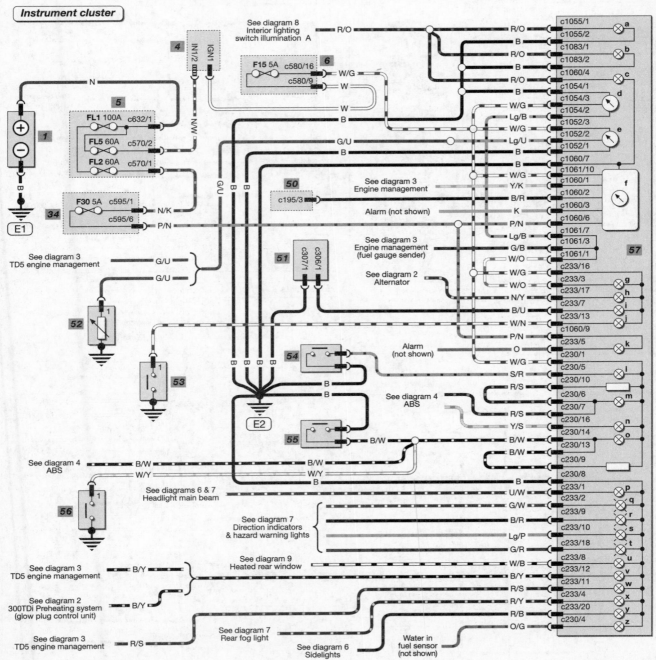

Wire colours

B	Black	P	Purple
G	Green	R	Red
K	Pink	S	Slate
Lg	Light green	U	Blue
N	Brown	W	White
O	Orange	Y	Yellow

Key to items

1 Battery
4 Ignition switch
5 Under seat fusebox
6 Passenger fusebox
12 Column switch
  b = headlight flasher
  c = dip/main switch
60 Stop light switch
61 Reversing light switch
62 High level stop light
63 Reversing light

64 Accessory socket
65 LH rear light unit
  a = stop light
  b = tail light
66 LH rear light unit
  a = stop light
  b = tail light
67 LH front side light
68 RH front side light
69 Number plate light
70 Light switch

71 Trailer socket
72 Diode
73 LH headlights
  a = main beam
  b = dipped beam
74 RH headlight
  a = main beam
  b = dipped beam
75 Headlight relay

Diagram 6

H33552

Stop & reversing lights

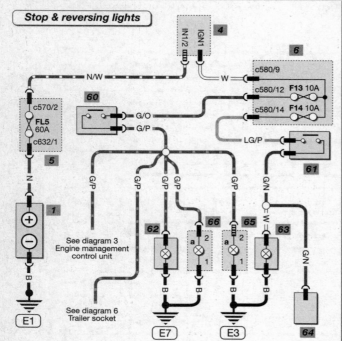

Trailer socket

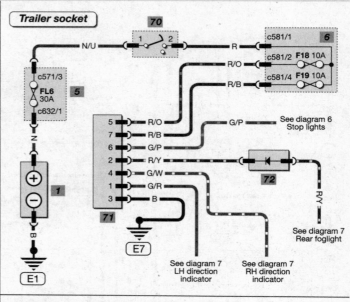

Side, tail & number plate lights

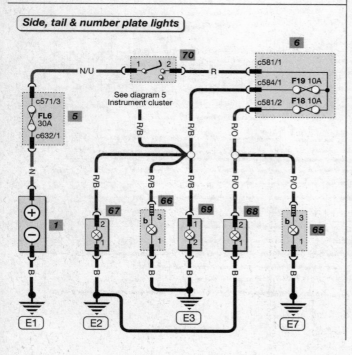

Headlights - without dim/dip

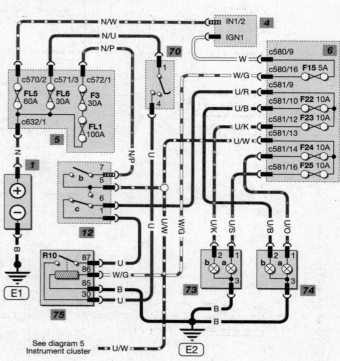

Wire colours

B	Black	P	Purple
G	Green	R	Red
K	Pink	S	Slate
Lg	Light green	U	Blue
N	Brown	W	White
O	Orange	Y	Yellow

Key to items

1 Battery
4 Ignition switch
5 Under seat fusebox
6 Passenger fusebox
12 Column switch
  b = headlight flasher
  c = dip/main
  d = direction indicator

34 Satellite fusebox
70 Light switch
73 LH headlights
  a = main beam
  b = dipped beam
74 RH headlight
  a = main beam
  b = dipped beam

75 Headlight relay
78 Dim/dip relay
79 Dim/dip resistor
80 Rear foglight switch
81 Rear foglight control unit
82 LH rear foglight
83 RH rear foglight
84 Hazard warning relay

85 Hazard warning switch
86 LH front direction indicator
87 LH indicator side repeater
88 LH rear direction indicator
89 RH front direction indicator
90 RH indicator side repeater
91 RH rear direction indicator

Diagram 7

H33553

Headlights - with dim/dip

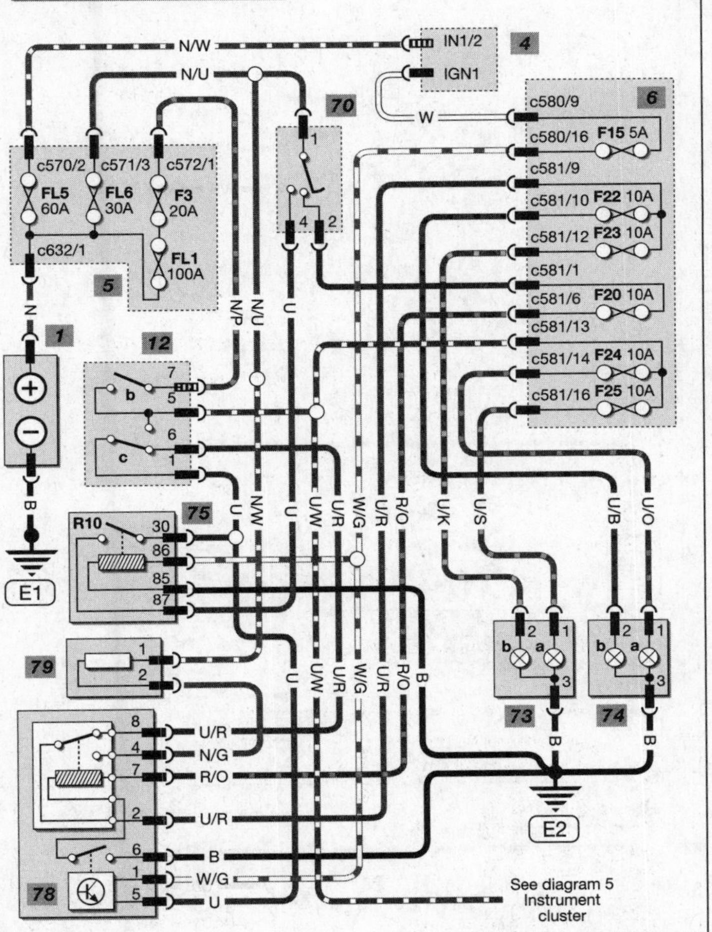

Direction indicators & hazard warning lights

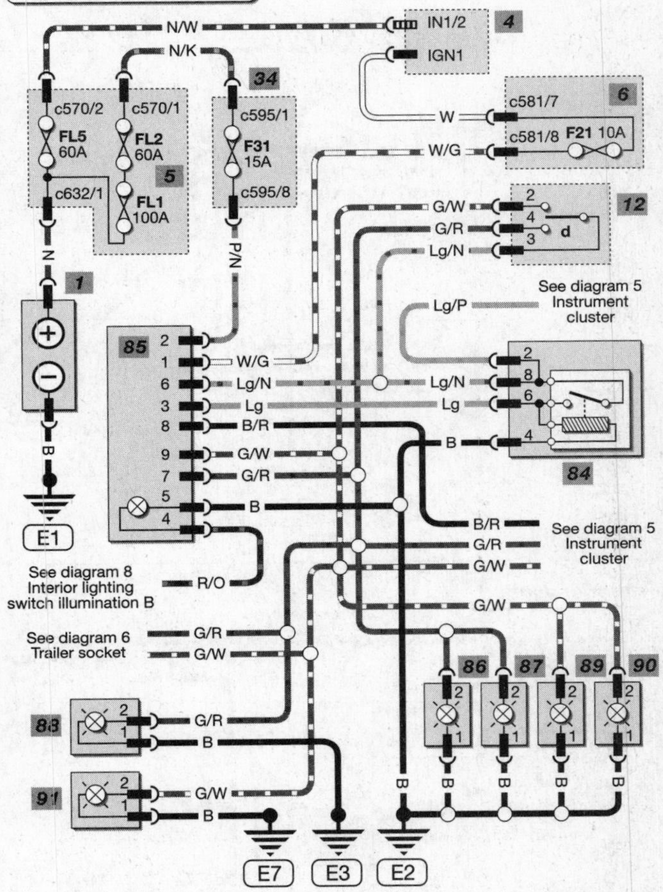

Rear foglights

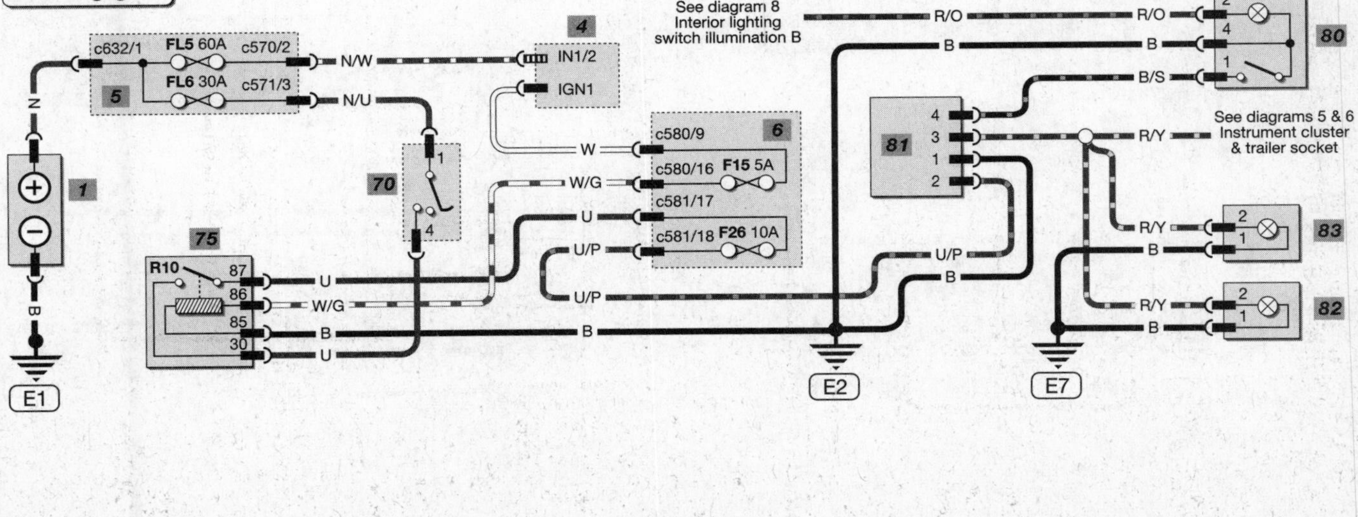

Wire colours

B	Black	**P**	Purple
G	Green	**R**	Red
K	Pink	**S**	Slate
Lg	Light green	**U**	Blue
N	Brown	**W**	White
O	Orange	**Y**	Yellow

Key to items

1 Battery
4 Ignition switch
5 Under seat fusebox
6 Passenger fusebox
34 Satellite fusebox
70 Light switch
93 Headlight levelling switch
94 LH headlight levelling motor
95 RH headlight levelling motor

96 Alarm control unit
97 LH front door switch
98 RH front door switch
99 LH rear door switch
100 RH rear door switch
101 Tailgate/boot switch
102 Interior light
103 Clock
104 Accessory socket

105 Heater blower motor
106 Heater blower switch
107 Seat heater/electric window relay
108 LH heated seat switch
109 RH heated seat switch
110 LH heated seat
111 RH heated seat

Diagram 8

H33554

Headlight levelling

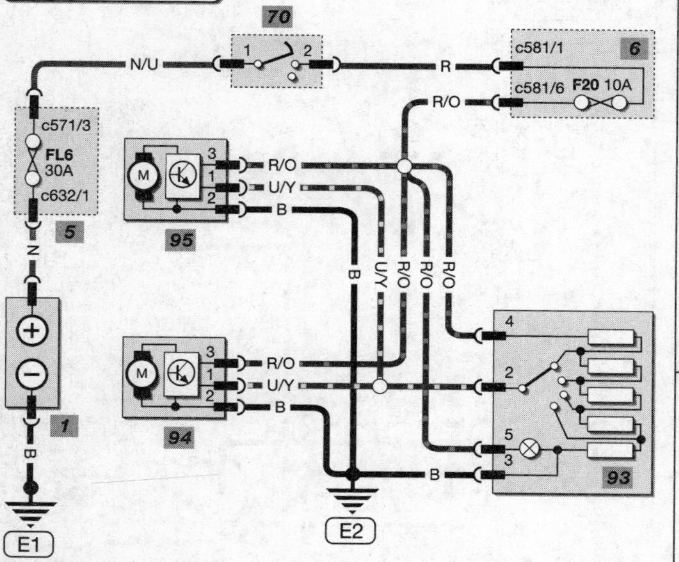

Interior lighting

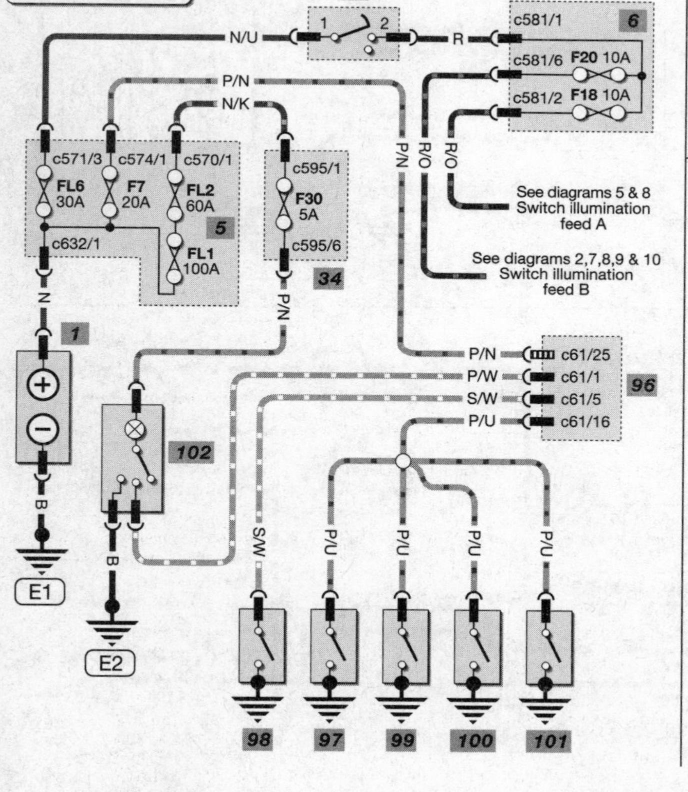

Clock & accessory socket

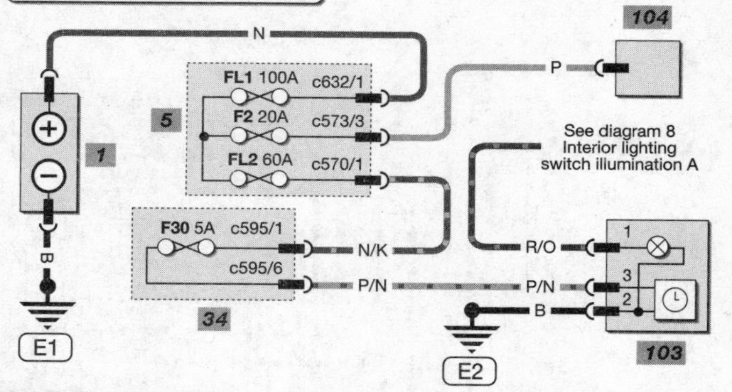

Heater blower

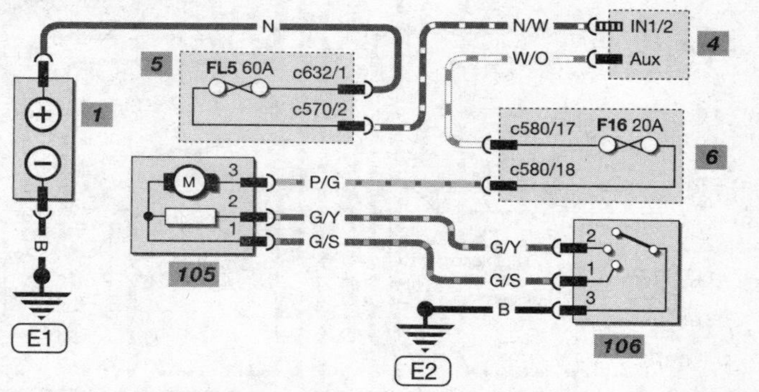

Heated seats

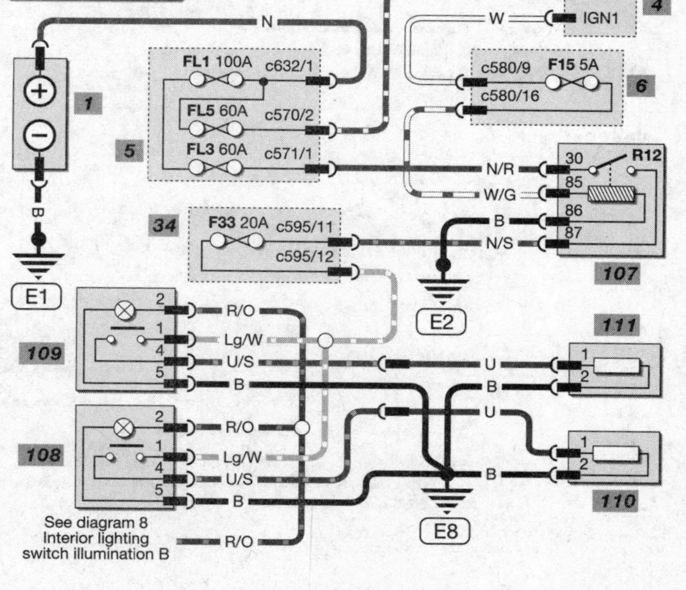

Wire colours

B	Black	**P**	Purple
G	Green	**R**	Red
K	Pink	**S**	Slate
Lg	Light green	**U**	Blue
N	Brown	**W**	White
O	Orange	**Y**	Yellow

Key to items

1	Battery	119	Heated rear window relay
4	Ignition switch	120	Heated rear window switch
5	Under seat fusebox	121	Heated rear window
6	Passenger fusebox	122	Front wiper relay
34	Satellite fusebox	123	Front wash/wipe switch
115	Heated front screen relay		a = wiper
116	Heated front screen timer relay		b = flick
117	Heated front screen switch		c = washer
118	Heated front screen	124	Front washer pump

125	Front wiper motor
126	Rear wiper motor
127	Rear wiper relay
128	Rear wiper switch
129	Rear washer switch
130	Rear washer pump

Diagram 9

H33555

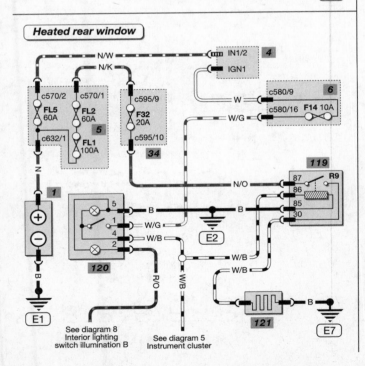

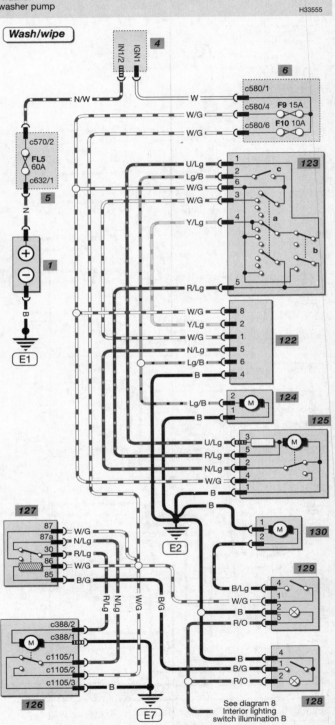

Wire colours

B	Black	P	Purple
G	Green	R	Red
K	Pink	S	Slate
Lg	Light green	U	Blue
N	Brown	W	White
O	Orange	Y	Yellow

Key to items

1 Battery
4 Ignition switch
5 Under seat fusebox
6 Passenger fusebox
34 Satellite fusebox
96 Alarm control unit
97 LH front door switch
98 RH front door switch
99 LH rear door switch
100 RH rear door switch
101 Tailgate/boot switch
107 Seat heater/electric window relay
135 Radio/cassette player
136 CD player
137 LH front speaker
138 RH front speaker
139 LH front window switch
140 RH front window switch
141 LH front window motor
142 RH front window motor
143 Antenna
144 LH front door lock motor
145 RH front door lock motor
146 Tailgate lock motor
147 LH rear door lock motor
148 RH rear door lock motor

Diagram 10

H33556

Audio system

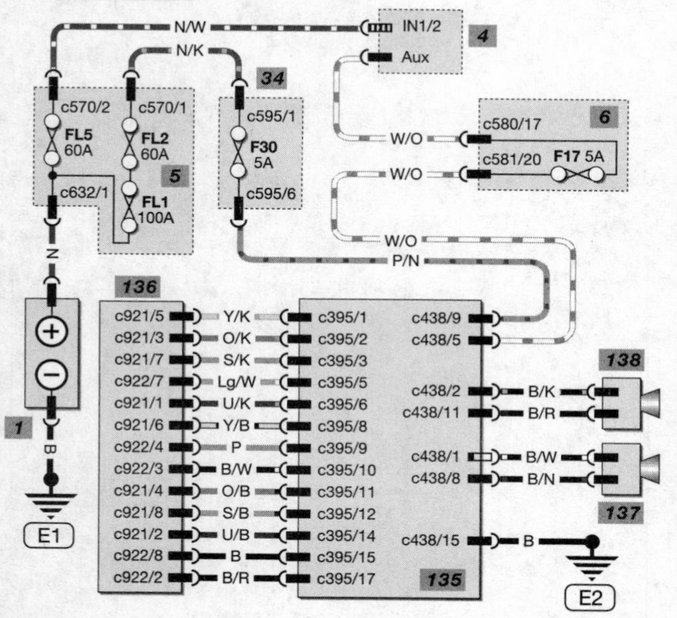

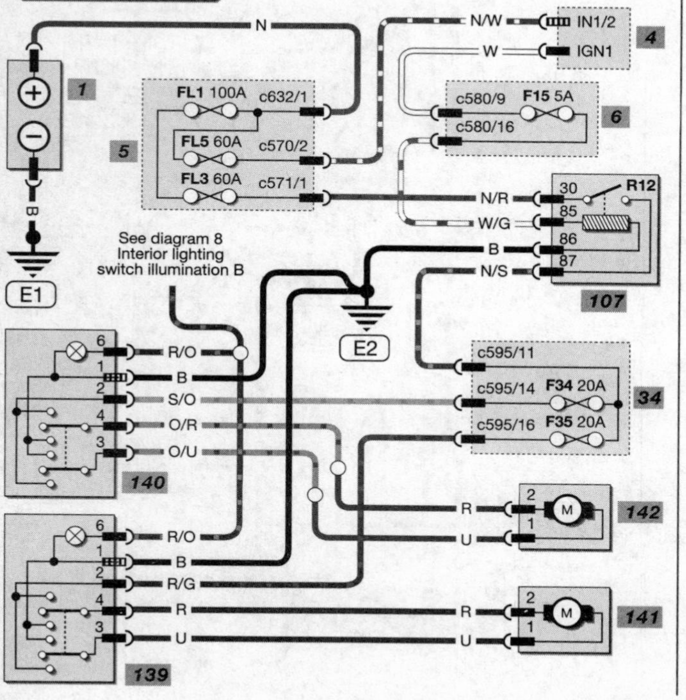

Central locking

Electric windows

See diagram 8
Interior lighting
switch illumination B

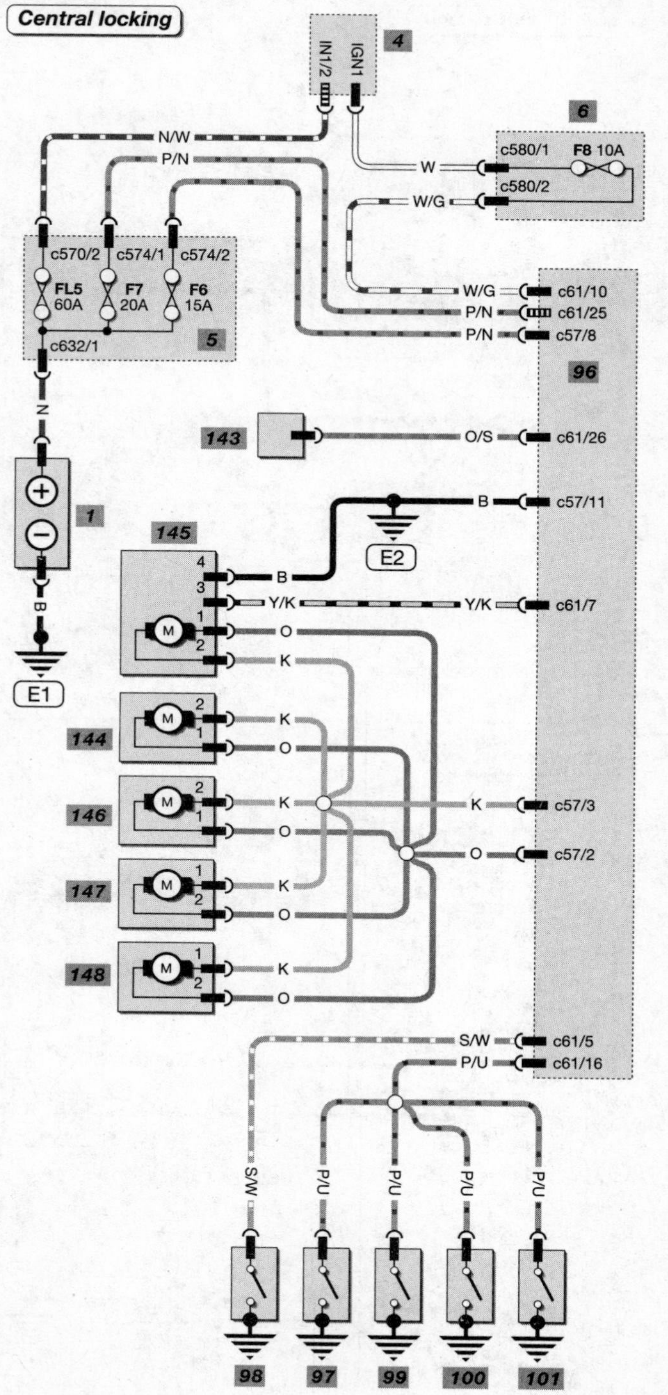

General dimensions and weights . . . . **REF•1**
Conversion factors . . . . **REF•2**
General repair procedures . . . . **REF•3**
Buying spare parts . . . . **REF•4**
Vehicle identification . . . . **REF•4**
Jacking and vehicle support . . . . **REF•6**

Radio/cassette unit anti-theft system –
  precautions . . . . **REF•6**
Tools and working facilities . . . . **REF•7**
MOT test checks . . . . **REF•9**
Fault finding . . . . **REF•13**
Glossary of technical terms . . . . **REF•22**
Index . . . . **REF•27**

General dimensions & weights

Note: *All figures are approximate, and may vary according to model. Refer to manufacturer's data for exact figures.*

Dimensions

Overall length:
  90 models:
    Soft-Top and Pick-Up models . . . . .3722 mm
    Hard-Top and Station Wagon models . . . . .3883 mm
  110 models:
    Soft-Top and Pick-Up models . . . . .4438 mm
    Hard-Top and Station Wagon models . . . . .4599 mm
    High Capacity Pick-Up models . . . . .4631 mm
  130 models . . . . .5132 mm
Overall width (all models) . . . . .1790 mm

Overall height*:
  90 models . . . . 1965 to 2000 mm
  110 models . . . . 2035 to 2079 mm
  130 models . . . . .2035 mm
Wheelbase:
  90 models . . . . .2360 mm
  110 models . . . . .2794 mm
  130 models . . . . .3226 mm
Front and rear track . . . . .1486 mm
* Overall height depends on suspension specification and load.

Weights

Kerb weight (approximate weights without options):
  90 models:
    Soft-Top . . . . .1643 kg
    Pick-Up . . . . .1661 kg
    Hard-Top . . . . .1685 kg
    Station Wagon . . . . .1727 kg
  110 models:
    Soft-Top . . . . .1742 kg
    Pick-Up . . . . .1743 kg
    Hard-Top . . . . .1796 kg
    Station Wagon . . . . .1906 kg
    High Capacity Pick-Up . . . . .1859 kg
  130 models:
    High capacity Pick-up . . . . .2120 kg
Maximum axle weights:
  Front axle:
    90 and 110 models . . . . .1200 kg
    130 models . . . . .1580 kg
  Rear axle:
    90 models:
      Standard suspension . . . . .1380 kg
      High-load suspension . . . . .1500 kg
    110 models:
      Standard suspension . . . . .1750 kg
      High-load suspension . . . . .1850 kg
    130 models . . . . .2200 kg

Maximum gross vehicle weight:
  90 models:
    Standard suspension . . . . .2400 kg
    High-load suspension . . . . .2550 kg
  110 models:
    Standard suspension . . . . .2950 kg
    High-load suspension . . . . .3050 kg
  130 models . . . . .3500 kg
Maximum roof load (including roof rack) . . . . .75 kg
Maximum towing weight:
  On-road:
    Unbraked trailer . . . . .750 kg
    Trailer with overrun brakes . . . . .3500 kg
    Fully-braked trailer*:
      Non-turbo models . . . . .3500 kg
      Turbo models . . . . .4000 kg
  Off-road:
    Unbraked trailer . . . . .500 kg
    Trailer with overrun brakes . . . . .1000 kg
    Fully-braked trailer . . . . .1000 kg

* Only applies to vehicles modified to accept coupled brakes.

Conversion factors

Length (distance)

Inches (in)	x 25.4	= Millimetres (mm)	x 0.0394	= Inches (in)
Feet (ft)	x 0.305	= Metres (m)	x 3.281	= Feet (ft)
Miles	x 1.609	= Kilometres (km)	x 0.621	= Miles

Volume (capacity)

Cubic inches (cu in; in^3)	x 16.387	= Cubic centimetres (cc; cm^3)	x 0.061	= Cubic inches (cu in; in^3)
Imperial pints (Imp pt)	x 0.568	= Litres (l)	x 1.76	= Imperial pints (Imp pt)
Imperial quarts (Imp qt)	x 1.137	= Litres (l)	x 0.88	= Imperial quarts (Imp qt)
Imperial quarts (Imp qt)	x 1.201	= US quarts (US qt)	x 0.833	= Imperial quarts (Imp qt)
US quarts (US qt)	x 0.946	= Litres (l)	x 1.057	= US quarts (US qt)
Imperial gallons (Imp gal)	x 4.546	= Litres (l)	x 0.22	= Imperial gallons (Imp gal)
Imperial gallons (Imp gal)	x 1.201	= US gallons (US gal)	x 0.833	= Imperial gallons (Imp gal)
US gallons (US gal)	x 3.785	= Litres (l)	x 0.264	= US gallons (US gal)

Mass (weight)

Ounces (oz)	x 28.35	= Grams (g)	x 0.035	= Ounces (oz)
Pounds (lb)	x 0.454	= Kilograms (kg)	x 2.205	= Pounds (lb)

Force

Ounces-force (ozf; oz)	x 0.278	= Newtons (N)	x 3.6	= Ounces-force (ozf; oz)
Pounds-force (lbf; lb)	x 4.448	= Newtons (N)	x 0.225	= Pounds-force (lbf; lb)
Newtons (N)	x 0.1	= Kilograms-force (kgf; kg)	x 9.81	= Newtons (N)

Pressure

Pounds-force per square inch (psi; lbf/in^2; lb/in^2)	x 0.070	= Kilograms-force per square centimetre (kgf/cm^2; kg/cm^2)	x 14.223	= Pounds-force per square inch (psi; lbf/in^2; lb/in^2)
Pounds-force per square inch (psi; lbf/in^2; lb/in^2)	x 0.068	= Atmospheres (atm)	x 14.696	= Pounds-force per square inch (psi; lbf/in^2; lb/in^2)
Pounds-force per square inch (psi; lbf/in^2; lb/in^2)	x 0.069	= Bars	x 14.5	= Pounds-force per square inch (psi; lbf/in^2; lb/in^2)
Pounds-force per square inch (psi; lbf/in^2; lb/in^2)	x 6.895	= Kilopascals (kPa)	x 0.145	= Pounds-force per square inch (psi; lbf/in^2; lb/in^2)
Kilopascals (kPa)	x 0.01	= Kilograms-force per square centimetre (kgf/cm^2; kg/cm^2)	x 98.1	= Kilopascals (kPa)
Millibar (mbar)	x 100	= Pascals (Pa)	x 0.01	= Millibar (mbar)
Millibar (mbar)	x 0.0145	= Pounds-force per square inch (psi; lbf/in^2; lb/in^2)	x 68.947	= Millibar (mbar)
Millibar (mbar)	x 0.75	= Millimetres of mercury (mmHg)	x 1.333	= Millibar (mbar)
Millibar (mbar)	x 0.401	= Inches of water (inH$_2$O)	x 2.491	= Millibar (mbar)
Millimetres of mercury (mmHg)	x 0.535	= Inches of water (inH$_2$O)	x 1.868	= Millimetres of mercury (mmHg)
Inches of water (inH$_2$O)	x 0.036	= Pounds-force per square inch (psi; lbf/in^2; lb/in^2)	x 27.68	= Inches of water (inH$_2$O)

Torque (moment of force)

Pounds-force inches (lbf in; lb in)	x 1.152	= Kilograms-force centimetre (kgf cm; kg cm)	x 0.868	= Pounds-force inches (lbf in; lb in)
Pounds-force inches (lbf in; lb in)	x 0.113	= Newton metres (Nm)	x 8.85	= Pounds-force inches (lbf in; lb in)
Pounds-force inches (lbf in; lb in)	x 0.083	= Pounds-force feet (lbf ft; lb ft)	x 12	= Pounds-force inches (lbf in; lb in)
Pounds-force feet (lbf ft; lb ft)	x 0.138	= Kilograms-force metres (kgf m; kg m)	x 7.233	= Pounds-force feet (lbf ft; lb ft)
Pounds-force feet (lbf ft; lb ft)	x 1.356	= Newton metres (Nm)	x 0.738	= Pounds-force feet (lbf ft; lb ft)
Newton metres (Nm)	x 0.102	= Kilograms-force metres (kgf m; kg m)	x 9.804	= Newton metres (Nm)

Power

Horsepower (hp)	x 745.7	= Watts (W)	x 0.0013	= Horsepower (hp)

Velocity (speed)

Miles per hour (miles/hr; mph)	x 1.609	= Kilometres per hour (km/hr; kph)	x 0.621	= Miles per hour (miles/hr; mph)

Fuel consumption*

Miles per gallon, Imperial (mpg)	x 0.354	= Kilometres per litre (km/l)	x 2.825	= Miles per gallon, Imperial (mpg)
Miles per gallon, US (mpg)	x 0.425	= Kilometres per litre (km/l)	x 2.352	= Miles per gallon, US (mpg)

Temperature

Degrees Fahrenheit = (°C x 1.8) + 32   Degrees Celsius (Degrees Centigrade; °C) = (°F - 32) x 0.56

It is common practice to convert from miles per gallon (mpg) to litres/100 kilometres (l/100km), where mpg x l/100 km = 282

Whenever servicing, repair or overhaul work is carried out on the car or its components, observe the following procedures and instructions. This will assist in carrying out the operation efficiently and to a professional standard of workmanship.

Joint mating faces and gaskets

When separating components at their mating faces, never insert screwdrivers or similar implements into the joint between the faces in order to prise them apart. This can cause severe damage which results in oil leaks, coolant leaks, etc upon reassembly. Separation is usually achieved by tapping along the joint with a soft-faced hammer in order to break the seal. However, note that this method may not be suitable where dowels are used for component location.

Where a gasket is used between the mating faces of two components, a new one must be fitted on reassembly; fit it dry unless otherwise stated in the repair procedure. Make sure that the mating faces are clean and dry, with all traces of old gasket removed. When cleaning a joint face, use a tool which is unlikely to score or damage the face, and remove any burrs or nicks with an oilstone or fine file.

Make sure that tapped holes are cleaned with a pipe cleaner, and keep them free of jointing compound, if this is being used, unless specifically instructed otherwise.

Ensure that all orifices, channels or pipes are clear, and blow through them, preferably using compressed air.

Oil seals

Oil seals can be removed by levering them out with a wide flat-bladed screwdriver or similar implement. Alternatively, a number of self-tapping screws may be screwed into the seal, and these used as a purchase for pliers or some similar device in order to pull the seal free.

Whenever an oil seal is removed from its working location, either individually or as part of an assembly, it should be renewed.

The very fine sealing lip of the seal is easily damaged, and will not seal if the surface it contacts is not completely clean and free from scratches, nicks or grooves. If the original sealing surface of the component cannot be restored, and the manufacturer has not made provision for slight relocation of the seal relative to the sealing surface, the component should be renewed.

Protect the lips of the seal from any surface which may damage them in the course of fitting. Use tape or a conical sleeve where possible. Lubricate the seal lips with oil before fitting and, on dual-lipped seals, fill the space between the lips with grease.

Unless otherwise stated, oil seals must be fitted with their sealing lips toward the lubricant to be sealed.

Use a tubular drift or block of wood of the appropriate size to install the seal and, if the seal housing is shouldered, drive the seal down to the shoulder. If the seal housing is unshouldered, the seal should be fitted with its face flush with the housing top face (unless otherwise instructed).

Screw threads and fastenings

Seized nuts, bolts and screws are quite a common occurrence where corrosion has set in, and the use of penetrating oil or releasing fluid will often overcome this problem if the offending item is soaked for a while before attempting to release it. The use of an impact driver may also provide a means of releasing such stubborn fastening devices, when used in conjunction with the appropriate screwdriver bit or socket. If none of these methods works, it may be necessary to resort to the careful application of heat, or the use of a hacksaw or nut splitter device.

Studs are usually removed by locking two nuts together on the threaded part, and then using a spanner on the lower nut to unscrew the stud. Studs or bolts which have broken off below the surface of the component in which they are mounted can sometimes be removed using a stud extractor. Always ensure that a blind tapped hole is completely free from oil, grease, water or other fluid before installing the bolt or stud. Failure to do this could cause the housing to crack due to the hydraulic action of the bolt or stud as it is screwed in.

When tightening a castellated nut to accept a split pin, tighten the nut to the specified torque, where applicable, and then tighten further to the next split pin hole. Never slacken the nut to align the split pin hole, unless stated in the repair procedure.

When checking or retightening a nut or bolt to a specified torque setting, slacken the nut or bolt by a quarter of a turn, and then retighten to the specified setting. However, this should not be attempted where angular tightening has been used.

For some screw fastenings, notably cylinder head bolts or nuts, torque wrench settings are no longer specified for the latter stages of tightening, "angle-tightening" being called up instead. Typically, a fairly low torque wrench setting will be applied to the bolts/nuts in the correct sequence, followed by one or more stages of tightening through specified angles.

Locknuts, locktabs and washers

Any fastening which will rotate against a component or housing during tightening should always have a washer between it and the relevant component or housing.

Spring or split washers should always be renewed when they are used to lock a critical component such as a big-end bearing retaining bolt or nut. Locktabs which are folded over to retain a nut or bolt should always be renewed.

Self-locking nuts can be re-used in non-critical areas, providing resistance can be felt when the locking portion passes over the bolt or stud thread. However, it should be noted that self-locking stiffnuts tend to lose their effectiveness after long periods of use, and should then be renewed as a matter of course.

Split pins must always be replaced with new ones of the correct size for the hole.

When thread-locking compound is found on the threads of a fastener which is to be re-used, it should be cleaned off with a wire brush and solvent, and fresh compound applied on reassembly.

Special tools

Some repair procedures in this manual entail the use of special tools such as a press, two or three-legged pullers, spring compressors, etc. Wherever possible, suitable readily-available alternatives to the manufacturer's special tools are described, and are shown in use. In some instances, where no alternative is possible, it has been necessary to resort to the use of a manufacturer's tool, and this has been done for reasons of safety as well as the efficient completion of the repair operation. Unless you are highly-skilled and have a thorough understanding of the procedures described, never attempt to bypass the use of any special tool when the procedure described specifies its use. Not only is there a very great risk of personal injury, but expensive damage could be caused to the components involved.

Environmental considerations

When disposing of used engine oil, brake fluid, antifreeze, etc, give due consideration to any detrimental environmental effects. Do not, for instance, pour any of the above liquids down drains into the general sewage system, or onto the ground to soak away. Many local council refuse tips provide a facility for waste oil disposal, as do some garages. If none of these facilities are available, consult your local Environmental Health Department, or the National Rivers Authority, for further advice.

With the universal tightening-up of legislation regarding the emission of environmentally-harmful substances from motor vehicles, most vehicles have tamperproof devices fitted to the main adjustment points of the fuel system. These devices are primarily designed to prevent unqualified persons from adjusting the fuel/air mixture, with the chance of a consequent increase in toxic emissions. If such devices are found during servicing or overhaul, they should, wherever possible, be renewed or refitted in accordance with the manufacturer's requirements or current legislation.

OIL CARE
FOLLOW THE CODE
OIL BANK LINE
0800 66 33 66
www.oilbankline.org.uk

Note: It is antisocial and illegal to dump oil down the drain. To find the location of your local oil recycling bank, call this number free.

Spare parts are available from many sources, including maker's appointed garages, accessory shops, and motor factors. To be sure of obtaining the correct parts, it will sometimes be necessary to quote the vehicle identification number. If possible, it can also be useful to take the old parts along for positive identification. Items such as starter motors and alternators may be available under a service exchange scheme – any parts returned should always be clean.

Our advice regarding spare part sources is as follows.

Officially-appointed garages

This is the best source of parts which are peculiar to your vehicle, and are not otherwise generally available (eg badges, interior trim, certain body panels, etc). It is also the only place at which you should buy parts if the vehicle is still under warranty.

Accessory shops

These are very good places to buy materials and components needed for the maintenance of your vehicle (oil, air and fuel filters, light bulbs, drivebelts, oils and greases, brake pads, touch-up paint, etc). Components of this nature sold by a reputable shop are of the same standard as those used by the car manufacturer.

Besides components, these shops also sell tools and general accessories, usually have convenient opening hours, charge lower prices, and can often be found not far from home. Some accessory shops have parts counters where the components needed for almost any repair job can be purchased or ordered.

Motor factors

Good factors will stock all the more important components which wear out comparatively quickly, and can sometimes supply individual components needed for the overhaul of a larger assembly (eg brake seals and hydraulic parts, bearing shells, pistons, valves, alternator brushes). They may also handle work such as cylinder block reboring, crankshaft regrinding and balancing, etc.

Tyre and exhaust specialists

These outlets may be independent or members of a local or national chain. They frequently offer competitive prices when compared with a main dealer or local garage, but it will pay to obtain several quotes before making a decision. When researching prices, also ask what 'extras' may be added – for instance, fitting a new valve and balancing the wheel are both commonly charged on top of the price of a new tyre.

Other sources

Beware of parts or materials obtained from market stalls, car boot sales or similar outlets. Such items are not invariably sub-standard, but there is little chance of compensation if they do prove unsatisfactory. In the case of safety-critical components such as brake pads, there is the risk not only of financial loss, but also of an accident causing injury or death.

Second-hand components or assemblies obtained from a car breaker can be a good buy in some circumstances, but this sort of purchase is best made by the experienced DIY mechanic.

Vehicle identification

Modifications are a continuing and unpublicised process in vehicle manufacture, quite apart from major model changes. Spare parts manuals and lists are compiled upon a numerical basis, the vehicle identification numbers being essential to correct identification of the component concerned.

When ordering spare parts, always give as much information as possible. Quote the vehicle model, year of manufacture, body and engine numbers as appropriate.

The *Vehicle Identification Number (VIN) plate* is riveted to the top of the brake pedal box in the engine compartment, and can be viewed once the bonnet is open **(see illustrations)**. The plate carries the VIN number, vehicle weight information, and paint and trim colour codes.

The *Vehicle Identification Number (VIN)* is given on the VIN plate, and is also stamped into front right-hand side of the chassis, forward of the coil spring mounting **(see illustration)**.

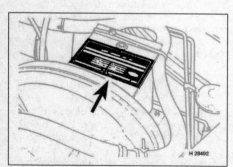

VIN plate location (arrowed)

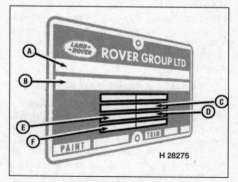

VIN plate information

A *Type approval number*
B *VIN (minimum 17 digits)*
C *Maximum permitted laden weight for vehicle*
D *Maximum vehicle and trailer weight*
E *Maximum road weight – front axle*
F *Maximum road weight – rear axle*

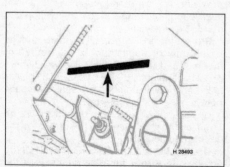

VIN stamped on right-hand side of chassis

The *engine number* is stamped into the cylinder block, and is located as follows, according to engine type:

a) Early 10J, 12J and 19J engines – the number is located on a machined surface on the left-hand side of the engine, adjacent to the exhaust manifold front flange *(see illustration)*.

b) Later 10J, 12J and 19J engines – the number is located on the right-hand side of the engine, above the fuel lift pump mounting plate *(see illustration)*.

c) 200 TDi and 300 TDi engines – the number is located on the right-hand side of the engine, above the engine breather cover plate *(see illustration)*.

d) TD5 engines – then number is located on the left-hand side of the engine block, just below the joint with the cylinder head *(see illustration)*.

The *main gearbox identification number* is stamped into a flat on the bottom right-hand side of the gearbox casing *(see illustration)*.

The *transfer gearbox identification number* is stamped into the lower left-hand side or lower right-hand side of the gearbox casing, or on the rear of the gearbox casing below the power take-off cover, depending on model *(see illustrations)*.

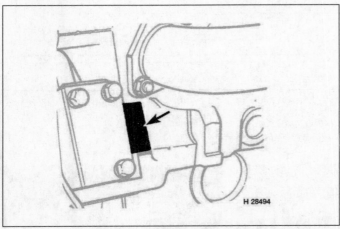

Engine identification number location (arrowed) – early 10J, 12J and 19J engines

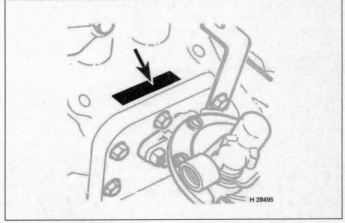

Engine identification number location (arrowed) – later 10J, 12J and 19J engines

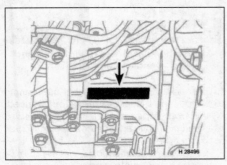

Engine identification number location (arrowed) – 200 TDi and 300 TDi engines

Engine identification number location (arrowed) – TD5 engines

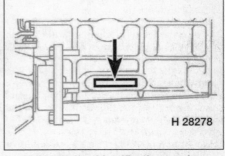

Main gearbox identification number location (arrowed)

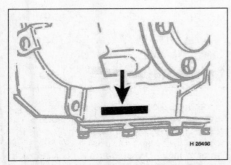

Transfer gearbox identification number location (arrowed) – LT230R-type transfer gearbox

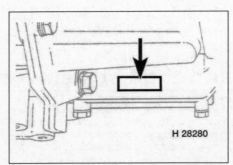

Transfer gearbox identification number location (arrowed) – early LT230T-type transfer gearbox

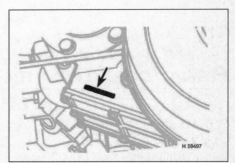

Transfer gearbox identification number location (arrowed) – later LT230TE-type transfer gearbox

⚠ *Warning: The handbrake acts on the transmission, not the rear wheels, and may not hold the vehicle stationary when jacking, unless the following procedure is followed precisely. If one front wheel and one rear wheel are raised, no vehicle holding or braking effect is possible using the handbrake, therefore the wheels must always be chocked (using the chock supplied in the tool kit). If the vehicle is coupled to a trailer, disconnect the trailer from the vehicle before commencing jacking. This is to prevent the trailer pulling the vehicle off the jack and causing personal injury.*

Note: *To raise the vehicle, a hydraulic jack with a minimum load capacity of 1500 kg must be used.* **Never** *work under a vehicle supported solely by a hydraulic jack – always supplement the jack with axle stands.*

1 The jack supplied with the vehicle tool kit should only be used for changing the roadwheels – see *Wheel changing* later in this Section. When carrying out any other kind of work, raise the vehicle using a hydraulic jack, and always supplement the jack with axle stands positioned under the axles or the chassis sidemembers **(see illustration)**. **Do not** jack the vehicle, or position axle stands under any of the following components:

a) *Body structure.*
b) *Bumpers.*
c) *Underbody pipes and hoses.*
d) *Suspension components.*
e) *Gearbox/transfer gearbox housings.*
f) *Engine sump.*
g) *Fuel tank.*

2 To raise the front or the rear of the vehicle, chock the appropriate roadwheels, then position the jack head under the front or rear differential casing, as appropriate **(see illustration)**. **Note:** *The differential casing is not in the centre of the axle, and the vehicle will tilt when jacked under the differential casing. This is particularly noticeable when jacking up the front of the vehicle.*

3 Operate the jack to raise the vehicle, then

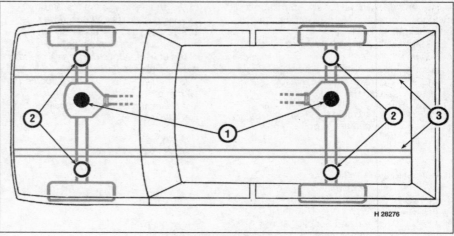

Vehicle jacking points

1 *Jacking points for use with hydraulic jack (under differential housing)*
2 *Support points for use with axle stands (under axle tubes)*
3 *Chassis side members*

Jack positioned under front differential casing

position an axle stand under the right-hand end of the axle **(see illustration)**.

4 Position an axle stand under the left-hand end of the axle, then carefully lower the jack until the axle is supported by both axle stands.

Axle stand positioned under right-hand end of front axle

5 Position axle stands under the appropriate axle tubes, or under the chassis, as required. **Never** *work under, around, or near a raised vehicle, unless it is adequately supported in at least two places.*

Radio/cassette unit anti-theft system – precautions

The radio/cassette unit fitted as standard equipment by Land Rover may be equipped with a built-in security code, to deter thieves. If the power source to the unit is cut, the anti-theft system will activate. Even if the power source is immediately reconnected, the radio/cassette unit will not function until the correct security code has been entered. Therefore,

if you do not know the correct security code for the radio/cassette unit, **do not** disconnect the battery negative terminal of the battery, nor remove the radio/cassette unit from the vehicle.

To enter the correct security code, follow the instructions provided with the radio/cassette player handbook.

If an incorrect code is entered, the unit will become locked, and cannot be operated.

If this happens or if the security code is lost or forgotten, seek the advice of your Land Rover dealer. On presentation of proof of ownership, a Land Rover dealer will be able to unlock the unit, and provide you with a new security code.

Introduction

A selection of good tools is a fundamental requirement for anyone contemplating the maintenance and repair of a motor vehicle. For the owner who does not possess any, their purchase will prove a considerable expense, offsetting some of the savings made by doing-it-yourself. However, provided that the tools purchased meet the relevant national safety standards and are of good quality, they will last for many years and prove an extremely worthwhile investment.

To help the average owner to decide which tools are needed to carry out the various tasks detailed in this manual, we have compiled three lists of tools under the following headings: *Maintenance and minor repair, Repair and overhaul,* and *Special*. Newcomers to practical mechanics should start off with the *Maintenance and minor repair* tool kit, and confine themselves to the simpler jobs around the vehicle. Then, as confidence and experience grow, more difficult tasks can be undertaken, with extra tools being purchased as, and when, they are needed. In this way, a *Maintenance and minor repair* tool kit can be built up into a *Repair and overhaul* tool kit over a considerable period of time, without any major cash outlays. The experienced do-it-yourselfer will have a tool kit good enough for most repair and overhaul procedures, and will add tools from the *Special* category when it is felt that the expense is justified by the amount of use to which these tools will be put.

Maintenance and minor repair tool kit

The tools given in this list should be considered as a minimum requirement if routine maintenance, servicing and minor repair operations are to be undertaken. We recommend the purchase of combination spanners (ring one end, open-ended the other); although more expensive than open-ended ones, they do give the advantages of both types of spanner.

☐ *Combination spanners:*
  Metric - 8 to 19 mm inclusive
☐ *Adjustable spanner - 35 mm jaw (approx.)*
☐ *Spark plug spanner (with rubber insert) - petrol models*
☐ *Spark plug gap adjustment tool - petrol models*
☐ *Set of feeler gauges*
☐ *Brake bleed nipple spanner*
☐ *Screwdrivers:*
  Flat blade - 100 mm long x 6 mm dia
  Cross blade - 100 mm long x 6 mm dia
  Torx - various sizes (not all vehicles)
☐ *Combination pliers*
☐ *Hacksaw (junior)*
☐ *Tyre pump*
☐ *Tyre pressure gauge*
☐ *Oil can*
☐ *Oil filter removal tool*
☐ *Fine emery cloth*
☐ *Wire brush (small)*
☐ *Funnel (medium size)*
☐ *Sump drain plug key (not all vehicles)*

Repair and overhaul tool kit

These tools are virtually essential for anyone undertaking any major repairs to a motor vehicle, and are additional to those given in the *Maintenance and minor repair* list. Included in this list is a comprehensive set of sockets. Although these are expensive, they will be found invaluable as they are so versatile - particularly if various drives are included in the set. We recommend the half-inch square-drive type, as this can be used with most proprietary torque wrenches.

The tools in this list will sometimes need to be supplemented by tools from the *Special* list:

☐ *Sockets (or box spanners) to cover range in previous list (including Torx sockets)*
☐ *Reversible ratchet drive (for use with sockets)*
☐ *Extension piece, 250 mm (for use with sockets)*
☐ *Universal joint (for use with sockets)*
☐ *Flexible handle or sliding T "breaker bar" (for use with sockets)*
☐ *Torque wrench (for use with sockets)*
☐ *Self-locking grips*
☐ *Ball pein hammer*
☐ *Soft-faced mallet (plastic or rubber)*
☐ *Screwdrivers:*
  Flat blade - long & sturdy, short (chubby), and narrow (electrician's) types
  Cross blade – long & sturdy, and short (chubby) types
☐ *Pliers:*
  Long-nosed
  Side cutters (electrician's)
  Circlip (internal and external)
☐ *Cold chisel - 25 mm*
☐ *Scriber*
☐ *Scraper*
☐ *Centre-punch*
☐ *Pin punch*
☐ *Hacksaw*
☐ *Brake hose clamp*
☐ *Brake/clutch bleeding kit*
☐ *Selection of twist drills*
☐ *Steel rule/straight-edge*
☐ *Allen keys (inc. splined/Torx type)*
☐ *Selection of files*
☐ *Wire brush*
☐ *Axle stands*
☐ *Jack (strong trolley or hydraulic type)*
☐ *Light with extension lead*
☐ *Universal electrical multi-meter*

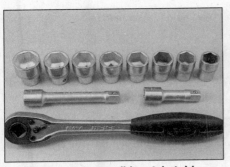

Sockets and reversible ratchet drive

Brake bleeding kit

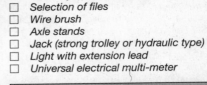

Torx key, socket and bit

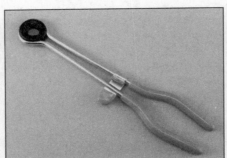

Hose clamp

Angular-tightening gauge

Special tools

The tools in this list are those which are not used regularly, are expensive to buy, or which need to be used in accordance with their manufacturers' instructions. Unless relatively difficult mechanical jobs are undertaken frequently, it will not be economic to buy many of these tools. Where this is the case, you could consider clubbing together with friends (or joining a motorists' club) to make a joint purchase, or borrowing the tools against a deposit from a local garage or tool hire specialist. It is worth noting that many of the larger DIY superstores now carry a large range of special tools for hire at modest rates.

The following list contains only those tools and instruments freely available to the public, and not those special tools produced by the vehicle manufacturer specifically for its dealer network. You will find occasional references to these manufacturers' special tools in the text of this manual. Generally, an alternative method of doing the job without the vehicle manufacturers' special tool is given. However, sometimes there is no alternative to using them. Where this is the case and the relevant tool cannot be bought or borrowed, you will have to entrust the work to a dealer.

☐ Angular-tightening gauge
☐ Valve spring compressor
☐ Valve grinding tool
☐ Piston ring compressor
☐ Piston ring removal/installation tool
☐ Cylinder bore hone
☐ Balljoint separator
☐ Coil spring compressors (where applicable)
☐ Two/three-legged hub and bearing puller
☐ Impact screwdriver
☐ Micrometer and/or vernier calipers
☐ Dial gauge
☐ Stroboscopic timing light
☐ Dwell angle meter/tachometer
☐ Fault code reader
☐ Cylinder compression gauge
☐ Hand-operated vacuum pump and gauge
☐ Clutch plate alignment set
☐ Brake shoe steady spring cup removal tool
☐ Bush and bearing removal/installation set
☐ Stud extractors
☐ Tap and die set
☐ Lifting tackle
☐ Trolley jack

Buying tools

Reputable motor accessory shops and superstores often offer excellent quality tools at discount prices, so it pays to shop around.

Remember, you don't have to buy the most expensive items on the shelf, but it is always advisable to steer clear of the very cheap tools. Beware of 'bargains' offered on market stalls or at car boot sales. There are plenty of good tools around at reasonable prices, but always aim to purchase items which meet the relevant national safety standards. If in doubt, ask the proprietor or manager of the shop for advice before making a purchase.

Care and maintenance of tools

Having purchased a reasonable tool kit, it is necessary to keep the tools in a clean and serviceable condition. After use, always wipe off any dirt, grease and metal particles using a clean, dry cloth, before putting the tools away. Never leave them lying around after they have been used. A simple tool rack on the garage or workshop wall for items such as screwdrivers and pliers is a good idea. Store all normal spanners and sockets in a metal box. Any measuring instruments, gauges, meters, etc, must be carefully stored where they cannot be damaged or become rusty.

Take a little care when tools are used. Hammer heads inevitably become marked, and screwdrivers lose the keen edge on their blades from time to time. A little timely attention with emery cloth or a file will soon restore items like this to a good finish.

Working facilities

Not to be forgotten when discussing tools is the workshop itself. If anything more than routine maintenance is to be carried out, a suitable working area becomes essential.

It is appreciated that many an owner-mechanic is forced by circumstances to remove an engine or similar item without the benefit of a garage or workshop. Having done this, any repairs should always be done under the cover of a roof.

Wherever possible, any dismantling should be done on a clean, flat workbench or table at a suitable working height.

Any workbench needs a vice; one with a jaw opening of 100 mm is suitable for most jobs. As mentioned previously, some clean dry storage space is also required for tools, as well as for any lubricants, cleaning fluids, touch-up paints etc, which become necessary.

Another item which may be required, and which has a much more general usage, is an electric drill with a chuck capacity of at least 8 mm. This, together with a good range of twist drills, is virtually essential for fitting accessories.

Last, but not least, always keep a supply of old newspapers and clean, lint-free rags available, and try to keep any working area as clean as possible.

Micrometers

Dial test indicator ("dial gauge")

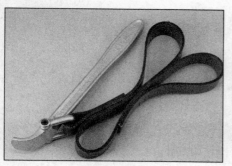
Strap wrench

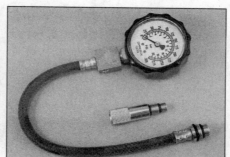
Compression tester

Fault code reader

This is a guide to getting your vehicle through the MOT test. Obviously it will not be possible to examine the vehicle to the same standard as the professional MOT tester. However, working through the following checks will enable you to identify any problem areas before submitting the vehicle for the test.

It has only been possible to summarise the test requirements here, based on the regulations in force at the time of printing. Test standards are becoming increasingly stringent, although there are some exemptions for older vehicles.

An assistant will be needed to help carry out some of these checks.

The checks have been sub-divided into four categories, as follows:

1 Checks carried out **FROM THE DRIVER'S SEAT**

2 Checks carried out **WITH THE VEHICLE ON THE GROUND**

3 Checks carried out **WITH THE VEHICLE RAISED AND THE WHEELS FREE TO TURN**

4 Checks carried out on **YOUR VEHICLE'S EXHAUST EMISSION SYSTEM**

---

1 Checks carried out **FROM THE DRIVER'S SEAT**

Handbrake

☐ Test the operation of the handbrake. Excessive travel (too many clicks) indicates incorrect brake or cable adjustment.
☐ Check that the handbrake cannot be released by tapping the lever sideways. Check the security of the lever mountings.

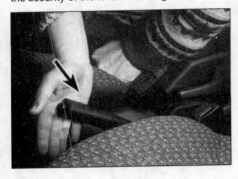

Footbrake

☐ Depress the brake pedal and check that it does not creep down to the floor, indicating a master cylinder fault. Release the pedal, wait a few seconds, then depress it again. If the pedal travels nearly to the floor before firm resistance is felt, brake adjustment or repair is necessary. If the pedal feels spongy, there is air in the hydraulic system which must be removed by bleeding.

☐ Check that the brake pedal is secure and in good condition. Check also for signs of fluid leaks on the pedal, floor or carpets, which would indicate failed seals in the brake master cylinder.
☐ Check the servo unit (when applicable) by operating the brake pedal several times, then keeping the pedal depressed and starting the engine. As the engine starts, the pedal will move down slightly. If not, the vacuum hose or the servo itself may be faulty.

Steering wheel and column

☐ Examine the steering wheel for fractures or looseness of the hub, spokes or rim.
☐ Move the steering wheel from side to side and then up and down. Check that the steering wheel is not loose on the column, indicating wear or a loose retaining nut. Continue moving the steering wheel as before, but also turn it slightly from left to right.
☐ Check that the steering wheel is not loose on the column, and that there is no abnormal

movement of the steering wheel, indicating wear in the column support bearings or couplings.

Windscreen, mirrors and sunvisor

☐ The windscreen must be free of cracks or other significant damage within the driver's field of view. (Small stone chips are acceptable.) Rear view mirrors must be secure, intact, and capable of being adjusted.

290mm

☐ The driver's sunvisor must be capable of being stored in the "up" position.

Seat belts and seats

Note: *The following checks are applicable to all seat belts, front and rear.*

☐ Examine the webbing of all the belts (including rear belts if fitted) for cuts, serious fraying or deterioration. Fasten and unfasten each belt to check the buckles. If applicable, check the retracting mechanism. Check the security of all seat belt mountings accessible from inside the vehicle.

☐ Seat belts with pre-tensioners, once activated, have a "flag" or similar showing on the seat belt stalk. This, in itself, is not a reason for test failure.

☐ The front seats themselves must be securely attached and the backrests must lock in the upright position.

Doors

☐ Both front doors must be able to be opened and closed from outside and inside, and must latch securely when closed.

2 Checks carried out WITH THE VEHICLE ON THE GROUND

Vehicle identification

☐ Number plates must be in good condition, secure and legible, with letters and numbers correctly spaced – spacing at (A) should be at least twice that at (B).

☐ The VIN plate and/or homologation plate must be legible.

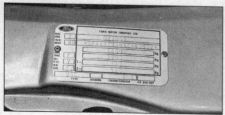

Electrical equipment

☐ Switch on the ignition and check the operation of the horn.

☐ Check the windscreen washers and wipers, examining the wiper blades; renew damaged or perished blades. Also check the operation of the stop-lights.

☐ Check the operation of the sidelights and number plate lights. The lenses and reflectors must be secure, clean and undamaged.

☐ Check the operation and alignment of the headlights. The headlight reflectors must not be tarnished and the lenses must be undamaged.

☐ Switch on the ignition and check the operation of the direction indicators (including the instrument panel tell-tale) and the hazard warning lights. Operation of the sidelights and stop-lights must not affect the indicators - if it does, the cause is usually a bad earth at the rear light cluster.

☐ Check the operation of the rear foglight(s), including the warning light on the instrument panel or in the switch.

☐ The ABS warning light must illuminate in accordance with the manufacturers' design. For most vehicles, the ABS warning light should illuminate when the ignition is switched on, and (if the system is operating properly) extinguish after a few seconds. Refer to the owner's handbook.

Footbrake

☐ Examine the master cylinder, brake pipes and servo unit for leaks, loose mountings, corrosion or other damage.

☐ The fluid reservoir must be secure and the fluid level must be between the upper (**A**) and lower (**B**) markings.

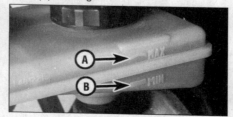

☐ Inspect both front brake flexible hoses for cracks or deterioration of the rubber. Turn the steering from lock to lock, and ensure that the hoses do not contact the wheel, tyre, or any part of the steering or suspension mechanism. With the brake pedal firmly depressed, check the hoses for bulges or leaks under pressure.

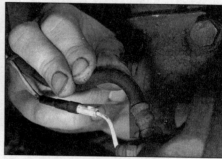

Steering and suspension

☐ Have your assistant turn the steering wheel from side to side slightly, up to the point where the steering gear just begins to transmit this movement to the roadwheels. Check for excessive free play between the steering wheel and the steering gear, indicating wear or insecurity of the steering column joints, the column-to-steering gear coupling, or the steering gear itself.

☐ Have your assistant turn the steering wheel more vigorously in each direction, so that the roadwheels just begin to turn. As this is done, examine all the steering joints, linkages, fittings and attachments. Renew any component that shows signs of wear or damage. On vehicles with power steering, check the security and condition of the steering pump, drivebelt and hoses.

☐ Check that the vehicle is standing level, and at approximately the correct ride height.

Shock absorbers

☐ Depress each corner of the vehicle in turn, then release it. The vehicle should rise and then settle in its normal position. If the vehicle continues to rise and fall, the shock absorber is defective. A shock absorber which has seized will also cause the vehicle to fail.

Exhaust system

☐ Start the engine. With your assistant holding a rag over the tailpipe, check the entire system for leaks. Repair or renew leaking sections.

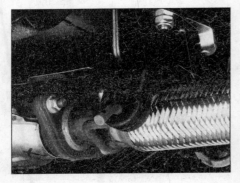

3 Checks carried out WITH THE VEHICLE RAISED AND THE WHEELS FREE TO TURN

Jack up the front and rear of the vehicle, and securely support it on axle stands. Position the stands clear of the suspension assemblies. Ensure that the wheels are clear of the ground and that the steering can be turned from lock to lock.

Steering mechanism

☐ Have your assistant turn the steering from lock to lock. Check that the steering turns smoothly, and that no part of the steering mechanism, including a wheel or tyre, fouls any brake hose or pipe or any part of the body structure.

☐ Examine the steering rack rubber gaiters for damage or insecurity of the retaining clips. If power steering is fitted, check for signs of damage or leakage of the fluid hoses, pipes or connections. Also check for excessive stiffness or binding of the steering, a missing split pin or locking device, or severe corrosion of the body structure within 30 cm of any steering component attachment point.

Front and rear suspension and wheel bearings

☐ Starting at the front right-hand side, grasp the roadwheel at the 3 o'clock and 9 o'clock positions and rock gently but firmly. Check for free play or insecurity at the wheel bearings, suspension balljoints, or suspension mountings, pivots and attachments.

☐ Now grasp the wheel at the 12 o'clock and 6 o'clock positions and repeat the previous inspection. Spin the wheel, and check for roughness or tightness of the front wheel bearing.

☐ If excess free play is suspected at a component pivot point, this can be confirmed by using a large screwdriver or similar tool and levering between the mounting and the component attachment. This will confirm whether the wear is in the pivot bush, its retaining bolt, or in the mounting itself (the bolt holes can often become elongated).

☐ Carry out all the above checks at the other front wheel, and then at both rear wheels.

Springs and shock absorbers

☐ Examine the suspension struts (when applicable) for serious fluid leakage, corrosion, or damage to the casing. Also check the security of the mounting points.

☐ If coil springs are fitted, check that the spring ends locate in their seats, and that the spring is not corroded, cracked or broken.

☐ If leaf springs are fitted, check that all leaves are intact, that the axle is securely attached to each spring, and that there is no deterioration of the spring eye mountings, bushes, and shackles.

☐ The same general checks apply to vehicles fitted with other suspension types, such as torsion bars, hydraulic displacer units, etc. Ensure that all mountings and attachments are secure, that there are no signs of excessive wear, corrosion or damage, and (on hydraulic types) that there are no fluid leaks or damaged pipes.

☐ Inspect the shock absorbers for signs of serious fluid leakage. Check for wear of the mounting bushes or attachments, or damage to the body of the unit.

Driveshafts (fwd vehicles only)

☐ Rotate each front wheel in turn and inspect the constant velocity joint gaiters for splits or damage. Also check that each driveshaft is straight and undamaged.

Braking system

☐ If possible without dismantling, check brake pad wear and disc condition. Ensure that the friction lining material has not worn excessively, (A) and that the discs are not fractured, pitted, scored or badly worn (B).

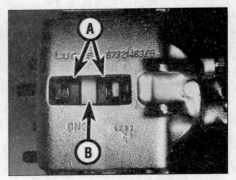

☐ Examine all the rigid brake pipes underneath the vehicle, and the flexible hose(s) at the rear. Look for corrosion, chafing or insecurity of the pipes, and for signs of bulging under pressure, chafing, splits or deterioration of the flexible hoses.

☐ Look for signs of fluid leaks at the brake calipers or on the brake backplates. Repair or renew leaking components.

☐ Slowly spin each wheel, while your assistant depresses and releases the footbrake. Ensure that each brake is operating and does not bind when the pedal is released.

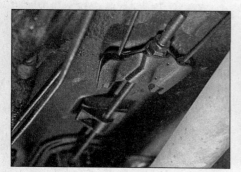

☐ Examine the handbrake mechanism, checking for frayed or broken cables, excessive corrosion, or wear or insecurity of the linkage. Check that the mechanism works on each relevant wheel, and releases fully, without binding.

☐ It is not possible to test brake efficiency without special equipment, but a road test can be carried out later to check that the vehicle pulls up in a straight line.

Fuel and exhaust systems

☐ Inspect the fuel tank (including the filler cap), fuel pipes, hoses and unions. All components must be secure and free from leaks.

☐ Examine the exhaust system over its entire length, checking for any damaged, broken or missing mountings, security of the retaining clamps and rust or corrosion.

Wheels and tyres

☐ Examine the sidewalls and tread area of each tyre in turn. Check for cuts, tears, lumps, bulges, separation of the tread, and exposure of the ply or cord due to wear or damage. Check that the tyre bead is correctly seated on the wheel rim, that the valve is sound and properly seated, and that the wheel is not distorted or damaged.

☐ Check that the tyres are of the correct size for the vehicle, that they are of the same size

and type on each axle, and that the pressures are correct.

☐ Check the tyre tread depth. The legal minimum at the time of writing is 1.6 mm over at least three-quarters of the tread width. Abnormal tread wear may indicate incorrect front wheel alignment.

Body corrosion

☐ Check the condition of the entire vehicle structure for signs of corrosion in load-bearing areas. (These include chassis box sections, side sills, cross-members, pillars, and all suspension, steering, braking system and seat belt mountings and anchorages.) Any corrosion which has seriously reduced the thickness of a load-bearing area is likely to cause the vehicle to fail. In this case professional repairs are likely to be needed.

☐ Damage or corrosion which causes sharp or otherwise dangerous edges to be exposed will also cause the vehicle to fail.

4 Checks carried out on YOUR VEHICLE'S EXHAUST EMISSION SYSTEM

Petrol models

☐ The engine should be warmed up, and running well (ignition system in good order, air filter element clean, etc).

☐ Before testing, run the engine at around 2500 rpm for 20 seconds. Let the engine drop to idle, and watch for smoke from the exhaust. If the idle speed is too high, or if dense blue or black smoke emerges for more than 5 seconds, the vehicle will fail. Typically, blue smoke signifies oil burning (engine wear); black smoke means unburnt fuel (dirty air cleaner element, or other fuel system fault).

☐ An exhaust gas analyser for measuring carbon monoxide (CO) and hydrocarbons (HC) is now needed. If one cannot be hired or borrowed, have a local garage perform the check.

CO emissions (mixture)

☐ The MOT tester has access to the CO limits for all vehicles. The CO level is measured at idle speed, and at 'fast idle' (2500 to 3000 rpm). The following limits are given as a general guide:
  At idle speed – Less than 0.5% CO
  At 'fast idle' – Less than 0.3% CO
  Lambda reading – 0.97 to 1.03

☐ If the CO level is too high, this may point to poor maintenance, a fuel injection system problem, faulty lambda (oxygen) sensor or catalytic converter. Try an injector cleaning treatment, and check the vehicle's ECU for fault codes.

HC emissions

☐ The MOT tester has access to HC limits for all vehicles. The HC level is measured at 'fast idle' (2500 to 3000 rpm). The following limits are given as a general guide:
  At 'fast idle' – Less then 200 ppm

☐ Excessive HC emissions are typically caused by oil being burnt (worn engine), or by a blocked crankcase ventilation system ('breather'). If the engine oil is old and thin, an oil change may help. If the engine is running badly, check the vehicle's ECU for fault codes.

Diesel models

☐ The only emission test for diesel engines is measuring exhaust smoke density, using a calibrated smoke meter. The test involves accelerating the engine at least 3 times to its maximum unloaded speed.

Note: *On engines with a timing belt, it is VITAL that the belt is in good condition before the test is carried out.*

☐ With the engine warmed up, it is first purged by running at around 2500 rpm for 20 seconds. A governor check is then carried out, by slowly accelerating the engine to its maximum speed. After this, the smoke meter is connected, and the engine is accelerated quickly to maximum speed three times. If the smoke density is less than the limits given below, the vehicle will pass:
  Non-turbo vehicles: 2.5m-1
  Turbocharged vehicles: 3.0m-1

☐ If excess smoke is produced, try fitting a new air cleaner element, or using an injector cleaning treatment. If the engine is running badly, where applicable, check the vehicle's ECU for fault codes. Also check the vehicle's EGR system, where applicable. At high mileages, the injectors may require professional attention.

Engine

- [ ] Engine fails to rotate when attempting to start
- [ ] Starter motor turns engine slowly
- [ ] Starter motor spins without turning engine
- [ ] Starter motor noisy or excessively-rough in engagement
- [ ] Engine rotates, but will not start
- [ ] Engine fires, but will not run
- [ ] Engine difficult to start when cold
- [ ] Engine difficult to start when hot
- [ ] Engine idles erratically
- [ ] Engine misfires at idle speed
- [ ] Engine misfires throughout the driving speed range
- [ ] Engine stalls
- [ ] Engine lacks power
- [ ] Oil pressure warning light illuminated with engine running
- [ ] Engine runs-on after switching off
- [ ] Engine noises

Cooling system

- [ ] Overheating
- [ ] Overcooling
- [ ] External coolant leakage
- [ ] Internal coolant leakage
- [ ] Corrosion

Fuel and exhaust systems

- [ ] Excessive fuel consumption
- [ ] Fuel leakage and/or fuel odour
- [ ] Excessive noise or fumes from exhaust system

Clutch

- [ ] Pedal travels to floor – no pressure or very little resistance
- [ ] Clutch fails to disengage (unable to select gears)
- [ ] Clutch slips (engine speed increases, with no increase in vehicle speed)
- [ ] Judder as clutch is engaged
- [ ] Noise when depressing or releasing clutch pedal

Manual gearbox

- [ ] Noisy in neutral with engine running
- [ ] Noisy in one particular gear
- [ ] Difficulty engaging gears
- [ ] Jumps out of gear
- [ ] Vibration
- [ ] Lubricant leaks

Transfer gearbox

- [ ] Noisy in neutral with engine running
- [ ] Noisy in Low or High positions
- [ ] Difficulty engaging ranges
- [ ] Jumps out of gear
- [ ] Vibration
- [ ] Lubricant leaks

Propeller shafts

- [ ] Knock or clunk when taking up drive
- [ ] Oil leak where propeller shaft enters transfer gearbox
- [ ] Oil leak where propeller shaft enters axle
- [ ] Metallic grating sound consistent with vehicle speed
- [ ] Scraping noise
- [ ] Vibration

Front and rear axles

- [ ] Vibration
- [ ] Noise on drive and overrun
- [ ] Noise consistent with road speed
- [ ] Knock or clunk when taking up drive
- [ ] Oil leakage

Braking system

- [ ] Vehicle pulls to one side under braking
- [ ] Noise (grinding or high-pitched squeal) when brakes applied
- [ ] Excessive brake pedal travel
- [ ] Brake pedal feels spongy when depressed
- [ ] Excessive brake pedal effort required to stop vehicle
- [ ] Judder felt through brake pedal or steering wheel when braking
- [ ] Brakes binding
- [ ] Rear wheels locking under normal braking

Suspension and steering systems

- [ ] Vehicle pulls to one side
- [ ] Wheel wobble and vibration
- [ ] Excessive pitching and/or rolling around corners, or during braking
- [ ] Wandering or general instability
- [ ] Excessively-stiff steering
- [ ] Excessive play in steering
- [ ] Lack of power assistance
- [ ] Tyre wear excessive

Electrical system

- [ ] Battery will not hold a charge for more than a few days
- [ ] Ignition/no-charge warning light remains illuminated with engine running
- [ ] Ignition/no-charge warning light fails to come on
- [ ] Lights inoperative
- [ ] Instrument readings inaccurate or erratic
- [ ] Horn inoperative, or unsatisfactory in operation
- [ ] Windscreen/tailgate wipers inoperative, or unsatisfactory in operation
- [ ] Windscreen/tailgate washers inoperative, or unsatisfactory in operation

Introduction

The vehicle owner who does his or her own maintenance according to the recommended service schedules should not have to use this section of the manual very often. Modern component reliability is such that, provided those items subject to wear or deterioration are inspected or renewed at the specified intervals, sudden failure is comparatively rare. Faults do not usually just happen as a result of sudden failure, but develop over a period of time. Major mechanical failures in particular are usually preceded by characteristic symptoms over hundreds or even thousands of miles. Those components which do occasionally fail without warning are often small and easily carried in the vehicle.

With any fault-finding, the first step is to decide where to begin investigations. Sometimes this is obvious, but on other occasions a little detective work will be necessary. The owner who makes half a dozen haphazard adjustments or replacements may be successful in curing a fault (or its symptoms), but will be none the wiser if the fault recurs, and ultimately may have spent more time and money than was necessary. A calm and logical approach will be found to be more satisfactory in the long run. Always take into account any warning signs or abnormalities that may have been noticed in the period preceding the fault – power loss, high or low gauge readings, unusual smells, etc – and remember that failure of components such as fuses or relays may only be pointers to some underlying fault.

The pages which follow provide an easy-reference guide to the more common problems which may occur during the operation of the vehicle. These problems and their possible causes are grouped under headings denoting various components or systems, such as Engine, Cooling system, etc. The general Chapter which deals with the problem is also shown in brackets; refer to the relevant part of that Chapter for system-specific information. Whatever the fault, certain basic principles apply. These are as follows:

Verify the fault. This is simply a matter of being sure that you know what the symptoms are before starting work. This is particularly important if you are investigating a fault for someone else, who may not have described it very accurately.

Don't overlook the obvious. For example, if the vehicle won't start, is there fuel in the tank? (Don't take anyone else's word on this particular point, and don't trust the fuel gauge either!) If an electrical fault is indicated, look for loose or broken wires before digging out the test gear.

Cure the disease, not the symptom. Substituting a flat battery with a fully-charged one will get you off the hard shoulder, but if the underlying cause is not attended to, the new battery will go the same way.

Don't take anything for granted. Particularly, don't forget that a 'new' component may itself be defective (especially if it's been rattling around in the boot for months), and don't leave components out of a fault diagnosis sequence just because they are new or recently fitted.

When you do finally diagnose a difficult fault, you'll probably realise that all the evidence was there from the start.

Diesel fault diagnosis

The majority of starting problems on diesel engines are electrical in origin. The mechanic who is familiar with petrol engines but less so with diesel may be inclined to view the diesel's injectors and pump in the same light as the spark plugs and distributor, but this is generally a mistake.

When investigating complaints of difficult starting for someone else, make sure that the correct starting procedure is understood and is being followed. Some drivers are unaware of the significance of the preheating warning light – many modern engines are sufficiently forgiving for this not to matter in mild weather, but with the onset of winter, problems begin.

As a rule of thumb, if the engine is difficult to start but runs well when it has finally got going, the problem is electrical (battery, starter motor or preheating system). If poor performance is combined with difficult starting, the problem is likely to be in the fuel system. The low-pressure (supply) side of the fuel system should be checked before suspecting the injectors and high-pressure pump. The most common fuel supply problem is air getting into the system, and any pipe from the fuel tank forwards must be scrutinised if air leakage is suspected. Normally the pump is the last item to suspect, since unless it has been tampered with, there is no reason for it to be at fault.

Engine

Engine fails to rotate when attempting to start

☐ Battery terminal connections loose or corroded (Chapter 1).
☐ Battery discharged or faulty (Chapter 5).
☐ Broken, loose or disconnected wiring in the starting circuit (Chapter 5).
☐ Defective starter solenoid or switch (Chapter 5).
☐ Defective starter motor (Chapter 5).
☐ Starter pinion or flywheel ring gear teeth loose or broken (Chapter 5 or Chapter 2A/B).
☐ Engine earth strap broken or disconnected (Chapter 5).

Starter motor turns engine slowly

☐ Partially-discharged battery (recharge, or use jump leads) (Chapter 5).
☐ Battery terminals loose or corroded (Chapter 1).
☐ Battery earth to body defective (Chapter 5).
☐ Engine earth strap loose (Chapter 5).
☐ Starter motor (or solenoid) wiring loose (Chapter 5).
☐ Starter motor internal fault (Chapter 5).

Starter motor spins without turning engine

☐ Starter motor reduction gears stripped (Chapter 5).
☐ Starter motor mounting bolts loose (Chapter 5).

Engine (continued)

Starter motor noisy or excessively-rough in engagement

- [ ] Starter pinion or flywheel ring gear teeth loose or broken (Chapter 5 and Chapter 2A/B).
- [ ] Starter motor mounting bolts loose or missing (Chapter 5).
- [ ] Starter motor internal components worn or damaged (Chapter 5).

Engine rotates, but will not start

- [ ] Fuel tank empty.
- [ ] Battery discharged (engine rotates slowly) (Chapter 5).
- [ ] Battery terminal connections loose or corroded (Chapter 1).
- [ ] Air in fuel (Chapter 4).
- [ ] Wax formed in fuel (in very cold weather).
- [ ] Faulty stop solenoid (Chapter 4).
- [ ] Low cylinder compressions (Chapter 2A or 2B).
- [ ] Fuel system or preheating system fault (Chapters 4 and 5).
- [ ] Major mechanical failure (eg camshaft drive) (Chapter 2A or 2B).

Engine fires, but will not run

- [ ] Preheating system fault (Chapter 5).
- [ ] Air in fuel (Chapter 4).
- [ ] Wax formed in fuel (in very cold weather).
- [ ] Other fuel system fault (Chapter 4).

Engine difficult to start when cold

- [ ] Battery discharged (Chapter 5).
- [ ] Battery terminal connections loose or corroded (Chapter 1).
- [ ] Air in fuel (Chapter 4).
- [ ] Air filter element dirty or clogged (Chapter 1).
- [ ] Wax formed in fuel (in very cold weather).
- [ ] Preheating system fault (Chapter 5).
- [ ] Other fuel system fault (Chapter 4).
- [ ] Low cylinder compressions (Chapter 2A or 2B).

Engine difficult to start when hot

- [ ] Battery discharged (Chapter 5).
- [ ] Battery terminal connections loose or corroded (Chapter 1).
- [ ] Air filter element dirty or clogged (Chapter 1).
- [ ] Air in fuel (Chapter 4).
- [ ] Low cylinder compressions (Chapter 2A or 2B).

Engine idles erratically

- [ ] Incorrectly-adjusted idle speed (Chapter 1).
- [ ] Air filter element clogged (Chapter 1).
- [ ] Incorrectly-adjusted valve clearances (Chapter 2A).
- [ ] Uneven or low cylinder compressions (Chapter 2A or 2B).
- [ ] Camshaft lobes worn (Chapter 2A or 2B).
- [ ] Timing chain/belt incorrectly tensioned (Chapter 2A or 2B).
- [ ] Incorrect fuel injection pump timing (Chapter 4).

Engine misfires at idle speed

- [ ] Air in fuel (Chapter 4).
- [ ] Wax formed in fuel (in very cold weather).
- [ ] Other fuel system fault (Chapter 4).
- [ ] Incorrectly-adjusted valve clearances (Chapter 2A).
- [ ] Uneven or low cylinder compressions (Chapter 2A or 2B).
- [ ] Disconnected, leaking or perished crankcase ventilation hoses (Chapters 1 and 4).
- [ ] Incorrect fuel injection pump timing (Chapter 4).

Engine misfires throughout the driving speed range

- [ ] Fuel filter choked (Chapter 1).
- [ ] Fuel tank vent blocked or fuel pipes restricted (Chapter 4).
- [ ] Uneven or low cylinder compressions (Chapter 2A or 2B).
- [ ] Incorrect fuel injection pump timing (Chapter 4).

Engine stalls

- [ ] Incorrectly-adjusted idle speed (Chapter 1).
- [ ] Fuel filter choked (Chapter 1).
- [ ] Fuel tank vent blocked or fuel pipes restricted (Chapter 4).

Engine lacks power

- [ ] Air in fuel (Chapter 4).
- [ ] Incorrect fuel injection pump timing (Chapter 4).
- [ ] Timing chain/belt incorrectly fitted or tensioned (Chapter 2A or 2B).
- [ ] Fuel filter choked (Chapter 1).
- [ ] Uneven or low cylinder compressions (Chapter 2A or 2B).
- [ ] Brakes binding (Chapters 1 and 9).
- [ ] Clutch slipping (Chapter 6).

Oil pressure warning light illuminated with engine running

- [ ] Low oil level or incorrect grade (Chapter 1).
- [ ] Faulty oil pressure switch (Chapter 5).
- [ ] Worn engine bearings and/or oil pump (Chapters 2, Parts A, B and C).
- [ ] High engine operating temperature (Chapter 3).
- [ ] Oil pressure relief valve defective (Chapter 2A or 2B).
- [ ] Oil pick-up strainer clogged (Chapter 2A or 2B).

Note: *Low oil pressure in a high-mileage engine at tickover is not necessarily a cause for concern. Sudden pressure loss at speed is far more significant. In any event, check the gauge or warning light sender before condemning the engine.*

Engine runs-on after switching off

- [ ] Faulty stop solenoid (Chapter 4).

Engine noises

Note: *To inexperienced ears, the diesel engine can sound alarming even when there is nothing wrong with it, so it may be prudent to have an unusual noise expertly diagnosed before making renewals or repairs.*

Whistling or wheezing noises

- [ ] Leaking manifold gasket (Chapter 4).
- [ ] Leaking vacuum hose (Chapters 1 and 4).
- [ ] Blowing cylinder head gasket (Chapter 2A or 2B).

Tapping or rattling noises

- [ ] Incorrect valve clearances (Chapter 2A).
- [ ] Worn valve gear or camshaft (Chapter 2A or 2B).
- [ ] Broken piston ring (ticking noise) (Chapter 2C).
- [ ] Ancillary component fault (water pump, alternator, etc) (Chapters 3 and 5).
- [ ] Worn timing chain – where applicable (Chapter 2A or 2B).

Knocking or thumping noises

- [ ] Air in fuel (Chapter 4).
- [ ] Worn drivebelt (Chapter 1 and Chapter 2A/B).
- [ ] Worn timing chain – where applicable (Chapter 2A or 2B).
- [ ] Fuel injector(s) leaking or sticking (Chapter 4).
- [ ] Worn big-end bearings (regular heavy knocking, perhaps less under load) (Chapter 2C).
- [ ] Worn main bearings (rumbling and knocking, perhaps worsening under load) (Chapter 2C).
- [ ] Piston slap (most noticeable when cold) (Chapter 2C).
- [ ] Ancillary component fault (alternator, water pump etc) (Chapters 3 and 5).

Cooling system

Overheating

- [ ] Insufficient coolant in system (Chapter 1).
- [ ] Thermostat faulty (Chapter 3).
- [ ] Radiator core blocked or grille restricted (Chapter 3).
- [ ] Cooling fan faulty (Chapter 3).
- [ ] Pressure cap faulty (Chapter 3).
- [ ] Timing belt worn, or incorrectly adjusted (Chapter 2A).
- [ ] Inaccurate temperature gauge sender unit (Chapter 3).
- [ ] Airlock in cooling system (Chapter 1).

Overcooling

- [ ] Thermostat faulty (Chapter 3).
- [ ] Inaccurate temperature gauge sender unit (Chapter 3).

Corrosion

- [ ] Infrequent draining and flushing (Chapter 1).
- [ ] Incorrect antifreeze mixture or inappropriate type (Chapter 1).

External coolant leakage

- [ ] Deteriorated or damaged hoses or hose clips (Chapter 1).
- [ ] Radiator core or heater matrix leaking (Chapter 3).
- [ ] Pressure cap faulty (Chapter 3).
- [ ] Water pump seal leaking (Chapter 3).
- [ ] Boiling due to overheating (Chapter 3).
- [ ] Core plug leaking (Chapter 2C).

Internal coolant leakage

- [ ] Leaking cylinder head gasket (Chapter 2A or 2B).
- [ ] Cracked cylinder head or cylinder bore (Chapter 2, Parts A, B and C).

Fuel and exhaust systems

Excessive fuel consumption

- [ ] Air filter element dirty or clogged (Chapter 1).
- [ ] Preheating system fault (Chapter 5).
- [ ] Incorrect idle speed (Chapter 4).
- [ ] Incorrect fuel injection pump timing (Chapter 4).
- [ ] Brakes binding (Chapter 9).
- [ ] Tyres under-inflated (Chapter 1).

Fuel leakage and/or fuel odour

- [ ] Damaged or corroded fuel tank, pipes or connections (Chapters 1 and 4).

Excessive noise or fumes from exhaust system

- [ ] Leaking exhaust system or manifold joints (Chapter 4).
- [ ] Leaking, corroded or damaged silencers or pipe (Chapter 4).
- [ ] Broken mountings causing body or suspension contact (Chapter 4).

Clutch

Pedal travels to floor – no pressure or very little resistance

- [ ] Leak in clutch hydraulic system (Chapter 6).
- [ ] Faulty hydraulic master or slave cylinder (Chapter 6).
- [ ] Broken clutch release bearing or fork (Chapter 6).
- [ ] Broken diaphragm spring in clutch pressure plate (Chapter 6).

Clutch fails to disengage (unable to select gears)

- [ ] Leak in clutch hydraulic system (Chapter 6).
- [ ] Faulty hydraulic master or slave cylinder (Chapter 6).
- [ ] Clutch disc sticking on gearbox input shaft splines (Chapter 6).
- [ ] Clutch disc sticking to flywheel or pressure plate (Chapter 6).
- [ ] Faulty pressure plate assembly (Chapter 6).
- [ ] Clutch release mechanism worn or incorrectly assembled (Chapter 6).

Clutch slips (engine speed increases, with no increase in vehicle speed)

- [ ] Clutch disc linings excessively worn (Chapter 6).
- [ ] Clutch disc linings contaminated with oil or grease (Chapter 6).
- [ ] Faulty pressure plate or weak diaphragm spring (Chapter 6).

Judder as clutch is engaged

- [ ] Clutch disc linings contaminated with oil or grease (Chapter 6).
- [ ] Clutch disc linings excessively worn (Chapter 6).
- [ ] Clutch cable sticking or frayed (Chapter 6).
- [ ] Faulty or distorted pressure plate or diaphragm spring (Chapter 6).
- [ ] Worn or loose engine or gearbox mountings (Chapter 2A or 2B).
- [ ] Clutch disc hub or gearbox input shaft splines worn (Chapter 6).

Noise when depressing or releasing clutch pedal

- [ ] Worn clutch release bearing (Chapter 6).
- [ ] Worn or dry clutch pedal bushes (Chapter 6).
- [ ] Faulty pressure plate assembly (Chapter 6).
- [ ] Pressure plate diaphragm spring broken (Chapter 6).
- [ ] Broken clutch disc cushioning springs (Chapter 6).

Manual gearbox

Noisy in neutral with engine running

☐ Input shaft and/or mainshaft bearings worn (noise apparent with clutch pedal released, but not when depressed) (Chapter 7A).*
☐ Clutch release bearing worn (noise apparent with clutch pedal depressed, possibly less when released) (Chapter 6).

Noisy in one particular gear

☐ Worn, damaged or chipped gear teeth (Chapter 7A).*

Difficulty engaging gears

☐ Clutch fault (Chapter 6).
☐ Worn or damaged gear linkage (Chapter 7A).
☐ Worn synchroniser units (Chapter 7A).*

Jumps out of gear

☐ Worn or damaged gear linkage (Chapter 7A).
☐ Incorrectly-adjusted gear linkage (Chapter 7A).
☐ Worn synchroniser units (Chapter 7A).*
☐ Worn selector forks (Chapter 7A).*

Vibration

☐ Lack of oil (Chapter 1).
☐ Worn bearings (Chapter 7A).*

Lubricant leaks

☐ Leaking oil seal (Chapter 7A).
☐ Leaking housing joint (Chapter 7A).*

Although the corrective action necessary to remedy the symptoms described is beyond the scope of the home mechanic, the above information should be helpful in isolating the cause of the condition, so that the owner can communicate clearly with a professional mechanic.

Transfer gearbox

Noisy in neutral with engine running

☐ Worn mainshaft or output shaft bearings (Chapter 7B).*

Noisy in Low or High positions

☐ Worn, damaged or chipped gear teeth (Chapter 7B).*

Difficulty engaging ranges

☐ Clutch fault (Chapter 6).
☐ Main gearbox fault (Chapter 7A).
☐ Worn selector fork (Chapter 7B).*

Jumps out of gear

☐ Worn or damaged gear linkage (Chapter 7B).*
☐ Worn selector fork (Chapter 7B).*

Vibration

☐ Lack of oil (Chapter 1).
☐ Worn bearings (Chapter 7B).*

Lubricant leaks

☐ Leaking oil seal (Chapter 7B).*
☐ Leaking housing joint (Chapter 7B).*

* Although the corrective action necessary to remedy the symptoms described is beyond the scope of the home mechanic, the above information should be helpful in isolating the cause of the condition, so that the owner can communicate clearly with a professional mechanic.

Propeller shafts

Knock or clunk when taking up drive

☐ Worn universal joint bearings (Chapter 8).
☐ Worn axle drive pinion splines (Chapter 9).
☐ Loose drive flange bolts (Chapter 8).
☐ Excessive backlash in axle gears (Chapter 9).

Metallic grating sound consistent with vehicle speed

☐ Severe wear in universal joint bearings (Chapter 8).

Vibration

☐ Wear in sliding sleeve splines (Chapter 8).
☐ Worn universal joint bearings (Chapter 8).
☐ Propeller shaft out of balance (Chapter 8).

Front and rear axles

Vibration

- [ ] Propeller shaft out of balance (Chapter 8).
- [ ] Worn hub bearings (Chapter 9).
- [ ] Wheels out of balance.
- [ ] Propeller shaft or halfshaft joints worn (Chapters 8 and 9).
- [ ] Suspension or steering fault (Chapter 11).

Noise on drive and overrun

- [ ] Worn crownwheel and pinion gears (Chapter 9).
- [ ] Worn differential bearings (Chapter 9).
- [ ] Lack of lubrication in axle or swivel pin housings (Chapters 9 and 11).
- [ ] Manual gearbox or transfer gearbox fault (Chapter 7).

Noise consistent with road speed

- [ ] Worn hub bearings (Chapter 9).
- [ ] Worn differential bearings (Chapter 9).
- [ ] Lack of lubrication in axle or swivel pin housings (Chapters 9 and 11).
- [ ] Manual gearbox or transfer gearbox fault (Chapter 7).

Knock or clunk when taking up drive

- [ ] Excessive crownwheel and pinion backlash (Chapter 9).
- [ ] Worn propeller shaft or halfshaft joints (Chapters 8 and 9).
- [ ] Worn halfshaft splines (Chapter 9).
- [ ] Halfshaft bolts or roadwheel nuts loose (Chapter 9).
- [ ] Broken, damaged, or worn suspension components or axle mountings (Chapters 11 and 9).
- [ ] Manual gearbox or transfer gearbox fault (Chapter 7).

Oil leakage

- [ ] Faulty differential pinion or halfshaft oil seals (Chapter 9).
- [ ] Blocked axle breather valve (Chapter 9).
- [ ] Damaged swivel pin housing or oil seal (Chapter 11).

Braking system

Note: *Before assuming that a brake problem exists, make sure that the tyres are in good condition and correctly inflated, the front wheel alignment is correct, and the vehicle is not loaded with weight in an unequal manner.*

Vehicle pulls to one side under braking

- [ ] Worn, defective, damaged or contaminated front or rear brake shoes/pads on one side (Chapter 10).
- [ ] Seized or partially-seized front or rear brake wheel cylinder or caliper piston (Chapter 10).
- [ ] A mixture of brake lining materials fitted between sides (Chapter 10).
- [ ] Brake caliper mounting bolts loose (Chapter 10).
- [ ] Worn or damaged steering or suspension components (Chapter 11).

Noise (grinding or high-pitched squeal) when brakes applied

- [ ] Brake friction lining material worn down to metal backing (Chapter 10).
- [ ] Excessive corrosion or wear of brake drum – where applicable (Chapter 10).
- [ ] Excessive corrosion of brake disc – where applicable. (May be apparent after the vehicle has been standing for some time (Chapter 10).

Excessive brake pedal travel

- [ ] Faulty master cylinder (Chapter 10).
- [ ] Air in hydraulic system (Chapter 10).
- [ ] Faulty vacuum servo unit (Chapter 10).
- [ ] Faulty brake vacuum pump (Chapter 10).

Brake pedal feels spongy when depressed

- [ ] Air in hydraulic system (Chapter 10).
- [ ] Deteriorated flexible rubber brake hoses (Chapter 10).
- [ ] Master cylinder mountings loose (Chapter 10).
- [ ] Faulty master cylinder (Chapter 10).

Excessive brake pedal effort required to stop vehicle

- [ ] Faulty vacuum servo unit (Chapter 10).
- [ ] Disconnected, damaged or insecure brake servo vacuum hose (Chapters 1 and 10).
- [ ] Faulty brake vacuum pump (Chapter 10).
- [ ] Primary or secondary hydraulic circuit failure (Chapter 10).
- [ ] Seized brake wheel cylinder or caliper piston(s) (Chapter 10).
- [ ] Brake shoes or pads incorrectly fitted (Chapter 10).
- [ ] Incorrect grade of brake shoes/pads fitted (Chapter 10).
- [ ] Brake shoes/pads contaminated (Chapter 10).

Judder felt through brake pedal or steering wheel when braking

- [ ] Excessive run-out or distortion of brake drum(s)/disc(s) (Chapter 10).
- [ ] Brake friction material worn (Chapter 10).
- [ ] Brake caliper mounting bolts loose – where applicable (Chapter 10).
- [ ] Wear in suspension or steering components or mountings (Chapter 11).
- [ ] ABS normal operation.

Brakes binding

- [ ] Seized brake wheel cylinder(s) or caliper piston(s) (Chapter 10).
- [ ] Faulty master cylinder (Chapter 10).

Rear wheels locking under normal braking

- [ ] Faulty brake pressure regulator (Chapter 10).

Suspension and steering systems

Note: *Before diagnosing suspension or steering faults, be sure that the trouble is not due to incorrect tyre pressures, mixtures of tyre types, or binding brakes.*

Vehicle pulls to one side

- [ ] Defective tyre (Chapter 1).
- [ ] Excessive wear in suspension or steering components (Chapter 11).
- [ ] Incorrect front wheel alignment (Chapter 11).
- [ ] Accident damage to steering/suspension components (Chapter 11).

Wheel wobble and vibration

- [ ] Front roadwheels out of balance (vibration felt mainly through the steering wheel) (Chapter 11).
- [ ] Rear roadwheels out of balance (vibration felt throughout the vehicle) (Chapter 11).
- [ ] Roadwheels damaged or distorted (Chapter 1).
- [ ] Faulty or damaged tyre (Chapter 1).
- [ ] Worn steering or suspension joints, bushes or components (Chapter 11).
- [ ] Wheel nuts loose (Chapter 11).

Excessive pitching and/or rolling around corners, or during braking

- [ ] Defective shock absorbers (Chapter 11).
- [ ] Broken or weak coil spring and/or suspension component (Chapter 11).
- [ ] Worn or damaged anti-roll bar or mountings (Chapter 11).

Wandering or general instability

- [ ] Incorrect front wheel alignment (Chapter 11).
- [ ] Worn steering or suspension joints, bushes or components (Chapter 11).
- [ ] Roadwheels out of balance (Chapter 11).
- [ ] Faulty or damaged tyre (Chapter 1).
- [ ] Roadwheel nuts loose (Chapter 11).
- [ ] Defective shock absorbers (Chapter 11).

Excessive play in steering

- [ ] Worn steering column universal joint(s) or intermediate coupling (Chapter 11).
- [ ] Worn steering track-rod end balljoints (Chapter 11).
- [ ] Worn steering box (Chapter 11).
- [ ] Worn steering/suspension joints, bushes or components (Chapter 11).

Excessively-stiff steering

- [ ] Lack of steering gear lubricant (Chapter 11).
- [ ] Seized track-rod end balljoint (Chapter 11).
- [ ] Broken or incorrectly-adjusted power steering pump drivebelt (Chapter 1).
- [ ] Incorrect front wheel alignment (Chapter 11).
- [ ] Steering box or column damaged (Chapter 11).

Lack of power assistance

- [ ] Broken or incorrectly-adjusted power steering pump drivebelt (Chapter 1).
- [ ] Incorrect power steering fluid level (Chapter 1).
- [ ] Restriction in power steering fluid hoses (Chapter 1).
- [ ] Faulty power steering pump (Chapter 11).
- [ ] Faulty steering box (Chapter 11).

Tyre wear excessive

Tyre treads exhibit feathered edges

- [ ] Incorrect toe setting (Chapter 11).

Tyres worn in centre of tread

- [ ] Tyres over-inflated (Chapter 1).

Tyres worn on inside or outside edges

- [ ] Tyres under-inflated (wear on both edges) (Chapter 1).
- [ ] Incorrect camber or castor angles (wear on one edge only) (Chapter 11).
- [ ] Worn steering or suspension joints, bushes or components (Chapter 11).
- [ ] Excessively hard cornering.
- [ ] Accident damage.

Tyres worn on inside and outside edges

- [ ] Tyres under inflated (Chapter 1).
- [ ] Worn shock absorbers (Chapter 11).

Tyres worn unevenly

- [ ] Tyres out of balance (Chapter 1).
- [ ] Excessive wheel or tyre run-out (Chapter 1).
- [ ] Worn shock absorbers (Chapter 11).
- [ ] Faulty tyre (Chapter 1).

Electrical system

Note: *For problems associated with the starting system, refer to the faults listed under 'Engine' earlier in this Section.*

Battery will not hold a charge more than a few days

- ☐ Battery defective internally (Chapter 5).
- ☐ Battery electrolyte level low – where applicable (Chapter 1).
- ☐ Battery terminal connections loose or corroded (Chapter 1).
- ☐ Alternator drivebelt worn or incorrectly adjusted (Chapter 1).
- ☐ Alternator not charging at correct output (Chapter 5).
- ☐ Alternator or voltage regulator faulty (Chapter 5).
- ☐ Short-circuit causing continual battery drain (Chapter 5).

Ignition/no-charge warning light remains illuminated with engine running

- ☐ Alternator drivebelt broken, or incorrectly adjusted (Chapter 1).
- ☐ Alternator brushes worn, sticking, or dirty (Chapter 5).
- ☐ Alternator brush springs weak or broken (Chapter 5).
- ☐ Internal fault in alternator or voltage regulator (Chapter 5).
- ☐ Disconnected, or loose wiring in charging circuit (Chapter 5).

Ignition/no-charge warning light fails to come on

- ☐ Warning light bulb blown (Chapter 13).
- ☐ Disconnected or loose wiring in warning light circuit (Chapter 13).
- ☐ Alternator faulty (Chapter 5).

Lights inoperative

- ☐ Bulb blown (Chapter 13).
- ☐ Corrosion of bulb or bulbholder contacts (Chapter 13).
- ☐ Blown fuse (Chapter 13).
- ☐ Faulty relay (Chapter 13).
- ☐ Broken, loose, or disconnected wiring (Chapter 13).
- ☐ Faulty switch (Chapter 13).

Instrument readings inaccurate or erratic

Instrument readings increase with engine speed

- ☐ Faulty voltage regulator (Chapter 13).

Fuel or temperature gauge gives no reading

- ☐ Faulty gauge sender unit (Chapters 3 or 4).
- ☐ Wiring open-circuit (Chapter 5).
- ☐ Faulty gauge (Chapter 13).

Fuel or temperature gauge gives continuous maximum reading

- ☐ Faulty gauge sender unit (Chapters 3 or 4).
- ☐ Wiring short-circuit (Chapter 5).
- ☐ Faulty gauge (Chapter 13).

Horn inoperative, or unsatisfactory in operation

Horn operates all the time

- ☐ Horn push either earthed or stuck down (Chapter 13).
- ☐ Horn cable to horn push earthed (Chapter 13).

Horn fails to operate

- ☐ Blown fuse (Chapter 13).
- ☐ Cable connections loose, broken or disconnected (Chapter 13).
- ☐ Faulty horn (Chapter 13).

Horn emits intermittent or unsatisfactory sound

- ☐ Cable connections loose (Chapter 13).
- ☐ Horn mountings loose (Chapter 13).
- ☐ Faulty horn (Chapter 13).

Wash/wipe inoperative, or unsatisfactory in operation

Wipers fail to operate, or operate very slowly

- ☐ Wiper blades stuck to screen, or linkage seized or binding (Chapters 1 and 13).
- ☐ Blown fuse (Chapter 13).
- ☐ Cable connections loose, broken or disconnected (Chapter 13).
- ☐ Faulty relay (Chapter 13).
- ☐ Faulty wiper motor (Chapter 13).

Wiper blades sweep over too large or too small an area of the glass

- ☐ Wiper arms incorrectly positioned on spindles (Chapter 13).
- ☐ Excessive wear of wiper linkage (Chapter 13).
- ☐ Wiper motor or linkage mountings loose or insecure (Chapter 13).

Wiper blades fail to clean the glass effectively

- ☐ Wiper blade rubbers worn or perished (Chapter 1).
- ☐ Wiper arm springs broken, or arm pivots seized (Chapter 13).
- ☐ Insufficient windscreen washer additive to adequately remove road film (Chapter 1).

One or more washer jets inoperative

- ☐ Blocked washer jet (Chapter 13).
- ☐ Disconnected, kinked or restricted fluid hose (Chapter 13).
- ☐ Insufficient fluid in washer reservoir (Chapter 1).

Washer pump fails to operate

- ☐ Broken or disconnected wiring or connections (Chapter 13).
- ☐ Blown fuse (Chapter 13).
- ☐ Faulty washer switch (Chapter 13).
- ☐ Faulty washer pump (Chapter 13).

Washer pump runs for some time before jets operate

- ☐ Faulty one-way valve in fluid supply hose (Chapter 13).

A

ABS (Anti-lock brake system) A system, usually electronically controlled, that senses incipient wheel lockup during braking and relieves hydraulic pressure at wheels that are about to skid.

Air bag An inflatable bag hidden in the steering wheel (driver's side) or the dash or glovebox (passenger side). In a head-on collision, the bags inflate, preventing the driver and front passenger from being thrown forward into the steering wheel or windscreen.

Air cleaner A metal or plastic housing, containing a filter element, which removes dust and dirt from the air being drawn into the engine.

Air filter element The actual filter in an air cleaner system, usually manufactured from pleated paper and requiring renewal at regular intervals.

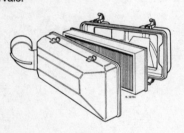

Air filter

Allen key A hexagonal wrench which fits into a recessed hexagonal hole.

Alligator clip A long-nosed spring-loaded metal clip with meshing teeth. Used to make temporary electrical connections.

Alternator A component in the electrical system which converts mechanical energy from a drivebelt into electrical energy to charge the battery and to operate the starting system, ignition system and electrical accessories.

Alternator (exploded view)

Ampere (amp) A unit of measurement for the flow of electric current. One amp is the amount of current produced by one volt acting through a resistance of one ohm.

Anaerobic sealer A substance used to prevent bolts and screws from loosening. Anaerobic means that it does not require oxygen for activation. The Loctite brand is widely used.

Antifreeze A substance (usually ethylene glycol) mixed with water, and added to a vehicle's cooling system, to prevent freezing of the coolant in winter. Antifreeze also contains chemicals to inhibit corrosion and the formation of rust and other deposits that would tend to clog the radiator and coolant passages and reduce cooling efficiency.

Anti-seize compound A coating that reduces the risk of seizing on fasteners that are subjected to high temperatures, such as exhaust manifold bolts and nuts.

Anti-seize compound

Asbestos A natural fibrous mineral with great heat resistance, commonly used in the composition of brake friction materials. Asbestos is a health hazard and the dust created by brake systems should never be inhaled or ingested.

Axle A shaft on which a wheel revolves, or which revolves with a wheel. Also, a solid beam that connects the two wheels at one end of the vehicle. An axle which also transmits power to the wheels is known as a live axle.

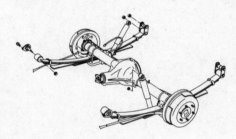

Axle assembly

Axleshaft A single rotating shaft, on either side of the differential, which delivers power from the final drive assembly to the drive wheels. Also called a driveshaft or a halfshaft.

B

Ball bearing An anti-friction bearing consisting of a hardened inner and outer race with hardened steel balls between two races.

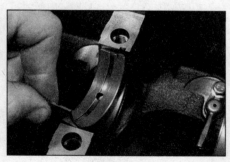

Bearing

Bearing The curved surface on a shaft or in a bore, or the part assembled into either, that permits relative motion between them with minimum wear and friction.

Big-end bearing The bearing in the end of the connecting rod that's attached to the crankshaft.

Bleed nipple A valve on a brake wheel cylinder, caliper or other hydraulic component that is opened to purge the hydraulic system of air. Also called a bleed screw.

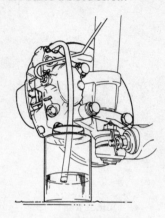

Brake bleeding

Brake bleeding Procedure for removing air from lines of a hydraulic brake system.

Brake disc The component of a disc brake that rotates with the wheels.

Brake drum The component of a drum brake that rotates with the wheels.

Brake linings The friction material which contacts the brake disc or drum to retard the vehicle's speed. The linings are bonded or riveted to the brake pads or shoes.

Brake pads The replaceable friction pads that pinch the brake disc when the brakes are applied. Brake pads consist of a friction material bonded or riveted to a rigid backing plate.

Brake shoe The crescent-shaped carrier to which the brake linings are mounted and which forces the lining against the rotating drum during braking.

Braking systems For more information on braking systems, consult the *Haynes Automotive Brake Manual*.

Breaker bar A long socket wrench handle providing greater leverage.

Bulkhead The insulated partition between the engine and the passenger compartment.

C

Caliper The non-rotating part of a disc-brake assembly that straddles the disc and carries the brake pads. The caliper also contains the hydraulic components that cause the pads to pinch the disc when the brakes are applied. A caliper is also a measuring tool that can be set to measure inside or outside dimensions of an object.

Camshaft A rotating shaft on which a series of cam lobes operate the valve mechanisms. The camshaft may be driven by gears, by sprockets and chain or by sprockets and a belt.

Canister A container in an evaporative emission control system; contains activated charcoal granules to trap vapours from the fuel system.

Canister

Carburettor A device which mixes fuel with air in the proper proportions to provide a desired power output from a spark ignition internal combustion engine.

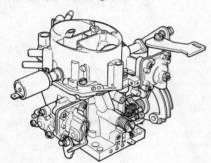

Carburettor

Castellated Resembling the parapets along the top of a castle wall. For example, a castellated balljoint stud nut.

Castellated nut

Castor In wheel alignment, the backward or forward tilt of the steering axis. Castor is positive when the steering axis is inclined rearward at the top.

Catalytic converter A silencer-like device in the exhaust system which converts certain pollutants in the exhaust gases into less harmful substances.

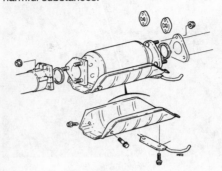

Catalytic converter

Circlip A ring-shaped clip used to prevent endwise movement of cylindrical parts and shafts. An internal circlip is installed in a groove in a housing; an external circlip fits into a groove on the outside of a cylindrical piece such as a shaft.

Clearance The amount of space between two parts. For example, between a piston and a cylinder, between a bearing and a journal, etc.

Coil spring A spiral of elastic steel found in various sizes throughout a vehicle, for example as a springing medium in the suspension and in the valve train.

Compression Reduction in volume, and increase in pressure and temperature, of a gas, caused by squeezing it into a smaller space.

Compression ratio The relationship between cylinder volume when the piston is at top dead centre and cylinder volume when the piston is at bottom dead centre.

Constant velocity (CV) joint A type of universal joint that cancels out vibrations caused by driving power being transmitted through an angle.

Core plug A disc or cup-shaped metal device inserted in a hole in a casting through which core was removed when the casting was formed. Also known as a freeze plug or expansion plug.

Crankcase The lower part of the engine block in which the crankshaft rotates.

Crankshaft The main rotating member, or shaft, running the length of the crankcase, with offset "throws" to which the connecting rods are attached.

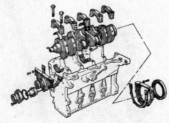

Crankshaft assembly

Crocodile clip See Alligator clip

D

Diagnostic code Code numbers obtained by accessing the diagnostic mode of an engine management computer. This code can be used to determine the area in the system where a malfunction may be located.

Disc brake A brake design incorporating a rotating disc onto which brake pads are squeezed. The resulting friction converts the energy of a moving vehicle into heat.

Double-overhead cam (DOHC) An engine that uses two overhead camshafts, usually one for the intake valves and one for the exhaust valves.

Drivebelt(s) The belt(s) used to drive accessories such as the alternator, water pump, power steering pump, air conditioning compressor, etc. off the crankshaft pulley.

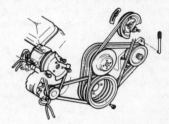

Accessory drivebelts

Driveshaft Any shaft used to transmit motion. Commonly used when referring to the axleshafts on a front wheel drive vehicle.

Driveshaft

Drum brake A type of brake using a drum-shaped metal cylinder attached to the inner surface of the wheel. When the brake pedal is pressed, curved brake shoes with friction linings press against the inside of the drum to slow or stop the vehicle.

Drum brake assembly

E

EGR valve A valve used to introduce exhaust gases into the intake air stream.

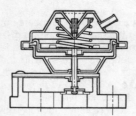
EGR valve

Electronic control unit (ECU) A computer which controls (for instance) ignition and fuel injection systems, or an anti-lock braking system. For more information refer to the *Haynes Automotive Electrical and Electronic Systems Manual*.

Electronic Fuel Injection (EFI) A computer controlled fuel system that distributes fuel through an injector located in each intake port of the engine.

Emergency brake A braking system, independent of the main hydraulic system, that can be used to slow or stop the vehicle if the primary brakes fail, or to hold the vehicle stationary even though the brake pedal isn't depressed. It usually consists of a hand lever that actuates either front or rear brakes mechanically through a series of cables and linkages. Also known as a handbrake or parking brake.

Endfloat The amount of lengthwise movement between two parts. As applied to a crankshaft, the distance that the crankshaft can move forward and back in the cylinder block.

Engine management system (EMS) A computer controlled system which manages the fuel injection and the ignition systems in an integrated fashion.

Exhaust manifold A part with several passages through which exhaust gases leave the engine combustion chambers and enter the exhaust pipe.

Exhaust manifold

F

Fan clutch A viscous (fluid) drive coupling device which permits variable engine fan speeds in relation to engine speeds.

Feeler blade A thin strip or blade of hardened steel, ground to an exact thickness, used to check or measure clearances between parts.

Feeler blade

Firing order The order in which the engine cylinders fire, or deliver their power strokes, beginning with the number one cylinder.

Flywheel A heavy spinning wheel in which energy is absorbed and stored by means of momentum. On cars, the flywheel is attached to the crankshaft to smooth out firing impulses.

Free play The amount of travel before any action takes place. The "looseness" in a linkage, or an assembly of parts, between the initial application of force and actual movement. For example, the distance the brake pedal moves before the pistons in the master cylinder are actuated.

Fuse An electrical device which protects a circuit against accidental overload. The typical fuse contains a soft piece of metal which is calibrated to melt at a predetermined current flow (expressed as amps) and break the circuit.

Fusible link A circuit protection device consisting of a conductor surrounded by heat-resistant insulation. The conductor is smaller than the wire it protects, so it acts as the weakest link in the circuit. Unlike a blown fuse, a failed fusible link must frequently be cut from the wire for replacement.

G

Gap The distance the spark must travel in jumping from the centre electrode to the side

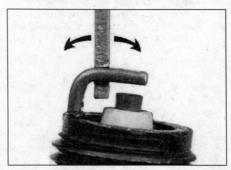
Adjusting spark plug gap

electrode in a spark plug. Also refers to the spacing between the points in a contact breaker assembly in a conventional points-type ignition, or to the distance between the reluctor or rotor and the pickup coil in an electronic ignition.

Gasket Any thin, soft material - usually cork, cardboard, asbestos or soft metal - installed between two metal surfaces to ensure a good seal. For instance, the cylinder head gasket seals the joint between the block and the cylinder head.

Gasket

Gauge An instrument panel display used to monitor engine conditions. A gauge with a movable pointer on a dial or a fixed scale is an analogue gauge. A gauge with a numerical readout is called a digital gauge.

H

Halfshaft A rotating shaft that transmits power from the final drive unit to a drive wheel, usually when referring to a live rear axle.

Harmonic balancer A device designed to reduce torsion or twisting vibration in the crankshaft. May be incorporated in the crankshaft pulley. Also known as a vibration damper.

Hone An abrasive tool for correcting small irregularities or differences in diameter in an engine cylinder, brake cylinder, etc.

Hydraulic tappet A tappet that utilises hydraulic pressure from the engine's lubrication system to maintain zero clearance (constant contact with both camshaft and valve stem). Automatically adjusts to variation in valve stem length. Hydraulic tappets also reduce valve noise.

I

Ignition timing The moment at which the spark plug fires, usually expressed in the number of crankshaft degrees before the piston reaches the top of its stroke.

Inlet manifold A tube or housing with passages through which flows the air-fuel mixture (carburettor vehicles and vehicles with throttle body injection) or air only (port fuel-injected vehicles) to the port openings in the cylinder head.

J

Jump start Starting the engine of a vehicle with a discharged or weak battery by attaching jump leads from the weak battery to a charged or helper battery.

L

Load Sensing Proportioning Valve (LSPV) A brake hydraulic system control valve that works like a proportioning valve, but also takes into consideration the amount of weight carried by the rear axle.

Locknut A nut used to lock an adjustment nut, or other threaded component, in place. For example, a locknut is employed to keep the adjusting nut on the rocker arm in position.

Lockwasher A form of washer designed to prevent an attaching nut from working loose.

M

MacPherson strut A type of front suspension system devised by Earle MacPherson at Ford of England. In its original form, a simple lateral link with the anti-roll bar creates the lower control arm. A long strut - an integral coil spring and shock absorber - is mounted between the body and the steering knuckle. Many modern so-called MacPherson strut systems use a conventional lower A-arm and don't rely on the anti-roll bar for location.

Multimeter An electrical test instrument with the capability to measure voltage, current and resistance.

N

NOx Oxides of Nitrogen. A common toxic pollutant emitted by petrol and diesel engines at higher temperatures.

O

Ohm The unit of electrical resistance. One volt applied to a resistance of one ohm will produce a current of one amp.

Ohmmeter An instrument for measuring electrical resistance.

O-ring A type of sealing ring made of a special rubber-like material; in use, the O-ring is compressed into a groove to provide the sealing action.

O-ring

Overhead cam (ohc) engine An engine with the camshaft(s) located on top of the cylinder head(s).

Overhead valve (ohv) engine An engine with the valves located in the cylinder head, but with the camshaft located in the engine block.

Oxygen sensor A device installed in the engine exhaust manifold, which senses the oxygen content in the exhaust and converts this information into an electric current. Also called a Lambda sensor.

P

Phillips screw A type of screw head having a cross instead of a slot for a corresponding type of screwdriver.

Plastigage A thin strip of plastic thread, available in different sizes, used for measuring clearances. For example, a strip of Plastigage is laid across a bearing journal. The parts are assembled and dismantled; the width of the crushed strip indicates the clearance between journal and bearing.

Plastigage

Propeller shaft The long hollow tube with universal joints at both ends that carries power from the transmission to the differential on front-engined rear wheel drive vehicles.

Proportioning valve A hydraulic control valve which limits the amount of pressure to the rear brakes during panic stops to prevent wheel lock-up.

R

Rack-and-pinion steering A steering system with a pinion gear on the end of the steering shaft that mates with a rack (think of a geared wheel opened up and laid flat). When the steering wheel is turned, the pinion turns, moving the rack to the left or right. This movement is transmitted through the track rods to the steering arms at the wheels.

Radiator A liquid-to-air heat transfer device designed to reduce the temperature of the coolant in an internal combustion engine cooling system.

Refrigerant Any substance used as a heat transfer agent in an air-conditioning system. R-12 has been the principle refrigerant for many years; recently, however, manufacturers have begun using R-134a, a non-CFC substance that is considered less harmful to the ozone in the upper atmosphere.

Rocker arm A lever arm that rocks on a shaft or pivots on a stud. In an overhead valve engine, the rocker arm converts the upward movement of the pushrod into a downward movement to open a valve.

Rotor In a distributor, the rotating device inside the cap that connects the centre electrode and the outer terminals as it turns, distributing the high voltage from the coil secondary winding to the proper spark plug. Also, that part of an alternator which rotates inside the stator. Also, the rotating assembly of a turbocharger, including the compressor wheel, shaft and turbine wheel.

Runout The amount of wobble (in-and-out movement) of a gear or wheel as it's rotated. The amount a shaft rotates "out-of-true." The out-of-round condition of a rotating part.

S

Sealant A liquid or paste used to prevent leakage at a joint. Sometimes used in conjunction with a gasket.

Sealed beam lamp An older headlight design which integrates the reflector, lens and filaments into a hermetically-sealed one-piece unit. When a filament burns out or the lens cracks, the entire unit is simply replaced.

Serpentine drivebelt A single, long, wide accessory drivebelt that's used on some newer vehicles to drive all the accessories, instead of a series of smaller, shorter belts. Serpentine drivebelts are usually tensioned by an automatic tensioner.

Serpentine drivebelt

Shim Thin spacer, commonly used to adjust the clearance or relative positions between two parts. For example, shims inserted into or under bucket tappets control valve clearances. Clearance is adjusted by changing the thickness of the shim.

Slide hammer A special puller that screws into or hooks onto a component such as a shaft or bearing; a heavy sliding handle on the shaft bottoms against the end of the shaft to knock the component free.

Sprocket A tooth or projection on the periphery of a wheel, shaped to engage with a chain or drivebelt. Commonly used to refer to the sprocket wheel itself.

Starter inhibitor switch On vehicles with an automatic transmission, a switch that prevents starting if the vehicle is not in Neutral or Park.

Strut See MacPherson strut.

T

Tappet A cylindrical component which transmits motion from the cam to the valve stem, either directly or via a pushrod and rocker arm. Also called a cam follower.

Thermostat A heat-controlled valve that regulates the flow of coolant between the cylinder block and the radiator, so maintaining optimum engine operating temperature. A thermostat is also used in some air cleaners in which the temperature is regulated.

Thrust bearing The bearing in the clutch assembly that is moved in to the release levers by clutch pedal action to disengage the clutch. Also referred to as a release bearing.

Timing belt A toothed belt which drives the camshaft. Serious engine damage may result if it breaks in service.

Timing chain A chain which drives the camshaft.

Toe-in The amount the front wheels are closer together at the front than at the rear. On rear wheel drive vehicles, a slight amount of toe-in is usually specified to keep the front wheels running parallel on the road by offsetting other forces that tend to spread the wheels apart.

Toe-out The amount the front wheels are closer together at the rear than at the front. On front wheel drive vehicles, a slight amount of toe-out is usually specified.

Tools For full information on choosing and using tools, refer to the *Haynes Automotive Tools Manual.*

Tracer A stripe of a second colour applied to a wire insulator to distinguish that wire from another one with the same colour insulator.

Tune-up A process of accurate and careful adjustments and parts replacement to obtain the best possible engine performance.

Turbocharger A centrifugal device, driven by exhaust gases, that pressurises the intake air. Normally used to increase the power output from a given engine displacement, but can also be used primarily to reduce exhaust emissions (as on VW's "Umwelt" Diesel engine).

U

Universal joint or U-joint A double-pivoted connection for transmitting power from a driving to a driven shaft through an angle. A U-joint consists of two Y-shaped yokes and a cross-shaped member called the spider.

V

Valve A device through which the flow of liquid, gas, vacuum, or loose material in bulk may be started, stopped, or regulated by a movable part that opens, shuts, or partially obstructs one or more ports or passageways. A valve is also the movable part of such a device.

Valve clearance The clearance between the valve tip (the end of the valve stem) and the rocker arm or tappet. The valve clearance is measured when the valve is closed.

Vernier caliper A precision measuring instrument that measures inside and outside dimensions. Not quite as accurate as a micrometer, but more convenient.

Viscosity The thickness of a liquid or its resistance to flow.

Volt A unit for expressing electrical "pressure" in a circuit. One volt that will produce a current of one ampere through a resistance of one ohm.

W

Welding Various processes used to join metal items by heating the areas to be joined to a molten state and fusing them together. For more information refer to the *Haynes Automotive Welding Manual.*

Wiring diagram A drawing portraying the components and wires in a vehicle's electrical system, using standardised symbols. For more information refer to the *Haynes Automotive Electrical and Electronic Systems Manual.*

Note: *References throughout this index are in the form* "**Chapter number**" • "**Page number**". *So, for example, 2A•15 refers to page 15 of Chapter 2A.*

A

ABS wheel speed sensor – 1•22
Accelerator cable – 4A•4
Accelerator mechanism – 1•21
Accelerator pedal – 4A•5, 4B•3
**Accelerator pedal position
   sensor** – 4A•21, 4B•8
Accessory shops – REF•4
Acknowledgements – 0•6
Air cleaner ducting – 4A•4, 4B•3
Air conditioning – 3•9
   drivebelt – 1•12, 1•13
Air filter – 1•19, 4A•4, 4B•3
Air pressure sensor – 4B•8
Air temperature sensor – 4B•8
Airbags – 0•5
Airflow sensor – 4B•8
Alarm handset battery – 1•24
Alternator – 5•4
   brushes – 5•5
   drivebelt – 1•11, 1•12, 1•13
**Ambient air pressure
   sensor** – 4B•8
Antifreeze – 0•10, 0•15, 1•27
**Anti-lock braking system
   (ABS)** – 10•18, 10•19
Anti-roll bar – 11•7, 11•10, 11•11
Anti-theft system – REF•6
Asbestos – 0•5
Auxiliary drivebelt – 1•11
Auxiliary light adjustment – 1•23
Axle – 9•7, 9•10, 9•13, 9•14
   breather – 1•16
   halfshaft – 9•2, 9•11
   oil – 0•15, 1•15, 1•24
   swivel pin housing – 9•7

B

Badges – 12•12
Battery – 0•5, 0•14, 5•2, 5•3
   alarm handset – 1•24
Big-end bearings – 2C•15

Bleeding

Bleeding
   brakes – 10•2
   clutch – 6•7
   fuel system – 4A•5, 4B•4
   power steering system – 11•17
Blower motor – 3•8
   switch – 13•4
Body corrosion – REF•12
Body electrical systems – 13•1 *et seq*
Bodywork and fittings – 12•1 *et seq*
Bonnet – 12•4
Boost pressure – 1•25
Braking system – 1•16, 10•1 *et seq*,
   REF•9, REF•10, REF•11
   drums – 1•10
   fault finding – REF•18
   fluid – 0•13, 0•15, 1•24
   light – 13•7
   pads – 1•10
   pedal – 10•13
   vacuum servo air filter – 1•27
   vacuum servo hose – 1•21
Bulbs – 13•5, 13•7
Bump stop – 11•8
Bumpers – 12•4
Burning – 0•5
Buying spare parts – REF•4

C

Cables
   accelerator – 4A•4
   bonnet release – 12•4
   handbrake – 10•16
   speedometer – 13•10
   windscreen wiper – 13•11
Calipers – 1•10, 10•8, 10•9
Cam followers – 2A•22
Camshaft – 2A•30, 2B•7
   front oil seal – 2A•29
   rear oil seal – 2B•15
   sprocket – 2A•14
Carpets – 12•2
Cassette player – 13•15
Central locking components – 13•15

Centre console – 12•14
Centrifuge rotor – 1•17
Charging – 5•2, 5•3
Cigarette lighter – 13•10
Clock – 13•8, 13•9
Clutch – 6•1 *et seq*
   fault finding – REF•16
   fluid – 0•15, 1•9
   pedal – 6•8
Clutch release mechanism – 6•3
Coil spring – 11•5, 11•9
Compression test – 2A•5, 2B•3
Condenser cooling fan – 3•5
Connecting rods – 2C•10, 2C•13, 2C•19
Console centre – 12•14
Conversion factors – REF•2
Coolant – 0•10, 0•15, 1•26
   pump – 3•5
   pump drivebelt – 1•11, 1•12, 1•13
   temperature gauge sender – 3•5
   temperature sensor – 4A•21
Cooling fan – 3•4, 3•5
   drivebelt – 1•11, 1•12, 1•13
***Cooling, heating and ventilation
   systems*** – 1•15, 3•1 *et seq*
   fault finding – REF•16
   hoses – 3•2
Courtesy light – 13•7
Crankcase – 2C•12
   breather hose – 1•10
   emissions control – 4A•20, 4A•21, 4B•11
Crankshaft – 2C•11, 2C•15, 2C•16
   front oil seal – 2A•27, 2B•15
   pulley – 2A•8, 2B•5
   rear oil seal – 2A•28, 2B•15
   speed and position sensor – 4B•8
   spigot bush – 2A•32, 2B•16
   sprocket – 2A•14
Crushing – 0•5
Cut-off switch – 4B•8
Cylinder block – 2C•12
Cylinder head – 2A•19, 2B•9, 2C•7,
   2C•8, 2C•9
   cover – 2B•4

Note: References throughout this index are in the form "Chapter number" • "Page number". So, for example, 2A•15 refers to page 15 of Chapter 2A.

D

Damper (steering) – 11•17
Defender Diesel – 0•6
Dents – 12•2
Diesel fault diagnosis – REF•14
Diesel injection equipment – 0•5
Diff lock switches – 7A•5
Differential overhaul – 9•14
Dim-dip lighting system – 13•15
Dimensions – REF•1
Direction indicator – 13•6, 13•7, 13•8
Discs – 1•10, 10•6, 10•7
Doors – 12•4, 12•5, 12•6, 12•8, 13•15, 13•16, REF•10
Drag link – 11•18
Drivebelt – 1•11
Driveshafts – REF•11
Drivetrain – 1•16
Drums – 1•10, 10•7

E

Earth fault – 13•2
EGR system – 4A•21, 4B•11
Electric shock – 0•5
Electrical equipment – 1•16, REF•10
Electrical system – 0•14
    fault finding – 13•2, REF•20
Electronic control unit
    ABS – 10•19
    central locking – 13•15
    fuel system – 4B•7
Emissions control systems – 4A•20, 4A•21, 4B•11, REF•12
Engine breather – 1•21
Engine electrical systems – 5•1 *et seq*
Engine fault finding – REF•14, REF•15
Engine management electronic components – 4B•7
Engine oil – 0•11, 0•15
Engine oil – 1•8, 1•9
Engine oil centrifuge rotor – 1•17
Engine removal and general overhaul procedures – 2C•1 *et seq*
Environmental considerations – REF•3
Exhaust emissions control – 4A•20, 4A•21, 4B•11
Exhaust gas recirculation system – 4A•20
Exhaust manifold – 4A•18, 4A•19, 4B•10
Exhaust specialists – REF•4
Exhaust system – 1•22, 4A•20, 4B•10, REF•11, REF•12

F

Facia panel – 12•15
    switches – 13•4
Fan – 3•4, 3•5
Fault finding – REF•13 *et seq*
    braking system – REF•18
    clutch – REF•16
    cooling system – REF•16
    electrical system – 13•2, REF•20
    front and rear axles – REF•18

fuel and exhaust systems – REF•16
    manual gearbox – REF•17
    propeller shafts – REF•17
    suspension and steering systems – REF•19
    transfer gearbox – REF•17
Filling – 12•3
Filter
    air – 1•19, 4A•4, 4B•3
    brake vacuum servo – 1•27
    fuel – 1•18, 4B•8
    oil – 1•8, 1•25
    vacuum servo – 1•28
Fire – 0•5
Fixed windows – 12•12
Fluids – 0•15
Flywheel – 2A•31, 2B•15
    housing – 1•22
Foglight – 13•9
Front and rear axles – 9•1 *et seq*
    fault finding – REF•18
Fuel cooler – 4B•4
Fuel cut-off switch – 4B•8
Fuel filter – 1•18
    water sensor – 4B•8
Fuel gauge sender unit – 4A•6, 4B•4
Fuel injection pump – 4A•10
    sprocket – 2A•15
Fuel injectors – 4A•15, 4B•5
    leak – 1•25
    sleeve – 2C•9
    spray pattern – 1•25
Fuel lift pump – 4A•8
Fuel pressure regulator/connector block – 4B•7
Fuel sedimenter – 1•16
Fuel system – REF•12
Fuel tank – 1•23, 4A•6, 4B•5
Fuel temperature sensor – 4B•7
Fuel, exhaust and emissions control systems – non-TD5 engines – 4A•1 *et seq*
Fuel, exhaust and emissions control systems – TD5 engines – 4B•1 *et seq*
Fuel and exhaust systems fault finding – REF•16
Fume or gas intoxication – 0•5
Fuses – 13•3

G

Gaiters
    propeller shaft – 8•4
Garages – REF•4
Gashes – 12•2
Gaskets – REF•3
Gauge illumination – 13•8
General repair procedures – REF•3
Glass (door) – 12•8
Glow plugs – 5•9
    wiring – 1•21

H

Halfshaft – 9•2, 9•11
Handbrake – 1•10, 10•15, 10•16, REF•9
    warning switch – 13•5

Handles (door) – 12•6
Headlight – 13•5, 13•8
    adjustment – 1•23, 13•9
    headlight-levelling switch – 13•5
    washer system – 13•15
Heating system – 3•7
    blower motor – 3•8
    blower motor switch – 13•4
    heater unit – 3•7
    hose – 1•15
    matrix – 3•8
High-level brake light – 13•7
Hinges – 1•10
Holes – 12•2
Horn – 13•10
Hose brake vacuum servo – 1•21
Hoses – 3•2, 10•3
    heater system – 1•15
Hub assembly – 9•3, 9•11
    bearing – 9•6, 9•13
Hydraulic adjusters – 2B•7
Hydraulic unit (ABS) – 10•19
Hydrofluoric acid – 0•5

I

Identifying leaks – 0•9
Idle speed – 4A•9
Idler pulley – 2A•15
Ignition switch – 11•12
In-car repair procedures non-TD5 engines – 2A•1 *et seq*
In-car repair procedures TD5 engine – 2B•1 *et seq*
Indicators – 13•6, 13•7, 13•8
Inertia fuel cut-off switch – 4B•8
Injection pump – 4A•10
    sprocket – 2A•15
Injection timing – 4A•13, 4A•14
Injectors – 4A•15, 4B•5
    leak – 1•25
    rocker shaft – 2B•9
    sleeve – 2C•9
    spray pattern – 1•25
Inlet manifold – 4A•18
Instrument panel – 13•9
    illumination – 13•7
Instruments – 1•16
Intake air temperature sensor – 4B•8
Intake manifold – 4B•10
Intercooler – 1•21, 4A•17, 4B•10
Intercooler element – 1•28

J

Jack security – 1•22
Jacking and vehicle support – REF•6
Joint mating faces – REF•3
Jump starting – 0•7

L

Land Rover 90/110 – 0•6
Leakdown test – 2A•5, 2B•3
Leaks – 0•9
    fuel injector – 1•25

Note: *References throughout this index are in the form* "**Chapter number**" • "**Page number**". *So, for example, 2A•15 refers to page 15 of Chapter 2A.*

Light units – 13•8
Lighting system – 13•15
Lights-on warning system – 13•10
Locknuts, locktabs and washers – REF•3
Locks – 1•10
  bonnet – 12•4
  central locking components – 13•15
  door – 12•6, 13•15, 13•16
  steering column – 11•12
  tailgate – 12•10, 13•16
Low detect switches – 7A•5
Lower link – 11•9, 11•10
Lubricants and fluids – 0•15

M

Main bearings – 2C•15
Main gearbox oil – 1•14, 1•23
Manifold absolute pressure sensor – 4B•8
Manifolds – 4A•18, 4B•10
Manual gearbox – 7A•1 *et seq*
  fault finding – REF•17
  oil – 0•15
Mass airflow sensor – 4B•8
Master cylinder
  brake – 10•10
  clutch – 6•5
Maximum engine speed – 4A•9
Mirrors – 12•12, REF•9
MOT test checks – REF•9 *et seq*
Motor factors – REF•4
Mountings – 2A•32, 2B•17

N

Non-return valves – 13•14
Number plate light – 13•7, 13•9

O

Oils
  axle – 0•15, 1•15, 1•24
  engine – 0•11, 0•15, 1•8, 1•9
  main gearbox – 0•15, 1•14, 1•23
  manual steering – 0•15
  steering box – 1•21
  swivel pin housing – 0•15, 1•15, 1•25
  transfer gearbox – 0•15, 1•14, 1•24
Oil centrifuge rotor – 1•17
Oil cooler – 2A•33, 2B•16
Oil filter – 1•8, 1•25
Oil pressure switch – 2B•17, 5•8
Oil pump – 2A•23, 2A•26, 2B•13
Oil seals – 2A•27, 2B•15, REF•3
  transfer gearbox – 7B•3
  valve stem – 2C•9
Oil strainer – 2A•26
Oil thermostat – 2A•33
Open-circuit – 13•2

P

Pads – 1•10, 10•3, 10•5

Panhard rod – 11•6
Parts – REF•4
Pedals
  accelerator – 4A•5, 4B•3
  accelerator position sensor – 4A•21, 4B•8
  brake – 10•13
  clutch – 6•8
Pipes – 10•3
Pistons – 2C•10, 2C•13, 2C•19
Plastic components – 12•3
Poisonous or irritant substances – 0•5
Power steering fluid – 0•15, 1•9
Power steering pump – 11•17
  drivebelt – 1•11, 1•12, 1•13
Preheating system – 5•8
  relay/timer unit – 5•10
Pressure-regulating valve (brake) – 10•17
Priming
  fuel system – 4A•5, 4B•4
Propeller shafts – 1•22, 8•1 *et seq*
  fault finding – REF•17
  grease – 0•15
  rubber gaiter – 8•4
Puncture repair – 0•8

R

Radiator – 1•21, 3•2
Radio – 13•15
  anti-theft system – precaution – REF•6
Radius arm – 11•6
Rear light – 13•6, 13•8
Regulator (window glass) – 12•8
Relays – 13•3
  preheating system – 5•10
Release mechanism – 6•3
Repair procedures – REF•3
Respraying – 12•3
Reversing light – 13•6, 13•9
  switch – 7A•2
Road test – 1•16
Rocker gear – 2A•16, 2B•7
Routine maintenance – bodywork and underframe – 12•1
Routine maintenance – upholstery and carpets – 12•2
Routine maintenance and servicing – 1•1 *et seq*

S

Safety first! – 0•5, 0•13
Scalding – 0•5
Scratches – 12•2
Screw threads and fastenings – REF•3
Seat belts – 1•23, 12•13
Seats – 12•12
Self-levelling unit – 11•12
Servo unit – 10•14, 10•15
  air filter – 1•27
  filter – 1•28
  hose – 1•21
Shock absorbers – 1•27, 11•5, 11•8, REF•10, REF•11
Shoes – 1•10, 10•5, 10•15
Short-circuit – 13•2

Sidelight – 13•6, 13•8
Skew gear – 2A•23
Slave cylinder (clutch) – 6•4
Spare parts – REF•4
Spare wheel – 1•23
Speakers – 13•15
Speed sensor – 7A•5
Speedometer cable – 13•10
Springs – 11•5, 11•9, REF•11
Sprockets – 2A•14, 2B•6
Starter motor – 5•7, 5•8
Starting system – 5•7
Start-up after overhaul – 2C•20
Steering – 1•16, 11•15, REF•10, REF•11
  angles – 11•19
  box – 11•15
  box drop arm – 11•16
  box oil – 1•21
  column – 11•13, REF•9
  column lock – 11•12
  column switches – 13•4
  damper – 11•17
  gear backlash – 1•21
  wheel – 11•12, REF•9
Stop solenoid – 5•10
Stop-light switch – 10•17
Storage box – 12•14
Stub axle – 9•7, 9•13
Sump – 2A•23, 2B•13
Suspension and steering – 1•16, REF•10, REF•11, 11•1 *et seq*
  fault finding – REF•19
Suspension upper link balljoint – 1•15
Swirl chamber – 2C•9
Switches – 13•4
  diff lock – 7A•5
  fuel cut-off – 4B•8
  ignition – 11•12
  low detect – 7A•5
  oil pressure – 2B•17
  oil pressure warning light – 5•8
  reversing light – 7A•2
  stop-light – 10•17
  pin housing – 9•7
  pin housing oil – 0•15, 1•15, 1•25

T

Tailgate – 12•10
  lock solenoid – 13•16
  washer jet – 13•14
  washer system components – 13•13
  window – 12•12
  wiper motor – 13•13
  wiper switch – 13•4
Temperature gauge sender – 3•5
Temperature sensor – 4A•21, 4B•7, 4B•8
Tensioner – 2A•14
Thermostat – 2A•33, 3•3
Throttle position sensor – 4A•21
Timing belt – 2A•12
  cover – 2A•9
  cover dust seal – 2A•27
  housing – 1•22
  housing gasket – 2A•29
  housing oil seal – 2A•28
  tensioner – 2A•16

Note: *References throughout this index are in the form* **"Chapter number"** • **"Page number"**. *So, for example, 2A•15 refers to page 15 of Chapter 2A.*

Timing chain – 2A•11, 2B•6
    cover – 2A•9, 2B•5
    tensioner – 2A•16
Timing (injection) – 4A•13, 4A•14
Timing sprockets – 2A•14, 2B•6
Tools and working facilities – 1•22, REF•3,
    REF•7 *et seq*
Top dead centre (TDC) for No 1 piston
    location – 2A•5, 2B•4
Towing – 0•8
    bracket – 1•23
Track rod – 11•18
Transfer gearbox – 7B•1 *et seq*
    fault finding – REF•17
    oil – 0•15, 1•14, 1•24
    rear oil seal – 7B•3
Trim panels – 12•5, 12•12, 12•14
Turbocharger – 4A•16, 4A•17, 4B•8, 4B•9
    boost pressure – 1•25
Tyres – 0•12, REF•12
    pressures – 0•15
    specialists – REF•4

U

Underframe – 12•1
Upholstery – 12•2
Upper link – 11•10

V

Vacuum pump – 10•18
Vacuum servo unit – 10•14, 10•15
    air filter – 1•27
    filter – 1•28
    hose – 1•21
Valves – 2C•8, 2C•9
    clearances – 1•18
    operating (rocker) gear – 2A•16
    springs – 2C•9
    stem caps – 2C•9
Valve cover – 2A•7
Vehicle identification
    numbers – REF•4, REF•10
Vehicle speed sensor – 7A•5
Vehicle support – REF•6
Ventilation system – 3•7

W

Warning lights – 13•8
Washer system – 13•15
    fluid – 0•14
    jet – 13•14, 13•15
    pump – 13•14
    reservoir – 13•13

Water pump – 3•5
    drivebelt – 1•11, 1•12, 1•13
Weekly checks – 0•10 *et seq*
Weights – REF•1
Wheels – REF•12
    alignment – 11•19
    bearing – 9•6, 9•13, REF•11
    changing – 0•8
    speed sensor – 1•22, 10•19
Wheel arch liners – 12•12
Wheel cylinder – 1•10, 10•10
Windows – 12•12
    glass and regulator – 12•8
Windscreen – 12•12, REF•9
    washer jet – 13•14
    washer system components – 13•13
    wiper motor and cable – 13•11
Wipers
    arm – 13•10
    blades – 0•14
    motor – 13•11, 13•13
    switch – 13•4
Wiring diagrams – 13•17
Working facilities – REF•8

Preserving Our Motoring Heritage

< The Model J Duesenberg Derham Tourster. Only eight of these magnificent cars were ever built – this is the only example to be found outside the United States of America

Almost every car you've ever loved, loathed or desired is gathered under one roof at the Haynes Motor Museum. Over 300 immaculately presented cars and motorbikes represent every aspect of our motoring heritage, from elegant reminders of bygone days, such as the superb Model J Duesenberg to curiosities like the bug-eyed BMW Isetta. There are also many old friends and flames. Perhaps you remember the 1959 Ford Popular that you did your courting in? The magnificent 'Red Collection' is a spectacle of classic sports cars including AC, Alfa Romeo, Austin Healey, Ferrari, Lamborghini, Maserati, MG, Riley, Porsche and Triumph.

A Perfect Day Out

Each and every vehicle at the Haynes Motor Museum has played its part in the history and culture of Motoring. Today, they make a wonderful spectacle and a great day out for all the family. Bring the kids, bring Mum and Dad, but above all bring your camera to capture those golden memories for ever. You will also find an impressive array of motoring memorabilia, a comfortable 70 seat video cinema and one of the most extensive transport book shops in Britain. The Pit Stop Cafe serves everything from a cup of tea to wholesome, home-made meals or, if you prefer, you can enjoy the large picnic area nestled in the beautiful rural surroundings of Somerset.

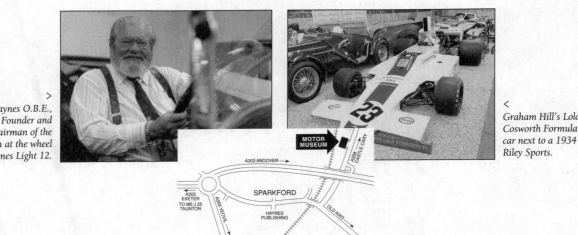

John Haynes O.B.E., Founder and Chairman of the museum at the wheel of a Haynes Light 12.

Graham Hill's Lola Cosworth Formula 1 car next to a 1934 Riley Sports.

The Museum is situated on the A359 Yeovil to Frome road at Sparkford, just off the A303 in Somerset. It is about 40 miles south of Bristol, and 25 minutes drive from the M5 intersection at Taunton.

Open 9.30am - 5.30pm (10.00am - 4.00pm Winter) 7 days a week, *except Christmas Day, Boxing Day and New Years Day*

Special rates available for schools, coach parties and outings Charitable Trust No. 292048

Title	Book No.
Peugeot 505 Petrol (79 - 89) up to G	0762
Peugeot 1.7/1.8 & 1.9 litre Diesel Engine (82 - 96) up to N	0950
Peugeot 2.0, 2.1, 2.3 & 2.5 litre Diesel Engines (74 - 90) up to H	1607
PORSCHE 911 (65 - 85) up to C	0264
Porsche 924 & 924 Turbo (76 - 85) up to C	0397
PROTON (89 - 97) F to P	3255
RANGE ROVER V8 Petrol (70 - Oct 92) up to K	0606
RELIANT Robin & Kitten (73 - 83) up to A *	0436
RENAULT 4 (61 - 86) up to D *	0072
Renault 5 Petrol (Feb 85 - 96) B to N	1219
Renault 9 & 11 Petrol (82 - 89) up to F	0822
Renault 18 Petrol (79 - 86) up to D	0598
Renault 19 Petrol (89 - 96) F to N	1646
Renault 19 Diesel (89 - 96) F to N	1946
Renault 21 Petrol (86 - 94) C to M	1397
Renault 25 Petrol & Diesel (84 - 92) B to K	1228
Renault Clio Petrol (91 - May 98) H to R	1853
Renault Clio Diesel (91 - June 96) H to N	3031
Renault Clio Petrol & Diesel (May 98 - May 01) R to Y	3906
Renault Clio Petrol & Diesel (June '01 - '05) Y to 55	4168
Renault Espace Petrol & Diesel (85 - 96) C to N	3197
Renault Laguna Petrol & Diesel (94 - 00) L to W	3252
Renault Laguna Petrol & Diesel (Feb 01 - Feb 05) X to 54	4283
Renault Mégane & Scénic Petrol & Diesel (96 - 99) N to T	3395
Renault Mégane & Scénic Petrol & Diesel (Apr 99 - 02) T to 52	3916
Renault Megane Petrol & Diesel (Oct 02 - 05) 52 to 55	4284
Renault Scenic Petrol & Diesel (Sept 03 - 06) 53 to 06	4297
ROVER 213 & 216 (84 - 89) A to G	1116
Rover 214 & 414 Petrol (89 - 96) G to N	1689
Rover 216 & 416 Petrol (89 - 96) G to N	1830
Rover 211, 214, 216, 218 & 220 Petrol & Diesel (Dec 95 - 99) N to V	3399
Rover 25 & MG ZR Petrol & Diesel (Oct 99 - 04) V to 54	4145
Rover 414, 416 & 420 Petrol & Diesel (May 95 - 98) M to R	3453
Rover 45 / MG ZS Petrol & Diesel (99 - 05) V to 55	4384
Rover 618, 620 & 623 Petrol (93 - 97) K to P	3257
Rover 75 / MG ZT Petrol & Diesel (99 - 06) S to 06	4292
Rover 820, 825 & 827 Petrol (86 - 95) D to N	1380
Rover 3500 (76 - 87) up to E *	0365
Rover Metro, 111 & 114 Petrol (May 90 - 98) G to S	1711
SAAB 95 & 96 (66 - 76) up to R *	0198
Saab 90, 99 & 900 (79 - Oct 93) up to L	0765
Saab 900 (Oct 93 - 98) L to R	3512
Saab 9000 (4-cyl) (85 - 98) C to S	1686
Saab 9-3 Petrol & Diesel (98 - Aug 02) R to 02	4614
Saab 9-3 Petrol & Diesel (02-07) 52 to 57	4749
Saab 9-5 4-cyl Petrol (97 - 04) R to 54	4156
SEAT Ibiza & Cordoba Petrol & Diesel (Oct 93 - Oct 99) L to V	3571
Seat Ibiza & Malaga Petrol (85 - 92) B to K	1609
SKODA Estelle (77 - 89) up to G	0604
Skoda Fabia Petrol & Diesel (00 - 06) W to 06	4376
Skoda Favorit (89 - 96) F to N	1801
Skoda Felicia Petrol & Diesel (95 - 01) M to X	3505
Skoda Octavia Petrol & Diesel (98 - Apr 04) R to 04	4285
SUBARU 1600 & 1800 (Nov 79 - 90) up to H *	0995

Title	Book No.
SUNBEAM Alpine, Rapier & H120 (67 - 74) up to N *	0051
SUZUKI SJ Series, Samurai & Vitara (4-cyl) Petrol (82 - 97) up to P	1942
Suzuki Supercarry & Bedford/Vauxhall Rascal (86 - Oct 94) C to M	3015
TALBOT Alpine, Solara, Minx & Rapier (75 - 86) up to D	0337
Talbot Horizon Petrol (78 - 86) up to D	0473
Talbot Samba (82 - 86) up to D	0823
TOYOTA Avensis Petrol (98 - Jan 03) R to 52	4264
Toyota Carina E Petrol (May 92 - 97) J to P	3256
Toyota Corolla (80 - 85) up to C	0683
Toyota Corolla (Sept 83 - Sept 87) A to E	1024
Toyota Corolla (Sept 87 - Aug 92) E to K	1683
Toyota Corolla Petrol (Aug 92 - 97) K to P	3259
Toyota Corolla Petrol (July 97 - Feb 02) P to 51	4286
Toyota Hi-Ace & Hi-Lux Petrol (69 - Oct 83) up to A	0304
Toyota RAV4 Petrol & Diesel (94-06) L to 55	4750
Toyota Yaris Petrol (99 - 05) T to 05	4265
TRIUMPH GT6 & Vitesse (62 - 74) up to N *	0112
Triumph Herald (59 - 71) up to K *	0010
Triumph Spitfire (62 - 81) up to X *	0113
Triumph Stag (70 - 78) up to T *	0441
Triumph TR2, TR3, TR3A, TR4 & TR4A (52 - 67) up to F *	0028
Triumph TR5 & 6 (67 - 75) up to P *	0031
Triumph TR7 (75 - 82) up to Y *	0322
VAUXHALL Astra Petrol (80 - Oct 84) up to B	0635
Vauxhall Astra & Belmont Petrol (Oct 84 - Oct 91) B to J	1136
Vauxhall Astra Petrol (Oct 91 - Feb 98) J to R	1832
Vauxhall/Opel Astra & Zafira Petrol (Feb 98 - Apr 04) R to 04	3758
Vauxhall/Opel Astra & Zafira Diesel (Feb 98 - Apr 04) R to 04	3797
Vauxhall/Opel Astra Petrol (04 - 08)	4732
Vauxhall/Opel Astra Diesel (04 - 08)	4733
Vauxhall/Opel Calibra (90 - 98) G to S	3502
Vauxhall Carlton Petrol (Oct 78 - Oct 86) up to D	0480
Vauxhall Carlton & Senator Petrol (Nov 86 - 94) D to L	1469
Vauxhall Cavalier Petrol (81 - Oct 88) up to F	0812
Vauxhall Cavalier Petrol (Oct 88 - 95) F to N	1570
Vauxhall Chevette (75 - 84) up to B	0285
Vauxhall/Opel Corsa Diesel (Mar 93 - Oct 00) K to X	4087
Vauxhall Corsa Petrol (Mar 93 - 97) K to R	1985
Vauxhall/Opel Corsa Petrol (Apr 97 - Oct 00) P to X	3921
Vauxhall/Opel Corsa Petrol & Diesel (Oct 00 - Sept 03) X to 53	4079
Vauxhall/Opel Corsa Petrol & Diesel (Oct 03 - Aug 06) 53 to 06	4617
Vauxhall/Opel Frontera Petrol & Diesel (91 - Sept 98) J to S	3454
Vauxhall Nova Petrol (83 - 93) up to K	0909
Vauxhall/Opel Omega Petrol (94 - 99) L to T	3510
Vauxhall/Opel Vectra Petrol & Diesel (95 - Feb 99) N to S	3396
Vauxhall/Opel Vectra Petrol & Diesel (Mar 99 - May 02) T to 02	3930
Vauxhall/Opel Vectra Petrol & Diesel (June 02 - Sept 05) 02 to 55	4618
Vauxhall/Opel 1.5, 1.6 & 1.7 litre Diesel Engine (82 - 96) up to N	1222
VW 411 & 412 (68 - 75) up to P *	0091
VW Beetle 1200 (54 - 77) up to S	0036
VW Beetle 1300 & 1500 (65 - 75) up to P	0039

Title	Book No.
VW 1302 & 1302S (70 - 72) up to L *	0110
VW Beetle 1303, 1303S & GT (72 - 75) up to P	0159
VW Beetle Petrol & Diesel (Apr 99 - 07) T to 57	3798
VW Golf & Jetta Mk 1 Petrol 1.1 & 1.3 (74 - 84) up to A	0716
VW Golf, Jetta & Scirocco Mk 1 Petrol 1.5, 1.6 & 1.8 (74 - 84) up to A	0726
VW Golf & Jetta Mk 1 Diesel (78 - 84) up to A	0451
VW Golf & Jetta Mk 2 Petrol (Mar 84 - Feb 92) A to J	1081
VW Golf & Vento Petrol & Diesel (Feb 92 - Mar 98) J to R	3097
VW Golf & Bora Petrol & Diesel (April 98 - 00) R to X	3727
VW Golf & Bora 4-cyl Petrol & Diesel (01 - 03) X to 53	4169
VW Golf & Jetta Petrol & Diesel (04 - 07) 53 to 07	4610
VW LT Petrol Vans & Light Trucks (76 - 87) up to E	0637
VW Passat & Santana Petrol (Sept 81 - May 88) up to E	0814
VW Passat 4-cyl Petrol & Diesel (May 88 - 96) E to P	3498
VW Passat 4-cyl Petrol & Diesel (Dec 96 - Nov 00) P to X	3917
VW Passat Petrol & Diesel (Dec 00 - May 05) X to 05	4279
VW Polo & Derby (76 - Jan 82) up to X	0335
VW Polo (82 - Oct 90) up to H	0813
VW Polo Petrol (Nov 90 - Aug 94) H to L	3245
VW Polo Hatchback Petrol & Diesel (94 - 99) M to S	3500
VW Polo Hatchback Petrol (00 - Jan 02) V to 51	4150
VW Polo Petrol & Diesel (02 - May 05) 51 to 05	4608
VW Scirocco (82 - 90) up to H *	1224
VW Transporter 1600 (68 - 79) up to V	0082
VW Transporter 1700, 1800 & 2000 (72 - 79) up to V *	0226
VW Transporter (air-cooled) Petrol (79 - 82) up to Y *	0638
VW Transporter (water-cooled) Petrol (82 - 90) up to H	3452
VW Type 3 (63 - 73) up to M *	0084
VOLVO 120 & 130 Series (& P1800) (61 - 73) up to M *	0203
Volvo 142, 144 & 145 (66 - 74) up to N *	0129
Volvo 240 Series Petrol (74 - 93) up to K	0270
Volvo 262, 264 & 260/265 (75 - 85) up to C *	0400
Volvo 340, 343, 345 & 360 (76 - 91) up to J	0715
Volvo 440, 460 & 480 Petrol (87 - 97) D to P	1691
Volvo 740 & 760 Petrol (82 - 91) up to J	1258
Volvo 850 Petrol (92 - 96) J to P	3260
Volvo 940 petrol (90 - 98) H to R	3249
Volvo S40 & V40 Petrol (96 - Mar 04) N to 04	3569
Volvo S40 & V50 Petrol & Diesel (Mar 04 - Jun 07) 04 to 07	4731
Volvo S60 Petrol & Diesel (01-08)	4793
Volvo S70, V70 & C70 Petrol (96 - 99) P to V	3573
Volvo V70 / S80 Petrol & Diesel (98 - 05) S to 55	4263

DIY MANUAL SERIES

Title	Book No.
The Haynes Air Conditioning Manual	4192
The Haynes Car Electrical Systems Manual	4251
The Haynes Manual on Bodywork	4198
The Haynes Manual on Brakes	4178
The Haynes Manual on Carburettors	4177
The Haynes Manual on Diesel Engines	4174
The Haynes Manual on Engine Management	4199
The Haynes Manual on Fault Codes	4175
The Haynes Manual on Practical Electrical Systems	4267
The Haynes Manual on Small Engines	4250
The Haynes Manual on Welding	4176

* Classic reprint

Haynes Manuals – The Complete **UK Car** List

Title	Book No.
ALFA ROMEO Alfasud/Sprint (74 - 88) up to F *	0292
Alfa Romeo Alfetta (73 - 87) up to E *	0531
AUDI 80, 90 & Coupe Petrol (79 - Nov 88) up to F	0605
Audi 80, 90 & Coupe Petrol (Oct 86 - 90) D to H	1491
Audi 100 & 200 Petrol (Oct 82 - 90) up to H	0907
Audi 100 & A6 Petrol & Diesel (May 91 - May 97) H to P	3504
Audi A3 Petrol & Diesel (96 - May 03) P to 03	4253
Audi A4 Petrol & Diesel (95 - 00) M to X	3575
Audi A4 Petrol & Diesel (01 - 04) X to 54	4609
AUSTIN A35 & A40 (56 - 67) up to F *	0118
Austin/MG/Rover Maestro 1.3 & 1.6 Petrol (83 - 95) up to M	0922
Austin/MG Metro (80 - May 90) up to G	0718
Austin/Rover Montego 1.3 & 1.6 Petrol (84 - 94) A to L	1066
Austin/MG/Rover Montego 2.0 Petrol (84 - 95) A to M	1067
Mini (59 - 69) up to H *	0527
Mini (69 - 01) up to X	0646
Austin/Rover 2.0 litre Diesel Engine (86 - 93) C to L	1857
Austin Healey 100/6 & 3000 (56 - 68) up to G *	0049
BEDFORD CF Petrol (69 - 87) up to E	0163
Bedford/Vauxhall Rascal & Suzuki Supercarry (86 - Oct 94) C to M	3015
BMW 316, 320 & 320i (4-cyl) (75 - Feb 83) up to Y *	0276
BMW 320, 320i, 323i & 325i (6-cyl) (Oct 77 - Sept 87) up to E	0815
BMW 3- & 5-Series Petrol (81 - 91) up to J	1948
BMW 3-Series Petrol (Apr 91 - 99) H to V	3210
BMW 3-Series Petrol (Sept 98 - 03) S to 53	4067
BMW 520i & 525e (Oct 81 - June 88) up to E	1560
BMW 525, 528 & 528i (73 - Sept 81) up to X *	0632
BMW 5-Series 6-cyl Petrol (April 96 - Aug 03) N to 03	4151
BMW 1500, 1502, 1600, 1602, 2000 & 2002 (59 - 77) up to S *	0240
CHRYSLER PT Cruiser Petrol (00 - 03) W to 53	4058
CITROËN 2CV, Ami & Dyane (67 - 90) up to H	0196
Citroën AX Petrol & Diesel (87 - 97) D to P	3014
Citroën Berlingo & Peugeot Partner Petrol & Diesel (96 - 05) P to 55	4281
Citroën BX Petrol (83 - 94) A to L	0908
Citroën C15 Van Petrol & Diesel (89 - Oct 98) F to S	3509
Citroën C3 Petrol & Diesel (02 - 05) 51 to 05	4197
Citroën C5 Petrol & Diesel (01-08) Y to 08	4745
Citroën CX Petrol (75 - 88) up to F	0528
Citroën Saxo Petrol & Diesel (96 - 04) N to 54	3506
Citroën Visa Petrol (79 - 88) up to F	0620
Citroën Xantia Petrol & Diesel (93 - 01) K to Y	3082
Citroën XM Petrol & Diesel (89 - 00) G to X	3451
Citroën Xsara Petrol & Diesel (97 - Sept 00) R to W	3751
Citroën Xsara Picasso Petrol & Diesel (00 - 02) W to 52	3944
Citroen Xsara Picasso (03-08)	4784
Citroën ZX Diesel (91 - 98) J to S	1922
Citroën ZX Petrol (91 - 98) H to S	1881
Citroën 1.7 & 1.9 litre Diesel Engine (84 - 96) A to N	1379
FIAT 126 (73 - 87) up to E *	0305
Fiat 500 (57 - 73) up to M *	0090
Fiat Bravo & Brava Petrol (95 - 00) N to W	3572
Fiat Cinquecento (93 - 98) K to R	3501
Fiat Panda (81 - 95) up to M	0793
Fiat Punto Petrol & Diesel (94 - Oct 99) L to V	3251
Fiat Punto Petrol (Oct 99 - July 03) V to 03	4066
Fiat Punto Petrol (03-07) 03 to 07	4746
Fiat Regata Petrol (84 - 88) A to F	1167
Fiat Tipo Petrol (88 - 91) E to J	1625
Fiat Uno Petrol (83 - 95) up to M	0923
Fiat X1/9 (74 - 89) up to G *	0273
FORD Anglia (59 - 68) up to G *	0001

Title	Book No.
Ford Capri II (& III) 1.6 & 2.0 (74 - 87) up to E *	0283
Ford Capri II (& III) 2.8 & 3.0 V6 (74 - 87) up to E	1309
Ford Cortina Mk I & Corsair 1500 ('62 - '66) up to D*	0214
Ford Cortina Mk III 1300 & 1600 (70 - 76) up to P	*0070
Ford Escort Mk I 1100 & 1300 (68 - 74) up to N *	0171
Ford Escort Mk I Mexico, RS 1600 & RS 2000 (70 - 74) up to N *	0139
Ford Escort Mk II Mexico, RS 1800 & RS 2000 (75 - 80) up to W *	0735
Ford Escort (75 - Aug 80) up to V *	0280
Ford Escort Petrol (Sept 80 - Sept 90) up to H	0686
Ford Escort & Orion Petrol (Sept 90 - 00) H to X	1737
Ford Escort & Orion Diesel (Sept 90 - 00) H to X	4081
Ford Fiesta (76 - Aug 83) up to Y	0334
Ford Fiesta Petrol (Aug 83 - Feb 89) A to F	1030
Ford Fiesta Petrol (Feb 89 - Oct 95) F to N	1595
Ford Fiesta Petrol & Diesel (Oct 95 - Mar 02) N to 02	3397
Ford Fiesta Petrol & Diesel (Apr 02 - 07) 02 to 57	4170
Ford Focus Petrol & Diesel (98 - 01) S to Y	3759
Ford Focus Petrol & Diesel (Oct 01 - 05) 51 to 05	4167
Ford Galaxy Petrol & Diesel (95 - Aug 00) M to W	3984
Ford Granada Petrol (Sept 77 - Feb 85) up to B *	0481
Ford Granada & Scorpio Petrol (Mar 85 - 94) B to M	1245
Ford Ka (96 - 02) P to 52	3570
Ford Mondeo Petrol (93 - Sept 00) K to X	1923
Ford Mondeo Petrol & Diesel (Oct 00 - Jul 03) X to 03	3990
Ford Mondeo Petrol & Diesel (July 03 - 07) 03 to 56	4619
Ford Mondeo Diesel (93 - 96) L to N	3465
Ford Orion Petrol (83 - Sept 90) up to H	1009
Ford Sierra 4-cyl Petrol (82 - 93) up to K	0903
Ford Sierra V6 Petrol (82 - 91) up to J	0904
Ford Transit Petrol (Mk 2) (78 - Jan 86) up to C	0719
Ford Transit Petrol (Mk 3) (Feb 86 - 89) C to G	1468
Ford Transit Diesel (Feb 86 - 99) C to T	3019
Ford Transit Diesel (00-06)	4775
Ford 1.6 & 1.8 litre Diesel Engine (84 - 96) A to N	1172
Ford 2.1, 2.3 & 2.5 litre Diesel Engine (77 - 90) up to H	1606
FREIGHT ROVER Sherpa Petrol (74 - 87) up to E	0463
HILLMAN Avenger (70 - 82) up to Y	0037
Hillman Imp (63 - 76) up to R *	0022
HONDA Civic (Feb 84 - Oct 87) A to E	1226
Honda Civic (Nov 91 - 96) J to N	3199
Honda Civic Petrol (Mar 95 - 00) M to X	4050
Honda Civic Petrol & Diesel (01 - 05) X to 55	4611
Honda CR-V Petrol & Diesel (01-06)	4747
Honda Jazz (01 - Feb 08) 51 - 57	4735
HYUNDAI Pony (85 - 94) C to M	3398
JAGUAR E Type (61 - 72) up to L *	0140
Jaguar MkI & II, 240 & 340 (55 - 69) up to H *	0098
Jaguar XJ6, XJ & Sovereign; Daimler Sovereign (68 - Oct 86) up to D	0242
Jaguar XJ6 & Sovereign (Oct 86 - Sept 94) D to M	3261
Jaguar XJ12, XJS & Sovereign; Daimler Double Six (72 - 88) up to F	0478
JEEP Cherokee Petrol (93 - 96) K to N	1943
LADA 1200, 1300, 1500 & 1600 (74 - 91) up to J	0413
Lada Samara (87 - 91) D to J	1610
LAND ROVER 90, 110 & Defender Diesel (83 - 07) up to 56	3017
Land Rover Discovery Petrol & Diesel (89 - 98) G to S	3016
Land Rover Discovery Diesel (Nov 98 - Jul 04) S to 04	4606
Land Rover Freelander Petrol & Diesel (97 - Sept 03) R to 53	3929
Land Rover Freelander Petrol & Diesel (Oct 03 - Oct 06) 53 to 56	4623

Title	Book No.
Land Rover Series IIA & III Diesel (58 - 85) up to C	0529
Land Rover Series II, IIA & III 4-cyl Petrol (58 - 85) up to C	0314
MAZDA 323 (Mar 81 - Oct 89) up to G	1608
Mazda 323 (Oct 89 - 98) G to R	3455
Mazda 626 (May 83 - Sept 87) up to E	0929
Mazda B1600, B1800 & B2000 Pick-up Petrol (72 - 88) up to F	0267
Mazda RX-7 (79 - 85) up to C *	0460
MERCEDES-BENZ 190, 190E & 190D Petrol & Diesel (83 - 93) A to L	3450
Mercedes-Benz 200D, 240D, 240TD, 300D & 300TD 123 Series Diesel (Oct 76 - 85)	1114
Mercedes-Benz 250 & 280 (68 - 72) up to L *	0346
Mercedes-Benz 250 & 280 123 Series Petrol (Oct 76 - 84) up to B *	0677
Mercedes-Benz 124 Series Petrol & Diesel (85 - Aug 93) C to K	3253
Mercedes-Benz A-Class Petrol & Diesel (98-04) S to 54	4748
Mercedes-Benz C-Class Petrol & Diesel (93 - Aug 00) L to W	3511
Mercedes-Benz C-Class (00-06)	4780
MGA (55 - 62) *	0475
MGB (62 - 80) up to W	0111
MG Midget & Austin-Healey Sprite (58 - 80) up to W *	0265
MINI Petrol (July 01 - 05) Y to 05	4273
MITSUBISHI Shogun & L200 Pick-Ups Petrol (83 - 94) up to M	1944
MORRIS Ital 1.3 (80 - 84) up to B	0705
Morris Minor 1000 (56 - 71) up to K	0024
NISSAN Almera Petrol (95 - Feb 00) N to V	4053
Nissan Almera & Tino Petrol (Feb 00 - 07) V to 56	4612
Nissan Bluebird (May 84 - Mar 86) A to C	1223
Nissan Bluebird Petrol (Mar 86 - 90) C to H	1473
Nissan Cherry (Sept 82 - 86) up to D	1031
Nissan Micra (83 - Jan 93) up to K	0931
Nissan Micra (93 - 02) K to 52	3254
Nissan Micra Petrol (03-07) 52 to 57	4734
Nissan Primera Petrol (90 - Aug 99) H to T	1851
Nissan Stanza (82 - 86) up to D	0824
Nissan Sunny Petrol (May 82 - Oct 86) up to D	0895
Nissan Sunny Petrol (Oct 86 - Mar 91) D to H	1378
Nissan Sunny Petrol (Apr 91 - 95) H to N	3219
OPEL Ascona & Manta (B Series) (Sept 75 - 88) up to F *	0316
Opel Ascona Petrol (81 - 88)	3215
Opel Astra Petrol (Oct 91 - Feb 98)	3156
Opel Corsa Petrol (83 - Mar 93)	3160
Opel Corsa Petrol (Mar 93 - 97)	3159
Opel Kadett Petrol (Nov 79 - Oct 84) up to B	0634
Opel Kadett Petrol (Oct 84 - Oct 91)	3196
Opel Omega & Senator Petrol (Nov 86 - 94)	3157
Opel Rekord Petrol (Feb 78 - Oct 86) up to D	0543
Opel Vectra Petrol (Oct 88 - Oct 95)	3158
PEUGEOT 106 Petrol & Diesel (91 - 04) J to 53	1882
Peugeot 205 Petrol (83 - 97) A to P	0932
Peugeot 206 Petrol & Diesel (98 - 01) S to X	3757
Peugeot 206 Petrol & Diesel (02 - 06) 51 to 06	4613
Peugeot 306 Petrol & Diesel (93 - 02) K to 02	3073
Peugeot 307 Petrol & Diesel (01 - 04) Y to 54	4147
Peugeot 309 Petrol (86 - 93) C to K	1266
Peugeot 405 Petrol (88 - 97) E to P	1559
Peugeot 405 Diesel (88 - 97) E to P	3198
Peugeot 406 Petrol & Diesel (96 - Mar 99) N to T	3394
Peugeot 406 Petrol & Diesel (Mar 99 - 02) T to 52	3982

* Classic reprint